£25

REDBRICK

Redbrick

A social and architectural history of Britain's civic universities

WILLIAM WHYTE

OXFORD
UNIVERSITY PRESS

Great Clarendon Street, Oxford, OX2 6DP,
United Kingdom

Oxford University Press is a department of the University of Oxford.
It furthers the University's objective of excellence in research, scholarship,
and education by publishing worldwide. Oxford is a registered trade mark of
Oxford University Press in the UK and in certain other countries

© William Whyte 2015

The moral rights of the author have been asserted

First Edition published in 2015

Impression: 1

All rights reserved. No part of this publication may be reproduced, stored in
a retrieval system, or transmitted, in any form or by any means, without the
prior permission in writing of Oxford University Press, or as expressly permitted
by law, by licence or under terms agreed with the appropriate reprographics
rights organization. Enquiries concerning reproduction outside the scope of the
above should be sent to the Rights Department, Oxford University Press, at the
address above

You must not circulate this work in any other form
and you must impose this same condition on any acquirer

Published in the United States of America by Oxford University Press
198 Madison Avenue, New York, NY 10016, United States of America

British Library Cataloguing in Publication Data
Data available

Library of Congress Control Number: 2014936757

ISBN 978–0–19–871612–9

Printed and bound by
CPI Group (UK) Ltd, Croydon, CR0 4YY

Links to third party websites are provided by Oxford in good faith and
for information only. Oxford disclaims any responsibility for the materials
contained in any third party website referenced in this work.

For Z. V. W.
For everything.

Preface

Redbrick has been more than ten years in the writing. I first began to gather material for it just as I finished my doctorate on the architect Thomas Graham Jackson. Jackson was a major figure at both Oxford and Cambridge in the last few decades of the nineteenth century; but he was never employed at the civic universities which were being established at the same time. Wanting to understand why, I looked for a book that might give me the answer. It soon transpired that no such volume existed. Indeed, the more I searched the more remarkable it seemed that the great foundations of the Victorian era lacked the attention that had been lavished on Oxbridge. This was all the more striking as my own family's move to Yorkshire a few years before had exposed me to a range of magnificent nineteenth- and twentieth-century buildings at the University of Leeds. Here, it seemed, was a truly wonderful subject, just ripe for research.

Of course there was a good reason that no one had yet written a book on the architecture of the civic universities. It is an enormous subject, and to do it justice, it would be necessary to visit dozens of institutions, to conduct fieldwork there and use their archives. The issues involved raise questions about civic life and national government; the history of education and the history of design. I soon realized, too, that a study of great architectural projects would be a partial and misleading one. There was a need to examine failures as well as successes; to look at what the buildings' inhabitants did with their surroundings as well as what the architects had intended them to do. Moreover, the more I read the more it became clear that the late-nineteenth century projects with which I began could only be understood as part of a much longer story—one that could be traced back to the late eighteenth century, and one that should be carried forward to the present day. Writing Redbrick back into history helped to revise the standard account of the post-war expansion of the university system and did something to explain our current dilemmas about higher education, not least worries about the social make-up of the student body.

In the current academic climate, many other institutions would quite reasonably have told me to focus on something smaller-scale and more manageable, something with a more predictable and timely outcome. I am enormously grateful that my two employers—the History Faculty at the University of Oxford and St John's College—were quite so indulgent. Words cannot express my gratitude to the Leverhulme Trust, whose Philip Leverhulme Prize enabled me to devote two years of full-time research to this project. The John Fell Fund and St John's College were also generous with their funding. My colleagues, especially Martin Ingram, Hannah Skoda, and Malcolm Vale, kindly tolerated my absences and compensated for my distraction. Sam Brewitt-Taylor, Jon MacDonagh, and Robert Saunders each superbly replaced me as a tutor at St John's, whilst Sam, together with Eve

Colpus, Edward Gillin, and Alana Harris, gave brilliant research assistance, making it possible for me to work on other projects as well as this one.

Within Oxford I have benefited from the professionalism of librarians in the History Faculty, St John's College, and the Upper Reading Room of the Bodleian. Like everyone there, I still miss Vera Ryhajlo. I am grateful for the help and advice of my colleagues especially Martin Conway, Louise Durning, Jane Garnett, Lawrence Goldman, Matthew Grimley, Dan Hicks, Simon Skinner, Alan Strathern, Selina Todd, Geoffrey Tyack, Mark Whittow, and Oliver Zimmer, all of whom shared ideas and several of whom also showed me their unpublished work. My students, undergraduate and graduate, have asked all the best questions, and I am particularly grateful to a host of exceptionally talented historians—including Matthew Andrews, Philip Aspin, Sam Brewitt-Taylor, Ursula DeYoung, Edward Gillin, Steve Greenwold, Dan Inman, Horatio Joyce, David Lewis, David McKinstry, and Neal Shasore—who have worked with me on their doctorates and contributed hugely to the development of my own thought as a result.

Not least of the appeals of *Redbrick*, however, has been that it has taken me out of Oxford. I am enormously grateful for the kindness shown to me by archivists, librarians, managers, and academics at innumerable institutions. I have tried out arguments in papers given in Belfast, Bristol, Colchester, Leicester, London, Southampton, and elsewhere, and benefited greatly from the subsequent comments and criticisms. I have been immeasurably aided by the professionalism and generosity of staff at the University, the City University, and at the Queen's Foundation in Birmingham; at the Universities of Cardiff, Dundee, Essex, Exeter, Keele, Leeds, Leicester, Liverpool, Loughborough, Manchester, Nottingham, Oxford Brookes, Reading, Salford, Sheffield, Southampton, and Sussex; at KCL and UCL, the Association of Commonwealth Universities, Modern College, Blackheath, the National Archives, and the University of London; and at the Modern Records Centre at the University of Warwick. I am thankful, too, to all these institutions for permission to use material held in their archives; and to those who have enabled me to reproduce images. For other images, I most gratefully acknowledge the British Museum, Roderick Bowen Library, Royal Institute of British Architects, and the Provincial Archivist of Nova Scotia. I am especially grateful to Martine Hamilton Knight and Michele Nastasi for allowing me to use their photographs.

Along the way, a whole host of people has supported me by reading my work or sending me theirs; by putting me up, our just putting up with me. I am especially thankful to Kester Aspden, Jeremy Black, Louise Campbell, Andrew Chandler, Joe Mordaunt Crook, Sophie Forgan, Elain Harwood, Margy and Peter Holden, Stuart Jones, Matt Kelly, Louis Nelson, Peter Nockles, Guy Ortolano, Tamson Pietsch, Roey Sweet, Michael Wykes, and Emma Cayley. At Oxford University Press, first Christopher Wheeler and then Robert Faber and Cathryn Steele were kindness and encouragement itself as editors, while Emma Slaughter, Kim Allen, and Nicola Sangster were immensely thorough and efficient at the production stage. I should also like to acknowledge the hard work and wisdom of the three anonymous readers of the text who immeasurably improved this volume.

Above all, I must thank my family for their love and support. My mother and father, my brother Alasdair and his family may have been bemused by my enthusiasm for all this; but they have been endlessly kind about it. So have my parents-in-law, Denis and Carole Waxman. *Redbrick* was under way well before my sons Nahum and Jacob were born and has been completed despite, rather than because of, their arrival. But they make my life more wonderful every day and they are far more amazing than anything I could ever think of, much less anything I've written here. And what can I say about Zoë Waxman, who has not only transformed my life and makes everything possible, but even read the text and improved it beyond all measure? I love her with all my heart—and dedicate this book to her. This is for her; for everything.

Contents

List of Abbreviations	xiii
List of Illustrations	xiv
Introduction	1

I. 1783–1843

Prologue	21
1. New Universities for a New Century	29
2. The People and Places of the University of London	51
Conclusion	67

II. 1843–1880

Prologue	71
3. Experiments in Ireland and England	78
4. Building the Mid-Victorian University	101
Conclusion	119

III. 1880–1914

Prologue	125
5. The Making of a Modern University	132
6. Life in a Modern University	147
Conclusion	171

IV. 1914–1949

Prologue	177
7. Redbrick Attacked	184
8. Redbrick Inhabited	205
Conclusion	217

V. 1949–1973

Prologue	221
9. The Expansion of Redbrick	229
10. Buildings and Battles	248
Conclusion	268

VI. 1973–1997

Prologue	273
11. Reshaping Higher Education	279
12. Students and Staff	290
13. Towards a New Architecture?	307
Conclusion	319
14. Epilogue: Redbrick since 1997	321
Bibliography	339
Index	381

List of Abbreviations

AUT	Association of University Teachers
BCA	Birmingham City University
Bodl.	Bodleian Library
BUA	Birmingham University Archive
CUA	Cardiff University Archive
CVCP	Committee of Vice Chancellors and Principals
DES	Department of Education and Science
DMU	De Montfort University Leicester
DUA	Dundee University Archive
EssUA	Essex University Archive
EUA	Exeter University Archive
HC DEB	House of Commons Debates
HL DEB	House of Lords Debates
KCL	King's College London
KUA	Keele University Archive
LeeUA	Leeds University Archive
LeiUA	Leicester University Archive
LivU	Liverpool University Archive
LonUA	London University Archive, Senate House
MIT	Massachusetts Institute of Technology
MUA	Manchester University Archive
NUS	National Union of Students
ODNB	*Oxford Dictionary of National Biography*
QCA	Queen's College Birmingham, Archive
RUA	Reading University Archive
SUA	Sheffield University Archive
SusUA	Sussex University Archive
THES	*Times Educational Supplement*
THE	*Times Higher Education Supplement* (*Times Higher Education* from 2008)
TNA	The National Archives
UCL	University College London
UEA	University of East Anglia
UGC	University Grants Committee
ULouA	University of Loughborough Archive
USA	University of Southampton Archive
WMRC	University of Warwick Modern Records Centre

List of Illustrations

1. 'The Cathedral of Rheims furnished the first hint of this elevation . . . I have, however, engrafted some alterations, which it is hoped will be considered as improvements': the University Church in Kelsall's *Phantasm of an University* (London, 1814) 2
2. '*The mother of an University*': King's College Windsor in the early nineteenth century 22
3. Charles Cockerell's design for Lampeter. Essentially an Oxbridge college in conception, the design was much simplified in construction 34
4. George Cruickshank, 'The political, toy-man' (1825). Brougham is shown carrying a Gothic college round Lincoln's Inn as he solicits subscriptions 42
5. 'The grandest entrance in London with nothing behind it': University College London 52
6. 'Contrasted College Gateways'. Pugin mocks the anonymity of King's College London when compared with the grand—if uncompleted— entrance to Christ Church, Oxford 58
7. The importance of buildings to institutional identity is made plain in the *London University Magazine* of 1829 62
8. 'How many have been ruined, as this College has been, by masses of unremunerative bricks and mortar piled up for show.' Queen's College Birmingham in 1843 86
9. A 'small dingy building in one of the worst parts of town': the original home of Owens College Manchester 92
10. Designed 'to harmonize with and advance the objects of the higher mental culture for which the University exists': the University of Bombay 102
11. 'A rather forbidding and comfortless place': Queen's College Belfast 103
12. 'Worthy to stand in the High Street of Oxford': the visit of Queen Victoria to Cork in 1849 103
13. 'The first building in the province of Connaught'? Queen's College Galway 104
14. Rectifying 'the *absence of external symbolism*': the new Owens College Manchester 108
15. Inspired by Vassar, Royal Holloway College was also intended to be a monument 'more lasting than the pyramids' 116
16. 'I should like to say I have found it next to impossible if not altogether so to carry out all the suggestions made to me': Waterhouse on the Owens College Manchester 117

List of Illustrations   xv

17. 'It is for us, the middle class . . . to resolve that we will, instead of falling into the back rank, maintain our position of influence in the country': plans for Bristol University College   118
18. 'The finest building in the city': Mason College Birmingham   120
19. 'Like a thrawn tree on a West Riding moor': the south elevation of the University of Leeds   131
20. Gender at work: the Liverpool Guild of Students uses a Baroque idiom for the men's side and a more refined Regency for the women's   138
21. 'The majesty of learning' embodied in the Wills Tower at the University of Bristol   140
22. 'Like an illegitimate child of the London Law Courts': University College Aberystwyth   159
23. A 'reference to that earlier and greater extension of the Universities when Colet lectured at Oxford and Erasmus led the new learning of Europe from his little cell at Queen's': C. R. Ashbee's design for a University Extension College   162
24. 'The court-yard—sacred to the collegers themselves': University College Cardiff   163
25. 'Amorphous as it might be, there was in it a reminiscence of the wondrous, cloistral origin of education': University College Nottingham   164
26. 'The Tudor Style, of which there are many examples in the Colleges of Oxford and Cambridge, and which by association and appropriateness gives a Collegiate character to the building': Western Bank, University of Sheffield   165
27. 'Give people something to see, and I will get . . . half a million without delay': Joseph Chamberlain at the University of Birmingham   166
28. 'The competitors seem to have taken different views of the precise meaning to be attached to the term University College. Some seem to place the accent on the University, and show the departments arranged in separate buildings with carriage drives between them; others place it on the college and, connecting their departments, group them as a single building round one or more quadrangles': Clyde and East's winning design for University College Southampton   170
29. Built 'most grand and cakeily': the new University College Nottingham   178
30. 'In every respect modern': Rutland Hall, Loughborough   181
31. 'A tremendous departure in style and tradition': the New Arts Faculty at the University of Liverpool   192
32. 'To dominate the neighbourhood and be seen from all directions and symbolise the University': the Parkinson Building, University of Leeds   194
33. 'How can we achieve a University atmosphere with a motley collection of buildings better suited to a factory yard?': the Hartley Library, Southampton   195
34. 'Help Youth to Realise Ambition,—Therein Lies Efficiency and the Nation's Destiny': appeal poster, University of Liverpool, 1920   200

35. 'A physical environment so mediocre that it belies the experiment of the university itself': Keele in the early 1960s ... 225
36. '60,000 square feet of progress. Progress which will itself induce progress and achievement': the Electrical Engineering and Architecture Building, University of Nottingham ... 256
37. 'Our First Contemporary Urban University': Mathematics, Earth Sciences and Computer Sciences Building, University of Leeds ... 257
38. 'Like some Dalek stronghold in Doctor Who': Langwith College, University of York ... 258
39. 'The writer receiving the most votes was Kafka': Towers at the University of Essex by Rwendland ... 259
40. 'A symbol of all this University doesn't stand for': Meeting House, University of Sussex ... 262
41. 'Bizarre... angry... controversial... rubbery and man-hating': James Stirling's engineering department, Denys Lasdun's Charles Wilson Building, and Ove Arup's Attenborough Building at the University of Leicester ... 264
42. 'Auschwitz with carpets'? The University of East Anglia Campus, Norwich ... 269
43. 'A major industrial undertaking, not a service run by gentleman for the few': Cedric Price's Potteries Thinkbelt ... 270
44. 'Its self-appointed task is to gobsmack'. The Queens Building, De Montfort University Leicester ... 308
45. One of 'The very best sort of buildings at the very worst sort of time': the Arts and Social Sciences Library, University College Cardiff ... 312
46. 'The most significant building in Britain for a quarter of a century': the Sainsbury Centre for the Visual Arts, University of East Anglia ... 313
47. The first entirely new university campus created since the 1960s: the University of Lincoln ... 317
48. 'England with palm trees': the University of Nottingham Ningbo ... 332
49. 'The building liberates modern university architecture from its redbrick, tower-block image, away from a tradition of mere functionality over form.' The Graduate Centre, London Metropolitan University ... 334
50. One answer to the question 'What is a civic university?' Staffordshire University Science Centre, Stoke on Trent ... 336

There are few earthly things more beautiful than a University.

> John Masefield
> Lines delivered at the University of Sheffield
> 25 June 1946

Introduction

Opening the battered Bodleian library box that holds it, the first thing that strikes any reader about the *Phantasm of an University* is its opulence (Figure 1). Even after two centuries it is still a handsome bit of work: a hand-printed, hand-bound quarto edition, about twelve by nine and a half inches across, with a beautifully embossed and gilded cover. It looks expensive and has always been pricey, costing £5 5s in 1814 when it was first published, a sum that would have taken an ordinary worker a month and half to earn.[1] As you turn its pages, you can see why it was so costly. Print after print after print, some of them engraved by the great masters of the London publishing world, depicts a series of fantastical buildings in Greek, Roman, Gothic, and Romanesque styles. Accompanying these gorgeous images is a no less elaborate text: nearly 200 pages of polemic, poetry, and philosophy. It is, as a nineteenth-century American critic observed, 'a fanciful work, gotten up with a great expense of beautiful but impracticable architectural designs'.[2] As the title suggests, this was indeed a fantastic dream—a £5 million fantasy in an age in which three-quarters of the population earned less that £200 a year.[3] Complete with plans for a 'Ménagerie' which was to include 'Boas' and 'Oran-outangs', it was a utopian plan for a new sort of university.[4]

The author of this remarkable book, Charles Kelsall, was an extraordinary individual; so strange that his Hampshire neighbours believed that he worshipped the devil.[5] So far as we know, he did not, but he looked as though he might, and he was undoubtedly possessed; someone who, as the historian David Watkin disparagingly puts it, 'could not observe any facet of human existence without wishing to liberalize and modernize it'.[6] He wrote books advocating church reform and proposing that Windsor Castle should be rebuilt in a fashionable neo-classical style.[7] He vehemently advocated the cause of Greek independence, passionately condemned the Papacy,

---

[1] *New Monthly Magazine* 1 (1814), p. 352.
[2] J. M. Wainwright, *Collegiate Education: an address pronounced before the House of Convocation of Trinity College, Hartford, August 4th, 1847* (Hartford, 1847), p. 8.
[3] P. K. O'Brien, 'British Incomes and Property in the Early-Nineteenth Century', *Economic History Review* 12 (1959), pp. 255–67.
[4] Charles Kelsall, *Phantasm of an University* (London, 1814), p. 171.
[5] Morden College, Biographical File: Charles Kelsall, E. Bromfield to R. Saw (23 August 1959).
[6] David Watkin, 'Charles Kelsall: the quintessence of neo-classicism', *Architectural Review* 140 (1966), pp. 109–12, p. 11.
[7] [Charles Kelsall] Mela Britannicus, *Horæ Viaticæ* (London, 1836), pp. 227–411 and *A Letter to the Society of the Dilettanti on the Works in Progress at Windsor Castle by Mela Britannicus* (London, 1827).

Fig. 1. 'The Cathedral of Rheims furnished the first hint of this elevation...I have, however, engrafted some alterations, which it is hoped will be considered as improvements': the University Church in Kelsall's *Phantasm of an University* (London, 1814)

Reproduced with the permission of the President and Fellows of St John's College, Oxford.

and fervently argued for political change in Britain, America, and Sicily.[8] A much-travelled man, he wrote with equal expertise on the affairs of France and Russia, Italy and Spain.[9] Yet he quite rightly saw the *Phantasm* as his greatest work, taking it with him to Paris on the off-chance that he could persuade the French government to adopt his plan,[10] and sending a copy to James Madison in hope that it would help shape the newly established University of Virginia.[11] It was surely Kelsall, too, who persuaded his friend Abraham Valpy to dispatch yet another copy to the founders of what was to become University College London.[12] However unlikely it may seem, he evidently believed that his apparently unrealizable dream could and would be made reality.

Indeed, Kelsall felt that his new idea for a new sort of institution was not merely desirable, but a burning necessity, especially given what he saw as the weakness of contemporary higher education. A product of Eton and Trinity College Cambridge, he had left university without a degree and remained unhappy at his experience as an undergraduate. Nor did he believe that life in Oxford was much better than that in his own *alma mater*. Both offered, he argued, too narrow a curriculum, focusing as they did on classics and mathematics. This was damaging for the students. 'No parents of good sense would encourage a poetical vein in a child', he observed, so why would a university insist that young men devote themselves to the study of Latin and Greek verse? Worse still, such single-mindedness threatened the country as whole. It neglected political science, moral philosophy, 'Agriculture, Commerce, and Manufactures, the main bulwarks of the nation, the pride and glory of the English people.' Oxford and Cambridge, Kelsall concluded, were thus not in fact universities at all, for

> A University should be able to face, and confer rewards on every candidate in every department of science and art; she should be to a nation, what the sun is to our system, the grand centre, from which the rays of universal knowledge should emanate, and by which the career of all the luminaries of science should be regulated and directed.

Unless this change could be effected, he went on to argue, not only would Oxford and Cambridge continue to be little more than parodies of a university, they would be unable to withstand 'that amazing display of talent in France, which is ever busy in contriving the ruin of that beautiful fabric, the English Constitution'.[13] Published in the months between Napoleon's first abdication and his return to power and eventual defeat, this was a serious threat indeed.

---

[8] Charles Kelsall, *Letter from Athens* (London, 1812), *Classical Excursion from Rome to Arpino* (Geneva, 1820), *The Last Two Pleadings of Marcus Tullius Cicero against Cauis Verres* (London, 1812), pp. 347–65; as Junius Secundus, *Constantine and Eugene, or an evening at Mount Vernon* (Brussels, 1828); as Mela Britannicus, *Remarks touching geography specially that of the British isles, comprising strictures on the hierarchy of Great Britain* (London, 1825).

[9] [Charles Kelsall], *Esquisse de mes travaux, de mes voyages et de mes opinions* (London, 1830).

[10] [Kelsall], *Esquisse de mes travaux*, p. 45.

[11] *Calendar of the Correspondence of James Madison* (Washington, DC, 1894), p. 441.

[12] UCL, Misc. Committee Minutes 1826–27, p. 4 (18 March 1826). Valpy was Kelsall's editor at the *Classical Journal*. See also the inscription in Kelsall's copy of Valpy's *Poemata, quae de praemio Oxoniensibus posito anno 1806, 1807, et 1808* (London, 1809), held at Morden College.

[13] Kelsall, *Phantasm*, pp. 3, 24, 38, 39.

The *Phantasm* was couched as a plea to England's two ancient universities: 'Come Oxonia, come my *alma mater* Cantabrigia, let us see whether, by trenching the earth a little, the plants which you cherish may not be made to shoot with more vigour, and produce a richer and more vigorous display of fruit.' He argued that they should turn each college into a different department of study. In Cambridge, for example, Trinity would specialize in 'Civil Polity and Languages', St John's in moral philosophy, Downing in the fine arts, and Queens' in natural philosophy, with Peterhouse becoming the home of 'Agriculture and Manufactures', and King's forming a college of mathematics. It was only in the entirely predictable circumstances that these reforms were rejected that Kelsall was willing to contemplate the necessity of establishing a wholly new institution, a massive 'metropolis of science and art', consisting of no fewer than seven quadrangles somewhat larger than Lincoln's Inn Fields, London's largest public square. There would be a museum and a university press, a Senate House, a university church inspired by the cathedral at Rheims, a 'Grove' of trees and beautiful walks, and a library full of books. But the heart of the project consisted of seven enormous colleges, each one pursuing its own subject. Such an undertaking, Kelsall was clear, would be expensive. It would also need plenty of space. 'For the situation of the new University,' he concluded, 'let a healthy and cheerful spot be chosen in the county of Stafford; and let the silver Trent mæander at the end of the University Grove.'[14]

Although his book was unique in its scale, Charles Kelsall was far from alone in proposing a new sort of university in a new sort of location teaching a new set of subjects. As Part I will show, the late-eighteenth and early-nineteenth centuries witnessed a now-forgotten welter of books, articles, and pamphlets, all of them imagining significant reforms to higher education. Small wonder; for although the world had changed—with a growing population, increasing industrialization, a new sense of globalization—Britain's university system had not.[15] England in 1814 possessed only the two universities that Kelsall decried, Oxford and Cambridge, each already 600 years old. The situation in Scotland was different, with five institutions. But the youngest of these, Edinburgh and Marischal College, Aberdeen had been established as long ago as the sixteenth century. Wales had no university of its own and Ireland had only one: Trinity College Dublin, founded in 1592.[16] Even together, these universities could educate only a tiny minority of the population—rather less than 1 per cent in England and Ireland, and a little more than 2 per cent in Scotland.

Moreover, with the exception of the Scottish foundations, which were open to all comers, entrance to each of the English and Irish institutions was restricted on the grounds of expense and belief.[17] Undergraduates at Oxford were compelled to

---

[14] Kelsall, *Phantasm*, pp. 13, 118, 127–74.

[15] See C. A. Bayly, *The Birth of the Modern World, 1780–1914* (Oxford, 2004).

[16] The best introduction to these institutions is Robert Anderson, *British Universities: past and present* (London, 2006).

[17] Confessional oaths taken by professors in Scotland were apparently unproblematic. See R. D. Anderson, *Education and Opportunity in Victorian Scotland: schools and universities* (Oxford, 1983), p. 53.

subscribe to the Church of England's statement of faith, the 39 Articles.[18] At Cambridge, all graduates were similarly expected to conform, and if they would not, they received no degree.[19] Reform in the 1790s made Trinity College Dublin, less sectarian than it had been. Yet it remained the case that Roman Catholics could not win academic prizes or, more importantly, hold any office.[20] Not everyone— not even all reformers—believed that such restrictions were problematic. Nonetheless, even conservatives acknowledged that there was a need for less expensive, less exclusive institutions.[21]

Prospective students who were excluded by their religion or lack of wealth from attendance at England's two ancient universities could go to Scotland—and some did. There were also Academies set up by Protestant Non-Conformists, which often offered a more rigorous and wide-ranging education than anything provided by the universities.[22] Some likewise looked further afield. By the second decade of the nineteenth century, there were 200 British medical students in Paris alone, whilst others attended German universities.[23] One traveller in 1819 found that 10 per cent of students at Göttingen and nearly a quarter of those at Würzburg were foreigners, many of them British.[24] Yet, as we will see, the cheaper, less exclusive Scottish universities were not without their critics, and the Dissenting Academies were, in many respects, struggling to maintain momentum.[25] Both sorts of institution found it hard to keep up with new intellectual developments, and each was increasingly the subject of complaint.[26] Moreover, although a foreign education remained attractive throughout the nineteenth century, not everyone could or would take advantage of it.[27]

Charles Kelsall believed that he had solved all these problems—and there are hints that some others agreed. Across the Atlantic James Madison did indeed send his copy of the *Phantasm* to Thomas Jefferson as he designed the University of Virginia.[28] The book may also have later helped shape the layout of Cornell in New

---

[18] L. S. Sutherland and L. G. Mitchell, eds, *The History of the University of Oxford: vol. v, the eighteenth century* (Oxford, 1986).
[19] Peter Searby, *A History of the University of Cambridge: vol. iii, 1750–1870* (Cambridge, 1997).
[20] R. B. McDowell and D. A. Webb, *Trinity College, Dublin, 1592–1952: an academic history* (1982; Dublin, 2002).
[21] Asa Briggs, 'Oxford and Its Critics, 1800–1835', in M. G. Brock and M. C. Curthoys, eds, *The History of the University of Oxford: vol. vi, nineteenth-century Oxford, part 1* (Oxford, 1997), pp. 134–46.
[22] H. McLachlan, *English Education Under the Test Acts: being the history of the Non-Conformist academies, 1662–1820* (Manchester, 1931); J. W. Ashley Smith, *The Birth of Modern Education: the contribution of the Dissenting Academies, 1660–1800* (London, 1954).
[23] Charles Singer and S. W. F. Holloway, 'Early Medical Education in Relation to the Pre-History of London University', *Medical History* 4 (1960), pp. 1–17, p. 1.
[24] Thomas Hodgskin, *Travels in the North of Germany* (London, 1820), pp. 290–1.
[25] Though see Boyd Hilton, *A Mad, Bad, and Dangerous People? England, 1783–1846* (Oxford, 2006), p. 169.
[26] Anderson, *Education and Opportunity*, p. 32.
[27] See, for example, the religious links brought out in Keith Robbins, *Foreign Encounters: English Congregationalism, Germany and the United States c.1850–c.1914* (London, 2006).
[28] William B. O'Neal, *Jefferson's Fine Arts Library for the University of Virginia* (Charlottesville, 1956), p. 15. On the university design, see Mary N. Woods, 'Thomas Jefferson and the University of

York State.²⁹ Kelsall himself claimed credit for the foundation of the University of London.³⁰ But, in reality, neither this, nor any other British university owed anything to his grandiose plans. The biggest impact that the *Phantasm* had in Kelsall's home country was to irritate Lord Byron with the predictably poor poem in his honour that it contained.³¹ For all Kelsall's optimism and enthusiasm, it is categorically clear that no one—absolutely no one—expected to see the *Phantasm* realized in stone, much less in Staffordshire.³²

In part, this was a product of Kelsall's own isolation. As a dilettante traveller, he was scarcely in a position to influence the sorts of people who could make his *Phantasm* a reality. In part, it was due to his utopianism. The new institutions that actually emerged in the decades immediately after he wrote owed little to the ambitious, state-sponsored sort of reforms Kelsall imagined. Rather, they were the product of private enterprise. Some founders were staunch reformers; others conservatives of the deepest Tory-blue hue. Almost all were members of a newly emergent and increasingly ambitious middle class—or sought to serve that important new demographic. They tended to be urban, too; or at least to recognize that the real need for higher education was in the towns; and so Kelsall's vision of a rural idyll similarly did not fit with their lives or their ideals.

But this does not mean that Kelsall or his book should be dismissed or ignored, as they have been by almost all subsequent writers on the subject. His enthusiasm for change is noteworthy, as is his belief that educational and architectural reform would need to be coupled together. Indeed, with hindsight, it would turn out that he was too modest in his ambitions. The university he imagined would be dwarfed by the institutions that were eventually built all across the country. Kelsall envisaged a site of 77 acres. By the mid-twentieth century, this was less than half the 200-acre minimum that universities had come to expect.³³ The variety of architectural styles Kelsall sought to inspire would also be replicated in these big new campuses—though, as we will see, this was not quite in the way that he had expected, or their own founders had hoped.

For all his oddness, then, Kelsall provides a useful *entrée* into the world of new universities which was inaugurated at the turn of the nineteenth century. What he does not do—what he could not be expected to have done—is to envisage the Redbrick universities which were the ultimate consequence of this debate. What, though, was Redbrick? What did it—indeed, what does it—mean? It was not a term used by Kelsall or his contemporaries. As a general description it dates, very

---

Virginia: planning the academic village', *Journal of the Society of Architectural Historians* 44 (1985), pp. 266–83.

²⁹ Kermit C. Parsons, 'The Quad on the Hill: an account of the first buildings at Cornell', *Journal of the Society of Architectural Historians* 22 (1963), pp. 199–216.

³⁰ Morden College, 'Post Obit Memorial addressed to the Trustees of Morden College by Charles Kelsall' (December 1844). See also his notes in his own copy of the *Phantasm* kept at the College.

³¹ Morden College, Kelsall's copy of *The Works of Lord Byron* (London, 1837) contains a note to that effect.

³² David Watkin, *Thomas Hope and the Neo-Classical Idea* (London, 1968), pp. 77, 82.

³³ William Holford, *Proposals for the Development of a Site for the University of Liverpool* (Liverpool, 1949), p. 8.

precisely, from the summer of 1943, when Faber and Faber published a book called *Redbrick University*.[34] This was an instant *cause célèbre*, not least because its author concealed his identity behind the pseudonym Bruce Truscot.[35] For those who were not in on the secret—and only very few were—identifying Truscot and the university he described became a subject of real fascination.[36] The author was in fact Edgar Allison Peers, professor of Spanish at Liverpool, a deeply idiosyncratic but nonetheless major scholar. Possessed with the manner of a public school headmaster, he combined a profound knowledge of Hispanic literature, especially Spanish mysticism, with an admirable practicality.[37] When his annual summer school in San Sebastiàn was threatened by the start of the Spanish Civil War, for example, he simply arranged for the British navy to provide a destroyer which collected the students involved.[38] This was not the sort of man who would disguise his identity simply out of a desire to intrigue or to avoid offending his colleagues. Rather, as 'Bruce Truscot' later explained, *Redbrick University* was intended to describe all of Britain's 'modern' universities: Leeds as much as Liverpool; Manchester as much as Leeds; Birmingham, Bristol, Sheffield, and Reading as much as Manchester.[39] By refusing to name one, he hoped to imply all of those institutions founded in the nineteenth and made universities in the first half of the twentieth century. Truscot's subject was, in other words, what other authors would have called the civic university.

It is the rise of this new sort of institution that *Redbrick* seeks to explore. But whilst Peers concentrated his attention on the English nineteenth-century foundations he knew so well, this book will go further. It will trace the pre-history of debates about higher education: exploring the ways in which developments in London and across the British Empire made possible the creation of new universities in the great manufacturing centres of England. It will also examine other, failed experiments as well as going on to outline how the civic university tradition evolved after 1943. Redbrick, it will argue, was the single biggest influence on the creation of new universities in the 1950s and 1960s. It, too, was the model to which the polytechnics—originally envisaged as a rival system—came to cleave. Moreover, this is not just a story about England. Although the majority of new foundations were established there, the creation of new universities in Ireland in the 1840s and Wales in the 1880s is an integral part of the development—or series

---

[34] Though the Birmingham Guild of Students' newspaper, *Red Brick*, predates this, having been founded in 1936.
[35] LivUA, D265/1/2, Letters to Bruce Truscot.
[36] Ann L. Mackenzie, 'Introduction', to E. Allison Peers, *Redbrick University Revisited*, ed. Ann L. Mackenzie and Adrian R. Allen (Liverpool, 1996), pp. 1–34, pp. 2–5; H. C. Dent, 'Bruce Truscot', *Universities Quarterly* 7 (1952–3), pp. 326–32, p. 326. More generally, see Harold Silver, 'The Universities' Speaking Conscience: "Bruce Truscot" and Redbrick university', *History of Education* 28 (1999), p. 173–89.
[37] Though see Tom Buchanan, *Britain and the Spanish Civil War* (Cambridge, 1997), pp. 151–2, for Peers' misreading of the Spanish Civil War.
[38] LivUA, D265/3/2/3, Amy Hollins, 'Recollections involving Professor E. Allison Peers'; D265/3/2/4, Patrick Nield, 'When Adam Walked in Eden Young. Personal Reminiscences of E. Allison Peers'.
[39] 'Bruce Truscot', *Red Brick University* (London, 1951), p. 16. For his definition of 'modern university', see 'Bruce Truscot', *Red Brick University* (London, 1943), p. 16.

of developments—that this book seeks to explore. Even in Scotland, where the pre-existence of a handful of universities meant that the evolution of higher education was rather different and the number of new institutions rather fewer, Redbrick had its effect. The creation of a university for Dundee, for instance, exemplifies all the idealism that Redbrick inspired in dozens of cities across Britain—an idealism that would change British education, and help to change Britain itself.

In the 1920s prime minister Stanley Baldwin confidently claimed that the civic universities were a development 'which historians of the future would regard as a Renaissance . . . as genuine and as pregnant in its possibilities as the Renaissance of the fifteenth century'.[40] Nor was Baldwin wholly absurd in making this claim. By the start of the twentieth century Redbrick had indeed transformed the intellectual and social life of the country: providing access to university for those who had previously been excluded by their class, beliefs, or gender; taking higher education to places which would otherwise not have encountered it. They would, as this book seeks to show, continue to do so.

As it turned out, Baldwin was too sanguine in his predictions. This has become an almost forgotten revolution, a Renaissance that nobody now notices. In reality, almost nothing has been made of this history; almost no one has sought to tell this story.[41] Since Baldwin spoke and Truscot wrote, indeed, there has only been a single book devoted to the subject as whole: Harry Armytage's *Civic Universities: aspects of a British tradition*—a cheerful romp through a thousand years of history—published as long ago as 1955.[42] Instead of Redbrick, historians have been obsessed with Oxbridge: studying England's ancient universities and tending to ignore Britain's alternative history of higher education.[43] Although individual institutions have inspired some important studies, the significance of the civic universities as a whole has been downplayed.[44] Worse still, this remarkably single-minded focus on Oxford and Cambridge has had a disastrous effect on those few historians who have dealt with the civic universities, and who have tended to conclude that Redbrick

---

[40] Quoted in H. J. W. Hetherington, 'The History and Significance of the Modern Universities', in Hugh Martin, ed., *The Life of the Modern University* (London, 1930), pp. 9–20, p. 12.

[41] Though the foundation of three of the universities is discussed in David R. Jones, *The Origins of Civic Universities: Manchester, Leeds, and Liverpool* (London, 1988). See also Brian Simon, *The Two Nations and the Educational Structure, 1780–1870* (London, 1974); Anderson, *British Universities*; Michael Sanderson, 'The English Civic Universities and the "Industrial Spirit", 1870–1914', *Historical Research* 61 (1988), pp. 90–104; Michael Shattock, 'The Transformation of the Civic Universities', *History of Education* 31 (2002), pp. 623–34, for some other aspects of this tradition.

[42] W. H. Armytage, *Civic Universities: aspects of a British tradition* (London, 1955). Though see Roy Lowe, 'The Changing Role of the Academic Journal: the coverage of higher education in *History of Education* as a case study, 1972–2011', *History of Education* 41 (2012), pp. 103–15, p. 106, for a more optimistic view of its impact.

[43] Oxford has an 8-volume official history; Cambridge has 4 volumes. But there are numerous unofficial histories, most recently G. R. Evans, *The University of Cambridge: a new history* (London, 2009) and *The University of Oxford: a new history* (London, 2010).

[44] See, for example, Eric Ives, Diane Drummond, and Leonard Schwartz, *The First Civic University: Birmingham, 1880–1980* (Birmingham, 2000); Thomas Kelly, *For Advancement of Learning: the University of Liverpool, 1881–1981* (Liverpool, 1981); Helen Mathers, *Steel City Scholars: the centenary history of the University of Sheffield* (London, 2005).

was nothing more than a pale and failed imitation of Oxbridge.[45] This book will argue otherwise. It will not only outline the history of the civic universities, but also seek to demonstrate their distinctiveness; to argue that we must take the Redbricks every bit as seriously as Armytage, Truscot, and for that matter Stanley Baldwin suggested we should.

This book is thus not only the first history of the civic universities for sixty years. It is also an attempt to present a rather different account from that suggested by previous writers. Part I examines the debate that Kelsall contributed to, and draws attention to the numerous new institutions founded and proposed between 1783 and 1843. It looks at the important links which bound together contemporary religious and political debates with the foundation of universities: something that can be seen from Canada to India, and which was especially evident in the creation of a new university for London. In the next part, which explores the period from 1843 to 1880, we will see that religious controversy was never very far away from discussion about universities, but that increasingly new foundations were the product of civic rather than denominational rivalry. The next two parts, which discuss the development of these institutions from 1880 to 1949, cover a time which many historians have seen as witnessing the decline and fall of Redbrick.[46] In fact, I shall argue, it was precisely in these years that the new civic universities established their identity and consolidated their distinctive way of university life. Part V thus explores the implications of this in the post-war period, not least by demonstrating the ways in which the Redbrick tradition influenced the development of higher education more broadly. In Part VI, we will trace the story between the mid-1970s to the mid-1990s: an era of expansive and remarkable change, but also some intriguing continuities; an age, which for all its difficulties, saw the final triumph of the civic university model. Finally, in an epilogue, I will explain how the last two decades of continued evolution have not only reshaped higher education, but also—however surprisingly—re-emphasized the continued centrality of Redbrick to the British understanding and experience of the university.

In writing such a history, I have necessarily drawn on a wide variety of sources. Indeed, I have travelled hundreds of miles and read thousands of pages of evidence, exploring everything from buildings to books; from photographs to apparently intractable sets of annual accounts. I have visited scores of institutions, surveyed their sites, and used documents ranging from the numerous official publications issued by government to the *samizdat* leaflets produced by rebellious students. I have mined the archives of organizations like the Committee of Vice Chancellors and Principals, the National Union of Students, and the Association of University

---

[45] Elizabeth J. Morse, 'English Civic Universities and the Myth of Decline', *History of Universities* 9 (1992), pp. 177–204; Sarah V. Barnes, 'England's Civic Universities and the Triumph of the Oxbridge Ideal', *History of Education Quarterly* 36 (1996), pp. 271–305; A. H. Halsey, 'Oxford and the British Universities', in Brian Harrison, ed., *The History of the University of Oxford: vol. viii, the twentieth century* (Oxford, 1994), pp. 577–606. See also T. W. Heyck, 'The Idea of a University in Britain, 1870–1970', *History of European Ideas* 8 (1987), pp. 205–19.

[46] See, for example, Halsey, 'Oxford and the British Universities', and Morse, 'English Civic Universities'.

Teachers, as well as more international bodies, including the Association of Commonwealth Universities, and more official outfits, like the University Grants Committee. Above all, I have been especially keen to exploit the archival holdings of the universities themselves—and pursued a method of sampling intended to produce a representative range of institutions.

This meant exploring the archives of the first wave of foundations: places like Birmingham, Bristol, Dundee, Leeds, Liverpool, Manchester, Reading, and Sheffield; as well as papers from the early years of the University of London. It also meant examining material held by a second tranche of universities which were chartered in the first half of the twentieth century: Exeter, Leicester, Nottingham, and Southampton. From the post-Second World War period, I selected Essex, Keele, Sussex, and—as representatives of the technological universities established in the 1960s—Loughborough and Salford. For the polytechnics, I used materials held by De Montfort, Birmingham City, and Oxford Brookes. Very often, I have been the only researcher using the archives of the institution I was studying. At several universities, I was the very first person ever to consult their records. In one, they bought a brand-new visitor's book to mark the occasion.

Such an approach differs markedly from any previous study of the universities, most of which utilize the holdings of a single institution or organization; and many of which rely almost entirely on materials already in the public domain.[47] My approach to these sources is also, I hope, original. This book is not an administrative history, except inasmuch as administrative structures helped to mould university life.[48] Nor is it an intellectual history; though, of course, developments in the history of thought necessarily helped to shape the institutions in question.[49] Rather, it is an attempt to go beyond these more well-trodden topics: to escape, in Anthony Grafton's memorable phrase, 'the clouds of flatulent rhetoric in which administrators hide like squids projecting ink; the taciturnity of teachers and students about just what they do all day in study and classroom'.[50] In seeking to understand civic universities in the round, this is instead a social and architectural history. Both terms deserve some further explanation.

---

[47] Recent exceptions include Caroline M. Hoefferle, *British Student Activism in the Long Sixties* (New York and London, 2013) and Michael Shattock, *Making Policy in British Higher Education, 1945–2011* (Buckingham, 2012), though they cover a very much shorter period and do not explore such a variety of sources.

[48] For exemplary administrative histories, see for example, F. M. G. Willson, *Our Minerva: the men and politics of the University of London, 1836–58* (London, 1995); John Carswell, *Government and the Universities in Britain: programme and performance, 1960–1980* (Cambridge, 1985); and the many works of Michael Shattock listed in the Bibliography.

[49] See, for example, Michael J. Hofstetter, *The Romantic Idea of the University in England and Germany, 1770–1850* (Basingstoke, 2001); Frank M. Turner, ed., *The Idea of the University: John Henry Newman* (New Haven and London, 1996); and the important works of Sheldon Rothblatt, especially his *The Modern University and Its Discontents: the fate of Newman's legacies in Britain and America* (Cambridge, 1997).

[50] Anthony Grafton, 'Civic Humanism and Scientific Scholarship at Leiden', in Thomas Bender, ed., *The University and the City: from medieval origins to the present* (New York and Oxford, 1988), pp. 59–78, p. 60.

This is a social history in three respects. In the first place it approaches universities as societies in their own right; the word university, after all, means just that: a society. More than this, universities, as Pierre Bourdieu has shown, produce cultures that are every bit as complex as any other society, and they deserve to be studied with the same seriousness and attention to detail.[51] The following chapters will explore the divisions within these societies—divisions of gender, discipline, class, and much else besides—as well as exploring common experiences and the growth of a wider Redbrick culture. It will also—again, following the cue provided by Bourdieu—consider the extent to which the civic universities reproduced existing social structures.[52] These were bourgeois universities from the first. *Redbrick* will show that they have, on the whole, remained faithful to their origins and thereby encouraged their imitators, more newly-established institutions like the former polytechnics, to become ever-more middle class themselves.

As this suggests, in the second place, this book seeks to place Redbrick within a wider social history, relating developments in higher education to life beyond the academy. However much they may be seen and sometimes seek to serve as refuges from the 'real world', universities are in fact products of the environment in which they work: linked to it by strong, but by no means simple, political, economic, and cultural ties.[53] As Lawrence Stone observed forty years ago, the interaction between the university and society is 'one of the most potentially illuminating, but most practically obscure, aspects of the process of historical change'.[54] This is particularly the case when one considers the question of government involvement in higher education. The conventional account of British higher education is one that sees the state as an essentially absent figure in the nineteenth century, becoming ever more engaged—indeed, becoming the central determinant of university life—in the second half of the twentieth century.[55] By focusing on the civic universities, however, this book will show not just that the state was involved and often highly *dirigiste* long before most commentators have noticed it; but also that more recent developments which have often been attributed solely to executive fiat were actually the outcome of pressures on government, not least from the universities themselves.

Thirdly, and perhaps above all, this is a social history in terms rather similar to those recently outlined by Patrick Joyce: one that sees the social as something 'performed by material things just as much as by humans'.[56] It was Bruno Latour, in his *Reassembling the Social*, who used the university lecture room as a classic—though 'trivial enough'—example of the sort of 'structure' which helped shape

---

[51] Pierre Bourdieu, *Homo Academicus*, trans. Peter Collier (Cambridge, 1988); *The State Nobility: elite schools in the field of power*, trans. Lauretta C. Clough (Cambridge, 1996).

[52] Pierre Bourdieu and Jean-Claude Passeron, *Reproduction in Education, Society and Culture*, trans. Richard Nice (2nd edn; London, 1977).

[53] For an exemplary set of reflections on this theme, see Thomas Bender, ed., *The University and the City: from medieval origins to the present* (New York and Oxford, 1988).

[54] Lawrence Stone, 'Introduction to Vols. I & II', in Lawrence Stone, ed., *The University in Society* (2 vols; London, 1975), vol. i, pp. v–vii, p. v.

[55] Brian Salter and Ted Tapper, *The State and Higher Education* (London, 1994).

[56] Patrick Joyce, 'What is the Social in Social History?', *Past and Present* 206 (2010), pp. 213–48, p. 227.

individual and social behaviour.[57] This is an undeniably intriguing invitation to further research for any historian of higher education. Although the idea that buildings are 'actors', somehow capable of agency, is a problematic—indeed, an objectionable—one, the notion that the social is constituted by things as well as people informs the whole of this book.[58]

As an architectural history, too, *Redbrick* is intended to achieve three ends. Most obviously, it is designed to draw attention to a neglected field of research.[59] The university as a built environment has very rarely been the subject of serious discussion by architectural historians: strikingly it was one of the categories wholly disregarded by Nikolaus Pevsner in his *History of Building Types*, for example.[60] When universities have been studied, they have been valued for the ways in which they exhibit 'a special kind of physical coherence and continuity',[61] a 'lucid, connected whole'.[62] The civic universities, which often display no such coherence and which seem, to the unsympathetic, 'often indistinguishable' from other public buildings, do not live up to these ideals.[63] For many historians, the civic universities have consequently not been worth studying because their architecture is not thought to be either distinctive or distinguished enough.[64] Encountering the University of Liverpool—Truscot's original Redbrick—in 1969, Pevsner observed that 'The whole is not a whole but a zoo, with species after species represented.'[65] Such an attitude has understandably discouraged those writers on university architecture who are, in their own words, 'in search of perfection'.[66]

Yet to turn away from the physical form of Redbrick because it is not a coherent whole means ignoring an extraordinarily rich seam of evidence about British universities. These sites are a sort of palimpsest, overwritten by each generation's attempt to build a new sort of institution. Master plan follows master plan, building follows building. At Birmingham alone, there were at least half a dozen different campus layouts proposed between 1925 and 1957. None of them was ever satisfactorily completed.[67] At Leeds, successive plans from the foundation onwards sought to hide, replace, or demolish what had been built before, as new needs, new fashions, and new beliefs about the university rendered the existing fabric

---

[57] Bruno Latour, *Reassembling the Social: an introduction to actor-network-theory* (Oxford, 2005), pp. 194–5.

[58] On this, see William Whyte 'What Can Buildings Do?', lecture at the Buildings in Society International Conference, Queen's University, Belfast, June 2014.

[59] Though see Martin Pearce, *University Builders* (Chichester, 2001), pp. 11–12.

[60] Nikolaus Pevsner, *A History of Building Types* (London, 1976). See also Susie Harries, *Nikolaus Pevsner: the life* (London, 2011), p. 715.

[61] Turner, *Campus*, p. 304.

[62] Jonathan Coulson, Paul Roberts, and Isabelle Taylor, *University Planning and Architecture: the search for perfection* (Abingdon, 2011), p. 237. See also, Thomas A. Gaines, *The Campus as a Work of Art* (London, 1991).

[63] Gaines, *The Campus as a Work of Art*, p. 20.

[64] Laurence Brockliss, 'Gown and Town: the university and the city in Europe, 1200–2000', *Minerva* 38 (2000), pp. 147–70, pp. 161–4.

[65] Nikolaus Pevsner, quoted in Joseph Sharples, *Liverpool* (New Haven and London, 2004), p. 214.

[66] Coulson et al., *University Planning and Architecture*.

[67] Ives et al., *The First Civic University*, pp. 430–40.

apparently obsolete.⁶⁸ By studying these plans and the changes of mind that they reveal, we can learn how the civic universities imagined themselves and sought to realize these dreams in concrete reality.

Redbrick is thus, secondly, an exploration of how architects and their clients sought to provide buildings which not only solved practical problems but also gave physical expression to an institution's ideals. The notion that a university's identity could be embodied in its architecture is one that runs throughout the period covered by this book. It was present in the ancient universities, especially Oxford and Cambridge; and it also shaped buildings and plans for the newer, civic institutions.⁶⁹ It is captured in this volume's epigraph, taken from a poem delivered by the poet laureate John Masefield at the University of Sheffield in 1946,⁷⁰ and it can be seen in comments made by writers as varied as the nineteenth-century historian Thomas Macaulay and the twentieth-century social reformer William Beveridge.⁷¹ Yet despite this remarkable consensus across time, no book has ever attempted to explore its implications.⁷² Indeed, on those rare occasions when the architecture of the civic universities has been discussed, Redbrick has tended to be dismissed either as an architectural imitation of Oxbridge or, worse still, as an institution with no distinctive architecture of its own.⁷³

This is also an architectural history in a third, rather different sense. 'Architectural history,' as J Mordaunt Crook has observed, 'is a fairly new discipline; the social history of architecture is newer still'.⁷⁴ *Redbrick* is a contribution to that newer discipline. It is an attempt to write not (as most architectural historians do) simply about the production of buildings, but also about their use and reuse, and about the ways in which architecture was reinterpreted and reshaped by those who

---

⁶⁸ William Whyte, 'The Modernist Moment at the University of Leeds, 1957–1977', *Historical Journal* 51 (2008), pp. 169–93.

⁶⁹ I have explored this theme in nineteenth- and twentieth-century Oxford and Cambridge in my *Oxford Jackson: architecture, education, status and style, 1835–1924* (Oxford, 2006), ch. 3 and 5 and in '"A pastiche or a packing case": building in twentieth-century Oxford and Cambridge', *Twentieth-Century Architecture* 11 (2013), pp. 16–29.

⁷⁰ John Masefield, *There are Few Earthly Things More Splendid than a University* (Providence, RI, 1969).

⁷¹ See, for example, [T. B. Macaulay], *Edinburgh Review* 43 (1826), pp. 315–41, p. 316; William Beveridge, *The Physical Relation of a University to a City* (London, 1928). See also Albert Sloman, *A University in the Making* (London, 1963), p. 68.

⁷² Though for some examples from London, see Margaret Birney Vickery, *Buildings for Bluestockings: the architecture and social history of women's colleges in late Victorian England* (London, 2000); J. Mordaunt Crook, 'The Architectural Image', in F. M. L. Thompson, ed., *The University of London and the World of Learning, 1836–1986* (London, 1990), pp. 1–34. The University of Nottingham and both universities in Leicester also have architectural histories of their own: Peter Fawcett and Neil Jackson, *Campus Critique: the architecture of the University of Nottingham* (Nottingham, 1998); Arthur Lyons, *The Architecture of the Universities of Leicester* (Leicester, 2010).

⁷³ R. A. Lowe and Rex Knight, 'Building the Ivory Tower: the social functions of late-nineteenth-century collegiate architecture', *Studies in Higher Education* 7 (1982), pp. 81–91; Sarah V. Barnes, 'Lessons in Stone: architecture and academic ethos in an urban setting', in Debra N. Mancroft and D. J. Trela, eds, *Victorian Urban Settings: essays on the nineteenth-century city and its contexts* (New York and London, 1996), pp. 214–29.

⁷⁴ J. Mordaunt Crook, *The Rise of the Nouveaux Riches: style and status in Victorian and Edwardian Architecture* (London: John Murray, 1999), p. 2.

inhabited it.[75] In that sense, it is closer to the work of archaeologists,[76] or historians and theorists of science,[77] than it is to much of what is currently described as architectural history—although it is perhaps similar to the social and architectural history of Cambridge University that Robert Willis took up, and then abandoned, in the 1840s.[78] Nonetheless, such an approach is even distinct from the pioneering books on the architecture of American universities produced by writers like Paul Venable Turner and Helen Lefkowitz Horowitz. Turner, like most architectural historians, outlines a story about design rather than seeking to explore how buildings were used.[79] Horowitz, still more tellingly, divides her account into two separate volumes: one on design and the other on student life.[80] This book, by contrast, attempts to explore the links between both.

What unites these two strands of social and architectural history is an understanding of the university as a place.[81] As Christopher Driver once put it: 'Universities are, before anything else, places: populated packages of bricks and concrete and Gothic mouldings and flowering shrubs, set down in a particular park, suburb, or city, at the bidding of a particular civilisation, to grow up in their own way.'[82] This is particularly true of British universities, for, as Sheldon Rothblatt has observed, it is in Britain that the notion of the university as 'a *place* for the dissemination of universal learning' has had an especial purchase.[83] It is also true

---

[75] On the social history of architecture, see Dana Arnold, *Reading Architectural History* (London and New York, 2002), pp. 127–42. Mark Girouard, *Life in the English Country House: a social and architectural history* (New Haven and London, 1978) provides a wonderful example of a somewhat similar approach. See also his *Town and Country* (New Haven and London, 1992), pp. 9–10.

[76] Laurie Wilkie, *The Lost Boys of Zeta Psi: a historical archaeology of masculinity at a university fraternity* (Berkeley, 2010).

[77] Thomas F. Gieryn, 'What Buildings Do', *Theory and Society* 31 (2002), pp. 35–74; Crosbie Smith and Jon Agar, eds, *Making Space for Science: territorial themes in the shaping of knowledge* (Basingstoke, 1998), pp. 149–80; Albena Yaneva, 'Is the Atrium More Important than the Lab? Designer buildings for new cultures of creativity', in Peter Meusberger, David N. Livingstone, and Heike Jöns, eds, *Geographies of Science* (Loughborough, 2010), pp. 19–50. The work of Sophie Forgan has been extremely important for this project: see especially her 'The Architecture of Science and the Idea of a University', *Studies in the History and Philosophy of Science* 20 (1989), pp. 405–34; 'Bricks and Bones: architecture and science in Victorian Britain', in Peter Galison and Emily Thompson, eds, *The Architecture of Science* (Cambridge, MA, and London, 1999), pp. 181–208; and with Graeme Gooday, 'Constructing South Kensington: the buildings and politics of T. H. Huxley's working environments', *British Journal for the History of Science* 29 (1986), pp. 435–68.

[78] Alexandrina Buchanan, *Robert Willis and the Foundation of Architectural History* (Woodbridge, 2013), p. 343.

[79] Paul Venable Turner, *Campus: an American planning tradition* (Cambridge, MA, and London, 1984).

[80] Helen Lefkowitz Horowitz, *Alma Mater: design and experience in the women's college from their nineteenth-century beginnings to the 1930s* (Boston, 1984); *Campus Life: undergraduate cultures from the eighteenth century to the present* (Chicago, 1988).

[81] Alan R. H. Baker, *Geography and History: bridging the divide* (Cambridge, 2003), pp. 67–8. For a recent book which provides a marvellous example of a historian taking place very seriously, see Alexandra Walsham, *The Reformation of the Landscape: religion, identity, and memory in early-modern Britain and Ireland* (Oxford, 2011). I must also acknowledge the influence of Oliver Zimmer's work on my thinking. See his *Remaking the Rhythms of Life: German communities in the age of the nation state* (Oxford, 2013).

[82] Christopher Driver, *The Exploding University* (London, 1971), p. 25.

[83] Sheldon Rothblatt, *The Modern University and Its Discontents: the fate of Newman's legacies in Britain and America* (Cambridge, 1997), p. 53.

in a more general sense. Indeed, for the geographer Robert Sacks, 'universities are the archetypal place for the creation of meaning and the search for truth'.[84] Yet although this truth has been all but universally acknowledged, little analytical use has been made of it by historians.[85] It remains the case, in the words of the philosopher Edward Casey, that 'no systematic effort has been made to account for the indispensability of place in the evolution and presentation of cultural institutions'; even though, as he goes on to argue, culture 'exists more concretely and completely in places than in minds or signs'.[86]

Instead of focusing on place, most previous writers have conceived of the university as an institution characterized by a 'sort of placelessness and abstraction';[87] not a distinct locale, but an intangible idea.[88] Indeed, John Henry Newman's lectures on *The Idea of the University*, given in Dublin in the 1850s, have become the touchstone for contemporary debate about higher education, quoted—often wildly out of context—by almost everyone who has something to say about universities.[89] Newman's thought is indeed hugely interesting and creative and worth further exploration.[90] Yet although he himself did not ignore the importance of place in his disquisition, subsequent readers have disregarded this part of his work, and focused only on the philosophical claims that he made.[91] This has had the unfortunate effect of reifying the university—making a mental construct fixed and apparently unchangeable, turning it from a real place into an imagined idea. Little wonder, then, that writers on higher education are prone to nostalgia and the search for a lost golden age of the university.[92] Little wonder, too, that there is a constant sense that the university is in crisis, failing to live up to this exalted, fixed, and fictive idea.[93]

---

[84] Robert David Sack, *Homo Geographicus: a framework for action, awareness, and moral concern* (Baltimore and London, 1997), p. 69.

[85] Krishnan Kumar, 'The Need for Place', in Anthony Smith and Frank Webster, *The Postmodern University? Contested visions of higher education in society* (Buckingham, 1997), pp. 27–35; Frances Halsband, 'Campuses in Place', *Places* 17 (2005), pp. 4–11. On the role of place in the history of education more generally, see Catherine Burke, Peter Cunningham, and Ian Grosvenor, 'Putting Education in its Place: space, place, and materialities in the history of education', *History of Education* 39 (2010), pp. 677–80.

[86] Edward S. Casey, 'How to Get from Space to Place in a Fairly Short Stretch of Time: phenomenological prolegomena', in Steven Feld and Keith H. Basso, eds, *Senses of Place* (Santé Fe, NM, 1996), pp. 13–52, p. 33. See also his, *The Fate of Place: a philosophical history* (Berkeley, 1997), pp. 313, 320.

[87] Stephen C. Ferruolo, '*Parisius-Paradisus*: the city, its schools, and the origins of the University of Paris', in Bender, ed., *The University and the City*, pp. 22–46, p. 25.

[88] Thomas William Heyck, 'The Idea of a University in Britain, 1870–1970', *History of European Ideas* 8 (1987), pp. 205–19.

[89] Rothblatt, *Modern University*, ch. 1.

[90] Though see Chapter 3 for the failure of Newman's plans for a university.

[91] Frank M. Turner, ed., *The Idea of the University: John Henry Newman* (New Haven and London, 1996), pp. 77–8, 105–6.

[92] Malcolm Tight, 'The Golden Age of Academe: myth or memory?', *British Journal of Educational Studies* 58 (2010), pp. 105–16.

[93] Stefan Collini, *What Are Universities For?* (London, 2012), pp. 21, 118.

Against the messy reality of everyday life, the purity of an idea seems highly attractive. But it is also illusory—and, worse still, it conceals more than it reveals. What is the idea of a university? asks a recent writer:

> Agreeing to affirm the intrinsic values of a university is one thing; agreeing what those values are is quite another. It might be doubted whether there really is anything distinctive that universities are for: students may see them as places to escape their parents, lose their virginity, and make friends for life; parents may see them as places to fit their offspring for financial independence; researchers may see them as places to be paid to do what they want; politicians may see them as places to keep the unemployment figures down; philanthropists may see them as places to be fawned on by the same dons who treated them so superciliously when they were students. Universities are all of these things and more; are they intrinsically any one thing in particular?[94]

This is an important point. There is not, and never has been, a single idea of a university; attempts to find one are doomed to failure from the start.[95]

To think about the university as a definite place, therefore, is to do more than just state the obvious. It means analysing the university as a location: a collection of people and buildings, where staff and students, visitors and interlopers live and work as well as think.[96] Such an approach helps to reconceptualize the history of higher education: rejecting the sort of narrow taxonomies that have characterized much previous writing in favour of a more fluid, subtle approach. Redbrick was not a predetermined type of university. It evolved, often haphazardly, to become what it is and includes several different forms of legal entity.[97] Indeed, far from being the outworking of an idea, Redbrick is a different sort of place: different, both in the ways it was made and the ways it was experienced.

As this suggests, place is likewise not simply a description, a way of saying where something is. It is also about meaning: how we, as humans, make sense of the world.[98] Teachers and taught, benefactors and administrators alike all vest their environment with significance: defining their identities with things.[99] In making a university, they attempt to create *somewhere* as well as *something*.[100] Exploring place similarly enables us to uncover the ways in which universities use their sites to

---

[94] Paul Seabright, 'How to defend universities', *Times Literary Supplement*, 9 March 2012.
[95] See also Susan Howson, *Lionel Robbins* (Cambridge, 2011), p. 862.
[96] Peter Jamieson, Kenn Fisher, Tony Golding, and A. C. F. Trevitt, 'Place and Space in the Design of New Learning Environments', *Higher Education Research and Learning* 19 (2000), pp. 221–36.
[97] For a useful survey of taxonomies, see Andrew McGettigan, *The Great University Gamble: money, markets, and the future of higher education* (London, 2013), pp. 128–9.
[98] Yi-Fu Tuan, *Space and Place: the perspective of experience* (Minneapolis, 1977); David Ley, *A Social Geography of the City* (London, 1983), p. 133. See also Amos Rappoport, *The Meaning of the Built Environment: a nonverbal communication approach* (Tucson, 1990).
[99] Ira Silver, 'Role Transitions, Objects, and Identity', *Symbolic Interaction* 19 (1996), pp. 1–20; Michael Moffatt, *Coming of Age in New Jersey: college and American culture* (New Brunswick and London, 1989), pp. 79–83.
[100] William Whyte, ' "Redbrick's unlovely quadrangles": reinterpreting the architecture of the civic universities', *History of Universities*, 21 (2006) pp. 151–77. For an intriguing example of how even cartography plays into this theme, see E. Lisa Panayotidis and Paul Storz, 'Intellectual Space, Image, and Identities in the Historical University campus: Helen Kemp's map of the University of Toronto, 1932', *Journal of the Canadian Historical Association* 15 (2004), pp. 123–52.

manifest authority, expressing and reinforcing divisions of status, gender, educational attainment: excluding some, including others; preventing different groups from meeting on terms of equality. It also invites us to consider the moments when this process is challenged and overturned, with boundaries subverted or broken, as well as those occasions when hierarchies are successfully sustained and even entrenched.[101]

Looking at place, moreover, does not mean ignoring the wider world, or pursuing a narrowly parochial approach to the subject. For as the geographer Doreen Massey has most persuasively argued, to take place seriously one has to acknowledge that it does not exist in isolation, separated from developments elsewhere. Rather, it is 'constructed out of a particular constellation of social relations, meeting and weaving together at a particular locus'.[102] A university brings together people from all over the world, and even its buildings reflect influences from well beyond the immediate vicinity.[103] As one observer accurately noted in the early-1960s: 'The building of universities is almost unique in that six parties are involved. One person or firm designs for a second party to build, to the requirements of a third, for a fourth to live and work in. A fifth provides the money out of public funds and the building is maintained and reviewed by a sixth.'[104] This particular model was not always true, but the general point still stands. The university is best analysed as a place not least because it is a location in which multiple forces and a variety of people meet. In that sense, place is not marginal but central to the history of universities—especially their social and architectural history.

Finally, a focus on place also enables the historian to uncover the emotions that have been evoked by the university, especially the anxieties—social, personal, and political—they have inspired. Universities are an emotional landscape. Psychologists have shown that the transition to university life results in 'a rise in psychological disturbance' for all students.[105] The pressures of work and of socializing; the role of the university as a locus for rites of passage; the widespread fear of the future that follows undergraduate life: all this makes it an institution freighted with strong feelings. A succession of novels—not least John Williams' recently rediscovered and acclaimed *Stoner*—has sought to explore the same experience for university staff,

---

[101] See, for example, William Whyte, 'Halls of Residence at the British Civic Universities, 1870–1970', in Jane Hamlett, Lesley Hopkins, and Rebecca Preston, eds, *Residential Institutions in Britain, 1725–1950: inmates and environments* (London, 2013), pp. 155–66; Haim Yacobi, 'Academic Fortress: the case of Hebrew University on Mount Scopus, Jerusalem', in Wim Wiewal and David C. Perry, eds., *Global Universities and Urban Development* (New York, 2008), pp. 257–72.

[102] Doreen Massey, 'A Global Sense of Place', *Marxism Today* 38 (1991), pp. 24–9, p. 28.

[103] Rainer Knapas, 'An Intellectual Space: codes of early-nineteenth-century university architecture in Northern Europe', in Märtha Norrback, Kristina Ranki, Helga Robinson-Hammertsein, and Rainer Knapas, eds., *University and Nation: the university and the making of the nation in Northern Europe in the 19th and 20th centuries* (Helsinki, 1996), pp. 45–50.

[104] Christopher Reeve, '"Keele in Context": architecture and the University', *Cum Grano* 21 (December 1962), pp. 35–51, p. 43.

[105] Shirley Fisher and Bruce Hood, 'The Stress of the Transition to University: a longitudinal study of psychological disturbance, absent-mindedness and vulnerability to homesickness', *British Journal of Psychology* 78 (1987), pp. 425–41, p. 436.

whose emotional lives are framed by the place in which they work.[106] More strikingly still, throughout the two centuries and more covered by this book, fears about moral degeneration, economic decline, and social fragmentation have all been focused on the university. It has been seen sometimes as the cause and often as the solution to these wider problems. And so, people have reformed and rebuilt it again and again. The campuses *Redbrick* explores are monuments to hope and fear: the architecture of anxiety as well as of ambition.

Little wonder, then, that for all his peculiarities, Charles Kelsall is the ideal starting point for any study of the civic universities. Not only does he illustrate the ways in which his contemporaries and his successors sought to create a higher education fit for the modern world—a higher education distinctively different from that offered by the ancient universities. He also highlights the importance of place in that history. His plan may have been fantastic, but it was not an ethereal, disembodied idea of a university. For Kelsall, a university was above all else a building—or, rather, a series of buildings, in which the students would learn as much from their surroundings as they did from their lectures. It was also an institution rooted in its locality: set down in Staffordshire, by the side of the River Trent.[107] The *Phantasm of an University* is an important reminder that universities—even new universities—have a social and architectural history, a history that this book will seek to uncover.

---

[106] John Williams, *Stoner: a novel* (1963; London, 2012).
[107] Kelsall, *Phantasm*, p. 165.

PART I
1783–1843

Prologue

The conventional start to the story of Britain's modern universities is in 1825, with the first stirrings of interest in what was founded as the University of London and would eventually become University College London (UCL). And there are good reasons for beginning there. UCL, with its middle-class founders, apparently utilitarian inspiration, and ostensibly secular curriculum does represent an important innovation in higher education.[1] But this section will start somewhat earlier: in the 1780s, not the 1820s; and in New York, rather than in London. More precisely, it will begin in the burnt-out remains of Broadway at the end of the American War of Independence. For it was there, rather than in Bloomsbury, that the first British university college of the modern age—King's College Windsor—was planned (Figure 2). As its name suggests, the conservative, clerical institution that emerged from the ashes of loyalist New York was very different from the college later founded in confident, commercial, and progressive London. It was also very much less successful. But it bears examination nevertheless. It provides evidence of an alternative history of higher education—one that stresses continuities as much as change. It also helpfully situates the establishment of UCL within a wider historical picture: revealing its resemblances to other, often apparently different, foundations. Above all, the history of King's College Windsor—just as much as the history of University College London—highlights just how important higher education became to people of all political persuasions in the late-eighteenth and early-nineteenth centuries.

King's College was, of course, scarcely the first institute of higher education to be established in North America. Between the foundation of Harvard in 1636 and the creation of Brown in 1764, no fewer than nine colleges were granted Royal charters in the American colonies. A smattering of other unchartered institutions—like the future University of Delaware, established as the New London Free School in 1743—completed a pattern of higher learning, at least until the Revolution. King's was not even the first college to be founded in New York: that honour goes to another King's College, which was chartered in 1754 and eventually became Columbia University.[2] What marks King's College Windsor out from amongst these foundations is that it was always intended to be, as its statutes put it, not just a

---

[1] Brian Simon, *The Two Nations and the Educational Structure, 1780–1870* (1960; London, 1976), p. 124.
[2] Robert A. McCaughey, *Stand, Columbia: a history of Columbia University in the city of New York, 1754–2004* (New York, 2003).

Fig. 2. '*The mother of an University*': King's College Windsor in the early nineteenth century
Reproduced with the permission of the Provincial Archivist of Nova Scotia.

college, but a place which would become '*the mother of an University*'.³ Moreover, unlike these previous establishments—and even unlike the abortive attempt to create a University of Bermuda in the 1720s—this pioneering effort to found the first new university in the British Empire came just as the British Empire appeared to be collapsing.⁴ Indeed, it was brought into being precisely because the Empire was under threat.⁵

The founders of King's College were a group of ambitious Anglican clergy—and, in particular, the indomitable and upwardly-mobile Charles Inglis.⁶ Inglis came from a family of impoverished Church of Ireland ministers and in 1754 immigrated to the new world to make his fortune. Such was his poverty that he made the journey as an indentured servant, but within a decade he had attached himself to a group of New York Anglicans who were pushing hard to achieve three broad and interlinked goals.⁷ First, they wanted to establish a university in New York. In the second place, they intended to found a colonial bishopric centred on the city; indeed, they hoped that the existence of a university would reinforce the exclusive

---

³ *The Statutes, Rules and Ordinances of the University of King's College at Windsor* (Halifax, NS, 1821), p. 1.
⁴ W. H. G. Armytage, *Civic Universities: aspects of a British tradition* (London, 1955), p. 138.
⁵ Henry Roper, 'Aspects of the History of a Loyalist College: King's College, Windsor, and Nova Scotian higher education in the nineteenth century', *Anglican and Episcopal History* 60 (1991), pp. 443–59.
⁶ On Inglis, see, Brian Cuthbertson, *The First Bishop: a biography of Charles Inglis* (Halifax, NS, 1987).
⁷ Bruce E. Steiner, *Samuel Seabury, 1729–1796: a study in the high church tradition* (Athens, Ohio, 1971), p. 100.

claim of New York as the home for this first American see.[8] Thirdly, and most importantly, they intended to use both episcopacy and university alike to redefine the Anglican Church in America: providing it with real authority, and—as a coincidental benefit, no doubt—allowing them to dominate ecclesiastical life, ensuring that they obtained preferment for themselves and were able to reposition the centre of power within the Church from New England to New York.[9] To this end, they had established the exclusively Anglican King's College on Madison Avenue in 1754, and in 1771 they tried to obtain a charter for it as the first British university overseas.

It was an undeniably controversial campaign: one that provoked many Anglicans as well as outraging members of other denominations, who felt themselves unjustly excluded from the opportunities that King's College New York was intended to provide.[10] Nevertheless, the campaign for an American bishop, an American university, and jobs for the boys steadily grew in strength.[11] And as the agitation continued, so Charles Inglis steadily improved his place in society. Between 1771 and 1773, he acted as President of King's College. In 1777, he was promoted to the prestigious role of Rector at Trinity Church, Wall Street. A year later, this former semi-slave, whose family had been too poor to send him to Trinity College Dublin, was awarded an honorary doctorate by the University of Oxford.

Yet even as Charles Inglis rose, the success he and his allies hoped for receded further and further from their grasp. The year he stepped down as acting President of King's College was also the year of the Boston Tea Party. Inglis became Rector of Trinity months after the North American colonies had declared themselves independent—and he continued to agitate for the loyalist cause even after New York was taken by rebels and he was attainted for treason.[12] Far from being chartered as a university, King's College was closed in 1776 and looked as though it would never reopen.[13] As for the city itself, by the late-1770s much of it lay in ruins: no longer the prospective home for the first American bishop, but the dwelling place for thousands of refugees, all living in the makeshift and insanitary tents that made up 'Canvas Town'.[14] In the latter months of the war it became inescapably apparent that all the hopes of these ambitious Anglican loyalists were doomed. There would be no university, no episcopacy, and no future for them in the new and independent United States. They were threatened with treason trials, the confiscation of their property, and the loss of their livelihoods. Although Charles Inglis struggled to hang on in New York, the peace treaty between the

---

[8] McCaughey, *Stand, Columbia*, pp. 14–15.
[9] Steiner, *Seabury*, pp. 99, 101.
[10] David C. Humphrey, *From King's College to Columbia, 1746–1800* (New York, 1976), pp. 71, 140.
[11] Humphrey, *From King's College to Columbia*, p. 151.
[12] Charles Inglis, *Letters of Papinian* (New York, 1779), *The Duty of Honouring the King* (New York, 1780).
[13] McCaughey, *Stand, Columbia*, p. 50.
[14] Edwin G. Burrows and Mike Wallace, *Gotham: a history of New York City to 1898* (New York, 1999), p. 251. See also Benjamin L. Carp, 'The Night the Yankees Burned Broadway: the New York City Fire of 1776', *Early American Studies* 4 (2006), pp. 471–511.

rebels and the British sealed his fate. By 1783, his only hope was to escape, and on 21 October he preached his last sermon, setting sail a few days later.[15]

This ignominious end to the New York loyalists' plans did not, however, stop them plotting. Even as they deliberated on their escape, they envisaged new ways of bringing higher learning and High Church theology to North America. Indeed, they came to believe that the Revolution only strengthened their claims. The need for a new sort of university—one which would teach nothing 'repugnant to the constitution of Great Britain as a monarchy'—was, to them, self-evident. It was the existence of colleges in America which had failed to inculcate these teachings, they argued, that had 'proved one of the most obvious and immediate causes of the subversion of that happy system by which the country was so eminently blest'.[16] In March and again in October 1783, Inglis was amongst those who petitioned the British government for support to develop a loyalist university in Nova Scotia. Ever optimistic, and always on the make, Inglis and his allies looked on this new New York as an opportunity to start again, avoiding the errors that had plunged the old New World into chaos. To that end, they reasserted the importance of a North American Established Church, bishop, and university. On 18 October 1783, just days before Inglis finally fled Manhattan, his name led the list of five clergymen who wrote to the British government urging the need for a new and loyalist college.[17]

Charles Inglis reiterated these points in a pamphlet of 1786 and, although the government did not immediately pick up on the idea, there were some encouraging signs that people were starting to listen.[18] At the same time, the pamphleteer William Knox and the bishop of Salisbury, Shute Barrington, each precisely echoed the words of Inglis' letter of three years before, calling for the creation of colleges in Nova Scotia that would 'diffuse Literature, Loyalty, and good Morals among the colonists'.[19] Moreover, in 1787, a diminutive King's College was in fact established in Fredericton, New Brunswick; though it remained essentially nothing more than a school for decades.[20] That August, after much wrangling, Inglis finally achieved two of his goals: at one and the same time ensuring the establishment of a bishopric in Nova Scotia and, still more gratifyingly, being elevated to the see himself. It could not be long before he achieved his third, interlinked ambition—the creation of an Anglican university. Indeed, in 1789, the Nova Scotia Assembly passed an Act

[15] Maya Jasanoff, *Liberty's Exiles: the loss of America and the remaking of the British empire* (London, 2011), pp. 147–51.
[16] 'E. P.', 'A Plan of Religious and Literary Institution for the Province of Nova Scotia' (8 March 1783), in 'King's College and Episcopate in Nova Scotia', *Collections of the Nova Scotia Historical Society* 6 (1887–8), pp. 123–35, pp. 125–30, p. 129.
[17] Letter to Sir Guy Carleton (18 October 1783), in 'King's College and Episcopate in Nova Scotia', pp. 123–4, p. 123.
[18] Cuthbertson, *First Bishop*, p. 138.
[19] William Knox, quoted in Judith Fingard, *The Anglican Design in Loyalist Nova Scotia, 1783–1816* (London, 1972), p. 149. See also, pp. 150–1.
[20] Alfred G. Bailey, 'Early Foundations, 1783–1829', in Alfred G. Bailey, ed., *The University of New Brunswick: memorial volume* (Fredricton, NB, 1950), pp. 15–21, p. 16. See also Robin S. Harris, *A History of Higher Education in Canada, 1663–1960* (Toronto and Buffalo, 1976), p. 28.

which would not only found a college, but also endow it with a perpetual grant of money. Still more remarkably, a year later, the British prime minister, William Pitt the Younger, was dragged into Inglis' scheme, producing his own suggestions for a link between this boreal college and England's ancient universities and preparing the Treasury to pay for the experiment.[21] In 1791, the corner stone for Inglis' institution was laid and in 1795 it finally opened.[22]

The place chosen for this new university was not, at first sight, all that prepossessing. Fewer than 300 people lived in Windsor, Nova Scotia. It did not rate a mention in guides to the area, and contemporaries were clearly unconvinced that the small town had a future.[23] In 1785, the Rev George Gilmore left Windsor and walked forty miles to the provincial capital Halifax in the hope of buying provisions. He offered all his land and his home as security for one barrel of flour and another of pork—and was refused any credit whatsoever.[24] Armed with a grant of £360 from the Assembly to buy the site and £4000 from the British government to erect a building, Inglis was, however, undeterred.[25] There were no architects—so he designed the college himself; and no stone—so he determined it should be built in wood. The result was 'the largest structure then erected in the province': a neo-classical, neo-colonial college set down in the middle of nowhere.[26]

Both the building and the institution itself were based on the King's College, New York that Inglis knew so well; even the little octagonal belvedere that crowned the roof was copied from the same metropolitan model. But Inglis was determined that this foundation would withstand the threat of rebellion that had overwhelmed the New York college.[27] To that end, it would be residential, with students living in small apartments on site.[28] It would also be exclusively Anglican, with pupils and teachers each swearing oaths to the Church of England and compelled to attend chapel. In 1802, Inglis finally achieved his ambition, as King's College Windsor was granted a charter by George III and with it the right to offer its own degrees. Its patron would be the Archbishop of Canterbury and it would receive £1,000 a year from the British Treasury to sustain its work. The college seemed well on its way to becoming the first new university, and—what's more—a truly loyalist university in which 'No Professor, directly or indirectly, shall teach, or maintain, any atheistical, deistical, or democratical principles, or

---

[21] Vincent T. Harlow, *The Founding of the Second British Empire, 1763–1793* (2 vols; London, 1964), vol. ii, pp. 740–1.
[22] Reginald V. Harris, *Charles Inglis: missionary, loyalist, bishop (1734–1816)* (Toronto, 1937), pp. 115–16.
[23] See, for example, S. Hollingsworth, *An Account of the Present State of Nova Scotia* (London, 1786).
[24] Neil MacKinnon, *This Unfriendly Soil: the loyalist experience in Nova Scotia, 1783–91* (Kingston and Montreal, 1986), p. 47.
[25] *Statutes, Rules, and Ordinances of the University of King's College*, p. 1.
[26] Cuthbertson, *The First Bishop*, p. 143.
[27] Roper, 'Aspects of the History of a Loyalist College', p. 443.
[28] There is a useful description of the accommodation in Thomas Chandler Haliburton, *A General Description of Nova Scotia* (London, 1823), p. 157.

any doctrines contrary to the Christian faith, or to good morals, or subversive of the British constitution', as the statutes put it.[29]

Nonetheless, as with so much of Charles Inglis' life, even this triumph was only partial and short lived. He soon fell out with the college authorities and found that the people of Nova Scotia were less appreciative of the benefits of higher education than he had hoped. As early as 1798, the problem of recruitment was self-evident. 'The College at Windsor is a large commodious building, with Governors, Professors, and a Steward—indeed, every thing but Students', observed Edward Willoughby, vicar of the neighbouring town.[30] In the years that followed, enrolments actually fell, with fewer than four matriculating annually between 1803 and 1810.[31] Nova Scotia turned out to be far from the Establishment Eden that loyalist exiles had imagined. As many as 20,000 moved there after the American Revolution, but within less than a decade the exodus of the disappointed had grown so great that the provincial Assembly attempted to enforce a ban on further emigration.[32]

To make matters worse, close to three-quarters of those who remained in Nova Scotia were not members of the Church of England—and were thus not entitled to take advantage of the strictly confessional Anglican College.[33] Moreover, Inglis' building proved a failure: its flat roof leaked, its wood decayed, and without many of the expensive decorative features he had planned for, 'it looked more like a barracks' than an institute of higher education.[34] Even the tens of thousands of pounds ploughed into the college by the missionary Society for the Propagation of the Gospel could not disguise the awful reality that this *mother of an University* was in trouble. When the lieutenant-governor of Nova Scotia, Lord Dalhousie, visited in 1817 he found only two professors—each at war with the other, fourteen 'unruly and rebellious' students, and a 'ruinous' building. 'In short', he recorded, 'there are a thousand objections to it, and reasons why it should not prosper in its present situation, laws and conduct.'[35] Small wonder that his legacy to the province was a new non-denominational college in Halifax; although it, too, would take years to acquire any students whatsoever, and decades more to establish itself as Dalhousie University.[36]

King's College still exists—just not in the form, or serving the function, or situated in the place that Inglis intended. In 1829 it dropped the demand that its students conform to the Church of England. Almost a hundred years later, in 1920, Inglis' wooden building was destroyed by fire. The college subsequently abandoned Windsor, moving to Halifax, where it became associated with the neighbouring,

---

[29] *Statutes, Rules, and Ordinances of the University of King's College*, p. 13.
[30] Quoted in, Fingard, *Anglican Design*, p. 151.
[31] Henry Yorke Hind, *The University of King's College, 1790–1890* (New York, 1890), p. 46.
[32] MacKinnon, *Unfriendly Soil*, pp. 165, 174.
[33] Hind, *University of King's College*, p. 49.
[34] Harris, *Charles Inglis*, p. 116. See also *Memorial Received from the Governors of King's College at Windsor, Nova Scotia* (London, 1822), p. 6.
[35] Marjory Whitelaw, ed., *The Dalhousie Journals* (Ottowa, 1978), pp. 62–3.
[36] P. B. Waite, *The Lives of Dalhousie University: vol. one, 1818–1925, Lord Dalhousie's university* (Montreal and Kingston, 1994), pp. 12–49.

non-denominational Dalhousie University. It claims to be 'Canada's oldest chartered university' and does go down, at least in some histories, as the originator of Canadian ice hockey.[37] This is something—though, of course, it is not at all what its founders had planned.

While King's did not become the bastion of the Established Church—much less the alternative to seditious Harvard and rebellious Yale—that Charles Inglis hoped it would be, the college does exemplify some the key themes of this section. In the first place, it reveals the surprising involvement of the British state in higher education long before most modern histories would suggest it played any significant role.[38] Not only did the British government take a remarkably detailed interest in the structure and working of the college, it also spent an extraordinary amount of money on it: investing no less than £37,000 between 1790 and 1834.[39] Secondly, the story of King's College Windsor exposes the central significance of religion in contemporary debates about higher education. The university and the Church were believed by many to be inseparably linked. Inglis was neither unique nor anachronistic in his perspective; indeed, throughout the nineteenth century, other new universities would be founded on this assumption, not least Newman's Catholic University in Ireland, the inspiration for his seminal lectures on the *Idea of a University*.[40] In the third place, Inglis' Nova Scotian failure illuminates a more prosaic reality about university life at this time: the lack of demand for degrees. It was not just in Canada and not only at the turn of the nineteenth century that institutions struggled to recruit. Nor was it solely denominational institutions that failed to attract enough undergraduates: secular colleges, like Dalhousie, would also face this problem too. As one historian has noted, underlying many of the most important developments in the higher education of this period was the 'small size of the applicant pool'.[41] All the institutions dealt with in this section struggled to survive—and many simply failed to make the grade.

Above all, as this disjunction between the ambitions of those who created colleges and the actual needs of potential students makes clear, almost none of the new foundations in this era were, in fact, the product of popular demand. Rather, they chiefly reflected the ideas and ideologies of those who established them. They were instruments of social, political, or theological transformation, the focus for the ambitions and anxieties of reformers, as much as they were locations for learning. Just as Charles Inglis sought to create a loyalist, royalist, Anglican community in Nova Scotia through his King's College, so other founders hoped to

---

[37] <http://www.ukings.ns.ca/>; <http://www.birthplaceofhockey.com/index.html> (accessed 6 June 2011). The actual origin of the modern game appears to be Montreal.

[38] C.f. Sheldon Rothblatt and Martin Trow, 'Government Policies and Higher Education: a comparison of Britain and the United States, 1630–1860', in Colin Crouch and Anthony Heath, eds, *Social Research and Social Reform: essays in honour of A. H. Halsey* (Oxford, 1992), pp. 173–216, p. 119.

[39] Fingard, *Anglican Design*, p. 154.

[40] T. W. Moody, 'The Irish University Question of the Nineteenth Century', *History* 43 (1958), pp. 90–109. See also Senia Pašeta, *Before the Revolution: nationalism, social change and Ireland's Catholic elite, 1789–1922* (Cork, 1999), ch. 1.

[41] Sheldon Rothblatt, *The Modern University and Its Discontents* (Cambridge, 1997), p. 264.

inculcate their own values through the institutions they established. The development of higher education in the early-nineteenth century consequently cannot be reduced to a simple story in which the forces of progress—the rising middle classes and the growth of an industrial economy—inevitably and irresistibly created a new and modern sort of university. There were many different visions of the new society being built—and many who hoped to use universities as a means of resisting the changes they saw around them. King's College Windsor, for all its problems, is therefore an important reminder of an alternative history of higher education: one in which there is room for a multitude of competing visions, rather than a simplistic story of reaction being overcome by reform.

1
New Universities for a New Century

King's College Windsor was founded at a period of enormous creativity for higher education in the British Empire. Although it has tended to be ignored by historians—who have focused on the apparently more fertile Victorian era—the late-eighteenth and early-nineteenth centuries in reality witnessed an efflorescence of debate about universities.[1] This was not, of course, the first time that the British had tried to establish new foundations: the mid-seventeenth century had seen several abortive attempts, and in 1742 it was actually announced that a University of London was soon to open.[2] The Dissenting academies, which provided first-rate advanced teaching for those unable or unwilling to attend the ancient universities, owed their origins to the 1660s.[3] But the years after 1780 were marked by a new and widespread determination to reshape higher learning, an enthusiasm exemplified in Wordsworth's image of the ideal university—'a sanctuary for our country's youth'—in book three of his *Prelude* (1805).[4] In Manchester, for example, a College of Arts and Sciences designed 'to give a young man some taste for SUPERIOR KNOWLEDGE' was opened in 1783 and an Academy for non-conformist ministers was established three years later in 1786.[5] This was just one of several new academies started in that period—from Hoxton (1778) to Newport Pagnell (1783), Gosport (1789) to Hackney (1803).[6] More ambitiously still, proposals for a university of Armagh were debated in the Irish parliament in 1787 and further attempts to establish it would be made in 1794, 1826, and again in 1845.[7]

---

[1] For a rare exception, which provides a wider context for these developments, see Joanna Innes, 'L'« éducation nationale » dans les îles Britanniques, 1765–1815: variations britanniques et irlandaises sur un thème européen', *Annales: Histoire, Science Sociales* 65 (2010), pp. 1087–116.

[2] W. H. G. Armytage, *Civic Universities: aspects of a British tradition* (London, 1955), pp. 138, 144.

[3] H. McLachlan, *English Education Under the Test Acts: being the history of the Non-Conformist academies, 1662–1820* (Manchester, 1931); J. W. Ashley Smith, *The Birth of Modern Education: the contribution of the Dissenting Academies, 1660–1800* (London, 1954).

[4] William Knight, ed., *The Poetical Works of William Wordsworth* (8 vols; London, 1896), vol. iii, book 3, line 341.

[5] Thomas Barnes, 'Proposals for Establishing in Manchester a Plan of Liberal Education for Young Men designed for civil and active life, whether in trade, or in any of the professions', *Memoirs of the Literary and Philosophical Society of Manchester* 2 (1789), pp. 30–41, p. 36. See also Joseph Thompson, *The Owens College: its foundation and growth, and its connection with the Victoria University, Manchester* (Manchester, 1886), pp. 6–10.

[6] Geoffrey F. Nuttall, *The Significance of Trevecca College, 1768–91* (London, 1969), pp. 11–17.

[7] T. G. F. Paterson, 'Proposals for a University of Armagh', *Ulster Journal of Archaeology* 3rd series 8 (1945), pp. 5–13. There was also a short-lived attempt to transplant the Geneva Academy to Waterford: see Jennifer Powell McNutt and Richard Whatmore, 'The Attempts to Transfer the

As this suggests, whilst the French Revolution and ensuing global conflict left European universities devastated, declining in number from 143 in 1798 to only 83 in 1815, numerous projects were promulgated within the English-speaking world even in the midst of war.[8] Thus it was that plans were hatched for a new Non-Conformist English university in 1812 and 1820,[9] and a non-sectarian college—the Royal Belfast Academic Institution—was founded in 1810, having been first mooted as early as 1782.[10] Indeed, the French Revolutionary wars actually had the unexpected effect of increasing the country's provision of further and higher education. The closure of seminaries on the continent forced fleeing Roman Catholic priests to seek sanctuary in Britain and Ireland. The consequence was the creation of new schools and colleges, like Oscott in the West Midlands (1794) and Ampleforth in Yorkshire (1802).[11] The foundation of Ireland's Roman Catholic Maynooth College in 1795 was even underwritten by the Irish government, which remarkably offered a £10,000 grant to establish the place and then instituted annual payments of £1,000 from 1801.[12] In a striking anticipation of later developments, Maynooth was not only dependent on the government for funding, but structured its finances in such a way that was principally intended to demonstrate compliance with state strictures.[13] For a Roman Catholic seminary in an ostensibly Protestant polity, this was no small concession.

With the advent of peace in 1815, European universities recovered. What had looked, in one historian's words, 'like a doomed species' was now revived by the conservative reaction which spread across the continent.[14] The newly-founded University of Berlin on the one hand; the reformed and centrally-managed French system on the other: each approach to higher education spawned imitations throughout Europe and beyond.[15] Within the British world, too, the years after the Napoleonic Wars also saw a series of new projects and new foundations. The Church of England established seminaries of its own—from St Bees in Cumbria, opened in 1816, to Bishop's College in Calcutta, opened in 1819 and intended to

---

Geneva Academy to Ireland and to America, 1782–1795', *Historical Journal* 56 (2013), pp. 345–68, pp. 354–5.

[8] Walter Rüegg, 'Themes', in Walter Rüegg, ed., *A History of the University in Europe: vol. iii— universities in the nineteenth and twentieth centuries (1800–1945)* (Cambridge, 2004), pp. 3–32, p. 3.

[9] H. Hale Bellot, *University College, London, 1826–1926* (London, 1929), pp. 20–1.

[10] *An Account of the System of Education in the Belfast Academical Institution* (Belfast, 1818), pp. 3–4. See also, Joseph R. Fisher and John H. Robb, *Royal Belfast Academical Institution: centenary volume, 1810–1910* (Belfast, 1913) and Robert Allen, *The Presbyterian College, Belfast, 1853–1953* (Belfast, 1954), pp. 22–3, 37–8.

[11] Judith F. Champ, *Oscott* (Birmingham, 1987); Anthony Marrett-Crosby, *A School of the Lord's Service: a history of Ampleforth* (Ampleforth, 2002), pp. 14–17.

[12] Patrick J. Corish, *Maynooth College, 1795–1995* (Dublin, 1995), pp. 6–24.

[13] Creide O'Brien, *The Development of Accounting in Ireland—the accounts of Maynooth College, 1795–1832*, Maynooth Economics Department Working Papers N96/11/99 (1999), p. 9.

[14] L. W. B. Brockliss, 'The European University in the Age of Revolution, 1789–1850', in M. G. Brock and M. C. Curthoys, eds, *The History of the University of Oxford vol. vi: the nineteenth century part I* (Oxford, 1997), pp. 77–133, p. 100. See also Michael J. Hofstetter, *The Romantic Idea of the University in England and Germany, 1770–1850* (Basingstoke, 2001).

[15] Christophe Charle, 'Patterns', in Rüegg, ed., *History of the University in Europe*, pp. 33–81, esp. pp. 44–53.

provide an 'English collegiate education, with such modifications as may best suit the circumstances of those who are to teach Christianity in a heathen country.'[16] In 1825 there were proposals for a university in York;[17] a year later suggestions were made for one in Leeds;[18] in 1831 there was discussion about a University of Dumfries.[19] These were followed by rival schemes for both an Anglican and a Roman Catholic university on the outskirts of Bath,[20] proposals for a college at Newcastle,[21] and a *Plan of a University for the Town of Manchester*—amongst several others.[22]

Across the empire, too, a variety of institutions were granted charters: McGill (1821); the future University of Toronto (1827); the future University of New Brunswick (1829).[23] In 1824 a still more remarkable event occurred with the inauguration of the Ionian Academy on British-ruled Corfu, founded by the fifth earl of Guilford.[24] Philhelline, Orthodox convert, a travelling companion of Charles Kelsall and a man even more eccentric than the author of the *Phantasm of an University*, Guilford sought to recreate the intellectual atmosphere of ancient Athens, and even designed robes to help staff and students live his dream. 'He goes about dressed up like Plato,' observed one unimpressed visitor, 'with a gold band around his mad pate and flowing drapery of purple hue.'[25] The Academy did not long outlive him.

In Oxford, Cambridge, Dublin, and in the Scottish Universities, the first few decades of the nineteenth century also marked a period of great change. At one level, things had never been better. Student numbers rose and rose.[26] Trinity College Dublin was typical in seeing its annual intake more than treble between 1800 and 1830, rising to the giddy height of 466 in 1824.[27] Yet at the same time these ancient universities were also subject to an unprecedented range of criticism.

---

[16] S. C. Malan, *An Outline of Bishop's College* (London, 1843), p. 8; Trevor Park, *St Bees College 1816–1895* (Dalton-in-Furness, 1982). See also, David Dowland, *Nineteenth-Century Anglican Theological Training: the Redbrick challenge* (Oxford, 1997).

[17] *British Critic* 1 (1827), p. 187, notes a plan by Lord Fitzwilliam; *Quarterly Review* 32 (1825–6), p. 127, notes that 'a lady' had offered money for a Yorkshire university.

[18] A. N. Shimmin, *The University of Leeds the First Half Century* (Leeds, 1954), p. 3.

[19] *Report of the Royal Commission of Enquiry into the State of the Universities of Scotland* PP 1831 (310), pp. 85–9.

[20] Vincent Alan McClelland, *English Roman Catholics and Higher Education, 1830–1903* (Oxford, 1973), pp. 10–16; *The Mirror of Literature, Amusement and Instruction* 34 (1839), p. 202.

[21] Sophie Forgan, 'The Architecture of Science and the Idea of a University', *Studies in the History and Philosophy of Science* 20 (1989), pp. 405–34, p. 413.

[22] Harry Longueville Jones, *Plan of a University for the Town of Manchester* (Manchester, 1836).

[23] Martin L. Friedland, *The University of Toronto: a history* (Toronto, 2002); Stanley Brace Frost, *McGill University: for the advancement of learning: vol. i, 1801–1895* (1980; Kingston and Montreal, 1985); Bailey, *University of New Brunswick*.

[24] G. P. Henderson, *The Ionian Academy* (Edinburgh, 1988).

[25] Sir James Napier, quoted in Z. D. Feriman, *Some English Philhellenes vol. vi: Lord Guilford* (London, 1919), p. 94.

[26] Gillian Sutherland, 'Education', in F. M. L. Thompson, ed., *Cambridge Social History of Britain, 1750–1950* (3 vols; Cambridge, 1990), vol. iii, pp. 119–70, pp. 137–8. See also Sheldon Rothblatt, *The Modern University and Its Discontents* (Cambridge, 1997), pp. 135, 349.

[27] R. B. McDowell and D. A. Webb, *Trinity College, Dublin 1592–1952* (1982; Dublin, 2004), p. 86.

Oxford and Cambridge were attacked for the narrowness of their curriculum and the exclusiveness of their admissions.[28] Such was the atmosphere of antagonism that one critic even seized on the tragic and drunken death of a Cambridge student to preach against the university, condemning its *'laxity of discipline'*, its lack of intellectual seriousness, and also demanding that 'the disgraceful and licentious pictures exhibited in the Fitzwilliam Museum, be removed'. 'I am not at all prepared to say what might have been my own conduct, though I drank no wine, had the Museum existed during my Under-graduateship', concluded the outraged author.[29] Nor did the Scottish universities escape this rancour. By the early-nineteenth century, their glorious Enlightenment past seemed firmly behind them. As two of their historians have observed:

> there was widespread public and national concern over the declining status of the Scottish colleges; over indolence and corruption which inhibited their meeting the changed demands of a changed society; over national institutions apparently converted into private, secretive corporations; and over a national heritage so poorly cared for that buildings were crumbling, teaching was outdated and often perfunctory, the curriculum was limited, and remarkably few students were bothered to go through the full 'gowned' course and graduate.[30]

What was true of Scotland was true elsewhere—and the existing universities on both sides of the border would experience a series of reforms, enquiries, and Royal Commissions from the 1820s onwards.[31]

The most striking thing about these manifold ideas for new institutions and for university reform more generally is their variety. There was simply no one model for founders or reformers to follow. Some of these projects were confessional and others were not.[32] Some writers imagined new rural foundations and others argued that 'the largest towns and most populous districts are the fittest places for universities'.[33] Some violently condemned the ancient universities and others equally strongly defended them.[34] Some envisaged grand new buildings, designed

---

[28] See especially, W. Cockburn, *Strictures on Clerical Education in the University of Cambridge* (London, 1809); G. Dyer, *Academic Unity; being the substance of a general discussion contained in the privileges of the University of Cambridge* (London, 1827); William Hamilton, *Discussions on Philosophy and Literature, Education and University Reform* (London, 1853), pp. 401–78.

[29] F. H. Maberly, *The Melancholy and Awful Death of Lawrence Dundas Esq* (London, 1818), pp. 24–30. For a response, see, *An Answer to the Rev T. H. Maberly's Pamphlet on the Death of Lawrence Dundas, Esq* (London, 1818).

[30] Jennifer J. Carter and Donald J. Withrington, 'Introduction', to Jennifer J. Carter and Donald J. Withrington, eds, *Scottish Universities: distinctiveness and diversity* (Edinburgh, 1992), p. 3.

[31] R. D. Anderson, *Education and Opportunity in Victorian Scotland: schools and universities* (Oxford, 1983), pp. 38–54; M. G. Brock, 'The Oxford of Peel and Gladstone' and W. R. Ward, 'From the Tractarians to the Executive Commission', in Brock and Curthoys, *History of the University of Oxford vol. vi, part i*, pp. 7–71 and 306–37; Martha McMackin Garland, *Cambridge Before Darwin: the ideal of a liberal education, 1800–1860* (Cambridge, 1980).

[32] McClelland, *English Roman Catholics and Higher Education*, pp. 10–16; N. R. Tempest, 'An Early Scheme for an Undenominational University', *Universities Review* 32 (1960), pp. 45–9.

[33] [James Yates], *Thoughts on the Advancement of Academical Education in England* (London, 1826), p. 183; Charles Kelsall, *Phantasm of a University* (London, 1814), p. 170.

[34] *Edinburgh Review* 11 (1808), pp. 283–4; 14 (1809), pp. 432–3, 15 (1809), p. 51; [Edward Copleston], *A Reply to the Calumnies of the* Edinburgh Review *against Oxford* (Oxford, 1810); Henry

to achieve a sublime effect, and others maintained that efforts should be made to 'restrain the impetuosity of the founders of a new English University to expend their money in a magnificent edifice'.[35] Nor did the promoters of these projects always seem to be entirely clear about what they were doing. It is noteworthy, for example, that the Whig grandee Lord John Russell apparently set aside his passionate commitment to equal rights for all religions when he supported the abortive attempt to found Queen's College Bath in 1839.[36] Far from being a non-denominational establishment, as one might have imagined, it was intended to offer an education 'in conformity to the Christian principles of our National Church establishment'. But the great reforming Russell was nonetheless willing to present the plans, by local architect James Wilson, to Queen Victoria herself.[37]

In this mêlée of competing projects what distinguished success from failure was—above all else—the ability to obtain sufficient funds. In the glaring absence of significant benefactors, this often meant reliance on either the state or the Church.[38] From the Act of Union in 1707 onwards, the British government always supported the Scottish Universities. By the 1830s, they were in receipt of around £5,000–£6,000 a year.[39] Union with Ireland, as we have already seen, similarly brought with it financial responsibilities—first, for the Roman Catholic Maynooth, and then, somewhat more sporadically, for the non-denominational Academic Institution in Belfast.[40] In Wales, the government also gave a grant of £5,000 to help establish St David's College Lampeter, originally conceived in 1803 as a seminary for Anglican priests, and eventually opened in 1827 as a far more ambitious Welsh university college, complete with charter and a full academic curriculum (Figure 3).[41] In England, however, the state was much less generous—and the Church was very much richer. Thus it was that the first new university for almost 250 years was founded—and funded—by the amply endowed Bishop of Durham. Durham University was established by Act of Parliament in 1832 and granted a Royal Charter five years later in 1837. In this case, it appears to have been fear that the state would sequestrate Church funds that drove the whole project.[42] Yet, once it was begun, Durham sought to be a true university for the North: not only training Anglican clergy, but pioneering courses in subjects like civil engineering.[43]

Home Drummond, *Observations Suggested by the Strictures of the* Edinburgh Review *upon Oxford* (Edinburgh, 1810); Latham Wainewright, *The Literary and Scientific Pursuits which are Encouraged and Enforced in the University of Cambridge* (London, 1815), esp. pp. 80–3, 99.

[35] Kelsall, *Phantasm*, p. 129; Yates, *Thoughts*, p. 168.
[36] John Prest, *Lord John Russell* (London, 1972), pp. 33–5.
[37] *The Mirror of Literature, Amusement and Instruction* 34 (1839), p. 202.
[38] David Owen, *English Philanthropy, 1660–1960* (London, 1965), esp. pp. 347–64.
[39] Anderson, *Education and Opportunity in Victorian Scotland*, p. 36.
[40] T. W. Moody and J. C. Beckett, *Queen's, Belfast, 1845–1949* (2 vols; Belfast, 1959), vol. i., pp. xlviii–xlix.
[41] D. T. W. Price, *A History of St David's College, Lampeter, volume one: to 1898* (Cardiff, 1977), p. 25.
[42] C. E. Whiting, *The University of Durham, 1832–1932* (London, 1932), p. 31.
[43] See the on-going doctoral research of Matthew Andrews (Jesus College, Oxford) for more on this theme.

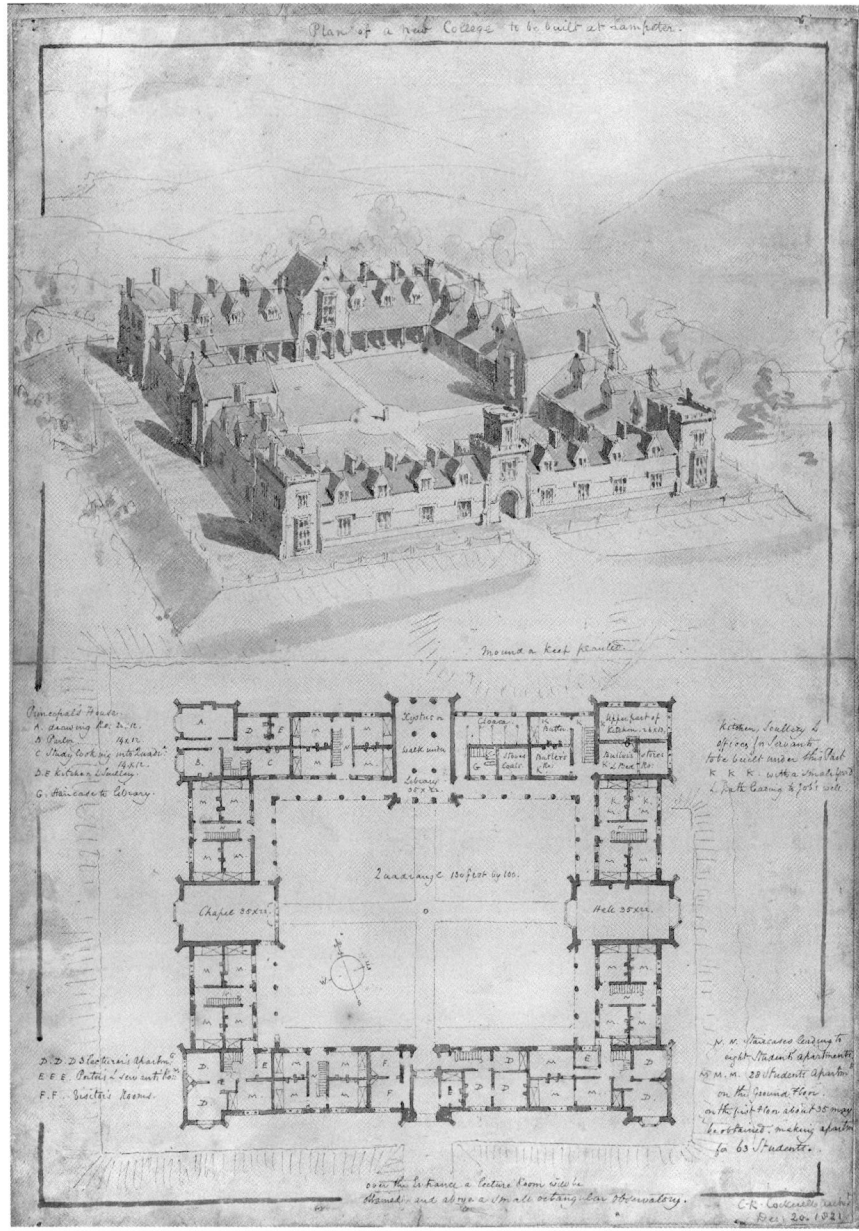

Fig. 3. Charles Cockerell's design for Lampeter. Essentially an Oxbridge college in conception, the design was much simplified in construction

The Roderic Bowen Library and Archives, University of Wales Trinity Saint David.

On its own, however, even subvention from Church and state was not enough to guarantee unmitigated triumph. Durham struggled to survive for most of the nineteenth century. Much like King's College Windsor, it was too expensive, too denominationally exclusive, and arguably in the wrong place.[44] By 1857, there was serious talk of closing it, and in 1862 a Royal Commission appointed to investigate its lack of success found only forty-four students rattling around the castle which had become its home.[45] Lampeter was an even more tragic case. Intended, in the words of one benefactor, to 'transplant the laurel and bay of the Cam and Isis to the banks of the Tivy', it signally failed to rise to the challenge. By 1836, only nine years after it was first opened, the Duke of Newcastle described as 'an apology for such an establishment'. The students were poor, the building was rotten, and its prospects were dire. It was only the government's annual grant of £400 that kept the place (barely) alive.[46]

It is a measure of the problems faced by any new college that, despite these setbacks, Lampeter and Durham can nonetheless be accounted as two of this period's successes—if only because they were successful in surviving. Sustained by external funding, they lasted when dozens of other projects failed to get off the ground. There was, then, lots of talk about new universities, lots of energy and plenty of excitement. But problems of finance and an apparent lack of student demand stymied even the best-supported schemes. Across the British Isles, the first few decades of the nineteenth century saw repeated calls for a new sort of higher education—and successive disappointments. It was against this atmosphere of expectation and in this uncertain environment that the founders of a new London university hatched their plans.

THE SYNAGOGUE OF SATAN

Attempts had been made to establish a university of London several times before. In some respects, the Inns of Court had indeed operated as 'the third university of England' in the Elizabethan era.[47] The eighteenth century also saw the capital become a major centre for medical education: 'the metropolis of the whole world for practical medicine', as one American student observed in the 1780s.[48] But by 1820, still no university existed. It was on a trip to Germany that year, in conversation with the professors of Bonn, that the Scottish poet, editor, and champion of Polish nationalism Thomas Campbell apparently resurrected the idea.[49] Four years later he returned to Germany in search of more detailed

[44] Rothblatt, *Modern University*, p. 21.
[45] *Report of the Commissioners Appointed for the Purposes of the Durham University Act, 1861*, PP 1863 (3137), p. 5; Whiting, *Durham*, p. 97.
[46] Price, *Lampeter*, pp. 46, 61, 83.
[47] J. H. Baker, *The Third University of England* (London, 1990), 3, 16, 21.
[48] Roy Porter, 'Medical Lecturing in Georgian London', *British Journal for the History of Science* 28 (1995), pp. 91–9, p. 93.
[49] William Beattie, *Life and Letters of Thomas Campbell* (3 vols; London, 1849), vol. ii., p. 355.

information about university life, and on 9 February 1825, he announced his intentions in a letter to *The Times*. 'The plan which I suggest', he wrote,

> is a great London University. Not a place for lecturing to people of both sexes (except as an appendage to the establishment), but for effectively and multifariously teaching, examining, exercising, and rewarding with honours in the liberal arts and sciences, the youth of our middling rich people, between the age of fifteen or sixteen and twenty, or later if you please.[50]

The initial response to his suggestion was discouraging. The editor of *The Times* pronounced the idea 'at once crude in conception, and meagre in development', concluding that 'there is very little in the letter itself worthy of public attention'.[51] In fact, this was the beginning of a new chapter in the history of British universities.

Each aspect of Thomas Campbell's proposal is worth examining in some detail. His journey to Germany hints at one important source of inspiration for the university: the higher education system first developed in Berlin, with its emphasis on the importance of research as well as of teaching. But his admiration even extended to the architecture of this Teutonic model, writing from Berlin in the autumn of 1825, 'the University is just such a building as I would wish for the London one'; 'I have taken the dimensions of its rooms, and got some books which give an account of its institutions.'[52] Campbell's Hibernian origins are also noteworthy. As a critic commented, his vision was 'something like a Scottish University in London, and a nursery for Scottish seedling merit'.[53] Non-residential and open to all, it certainly sounded more like Edinburgh than Oxford. It is also hard not to feel that the publication of Jefferson's plans for the University of Virginia in 1824 helped to encourage Campbell in his belief that new ways of imagining higher education were now possible.[54]

Yet his letter also reveals that still more important than these external influences was Campbell's immediate, metropolitan context. His insistence that it was 'not a place for lecturing to people of both sexes' undoubtedly reflects his desire to distinguish this institution from the popular 'Discourses' delivered each Friday at the Royal Institution in Albemarle Street. Open to any paying member, male or female, these scientific lectures were, in George Eliot's words, 'as fashionable an amusement as the Opera', but they did not provide a university education.[55] Campbell's desire to open the college only to those in their late teens is also telling. This would not merely make the institution far more like Oxford, which tended to admit older teenagers, than the Scottish universities, who very occasionally took in

---

[50] *The Times*, 9 February 1825, p. 4.
[51] *The Times*, 9 February 1825, p. 3.
[52] Letters of 5 October and 21 September 1825, in Beattie, *Thomas Campbell*, vol. ii, pp. 449 and 446.
[53] *Observations on the Probable Failure of the London University* (1825), quoted in Rothblatt, *Modern University*, p. 357.
[54] Bellot, *University College, London*, p. 11.
[55] Quoted in Ursula DeYoung, *A Vision of Modern Science: John Tyndall and the role of the scientist in Victorian culture* (London and New York, 2011), p. 15.

children as young as eight.⁵⁶ It also made it clear that he was not imagining a school, but rather a place to educate the sons of merchants and professional people who left school in their mid-teens and thereafter had no further training.⁵⁷ Indeed, his emphasis on 'the youth of our middling rich people' is perhaps the most noteworthy aspect of Campbell's letter, for this focus on the middle class was, as the historian Dror Wahrman has argued, a characteristic trope of writers in 1820s London and one that was laden with political as well as social significance.⁵⁸

It is also useful to note what it was that Campbell did not mention. Given the critical importance of both Church and state in underwriting other university experiments, it is striking that he did not discuss either. It is still more remarkable that he did not raise the all-important questions of religious teaching and religious tests in his embryo institution. But, of course, he was not being forgetful; as his opponents observed, he was deliberately avoiding these controversial issues.⁵⁹

Campbell's proposal was ostensibly an open letter to the Whig barrister and reformer Henry Brougham: a leading figure in the movement for non-denominational education, and a campaigner more generally for the abolition of religious discrimination.⁶⁰ Campbell, by contrast, was the editor of the Tory *New Monthly Magazine*, founded in 1814 to oppose the radical press.⁶¹ Brougham wanted to obtain the support of dissenters; Campbell sought to persuade Anglicans to underwrite the enterprise.⁶² There were also two other sets of interested observers whom he did not wish to alienate. On the one hand there was the small but vocal and influential group of thinkers who clustered round Jeremy Bentham. Ever since 1815, when he had published his vision of rational and useful learning, *Chrestomathia*, the Benthamites had cherished the idea of establishing a utilitarian and secular college.⁶³ On the other hand, there was the government: keen to underwrite Church building and the establishment of Anglican training colleges like Lampeter, this Tory administration could not be expected to look with enthusiasm on a university without firm religious teaching.⁶⁴ Given these competing interests, it is small wonder that *The Times* concluded it could 'say nothing... of the merits of the scheme itself, since we do not clearly see what it is'.⁶⁵

---

⁵⁶ Marjorie Harper, 'The Challenges and Rewards of Databases: Aberdeen University students, 1860–*c.*1880', in Carter and Withrington, eds, *Scottish Universities*, p. 149; see also Rothblatt, *Modern University*, p. 135.

⁵⁷ A point made as early as 1783 in Barnes, 'Proposals for Establishing in Manchester a Plan of Liberal Education'. It also inspired the foundation of a college for the East India Company on rather similar lines. See Imogen Thomas, *Haileybury, 1806–1987* (Hertford, 1987).

⁵⁸ Dror Wahrman, *Imagining the Middle Class: the political representation of class in Britain, c.1780–1840* (Cambridge, 1995), p 264.

⁵⁹ *Quarterly Review* 33 (1825–6), p. 259.

⁶⁰ C. H. New, *The Life of Henry Brougham to 1830* (Oxford, 1961), pp. 19–20.

⁶¹ Laurel Brake and Marysa Demoor, eds, *Dictionary of Nineteenth-Century Journalism in Great Britain and Ireland* (London, 2009), p. 443.

⁶² Beattie, *Campbell*, vol. ii, p. 440.

⁶³ Jeremy Bentham, *Crestomathia* (London, 1815).

⁶⁴ See Stewart J. Brown, *The National Churches of England, Ireland, and Scotland, 1801–1846* (Oxford, 2001); M. H. Port, *600 New Churches: the Church Building Commission 1818–1856* (Reading, 2006).

⁶⁵ *The Times*, 9 February 1825, p. 3.

The attempt to inspire a coalition of supporters for this new university project was made all the more difficult by the increasingly polarized politics of the period.[66] There was already a sharp division in debates about education for the working classes. Between 1811 and 1814, two rival organizations were founded which would battle for control of elementary schools for the rest of the century: on the one hand, the National Society for Promoting the Education of the Poor in the Principles of the Established Church and, on the other, the British and Foreign School Society, which supported undenominational teaching more acceptable to Dissenters.[67] In the 1820s, Mechanics' Institutes and the Society for the Diffusion of Useful Knowledge were also established to provide non-sectarian adult education for the lower orders.[68] All these progressive schemes were enthusiastically supported by Campbell's correspondent, Henry Brougham, and just as vociferously condemned by many Tories, who feared that they would alienate workers from Church and state.[69]

Campbell's call for a university for 'the middling rich—that is, all above the working classes and beneath the enormously rich' was also problematic.[70] For one thing, it went against Brougham's stated ambition of extending education to all classes.[71] More importantly still, it implicitly—and perhaps even accidentally—associated this project with a new understanding of society: one in which the middle class had come to be seen not as a bastion of stability, but as a threat to the establishment.[72] Whether Campbell intended to or not, he appeared to be siding with a particular set of values and a particular set of people, who saw themselves less as a social group than as 'the right-thinking, morally upright core of British society, untainted by the corruption of the old order'.[73] That he had published his proposals in *The Times*, which had become the advocate for just such an assumption, can only have confirmed the doubts of many conservatives.[74]

From the moment that Campbell first unveiled the idea of a London University, therefore, commentators started to impose their own ideas on the project. Those in favour often imagined that this was a more radical proposal than it actually was. Writing in the *Edinburgh Review*, for example, the historian Thomas Babington

---

[66] Boyd Hilton, *A Mad, Bad, and Dangerous People? England, 1783–1846* (Oxford, 2006), esp. pp. 4–6.

[67] John Hurt, *Education in Evolution: Church, state, society and popular education, 1800–1870* (London, 1971).

[68] Thomas Kelly, *George Birkbeck: pioneer of adult education* (Liverpool, 1957), book 2; Harold Smith, *The Society for the Diffusion of Useful Knowledge, 1826–1846: a social and bibliographical evaluation* (Halifax, NS, 1974).

[69] Hilton, *A Mad, Bad, and Dangerous People?*, p. 174.

[70] *The Times*, 9 February 1825, p. 4.

[71] New, *Henry Brougham*, p. 361.

[72] Wahrman, *Imagining the Middle Class*, pp. 236–66; though see p. 302, where he implies the foundation of UCL was less controversial than it actually was.

[73] Geoffrey Crossick, 'From Gentlemen to the Residuum: languages of social class in Victorian Britain', in Penelope J. Corfield, ed., *Language, History, and Class* (Oxford and Cambridge, Mass., 1991), pp. 150–78, p. 158.

[74] *The History of* The Times, *'The Thunderer' in the making, 1785–1841* (London, 1935), pp. 247–9.

Macaulay expressed surprise at the opposition the idea had engendered. As his father Zachary was on the founding committee, he was well placed to comment. But Macaulay's vision of the new university was of a wildly unorthodox place: a college that did not offer degrees; an institution with 'no ceremonial, no silver mace, no gowns either black or red, no hoods either of fur or satin'; an establishment in which 'nobody thought of emulating the cloisters, the organs, the painted glass, the withered mummies; the busts of great men and the pictures of naked women, which attract visitors from every part of the Island to the banks of the Isis and Cam'.[75] In fact, even as he wrote, the founders were drawing up plans for a vastly expensive building, complete with cloisters;[76] and lobbying for the right to grant degrees.[77] In 1850 they would even gain a withered mummy—in the shape of Jeremy Bentham.[78] It was all much less unconventional than Macaulay made it sound.

But if the supporters of the college occasionally got carried away, this was nothing compared to its opponents. In his novel *Vivian Grey* Disraeli captured the shock of many Tories, who could 'not exactly comprehend... the London University' and looked on the whole plan as 'a damnationed hoax'.[79] The Tory government refused to grant it a charter and the Tory press was savage in its attacks.[80] From Austria, the reactionary statesman Metternich wrote 'of my absolute conviction that the implementation of this plan would bring about England's ruin'.[81] The populist *John Bull* agreed, condemning this 'COCKNEY UNIVERSITY' as an absurdity—a place where 'each Dustman shall speak, both in Latin and Greek,/And Tinkers beat Bishops in knowledge'—and as an affront to decent society. The journal imagined a world turned upside down, with the radical university giving the lower orders ideas above their station:

> The rising of some, and the fall of the rest,
> Will bring things at last to their level;
> And just as in FRANCE, which has suffered the rest,
> OLD ENGLAND will go the *Devil*.[82]

In later articles, *John Bull* was still more specific though scarcely more lyrical, seeing the college established in Gower Street as literally 'godless', not least because it lacked the crucial support of the Church. Assuming—rather like the founders of King's College Windsor—that universities were political as much as educational institutions, *John Bull* envisaged that this new foundation would simply signal 'No CHURCH, no KING, no "*nothing else*"'.[83] Without state sanction, and

---

[75] [T. B. Macaulay], *Edinburgh Review* 43 (1826), pp. 315–41, p. 316.
[76] Negley Harte and John North, *The World of UCL, 1828–1990* (London, 1991), pp. 25–6.
[77] Bellot, *University College, London*, p. 49.
[78] Harte and North, *World of UCL*, p. 27.
[79] Benjamin Disraeli, *Vivian Grey* (2 vols; London, 1827), vol. ii, p. 166.
[80] Bellot, *University College, London*, pp. 216–18.
[81] Quoted in Negley Harte, *The University of London 1836–1986: an illustrated history* (London, 1986), p. 44.
[82] *John Bull*, 11 July 1825, p. 221.   [83] *John Bull*, 23 January 1826, p. 29.

lacking ecclesiastical support, the journal opined, 'it has no claim to the title of University'.[84]

The curriculum of the new college only exacerbated the outrage of the critics.[85] The course was intended to take four years and to include a far wider range of topics than the comparatively narrow degrees in Classics and mathematics offered at Oxford and Cambridge. The first and second years did cover Latin, Greek, and mathematics—but also offered options in French, German, and English. The third year took in logic and philosophy of mind, chemistry, biology, and physics (or natural philosophy, as it was called), and other optional courses. Finally, in the fourth year, students added jurisprudence, political economy, and—sometimes—modern history to the mix.[86] What shocked more conservative commentators was the absence of any theology. The proudly reactionary *British Critic* argued that it would even be better to 'see a "Dissenters' University" established in London . . . or even a "Deists' University"' instituted in the same way, than one, like the present, which professes to admit all the other ingredients of knowledge, and rejects religion as something unwholesome and unpalatable.[87] The Tory *Quarterly Review* agreed, asserting that a university without religious teaching was, quite simply, not a university.[88] The theologian Edward Irving went further still: such a secular institution would be 'the Synagogue of Satan'.[89]

The decision to omit theology was not, however, taken as a point of principle. Nor did it reflect the desire to create a solely secular institution. It was instead a desperate compromise. Initially, the plan had been to appoint professors of divinity. The problem was that the promoters of the college could not agree exactly what they should teach. The Non-Conformists were happy with a mixed economy: 'partly Church of England and partly Presbyterian'. The Anglican supporters, by contrast, could not accept this ecclesiastical confusion. They asserted that 'either the Church of England must predominate, or else there must be no church influence'.[90] In other words: it was Churchmen, rather than rationalists, who insisted that this new project should be secular—and they did so because they believed that theology was too important to be taught in a non-denominational institution, not because they believed that it should not be taught at all. Subsequent attempts to reopen the issue were firmly rebuffed, for fear that this delicate balance between different religious constituencies would be overturned.[91]

The corollary of this conclusion was that those attending the university would be taught religion elsewhere. It was hoped that halls of residence would be set up,[92] and in 1829 a group of evangelical Anglicans tried—and failed—to found a Church

---

[84] *John Bull*, 7 May 1827, p. 142.
[85] [F. D. Maurice], 'London University and King's College', *Athenaeum and Literary Chronicle* 51 (15 October 1828), pp. 799–800, provides an excellent contemporary analysis of this.
[86] Bellot, *University College, London*, p. 79.
[87] *British Critic* 1 (1827), p. 193.
[88] *Quarterly Review* 39 (1829), p. 129.
[89] Quoted in Harte, *University of London*, p. 64.
[90] Campbell, quoted in Beattie, ed., *Thomas Campbell*, vol. ii, p. 440.
[91] Bellot, *University College, London*, pp. 55–9.
[92] UCL, Council Minutes I (1825–29), Appendix Three, p. 6 (22 April 1826).

of England College for those attending UCL.[93] But it was assumed that most students would either live at home or in licensed lodging houses and receive exposure to religion there. A non-residential university was not, of course, unusual north of the border. By the 1820s, the last vestiges of student accommodation had been entirely removed from most Scottish institutions.[94] Advocates of this system made a virtue of bourgeois domestic life for undergraduates. 'If the student lives with his family,' wrote Macaulay, 'he will be under the influence of restraints more powerful and, we will add, infinitely more salutary and respectable, than those which the best disciplined colleges can impose.'[95]

For those used to the collegiate life of Oxford and Cambridge, however, this was just another provocation.[96] Suspicious enough of the project and doubtful about the political ambitions of the middle-class constituency it was intended to serve, the *British Critic* enjoyed the opportunity of sneering at both: 'the religion which is likely to be instilled at home, and under the supervision of parents, must be a sorry substitute for the legions of professed scholars', it declared.

> In general, and at best, they will be bankers, merchants, or tradesmen of respectability;—men who may be very sincere and very rational believers in Christianity, yet who will probably have taken up their system of faith upon practical grounds; and who will therefore be unable to refute scientific objections or to satisfy the scruples of young sceptics.[97]

Lacking residence, religion, links with the Church, or sanction from the state, the proposed University of London was thus in the minds of its critics nothing more than a contradiction in terms.

The new and somewhat experimental institution nonetheless opened in October 1828. Though it called itself the University of London, it was not a university because it had failed to obtain a charter of any sort from the Crown. But it overcame opposition from the government—and possibly sought to dodge any oversight by the state—by being established as a joint-stock company (Figure 4).[98] This was another striking innovation—and critics were quick to pick up on it, mocking the 'Share University' as a 'humbug joint stock subscription school for Cockney boys'.[99] To their consternation, however, this commercial innovation actually worked, and within two years almost £34,000-worth of shares had been sold.[100] Although this would in the event prove insufficient, it was almost as much as the state had spent sustaining King's College Windsor, and it seemed a sign that it was now possible to imagine a university which was not wholly dependent on government support or the financial resources of the Church. More than this, the

---

[93] Bellot, *University College, London*, p. 58.
[94] Anderson, *Education and Opportunity in Victorian Scotland*, p. 35.
[95] *Edinburgh Review* 43 (1826), p. 322.
[96] Christianus [George D'Oyly], *A Letter to the Right Hon. Robert Peel on the Subject of the London University* (London, 1828), pp. 26–7.
[97] *British Critic*, 1 (1827), pp. 200–1.
[98] Rothblatt, *Modern University*, p. 250.
[99] *John Bull*, 11 July 1825, p. 221 and 7 May 1827, p. 142.
[100] Bellot, *University College, London*, pp. 33–4.

Fig. 4. George Cruickshank, 'The political, toy-man' (1825). Brougham is shown carrying a Gothic college round Lincoln's Inn as he solicits subscriptions

Reproduced with the permission of the Trustees of the British Museum.

simple fact of the foundation itself was a challenge to its opponents. As the influential clergyman, George D'Oyly, observed, the very existence of a self-styled University of London had transformed the debate about higher education. It was no longer a question of whether there should be a metropolitan university, but what form one should take.[101]

---

[101] Christianus [George D'Oyly], *A Letter to the Right Hon. Robert Peel*, p. 37.

A BLIND TO THE PROTESTANT AND HIGH CHURCH PARTY

For D'Oyly, and for many others who opposed UCL, there was only one answer to this question: what was needed was a London university with proper connections to the Church and suitable support from the state: a *'purely and strictly defensive'* response to the godless institution in Gower Street.[102] Seizing on a sermon of 1826 by the High Church Hugh James Rose, which—conventionally enough—attacked materialism in education and called for a new focus on truly religious teaching, the Tory press pushed for some response.[103] Accordingly, even as the founders of UCL were drawing up detailed plans for their project, a rival group of impeccably orthodox Anglicans began plotting a college of their own. Amongst the leaders of this movement was George D'Oyly, one of Rose's patrons and a vocal opponent of the sort of non-denominational elementary schools that Brougham and his allies advocated. As a committee member of the Society for the Propagation of the Gospel, he was also involved in the running of King's College Windsor—for it was, of course, their money that kept the place going.[104] Writing as 'Christianus', he delivered an open letter to the Home Secretary Robert Peel, MP for Oxford University and outspoken defender of the Church. In it D'Oyly accepted the case for a London university, but went on to argue that UCL must be prevented from becoming any such thing. What was needed, he went on, was an Anglican university in the capital. 'While there is activity on one side, there must not want a corresponding activity on the other. The present is not a time when the friends of genuine Christianity, and of the Church of England, should slumber on their posts.'[105]

Proposing a response was one thing; actually founding a university was another. What should an Anglican university look like? Might it be like Oxford, with students required to swear an oath of loyalty to the Church as soon as they arrived? Or would it be like Cambridge, where the oath was not sworn until graduation? Or, then again, would it resemble Trinity College Dublin, where non-Anglicans were allowed to graduate, but could not receive prizes for their work or be appointed to any academic jobs? At both the existing English universities, the fellows of colleges also had to conform—and, in most cases, were required to be in holy orders. Would this also be appropriate for a new London college? Similar questions were being asked at exactly the same time in Canada, where another institution was being conceived: King's College York—the basis of the future University of Toronto. Founded by the Church, planned to provide a higher education for 'the children of

---

[102] *Remarks on the Objects of Public Education respectfully addressed to the provisional committee for conducting the intended establishment of King's College, London, by a subscriber* (London, 1828), p. 8.
[103] *British Critic* 1 (1827), pp. 175–210. See also, Hugh James Rose, *The Tendency of Prevalent Opinions about Knowledge Considered* (Cambridge, 1826).
[104] [Charles John D'Oyly], 'Memoir of the late Dr D'Oyly', in [Maria Francis D'Oyly] ed., *Sermons delivered at the Parish Church of St Mary, Lambeth by George D'Oyly DD FRS* (2 vols; London, 1847), vol. i., pp. xiii–xxxix.
[105] Christianus [George D'Oyly], *A Letter to the Right Hon. Robert Peel*, p. 39.

the farmer and the mechanic' who would otherwise not benefit from higher education, it was also intended to offset the pernicious influences of more seditious forms of teaching.[106] It was an Anglican college that followed the Dublin model: accepting students of any denomination, and requiring staff to conform; although for the provincial assembly even this was too restrictive and, from the moment of its foundation, efforts were made to make it still more liberal. The battle would last for decades.[107]

To make matters more intractable still, just as D'Oyly and his allies started to create King's College London (KCL) their religious and political world began to fall apart. The inaugural meeting to raise funds for the foundation was held on 23 June 1828, with the arch-Protestant prime minister, the Duke of Wellington, in the chair. The primates of England and Ireland—the Archbishops of Canterbury, York, and Armagh—were in attendance. Church and state were apparently at one.[108] Less than two weeks later, this comforting sense of cohesion collapsed. The illegal election of a Roman Catholic as MP for the Irish constituency of County Clare dramatically called into question the existing Protestant constitution, which prohibited Catholics from sitting in parliament. It was clear, as the anti-Catholic Lord Liverpool had observed three years before, that 'whenever the *crisis does* come, the *Protestants* must go to the *wall*'.[109] Now that crisis had arrived, Liverpool's prediction was proved correct. It forced Wellington's Tory government to consider the unthinkable: Catholic Emancipation, the removal of discriminatory legislation that made Roman Catholics second-class citizens.[110] So it was that the plans for King's College were developed and funds were raised in the midst of a political whirlwind. Worse still, many of the leading figures in the foundation were sucked into this vortex.

In March 1829, the same month that George IV granted Royal approval for the new college's site, Wellington and Peel announced that they were now, however reluctantly, committed to Catholic Emancipation. This sudden about turn from two of the Church's chief defenders was a terrible blow both to their authority and to the College they hoped to found. Previous supporters suddenly withdrew their money, condemning the 'Judas Isacariots' who had introduced 'The Bill for the Promoting of Papist Ascendancy'. At least Judas, one observed, had the grace to hang himself.[111] More dramatically, the fiercely pro-Protestant earl of Winchilsea connected the college and Catholic Emancipation in his attacks on the government. Wellington's involvement in King's, he alleged, 'was intended as a blind to the Protestant and high church party'. 'Under the cloak of some outward show of zeal for the Protestant religion', he went on, the prime minister had plotted 'insidious

---

[106] John Strachan, *An Appeal to the Friends of Religion and Literature in* [sic] *behalf of the University of Upper Canada* (London, 1827), pp. 7, 21.
[107] Martin L. Friedland, *The University of Toronto: a history* (Toronto, 2002), esp. pp. 8–29.
[108] *Statement of Proceedings towards the establishment of King's College, London* (London, 1830).
[109] Quoted in Hilton, *A Mad, Bad, and Dangerous People?*, p. 385.
[110] G. I. T. Machin, *The Catholic Question in English Politics 1820 to 1830* (Oxford, 1964), ch. 6.
[111] KCL, KA/IC/F2, B? Flounders to Secretary (2 April 1829).

designs for the infringement of our liberties, and the introduction of Popery into every department of the State'. The prime minister was bound to respond—and so he did. At 8 o'clock on the morning of 21 March, Winchilsea and Wellington met to fight a duel, perhaps the only one in history provoked by higher education.[112] Four days later, Winchilsea withdrew his support for the project for good.[113]

The college that finally opened on 8 October 1831 was consequently not quite what its founders had hoped for. The battle over Catholic Emancipation, in particular, left King's financially embarrassed, as anti-Catholics deserted in droves. It was not, as had been intended, chiefly residential—there was no money for sufficient rooms. It was not, as many supporters had hoped, exclusively Anglican—there were no religious tests for students, and chapel was not compulsory for everyone. Rather like Trinity College Dublin, there was a category of 'occasional' students who were able to attend class, but could duck any religious requirements.[114] In many respects, indeed, it was hard to distinguish between UCL and KCL. Both were joint-stock companies. Both seemed to be open to all-comers. Both relied on their students living at home or renting rooms nearby. In some respects, King's was actually more avant-garde than its supposedly more innovative rival. It pioneered the study of English literature, whilst it turned out that classics predominated in Gower Street.[115] The founders of UCL were so terrified of appointing a professor who would teach unorthodox doctrine that at its opening both the chairs in philosophy remained unfilled.[116] Yet the council at King's employed the controversial Charles Lyell to lecture on geology, despite their doubts about his orthodoxy—though it must be admitted that this was a short-lived experiment, as the ambitious scientist found that his pay was not worth the amount of work he was required to do.[117]

In the end, only two clear differences existed between the fundamentally rather conventional UCL and the surprisingly liberal KCL. In the first place, King's had a chapel; its staff were also required to conform to the Church of England. This was highly symbolically significant—and certainly marked it out from its unsectarian competitor. Secondly, it possessed a charter of incorporation.[118] This was something the founders of the self-proclaimed London University longed for—and something they were determined to achieve. Until they did, however, it was a unique advantage for King's, which—despite all its troubles—was the only recognized university college in the capital.

---

[112] *Annual Register* 1829, pp. 58–63.
[113] KCL, KA/C/M1, King's College Council Minute Book, 1828–9, p. 74 (26 March 1829).
[114] F. J. C. Hearnshaw, *The Centenary History of King's College, London, 1828–1928* (London, 1929), pp. 42, 51–7.
[115] Alan Bacon, 'English Literature Becomes a Subject: King's College, London, as pioneer', *Victorian Studies* 29 (1986), pp. 591–612; Rothblatt, *Modern University*, p. 362.
[116] Bellot, *University College, London*, p. 59.
[117] J. B. Morrell, 'London Institutions and Lyell's Career: 1820–41', *British Journal for the History of Science* 9 (1976), pp. 132–46.
[118] Hearnshaw, *King's College, London*, pp. 67–9.

A RAMBLING, FUMBLING SOLUTION

Within six years of Campbell's letter, London had acquired two new and important institutes of higher education. Yet the result of this sudden outbreak of educational initiative was not all that contemporaries had expected. The establishment choice—King's College—had a charter, it is true; but it also possessed almost no money. It remained financially vulnerable throughout the nineteenth century.[119] Its rival, the notoriously non-religious UCL, had no charter; but it did have more money: indeed, although it struggled to begin with, it soon acquired an endowment of no less than £10,000.[120] And even this was somewhat odd. At its foundation it had been suggested—in true utilitarian fashion—that the institution would survive on fee income alone and thus avoid the temptations of over-endowed Oxford, which, it had been claimed ever since Adam Smith's time, had fallen into corruption precisely because of its riches.[121] As Macaulay put it, 'A chartered and endowed college, strong in its wealth and in its degrees, does not find it necessary to teach what is useful, because it can pay men to learn what is useless.' At London, by contrast, 'To be prosperous, it must be useful.'[122] An endowment of any sort evidently undermined this assumption.

Nor were these the only surprises. Whilst King's saw its supporters desert in droves, UCL witnessed a slower, but no less significant process of attrition. Some withdrew their money because they had misunderstood the nature of the investment, assuming that shares in the joint-stock company would actually yield a profit.[123] Others—including some of the founding committee—resigned over matters of more substance. Even before the college had opened, the evangelical Anglican William Wilberforce withdrew his support because of the college's refusal to teach theology.[124] Later, the radical educational reformer George Birkbeck left in disgust, believing that the place was fatally mismanaged.[125] In turn, Leonard Horner, the man appointed to head the college as warden, was driven from office in 1831—and his post was never refilled.[126] The originator of the whole scheme, Thomas Campbell, also abandoned the project, apparently feeling excluded by Brougham.[127] More alarmingly, UCL struggled to attract students. It had been founded on the assumption that 2,000 would attend, but at its opening fewer than a third of that turned up. In each successive year, numbers fell further. The college responded in 1831 by reducing its four-year course to three—and even then not enough took it to make the place financially viable in the longer term.[128] Little wonder that by 1835 even Brougham was reduced to despair, declaring 'no plan in

---

[119] Rothblatt, *Modern University*, p. 301.   [120] *UCL Annual Report* 1840, p. 12.
[121] Adam Smith, *An Inquiry into the Nature and Causes of the Wealth of nations* (1776; Indianapolis, 1981), vol. ii, pp. 760–1.
[122] *Edinburgh Review* 43 (1826), pp. 319, 322.
[123] UCL, College Correspondence, 512, Thomas Strickland (8 February 1827).
[124] Bellot, *University College, London*, p. 58.   [125] Kelly, *George Birkbeck*, pp. 155–60.
[126] Bellot, *University College, London*, ch 6.   [127] New, *Henry Brougham*, pp. 372–3.
[128] Bellot, *University College, London*, pp. 74, 79.

which he had ever been engaged had *caused him so much mortification as the failure... of the University of London*.[129]

Both these new metropolitan colleges survived despite, rather than because, of their origin in the political battles of the 1820s and 1830s. Crucial to their continued existence was not a link with the Church or a rejection of denominational religious education. Instead, they became dependent on two sorts of teaching that were barely mentioned in the controversy which surrounded their foundation: secondary schools and medical schools.[130]

King's College School for boys was part of the initial plan, and was included in the Royal Charter of 1829.[131] It was initially regarded as little more than an effective way of recruiting future students, but within three years of opening it had enrolled twice as many boys as the college itself.[132] University College School was, by contrast, not considered an essential part of the original project, but its opening in 1832 turned out to be equally important—and in 1833 *The Times* observed that that it too had 'succeeded beyond any expectation'.[133]

Medical education was still more central to the colleges' survival—and became a crucial element in establishing their reputation too.[134] New legislation and new scientific discoveries each helped to reform doctors' training.[135] As a consequence, between 1824 and 1834 at least ten medical schools were set up in the provinces.[136] London was already the centre of British medical education. The increasing requirement that trainee medics should have some hospital experience only strengthened the claims of a city that had a long tradition of just that sort of teaching.[137] The founders of both UCL and KCL were consequently in a very strong position to capitalize on this demand—and they did so with alacrity, though this is not to say that they did not differ. King's would never have dreamt of naming hospital wards after George IV's disgraced ex-wife for example. Brougham, by contrast, had been her staunchest defender in the 1820s, so it was only appropriate that money was to be raised for 'Queen Caroline's Wards' at University College Hospital.[138] This emblematic difference aside, the contrast between the two institutions was apparently paradoxical. Although it was the chartered college, King's struggled to recruit; indeed its medical school continually threatened to

---

[129] Quoted in Rosemary Ashton, *Victorian Bloomsbury* (New Haven and London, 2012), p. 41.
[130] Ashton, *Victorian Bloomsbury*, pp. 93–130.
[131] Frank Miles and Graeme Cranch, *King's College School: the first 150 years* (London, 1979).
[132] *King's College Calendar* 1834–5, p. 96.
[133] Quoted in Bellot, *University College, London*, p. 170. See also G. G. H. Page, *An Angel Without Wings: the history of University College School, 1830–1980* (London, 1981).
[134] Charles Singer and S. W. F. Holloway, 'Early Medical Education in Relation to the Pre-History of London University', *Medical History* 4 (1960), pp. 1–17; Rothblatt, *Modern University*, p. 20.
[135] Irvine Loudon, 'Medical Education and Medical Reform', in Vivian Nulton and Roy Porter, eds, *The History of Medical Education in Britain* (Amsterdam, 1995), pp. 229–49, p. 232.
[136] Irvine Loudon, *Medical Care and the General Practitioner, 1750–1850* (Oxford, 1986), p. 49.
[137] Susan C. Lawrence, 'Private Enterprise and Public Interest: medical education and the Apothecaries' Act, 1780–1825', in Roger French and Andrew Wear, eds, *British Medicine in the Age of Reform* (London, 1991), pp. 45–73, pp. 46, 64–5; see also Ashton, *Victorian Bloomsbury*, ch. 4.
[138] UCL, MS Add 56, Notes from the Minutes of the General Meetings and Meetings of Council 1825–39, 1834.

become a liability.[139] UCL's training was more popular. Despite its lack of official recognition, by 1834 it was educating nearly 400 medical students. Nonetheless, it was unwilling to rethink the traditional approach to teaching—leading the distinguished surgeon Sir Charles Bell to resign from his chair, disappointed at the conservatism of the supposedly radical college.[140]

The two institutions consequently came to resemble one another; their differences in many respects outweighed by their similarities. Each jealously eyed the other and both were looked on with suspicion by the ancient universities and the London medical schools in their turn. Both also faced similar problems. They lacked money and sufficient well-qualified students. They also lacked status, for neither could award its own degrees. The only solution seemed to be a university charter, which would grant legitimacy and hopefully attract undergraduates. UCL tried again and again to achieve just that: in 1825, 1827, 1830, 1833, and 1834.[141] Each time, essentially the same arguments were trotted out against the College: it was ungodly; it could not be a university because it did not teach religion; it could not be recognized because it was nothing more than a joint-stock company. Above all, as one Oxford don put it, 'the chartering of a London University is the cutting of another tie between the state and Established religion'.[142] In a desperate attempt to block the charter, the fanatically anti-Catholic MP Sir Charles Wetherell made all these arguments to the Privy Council—and then went on to claim that the link between Church and university was so fundamental that only the Archbishop of Canterbury could grant a charter.[143] In many respects, the success of the medical school only made matters worse. It left the college open to ridicule as a hospital rather than a putative university, and also excited opposition from the many other institutions that trained doctors.[144] And so the debate went on, reaching into the heart of government. Indeed, in March 1835, Robert Peel's opposition to a charter for UCL was one of the underlying causes for his minority administration's collapse.[145]

The year of 1836 brought a resolution to this on-going problem. It was, in the words of one historian, a 'rambling, fumbling solution', but it did bring the uncertainty to an end—for the time being, at least.[146] Neither place would be chartered as a university. Rather, a new institution would be imposed above them. King's and the newly-named University College would teach students and a freshly-minted University of London would examine them. It was, to all intents and purposes, a government department, with the chancellor, vice-chancellor, and

---

[139] Hearnshaw, *King's College, London*, p. 114.
[140] Bellot, *University College, London*, pp. 145–51.
[141] Bellot, *University College, London*, ch. 7.
[142] William Sewell *A Second Letter to a Dissenter on the Opposition of the University of Oxford to the Charter of the London College* (Oxford and London, 1834), p. 48.
[143] *The Substance of the Speech of Sir Charles Wetherell before the Lords of the Privy Council on the subject of the Incorporating of London University* (London, 1834), p. 38.
[144] Sewell, *A Second Letter to a Dissenter*, p. 3.
[145] HC Deb 26 March 1835 vol. 27 cc279–301.
[146] Rothblatt, *Modern University*, p. 247.

thirty-seven members of the governing senate all appointed by the Crown.[147] It was also completely dependent on state funding; so much so, in fact, that it had to petition the Treasury each time it needed to purchase so much as a broom for the cleaner.[148] Even the curriculum was overseen by the state, with the Home Secretary amending courses and awarding scholarships apparently at will.[149]

The Times was outraged at the situation: 'Why was not the power of conferring degrees given to the Poor Law Commissioners, or to the Boards of Excise and Customs?' it mocked. 'Or why not have revived the Board of Hackney-Coach Commissioners for the purpose'.[150] Foreign commentators, like the German V. A. Huber, were shocked that a university should be no more than a 'mere piece of modern State machinery'.[151] There was also a peculiar irony that UCL had in many ways been created to oppose government control of universities, whilst KCL had been established to defend a very different sort of state. Yet both now found their work directly regulated by the Crown.

Nonetheless, no real alternative to this solution—'a university that bizarrely had neither students nor teachers'—could be found.[152] Even had the issue been less divisive, it is hard to imagine that the two rival institutions would have been able to agree on a curriculum, much less on how to mark it.[153] As it was, there were furious rows about whether the London BA should include religious subjects and whether clergymen should be allowed to examine them.[154] Above all, the compromise reflected the continuing problem of recruiting students—for there were, in fact, very few takers for the degree at all. In its first year, 1839, only seventeen graduated Bachelor of Arts (London). A year later, it was still only forty; little wonder that the chancellor, Lord Burlington, had time to sign all the certificates himself. Ten years after the foundation, in 1849, numbers had risen—but not by much. In that year fifty-three people obtained a BA.[155] The whole apparatus of setting, marking, and issuing degrees was only made possible by state subvention: in 1839–40 the University cost £4,563 to run, and only received £405 in examination fees.[156] Neither UCL nor KCL could afford to bleed money like that; so they were compelled to put up with the compromise.

---

[147] W. H. Allchin, *An Account of the Reconstruction of the University of London. Part I: from the foundation to the appointment of the first Royal Commission, 1825 to 1888* (London, 1905), pp. 4–5.
[148] LonUA, RO1/1/1, Letter Book, 1837–40, 110–11, Registrar to the Secretary to the Treasury (30 January 1839).
[149] LonUA, RO1/1/1, Letter Book, 1837–40, 47, Lord John Russell (1 August 1838); Harte, *University of London*, p. 98.
[150] *The Times*, 13 December 1836, p. 4.
[151] V. A. Huber, *The English Universities*, abridged and translated by Francis W. Newman (2 vols; London, 1843), vol. ii, p. 418.
[152] F. M. G. Willson, *Our Minerva: the men and politics of the University of London, 1836–58* (London, 1995), p. xv.
[153] Rothblatt, *Modern University*, pp. 263–4.
[154] Willson, *Our Minerva*, ch. 8.
[155] *University of London: the historical record* (London, 1912); LonUA, RO1/2/2, Letter Book, 1840–41, 90, Registrar to Chancellor (20 June 1840).
[156] Willson, *Our Minerva*, p. 145.

The University of London as established in 1836 was never popular. It was radically reformed in 1858, 1863, and again in 1900, and has been endlessly restructured throughout its life.[157] Yet it marked a milestone in the evolution of Britain's higher education. On the one hand, it showed that the role of the state in sustaining as well as regulating universities was still significant. This was to prove very important over the next decades. On the other hand, however, it revealed that change was possible: that one could imagine a very different form of university from the models presented by Oxford, Edinburgh, Dublin, or elsewhere. To be sure, the distinction between an examining university and a teaching college was implicit in England's ancient universities—indeed, the comparison with Cambridge was made at the time.[158] But the reality was that the London compromise looked, felt, and actually operated in a way that was very different.

Most importantly, this was a national solution to a local problem. KCL and UCL were not the only institutions allowed to enter students for London degrees: colleges across the country could also prepare their own candidates.[159] And they did. The Dissenting Academy at Trevecca, the Roman Catholic seminary at Stonyhurst, the University at Durham; institutions from Bath to Birmingham, Huddersfield to Newcastle: all signed up.[160] The University of London thus provided an opportunity for other towns and cities to found their own colleges, offer degrees to their own citizens, and dream of establishing their own institutions. It was an unhappy compromise—but, for the time being, it was a compromise that seemed to work.

[157] F. M. L. Thompson, ed., *The University of London and the World of Learning, 1836–1986* (London, 1990).
[158] Willson, *Our Minerva*, p. 14.
[159] Robert Bell and Malcolm Tight, *Open Universities: a British tradition?* (Buckingham, 1993), p. 1.
[160] LonUA, RO1/10/1, Home Office Letters 1838–69.

2

The People and Places of the University of London

This combination of high idealism and uncomfortable pragmatism played itself out in the architecture of the three new metropolitan institutions. Each one was given a home—and, especially in the case of the two rival colleges, that home was intended to express the identity and emphasize the importance of the place. The plans for UCL, in particular, were greeted by contemporaries with real enthusiasm. The building, wrote the critic John Britton in 1828, 'promises to present, when completed, one of the richest displays of Architecture in the metropolis'. It would, he imagined, be 'one of our most original and magnificent edifices'. (Figure 5)[1] Yet, the end results rarely lived up to these ambitions. The problems that attended the birth of each foundation were reflected in their homes. A lack of money, a need to compromise; overweening ambition and the parsimony of the state: all of these frustrated architects and clients alike. The result was a series of half-finished and sometimes half-furnished buildings. Indeed, UCL's front quadrangle, begun in 1827, was not completed until 1985.[2] To study the architecture of the University of London—built, unbuilt, and frankly unbuildable—is thus to explore the ways in which aspiration encountered reality; or, in the words of one historian, to discover 'an educational giant which has often given the impression of living in furnished lodgings'.[3]

Nowhere was this clearer than in the chartered University of London itself. As a department of state, it was given rooms in Somerset House, the home of the Inland Revenue. In the same building, taxes were calculated, moneys disbursed, and the perforation of stamps was eventually perfected.[4] It was not, in short, a glamorous location. To make matters worse, the university's complete dependence on the Crown meant that any improvements had to be cleared with the Treasury. Many vice-chancellors have doubtless felt impelled to expedite refurbishments personally. Few will have been forced to write, like Sir John Lubbock, first vice-chancellor of London, directly to the Chancellor of the Exchequer: 'Our apartments in Somerset

---

[1] John Britton, 'Remarks on New Buildings &c', in John Britton and A. C. Pugin, *Illustrations of the Public Buildings of London* (2 vols; London, 1828), vol. ii, pp. vii–xxxii, pp. xxvii–viii.
[2] Negley Harte and John North, *The World of UCL, 1828–1990* (London, 1991), p. 257.
[3] J. Mordaunt Crook, 'The Architectural Image', in. F. M. L. Thompson, ed., *The University of London and the World of Learning, 1836–1986* (London, 1990), pp. 1–33, p. 1.
[4] Ray Simpson and Peter Sargeant, *Stamp Perforation: the Somerset House years, 1848–1880* (London, 2006).

Fig. 5. 'The grandest entrance in London with nothing behind it': University College London

Reproduced with the permission of the Trustees of the British Museum.

House are in the hands of the painters and carpenters. If you could cause them to use greater despatch, you would much oblige us.'[5]

Even then, the end results were not encouraging. A year after the University had first opened, it still did not have enough chairs in its offices, and the level of comfort in its meeting rooms was not all that might be expected.[6] One of the first members of the governing Senate, the Anglican bishop Edward Maltby, complained that 'the *bare walls* of Somerset House was [*sic*] both inconvenient and unhealthy—I caught a cold, when I first attended there which confined me nearly two months.'[7] Nor did matters improve much in the years that followed. In the 1850s, the university was driven into even worse accommodation: a 'miserable garret' in Marlborough House.[8] Then it was transferred into part of another state-owned property, the east wing of Burlington House. Its travels subsequently continued with a move to 'an address more suitable to a gentleman tailor: 17 Savile Row'.[9] It is scarcely a surprise that these peregrinations were accompanied by the continual complaint that the university was hampered 'by want of an edifice' and that its role was undermined

---

[5] LonUA, RO1/2/1, 11, vice-chancellor to chancellor of the exchequer (21 November 1837).
[6] Negley Harte, *The University of London 1836–1986: an illustrated history* (London, 1986), p. 88.
[7] Quoted in F. M. H. Willson, *Our Minerva: the men and politics of the University of London, 1836–58* (London, 1995), p. 47.
[8] Harte, *The University of London 1836–1986*, p. 118.
[9] Crook, 'The Architectural Image', p. 7.

through its 'want of due prominence as a visible feature of the metropolis'.[10] Not until 1870 would it gain a building of its own.[11]

The conditions which produced the University of London were, of course, peculiar. They were the product of the bargain that had brought it into being—and, particularly, of the desire to avoid unnecessary expenditure. Put simply, the university was trapped between those MPs who were suspicious that it was nothing more than the Synagogue of Satan mark two and others who were happy to support it—so long as it was as cheap as possible.[12] Given the persistent battles over the government's subvention and the payment of examiners, not to mention struggles within the Senate itself about the possibility of some religious component in the syllabus, it is small wonder that the accommodation offered to the university was not a high priority for either its opponents or its supporters. Doubtless many agreed with the radical Unitarian James Yates who argued that money spent by universities on buildings was money wasted—at least while the institution was developing. Only once a university was paying its way should there be any investment in architecture, he argued. Until then, temporary accommodation was all that was needed.[13]

Yates was amongst the founders of University College, yet when it came to build a home for UCL, his advice was completely disregarded. Instead of eschewing magnificence, the youthful institution embraced it. Thomas Campbell, of course, had envied the University of Berlin's grand home: a princely palace on Unter den Linden.[14] Henry Brougham had compared the college to Edinburgh High School, which was concurrently erecting an extraordinary new Greek Revival edifice, an enlarged and (it was claimed) improved version of the Athenian Temple of Hephaestus.[15] At the first public meeting for the project's supporters, the Baptist minister F. A. Cox went even further still, envisaging 'a palace for genius... where future Ciceros should record their influence of that incitement which Tully declares he felt at Athens, when he contemplated the porticoes where Socrates sat'.[16]

A building for UCL also needed to establish the college's *bona fides*, for not only was the institution looked on with much suspicion, it was also located on an ill-favoured site. As the Tory press was only too willing to point out, the land bought for the upstart university was a rubbish dump.[17] Even once it had been cleared, it was scarcely a desirable address. In 1825, the Tory MP John Croker was still able to raise a laugh in the House of Commons by admitting that he 'did not profess to

---

[10] Harte, *University of London*, p. 116.
[11] Geoffrey Tyack, *Sir James Pennethorne and the Making of Victorian London* (Cambridge, 1992), pp. 290–304.
[12] *Copies of the Correspondence and Communications which have passed between the Treasury and the Chancellor of the Exchequer and the University of London*, PP 1842 (542). See also HC Deb 27 July 1840 vol. 55 cc1054–7.
[13] James Yates, *Thoughts on the Advancement of Academical Education in England* (London, 1826), p. 169.
[14] William Beattie, *Life and Letters of Thomas Campbell* (3 vols; London, 1849), vol. ii, pp. 449 and 446.
[15] H. Hale Bellot, *University College, London, 1826–1926* (London, 1929), p. 48.
[16] Bellot, *University College, London*, p. 27.
[17] *John Bull*, 26 December 1825, p. 413.

know exactly where Russell square was'.[18] Nearby Gower Street was still more *terra incognita* for the respectable. So it was that *John Bull* mockingly imagined 'a mother describing her son as having had an University education'.

> 'Which university, Madam, says a deeply interested friend, 'Oxford or Cambridge?'—'No, Sir,' says the lady, 'No. 37, Upper-Camarthen-street, Tottenham Court Road.'—the man stares—the lady continues—'Don't you know it? Dear me, it's the second door from the Lansdowne Arms, at the corner, on the left hand as you go out of the New Road.'[19]

The home for this parvenu institution needed to silence the critics and satisfy the ambitions of its founders. Temporary accommodation of the sort that Yates proposed would never do.

When looking for an architect, UCL consequently went to the top of the profession. Designs were solicited from such as luminaries as Jeffry Wyatville, who was just about to be knighted for his work on Windsor Castle, and C. R. Cockerell, who was building St David's College Lampeter, and had designed the National Monument in Edinburgh. Less well-known names included William Atkinson, architect to the Board of Ordnance; John Davies, designer of the dissenting academy at Highbury (1825–6); and John Gandy, who had made his name winning the competition for a new Bethlehem Hospital in 1810.[20] When invited to compete, William Wilkins responded that 'The names of the architects which have been mentioned to me are sufficient to inspire emulation and confer honor [*sic*]' on the architect who won.[21] As he was already responsible for designing a whole new Cambridge college—Downing—and for the East India Company's training school at Haileybury, this was no small admission.[22]

After much consideration, Wilkins won, having recommended himself to the committee with his obvious experience, his evident ability, and—perhaps most importantly—his apparent cheapness. The governing Council later announced that its intention was 'rather to select a great design suited to the wants, the wealth, and the magnitude of the population for whom the Institution is intended, than one commensurate with its present means'.[23] But it is evident that, in many respects, this was an *ex post facto* rationalization of a simple mistake. When reviewing the various entries, it was cost as much as convenience that determined their decision. Atkinson's grand Greek proposals, in a suitably scholarly Ionic order, were estimated at £104,360. Davies' design—also in Ionic—came in at £103,658. Cockerell offered no guide to the likely expense of his entry, but the whole scheme, complete with Doric propylaeum was clearly costly; whilst Wyatville's Corinthian

---

[18] HC Deb 28 March 1825 vol. 12 cc 1263–4.
[19] *John Bull*, 19 December 1825, p. 404.
[20] See H. M. Colvin, *A Biographical Dictionary of British Architects, 1600–1840* (New Haven and London, 2008).
[21] UCL, College Correspondence, Wilkins to Lord Auckland (1 November 1825).
[22] R. W. Liscombe, *William Wilkins, 1778–1839* (Cambridge, 1980).
[23] *Statement by the Council of the University of London, explanatory of the nature and objects of the Institution* (London, 1827), p. 43.

proposals were expected to set them back no less than £250,000. The runner-up, James Gandy, offered an Ionic screen and no fewer than two courtyards for between £75,000–£85,000. But it was Wilkins who appeared to provide the best deal: a grand new university for the knock-down price of £70,000.[24]

This must have seemed too good to be true. It was. Having been appointed, Wilkins admitted that his estimates were just that—estimates. Indeed, they were little more than guesses. Writing to Lord Auckland, chairman of the building committee, he observed that 'I find it difficult to give your Lordship that positive assurance, you appear to think essential, of the accuracy of my estimate'.[25] On further examination, the expected costs escalated: from £70,000 to £81,000; then from £108,000 to £129,000.[26] This was simply too much. UCL just could not afford it.

Yet the college Council was trapped. The minute they accepted Wilkins' plans, they had commissioned a lithograph of the grand new building they expected to erect.[27] It was published in the press; it was put on the front of the prospectus: it had become not just their future home, but also a promise of its present importance. It was indeed an immensely impressive plan. Passing through a Doric gateway, like the one that led to the acropolis, the visitor would encounter a massive, ten-columned portico modelled after the Temple of Jupiter Olympus in Athens. There was nothing quite like it anywhere else in England, and the whole effect, Wilkins asserted, was calculated to achieve 'magnificence'.[28]

Although the sheer enormity of the cost briefly led the college to consider abandoning the plans altogether, it was eventually decided to come up with a face-saving compromise.[29] Only one part—the central range, would be built. The gateway would be abandoned; the wings, with their museum, fifteen lecture rooms, and official residence for the warden, would be delayed. There was even talk of omitting the dome—so long as its absence would not 'materially diminish the beauty of the building'.[30] Every expedient was used to bring down the cost—and still it crept up, from £53,000 to £66,000.[31] The final bill came in at £86,000, plus the architect's 5 per cent commission.[32] UCL had undoubtedly acquired a remarkable home, but it had paid nearly a quarter more than it had expected to build two-thirds less than it had hoped. Moreover, the reduction in scale left the college lacking several rooms—including its great hall. The impressive portico thus became 'the grandest entrance in London with nothing behind it'.[33]

If the history of UCL's new building was one of thwarted ambitions and architectural disappointments, then this was nothing compared to the sad little

---

[24] UCL, College Correspondence, 167/15, analysis of plans.
[25] UCL, College Correspondence, ?32, Wilkins to Auckland (24 April 1826).
[26] UCL, Council Minutes 1, Appendix 4, 8 Report of Building Committee (29 April 1826); Minutes (19 September 1826).
[27] UCL, Council Minutes 1 p. 12 (15 April 1826); p. 15 (6 May 1826).
[28] UCL, College Correspondence, 1167/10 Wilkins (March 1826).
[29] UCL, College Correspondence, 18 Auckland to ?Coates (22 September 1826).
[30] UCL, Council Minutes 1, 19 September 1826.
[31] UCL, Miscellaneous Committee Minutes 1826–27, pp. 11 (29 April 1826, 1 December 1827).
[32] UCL, Letter Book 1828–31, p. 198 (8 February 1830).
[33] Quoted in Harte and North, *The World of UCL*, p. 45.

story of King's. In the first flush of enthusiasm, its founders were determined to match the infidel institution in Gower Street stone for stone—and hoped, in fact, to acquire a far more eligible site. Regent's Park; Kentish Town; the south bank opposite the Houses of Parliament: all of these (and more) were considered. One enthusiastic supporter wrote to urge that 'Buckingham Palace should be bought for the purposes of the College'.[34] None of these were considered suitable; indeed, residents near Regent's Park complained that a college would be 'far more turbulent, and vastly more mischievous than the bears, the kangaroos, the wolves, and the tiger-cat in the adjacent menagerie'.[35] In reality, none of these locations was remotely plausible, much less affordable, for the financial problems of the college extended to its accommodation. Years after the building was finished, indeed, King's would still be paying off debts accrued in its construction.[36]

Salvation—if indeed it was salvation—came in the shape of Somerset House; or, more precisely, the builders' yard on an uncompleted part of its site.[37] The government architect Sir Robert Smirke drew up plans for a building that could hold 2,000 students, complete with chapel, hall, and residence for the principal. But his estimate came in at £170,000, which was demonstrably too high.[38] Moreover, the locality was not popular with the college's supporters. A number withdrew their financial backing precisely because it was 'not placed on some elevated site near the Metropolis',[39] whilst others were shocked at the decision to build near the Strand, which was home not only to a number of theatres and pubs, but also 'the most infamous Women in London'.[40] The poet Robert Southey objected that 'the College ought to be a substantial edifice—not part of a great building'.[41] Smirke, however, responded quickly: radically retrenching and producing a design that could—he said—be built for less than £64,000.[42] It would only be part of his original plan, and costs would soon rise to something more like £80,000.[43]

Much of the accommodation was cramped and defective; a pupil at the school, which was crammed into the basement, recalled that 'The place exercised a depressing effect upon the sprits, and the boys in the playground appeared destitute of buoyancy of life, crushed by the subterranean nature of the school and the appalling ugliness of the buildings.'[44] The entrance from the Strand was comically anonymous: a gateway, wrote one critic, which 'might have been mistaken for one

[34] KCL, KA/C/M1/17 John Harrison Curtis (18 July 1828).
[35] *The Times*, 24 December 1828, p. 2.
[36] *King's College Calendar*, 1833–4, p. 64.
[37] J. Mordaunt Crook and M. H. Port, *The History of the King's Works vol. vi: 1782–1851* (London, 1973), pp. 481–3.
[38] KCL, KA/C/M1, Council Minute Book 1828–9, p. 100 (16 May 1829).
[39] KCL, KA/C/M1, Council Minute Book 1828–9, p. 104 (16 June 1829).
[40] KCL, KA/IC/A2/3, 'Subscriber and Friend to the Institution' (26 March 1829).
[41] KCL, KA/C/M1, loose typescript letter from Robert Southey (31 July 1828).
[42] KCL, KA/C/M2, Council Minute Book 1829–36, p. 2 (25 August 1829).
[43] F. J. C. Hearnshaw, *The Centenary History of King's College, London, 1828–1928* (London, 1929), p. 77.
[44] Sabine Baring-Gould, quoted in Frank Miles and Graeme Cranch, *King's College School: the first 150 years* (London, 1979), p. 19.

leading to some mews, or to a porter-brewery'.[45] Decades later, it would be seen as positively off-putting to prospective students.[46] Nonetheless, even with these problems, Smirke had provided King's with much of what it wanted—not least the sort of scholarly, solid Greek Revival structure that could be reproduced in lithographs to advertise the institution.[47]

That both King's and UCL ended up with similarly classical buildings should come as no shock. The 1820s and 1830s witnessed the triumph of the Greek Revival. Whilst the two colleges were being built, similarly Hellenistic edifices were going up all across London—from the National Gallery to the British Museum, the Post Office to St George's Hospital.[48] In Oxford, too, neo-classicism was still the dominant style for new university buildings—as witnessed by the neo-Roman University Press (1826–7); whilst in Cambridge, Wilkins' Downing College was an exceptionally pure example of Greek Revival taste.[49]

True enough, both Lampeter and Durham plumped for Gothic when building their colleges; but, of course, one was originally planned as a seminary and the other already occupied a castle. Their choice had, in a sense, already been made for them—and even then, when the architect of Durham was allowed free rein, he built a neo-classical observatory (1839–40).[50] Oddly, it was in New York that the neo-Gothic first triumphed over the neo-Greek for a university building—but even that was not until 1833, nearly a decade after the plans for UCL had been first mooted.[51] It was three years later, in 1836, that the manic Gothic propagandist, Augustus Pugin published his book *Contrasts*, an illustrated attack on the classicizing fashions of contemporary architecture. One of the telling juxtapositions he drew was between the nondescript entrance to King's College London and the great Gothic gate to Christ Church, Oxford. (Figure 6)[52] Yet most people objected to King's because it was undistinguished, not because it was neo-classical. It did not seem at all inappropriate for both London colleges to build in the Greek revival style.

Although some historians have endeavoured to find analogies between the architecture of King's and buildings at Oxbridge—seeing the dark and narrow court carved out of the former building yard as an 'archetypal college quadrangle'—the reality is that both London colleges resembled each other more than either aped

---

[45] *Library of the Fine Arts* (1831), quoted in Crook, 'The Architectural Image', p. 6.
[46] Thomas Hinde, *A Great Day School in London: a history of King's College School* (London, 1995), p. 39.
[47] See, for example, *Literary Gazette*, 8 May 1830, p. 306; *Saturday Magazine*, 21 December 1833, pp. 233–6.
[48] J. Mordaunt Crook, *The Greek Revival: neo-classical attitudes in British architecture, 1760–1870*, (London, 1972), p. 98.
[49] Geoffrey Tyack, *Oxford: an architectural guide* (Oxford, 1998), p. 199; David Watkin, ed., *The Age of Wilkins: the architecture of improvement* (Cambridge, 2000). I am grateful also to my doctoral student, Steve Greenwold, for sharing his work on the subject.
[50] David Watkin, *The Life and Work of C. R. Cockerell* (Cambridge, 1974); Jill Allibone, *Anthony Salvin: pioneer of Gothic Revival architecture* (Cambridge, 1987), pp. 128–34.
[51] Elon Danziger, 'A University Building for New York', *Burlington Magazine* 150 (2008), pp. 444–51.
[52] A. N. W. Pugin, *Contrasts: or, a parallel between the noble edifices of the middle ages and the corresponding buildings of the present day; shewing the present decay of taste* (London, 1836).

Fig. 6. 'Contrasted College Gateways'. Pugin mocks the anonymity of King's College London when compared with the grand—if uncompleted—entrance to Christ Church, Oxford

A. N. W. Pugin, *Contrasts* (London, 1841).

the ancient universities.[53] Partly, this was because both were conceived as independent institutions: unlike Oxbridge, where there was nominally a division of labour between college and university, these buildings had to contain everything necessary for higher learning. Whilst Oxford had the Bodleian, for example, there would be no autonomous University of London library until 1870; so both King's and UCL had to find room for their own collections.[54] The similarities between the two colleges were also the result of a shared approach to teaching. The core of the course at each place was not the more intimate tutorial, or even the class, but the lecture. Large lecture rooms and capacious corridors consequently took up a considerable proportion of the buildings—at UCL, for instance, there were four rooms each capable of holding 440, two which could seat 270, and five which were built for about 170.[55] At King's, there were ten lecture rooms, with a capacity of 2,000 in total.[56] In this emphasis on lecturing—and need for lecture halls—they were thus far closer to the Scottish universities than they were to either Oxford or Cambridge, and closer still to the European institutions which had so inspired Campbell in his vision of a university for London.

[53] Sheldon Rothblatt, *The Modern University and Its Discontents* (Cambridge, 1997), p. 73.
[54] Harte, *University of London*, p. 120.
[55] *Statement by the Council of the University of London*, p. 24.
[56] KCL, KA/C/M1/83, Smirke (9 April 1829).

Changing ideas about undergraduate life similarly shaped the two institutions. When University College was first being planned, it took little account of the social needs of students. Encouraged by the architect W. H. Playfair, who had worked at the University of Edinburgh, the building committee approached the project primarily thinking about discipline rather than the provision of facilities. 'There is one broad principle to be acted on in the whole arrangement of the Plan', he wrote; 'to remove all petty incitements to Levity or Disorder.' 'A fire place causes a crowd, and perhaps the application of a little gunpowder: dark and circuitous entrances to the Class Rooms incite a man to loiter and to take his seat after the commencement of the Lecture'.[57] Given these assumptions, there is little wonder that UCL was equipped with well-lit passages and impressive doorways—and precious few fireplaces for the application of gunpowder. It should come as no surprise, too, that the founders did not think to provide the students with any sort of social space. It was William Wilkins who insisted that 'rooms in which the Students may assemble previously to attending lectures' were 'absolutely required'.[58] Eventually these became student common rooms: a simple solution to the problems that arose within this non-residential academy; and one that was pioneered there, some forty years before Oxford acquired similar facilities.[59] By the time King's started to plan, only three years later, the provision of 'refreshment rooms' for the undergraduates was simply taken for granted in a metropolitan college—even if they struggled to fit them within the strictly circumscribed space provided.[60]

Above all, it was this lack of space—and, still more, a serious lack of money—that led King's to resemble UCL much more closely than was first intended. 'Grinding economy' left the college with a building far less exciting and with far fewer facilities than its founders had initially imagined.[61] There was no possibility of large-scale student or staff accommodation; even the provision of a home for the porter was a problem. 'He wants an additional room in which his *children* can sleep', wrote a shocked Robert Smirke in 1831.[62] The difference between the two colleges thus ultimately amounted to little more than this: King's built fourteen bedrooms for students to rent, an ill-attended hall for dinner, and a large, though barely-furnished chapel; while UCL did not.[63] However symbolically significant these were—and there can be little doubt that, in particular, the presence or absence of a chapel seemed extremely important at the time—the fact was that these two new colleges were both engaged in a similar process of architectural experimentation. Their façades and their plans and, above all, their range of

---

[57] UCL, College Correspondence, 1167/13, Playfair to John Murray (6 October 1825).
[58] UCL, College Correspondence, 1167/10, Wilkins to Committee (March 1826).
[59] UCL, Miscellaneous Committee Minutes 1828–9, 27 October and 13 November 1828; M. C. Curthoys, 'The Colleges in the New Era', in M. G. Brock and M. C. Curthoys, *The History of the University of Oxford, vol. vii: the nineteenth century part II* (Oxford, 2000), pp. 115–58, p. 151.
[60] KCL, KA/IC/S10, Smirke to Secretary (14 April 1832).
[61] Crook and Port, *King's Works*, p. 483.
[62] KCL, KA/IC/S6, Smirke to Secretary (6 October 1831).
[63] KCL, KA/CS/M/1 Special Committee Minutes, 1835–53, p. 2, Student's Rooms (14 October 1835); KA/C/M3, Council Minutes 1836–1842, p. 222 (11 February 1842).

amenities—with long, wide corridors opening onto large classrooms and the tentative yet innovative provision of student social space—was thoroughly different from the cloistered communities of the ancient universities. Each London college may have been a disappointment: a sign that one cannot, after all, achieve cut-price magnificence. But both showed that it was possible to imagine and to create a new sort of English, urban university.

IS THIS NOT ROBBERY?

Who were the people who inhabited these halls? Who were the staff and the students? Perhaps the most important point to note is that there were rather few of them. Each institution had, of course, been planned for thousands—indeed, UCL needed at least 1,000 paying students to balance the books. Unfortunately, only about half this number actually turned up.[64] Creative accountancy allowed King's to claim that it had over 900 students by 1832, but in fact a third of these were attending the school, and another third were medical students. This left just over 300 undergraduates attending lectures for the 'General Course of Study' that the college had been founded to teach, and of those only 109 were taking the full range offered.[65] At UCL, too, very few students bothered to attend all the classes even in those subjects which they had expressly chosen.[66] Nor did the advent of the University of London degree do much to change this. In 1839 fewer than 5 per cent of those enrolled as students at either college actually sat for a BA.[67] Now this freedom had clear advantages for some individuals, not least the small number of women who were not permitted to matriculate as students but who were nonetheless able to attend some lectures.[68] Still, the shifting constituency of the student body—which changed from term to term and from class to class—undoubtedly caused problems for the institutions themselves. Not only had they wildly under-recruited, but they could never be confident that they would achieve anything like financial stability.

The perpetual fluidity of the undergraduate population also made it hard to sustain any sort of student culture. At King's much emphasis was placed on the unifying effect of attending chapel and dining in hall.[69] But the college authorities in both institutions were unhappy about giving any sort of sanction to autonomous undergraduate activities. There was, in the 1820s and 1830s, still little sense that time at university formed a distinct stage in the life-course;[70] indeed, well into the 1840s Oxford colleges often sought to prevent undergraduates from participating

---

[64] Harte and North, *World of UCL*, p. 45.
[65] *King's College Calendar*, 1833–4, p. 55.
[66] Bellot, *University College, London*, p. 179.
[67] *UCL Annual Report* 1840, p. 8; *King's College Calendar* 1839–40, p. 96; Willson, *Our Minerva*, p. 179.
[68] Bellot, *University College, London*, p. 367; Hearnshaw, *King's College, London*, pp. 108–9.
[69] KCL, KA/C.M2, p. 136 (8 March 1833); KA/C/M3, p. 222 (11 February 1842).
[70] Rothblatt, *Modern University*, ch. 3.

in the organized sports, like rowing, which would later become synonymous with student life.[71] True to form, UCL forbade its students from becoming involved in collecting money for charity, or holding meetings to discuss current affairs.[72] The governing Council was horrified to discover that a *London University Magazine* had been founded, and they expressed themselves delighted to find that 'none of the present Students are connected with a publication tending to distract their attention from the prosecution of their prescribed studies and bring them prematurely before the publick' (Figure 7).[73]

Unofficially, and quite against both the spirit and the letter of college rules, however, a few students tried to create some sort of corporate spirit. The medics started to mark themselves off by wearing academic gowns.[74] It also transpired that the *London University Magazine* was in fact written by current students, and even some staff. Indeed, it was followed by a series of student publications: the *London University Chronicle*, the *London University Examiner*, the *London University Inquirer*, and *The Marauder*. None lasted long, but they were interesting experiments in the nature and form of undergraduate life—as were the handful of student societies that came into being.[75] By the early 1840s, they were imitated by King's College students, who also established a short-lived magazine and founded a series of clubs.[76] It was little enough—and did little to change the experience of student life—but these early efforts would prove to be influential in the longer term.

This energy was all the more impressive given the difficulties that students had to overcome. Most of them were young. At King's they entered the college at 16; at UCL some were even younger: the first year of entry included thirty under 15 and two who were only 11.[77] Those who sought qualifications studied relatively hard and would have had little energy for extra-curricular activities. At King's, the first lectures started at 8 a.m., and the last concluded at 9 p.m. 'Regular students' were expected to attend five-hours of classes six days a week as well as a daily service in chapel. Nor did Sunday bring any relief, for there was compulsory chapel then as well.[78] UCL undergraduates spent even longer in the classroom: one recalled attending 35 lectures a week.[79] They were also, of course, generally not living on site, but rather rented lodgings nearby or walked in from their parents' homes. For those who lived far away, this added hours to their day. As a student, the geologist Joseph Prestwich walked eight miles to and from his home in Lambeth.[80] Yet life in lodgings was far from ideal, too. Although landlords promised much to the

---

[71] See, for example, T. G. Jackson, *Recollections: the life and times of a Victorian architect*, ed. Nicholas Jackson (London, 2003), p. 35.
[72] Bellot, *University College, London*, p. 183.
[73] UCL, College Council Minutes 2, 1829–35 (18 June 1829).
[74] W. C. Williamson, *Reminiscences of a Yorkshire Naturalist* (London, 1896), p. 92. See also Harte and North, *The World of UCL*, p. 6.
[75] Bellot, *University College, London*, pp. 181–5.
[76] Hearnshaw, *King's College, London*, pp. 197–8.
[77] Bellot, *University College, London*, p. 180.
[78] *King's College Calendar*, 1833–4, pp. 5, 8, 15.
[79] Bellot, *University College, London*, p. 179; Harte and North, *The World of UCL*, p. 66.
[80] G. H. Prestwich, *Life and Letters of Sir Joseph Prestwich* (London, 1899), p. 23.

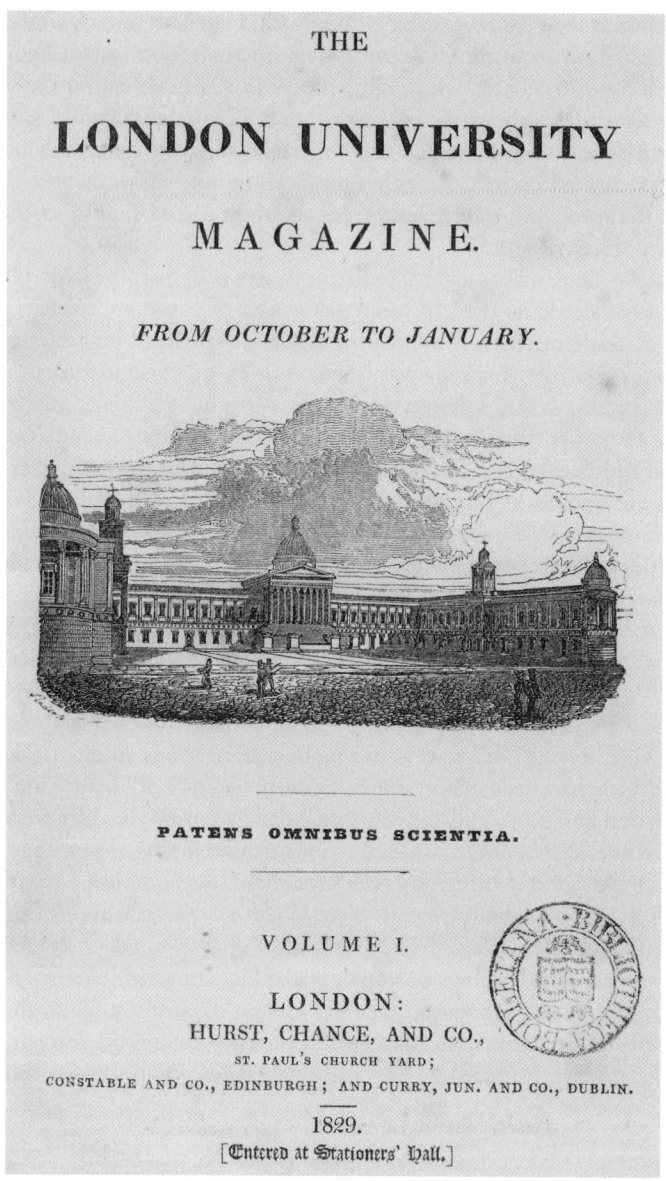

Fig. 7. The importance of buildings to institutional identity is made plain in the *London University Magazine* of 1829

Reproduced with the permission of the Bodleian Library, University of Oxford. Per. 2705 e.529/1.

students—not least 'a diligent attention to their moral and spiritual benefit'—the results did not always live up to expectations.[81] The young Robert Browning was so lonely in his Bedford Square accommodation that he moved home after a week.[82] Even those few undergraduates who rented rooms from King's College were not always happy; most of the rooms were tiny, and visitors were inclined to confuse their 'invisible bed-cubicle . . . for a closet'.[83] Certainly, there was no sense that this clutch of students formed the core of student life: regular attempts by the authorities to compel those living in Somerset House to attend both chapel and hall suggest that they similarly sought company and entertainment beyond the curtilage of the college.[84]

What can only have helped provide the little cohesion that existed amongst the students at either UCL or Kings was their shared social background. For Campbell's vision of a college for the middle class—the group that his ally James Mill called 'the glory of England'—was indeed fully realized at both institutions.[85] The sheer cost of sending a son to either would have deterred all but the most financially secure. A year's tuition would set one back rather more than £26; something like the annual salary of a clerk or a coachman. Discounts were available, it is true. Those people who bought £100 shares in the two colleges were entitled to nominate students and to a fifth off the price of lectures.[86] But, of course, £100 was an unimaginable amount for most people. Living expenses were also high: lunch at King's cost £15 a year; and its student rooms were rented out at between £30 and £90 per annum. Beyond the walls of the college, similar accommodation often cost even more.[87]

Little wonder the student body remained exclusive. Undergraduates came from similar sorts of homes in similar sorts of places. Southey even argued that King's should be sited in the east of the city, because the upmarket west was 'chiefly inhabited by a class of persons whose sons go regularly' to its rival.[88] Yet its eventual location actually placed it—just like UCL—within easy reach of the smarter parts of town. It was thus a work of special social outreach when King's imagined providing education for the sons of tradesmen—though, even then, it sought only to attract those 'who are designed for the higher branches of Commerce'.[89]

The men—and they were only men—who taught these upwardly-mobile undergraduates did not always share their advantages. UCL had been founded on the assumption that 'The salaries of the professors are to be very moderate, in order

---

[81] UCL, College Correspondence 222, Inigo Tudor to Leonard Horner (21 September 1827).
[82] John Maynard, *Browning's Youth* (Cambridge, MA, 1977), p. 268.
[83] Shephard T. Taylor, *The Diary of a Medical Student During the Mid-Victorian Period, 1860–1864* (Norwich, 1927), p. 2.
[84] KCL, KA/C/M3, pp. 83 (14 December 1838), 222 (11 February 1842).
[85] [James Mill], 'The State of the Nation', *Westminster Review* 6 (1826), pp. 249–78, p. 269.
[86] *King's College Calendar*, 1834–5, p. 74; Harte and North, *The World of UCL*, p. 67; *University of London Prospectus* (London, 1826).
[87] KCL, KA/C/M3, p. 7 (11 November 1836); KA/CS/M/1, p. 2 (14 October 1835).
[88] KCL, KA/CS/M/1, Southey (31 July 1828).
[89] *King's College Calendar*, 1834–5, p. 96.

that their emoluments may depend upon their classes'.[90] Put plainly: popular professors would earn more than those who failed to attract students. In this way, it was argued, the college would provide useful, modern learning, rather than the outdated, useless excuse for education offered at the ancient universities.[91] There was no expectation that these teachers would do research; indeed it is clear that Thomas Campbell saw the desire to write as a distinct disqualification for some candidates for chairs.[92] Nor were the teaching staff autonomous in their work: they were denied any collective authority to determine courses or become involved in the running of the college. Instead, they were to be overseen by a warden, who reported to the College Council; this in turn would be responsible to the proprietors—the people who had bought shares in the enterprise and were consequently believed to have its best interests at heart.[93] It was an entirely rational solution to the perceived problems of amply-endowed, self-governing Oxford and Cambridge, and it very soon collapsed. The desire to attract able lecturers came into conflict with the college's failure to enrol sufficient students: salaries had, as a result, to be paid. The Council also failed to hold its nerve, proving to be unwilling either to censor its professors' books or compel them to publish their lectures. It likewise abandoned its policy of refusing tenure to the teachers. This was, however, just the start.[94]

In 1829 a storm broke which was to transform the running of the college completely. It began with student complaints about the professor of anatomy, G. S. Pattison. He had shown, they said, '*unusual ignorance* of old notions, and *total ignorance of* and *disgusting indifference to* new anatomical views and researches'. Arguing that, as consumers, they had been let down, the medics demanded redress. 'We have paid freely all you demand, and we expect that you will provide... it is a bona fide contract between us, and that contract has been broken... Is this not robbery?' they asked.[95] This ostensibly trivial struggle soon became an existential crisis for the college, as the Council split and the staff turned on the warden.[96] Students were expelled, professors resigned, and the warden collapsed in nervous exhaustion.[97] In the end, the Council had to act—and Pattison was sacked. As the chairman put it:

> In the University there was no power over the Students, and therefore the Professors must be popular or the University could not flourish. It had been proved to the Council that Professor Pattison was not popular, and therefore the Council thought

---

[90] [Henry Brougham], 'The Proposals for Founding an University in London Considered', *Edinburgh Review* 42 (1825), pp. 346–66, p. 362.

[91] Macaulay, 'Thoughts', pp. 327–35.

[92] Bellot, *University College, London*, p. 51.

[93] *The Deed of Settlement of the University of London* (London, 1826); *Statement by the Council of the University of London, explanatory of the Nature and Objects of the Institution* (London, 1827).

[94] Bellot, *University College, London*, ch 6.

[95] 'Dissensions in the London University', *London Medical and Surgical Journal* 5 (1830), pp. 435–56, pp. 446–7.

[96] Leonard Horner, *Letter to the Council of the University of London* (London, 1830), p. 30.

[97] James Grieg, *Leonard Horner FRSE* (Edinburgh, 1982).

it was only discharging its duty to the Institution and the public by dismissing Professor Pattison.[98]

Yet the result of this contretemps was not the increased power of the council or the students, but a realization that the professoriate needed more autonomy. To that end, an academic senate was created and the office of warden abolished. In future, administrative work would be done by a secretary, and the academics would increasingly determine policy.[99] Bit by bit, authority passed from the shareholders and into the hands of the professors.

At King's, the struggle for control was less dramatic: a steady process of attrition rather than a full-blown battle. The low pay and hard work of the professors exacted a terrible toll. Of the first twelve appointed, fully five were dead within a few years of the foundation. Gilbert Burnett, the botanist, was the last to go. As the official historian of the college puts it: 'it must have been a strain to deliver lectures to medical students every day of the week, except Sunday, at eight o'clock in the morning; but probably what wore him out was the delivery of inaugural orations of inordinate prolixity— among the King's College papers there are no fewer than four'.[100] Resignations were also frequent. As tutors failed to fill their classes, fell out with the Council, or found other, more lucrative openings, so the list of the disappointed grew ever greater. By 1843 almost all the chairs had changed hands several times.

Nonetheless, slowly but surely, even the professors of King's saw their influence grow. The college Council was enormous and, in theory, all-powerful.[101] The perpetual members included the Lord Chief Justice, Home Secretary, Speaker of the House of Commons, Lord Mayor of London, and the Lord Chancellor. Indeed, in a delicious irony, Lord Brougham—the *eminence grise* of UCL—found himself *ex officio* chairman of King's when he sat on the woolsack in 1830. It hardly needs to be said, however, that such figures rarely had time to intervene in the affairs of the college. Indeed, scarcely any one of the Council members regularly attended meetings, and by the 1840s only the indefatigable bishop of London, Charles Blomfield, seems to have been directly involved in the day-to-day running of the place.[102] Although the Council remained sovereign, the academic staff were increasingly able to manage their own affairs.

In the great battle over the rights of the professors at UCL, complaint was made that university teachers were not treated with sufficient respect. As Anthony Panizzi, professor of Italian, put it:

> It is very hard for any man of education to see himself set down pêle mêle after the clerks, and with workers and servants, as if before the eyes of the Council there was no distinction between a man of European reputation . . . and any beadle or porter of the University.[103]

---

[98] Lord Ebrington, quoted in Bellot, *University College, London*, p. 211.
[99] *University of London. Proposed Plan for Future Management* (London, 1832).
[100] Hearnshaw, *King's College, London*, p. 105.
[101] Christine Kenyon Scott, *The Council: a portrait* (London, 2007).
[102] Hearnshaw, *King's College, London*, p. 200.
[103] Anthony Panizzi, quoted in New, *Henry Brougham*, p. 387.

Academics were indeed employees, and they were not, in general, very highly paid employees at that. Salaries ranged from £150 to £500 a year—or, in other words, from little more than the sum a clerk might earn to a little less than the minimum expected for a gentleman.[104] They were thus considerably less well off than their students, some of whom were renting rooms that cost more than half a lecturer's annual income. It is hardly surprising that the colleges saw a rapid turnover in staff, nor that many who stayed were evidently disgruntled.

Even Panizzi, however, ultimately concluded that the academics felt some sort of commitment to their role, despite the fact that he was forced to take a second job to make ends meet. 'In this noble institution', he wrote, 'the professors have by far a greater interest' than any shareholder.[105] Just like the student body—which was equally mercurial and often as dissatisfied—there were indications that the lecturers were increasingly coming to form a coherent community, brought together, not least, by adversity. Long before Oxford dons thought of themselves as professional academics, there were some signs that more metropolitan teachers were starting to think in precisely those terms.[106] The University of London—and its two component colleges—was starting, very slowly, to take root and to bear fruit. The ecology of higher education was becoming more diverse.

---

[104] Horner, *Letter*, pp. 32–3; Stefan Collini, *Public Moralists: political thought and intellectual life in Britain, 1850–1930* (Cambridge, 1991), pp. 35–7.
[105] Anthony Panizzi, quoted in New, *Henry Brougham*, p. 387.
[106] A. J. Engel, *From Clergyman to Don: the rise of academic profession in nineteenth-century Oxford* (Oxford, 1983).

Conclusion

The years between 1783 and 1843 were consequently a time of enormous hope and deep disappointment in the world of universities. Many plans were proposed and few were called into being. Those institutions which did open had to overcome enormous difficulties just to survive. Although separated by several decades and nearly 3,000 miles, both King's College London and King's College Windsor each faced the problem of financing an institution in an apparently hostile environment and amidst limited student demand. Both looked to the Church and the state for support, but what they got was never enough. Ostensibly very different, the place which became University College London also encountered obstacles. It too came to rely on the state, in the form of the *dirigiste* University of London. To that extent, at least, our four themes—the importance of the state, the significance of religion, the difficulty of recruiting undergraduates, and the ways in which individual institutions were founded to express an ideology as much as to respond to demand—hold true throughout this period.

Yet, at the same time, there were signs of change. For the first time, a boy's choice was no longer confined to the ancient English, Scottish, or Irish universities. The creation of new institutions by private individuals rather than rich bishops or state fiat was also significant. King's and UCL were as much companies as colleges, and yet they—eventually—received Royal charters. This is not how it had been done before, and it was certainly not how it was being done on the continent. Above all, however painful the births of these two colleges proved to be, the very fact that they had been brought to birth provided a precedent for others to do the same. In his proposals for the University of London, Brougham had argued that every town of at least 80,000 inhabitants should aspire to found a college.[1] A year later, in 1826, James Yates applauded these moves in the metropolis and concluded that others must now be created: 'First of all, the *North of England* claims our attention, and next the *West*.'[2]

It is with these new, non-metropolitan institutions that the remainder of this book is concerned. The enormous growth of London's university and the repeated attempts to reform—or even disband—it are not now our concern.[3] But the University of London will nonetheless continue to play an important part in this

---

[1] [Henry Brougham], 'The Proposals for Founding an University in London Considered', *Edinburgh Review* 42 (1825), pp. 346–66, p. 353.
[2] [James Yates], *Thoughts on the Advancement of Academical Education in England* (London, 1826), p. 184.
[3] For an excellent introduction to this, see the chapters in F. M. L. Thompson, ed., *The University of London and the World of Learning, 1836–1986* (London, 1990).

story. For it was not just the fact of a new sort of institution that would inspire others to establish their own, it was also the form that it had taken. That the University of London came to open its degrees up to anyone—even those outside the city—made it possible for provincial institutions to offer a real undergraduate education, and one that would result in a recognized qualification. University of London degrees would consequently be studied throughout the country and the British Empire. Redbrick would have been inconceivable without this. Thus, although the civic universities would differ substantially from the two rival colleges founded in the capital, they would all share a common debt to the 'rambling fumbling solution' to London's problems that had evolved in the 1830s.

PART II

1843–1880

Prologue

One of the more dispiriting lessons of history is the realization that the good are not always very nice, that the apparently selfless are frequently very selfish. As historians have frequently been forced to acknowledge, the motivations for philanthropy are very rarely pure.[1] This general truth is especially evident when examining two of the greatest patrons of higher education in mid-Victorian Britain. The first was a grasping, avaricious, bigoted reactionary, a man who died muttering 'I should have been kinder, I should have been more considerate and understanding.'[2] Yet he also gave £200,000 to charity, his cash was crucial in helping to bring higher education to Birmingham, and he was mourned as the exemplification of Christian philanthropy by at least some of those he left behind.[3] The second was a still more shadowy figure: a parsimonious, work-obsessed, easily-offended bachelor, who gave little to charity in his lifetime, who 'liked reading, but not to the extent of buying books', and who nonetheless bequeathed almost £100,000 to found what became the University of Manchester.[4] Samuel Warneford and John Owens—for these were the two individuals in question—were both disagreeable men, with deep pockets and few friends. Each, however, played an important role in expanding the world of universities in nineteenth-century Britain, establishing institutions—just as James Yates had hoped—to the north and west of London.[5]

The foundations that these two rich, strange men helped establish were very different from one another. Samuel Warneford's Queen's College Birmingham was part medical school, part seminary: exclusively Anglican and 'founded on a strictly Christian basis ... at time when Colleges, of which the tendency is at least to ignore Christianity, are being so widely founded throughout the country'.[6] In that respect, it is scarcely surprising to find that Warneford was a staunch supporter of King's

---

[1] Brian Harrison, 'Philanthropy and the Victorians', *Victorian Studies* 9 (1966), pp. 353–74, p. 361; F. K. Prochaska, 'Philanthropy', in F. M. L. Thompson, ed., *Cambridge Social History of Britain, 1750–1950* (3 vols; Cambridge, 1990), vol. iii, pp. 357–93, p. 386.
[2] Quoted in W. M. Priest, 'The Rev Samuel Warneford, MA LLD (1763–1855)', *British Medical Journal*, 6 September 1969, pp. 587–90, p. 589.
[3] [Thomas Vaughan], *Christian Philanthropy Exemplified in a Memoir of the late Rev Samuel Wilson Warneford LLD* (London, 1856).
[4] B. W. Clapp, *John Owens: Manchester merchant* (Manchester, 1965), p. 171.
[5] On Yates, see Part I.
[6] William Sands Cox, *Reprint of the Charter; Supplemental Charter; the Warneford Trust Deeds; and the Act of Parliament of the Queen's College, Birmingham* (Birmingham, 1873), p. i. See also Andrew Chandler, *'The Latter Glory of this House': a history of two Christian Commonwealths in Britain in the nineteenth and twentieth centuries, the Queen's and Handsworth Colleges in Birmingham, 1828–1980* (London, 2013), ch. 1.

College London, nor, for that matter that he gave money to support Charles Inglis's diocese of Nova Scotia; though it is nonetheless indicative of the kind of man he was that he regarded 'the subtle designs of the Jesuits, and the insidious intrusion of malignant dissenters' as a continual greatest threat to all his plans.[7]

Owens College Manchester, by contrast, was firmly established as a non-denominational institution, in which any student or staff member 'shall not be required to make any declaration to, or submit to any test whatsoever of, their religious opinions'. Indeed, Owens' bequest went further still, insisting that 'nothing shall be introduced in the matter or mode of education or instruction in reference to any religious or theological subject which shall be reasonably offensive to the conscience of any student, or of his relations, guardians, or friends'.[8] As a man who had stormed out of chapel, never to return, because someone had asked to share his pew, Owens knew well the problems that religion could cause.[9]

In some respects, then, Queen's College Birmingham and Owens College Manchester each reflect the influence of the two rival London colleges. Queen's, with its theological education, Anglican inflexion, and link with a medical school, does indeed sound rather like King's—and Warneford believed that 'the nearer we can approach to the regulations and privileges of King's College London, the better'.[10] For its part, the example of UCL was undoubtedly influential for the work of the Manchester college; after all, John Owens was a staunch supporter of the non-denominational elementary schools that were also created by the founders of that infidel institution in Gower Street.[11] Nor did the connections and continuities end there, for the problem of student enrolment had not gone away either. Until the 1870s, all the new institutions—from Durham to Dublin, from King's to Queen's—struggled to recruit. In 1858, the *Manchester Guardian* observed that Owens, which 'it was hoped would form the nucleus of a Manchester University, is a mortifying failure'.[12] Two years later, in 1860, the library of Queen's College was seized for debt by the bailiffs.[13] Frustrated by falling rolls, it seemed—in the words of one knowledgeable contemporary—as though 'the plan of a Midland University' would be delayed 'perhaps for half a century, perhaps for ever'.[14] A similar crisis at Durham led to a Royal Commission in 1861;[15] whilst the energetic, charismatic, and apparently saintly John Henry Newman signally failed to found a successful Catholic University for Ireland.[16]

---

[7] [Vaughan], *Christian Philanthropy Exemplified*, pp. 22–3; Cox, *Reprint*, p. 244.
[8] Manchester University Archive [MUA], OCA/5/1/1, Owens Trustees Minutes, 1849–55, p. 14.
[9] Edward Fiddes, *Chapters in the History of Owens College and of Manchester University, 1851–1914* (Manchester, 1927), p. 7.
[10] Warneford to Sands Cox (17 September 1847), in Cox, *Reprint of the Charter*, p. 247.
[11] Clapp, *John Owens*, pp. 171–2.
[12] *Manchester Guardian*, 9 July 1858, p. 2.
[13] Queen's College, Birmingham, 'Introductory Remarks and Index to Mr Martin's Report' (1860).
[14] Chancellor Law, *Materials for a Brief History of the Advance and Decline of the Queen's College, Birmingham* (Lichfield, 1869), p. 42.
[15] C. E. Whiting, *The University of Durham, 1832–1932* (London, 1932), ch. 4.
[16] Donal McCarthy, *UCD: a National Idea, a history of University College, Dublin* (Dublin, 1999), pp. 8, 15.

The government's continued interest in higher education also represents another important continuity. Between 1843 and 1880, the state in its various different forms was involved again and again in the foundation, reform, and funding of different institutions. Across the empire, colonial governments established a series of new universities: Sydney in 1850; Calcutta, Bombay, and Madras in 1857; the University of New Zealand in 1871, and several more besides.[17] Within the United Kingdom, successive Royal Commissions transformed Oxford and Cambridge, breaking down their old Anglican monopolies and opening them up to new subjects.[18] Similar interventions eventually reformed Durham, whilst an act of parliament created a unified University of Aberdeen out of two existing colleges in 1860.[19] The University of London not only remained a department of state, but one with which the government continually tinkered: revising the charter every decade.[20] In Wales, too, the lack of a national university became a serious political issue—and by 1880 almost every MP was elected on a pledge to obtain state support for Welsh higher education.[21] Another Royal Commission was the inevitable response.[22]

The practical needs of the imperial state also necessitated the establishment of government training schools, like the Royal Indian Engineering College, opened in 1872,[23] and embryo research institutes like the future Royal College of Chemistry (1845) and Government School of Mines (1851).[24] It was in Ireland, however, that the government showed its strongest interest—and, for a while, revealed the continuing salience of the connection between religion and universities. There, the funding of the Roman Catholic seminary at Maynooth and the foundation of three university colleges in Belfast, Cork, and Galway, created the perfect political storm—and one made all the more problematic by the complicated religious topography of the island.[25]

---

[17] Eric Ashby, *Universities: British, Indian, African, a study in the ecology of higher education* (London, 1966), remains a key introduction to this theme.

[18] Robert Anderson, *British Universities Past and Present* (London, 2006), ch. 3. See also Christopher Harvie, 'Reform and expansion, 1854–1871', in M. G. Brock and M. C. Curthoys, eds, *The History of the University of Oxford VI: nineteenth-century Oxford*, Part 1 (Oxford, 1997) and Christopher Harvie, *The Lights of Liberalism: university liberals and the challenge of democracy* (London, 1976).

[19] R. D. Anderson, *Education and Opportunity in Victorian Scotland: schools and universities* (Oxford, 1983), ch. 2. On Durham, I am grateful to Mr Matthew Andrews for sharing his on-going doctoral researches.

[20] Negley Harte, *The University of London: an illustrated history* (London, 1980).

[21] E. L. Ellis, *The University College of Wales, Aberystwyth, 1872–1972* (Cardiff, 1972), p. 63.

[22] *Report of the Committee Appointed to Inquire into the Condition of Intermediate and Higher Education in Wales*, PP 1881 C.3047.

[23] J. G. P. Cameron, *A Short History of the Royal Indian Engineering College, Coopers Hill* (Coopers Hill, 1960).

[24] W. J. Reader, *Professional men: the rise of the professional classes in nineteenth-century England* (London, 1966), pp. 139–42; Anna Guagnini, 'Worlds Apart: academic instruction and professional qualifications in the training of mechanical engineers in England, 1850–1914', in Robert Fox and Anna Guagnini, eds, *Education, Technology, and Industrial Performance in Europe, 1850–1939* (Cambridge, 1993), pp. 16–41, p. 17.

[25] See especially, T. W. Moody, 'The Irish University Question of the Nineteenth Century', *History* 43 (1958), pp. 90–109.

But, as the example of the two colleges in Birmingham and Manchester reveals, the story of higher education in this period is more complicated than a simple account of continuity.[26] They were, after all, new initiatives: pioneering provincial colleges, founded by benefaction rather than state subsidy, and designed to provide 'an incipient university' specifically for the industrializing cities in which they were built.[27] Unlike the metropolitan foundations, too, they were public corporations, not private companies. Moreover, they show that a generation after the University of London was founded, any remaining sense of a distinct opposition between the two London colleges had completely broken down. Although Owens superficially looked like a northern UCL, its most important influence was King's, whose principal provided assistance when the Manchester college was drawing up its own curriculum.[28] Indeed, when the professors subsequently tried to reform Owens, they argued that it should become still more like King's, which they saw as strikingly progressive in its willingness to allow students to specialize in science.[29]

By the same token, whilst non-denominational Owens may appear like an enlightened, forward-looking institution in comparison with the strictly orthodox Queen's, the reality was somewhat different. The course at Owens College was initially utterly traditional, focusing on classics and mathematics. In the critical words of the *Manchester Guardian*, its founder 'thought rather of making Manchester rival Oxford and Cambridge in ancient learning, than of suiting his College to the peculiarities of his fellow-citizens.'[30] In Birmingham, however, Queen's pioneered a professional education: offering courses for doctors, for the increasingly professionalized clergy, and for architects and engineers. In many ways, it was a far more inventive place with a much more imaginative syllabus than its ostensibly radical Manchester equivalent.[31] As the historian Robert Anderson puts it, Queen's 'has as good a claim as Owens to pioneering status'.[32]

Even the religious differences between Owens and Queens are not what they might first appear.[33] It is striking that contemporaries believed the initial failure of the former and the ultimate decline of the latter were both caused by their diametrically dissimilar theological positions. The problem with Owens, complained its future principal in 1856, was 'the completely unsectarian character of the foundation'. This, he went on,

---

[26] Samuel J. M. M. Alberti, 'Civic Cultures and Civic Colleges in Victorian England', in Martin Daunton, ed., *The Organisation of Knowledge in Victorian Britain* (Oxford, 2005), pp. 337–56, provides a good introduction to some important themes.
[27] Horace Faithfull Gray, 'Address', in *Annals of Queen's College, Birmingham* (4 vols; London, 1873), vol. ii., pp. 121–38, p. 129.
[28] MUA, OCA/5/1/1, 30 January 1849, pp. 47–109.
[29] MUA, OCA/5/1/2, Owens Trustees Minutes 1855–61, 20 May 1856, p. 53.
[30] *Manchester Guardian*, 9 July 1858, p. 2.
[31] Cox, *Reprint of the Charter*, p. 36.
[32] R. D. Anderson, *Universities and Elites in Britain since 1800* (Cambridge, 1992), p. 6.
[33] Though see Dennis Smith, *Conflict and Compromise: class formation in English society, 1830–1914* (London, 1982), pp. 148–50, for a rather different—and more schematic—interpretation of developments in Birmingham.

inevitably *limits* the area of the probable supporters of the college. Even at University College [London] which in this respect offers a natural parallel, with all the undoubted advantages there offered, it seems that in practice, the limit of numbers has already been reached.[34]

Nor was John Greenwood the only academic to hold such views. His colleagues appear generally to have agreed that a key weakness for the college was the 'want of identification with some one religious or political party'.[35] In other words: a lack of dogmatic religion was perceived to be a disability, rather than an advantage; something that 'offended Churchman and Dissenter alike'.[36] Yet at Queen's, and at about the same time, quite the contrary conclusion was reached. There, the college's failure to thrive was squarely blamed on its exclusive link with a single religious and political party. The admission of dissenters, concluded a report of 1860, was a necessary change if the place were to survive.[37]

All this begs a question: who was right? Was Owens too ecumenical or Queen's too exclusive? The problems in Birmingham and the collapse of projects like the Roman Catholic Kensington University College (1868–82) might suggest that the time for strictly denominational higher education was now over.[38] Yet the widely held doubts about non-denominational Owens, and the total failure of such explicitly secular endeavours as the Government School of Mines, which managed to recruit only six students in 1861, suggests that something more interesting was going on.[39]

The reality was that religion, which had been much the most important focus for university debates in the first half of the nineteenth century, gradually came to assume a less vital significance. As the earlier battles over the University of London and the sustained criticism of Oxford and Cambridge showed, the link between Church, state, and university had once been the pre-eminent bone of contention.[40] Increasingly, however, both the growing gap between Church and state and the reform of the ancient universities meant that these confessional conflicts did not need to be fought with the same ferocity.[41] Individuals might still suffer—as did the Anglican theologian F. D. Maurice in 1853 when he was required to resign from his post at King's College London because of his heterodox beliefs.[42] But for most institutions, faith became just one of a range of other debatable issues—and, for most students, not even the most important. It is noteworthy, for example, that such issues were almost never raised in student union discussions, which tended

---

[34] John Greenwood in MUA, OCA/5/1/2, 20 May 1856, p. 46.
[35] W. C. Williamson, in MUA, OCA/5/1/2, 20 May 1856, p. 50.
[36] A. C. Magian, 'An Outline of the History of Owen's College', *Old Owensian* 9 (1931), pp. 16–19, p. 16.
[37] Queen's College, Birmingham, 'Recapitulation of Mr Martin's Report' (March 1860).
[38] Tom Horwood, 'The Rise and Fall of the Catholic University College, Kensington, 1868–82', *Journal of Ecclesiastical History* 54 (2003), pp. 302–18.
[39] Margaret Reeks, *Register of the Associates and Old Students of The Royal School of Mines and History of the Royal School of Mines* (London, 1920), p. 99.
[40] See Chapter 1.
[41] R. D. Anderson, *European Universities from the Enlightenment to 1914* (Oxford, 2004), ch. 6.
[42] F. Maurice, *The Life of Frederick Denison Maurice*, (2 vols; London, 1884), vol. ii.

to focus on controversies over party politics and educational matters rather than religion.[43]

In its stead, the social, economic, and political forces that were reshaping Britain also reshaped British universities. In the first place, the nature of middle-class life was changing, as some form of further education became an increasingly important marker of bourgeois identity. A period at a university was no longer just the prerequisite of the aristocracy. This not only increased demand for student places, it also helped create a new and increasingly vibrant student culture, as the university became part professional academy and part finishing school.[44] As this suggests, underlying these developments was the growth of a newly professionalizing society, which increasingly used the university to provide validation for those entering the professions.[45]

Nor did this occur in insolation. The second great development which reshaped higher education was pressure from new groups which also sought an entrée to the university. No longer was the struggle primarily concerned with opening universities to non-Anglicans. Now, there were movements to extend access to working-class students—and to women.[46] In the third place, external factors, like the growing belief that Britain was falling behind its industrial competitors made higher education—and the research done by institutes of higher education—seem ever more crucial.[47] In that sense, the very purpose of the university, and especially of the new universities, came to be seen less as a theological and more as a technological matter.[48] Finally, the rising power and increasing ambition of local government was reflected in councils' willingness to support civic university foundations. By the end of this period, indeed, a trip to Owens College was an essential (and inevitable) part of a visiting dignitary's tour of Manchester. Just like the town hall, it was considered one of the city's 'official institutions', and was celebrated as such.[49]

Hence, although religious difference did not stop being significant, its impact was mediated by other, increasingly important forces. These other issues created their own problems, too. The professionalization of Victorian society did not

---

[43] See, for example, *Owens College Magazine* 1 (1868), p. 94.

[44] For a useful discussion of this in the world of American universities, see Helen Lefkowitz Horowitz, *Campus Life: undergraduate cultures from the end of the eighteenth century to the present* (Chicago, 1987), ch. 1.

[45] Though see, Harold Perkin, *Origins of Modern English* Society (1969; London and New York, 1996), pp. 298–9 and *The Rise of Professional Society: England since 1880* (London and New York, 1989), pp. 199–21, who would place this change later.

[46] Generally, see Gillian Sutherland, 'Education', in Thompson, ed., *Cambridge Social History of Britain, 1750–1950*, vol. iii, pp. 119–70, pp. 154–8. See also Lawrence Goldman, *Dons and Workers: Oxford and adult education since 1850* (Oxford, 1995).

[47] Peter Alter, *The Reluctant Patron: science and the state in Britain, 1850–1920* (Oxford, 1987), p. 101.

[48] Though see, David R. Jones, *The Origins of Civic Universities: Manchester, Leeds, and Liverpool* (London, 1988), p. 18, for some scepticism about the real importance of this.

[49] Simon Gunn, 'Ritual and Civic Culture in the English Industrial City, *c.* 1835–1914', in Robert J. Morris and Richard H. Trainor, eds, *Urban Governance: Britain and beyond since 1750* (Aldershot, 2000), pp. 225–41, p. 230.

always mean that people looked to higher education to provide a route into the professions. Part of the problem for Queen's College Birmingham, for the University of Durham, and for other struggling institutions was that their ambitious and pioneering courses for architects and engineers actually attracted very few takers: the way into these vocations was through apprenticeship, not a degree.[50] Equally, although there was tremendous interest in scientific education, this did not always translate into demand for technical courses or benefactions to provide appropriate facilities.[51] Nor was the support of municipal corporations always quite what might have been hoped for: it could be a hindrance as much as a help. Just like the sepulchral City Museum in Bristol—founded with only a dozen paintings and no money to buy any more—universities were often established simply as symbols of civic pride rather than founded as fully functioning institutes of higher education.[52]

All this meant that the environment in which institutions like Owens and Queen's had to operate was constantly changing—and often hard to navigate. As the quite contradictory analyses of their apparent decline suggests, even contemporaries were not always sure what was happening. Just as some firmly believed that religious exclusivity was destroying the Birmingham college, others were arguing equally fiercely that the lack of a confessional identity was undermining its Manchester rival. Similar arguments were repeated almost everywhere; indeed, at about the same time, campaigners for a Welsh university were also pondering 'the necessity of its being *unsectarian*, and the necessity of its being *religious*'.[53] Wider social changes, not least the growing power of local government and increasing influence of the professional middle class, only made the situation still more unpredictable for those seeking to establish and sustain university life. But out of this confusion came enormous energy, as new campuses were created throughout the empire and, in 1880, a new university was finally established in England itself. At one level, this was the culmination of a campaign—or series of campaigns—that stretched back to the beginning of the century. More importantly, though, it reflected the fact that the world of universities had changed, and changed for good.

---

[50] Mark Crinson and Jules Lubbock, *Architecture: art or profession? Three hundred years of architectural education in Britain* (Manchester and New York, 1994), ch. 2; Guagnini, 'Worlds Apart', pp. 23–30.
[51] Jones, *The Origins of Civic Universities*, pp. 18, 65.
[52] Helen Meller, *Leisure and the Changing City, 1870–1914* (London, 1976), pp. 65–71, 62.
[53] Ben T. Williams, *The Desirableness of a University for Wales* (London, 1853), p. 17.

3

Experiments in Ireland and England

None of these changes seemed likely at the start of this period. In 1843, when Queen's College Birmingham received its Royal Charter, and even five years later in 1848, when its position as a leading provider of higher learning was affirmed by its depiction in the *University of London Almanac*, it rather looked as though it was nothing more than business as usual in the world of universities.[1] 'A general air of poverty and depression' continued to hang over King's College London, which remained impecunious and uncertain of itself.[2] UCL was also small and surprisingly insubstantial. 'The College is far from having yet answered the great purposes originally announced', observed one of its founders in 1852.[3] The Scottish universities were still thwarting reorganization,[4] and Oxford, in particular, was convulsed by religious controversy—'a nightmare which... oppressed Oxford for fifteen years', and prevented anything like serious reform.[5]

What change there was looked very familiar, as did many of the debates that surrounded it. In Canada, denominational disputes continued to promote the proliferation of colleges that had begun as far back as the 1790s.[6] In Australia, the new University of Sydney was established to educate a conservative elite, with its professors taken from Oxbridge, and its grand Gothic buildings erected out of reach of both the radical city council and any students hoping to attend on foot. For years, as the historian W. J. Gardner notes, it was so exclusive that the gargoyles outnumbered the students.[7]

Above all, in Ireland, the 1840s witnessed another series of monumental rows about the relationship between religion and higher education: a re-enactment of the battles of the 1820s made all the more acrimonious by an intractable mixture of faith and nationalism, and the unfortunate fact that in this case the Established Church served only the smallest proportion of people whilst possessing the largest

---

[1] Negley Harte, *The University of London 1836–1986: an illustrated history* (London, 1986), p. 97.
[2] F. J. C. Hearnshaw, *The Centenary History of King's College, London, 1828–1928* (London, 1929), p. 206.
[3] Henry Crabb Robinson, quoted in H. Hale Bellot, *University College, London, 1826–1926* (London, 1929), p. 249.
[4] Robert Anderson, *Education and Opportunity in Victorian Scotland; schools and universities* (Oxford, 1983), pp. 48–54.
[5] Mark Pattison, *Memoirs* (London, 1885), p. 236.
[6] Martin L. Friedland, *The University of Toronto: a history* (Toronto, 2002), pp. 26–9; J. L. H. Henderson, 'The Founding of Trinity College, Toronto', *Ontario History* 44 (1952), pp. 7–14.
[7] W. J. Gardner, *Colonial Cap and Gown: studies in the mid-Victorian universities of Australasia* (Canterbury NZ, 1979), pp. 13–18.

endowment of income. As if things could not get worse, all the parties involved were split down the middle, with separate factions each advocating different—and sometimes mutually contradictory—solutions.

The reforms of the late-eighteenth and early-nineteenth centuries had, of course, opened Trinity College Dublin to non-Anglicans. The Roman Catholic seminary at Maynooth had been established, and continued to receive subventions from the government. In Belfast, further non-denominational education was provided by the state-sponsored Royal Academic Institution. Yet it was clear that this pattern of provision was simply unsustainable. Trinity College remained an Anglican redoubt.[8] The Belfast Institution was riven by dissent amongst the Ulster Presbyterians.[9] And there was trouble in Maynooth, too. By 1841 it was deeply in debt and falling apart.[10] Visiting it a year later, William Thackeray observed that a workhouse was 'a palace' compared to it: 'Ruin so needless, filth so disgusting, such a look of lazy squalor, no Englishman who has not seen it can conceive.'[11] He assumed it was Irish indolence that explained the problem but, in fact, as even the seminary's harshest critics conceded, it was the 'niggardly' government grant that left it so exposed.[12] Most importantly, there remained the problem of the Roman Catholic laity: unwelcome in Dublin and Belfast, and un-catered for by Maynooth. Such a congeries of trouble was irresistible to the perennially improving Prime Minister Robert Peel. On 11 February 1844, he announced to his cabinet that he intended to reform Maynooth. A week later, he had determined to transform Irish higher education as a whole.[13] It was a bold move; one his critics would dub 'Madness little short of high treason against heaven'.[14]

Robert Peel's decision to reform the Irish universities was born of pragmatism and political calculation. He had staked his political career on his ability to combine 'with the firm maintenance of established rights, the correction of proved abuses, and the redress of real grievances'.[15] This seemed like an opportunity to resolve the proved abuse that was Maynooth, the real grievance of Catholic laymen, and—in the process—defend both the Church of Ireland and Union with Britain.[16] Maynooth, he was sure, had not worked. It had attracted the wrong sort of people—those connected 'with the lower classes of society, rather than with the aristocracy or gentry'. The financial problems of the college and the 'insufficient' sums of money offered by the government had resulted in 'a priesthood embittered

---

[8] R. B. McDowell and D. A. Webb, *Trinity College, Dublin, 1592–1952: an academic history* (1982; Dublin, 2004), ch. 7.
[9] T. W. Moody and J. C. Beckett, *Queen's, Belfast 1845–1949* (2 vols; Belfast, 1959), vol. i., pp. xlix–liii.
[10] Patrick J. Corish, *Maynooth College, 1795–1995* (Dublin, 1995), p. 97. Though see also, *Facts and Observations Relating to the Popish College of St Patrick* (London, 1845), p. 7.
[11] William Makepeace Thackeray, *An Irish Sketchbook* (1843; New York, 1848), p. 155.
[12] W. E. Gladstone, *The State in Its Relations with the Church* (London, 1838), p. 252.
[13] Charles Stuart Parker, ed., *Sir Robert Peel from His Private Papers* (3 vols: 1899; New York, 1970), vol. ii, pp. 101–3, 105–7.
[14] J. P. Plumptre, quoted in A. S. Thelwall, ed., *Proceedings of the Anti-Maynooth Conference of 1845* (London, 1845), p. vii.
[15] Robert Peel, *Address to the Electors of the Borough of Tamworth* (London, 1834), p. 8.
[16] See Donal A. Kerr, *Peel, Priests, and Politics* (Oxford, 1982), pp. 6–7.

rather than conciliated by the aid granted by the State for their education'.[17] As for the laity, he asked, was it not possible to establish new colleges 'which might be *accessible* to Roman Catholics intended for the Church, and might combine with them, as at Oxford and Cambridge, young men destined for secular pursuits?'[18] It seemed an eminently sensible set of suggestions: something Irish Catholics had been demanding for decades;[19] and a policy that was quickly embraced by several leading cabinet colleagues, including the Home Secretary, Sir James Graham, and Colonial Secretary, Lord Stanley.[20] Education, asserted Stanley, was the key point on which the Roman Catholics should be conciliated, and the peace of Ireland be thus assured.[21]

It was not, however, merely an eye for the main chance that drove Peel's programme of Irish university reform: there was an idealistic element to the whole scheme too. Just as he had dreamt of shoring up the Established Church in the 1820s through his support of King's College London, so now he hoped to effect a transformation in the condition of Ireland with another educational project. Opening a library in his own home constituency of Tamworth in 1841, Peel had quoted some words from the appropriately grand and safely dead former President of the Royal Society, Sir Humphry Davy. The truly enlightened man, he claimed, was not only mentally but ethically improved: 'in becoming wiser, he will become better; he will rise at once in the scale of intellectual and moral existence'.[22]

Such a proposition doubtless sounded simply conventional to many of Peel's audience. But to one of his readers, it was a provocation that demanded a response. Writing pseudonymously, and significantly, as 'Catholicus', John Henry Newman sought to reprise the role he had assumed back in 1829, when he had led academic opposition to Peel's U-turn on Catholic Emancipation.[23] In a series of letters to *The Times*, he likened the speech at the opening of the library to Brougham's address at the opening of UCL, arguing that Peel was making precisely the same utilitarian arguments about learning: seeing mere education as a substitute or even replacement for Christian faith.[24] This was scarcely fair—either to Brougham or Peel; and it was especially unkind to the latter, who had made it clear that this was precisely not what he was arguing. Newman was right, nonetheless, to see Peel as a true believer in the power of education. He hoped, in Ireland, to effect a reform of the Roman Catholic population: 'to wean them from vicious habits, to substitute

---

[17] Parker, ed., *Peel from His Private Papers*, vol. iii, p. 101.
[18] Parker, ed., *Peel from His Private Papers*, vol. iii, p. 106.
[19] See Winifride M. Wyse, *Notes on Education Reform in Ireland During the First half of the Nineteenth Century: compiled from speeches, letters, &c contained in the unpublished memoirs of the Rt Hon Sir Thomas Wyse KCB* (Waterford, 1901), pp. 17–24, 40.
[20] Charles Stuart Parker, *Life and Letters of Sir James Graham* (2 vols; London, 1907), vol. ii, pp. 8–14.
[21] Parker, ed., *Peel from His Private Papers*, vol. iii, pp. 107–8.
[22] *An Inaugural Address Delivered by the Right Hon Sir Robert Peel Bart. MP, President of the Tamworth Library and Reading Room* (London, 1841), p. 42.
[23] Jerry Coates, 'John Henry Newman's "Tamworth Reading Room": adjusting rhetorical approaches for the periodical press', *Victorian Periodicals Review* 24 (1991), pp. 173–80, p. 175.
[24] 'Catholicus' [John Henry Newman], *The Tamworth Reading Room: letters on an address delivered by Sir Robert Peel Bart. MP on the establishment of a reading room at Tamworth* (London, 1841).

knowledge for idleness and profligacy'.[25] He aimed, in other words, to use new universities to solve the Irish question by reforming the character of the Irish themselves.

Two proposals were presented to parliament in 1845. Maynooth's grant was to be increased from nearly £9,000 a year to more than £26,000. At the same time, three new colleges were to be founded: one in Cork, one in Belfast, and one at a location yet to be determined. Each element of these plans was objectionable to a different group. There were those like Thomas Macaulay who saw the whole thing as yet another *volte-face* by Peel: the adoption of Whig policies he had opposed in the 1830s.[26] There were those like William Gladstone who interpreted the increased Maynooth Grant as an abandonment of the Church, a rejection of established religion.[27] There were those like the Baptist preacher J. P. Mursell who took the opposite view, and perceived it as the beginnings of a dangerous new Church establishment.[28] The three new colleges were equally problematic.[29] With their religious identity too controversial an issue to resolve, the government suggested that no theological teaching would be paid for by the state, but that each denomination would be invited to endow professorships. Not only was this nothing like the proposals put forward by the Irish campaigners for higher education, it also left the proposal open to the accusation that this was 'a gigantic scheme of Godless education'.[30] It was consequently opposed by many of those who had agitated for reform,[31] rejected by many Irish Presbyterians, who were seeking more theological control, not less,[32] and, in 1846, very publicly and pointedly condemned by the Vatican.[33]

In Britain, Maynooth was 'the great political controversy of the year—the subject on which society seemed to be going mad', as Harriet Martineau put it.[34] It split the ruling Conservative Party right down the middle, drove Gladstone from government, and led Peel and his ministers to contemplate resignation.[35] In Ireland, the three 'Godless' colleges were the chief focus of discontent. They smashed the nationalist movement in two, divided the Roman Catholic bishops amongst themselves, and led to schism after schism amongst the Presbyterians.[36]

---

[25] Parker, ed., *Peel from His Private Papers*, vol. iii, p. 177.
[26] HC Deb 14 April 1845 vol. 79 cc. 650–65. See also Jonathan Parry, *The Politics of Patriotism: English liberalism, national identity and Europe, 1830–1886* (Cambridge, 2006), pp. 130–44, 166–8.
[27] H. C. G. Matthew, *Gladstone, 1809–1898* (Oxford, 1997), pp. 68–73.
[28] Simon Skinner, 'Protestants Disunited: Britons and the Maynooth Grant'. I am grateful to Dr Skinner for sharing this unpublished essay.
[29] See Moody and Beckett, *Queen's*, vol. i., part 1.
[30] Parker, *Life and Letters of Sir James Graham*, vol. ii., p. 11.
[31] Kerr, *Peel, Priests, and Politics*, pp. 293–302.
[32] Richard Dill, *On the Importance and Necessity of establishing a Presbyterian College in Ireland* (Belfast, 1846), pp. 4, 7, 9, 20.
[33] Kerr, *Peel, Priests, and Politics*, p. 348.
[34] Quoted in Skinner, 'Protestants Disunited'.
[35] Thelwall, ed., *Proceedings of the Anti-Maynooth Conference*, pp. lxiv, cxxii; Parker, ed., *Sir James Graham*, vol. ii, p. 14.
[36] Wyse, *Notes on Education Reform in Ireland*, pp. 97–9; Richard Dill, *Prelatico-Presbyterianism: or, curious chapters in the recent history of the Irish Presbyterian Church* (Dublin, 1856).

Yet out of this cacophony of competing views, there nonetheless emerged a new higher education system. In 1844, the leading campaigner Thomas Wyse had complained that Ireland had fewer universities per head of population than any other country in Europe.[37] Within a few years, this was certainly no longer the case. Maynooth was reformed and, with the help of a £30,000 grant, extensively rebuilt.[38] Although state support for the Belfast Academical Institution ceased, two independently-funded Presbyterian institutions eventually took its place: Assembly's College in Belfast (1853), and Magee College in Derry (1865).[39] The government established its new, neutral foundations in Belfast, Cork, and—after some debate—in Galway. Collectively, these three colleges formed the Queen's University of Ireland. Chartered in 1850, this was a truly federal institution, governed by representatives of each institution; it was also wholly centralized, examining only those who were members of the three colleges. In that sense, the product of all this dissension was a far more cohesive and coherent entity than the University of London.[40]

Although both colleges in Cork and Galway were headed by practising Roman Catholics—the latter by the Rev. Joseph Kirwan, who had narrowly failed to become Bishop of Galway, the Vatican continued to fulminate against Peel's reforms, publishing further condemnations in 1847, 1848, and 1850.[41] On 22 August 1850, the Irish Catholic hierarchy met together for their first full formal meeting since the twelfth century. The Synod of Thurles was the moment when the Queen's Colleges were finally declared, as it were, beyond the pale. The bishops were still split, and a minority appealed to Rome against the decision. But the verdict had been pronounced and the majority wanted death, hoping through their prohibitions to kill off the 'Godless' colleges altogether.[42]

This still left the problem of Irish Catholic higher education unresolved, however, and to provide a solution the bishops turned to Peel's most eloquent opponent, John Henry Newman. He was the most famous Roman Catholic convert in the empire, a first-rate scholar, and well known for his past influence as an Oxford tutor.[43] In 1851, he was appointed Rector of what was to be called the Catholic University.[44] A year later he delivered a series of lectures setting out his vision of the place: on 3 November 1854, he welcomed its first twenty students, inauspiciously quoting from *Henry V*: 'We few, we happy few, we band

---

[37] Thomas Wyse, *Speech on the Extension and Improvement of Academic, Collegiate, and University Education in Ireland at the Meeting Held for the Purpose at Cork* (London, 1845), p. 26.
[38] Corish, *Maynooth*, pp. 103–4.
[39] Robert Allen, *The Presbyterian College, Belfast, 1853–1953* (Belfast, 1954), ch. 2; William Logan, *The Story of Magee College* (Londonderry, 1989), p. 45.
[40] Moody and Beckett, *Queen's, Belfast*, vol. i., pp. 70–7.
[41] Kerr, *Peel, Priests, and Politics*, pp. 316–49.
[42] J. C. Barry, 'The Legislation of the Synod of Thurles, 1850', *Irish Theological Quarterly* 26 (1959), pp. 131–66, p. 159.
[43] On Newman at Oxford, see Peter Nockles, 'Oriel's Religious History in an Era of Intellectual Ascendancy'. I am grateful to Dr Nockles for allowing me to see this chapter for the college history in an early draft.
[44] Ian Ker, *John Henry Newman* (Oxford, 2009), pp. 9–11.

of brothers'.[45] As Henry's only experience of Ireland was as a hostage in Dublin, it was an ill-omened choice of words.

Newman came to the job with clear ideas about education and some definite notions about the university he was to create. As his attack on Peel revealed, he was utterly opposed to any system that instrumentalized learning and had set himself wholly against any institution that sought to make study a substitute for faith. He also possessed a romantic attachment to his *alma mater*, despite—indeed, of course, because of—the fact that he had been driven from it on his conversion to Roman Catholicism. When asked to establish a new university, he thought immediately of his old experiences: 'Curious it will be if Oxford is imported into Ireland, not in its members only, but its methods, ways, and arguments.'[46] His lectures on *The Idea of a University* went further still, depicting a place of liberal education designed to produce gentlemen. In many ways, he sounded like those apologists for the ancient universities that had written to defend Oxbridge in the 1810s and 1820s.[47] The institution that eventuated was ostensibly based on the appropriately pious Catholic University of Louvain, which had been re-founded in 1834. But it was in fact, as Newman hoped, a sort of Celtic Oxford, complete with tutorial system, embryonic colleges, and compulsory chapel.[48] It was also, in Newman's mind, not an exclusively Irish establishment at all, but was intended to be 'the Catholic University of the English tongue for the whole world'.[49]

Looking back on his experiences in Dublin, Newman later reflected that had the Vatican understood the situation in Ireland, it would have never have permitted the establishment of a Catholic University in the first place.[50] It is hard not to feel that had the Irish hierarchy understood Newman better, they would never have thought him a suitable founder for their new college. This was not because he lacked commitment or energy, or because he was unwilling to dirty his hands with the messy business of educational administration—indeed, as the historian Donal McCartney observes, 'at times Newman was obliged to behave more like the harassed house-master in a boarding school than as the rector of a new university'.[51] But his *Idea* was fundamentally ill suited to its environment. Newman's vision of a university open to Roman Catholics from throughout the empire dissatisfied those who wanted a truly Irish university. His defence of liberal education was rejected by those who sought a professional training, and his praise for the gentlemanly ideal sounded suspiciously secular to those who wanted a more dogmatic institution. He could not overcome many laymen's doubts about a university run by priests, nor heal the rift amongst the bishops; and his lectures left many baffled rather

---

[45] McCartney, *UCD*, p. 5.   [46] Quoted in Ker, *Newman*, p. 377.
[47] The standard edition of these is Ian Ker, ed., John Henry Newman, *The Idea of a University: defined and illustrated* (Oxford, 1976). For a very valuable set of essays on the *Idea*, see Frank Turner, ed., *The Idea of a University: John Henry Newman* (New Haven and London, 1996).
[48] A. Dwight Culler, *The Imperial Intellect: a study of Newman's educational ideal* (New Haven, 1955), pp. 158, 166–7.
[49] Quoted in Ker, *Newman*, p. 376.   [50] Ker, *Newman*, p. 462.
[51] McCartney, *UCD*, p. 6.

than inspired.[52] It was with some relief on both sides that Newman resigned as rector on 12 November 1858.

The Catholic University never recovered from its disappointing start. Throughout the next few decades, it barely managed an annual intake of twenty, and by 1879 there were only three students on the books.[53] The central problem was that there was simply not enough demand for it. Newman alienated some potential supporters; the Roman Catholic hierarchy alienated others. But even without these difficulties, it is hard to see how the self-styled university could have done much better. As he assumed office as Rector, Newman had spoken to the head of the Irish Jesuits, Fr. John Curtis. Curtis had warned that it would be impossible to find enough students: 'the middle class was too poor', while 'the gentleman class wished a degree for their sons, and sent them to Trinity College: and the upper class, who were few, sent their sons to English Universities'.[54] Lacking a charter, and thus without the authority to grant degrees, the Catholic University could never satisfy the needs of those who were its intended members.[55] Moreover, as Newman's biographer observes, 'The educated laity were especially opposed to the project. An exclusively Catholic university was seen as impractical, undesirable and unnecessary in a mixed Catholic-Protestant community.'[56] Even in Ireland, therefore, where religious difference would continue to shape all the debates about higher education, experience showed that universities could not rely solely on denominational loyalty to sustain themselves. Students and their families placed a higher value on obtaining an appropriate education than they did on attending a strictly orthodox institution.

This did not mean that the non-denominational Queen's Colleges found life easy. They remained the subject of severe criticism and repeated reform. The Queen's University itself was replaced in 1881 by the Royal University, which extended the institution's embrace to include Presbyterian Magee College, and the resurrected remains of Newman's Catholic University, now renamed University College Dublin. In 1908 the Royal University was in its turn replaced by the National University of Ireland, with Queen's College Belfast, splitting off to become a separate university in its own right.[57] Without massive government subsidy—amounting to no less than £367,000 between 1846 and 1859 alone—the whole system would have collapsed.[58]

But it is wrong to see the three colleges, as some writers do, as 'a colossal and expensive failure'.[59] Nor is it right to imagine that the Roman Catholic hierarchy

---

[52] Vincent Alan McClelland, *English Roman Catholics and Higher Education, 1830–1903* (Oxford, 1973), pp. 103–9; Fergal McGrath, *Newman's University: idea and reality* (London, 1971), pp. 497–504.

[53] McCarthy, *UCD*, pp. 8, 15.   [54] Quoted in Ker, *Newman*, p. 407.

[55] McGarth, *Newman's University*, p. 497–8.   [56] Ker, *Newman*, p. 407.

[57] Senia Pašeta, *Before the Revolution: nationalism, social change, and Ireland's Catholic elite, 879–1922* (Cork, 1999), ch. 1.

[58] *Queen's Colleges, Ireland*, PP. 1859 Session 1 (168) XXI Pt.II.415.

[59] McClelland, *English Roman Catholics*, p. 93.

was successful in its attempts to kill them off.[60] More than half of the nearly 1,900 students who matriculated at Cork and Galway in the first decade were Catholics, as were about 10 per cent of the almost 1,900 who attended predominantly Protestant Belfast over the same period.[61] True enough, only one in ten undergraduates actually graduated. Yet this was, after all, at a time when even the University of London produced only a few score of graduates per annum.[62] Moreover, the 119 matriculated students at Belfast, 125 at Cork, and even 92 at Galway in 1857–8 compared very favourably with the 34 recruited by Owens College Manchester, in the very same year.[63] The tangible achievements of the Queen's University were also recognized beyond Ireland, with its curriculum imitated at the newly founded University of Melbourne in 1853,[64] and its example cited as inspiration for a new university of Wales ten years later.[65] In many respects, indeed, the structure of the University would be more influential on the first Redbrick foundations than its London equivalent ever was.

Peel's plan had not solved the Irish question. It had not even solved the question of Irish higher education. Indeed, the disputes that his proposals engendered rumbled on for years, with each issue generating new controversies. The Queen's Colleges led inexorably to the Synod of Thurles; the Synod of Thurles provoked anti-Catholic legislation at Westminster; the anti-Catholic legislation further embittered those against whom it was directed.[66] But the outcome was not the disaster that Peel's critics predicted and Newman had counted on. Sustained by state subsidy and encouraged by popular demand, the three 'Godless' colleges survived and grew. Increasingly, they enrolled Roman Catholic students attracted by the vocational courses they offered.[67] No longer would the Maynooth grant be the focus for discontent in Ireland or Westminster—and the seminary itself became a more comfortable and conformist institution, producing priests (just as Peel had hoped) who often spoke up for the Union.[68] Above all, the development of higher education in Ireland in the 1840s reveals the ambivalent place of religion within the world of nineteenth-century universities. It was the subject of fierce debate, but was also of diminishing importance in determining which students would attend what institution. What was true in Ireland was still more apparent in Britain—as the case of Owens College Manchester, and Queen's College Birmingham, makes clear (Figure 8).

---

[60] McGrath, *Newman's University*, p. 81.
[61] *Queen's Colleges, Ireland*, PP. 1859 Session 1 (168) XXI Pt.II.415.
[62] F. M. G. Willson, *Our Minerva: the men and politics of the University of London, 1836–58* (London, 1995), p. 179.
[63] MUA, OCA/2/2, Owens College, Manchester, Annual Report, July 1858, p. iii.
[64] Eric Ashby, *Universities: British, Indian, African, a study in the ecology of higher education* (London, 1966), pp. 43–4.
[65] Thomas Nicholas, *Middle and High Schools and a University for Wales* (London, 1863), p. 34.
[66] McClelland, *English Roman Catholics*, pp. 91–2.
[67] Pašeta, *Before the Revolution*, p. 9.
[68] See, for example, Don Boyne, *I Remember Maynooth* (London, 1937); Walter McDonald, *Reminiscences of a Maynooth Professor* (London, 1925).

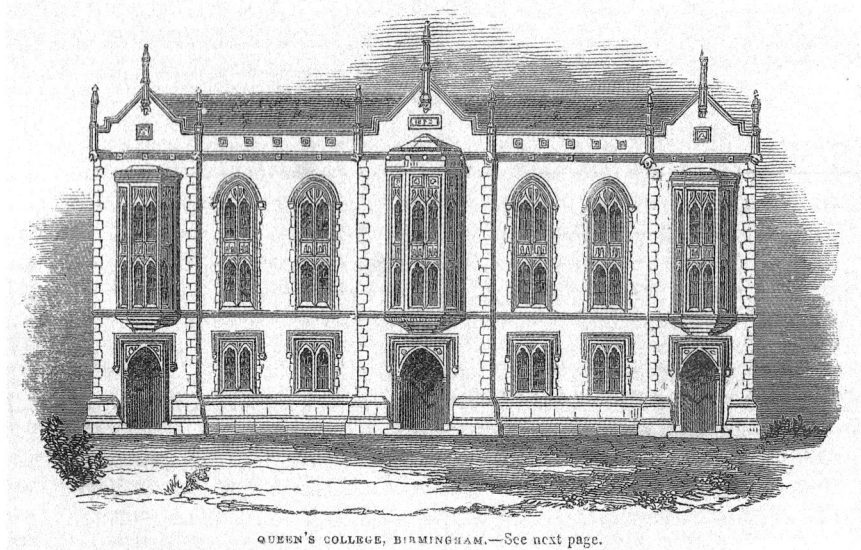

Fig. 8. 'How many have been ruined, as this College has been, by masses of unremunerative bricks and mortar piled up for show.' Queen's College Birmingham in 1843

Illustrated London News, 1843.

OH! AMBITION! AMBITION! THOU CURSE OF THE NOBLEST MINDS!

To move from the drama of the Irish colleges, to the outwardly sober, civic story of two provincial English institutions might seem to be like the transition from Technicolor to greyscale. Yet the struggles in Birmingham and Manchester were every bit as intense and often just as existential as anything that occurred across the Irish Sea. Moreover, whilst the Queen's Colleges in Ireland could count on large subsidies from the state, Owens in Manchester and Queen's in Birmingham were wholly dependent on benefactions and student fees. The possibility of total failure—of bankruptcy and closure—was never very far away. At the same time, however, the opportunities for a putative university presented by two of the greatest industrial cities of the world were also far more substantial than Ireland, with its relatively low level of education and small middle class, could possibly offer.[69]

By the mid-nineteenth century, it was noteworthy that there were now many more universities in the empire than there were in England.[70] 'I wish we had several more universities: our material progress has outrun our intellectual', observed the

---

[69] McGrath, *Newman's University*, p. 82.
[70] Edward Shils and John Roberts, 'The Diffusion of European Models Outside Europe', in Walter Rüegg, ed., *A History of the University in Europe: vol. iii—universities in the nineteenth and early twentieth centuries (1800–1945)* (Cambridge, 2004), pp. 163–230, p. 213.

great English imperialist Sir John Seeley in 1867.[71] If there was to be an expansion, where better to have it than the heartlands of the imperial economy? Moreover, the intense competition between the great cities of the Victorian era often found its expression in great public works, like town halls, schools, and hospitals.[72] Why should this munificence not extend to universities? It certainly did in the colonies.[73] Should it not at home? The two rival colleges in Birmingham and Manchester were consequently opened and operated at a time of immense uncertainty, and apparently limitless hope. Their different stories reflect both the trials and triumphs of the era.

That several decades had passed since the foundation of London University without seeing the creation of further new English institutions came as a something of a surprise even to contemporaries.[74] After all, Scotland had possessed its own little clutch of universities for centuries, and after 1850 the Irish possessed at least two of their own. New universities were springing up all across the globe, with the proliferation of American colleges becoming particularly notorious.[75] Nor had people stopped planning innovative English institutions. A variety of proposals continued to be presented in this period, including tangible efforts to create a centre for higher learning in Southampton from the 1840s, and more speculative attempts to inspire the establishment of a federal university to serve the agricultural counties in the 1860s.[76]

The failure to found a new English university was all the more striking given the remarkable vitality of the country's great cities. By 1850, England was the most urban society on earth, with more than half the population living in towns.[77] Moreover, those towns were themselves growing larger and life within them was taking on its own particular and distinctive *timbre*.[78] As provincial cities increased in size and confidence, so the cultural centrality of London declined, leaving places like Manchester, Birmingham, Liverpool, and Leeds as major centres for art, education, science, and literary life in their own right.[79] From the 1780s onwards, Manchester in particular had acquired a raft of foundations devoted to study and debate: the Literary and Philosophical Society (founded 1781), the Natural History

---

[71] Quoted in Charles Grant Robertson, *The British Universities* (London, 1930), p. 33.
[72] William Whyte, 'Building the Nation in the Town: Architecture and National Identity in Urban Britain, 1848–1914', in William Whyte and Oliver Zimmer, eds, *Nationalism and the Reshaping of Urban Communities, 1848–1914* (Basingstoke, 2011), pp. 204–33.
[73] Gardner, *Colonial Cap and Gown*, p. 12.
[74] V. A. Huber, *The English Universities*, trans. Francis W. Newman (2 vols; London, 1843), vol. ii., p. 416.
[75] Matthew Arnold, *Schools and Universities on the Continent* (London, 1868), pp. 272, 290.
[76] A. Temple Patterson, *The University of Southampton* (Southampton, 1962), ch. 2; Earl Fortescue, *Public Schools for the Middle Classes* (London, 1864), pp. 9–13.
[77] C. M. Law, 'Growth of the Urban Population in England and Wales, 1801–1911', *Transactions of the Institute of British Geographers* 41 (1967), pp. 125–43, p. 130.
[78] F. M. L. Thompson, 'Town and City', in Thompson, ed., *Cambridge Social History*, vol. 1, pp. 1–86. See also Patrick Joyce, *Visions of the people: industrial England and the question of class, 1848–1914* (Cambridge, 1991), esp. pp. 180–3.
[79] Simon Gunn, *The Public Culture of the Victorian Middle Class: ritual and authority in the English industrial city, 1840–1914* (Manchester and New York, 2000), p. 7. See also Andrew Lees and Lynn Hollen Lees, *Cities and the Making of Modern Europe, 1750–1914* (Cambridge, 2007), pp. 133–4.

Society (1821), the Royal Manchester Institution (1823), the Botanical Society (1827), the Statistical Society (1834), the Medical Society (1834), the Geological Society (1838), the antiquarian Chetham Society (1843), the Literary Club (1862), and the Athenaeum (1835), intended to be 'a magnificent home for the mind—a university in itself, of art, science and literature, and of every rational recreation'.[80] Yet despite all this, still no new university had been created.

The formal further education that existed in these cities tended to be chiefly vocational, especially focusing on theology and medicine. The Dissenting Academies remained important for the training of budding preachers and pastors, with each year seeing a series of mergers and moves and new beginnings.[81] Seven theological colleges were opened in Manchester alone in the four decades after 1840,[82] while the Independent Academy established at Manchester in 1786 moved to York in 1803, returned to Manchester in 1840, and went off to London in 1853, before finally settling as an Oxford college in 1889.[83] These towns were also home to a series of successful medical schools, with almost a dozen established outside London in the decade before 1834.[84] Two of these were in Manchester whilst Birmingham obtained a medical school of its own in 1828.[85]

The achievements of these medical and theological colleges reflected their capacity to cater for a very particular set of requirements. The first half of the nineteenth century witnessed a renewed emphasis on the need for specially-trained ministers to serve Non-Conformist congregations of all types. Employment as a pastor was, as a result, increasingly contingent on time spent in an Academy.[86] Legislation like the 1815 Apothecaries Act and 1858 Medical Act likewise placed a premium on appropriate qualifications for doctors too.[87] Put simply, the professionalization of both general practice and the Non-Conformist ministry each created a demand for college education. Yet these institutions' frequent changes of name and address also reflected their vulnerability. Utterly dependent on student fees, a religious upheaval—like the schism that split the two Presbyterian Colleges

---

[80] Quoted in Michael E. Rose, 'Culture, Philanthropy, and the Manchester Middle Classes', in A. J. Kidd and K. W. Roberts, eds, *City, Class, and Culture: studies of cultural production and social policy in Victorian Manchester* (Manchester, 1985), pp. 102–19, p. 112. See also Arnold Thackeray, 'Natural Knowledge in Cultural Context: the Manchester model', *American Historical Review* 79 (1974), pp. 672–709.

[81] Geoffrey Nuttall, *New College, London and its Library* (London, 1977), pp. 5–6; Kenneth W. Wadsworth, *Yorkshire United Independent College* (London, 1954), pp. 123–4, 139.

[82] Edward Fiddes, 'The University Movement in Manchester (1851–1903)', in J. G. Edwards, V. H. Galbraith, and E. F. Jacob, eds, *Historical Essays in Honour of James Tait* (Manchester, 1933), pp. 97–110, p. 106.

[83] Barbara Smith, ed., *Truth, Liberty and Religion: Essays Celebrating Two Hundred Years of Manchester College* (Oxford, 1986).

[84] Irvine Loudon, *Medical Care and the General Practitioner, 1750–1850* (Oxford, 1986), p. 49.

[85] *History of the Birmingham Medical School, 1825–1915* (Birmingham, 1925), pp. 19–28; P. J. Hartog, *The Owens College Manchester (founded 1851): a brief history of the college and description of its various departments* (Manchester, 1900), p. 1.

[86] Kenneth D. Brown, *A Social History of the Nonconformist Ministry in England and Wales, 1800–1930* (Oxford, 1988), ch. 2.

[87] Irvine Loudon, 'Medical Education and Medical Reform', in Vivian Nulton and Roy Porter, eds, *The History of Medical Education in Britain* (Amsterdam, 1995), pp. 229–49.

in Ireland,[88] or the appearance of a rival institution—like the competing medical schools in the Manchester of the 1820s,[89] could prove a terrible threat. These establishments stayed alive, in Sheldon Rothblatt's term, 'chameleon fashion', reshaping themselves to their surroundings. Those that could not adapt did not last.[90]

Queen's College grew out of one of the Birmingham medical schools.[91] Its founder was the energetic, enterprising, mercurial, and often irascible doctor William Sands Cox, himself the son of a leading Birmingham surgeon.[92] Sands Cox was educated in London and then Paris, one of the hundreds of British medical students who headed to the French capital for medical training.[93] On his return, newly qualified and not yet 24 years old, he began lecturing in a back room of his father's home in Temple Row, the fashionable street for Birmingham doctors.[94] Over the next few years, he visited the medical schools of Manchester, Edinburgh, Dublin, and Glasgow, as well as some of their continental equivalents, looking for inspiration. In 1828 he established his own institution, which was an instant success. Although he faced significant opposition from competing schools, within four years no fewer than eighty-three students had registered. Sands Cox was thus able to move his classes into their own premises, and was then forced to find still larger accommodation. To this end, he acquired a site in Paradise Street, opposite Birmingham's brand new town hall, and set about building a state-of-the-art medical school. Less than a decade after he had first lectured in his father's house, Sands Cox found himself presiding over a popular institution in a prime location. Here was triumph indeed—and in 1836, his school even gained a royal patron, in the person of King William IV.[95]

Only two years later, the newly-ennobled Birmingham Royal Medical School acquired something still more useful: a financial backer, in the shape of Samuel Warneford. Over the next seventeen years, he gave almost £30,000, helped the medical school acquire a Charter, and oversaw its transformation into the Queen's College. Warneford was a great medical benefactor: the Oxford mental health hospital is still named after him, and the wall he built to contain its inmates and prevent curious onlookers from 'exciting' them, still stands to this day, as does a statue commemorating his £70,000 bequest to the place.[96] Warneford was not, however, only interested in patients; he was also deeply concerned about the probity and

---

[88] Dill, *Prelatico-Presbyterianism*, pp. 392–4, notes that the legal costs alone ran into thousands.
[89] F. W. Jordan, *Life of Joseph Jordan, Surgeon* (London, 1904).
[90] Sheldon Rothblatt, *The Modern University and Its Discontents: the fate of Newman's legacies in Britain and America* (Cambridge, 1997), p. 301.
[91] Andrew Chandler, *'The Latter Glory of this House': a history of two Christian Commonwealths in Britain in the nineteenth and twentieth centuries, the Queen's and Handsworth Colleges in Birmingham, 1828–1980* (London, 2013), ch. 1.
[92] J. T. J. Morrison, *William Sands Cox and the Birmingham Medical School* (Birmingham, 1926).
[93] Charles Singer and S. W. F. Holloway, 'Early Medical Education in Relation to the Pre-History of London University', *Medical History* 4 (1960), pp. 1–17, p. 1.
[94] *History of the Birmingham Medical School*, p. 19.
[95] Bodl. MS Top Warw d.1, Papers Relating to Queen's College, 1838–52.
[96] Brenda Parry-Jones, *The Warneford Hospital, Oxford, 1826–1976* (Oxford, 1976), pp. 12, 17.

piety of physicians. He feared that medical students were ill disciplined and often immoral, and that many doctors were materialists at best and atheists at worst.[97] Without a doubt, Warneford was a peculiar and difficult man, endlessly on the watch for the threat of what he described as 'future satanic subtlety', but his views were not, in this case, ill-founded.[98] As Adrian Desmond has shown, many of the most radical thinkers of the Victorian era had a medical background,[99] whilst even students were sometimes shocked by the scatological and 'facetious' remarks made in medical lectures, where many professors were reported 'revelling in indecencies'.[100] Queen's College Birmingham was to be the balm to all these provocations. It was to provide a new, a religious, an exclusively Anglican type of medical training.

Samuel Warneford described himself as 'a miser—a calculating miser'.[101] Despite his enormous wealth, he lived in squalor: his rooms uncleaned, his windows unopened, and his possessions becoming increasingly threadbare. Even his carriage was notoriously shabby.[102] He was not interested in money for its own sake, but for the power it gave him; and he used his financial clout to reward those he approved of and punish those he did not. Thus, although he was rector of the little Wiltshire Parish of Lydiard Millicent for forty-six years, he never forgave the inhabitants for resisting his attempts to increase their tithe payments, and failed to fulfil his obligation to keep the parish church in good repair. Despite the fact that he owed his enormous wealth to the money he had inherited from relatives, he refused to give any to his own family—and spent years in dispute with his brother-in-law over the latter's rent arrears.[103] Warneford saw in William Sands Cox a man whose views accorded with his own. Here was a dynamic doctor who was suitably Anglican, suitably Tory, and even suitably dressed—for he was always attired 'like a well-to-do English country clergyman'.[104]

Yet Sands Cox was not entirely what he seemed. He was certainly a brilliant surgeon, but he was also an appalling manager.[105] He was undoubtedly a thorough conservative, but he was not the fierce Churchman that Warneford imagined. Sands Cox's initial inspiration for the Birmingham medical school had been his own training at London's Webb Street School of Anatomy.[106] This was a place so

---

[97] Vaughan, *Christian Philanthropy Exemplified*, p. 4.
[98] Quoted in Cox, *Reprint*, p. 243.
[99] Adrian Desmond, *The Politics of Evolution: morphology, medicine, and reform in radical London* (Chicago, 1989).
[100] Shephard T. Taylor, *The Dairy of a Medical Student During the Mid-Victorian Period, 1860–1864* (Norwich, 1927), pp. 30, 84.
[101] E. G. C. Beckwith, *Samuel Wilson Warneford, LL.D (1763–1855): rector extraordinary* (Bourton-on-the-Hill, 1974), p. 28.
[102] Priest, 'Warneford', p. 589. See also Mary Gibson, *Warneford: being the life and times of Harriet Elizabeth Wetherell Warneford* (Bournemouth, 1966).
[103] Beckwith, *Warneford*, pp. 12, 41, 20–1.
[104] Eliezer Edwards, *Personal Recollections of Birmingham and Birmingham Men* (Birmingham, 1877), p. 83.
[105] See W. H. McMenemey, 'William Sands Cox and the Stoicism of Elizabeth Powis', *Medical History* 2 (1958), pp. 109–13.
[106] T. H. Barker, 'William Sands Cox', in *Annals of Queen's College, Birmingham*, vol. iv, pp. 155060, p. 155.

radical that it was selected as the site for the atheist Jeremy Bentham's autopsy, an operation carried out by the school's Unitarian lecturer in anatomy Southwood Smith. Smith was himself a man so heterodox in his opinions that even UCL would not employ him.[107] Sands Cox posed as a parson, yet he apparently took no interest in the moral condition of his students.[108] He prided himself on his probity, yet funded his college through 'expedients of doubtful propriety'.[109] He was, in other words, a chancer, who sought to use Warneford even as Warneford sought to use him.

Somewhat surprisingly, the relationship between the tyrannical Warneford and slippery Sands Cox worked well. The rich old man funded a series of essay prizes intended to counteract any incipient materialism amongst the students.[110] In 1839 the subject was 'The Valvular Structure of the Veins, Anatomically and Pathologically considered, with a view to exemplify or set forth, by instance or example, the wisdom, power, and goodness of GOD, as revealed and declared by Holy Writ'. In 1840 essayists were asked to consider the same question, but with reference to 'the Aortic Circulation'. A year later, it was the heart; a year after that, the arteries; a year after that, the nerves of the chest. As time rolled on, every aspect of human anatomy would be found to illustrate divine providence.[111] Nor did Warneford stop there. His money helped establish the Queen's Hospital in Birmingham—an essential requirement for a growing medical school.[112] He also helped pay for an extension to the college premises, providing accommodation (and with it, he hoped, better oversight and improved discipline) for the students. He endowed a number of chairs and employed a chaplain for both medical school and hospital.[113] It was Warneford who, above all, worked to obtain the charter which dignified the institution, and enabled it to build up an endowment.[114] Throughout, he was clear: the '*inculcation of sound religious principles has been, and is, the basis of my donations either to your Hospital or your College...All other objects are to me of secondary consideration*'.[115]

Sands Cox, however, had a way of coaxing money out of the tightest purse, and he played his man well. Having persuaded the calculating miser to underwrite a medical school and build a hospital, his ambition had grown still greater: he now wanted to establish a university. First, he suggested that Queen's College should train Anglican clergymen. Then, he turned his attention to the other great profession, law. Birmingham, he wrote, had recently acquired a Bankruptcy Court, would soon possess a County Court, and could reasonably expect to gain an Assize Court in due course. 'May we not look forward to educate the law student?'

---

[107] Desmond, *Politics of Evolution*, pp. 163–4.
[108] Testimony of Archdeacon Sandford, in QCA, Queen's College, 'Introductory Remarks'.
[109] Report of Charities Commissioner (1860), in QCA, Queen's College, 'Introductory Remarks'.
[110] Vaughan, *Christian Philanthropy*, p. 6.
[111] Bodl. MS Top Warw d.1, Papers Relating to Queen's College, 1838–52; Vaughan, *Christian Philanthropy*, pp. 123–39.
[112] Vaughan, *Christian Philanthropy*, pp. 16, 38.
[113] F. O. Martin, 'Report', in QCA, Queen's College, 'Introductory Remarks'.
[114] Law, *Queen's College*; Vaughan, *Christian Philanthropy*, p. 8.
[115] Quoted in Cox, *Reprint*, p. 243 (italicized in the original text).

Fig. 9. A 'small dingy building in one of the worst parts of town': the original home of Owens College Manchester

Reproduced with the permission of the University of Manchester.

he asked.[116] More than this, Sands Cox hoped to open a 'Department of General Literature', and another teaching civil architecture and engineering.[117] He wanted, in other words, to 'lay the foundation of a great central University, based on sound Church of England principles', and he promised to do so 'without any great increase of capital'.[118] Warneford was hooked, and in 1851 the college's charter was changed to enable it to teach theology, architecture, and engineering.[119] What would come to be thought of as 'the Queen's University for the Midland Counties of England' was taking shape in Birmingham.[120]

The year 1851, celebrated for the success of the Great Exhibition, was an important moment for British higher education, for it also witnessed the opening of another ambitious institution in Manchester: Owens College (Figure 9). This owed its existence to a bequest from John Owens, who had died some five years previously, leaving almost all his money to establish

---

[116] Quoted in Cox, *Reprint*, pp. 244–7.   [117] Cox, *Reprint*, pp. 32–6.
[118] Quoted in Cox, *Reprint*, p. 247.   [119] Law, *Queen's College*.
[120] John K. Booth, 'Address', in *Annals of Queen's College, Birmingham*, vol. ii, pp. 181–93, p. 185.

an Institution for providing or aiding the means of instructing and improving young persons of the male sex (and being of an age not less than fourteen years) in such branches of learning and science as are now and may be hereafter usually taught in the English Universities.[121]

It is not at all clear why he did this. Unlike Warneford, Owens was not a great philanthropist in his own lifetime. His few donations were small, sporadic and apparently not driven by any single, overarching ideal.[122] Also unlike Warneford, Owens does not appear to have been motivated by a definite religious impulse. Born a Congregationalist, he became a nominal Anglican; but he was insistent that his college should have no religious tests and impose no theological dogmas on its students.[123] Whilst Warneford had studied at Oxford, Owens had no experience of university life. And whilst Warneford would not shut up about his plans, Owens seems to have told almost no one about them. His political views are also puzzling: outwardly, he was a Liberal, even a radical, but his closest friends were staunch Tories.[124] An apparently stereotypical Manchester merchant, he supported the free-trading Anti-Corn Law League in 1839, but perversely seems to have lost interest as they became more successful.[125] His personality remains similarly opaque. He lived thriftily, worked a twelve-hour day overseeing the family business (though he had no children to pass it on to), and enjoyed a good book.[126] Beyond that we know no more.

It is perhaps an index of the surprise with which Owens' benefaction was greeted that the trustees he named to carry out his wishes did not meet until two years after his death. True to his ecumenical impulses, they included Tories and Liberals; Anglicans and Non-Conformists; merchants, lawyers, parsons, and politicians.[127] The leading member of this variegated crew was Owens' best friend, the industrialist George Faulkner, a convinced Conservative and devout Anglican. He would in his turn give thousands of pounds to the fledgling institution.[128] Together with the other trustees, Faulkner applied himself seriously to carry out Owens' wishes. Although only three of them had any experience of university life whatsoever, they took legal advice, read the report of the 1826 Royal Commission on the Scottish Universities, and wrote to dozens of experts.[129] This proved less useful than they had hoped, as almost no one replied—and those that did included the Provost of Trinity College Dublin, who sent a letter 'containing nothing further than reference to the University Calendar from which we have not derived any material information'.[130] Nonetheless, the trustees soon developed a good idea about the sort of institution they hoped to establish.

---

[121] MUA, OCA/5/1/5, p. 14.   [122] Clapp, *John Owens*, p. 171.
[123] MUA, OCA/5/1/5, p. 14; Fiddes, *Chapters*, p. 7.
[124] Joseph Thompson, *The Owens College: its foundation and growth; and its connection with the Victoria University, Manchester* (Manchester, 1886), p. 42.
[125] Clapp, *John Owens*, p. 140.   [126] Clapp, *John Owens*, pp. 162–71.
[127] Thompson, *Owens College*, Ch. 3.
[128] *Manchester Guardian*, 28 February 1862, p. 2.
[129] H. B. Charlton, *Portrait of a University, 1851–1951* (Manchester, 1951), p. 26.
[130] MUA, OCA/5/1/1, p. 48.

Owens had insisted that there should be no religious tests—so there would be none. He had also been clear that the education offered should be that which was currently provided by the English universities. Oxford had just resolved to expand its curriculum, including such novel subjects as history and natural sciences, but still did not teach either.[131] The trustees consequently made London their model, concluding that the college would offer classes in Classics, mathematics, natural philosophy, and English. There would also be teaching in history, chemistry, and natural history; students could additionally opt to study French, German, arithmetic, and bookkeeping. Such a syllabus, they felt, would provide

> facilities for advancing the education of young men in those leading branches of general knowledge and science which experience has approved as best adapted to the development and improvement of the intellectual faculties, as in further subjects of information which . . . may be of practical value for the Students in their future life.[132]

One question, of course, remained: would this training also include theology? The trustees answered yes. Despite the condemnations of many commentators, and in spite of Owens' apparent injunctions against it, they resolved to provide optional classes on the Old and New Testaments, and a series of lectures on 'The Influence of Religion in Relation to the Life of the Scholar.'[133] They aimed, in other words, to be a university in embryo; a place where, as a local guidebook put it, 'at the fractional part of the cost, the sons of tradesmen may obtain an education equal to that furnished at universities'.[134]

Yet, in two respects, Owens was different from the other modern foundations. In the first place, any hopes of linking the college to the thriving local medical school soon came to nothing.[135] Secondly, attempts to forge a connection with the Unitarians' Independent Academy, which had only recently returned to the city, also foundered. The Academy resolved that Owens was just too small and too orthodox for its purposes, and headed off to London to seek a link with UCL.[136] As a result, the college was unable to offer either clerical or medical training. 'Few are aware how novel is the experiment here making of a College entirely unprofessional in its provisions', observed the principal in 1853.

> Durham is Theological. University College, London, qualifies for the professions of Medicine and of Law. King's College for Law, Medicine, and Divinity. In America, are several Colleges giving general education only. In England, Owens College stands alone in this respect.[137]

---

[131] W. R. Ward, 'From the Tractarians to the Executive Commission', in Brock and Curthoys, *History of the University of Oxford vol. vi, part i*, pp. 306–38, pp. 313–16.
[132] MUA, OCA/5/1/1, p. 39.
[133] Thompson, *Owens College*, pp. 125–31. See also MUA, OCA/5/1/1, p. 71.
[134] *Varley and Robinson's Guide for the Stranger in Manchester* (Salford, 1857), p. 9.
[135] MUA, OCA/2/2, Annual Report (July 1856), p. vii.
[136] Thompson, *Owens College*, pp. 29–32, 131.
[137] MUA, OCA/2/1, Annual Report (1 July 1853), p. v.

Indeed, it would stand or fall solely on its provision of a liberal—rather than a vocational, much less a technical—education.[138]

'An assembly of the learned, the lovely, the rich, the reverend, and the influential' gathered for the opening of Owens College.[139] Its students also included some impressive figures, like James Picton, a prospective Liberal MP, and the future social reformer Percy Bunting, both of whom won academic prizes in the college's first few years. Several students stayed at Owens to take University of London degrees, whilst others used the course as a preparation for study at Oxford or Cambridge.[140] Quantity, though, was as important as quality for the tyro institution, and initially at least numbers did not disappoint. True enough, not all classes worked. The lectures on Biblical Greek attracted no students at all, perhaps—as the principal put it—because they were seen as 'a professional study, rather than an essential branch of a liberal education'.[141] But, within a year, there were more than sixty students: three times as many as Newman first greeted at Dublin, and about the same number that had started at King's College London when it opened twenty years before.[142] It looked as though Owens had pulled it off: managing, finally, to create a college in Manchester; disproving, undeniably, those doubters, like the head of the Belfast Academical Institution, who argued that that no college could succeed 'that has not a body of students pursuing a course of study for professional objects'.[143]

Just a few years into the experiment, however, it became clear that these hopes were illusory. Numbers fell, and fell again, and showed no sign of stabilizing, much less recovering. By December 1857, there were only twenty-seven full-time students: the college had shrunk by half.[144] Even before that, the trustees had become alarmed that their plans were unravelling. On 20 May 1856, just five years after the college had first opened, they summoned the academics to explain their failure. Each reached a different set of conclusions, but the general trend was clear. The professors blamed the poor education of the local boys and limited academic aspirations of Manchester parents. Doubtless drawing on the example of the two London colleges, they called for the foundation of a school to prepare students for higher education. At the same time, they suggested that discipline within the college must be improved and a coherent syllabus be developed for all their pupils to follow. Several also complained that the want of a clear denominational character had alienated both Churchmen and Dissenters alike. Above all, they argued that Owens was failing because it lacked links to the professions and did not provide its students with the sort of vocational education that they required.[145]

---

[138] See A. J. Scott, 'On University Education', in *Introductory Lectures on the Opening of Owens College Manchester* (2nd edn; London, 1852), pp. 1–26.
[139] *Manchester Examiner and Times*, quoted in Fiddes, 'University Movement', p. 100.
[140] MUA, OCA/2/2, Annual Report (June 1859), p. vi.
[141] MUA, OCA/2/1, Annual Report (2 July 1852).
[142] MUA, OCA/2/1, Annual Report (2 July 1852); Hearnshaw, *King's College, London*, p. 104.
[143] Quoted in MUA, OCA/5/1/1, p. 96.
[144] MUA, OCA/5/1/2, Owens Trustees Minutes 1855–61, p. 152.
[145] MUA, OCA/5/1/2, Owens Trustees Minutes 1855–61, pp. 36–57.

They maintained, in other words, that Owens should become rather more like the professional, denominational, residential Queen's College Birmingham.

Yet in Birmingham, at exactly the same time, Queen's was also falling apart. Numbers were up, fuelled mainly by a surge of students who wanted to qualify as doctors before the bar to entry was set higher by much-anticipated legislation.[146] Financially, though, this made very little difference to the college, whose expenditure always exceeded its income, and which had become dependent on the moneys it received from Samuel Warneford. At his death in 1855 it lost the regular flow of income he had previously provided. Worse still, when his will was read, it made no mention of Queen's. One supporter, James Law, Chancellor of the Diocese of Lichfield, recalled that 'his heart shrank within him' when he learnt the news, for the college had expanded in expectation of a large bequest.[147] The consequences were disastrous: a debt of nearly £7,000 by 1859.[148] As Law put it, they 'had erected buildings adapted to a university, with no corresponding income'.[149] The staff went unpaid, rain came through the roof, and—eventually—the debt collectors arrived.[150] The chaos of these years, as Queen's suffered resignations, legal cases, investigation by the Charity Commissioners, and a series of other petty dramas is made painfully clear by the college's minute books, which reveal an institution in crisis, uncertain about its student numbers, unable to keep a proper record of decisions taken, unsure of the way forward; even the Common Seal—the legal badge of its incorporation—had been lost.[151] 'Oh! Ambition, Ambition! Thou curse of the noblest minds!' wrote Chancellor Law. 'How many have been ruined, as this College has been, by masses of unremunerative bricks and mortar piled up for show.'[152]

By 1860, Owens had money and no students; Queen's had students but no money. What was to be done? Both institutions took time to evolve a solution, yet slowly, fitfully, often resentfully, but nonetheless irrevocably, they spent much of the next decade transforming themselves. The most traumatic change took place in Birmingham, where Sands Cox was pressured to resign in 1859, 1860, and again in 1863.[153] When challenged, he began to channel Warneford, accusing his persecutors of 'making an insidious attempt to introduce papists, Dissenters, and Infidels' into the college, and attacking one critic as 'an emissary of Satan and a Jesuit'.[154] But, in truth, he knew he was beaten. The college and the hospital were forcibly separated, and Sands Cox grudgingly handed over control of first one and then the other, retiring to the rural splendour of the early-Georgian Bole Hall, the 'best house' in Tamworth.[155] His disappearance proved too late to save Queen's,

---

[146] QCA, Queen's College, 'Introductory Remarks'; Reader, *Professional Men*, p. 66.
[147] Chancellor Law, quoted in Queen's College, 'Introductory Remarks'.
[148] QCA, Queen's College, 'Introductory Remarks', pp. 40–5.
[149] QCA, Council Minute Book 1858–1867, Statement (6 October 1863).
[150] QCA, Queen's College, Birmingham, 'Introductory Remarks'.
[151] QCA, Council Minute Book 1858–1867.
[152] Law, *Queen's College, Birmingham*.
[153] *History of the Birmingham Medical School*, pp. 32–3.
[154] QCA, Queen's College, 'Introductory Remarks'.
[155] *ODNB*; Nikolaus Pevsner, *Buildings of England: Staffordshire* (London, 1972), p. 279.

however. In 1865 it was finally declared bankrupt and closed, by order of the Attorney General. Two years later, what remained of the institution was dismembered. The medical school and the theology department were severed from one another: the former merged with a rival institution, the non-denominational Sydenham College; and the latter was established as an autonomous college in its own right.[156] Not all was lost. As late as 1868, the historian Goldwin Smith still imagined that Queen's could be made an outpost of the University of London.[157] But in fact, Queen's College Birmingham would face the future as a seminary, not a university. Sands Cox would be forgotten and Warneford eventually memorialized with a seminar room in a bland, brick building set up in a Birmingham suburb.[158] Doubtless to his horror, Queen's is now a proudly ecumenical theological college, welcoming people of all Christian denominations—and even educating non-Christians too.[159]

The transformation at Manchester was less dramatic, though no less decisive. Out went the principal, A. J. Scott. He was an immensely charismatic figure: a hugely influential Non-Conformist theologian, an inspirational speaker and writer.[160] But he was a hopeless administrator, unwilling to allow any interruptions to his afternoon nap and unclear about the solution to the college's problems.[161] When asked what changes should be made to improve its position, he argued that a certain decline in student numbers was probably inevitable and that the trustees should simply hold their nerve.[162] He may not have been entirely wrong, but it was not what his employers wanted to hear. In June 1857 he resigned, pleading ill health as his excuse—though he remained professor of logic. 'It is sufficient that I ought to hold office no longer,' he wrote, 'after I despair of discharging its functions, in a manner satisfactory to my own conscience.'[163] Scott's replacement could not have been more different. John Greenwood, the professor of classics, was born to run a university. He was brimming over with ideas about how to reform the college.[164] Better still, he loved committees—the longer the agenda the better—greeting especially lengthy ones by rubbing his hands together and declaring 'an excellent bill of fare today, gentlemen!'[165]

Owens had already tried and failed to obtain state support for its work, seeking a government grant in 1852.[166] At its nadir, another approach was contemplated: turning the college into a teacher-training academy and relying on the state funding

[156] Morrison, *William Sands Cox*, pp. 121–32.
[157] Goldwin Smith, *The Reorganization of Oxford University* (Oxford and London, 1868), p. 54.
[158] Albeit one designed by the Birmingham modernist John Madin. See Alan Clawley, *John Madin* (London, 2011), pp. 45, 132.
[159] See Chandler, *'The Latter Glory of this House'*.
[160] J. Philip Newell, 'The Other Christian Socialist: Alexander John Scott', *Heythrop Journal* 24 (1983), pp. 278–89. On his teaching see, Joseph Thompson, 'Recollections of the Old College', in *The Owens College Jubilee* (Manchester, 1901), pp. 41–3, p. 41.
[161] Fiddes, *Chapters*, p. 34.
[162] MUA, OCA/5/1/2, Owens College Trustees Minutes 1855–61, pp. 37–45.
[163] MUA, OCA/5/1/2, Owens College Trustees Minutes 1855–61, p. 110.
[164] MUA, OCA/5/1/2, Owens College Trustees Minutes 1855–61, pp. 46–9; 167–73.
[165] Fiddes, *Chapters*, p. 38.
[166] MUA, OCA/5/1/1, Owens Trustees Minutes 1849–55, p. 269.

this would bring in from the Education Department.[167] Greenwood also hoped finally to achieve a link between Owens and the medical school, and thus attract students who sought a professional training, rather than a liberal education.[168] In the end, nothing came of these proposals, nor the suggestion that a school should be founded to raise the educational tone of the city.[169]

Instead, Greenwood settled for a less all-encompassing, though no less significant, set of internal reforms, hoping to make the college more attractive to students and their parents alike. For the parents, he offered a new and stricter disciplinary code, with monthly reports on their sons' progress. For the students, he created a common room and daily college dinner.[170] Within years, each became extremely popular, with the formal evening meal attended regularly by a healthy proportion of students and the common room hosting everything from serious discussions to the sort of horseplay that generated loud explosions and broken chairs.[171] Still more importantly in the short term, he attempted to widen the appeal of the evening classes, which had often been cancelled due to lack of interest, by uniting Owens with the recently-founded (and equally underperforming) Working Men's College. Characteristically punctilious, he sought to encourage attendance by guaranteeing that coffee would be served at each lecture.[172] Above all, Greenwood hoped to make the college's teaching more coherent and better focused. In addition to the 'occasional' students, who paid for individual classes as and when they wanted, the Owens now enrolled 'regular' students who would follow a fixed curriculum either in 'General Literature and Science' or 'Theoretical and Applied Science'.[173]

Initially, the results of these reforms were disappointing. Although the evening classes, and their complimentary cups of coffee, proved a hit, with more than 300 attending by 1861, the college was remarkably quiet during the day.[174] In 1858, there were only 14 regular and 26 occasional students, making a grand total of 40 in all. A year later, there were 57: 18 regular and 39 occasional. The year after that, there were 21 regular and 48 occasional, making 69 in total.[175] It was an increase, but it was not a dramatic turn-around. At this rate, Owens could not hope to remain open. Small wonder that when the new professor of chemistry Henry Roscoe arrived, he found it hard to obtain accommodation: landlords were unwilling to rent to someone employed by an institution they did not expect to survive. Standing on the steps of the college, he was greeted by a tramp who asked whether this was the night shelter for vagrants. 'No,' Roscoe replied, 'but if things go on as

---

[167] A. C. Magian, 'An Outline of the History of Owens College', *Old Owensian* 10 (1931), pp. 16–19, p. 19.
[168] MUA, OCA/5/1/2, Owens Trustees Minutes, 1855–61, p. 167.
[169] MUA, OCA/5/1/2, Owens Trustees Minutes, 1855–61, pp. 147–9, 227.
[170] MUA, OCA/5/1/2, Owens Trustees Minutes, 1855–61, pp. 137, 143, 145, 153, 314.
[171] J. Kentish Wright, 'Owens in the Sixties', in *Owens College Jubilee*, pp. 46–9; MUA, OCA/27/3, Dinner Lists (1864–5). By 1867 demand was so high that no more students were able to dine. See *Owens College Magazine* 1 (1868), p. 7.
[172] MUA, OCA/5/1/2, Owens Trustees Minutes, 1855–61, p. 410.
[173] MUA, OCA/5/1/2, Owens Trustees Minutes, 1855–61, p. 106.
[174] Thompson, *Owens College*, pp. 244–5.
[175] MUA, OCA/5/1/3, Owens Trustees Minutes, 1861–5, p. 120.

they are doing, it soon will be.'[176] Little by little, however, things looked up. The regular students remained a tiny minority, but the number of occasional and evening students grew and grew. By 1864, there were 439 students in total, twenty more than attended UCL in the same year. This created a new and welcome problem: overcrowding; and the scientists were quick to point out that the lecture rooms and laboratories were now so full that the air they contained was actively injurious to health.[177]

It has often been suggested—not least by Henry Roscoe himself—that the revival of the college was due directly to the success of his chemistry teaching.[178] And it is certainly true that Roscoe recruited far more students than his predecessor, Edward Frankland, who was often forced to cancel classes due to lack of interest.[179] But the idea that Owens was saved by abandoning a liberal education in favour of the practical sciences simply does not hold true.[180] Prospective parents and students do not appear to have wanted a chiefly vocational training: hence the failure of plans to create a regular course of instruction for those entering commerce or the civil service.[181] In fact, student numbers rose for all classes in the 1860s—and not just for the sciences. By 1865 there were nine day students taking advanced classes in chemistry, fourteen in classics, and fifteen in Greek New Testament. Strikingly, just as Frankland had been forced to do, Roscoe cancelled a series of evening classes on chemistry that year because he could not attract enough students.[182] In many respects, indeed, there was little to distinguish Roscoe from his predecessor, who had also attempted to interest the people of Manchester in applied science.[183] Quite contrary to the myth that technical education saved Owens, what had changed was the college as a whole—and, more importantly, the environment in which it operated.

The increased demand continued, as did the overcrowding, with nearly 700 students filling the building by 1868. In that year another application for state funding was turned down once again, this time after a personal appeal to the somewhat congested Chancellor of the Exchequer, Benjamin Disraeli, who capitalized on his cold, using a large handkerchief 'as a lady would use her fan, as a valuable aid to effect'.[184] It was thus evident that the college would have to raise its own money for new and better buildings. At the same time, the academic staff

[176] Henry Enfield Roscoe, *Life and Experiences* (London, 1906), pp. 102–3.
[177] MUA, OCA/5/1/3, Owens Trustees Minutes, 1861–5, pp. 349–56; Thompson, *Owens College*, p. 247.
[178] Henry Enfield Roscoe, *Record of Work Done in the Chemical Department of the Owens College, 1857–1887* (London, 1887), pp. 1–9; James Sumner, 'Halls of Resonance: institutional history and the buildings of the University of Manchester', *Studies in the History and Philosophy of Science* 44 (2013), pp. 700–15, p. 705; Charlton, *Portrait of a University*, p. 54; Fiddes, *Chapters*, pp. 63–4.
[179] Robert H. Kargon, *Science in Victorian Manchester: enterprise and expertise* (Manchester, 1977), pp. 161–6, 175–80.
[180] Jones, *Origins of Civic Universities*, pp. 65–7.
[181] *Owens College Prospectus* 1858–9, p. 5.
[182] MUA, OCA/5/1/4, Owens College Trustees Minutes 1865–9, pp. 55–6.
[183] Colin A. Russell, *Edward Frankland: chemistry, controversy and conspiracy in Victorian England* (Cambridge, 1996), pp. 160–5.
[184] Thompson, *Owens College*, p. 330; MUA, OCA/7/2/9, Appeal for Government Aid, 1868.

began to agitate for changes in the composition of the college. They wanted to offer a wider curriculum, including vocational education: teaching medicine, civil engineering, surveying, architecture, and mining. Success, in other words, had inspired a turn towards more professional training, rather than a turn towards professional training inspiring success. But their ambitions were greater even than this. They wanted halls of residence, too; and, increasingly, they wanted to teach women as well as men.[185] All this would require a radical restructuring of the college. Indeed, it would necessitate not one, but two, acts of parliament—not least because John Owens' will had specifically directed his bequest to provide for students 'of the male sex'.[186]

Extraordinarily, and due in no small part to the remarkable energies of the now long-forgotten John Greenwood, the legislation was passed, the reforms were effected, the money was raised, and new buildings erected. By 1877, subscriptions totalled nearly £250,000; student numbers had reached almost 1,400 in all; Owens had absorbed the Manchester medical school and established a college for women.[187] What's more, their grand new home in Oxford Road had inspired a still more remarkable aspiration: the campaign had begun for a true University of Manchester.[188]

---

[185] MUA, OCA/5/1/4, Owens College Trustees Minutes 1865–9, pp. 207–10.
[186] MUA, OCA/7/2/47, Owens College Extension and Amalgamation.
[187] MUA, OCA/7/2, Reports, memoranda, circulars, and related papers concerning the extension campaign 1865–77, list of subscriptions (January 1877); *Owens College Calendar* 1878–9, p. 156; Mabel Tylecote, ed., *The Education of Women at Manchester University* (Manchester, 1941), p. 9.
[188] Henry Enfield Roscoe, 'Original Research as a Means of Education', in Owens College, *Essays and Addresses by Professors and lecturers of the Owens College, Manchester* (London, 1874), pp. 40, 51.

4
Building the Mid-Victorian University

The new home for Owens College was not built simply to solve the problem of overcrowding. It was also meant to resolve a more intangible difficulty: what the professor of natural history, W. C. Williamson, described in 1856 as the 'absence of *external symbolism* of Collegiate life, such as the *want of a Collegiate building* and of a *Collegiate costume for our Students*.'[1] At the same time, the enlarged accommodation it offered was intended to provide improved facilities of every sort.[2] The college's change of location was also significant, taking Owens from the disreputable city centre—filled, as one student recalled, with 'vileness of every sort'—and out into the salubrious suburbs.[3]

The idea that an educational institution needed appropriate buildings, in a respectable location, evoking a set of suitable ideals through its architecture was not, of course, all that new or, for that matter, entirely remarkable. After all, similar ideas had shaped the architecture of the two London colleges several decades before, and simultaneously drove building at the University of Bombay, which demanded a design to 'harmonize with and advance the objects of the higher mental culture for which the University exists'.[4] Indeed, in Bombay, the architect George Gilbert Scott went far further than Manchester managed, erecting a structure that did not just represent the institution, but the empire as a whole (Figure 10). Larded with statues intended to capture the ethnic mix of the city—'the mild Hindu; the shrewd Kutchi; the traditionally fierce Rajput...a praying Parsee...a sleek high caste Brahmin'—this was a solid symbol of imperial harmony; something that even Mancunians could scarcely compete with.[5]

In Ireland, too, the need to find suitable accommodation for the new Queen's colleges led the government to spend no less than £100,000 erecting three distinctive—though scarcely mould-breaking—buildings, each of which owed much to the example of the ancient English universities.[6] Just as Peel had first intended, these were to be a little bit of Oxford set down across the Irish Sea. In Belfast, Charles Lanyon, architect of the city's court house, gaol, and customs

---

[1] MUA, OCA/5/1/2, Owens Trustees Minutes, 1855–61.
[2] MUA, OCA/7/1/3, Owens College, Minutes of sub-committees, 1867–73, p. 47.
[3] E. Armitage, in *Old Owensian* 1 (1923), p. 50.
[4] Quoted in S. R. Dongerkery, *A History of the University of Bombay, 1857–1957* (Bombay, 1957), p. 20.
[5] James Mackenzie Maclean, *A Guide to Bombay: historical, statistical, descriptive* (Bombay, 1889), p. 208.
[6] *Queen's Colleges, Ireland*, PP. 1859 Session 1 (168) XXI Pt.II.415.

Fig. 10. Designed 'to harmonize with and advance the objects of the higher mental culture for which the University exists': the University of Bombay

RIBA Photographs Collection.

house, erected a sturdy Gothic college, which, although built in a brick reminiscent of Cambridge, drew heavily on the architecture of Oxford's Magdalen College (Figure 11).[7] In Cork, the equally admired—and just as appropriately Tory— Thomas Newenham Deane designed another mock-medieval edifice: 'worthy', as Macaulay put it, 'to stand in the High Street of Oxford';[8] and intended, as the architect himself observed, 'to inculcate...Loyalty' through its use of English Gothic forms.[9] To that end its plans were drawn up after Deane had pored over a collection of Oxonian images, specially borrowed from a friend for the purpose (Figure 12). Again, the influence of Magdalen is unmistakable; though the hall is derived from the example of Christ Church.[10] The entrance to Christ Church was also crucial for the extraordinary college in Galway, designed by John Benjamin Keane, which looked as though Christopher Wren's Tom Tower had miraculously

---

[7] David Evans and Paul Larmour, *Queens, an architectural legacy* (Belfast, 1995), p. 11.

[8] T. B. Macaulay, *The History of England from the Accession of James II* (1848–55; 3 vols; London, 1906), vol. ii, p. 244.

[9] Quoted in Brian Hanson, *Architects and the 'Building World' from Chambers to Ruskin: constructing authority* (Cambridge, 2003), p. 213.

[10] Frederick O'Dwyer, *The Architecture of Deane and Woodward* (Cork, 1997), pp. 65, 76.

Building the Mid-Victorian University 103

Fig. 11. 'A rather forbidding and comfortless place': Queen's College Belfast
Illustrated London News, 1851.

Fig. 12. 'Worthy to stand in the High Street of Oxford': the visit of Queen Victoria to Cork in 1849

Reproduced with the permission of the archivist. IE UC/PH/LDSCAPE/02, University Archives, University College Cork, Ireland.

flown from Oxford, only to crash land on an Irish country house.[11] Arriving there as a student, the Fenian autodidact James Mullin was overwhelmed by a building he thought 'the most beautiful I had ever seen'.[12]

Galway may have blown away James Mullin, who claimed it as 'the first building in the province of Connaught'. But he was a poor and poorly-educated man, who turned up to college on his first day clad in a gown, frockcoat, bowler hat, collarless shirt, red cravat, waistcoat, and 'nondescript' trousers, presenting 'as bizarre appearance as ever figured on a variety stage'.[13] For the *cognoscenti* it was a little less impressive (Figure 13). Even as these hybrid buildings were being erected, indeed, attitudes towards architecture were changing.[14] In particular,

Fig. 13. 'The first building in the province of Connaught'? Queen's College Galway
James Hardiman Library, NUI Galway.

---

[11] James Mitchell, 'Queen's College, Galway 1845–1858: from site to structure', *Journal of the Galway Archaeological and Historical Society* 50 (1998), pp. 49–89, pp. 58–61.
[12] James Mullin, *The Story of a Toiler's Life* (Dublin and London, 1921), p. 96.
[13] Mullin, *Story of a Toiler's Life*, pp. 96, 94.
[14] Chris Brooks, *The Gothic Revival* (London, 1999). See also J. Mordaunt Crook, *The Dilemma of Style: architectural ideas from the picturesque to the post-modern* (London, 1987), pp. 115–19, 132, 174; William Whyte, 'Sacred Space as Sacred Text: church and chapel building in Victorian Britain', in Joe Sterrett and Peter Thomas, *Sacred Text-Sacred Space: architectural, literary, and spiritual convergences in England and Wales* (Leiden, 2011), pp. 247–67.

many commentators—and still more architects—were coming to believe that Gothic architecture possessed a clear superiority over any of its rivals. Only this medieval style, they argued, could truly embody the reality—the 'truth'—of a church, a school, or a university.[15] Indeed, this was not so much an argument about the intrinsic beauty of Gothic architecture—though it was argued that the coherence of real medieval architecture made it more attractive. It was, above all, a claim about the moral authority of the style.[16] For Gilbert Scott, architect of the universities of Glasgow and Bombay (and much more besides), the realization that only Gothic—and only a particular period of Gothic—would do came upon him with the force of a religious conversion, leaving him 'morally awakened', 'excited . . . almost to fury'.[17] He was not alone. In the 1840s, architects all over Britain and Ireland were similarly seized by this great Gothic awakening, coming to accept the absolute priority of a medieval approach to modern building.[18]

One of the leading figures in this aesthetic revolution was the architect and Roman Catholic convert, Augustus Pugin. It was his writings that effected Gilbert Scott's conversion, and his example that led to the foundation of campaigning pro-Gothic organizations like the Ecclesiological Society, established in 1839, which used its journal, *The Ecclesiologist*, to advocate the universal adoption of medieval building practices.[19] Pugin argued that only Gothic architecture was truly Christian architecture, and it was on that basis had he sneered at the neo-classical King's College London, depicting it as an anonymous mews building offering 'Cheap Knowledge Lectures', and contrasting it unfavourably with the sixteenth-century entrance to Christ Church (Figure 8).[20] Pugin would fail to build in Oxford and Cambridge where his religious identity made him *persona non grata* to many fiercely Anglican dons.[21] He was, nonetheless, the natural—perhaps inevitable—choice for the expanded, extended and improved Maynooth. Given a government grant equal to that offered to the three 'Godless' colleges, Pugin consequently proposed another quadrangular, Gothic scheme. But it was to be grander, plainer, and built within the spirit of the Gothic Revival.[22] Unlike Belfast, Cork, or Galway, this would be a project which did not simply steal details from existing buildings and apply

---

[15] Philip Aspin 'Architecture and Identity in the English Gothic Revival, 1800–1850' (Oxford University DPhil, 2013).
[16] James A. Schmiechen, 'The Victorians, the Historians, and the Idea of Modernism', *American Historical Review* 93 (1988), pp. 287–316.
[17] George Gilbert Scott, *Personal and Professional Recollections*, ed. Gavin Stamp (1879; Stamford, 1995), pp. 88. See also Geoffrey Tyack and William Whyte, eds, *George Gilbert Scott: an architect and his influence* (Donington, 2014).
[18] Though see William Whyte, 'Restoration and Recrimination: the Temple Church in the nineteenth century', in Robin Griffith-Jones and David Park, eds, *The Temple Church: history, art, and architecture* (Woodbridge, 2010), pp. 195–210, for some qualifications to this point.
[19] James F. White, *The Cambridge Movement: the Ecclesiologists and the Gothic Revival* (Cambridge, 1962); Christopher Webster and John Elliott, eds, *'A Church as it should be': the Cambridge Camden Society and its Influence* (Stamford, 2000).
[20] A. W. N. Pugin, *Contrasts* (1841; Reading, 2003).
[21] Howard Colvin, *Unbuilt Oxford* (New Haven and London, 1983), pp. 101–12.
[22] Frederick O'Dwyer, 'A. W. N. Pugin and St Patrick's College, Maynooth', *Irish Arts Review Yearbook* 12 (1996), pp. 102–9.

them willy-nilly. It was intended to be a true Gothic—in Pugin's terms, a truly Christian—college.

Despite Pugin's obvious importance and the ostensibly perfect fit between his own enthusiasms and the college's declared purposes, the end result was—even in his own eyes—disappointing.[23] His proposals were just too ambitious: eventually coming to cost more than twice the amount initially given to pay for them. As a result the building remained unfinished for decades.[24] Moreover, his plans were attacked by an apparently unlikely set of critics: the editors of *The Ecclesiologist*, who condemned them as dull. Still, this was better than the treatment that the notoriously intemperate journal meted out to the architects of the three 'Godless' colleges. Their work was written off as 'positively bad'; not Gothic at all, but a poor pastiche.[25] Given the heightened rhetoric of architectural criticism at the time—in which bad architecture was seen not simply as ugly but morally degraded, and in which pseudo-Gothic buildings were believed to be actually sinful—this was a seriously damning attack in every sense.

Naturally, not everyone accepted the analysis offered by Pugin, much less the sniping regularly published in the pages of the *Ecclesiologist*. There were those who actively opposed these attempts to conflate ethics and aesthetics.[26] Nonetheless, the sense that architecture was supremely a matter of morality dominated architectural debates in the mid-nineteenth century. This was especially true for those buildings—like churches, schools, or universities—which were intended to have a significant psychological impact on those who used them. Thus it was that headmasters, for example, publicly declared that buildings 'should tell no lie, but speak the truth, the honourable truth' about their purposes; with one individual even going so far as to suggest that the design of his school, including the carpets, was wholly dependent on the teachings of the Athanasian Creed.[27]

Owens College had thus decided to build at precisely the moment in which architecture was freighted with significance as never before. It needed to escape the failings of the London College of Health, whose building, Matthew Arnold complained, actually impaired the taste of the observer, 'by making us forget what more grandiose, noble, or beautiful character properly belongs to a public institution'.[28] It also had to avoid the dangers identified by Thomas Huxley at the opening of Johns Hopkins. 'Great educational funds', he warned, have a tendency 'to fossilize into mere bricks and mortar, with nothing left to work the institution that they were intended to support.'[29]

---

[23] Rosemary Hill, *God's Architect: Pugin and the building of romantic England* (London, 2007), pp. 417–18.

[24] O'Dwyer, 'A. W. N. Pugin and St Patrick's College', p. 107.

[25] *Ecclesiologist* 9 (1849), pp. 289–90.

[26] Crook, *Dilemma of Style*, p. 42.

[27] Edward Thring, quoted in William Whyte, 'Building a Public School Community, 1860–1910', *History of Education* 32 (2003), pp. 601–26, p. 619. On the headmaster who claimed that the Athanasian Creed influenced his school, see p. 618.

[28] Matthew Arnold, *Essays In Criticism: first series* (London, 1900), p. 33.

[29] T. H. Huxley, *Education and Science: essays* (1893; n.p, 2008), p. 145.

At the same time, it remained imperative to overcome the many practical problems that faced university builders. The Queen's Colleges in Ireland were all in many respects substandard: cold, leaky, and lacking in comfort; at Galway, indeed, books rotted on the library shelves for want of proper weather-proofing.[30] Queen's College in Birmingham was even worse, exemplifying all the problems that such an institution might encounter. Not only was its home ruinously expensive and built in the sort of Tudor Gothic style that *The Ecclesiologist* so forcefully condemned in the Irish colleges; it also turned out to be structurally unsound. The plan, with an anatomy theatre backing on to the chapel, and the engineering workshop condemned to the basement below the anatomical museum, attempted to cram far too much into far too little space. It resulted in a 'gloomy' quadrangle overlooked by 'small and cheerless' students' rooms.[31] More disastrously still, the building was not water-tight, leaving the contents of the museum sodden and the inhabitants cold and sickly. 'His health suffers materially when residing in College', wrote one concerned father about his undergraduate son, having noticed 'how thin and ill he...appeared' after a term residing there.[32] Neither fashionable nor functional, Queen's building became a problem long before the place closed.

The solution to these multiple dilemmas came in the shape of Alfred Waterhouse, a serious, meticulous, utterly professional Manchester architect; a great admirer of Pugin's and a scholarly advocate of Gothic design. He had made his name with a series of brilliantly planned local public buildings: the Salford Assize Court, Strangeways Gaol, and Manchester Town Hall amongst them.[33] Indeed, it was only two months after the foundation stone for the latter building had been laid that he was appointed to work for Owens. As the committee that chose him put it, in Waterhouse they had found 'a gentleman already well known in Manchester for the ingenuity and convenience of his plans and the elegance of his designs'.[34] But the importance of the new building meant that even this safe pair of hands was not allowed to work alone. Advice was sought from across the country about best practice, with every institution that had recently been built being contacted—from Oxford, to Glasgow, to Queen's College Cork.[35] The principal and two senior professors were also sent on a tour of German universities, seeking inspiration from what were widely considered the most up-to-date laboratories in the world.[36]

When plans were eventually produced, copies were given to every academic, each of whom predictably enough had improvements of their own to make. Even the

---

[30] Mitchell, 'Queen's College, Galway', pp. 82–4.
[31] QCA, Queen's College, 'Introductory Remarks and Index to Mr Martin's Report'.
[32] QCA, Council Minute Book 1858–67, 26 July 1864. Letter from Edward Bennett.
[33] Colin Cunningham and Prudence Waterhouse, *Alfred Waterhouse, 1830–1905: biography of a practice* (London, 1992).
[34] MUA, OCA/7/1/, Owens College Extension Committee Minutes, vol, i. p. 112 (30 December 1868), p. 184 (3 December 1869).
[35] MUA, OCA/7/1/3, Owens College Extension Subcommittee Minutes (1867–73), 8 (25 March 1867).
[36] MUA, OCA/7/2, Reports, Memorials, Circulars and Related papers Concerning the Extension Campaign, Report to Extension Committee (December 1868).

normally unflappable Waterhouse, who was famous for his adaptability and willingness to listen, found the process trying: 'I should like to say I have found it next to impossible if not altogether so to carry out all the suggestions made to me', he complained.[37] Innumerable meetings, still more letters, and half-a-dozen complete revisions nevertheless produced a proposal that all were apparently satisfied with: modern, expertly arranged, and designed to be built in sections as money allowed. This was no simple copy of an existing structure, but an exercise in non-historicist Gothic, taking some details from the Early English style, others from continental buildings of the high middle ages, and still others from the architect's own fertile mind (Figure 14).[38] Waterhouse's buildings were, in one admirer's words 'worthy both of his reputation and of the purpose for which they were designed'.[39]

Fig. 14. Rectifying 'the *absence of external symbolism*': the new Owens College Manchester
Reproduced with the permission of the University of Manchester.

[37] MUA, OCA/7/1/3, p. 54 (14 July 1869).
[38] Sarah V. Barnes, 'Lessons in Stone: architecture and academic ethos in an urban setting', in Debra N. Mancoff and D. J. Trela, eds, *Victorian Urban Settings: essays on the nineteenth century city and its contexts* (New York and London, 1996), 214–29, p. 224.
[39] Sir Thomas Beazley, 'Shall Manchester have a University', *Nineteenth Century* 2 (1877), pp. 113–23, p. 115.

Waterhouse's plan provided for increased and improved accommodation: newer, bigger, better laboratories; larger classrooms and a capacious library. It also presented a more impressive public face than one which a professor described as the 'small dingy building in one of the worst parts of town' which had previously been the college's home.[40] The call for *external symbolism* had finally been answered. Less obviously, but no less importantly, the new building's specifications spoke of changed ideas about university life. The two London colleges had been built—partly by design and partly as a result of poverty—as places for lecturing and little else. Even at King's, the provision of social space was nugatory and sometimes, like the much-loathed mandatory prayer meetings in chapel, probably counterproductive.[41] Any corporate student life that existed happened despite rather than because of official sanction.

In the three Irish colleges similar attitudes prevailed. Queen's Belfast, as one student recalled, was 'a rather forbidding and comfortless place'. There was no contact with the professors, who arrived five minutes before lectures and left immediately afterwards. There were no laboratories or places for practical work, even for the scientists, and 'If you were adrift between lectures, the only place where you could even sit down was on a wooden bench in a small severe room off the main hall.'[42] At Cork, the only concession to comfort seems to have been a 'barrow with refreshments', acquired in 1856 to discourage the students from visiting the pub.[43] In Birmingham, too, despite the claims made for the richness of its collegiate life, Queen's provided few useful facilities for staff or students. There was a hall for dinner, and a smoking room in the basement; there was also some residential accommodation. But the undergraduates found it 'cheaper as well as more agreeable to live out of college' and only the chapel was ever made much use of—and then solely because it was compulsory.[44]

At the new Owens, by contrast, both teachers and taught were to have purpose-built rooms from the start. Although it took time to acquire them, the declared intention was always to provide common rooms and dining rooms, offices for the professors and reading rooms for their pupils.[45] The social spaces were designed to foster the sense of community that Greenwood had placed at the heart of his reforms within the college, providing places for relaxation and conversation, and homes for the societies and clubs that he saw as an essential part of collegiate life. In contrast to the London colleges, Manchester's students would be encouraged to use the building for entertainment as well as formal education.[46]

---

[40] [Harriet A. Jevons, ed.], *Letters and Journals of W. Stanley Jevons* (London, 1886), p. 231.
[41] Taylor, *Diary of a Medical Student*, p. 3.
[42] Robert Lloyd Praeger, *The way that I went: an Irishman in Ireland* (Dublin and London, 1937), pp. 7–8.
[43] K. O'F, 'Random Notes from QCC in the Fifties', *Cork University Record* 10 (1947), pp. 26–8, p. 26.
[44] Edward St John Parry, quoted in Queen's College Birmingham, Mr Martin's Report.
[45] Thompson, *Owens College*, pp. 619–20.
[46] 'The Owens College Union, Past and Present, by an Old Student', *Owens College Magazine* 13 (1880–81), pp. 15, p. 2.

The work space—especially the professors' studies—served another purpose: enabling the academics to do research. This was by no means a revolution; after all, at its opening Owens had spent thousands of pounds providing a research laboratory for Edward Frankland.[47] But it was an important intensification of this ideal and one that distinguished Owens both from its predecessors and some other contemporary institutions. In 1870, for example, the professor of mathematics at UCL, Thomas Hirst, resigned his chair to become assistant registrar at the University of London. It was only by assuming this 'appointment of an inferior order', he argued, that he would escape the intolerable burden of too much teaching and find time for research.[48] Two years later in Manchester, by contrast, Henry Roscoe turned down the invitation to become professor of chemistry at Oxford because he believed that the facilities he possessed and the encouragement to engage in research he received at Owens were simply superior.[49] Certainly, it is true to say that his new laboratories served as a model for all others built in Britain in the next few years.[50] In that way, the new college did not just symbolize altered ideas about academic life, it actually contributed to that change: establishing once and for all that a civic institution must also be a social centre for its students, and that its staff should be encouraged to do research as well as required to teach.

A WHIRLPOOL OF PEOPLE AND APPARATUS

As this suggests, these developments were not confined to Manchester but reflected wider shifts in Victorian society. The individuals that the new Owens accommodated—some 392 day students, 232 medical students, and 855 evening students by 1880—were at the vanguard of changes that would affect almost every major city in the country.[51] It was a process revealed in a sudden efflorescence of foundations, with putative universities opened at Newcastle in 1871, Aberystwyth in 1872, Leeds in 1875, Bristol in 1876, Nottingham and Sheffield in 1879, and Liverpool in 1882. In 1880, Manchester became a fully chartered university in its own right: the Victoria University; another federal structure, rather like its Irish equivalent, that would come to incorporate both Liverpool and Leeds.[52] Such was its appeal that some even seriously proposed that UCL should break with the University of London and affiliate with the new northern federation.[53]

---

[47] Edward Frankland, 'Reminiscences of the Owens College, Manchester', *Journal of the Old Owensian and Manchester University Old Student Association* 22 (1934), pp. 39–46, p. 43.

[48] Roy M. McLeod, 'Resources of Science in Victorian England: the endowment of science movement, 1868–1900', in Peter Mathias, ed., *Science and Society, 1600–1900* (Cambridge, 1972), pp. 111–66, p. 122.

[49] Roscoe, *Life and Experiences*, p. 147.

[50] Edward Thorpe, *The Right Honourable Henry Enfield Roscoe: a biographical sketch* (London, 1916), p. 44.

[51] Jones, *The Origins of Civic Universities*, p. 63.

[52] MUA, OCA/23/24, Suggestions as to the basis for the Constitution of a New University (27 January 1879).

[53] Thomas Lloyd Humberstone, *University Reform in London* (London, 1926), p. 48.

It is important, of course, not to exaggerate either the coherence or the immediacy success of all this. Each of these newly established colleges struggled, short of cash and sometimes shorter still of students.[54] Each differed in its origins and its purposes, with a survey of 1878 concluding that 'no two of these Institutions are alike.'[55] But the fact remains that an unprecedentedly large number of new colleges was established, all seeking, as Lord Frederick Cavendish, president of the Yorkshire College put it, 'to see if they could not do something of the same sort' as Owens.[56] Indeed, at Liverpool and Leeds, the desire to keep up was so strong that both employed Waterhouse as their architect, ensuring that each of the three colleges which made up the Victoria University would share a family resemblance.

The demand for new colleges was driven, in large part, by the changing nature of the middle class. 'A new stratum of society, and a constantly increasing one, has been opened to the influence of University life', observed the promoters of the Manchester scheme in 1876.[57] It was that provincial, bourgeois constituency which the new foundations sought to serve. After all, something like three quarters of Manchester undergraduates were previously educated in public schools for the middle classes.[58] But one should not be misled into thinking that developments in higher education were the inevitable outcome of a massive growth in the size of the bourgeoisie. For one thing, the middle class remained relatively stable and small in numbers throughout this period, comprising less than a fifth of the population nationally and somewhat less than 3 per cent of inhabitants in many large industrial cities.[59] Professional men, of the sort that universities were set up to produce, actually constituted a diminishing proportion of this number.[60] Rather, it was the increased intensity of competition within this small sector of the community that produced a rise in demand for higher education. The need to pass competitive examinations, the requirement—sometimes statutory—to join a professional organization, the basic necessity of distinguishing oneself from other candidates for a job: these were the key forces of change.[61] 'From being a necessary but comparatively unimportant incident in University education', complained the *Examiner* in 1878, a degree was 'now generally regarded as an end in itself—a coveted prize eagerly sought after by numerous competing candidates'.[62] Moreover, the pressures did not only come from within the bourgeoisie. The extension of the franchise to some working-class men in 1867 and the advent of elementary education for all working-class children from 1870 both increased the competition

---

[54] James Jackson Walsh, 'The University Movement in the North of England at the End of the Nineteenth century', *Northern History* 46 (2009), pp. 113–31.
[55] LivUA, P3/34, University College Public Meeting (24 May 1878), p. 1.
[56] *Yorkshire College Annual Report*, Inauguration Ceremony Special Edition (6 October 1875), p. 6.
[57] MUA, UA/6/4/4, Proposed University of Manchester (3 March 1876).
[58] Jones, *The Origins of the Civic Universities*, p. 31.
[59] K. Theodore Hoppen, *The Mid-Victorian Generation, 1846–1886* (Oxford, 1998), pp. 31–45.
[60] F. Musgrove, 'Middle-Class Education and Employment in the Nineteenth Century', *Economic History Review* 12 (1959), pp. 99–111.
[61] John Roach, *Public Examinations in England, 1850–1900* (Cambridge, 1971); Reader, *Professional Men*, esp. pp. 51–71.
[62] *Examiner*, 3 November 1878, p. 1483.

from below as well. 'It is for us, the middle class . . . to resolve that we will, instead of falling into the back rank, maintain our position of influence in the country,' argued the Liberal MP Samuel Morley at a meeting held to create a college in Bristol. 'This we can only do by promoting the culture and intellectual advancement of our sons and daughters.'[63]

The supply of new colleges was also promoted by the changing role of the middle class. A potentially radical group, often seen as politically destabilizing in the early years of the century, the middle class became less and less threatening to conservatives as the Victorian era went on.[64] It grew more homogenous, less divided by the party political and denominational differences that distinguished the promoters of the two London colleges in the 1820s, and still separated individuals like Warneford and Owens in the 1840s. It also grew more ambitious for its sons. In the first half of the century, they would have gone straight into business. Now, this was considered inappropriate for the future leaders of local society.[65] 'It is necessary', wrote the historian Goldwin Smith in 1878, 'that the chiefs of English industry should have culture.'[66] But where were they to get it? Universities, it was hoped, would solve the problem of what to do with the large numbers of young, educated, middle-class men who had left school but were yet to find a role in society. Families feared, as Lord Frederick Cavendish observed at the opening of Leeds, that sending their sons to aristocratic Oxbridge was 'dangerous'. 'They had known instances in which, when the young men came back, they had rather looked down upon the occupation of their fathers.'[67] A local college would thus not only demonstrate their munificence, but also serve a practical—indeed, a patriarchal—purpose.

Novel ideas about the education of women also helped to inspire interest in the new civic colleges. When Owens opened it was a sign of its seriousness that, like the two London colleges, it was closed to women. Just as the outwardly progressive mid-Victorian scientist Thomas Huxley sought to exclude 'ladies' from learned societies not because he believed them to be stupid, but because he thought them ill-educated; so John Owens decided to found a college for 'young persons of the male sex' because he hoped to establish an institution of real educational value instead of a place of passing interest to a merely miscellaneous public.[68] The foundation of new girls' schools and the success of new women's colleges, however,

---

[63] *Report of a Public Meeting held at the Victoria Rooms, Clifton, on 11th of June 1874, to promote the establishment of a College of Science and Literature for the West of England and South Wales* (Bristol, 1874), p. 41.

[64] Dror Wahrman, *Imagining the Middle Class: the political representation of class in Britain, c.1780–1840* (Cambridge, 1995), pp. 236–45, 251–66.

[65] Simon Gunn, *The Public Culture of the Victorian Middle Class: ritual and authority in the English industrial city, 1840–1914* (Manchester and New York, 2000), pp. 69–70.

[66] Goldwin Smith, 'University Extension', *Fortnightly Review* 23 (1878), pp. 85–93, p. 89.

[67] *Yorkshire College Annual Report*, Inauguration Ceremony Special Edition (6 October 1875), p. 6.

[68] Eveleen Richards, 'Huxley and Women's Place in Science: the "woman question" and the control of Victorian anthropology', in James R. Moore, ed., *History, Humanity, and Evolution: essays for John C. Greene* (Cambridge, 1989), pp. 253–84.

increasingly raised questions about the validity of these assumptions.[69] By the 1860s there was also an increasing number of middle-class women both ready and willing to agitate for access to university. In 1866, Emily Davies published her pioneering work on *The Higher Education of Women*.[70] A year later, the North of England Council for Promoting the Higher Education of Women was founded to provide lectures in Manchester, Liverpool, Leeds, Newcastle, and Sheffield.[71]

Underlying these developments was the growing belief amongst middle-class families that their daughters needed to receive some form of advanced education. The motives for this were two-fold.[72] For some, fear of the future drove demand. Women's lives were tightly circumscribed by the expectation of marriage, yet there were hundreds of thousands more women than men—and thus potentially millions of spinsters. What to do with these so-called 'surplus women' was a serious problem. If they were to escape poverty or dependency on relatives, they would need somehow to be able to support themselves.[73] The opportunities higher education opened up were thus potentially transformative, offering middle-class women the chance of a career like teaching, which was both proper and potentially profitable.[74] Other, more financially secure families from the upper-middle classes, by contrast, could afford to indulge simple intellectual curiosity. At Bristol, for example, Lady Jebb recalled attending economics lectures, hoping to pick up details that she could use in after-dinner conversation.[75] She was certainly not alone: one of many women brought to college by curiosity rather than pressing need.[76]

Surprisingly enough, efforts to offer lectures to middle-class ladies also helped provide opportunities for working-class men. The success of the North of England Council for Promoting the Higher Education of Women inspired philanthropists to stage additional events in a slew of factory towns. At Rochdale in 1868 'upwards of a thousand' attended public lectures, encouraging organizers to imagine a vast, untapped demand for advanced learning.[77] Cambridge in 1873 and Oxford in

---

[69] Gillian Sutherland, 'The Social and Intellectual Context of the Movement for Women's Higher Education', in P. J. Waller, ed., *Politics and Social Change in Modern Britain: essays for A. F. Thompson* (Brighton, 1987), pp. 99–116; Christina de Bellaigue, *Educating Women: schooling and identity in England and France, 1800–1867* (Oxford, 2007), ch. 1; Deidre Rafferty, 'The Opening of Higher Education to Women in Nineteenth-Century England: "unexpected revolution" or inevitable change?', *Higher Education Quarterly* 56 (2002), pp. 327–450.

[70] Emily Davies, *The Higher Education of Women* (London, 1866).

[71] Gillian Sutherland, *Faith, Duty, and the Power of Mind: the Cloughs and their circle, 1820–1960* (Cambridge, 2006), pp. 78–83.

[72] This paragraph owes much to Mark Curthoys and Janet Howarth, 'The Political Economy of Women's Higher Education in Late-Nineteenth and Twentieth-Century Britain', *Historical Research* 60 (1987), pp. 208–31, pp. 215–21.

[73] Kathrin Levitan, 'Redundancy, the "Surplus Woman" Problem, and the British census', *Women's History Review* 17 (2008), pp. 359–76, pp. 363–4.

[74] See also Judith Worsnip, 'A Re-evaluation of "the problem of surplus women" in nineteenth-century England: the case of the 1851 census', *Women's Studies International Forum* 13 (1990), pp. 21–31, p. 23.

[75] Curthoys and Howarth, 'The Political Economy of Women's Higher Education', p. 221.

[76] Carol Dyhouse, *No Distinction of Sex? Women in British universities, 1870–1939* (London, 1995), pp. 23–8.

[77] James Stuart, quoted in Lawrence Goldman, *Dons and Workers: Oxford and adult education since 1850* (Oxford, 1995), p. 14.

1878 each established 'university extension classes' to cater for this previously undiscovered public. Lecturers were sent up and down the country, driven by a genuine sense of idealism. It was exhausting work—'I have been in a whirlpool of people and apparatus', observed an exhausted Edward Carpenter after a strenuous season of teaching.[78] It was also, truth be told, not nearly as successful as its promoters had imagined it would be.[79] While the middle class, with their sights set on the professions, could increasingly see the point of investing their money in tuition fees, those lower down the social hierarchy could neither afford expensive classes nor expect to see their investments in education make any real return. Although thousands started, only a few hundred stayed the course—and numbers declined year on year.[80]

Within the civic colleges integrating these disparate groups also proved problematic, with most institutions consisting of

> a motley mixture of young ladies attending afternoon lectures on Renaissance Art, foremen from the steelworks or laboratory assistants from the dye works taking night classes in chemistry, possibly for a City and Guilds examination, schoolboys getting up some science before taking an Oxford or Cambridge scholarship, intending school teachers in training, and the hard core of the dedicated studying for a London external degree.[81]

Nonetheless, the twin campaigns for women's higher education and university extension for working-class men did doubtless help to remould the educational landscape. New institutions—from Liverpool, which grew out of the work of the North of England Council, to Nottingham, which owed its genesis to Cambridge's university extension lectures—would not have taken shape without their influence.[82]

The need to found new colleges was given added urgency by a general belief in England's industrial decline. The Paris international exhibition of 1867 was in particular seized upon by critics, like the scientist Lyon Playfair, as evidence of the nation's decadence and technological backwardness. Seen in this global forum, he argued, the inferiority of British products was embarrassingly evident. Not everyone agreed, and historians have subsequently taken Playfair to task for the highly selective way in which he interpreted the event.[83] But the notion spawned an

---

[78] Quoted in Sheila Rowbotham, *Edward Carpenter: life of liberty and love* (London, 2008), p. 58.

[79] Sheila Rowbotham, 'Travellers in a strange country: responses of working-class students to the University Extension Movement—1873–1910', *History Workshop Journal* 12 (1981), pp. 62–95.

[80] J. G. Fitch, 'University Work in Great Towns', *Nineteenth Century* 4 (1878), pp. 889–909, pp. 890–1.

[81] Michael Sanderson, *The Universities and British Industry, 1850–1970* (London, 1972), p. 97.

[82] See *Transactions of the National Association for the Promotion of Social Science 1878* (London, 1879), pp. 368–73.

[83] 'The Paris Exhibition and Industrial Education', *Journal of the Royal Society of Arts* 15 (1867), pp. 477–9; Graeme Gooday, 'Lies, Damned Lies, and Declinism: Lyon Playfair, the Paris Exhibition and contested rhetorics of scientific education and industrial performance', in Ian Inkster, ed., *The Golden Age: essays in British social and economic history, 1850–1870* (Aldershot, 2000), pp. 105–20.

extensive literature and a Royal Commission.[84] It also provoked much talk about the need for new scientific institutions. The 'Yorkshire College of Science', as the future University of Leeds was initially known, was explicitly founded to help God's own county keep up with foreign competition.[85] Tellingly, Lyon Playfair was present at its opening.[86] Similar motivations led to the creation of a college of science at Newcastle.[87]

All these anxieties—the urgent need for improved middle-class higher education, the pressing demand for women's classes, and the fear of Britain's industrial decline—in many ways came together most pointedly in the campaign for a college in Bristol. Founded in collaboration with Oxford; open to women as well as men; seeking to educate 'our manufacturing, commercial, and industrial classes': the new institution was also intended to ensure that 'we should not drop behind in the race with other countries'.[88] In this way, the particular concerns of a specific social group and the more general unease about international trade each equally fostered an atmosphere in which the obvious thing to do was establish yet another embryonic university.

Talking about this was one thing, of course; raising the funds to pay for it was another. Yet the environment was such that a multiplicity of financial backers was found. Individual benefactors played a part; perhaps seeking, like the founder of Vassar, to build a monument 'more lasting than the pyramids' to themselves.[89] Certainly Vassar was the inspiration for the London women's college, Royal Holloway, built in an extraordinary red-brick Renaissance Revival by a man who had grown rich selling quack remedies (Figure 15).[90] All the new institutions of this period depended on philanthropy, but none could match the nearly £700,000 raised for Owens (Figure 16).[91] Most consequently relied on both private donations and, more importantly still, subsidies from local government. At Nottingham, for example, the £10,000 gift from a local worthy intended to establish a college was dwarfed by the £100,000 spent by the town council actually building the place. Moreover, the corporation also agreed to grant £6,000 a year to sustain its work.[92] Nottingham council was unusual in the scale of its support, but it was entirely unremarkable in its decision to offer money. Without the financial aid offered by

---

[84] *Royal Commission on Scientific Instruction and the Advancement of Science* PP 1872 c. 536.
[85] A. J. Taylor, 'County College and Civic University: an introductory essay', in P. H. J. H. Gosden and A. J. Taylor, eds, *Studies in the History of a University 1874–1974* (Leeds, 1975), pp. 1–42, p. 2.
[86] *Yorkshire College Annual Report*, Inauguration Ceremony Special Edition (6 October 1875).
[87] E. M. Bettensen, *The University of Newcastle Upon Tyne: a historical introduction, 1834–1971* (Newcastle, 1971), p. 21.
[88] *Report of a Public Meeting held at the Victoria Rooms, Clifton*, pp. 1, 10.
[89] Milo P. Jewett, quoted in Helen Lefkowitz Horowitz, *Alma Mater: design and experience in the women's colleges from their nineteenth-century beginnings to the 1930s* (Boston, MA, 1984), p. 31.
[90] Caroline Bingham, *The History of Royal Holloway College, 1886–1986* (London, 1987), pp. 43–6.
[91] Jones, *The Origins of Civic Universities*, ch. 5; David Owen, *English Philanthropy 1660–1960* (London, 1965), p. 364.
[92] Roy Church, *Economic and Social Change in a Midland Town: Victorian Nottingham, 1815–1900* (1966; London and New York, 2006), p. 364.

Fig. 15. Inspired by Vassar, Royal Holloway College was also intended to be a monument 'more lasting than the pyramids'

Eric de Mare/RIBA Photographs Collection.

municipalities throughout the land, none of the new colleges would ever have been built.

City councils' sudden enthusiasm for higher education grew out of the movement for urban reform that profoundly reshaped English towns from the 1860s onwards. It was no coincidence that new colleges were established in precisely those places that had also established new libraries, galleries, concert halls, and parks. These were all signs of a changing sense of the city—and of a new belief that

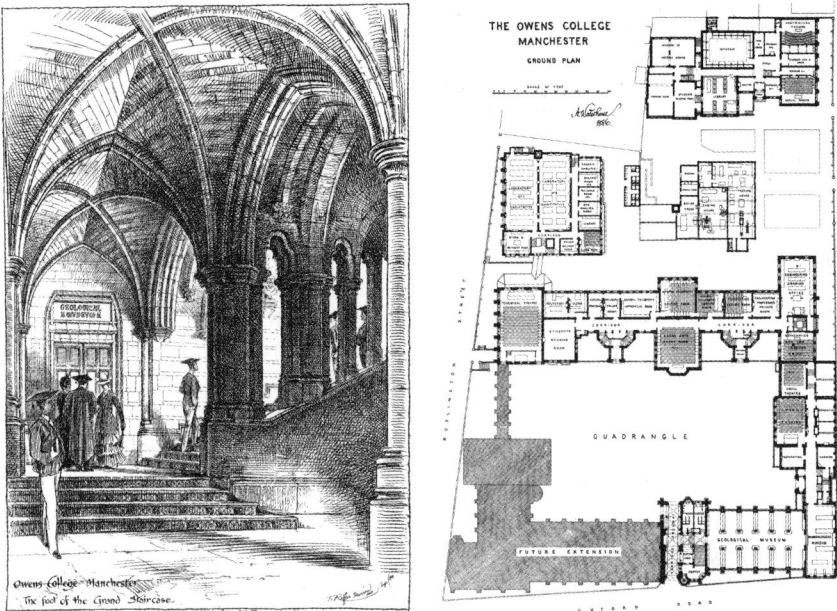

Fig. 16. 'I should like to say I have found it next to impossible if not altogether so to carry out all the suggestions made to me': Waterhouse on the Owens College Manchester

Building News, 21 January 1887.

the council had a responsibility for promoting culture.[93] In Leeds, the Yorkshire College was just one of a series of major building projects sponsored by the corporation, following the town hall and central library and followed by an art gallery and the laying out of a city square.[94] In Bristol, as the historian Helen Meller puts it, 'The founding of the University College marked a climax in the "cultural renaissance" of the decade 1865–75.' (Figure 17)[95] Yet, even these civic improvements were not wholly disinterested. The changing role of the council reflected its increasing dominance by the middle classes, who had assumed control of local politics and now sought to remake the city in their own image.[96] They thus built

---

[93] Hamish Fraser, 'Municipal Socialism and Social Policy', in R. J. Morris and Richard Rodger, eds, *The Victorian City: a reader in British urban history* (London and New York, 1993), pp. 258–80, esp. p. 263.

[94] R. J. Morris, 'Middle-Class Culture, 1700–1914', in Derek Fraser, ed., *A History of Modern Leeds* (Manchester, 1980), pp. 200–22, p. 219. Though see E. P. Hennock, *Fit and Proper Persons: ideal and reality in nineteenth-century urban government* (London, 1973), pp. 172, 223–4, 275–83, for another view.

[95] Helen Meller, *Leisure and the Changing City, 1870–1914* (London, 1976), p. 62.

[96] R. J. Morris, 'Structure, Culture, and Society in British Towns', in Martin Daunton, ed., *The Cambridge Urban History of Britain, vol. ii: 1800–1950* (Cambridge, 2000), pp. 395–426, p. 415; Richard Trainor, 'The Middle Class', in Daunton, *The Cambridge Urban History of Britain, vol. ii: 1800–1950*, pp. 673–713, p. 703.

Fig. 17. 'It is for us, the middle class... to resolve that we will, instead of falling into the back rank, maintain our position of influence in the country': plans for Bristol University College

University of Bristol Library, Special Collections (DM485).

colleges as symbols of their own importance and as places where their children could be educated, as well as institutions that would help reform their town. Public good promoted private gain. Small wonder that the term 'middle class' in this period became synonymous with selfishness.[97]

[97] Gunn, *Public Culture of the Victorian Middle Class*, p. 17.

Conclusion

The campaign for a university in Manchester was welcomed by some and condemned by others.[1] Commentator battled commentator, academic contended with academic.[2] For every argument that this would be a slippery slope, leading in time to the absurdity of a 'University of Leeds, of Bristol, or of Newcastle', counter-claims were made for the uniquely impressive facilities at Owens.[3] For every writer who maintained that it was too soon for such a change, or that Manchester was too small for such an institution, or that the country already had too many universities, others could be found to argue against them.[4] By 1878 the *Examiner* concluded that the question 'may now be said to have been fully discussed from every possible point of view'.[5] Nor did opposition come only from the metropolitan literati. Other, rival towns feared the possibility of Manchester stealing a march on them. Leeds was one of several councils to campaign against the proposed university on just these grounds.[6] By 1880, however, a compromise had been found. The federal Victoria University was created and Owens formed its first constituent college.

This solution left many questions unanswered. The majority of students at Owens had always been younger than those at more established institutions. By 1871, the average age of London undergraduates was 25.[7] At the same time in Manchester, nearly half were under 18.[8] Could this situation be tolerated in a university? It remained to be seen. The place of women was equally unclear. The foundation of an associated women's college in 1877 granted the ladies of

---

[1] MUA, UA/6/4/5B, letters in response to memorandum. See also *Transactions of the Social Science Association 1878*, pp. 338–84.
[2] A list of articles both for and against can be found in MUA, UA/6/4/8.
[3] *Saturday Review*, 12 August 1878, p. 648. See also *Examiner*, 7 December 1878, pp. 1546–7 and the exchange between Goldwin Smith and William Jack in the *Fortnightly Review* 23 (1878), pp. 85–93, 631–8.
[4] Robert Lowe, 'Shall We Create Another University?', *Fortnightly Review* 27 (1877), pp. 160–71 is an especially important attack. For further debate see also Sir Thomas Bazley, 'Shall Manchester have a university?', *Nineteenth Century* 2 (1877), pp. 113–23; *British Architect and Northern Engineer* 6 (1876), p. 1; *British Quarterly Review* 134 (1878), pp. 445–61; Jas. A Cotton, 'The Proposal to ask a University Charter for Owens College, Manchester', *Academy*, 8 July 1876, p. 37; E. A. Freeman, 'Owens College and Mr Lowe', *Macmillan's Magazine* 35 (1877), pp. 407–16; James Heywood, 'The Owens College, Manchester, and a Northern University', *Journal of the Statistical Society of London* 41 (1878), pp. 536–48; J. Bass Mullinger, 'The Multiplication of Universities', *Fraser's Magazine* 18 (1878), pp. 279–95; *Saturday Review*, 12 August 1878, p. 204.
[5] *Examiner*, 23 November 1878, p. 1482.
[6] MUA, OCA/23/31, Yorkshire College memorial to the Privy Council (15 May 1879).
[7] Lyon Playfair, *On Teaching Universities and Examining Bodies* (Edinburgh, 1872), p. 15.
[8] *Royal Commission on Scientific Instruction* PP 1872 *c.* 536, p. 497.

Fig. 18. 'The finest building in the city': Mason College Birmingham
Cadbury Research Library: Special Collections, University of Birmingham.

Manchester some access to higher education, but it was of a semi-detached and second-rate nature.[9] Even their advocates within Owens were half-hearted. Roscoe hoped women would be accepted, to be sure, but he nonetheless trusted they would not become all that easily assimilated: 'the prospect of the ladies "eight", of the ladies inter-university billiard match, and of the "ladies union" of the "ladies clubs" becomes so appalling that we willingly drop the curtain over what might be'.[10] Nonetheless, with women accepted as of right in the other civic colleges, could Manchester really continue to hold out? This, too, would have to be resolved.

But the fact remained that the little college in Manchester had survived, thrived, and turned into a university. Housed in its increasingly magnificent Gothic home, with its charter and its grant of arms, Owens College of the Victoria University was a model to be imitated in towns throughout England—and beyond. Here was a civic institution: one that was breaking free from the University of London's tutelage and control; one that its promoters believed would be shaped by local needs, local benefactors, and local government; one that would increasingly be moulded by the academics who were now able to determine its curriculum.[11] There was nothing inevitable about this achievement, although it was made possible by a

---

[9] Edward Fiddes, in Mabel Tylecote, *The Education of Women at Manchester University* (Manchester, 1941), pp. 7–13.

[10] H. E. Roscoe, 'Women at College', *Owens College Magazine* 2 (1869–70), pp. 129–33, p. 132.

[11] Stuart Jones, 'Mark Pattison and the Idea of the University Revisited' (unpublished paper). I am grateful to Professor Jones for allowing me to read this.

series of changes that were reshaping Victorian society more generally. In particular, as the middle class grew in cohesion and in competiveness, so they increasingly needed institutions like Owens. And as their demand grew, so the petty restrictions and theological battles of previous generations came to seem irrelevant.

Meanwhile, in Birmingham, the success of Manchester's great higher education experiment did not go unnoticed. Across the square from the old Queen's College, close to the brand new city hall, and near the recently erected public library, another foundation was growing up. Incorporated in 1870, with new buildings opened in 1880, Mason College was established to teach science, but soon embraced the more encompassing curriculum pioneered in Manchester (Figure 18). Founded by a wealthy philanthropist, it was sustained by subventions from the local council.[12] It was open to women and men; would avoid religious teaching; and with its elaborate Gothic façade was evidently intended to be a great civic monument as well as a serious educational advance.[13] The *Birmingham Daily Post* observed that it was 'the finest building' in the city.[14] Its existence was an acknowledgement of the evident success of the Owens model, and it was proof, too, that the story of Birmingham's higher education did not end with the collapse of Queen's.

---

[12] Diane K. Drummond, 'The University of Birmingham and the Industrial Spirit: reasons for the local support of Joseph Chamberlain's campaign to found the university, 1897–1900', *History of Universities* 14 (1995–6), pp. 247–63.

[13] Eric Ives, 'Josiah Mason', in Eric Ives, Diane Drummond, and Leonard Schwartz, *The First Civic University: Birmingham 1880–1980* (Birmingham, 2000), pp. 3–20.

[14] *Birmingham Daily Post*, 13 September 1880.

PART III
1880–1914

Prologue

On 23 June 1994, a Blackburn optician called Peter Worden returned home from an evening at one of the Italian tenor Pavarotti's concerts to find an intriguing message on his answer phone. Some builders, he was told, had discovered three large metal canisters in the cellar of a disused shop. On opening them, they had found roll upon roll of old and fragile film. Knowing he was interested in such things, the builders wondered if he wanted them; if not, they said, it would all go to the tip. Painstakingly restored over the next three months, these films revealed themselves to be an unrivalled archive of Edwardian life. They were almost all that remained of the pioneering partnership of Sagar Mitchell and James Kenyon, two filmmakers based in Blackburn from 1897 onwards. Although they also filmed fictionalized documentaries, Mitchell and Kenyon mainly made their money recording ordinary life, turning up at factory gates or setting up in the streets and selling the resulting films to local showmen who would charge people to watch themselves on the screen. As a result, these three drums of film are the closest to seeing turn-of-the-century Britain and to experiencing both its day-to-day existence and its more out-of-the-way events that we will ever get.[1] Amongst the many images this allows us to experience is degree day at the University of Birmingham on 6 July 1901.

Filmed by Arthur Thomas, a somewhat shady showman who preferred to be known as Thomas Edison or even Phineas T. Barnum, this short sequence lasts little longer than two minutes, but gives a striking snapshot of what was becoming an increasingly familiar scene in the streets of Britain's larger cities.[2] Clad in their academic robes, the subject of intense scrutiny by hundreds if not thousands of onlookers, and marshalled by attentive policemen, the scholars and staff of the university process ponderously along the road. Some smile, some wave; some even see and react to the camera: but most seem aware of the seriousness—the importance—of their performance. Here is the university in all its majesty, awarding its degrees to those who have worked so hard to achieve them. Without a doubt, the ceremony owed much to older models—to Encaenia at Oxford and the degree days of still more ancient institutions. The gowns the students wore were

---

[1] Vanessa Toulmin, *Electric Edwardians: the story of Mitchell and Kenyon* (London, 2006), ch. 1. See also Vanessa Toulmin, Patrick Russell, and Simon Popple, eds, *The Lost World of Mitchell and Kenyon: Edwardian Britain on film* (London, 2004).

[2] On Thomas, see Toulmin, *Electric Edwardians*, pp. 75–9.

themselves the descendants of medieval academic dress.³ But although much of this procession would have seemed reassuringly familiar—traditional, even—still more was remarkably new. In 1901, Birmingham, which had grown out of Mason College, had been a university for only a year. This was its first ever graduation; a sign that after more than six decades the dream of a great Midlands university had finally been realized.⁴ Moreover, although this ceremony was patterned after older models, the very fact that it was taking place in the streets of an industrial city and involved women as well as men marked it out from the still all-male events that took place in the ancient university towns of Oxford and Cambridge.⁵ This was a modern university in a modern city. Above all, this graduation was a civic as well as an academic occasion. Arthur Thomas was filming it precisely because the people of Birmingham as a whole wanted to see what was going on at their university.

Graduation day at Birmingham was an important event. It was important for the graduates, obviously; and they look suitably impressed by what even *The Times* agreed was 'an imposing ceremonial'.⁶ But it was also important for the institution as a whole. 'The procession of the University officers and graduates in robes of gold and scarlet', wrote one student of a later celebration, 'will awaken a thrill of enthusiasm which will never be forgotten'.⁷ Within a few years, indeed, the Birmingham Guild of Students was producing a printed songbook to accompany the festivities.⁸

The whole event had a two-fold function. In the first place, it was a corporate celebration—a chance for the students and staff alike to affirm their achievements and express their identity. Secondly, it was an opportunity for the institution to stress its continued centrality to the city that had created it. Writing in 1902, the vice-chancellor Sir Oliver Lodge argued that the university must constantly seek to bring its existence 'before the eyes of the citizens' of Birmingham.⁹ The procession was a perfect opportunity for this. Indeed, as a local paper observed just a few years later, it was degree days which reminded Brummies 'that there is in our midst one of the most important educational institutions in the country.'¹⁰ Certainly, they caused comment and drew attention to the university. More than thirty years later, Vero Garratt, the son of an impoverished Birmingham glassblower, could still recall Sir Oliver's public appearances. 'Enrobed in a scarlet academic gown,' he wrote, Lodge's 'massive form and Socratic appearance were in keeping with the giant-like

---

³ W. N. Hargreaves-Mawdsley, *A History of Academic Dress in Europe until the End of the Eighteenth Century* (Oxford, 1963). See also, David A. Lockmiller, *Scholars on Parade: universities, scholars, and degrees* (London, 1969).
⁴ Eric Ives, Diane Drummond, and Leonard Schwarz, *The First Civic University: Birmingham, 1880–1980* (Birmingham, 2000).
⁵ *Birmingham Pictorial and Post*, 12 July 1901. See also *Mason College Magazine* 6 (1888), p. 76.
⁶ *The Times*, 8 July 1901, p. 7.
⁷ *The Mermaid*, Supplement (March 1906), p. 16.
⁸ BUA, UC/8/vi/2/16, Guild of Undergraduates, 'Degree Day Song Book' (July 1914).
⁹ [Oliver Lodge], *University of Birmingham: University Development by the Principal* (Birmingham, 1902), p. 6.
¹⁰ *Birmingham Pictorial and Dart*, 2 December 1904, p. 3.

nature of his erudition'.[11] For Garratt, like many others, the university was not something distant or something irrelevant; much less something closed to them. It, and the figures who ran it, were an impressive and influential part of city life.

Ceremonies, though, do not only illuminate consensus. They also often reveal conflict—and there were certainly tensions underlying even this most festive of events.[12] For one thing, the procession was an exclusive one, with members of the university clearly marked out by academic gowns and hoods. Ordinary members of the public, in their work-a-day suits and hats, could only stand and watch. They were spectators, not participants in this new form of academic life. Unseen by this film, the university was also already changing in ways that many disapproved of. A grand new edifice was being built outside the city in the leafy suburb of Egbaston. Designed by a leading architect, equipped with the latest facilities, it was intended to replace the now-cramped college at the heart of the city.[13] But not everyone approved of the proposal. Oliver Lodge was especially concerned that taking the university out of the centre might cause a 'lukewarmness and slackness of co-operation between the city magnates and the University staff'. Pointing to the success of the first ever degree day in 'bringing the existence of a local university before the eyes of the citizens', he feared that a graduation held out in the suburbs 'would be shorn of some portion of its usefulness'.[14] Yet Lodge's words did not carry the day because he had been outflanked by a still more important individual, the cabinet minister and pre-eminent local politician Joseph Chamberlain.[15] This struggle between an academic and a local worthy is noteworthy, not least because it would be replayed across the country. As the civic universities grew, so they had to learn how to reconcile being universities with being civic—and it was a learning process not without its problems. Finally, and again invisible to the lens of the film camera, there was another dimension to the developments in Birmingham. For the university did not just depend on local support. Increasingly, it would turn to national government for aid. Inevitably, this too produced its own tensions, raising important questions about the nature of Redbrick university life.

Above all, these new institutions needed to define a role for themselves. No longer colleges, they were now increasingly likely to be chartered as universities. This meant a rise in status and in dignity. But what did it mean in practice? Were they rivals or alternatives to England's ancient universities? Or were they, as some feared, simply pale imitations? Were they doing something new, or—as some argued—simply reviving the 'mediaeval conception of the "Civic" university'?[16] It was all very well for Oliver Lodge to declare to Birmingham's first university students that 'We stand for the education of the future', but what did that actually

---

[11] V. W. Garratt, *A Man in the Street* (London, 1939), p. 105.
[12] See, for example, Elizabeth Hammerton and David Cannadine, 'Conflict and Consensus on a Ceremonial Occasion: the diamond jubilee in Cambridge in 1897', *Historical Journal* 24 (1981), pp. 111–46.
[13] Eric Ives, 'A new campus', in Ives et al., *The First Civic University*, pp. 111–30.
[14] [Lodge], *University of Birmingham*, pp. 5–6.
[15] Julian Amery, *The Life of Joseph Chamberlain, vol. iv* (London 1951), pp. 214–21.
[16] *Mermaid* II (1905–6), p. 132.

mean in practice?[17] Innumerable speeches and articles and pamphlets and books were devoted to solving this conundrum. At Birmingham the discussion began decades before the university received a charter and continued long after the first graduation ceremony. The pages of the college magazine from the early 1880s onwards throng with rival propositions.[18] The publications produced by students of the newly-chartered university show a similar search, as people repeatedly sought, often in wildly contradictory ways, to articulate an organizing principle for the modern university.[19]

The competing claims of academics and laymen, of local and national government, of the civic ideal and the autonomy of the university, of those who would reject Oxbridge and others who hoped to embrace it, understandably inspired huge tensions in this period. But these tensions were creative, helping to shape an increasingly confident and self-consciously different sort of British university, of which Birmingham was just one example. Indeed, the success of this civic ideal could be measured in the growing number of institutions which helped to articulate it. In 1880 England still only possessed five universities: Oxford, Cambridge, Durham, London, and the Victoria University, which encompassed colleges in Manchester, Liverpool, and Leeds. Within the next decade, that number more than doubled. Birmingham, Sheffield, and Bristol were chartered in 1900, 1903, and 1909 respectively. In 1903, the Victoria University disbanded, and each of its component colleges became universities in their own right.[20] At the same time, the University of London was reformed, becoming a truly federal structure, finally free of direct government control.[21] At the same time, new civic colleges were opened in Nottingham (1881), Reading (1892), Exeter (1901), and Southampton (1902).

Nor was this process confined to England. The University of Wales was formed in 1893 by the union of the three newly established colleges of Aberystwyth (founded in 1872), Bangor (1884), and Cardiff (1883). Swansea would gain a college in 1920.[22] Across the sea in Ireland, university reform also proceeded. The Queen's University of 1850 was transformed into the Royal University in 1881 and then the National University in 1908.[23] This was more than just a change of name: the nature of the institution also changed. The Royal University no longer restricted degrees to members of the Queen's Colleges in Belfast, Cork, and Galway, and was consequently intended to allow more pious Roman Catholics as well as Protestants and freethinkers to obtain qualifications whilst studying at other, officially sanctioned institutions.[24] The National University included the Catholic

---

[17] BUA, UC/7/iv/8/32, Oliver Lodge, *Address to Students During the First University Session* (Birmingham, 1900), p. 21.
[18] BUA, UC/9/i/1.   [19] BUA, UC/i/9/3.
[20] Robert Anderson, *British Universities Past and Present* (London, 2006), ch. 5.
[21] Negley Harte, *The University of London 1836–1986: an illustrated history* (London, 1986), p. 158.
[22] J. Gwynn Williams, *The University Movement in Wales* (Cardiff, 1993).
[23] Tom Dunne, John Coolahan, Maurice Manning, and Gearoid O Tuathaigh, eds, *The National University of Ireland 1908–2008: centenary essays* (Dublin, 2008).
[24] Susan Parkes, 'Higher Education, 1793–1908', in W. E. Vaughan, ed., *A New History of Ireland, vol. vi—Ireland under the Union ii, 1870–1921* (Oxford, 1996), pp. 539–70.

University College Dublin, but excluded the Loyalist Queen's College Belfast, which thus became a university in its own right.[25] Even in Scotland, there was a new kid on the block. The foundation of University College Dundee, in 1883, marked a Scottish variation on a common theme. Although the existence of universities in Edinburgh, Glasgow, St Andrews, and Aberdeen, meant that the Redbrick tradition was never as important in Scotland as it was to be in England, the creation of a college in one of Scotland's major manufacturing centres nonetheless revealed that even north of the border, the developments outlined here had some effect.

By any measure, this was a remarkable record of educational change. 'Future historians of England', claimed one author in 1921, 'will regard the foundation of its ... new universities as the most noteworthy incident that has marked the opening of the twentieth century.'[26] Yet historians have done no such thing. They have tended to side with the Redbricks' contemporary critics, seeing them (in the words of the Liberal politician Lord Bryce) as nothing more than 'Lilliputian Universities'.[27] Not only have they been generally ignored, but when they have been studied, they have frequently been written off as little more than a pale imitation of England's ancient universities. Founded as technical and scientific institutions, argues the historian Roy Lowe, they were soon 'colonised' by Oxbridge dons and began 'to imitate the teaching and collegiate style of Oxford and Cambridge'.[28] In his view, indeed, the 'complete transformation' of higher education in this period was nothing more than a failed revolution, in which the new institutions were held hostage by the insidious prestige of the old.[29]

Looking at the environment that shaped the new universities and colleges in this era, this section will reach a completely contrary conclusion. To be sure, Oxbridge undoubtedly retained its social distinction—a distinction bolstered by the educational reforms that it undertook. 'Don't send him here,' advised a UCL secretary when the subject of a boy's education was brought up; 'send him to either Oxford or Cambridge—you get a *cachet* there which you never get here and this is not a place for people of our class.'[30] Increasingly, however, it was not at all clear that the ancient universities were quite as intellectually superior. More importantly, it

---

[25] Senia Pašeta, 'The Catholic Hierarchy and the Irish University question, 1880–1908', *History* 85 (2000) pp. 268–84.
[26] Arthur Smithells, *From a Modern University, some aims and aspirations of science* (Oxford, 1921), p. 9. See also Arthur F. Leach, *Educational Charters and Documents 598–1909* (Cambridge, 1911), p. lii.
[27] Quoted in Don Carleton, *A University for Bristol: an informal history in text and pictures* (Bristol, 1984), p. 13.
[28] Roy Lowe, 'English Elite Education in the Late-Nineteenth and Early-twentieth Centuries', in Werber Lonze and Jürgen Kocha, eds, *Bildungsbürgertum in 19. Jahrhundert* (Stuttgart, 1985), pp. 17–62, p. 155.
[29] Roy Lowe, 'Structural Change in English Higher Education, 1870–1920', in Detlef K. Müller, Fritz Ringer, and Brian Simon, eds, *The Rise of the Modern Educational System: structural change and social reproduction, 1870–1920* (Cambridge and Paris, 1987), pp. 163–78.
[30] Margaret Murray, *My First Hundred Years* (London, 1963), p. 154.

was evidently true that in their antiquity, financial resources, governing structures, and the sorts of students they were able to attract, the ancient English universities were so profoundly unlike the new civic foundations that they could offer no useful example, much less a model to be imitated.[31] Even before Mason College had been transformed into the University of Birmingham this was clear. As Joseph Chamberlain himself put it

> Any new university... will not be in any sense a competitor with the old universities of Oxford and Cambridge. They appeal necessarily to classes many of whom we cannot expect to touch, and they offer associations which we could not under any circumstances attempt or hope to emulate... when we come to create new universities in these modern times, and under modern conditions, it is something rather different that we have in view.[32]

The institution that eventuated was not merely a provincial attempt to ape Oxbridge, it was rather the product of cooperation and competition between local and national government, private benefactors and public bodies, academics and the people they taught. The result was not an old idea reheated, but a new sort of British university.

This section therefore concerns the creation of a culture: a culture that would become characteristic of civic colleges in this period, and which endured long into the twentieth century, shaping the lives of many thousands. It was a culture that left varied traces: in the books and buildings of the universities and colleges; in the memoirs of their students and their scholars; in the student magazines, the official records, and even—as we have already seen—occasionally on film. As Michael Sadler, vice-chancellor of Leeds, recalled of his own, entirely typical university:

> hampered by poverty, [it] had to put up with unworthy buildings, with an almost slum lay-out for some of its extensions, with pinched salaries, with a starved library, with a makeshift refectory and common room, with a third-rate athletic field. Nevertheless, by sheer weight of character, of brain power and public spirit the University won through. But to the end of its life it will bear marks of struggle, like a thrawn tree on a West Riding moor.[33]

Local universities and colleges, the product of local pride and home of local students, were getting more and more ambitious; competing with one another, and coming increasingly to resemble one another. This was clear in their work and their student life, in their self-image and their self-presentation. It was clear, perhaps above all, as Sadler suggests, in their architecture (Figure 19).

---

[31] See, for example, the analysis of the University of Wales provided by the 1907 Raleigh Commission; J. Gwynn Williams, *The University of Wales 1893–1930* (Cardiff, 1994), p. 41.

[32] *Mason University College Magazine* extra number 1898, p. 17.

[33] Quoted in Lynda Grier, *Achievement in Education: the work of Michael Ernest Sadler, 1885–1935* (London, 1952), p. 168.

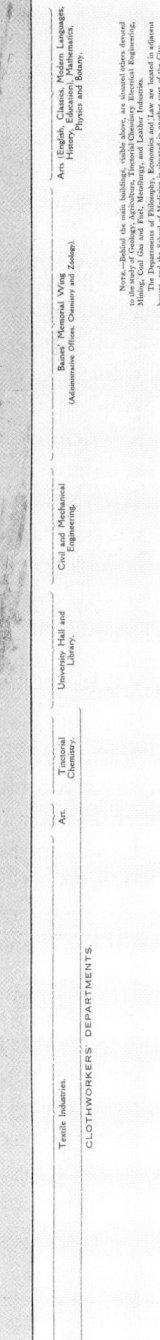

Fig. 19. 'Like a thrawn tree on a West Riding moor': the south elevation of the University of Leeds

5

The Making of a Modern University

In May 1908 the editor of the *Bristol University College Gazette* posed an important question: 'What is a modern university?' Coming only a year before Bristol was transformed into just such an institution, this was doubtless an issue that was being pretty generally debated and the answer which the *Gazette* supplied was very full. A 'modern university', it wrote, is a local institution, governed by a mixture of academics and lay people. It is democratic. It provides training in modern disciplines—'a training which the older Universities, remote from the great centres of industry cannot provide.' It is a hub of culture and enlightenment within its community. It serves its local population. It carries out useful research—indeed, it concluded, 'Research is the keynote of a modern University.'[1]

Although the *Bristol University College Gazette* was prompted to ask this question by very specific circumstances, and no doubt answered its enquiry with particular reference to Bristol's own ambitions, this definition was pretty widely shared.[2] What is noteworthy about this vision of a modern university is the way in which it was often defined against the ancient universities of Oxford and Cambridge. Whilst they were elitist, it was suggested, the modern university was democratic. Whilst they were national, the modern university was rooted in its locality. Whilst they concentrated on the liberal arts, the modern university taught practical and professional subjects. Whilst they were almost exclusively focused on teaching, the modern university also conducted serious research. Here was a place for those students who could not afford a more expensive education, for those people who wanted a useful training, and for those scholars who really wanted to do original work.

Of course, the distinction between Oxbridge and Redbrick can be too sharply drawn. The Oxford extension courses and summer schools, the foundation of women's colleges and the provision of teaching for those unable to afford collegiate life, all meant that the ancient universities were more open to the modern world than was sometimes admitted.[3] Likewise, an increasing emphasis on a wider curriculum and on serious scientific research ensured that, by 1921, Cambridge, at least, claimed to possess a 'finer set of laboratories . . . than any other University

---

[1] *The Bristol University College Gazette* 1 (1908), p. 37.
[2] See also W. M. Childs, 'The Essentials of a University Education', *Hibbert Journal* 10 (1912), pp. 581–98, p. 595.
[3] Lawrence Goldman, *Dons and Workers: Oxford and adult education since 1850* (Oxford, 1995); M. G. Brock and M. C. Curthoys, eds, *History of the University of Oxford, vol. vii: nineteenth-century Oxford, part two* (Oxford, 2000); Christopher N. L. Brooke, *A History of the University of Cambridge: vol. iv, 1870–1990* (Cambridge, 1993).

in the Empire'.[4] During this period, both Oxford and Cambridge underwent immense change, with the latter smugly celebrated as a university

> accommodating itself with flexibility and readiness to requirements the most diverse, appointing new teachers in departments of study the most remote... flinging open doors to all comers, regardless of sex, creed, or nationality, and thronged with students.[5]

This was not revolution—after all, women could still not receive degrees at either Oxford or Cambridge. But it was change; and it did leave Oxbridge less unlike Redbrick than before.

Equally, the modern universities were not just training grounds for future clerks and apprentice brewers. Oxford students might well sing, 'He gets a degree in making jam/At Liverpool and Birmingham'; journalists might well ask 'what special advantages can a Reading Degree confer, unless a "D.B."—Doctor of Biscuits—is established'.[6] But in fact Liverpool, Birmingham, and Reading each had distinguished professors of liberal arts, and at Manchester the classical lecturers were, tellingly, paid more than their scientific colleagues.[7] True enough, in many institutions the scientists pre-dominated, but they were not, on the whole, exclusively technical in their interests. The list of 100 best books drawn up by the students of Birmingham's Mason College in 1886 included only four scientific works—Lyell on Geology, Huxley on Zoology, Roscoe and Scholemmer on Chemistry, and Tilden on Chemical Philosophy. The rest of the list was overwhelmingly literary, with Ruskin's *Sesame and Lillies* and George Eliot's *Mill on the Floss* and *Romola* proving by far the most popular.[8] This was typical. Indeed, in the 1870s, when Oliver Lodge was himself a science student, he exchanged a prize from the Society for Telegraph Engineers for both a registering barometer and the *Works* of John Ruskin.[9] When vice-chancellor of Birmingham, he was a member of the multi-disciplinary Synthetic Society, and counted amongst his friends not only other scientists but also theologians, philosophers, journalists, and politicians.[10] As this suggests, Redbrick was never crudely antithetical to Oxbridge or the arts.

Nonetheless, it is clear that Birmingham and Bristol, Liverpool, Leeds, and the others were perceived, and self-consciously defined, as 'modern' in opposition to

---

[4] Arthur E. Shipley, 'Historical Introduction', to Alan E. Munby, *Laboratories, their plannings and fittings* (London, 1921), p. xiii.

[5] John Willis Clark, *Old Friends at Cambridge and Elsewhere* (London and Cambridge, 1900), p. 13.

[6] Quoted in Diane Drummond, 'The New University', in Eric Ives, Diane Drummond, and Leonard Schwartz, eds, *The First Civic University: Birmingham, 1880–1980* (Birmingham, 2000), p. 143; *Pall Mall Gazette*, 7 September 1912, quoted in *Tamesis* 11 (1911–12), p. 3.

[7] As W. C. Williamson complained in his *Reminiscences of a Yorkshire Naturalist* (London, 1896), p. 139.

[8] *Mason College Magazine* 4 (1886), pp. 32–5. This list of recommended reading was, as they admitted, inspired by Sir John Lubbock's own initial selection; for which, see Philip Waller, *Writers, Readers, and Reputations: literary life in Britain, 1870–1918* (Oxford, 2006), ch. 3.

[9] Oliver Lodge, *Past Years* (London, 1931), p. 105.

[10] William Whyte, 'The Intellectual Aristocracy Revisited', *Journal of Victorian Culture* 10 (2005), pp. 15–45.

the 'ancient' universities. Whilst the latter were seen as elitist and Arcadian, the former were portrayed as democratic and urban—sometimes very urban.[11] As the students at Liverpool sang:

> Not ours the groves of Academe,
> Where learned pedants drowse and dream;
> Not ours the cloistered calm retreat,
> Around us roars the city street,
> Whose surging tides of ceaseless strife
> Sound like a bugle call to life.[12]

A similar theme was taken up by Hastings Rashdall, a distinguished historian of the medieval university, in his talk on 'The Functions of a University in a Commercial Centre' which he delivered in Liverpool and Birmingham at the turn of the century—though, as an Oxford don, he stressed collaboration rather than competition. 'New universities', he said

> Bring university education within the reach of localities, of individuals, and of classes, which could not otherwise enjoy them; they multiply and increase the order, so deficient in England, of professional scholars and men of science; they introduce other ideals of culture and of life into communities apt to be too exclusively absorbed with the material side of things; they vary and diversify the education which is apt, when one or two universities enjoy a monopoly, to run into grooves.[13]

In other words, the Redbrick universities were expected to provide a very different sort of education, to a very different type of student, in a very different kind of environment. These new universities had, as the University of Sheffield proudly boasted, 'given to the old word a new meaning'.[14]

Even new and modern institutions did, of course, have a history. Some, like Manchester, grew out of older existing foundations. Others, like Bristol, were the products of cooperation between local worthies and one or other of the two ancient universities. All these places also shared a debt to the University of London. Indeed, Dundee, the sole Scots' civic college founded in this period, was created in part precisely because of the local demand for London degrees.[15] Even after the Victoria University was created, some students at Manchester, Liverpool, and Leeds continued to sit for London qualifications, whilst the University of London matriculation exam became the standard end-of-school test for tens of thousands of pupils.[16] Moreover, the lecture-based system of the older Scottish universities

---

[11] See also DUA, UR-DUSA/646/1, *The Meal-Poke* (1903), pp. 89–90; [Maureen Boylan], *The University of Sheffield: a pictorial history* (Sheffield, 1985), p. 1.

[12] *Liverpool Students' Song Book* in Ann L. Mackenzie and Adrian R. Allan, eds, *Redbrick University Revisited* (Liverpool, 1996), p. 391.

[13] Hastings Rashdall, 'The Functions of a University in a Commercial Centre', *Economic Review* 12 (1902), pp. 60–79, pp. 64–5.

[14] SUA, US/CHA/5/3, Opening of the Department of Applied Science (25 October 1913).

[15] R. D. Anderson, *Education and Opportunity in Victorian Scotland: schools and universities* (Oxford, 1989), p. 82.

[16] F. M. G. Willson, *The University of London 1858–1900: the politics of Senate and Convocation* (Woodbridge, 2004), pp. 4–5.

also remained important, as it had done since the founding of UCL—not least in providing a relatively inexpensive means of mass teaching.[17]

Nor were the new universities afraid to look abroad. In 1899, for example, a group of Birmingham lecturers toured North America, visiting Harvard and Toronto, Johns Hopkins and MIT, and several other institutions; concluding that in engineering the university should follow Cornell and in mining and metallurgy the model should be Boston and Montreal.[18] Some writers went further still. Comparing British universities with their transatlantic counterparts in 1905, H. R. Reichel, principal of Bangor, told the graduates of Aberystwyth that American State universities were 'most analogous to our own system in Wales'. They too, he went on, were co-educational, predominantly non-residential, with a flexible curriculum, and a system of accreditation which allowed schools to send students without requiring them to take additional exams.[19] Europe likewise offered models for a modern university. At Birmingham, Oliver Lodge made this quite plain. 'When you were looking over the buildings of the University, some of your Members said it was hardly up to Oxford', he complained to a touring group from the association of booksellers in 1910. 'We are not up to Oxford', he went on,

> and we shall never be anywhere near either Oxford or Cambridge, because we are not aiming in that direction. British people when they think of a University always think of those two. But I want everyone to realise that those two are quite exceptional in the world. As Universities they are unique. The Universities in the world... are all of the type of the German University, the Scotch University, and, to some extent, the American University. But take especially the Scotch, as we know it best, and the German—that is the type at which we are aiming, that is the ordinary university type.[20]

With the Scottish system of teaching through lectures, the German emphasis on the importance of research, and the American idea of the university as a civic institution to the fore, it is little wonder that Oxbridge was less of an example than an irrelevance.

Above all, though, the Redbrick colleges and universities continued to be influenced by one of their own: Manchester. It was, as a vice-chancellor of Birmingham put it, 'both the model and the inspiration to other important and developing industrial centres'.[21] Manchester was, of course, the first of the old civic colleges to be granted university status, and was also for many years the largest of the Redbricks, with over 1,000 students by 1901.[22] It was also highly successful: a true rival, and even—in some areas—superior, to Oxbridge. Noting a substantial

---

[17] David R. Jones, *The Origins of Civic Universities: Manchester, Leeds, and Liverpool* (London, 1988), p. 161.
[18] BUA, UC/4/iii/10, Report of a Visit to Colleges and Universities in the United States and Canada made in November 1899 on the Suggestion of Mr Carnegie, pp. 1–11.
[19] H. R. Reichel, *Some Interesting Features of American Universities* (Cardiff, 1905), p. 6.
[20] J. H. Poynting, *Sir Oliver Lodge: a biographical sketch* (London, 1910), p. 13.
[21] Charles Grant Robinson, quoted in H. B. Charlton, *Portrait of a University, 1851–1951* (Manchester, 1951), pp. 128–9.
[22] F. E. Weiss, 'The University of Manchester', in W. H. Brindley, ed., *The Soul of Manchester* (Manchester, 1929), pp. 62–76, p. 63.

benefaction to Manchester in 1887, the *Oxford Magazine* complained that 'Oxford is a poor university with an expenditure exceeding its income: will any wealthy person take the hint?'[23] Over a decade later, in 1903, the other ancient English university felt a similar sense of envy, with one writer noting that Manchester had been so successful in raising money and building laboratories that 'Cambridge, fearing for her laurels, has had, in order to maintain her position, greatly to extend her science schools'.[24] Sure enough, when Wittgenstein travelled to England in 1908 to continue his training in engineering, it was to well-equipped Manchester rather than inadequate Oxbridge that he went.[25] Even the vice-chancellor of Leeds—the obvious, Yorkshire rival to this Lancastrian foundation—acknowledged the importance of Manchester. Michael Sadler paid tribute to the 'profound influence' it had had on universities throughout the empire.[26] Likewise, in Dundee the new college was not to be based on any existing Scottish foundation, but was intended to be 'similar or nearly similar to Owens College at Manchester.'[27]

In the Redbrick pantheon, then, Manchester was always accorded a position of prominence. But gradually even this came to be challenged. As the civic universities and colleges grew more confident, competition rather than emulation characterized their relationship. For Sheffield, in 1905, the 'other three universities' were Leeds, Manchester, and Liverpool.[28] Two years earlier, the university's building fund was launched with the ringing declaration: 'Come what may, we must be on an equality with Leeds (loud applause)'.[29] This competition gradually but inexorably created institutions with important similarities: modern universities that were self-consciously egalitarian, keen to pursue a wide range of studies, and to admit men and women who would otherwise not receive a higher education. Imitation and competition together produced a definition of what a modern university ought to be, what it ought do, and how it ought work. Willing to learn from America, from Europe, and from Scotland, these new colleges looked everywhere for inspiration except to Oxford and Cambridge. 'Have the [older] Universities created a Frankenstein that will threaten his makers?' asked Lewis Campbell in 1901; 'Will the newer growths ultimately supersede the old?'[30] Only time would tell.

A GLORIFIED NIGHT SCHOOL

Speaking at the *Congress of the Universities of the Empire* in 1912, Lord Rosebery gave voice to the general amazement at the number of colleges that now existed. In

---

[23] *Oxford Magazine* 6 (1887–8), p. 4.
[24] A. H. Leahy, *The Work of a University and of a College* (Sheffield, 1903), p. 9.
[25] R. D. Anderson, 'Universities and Elites in Modern Britain', *History of Universities* 10 (1991), pp. 225–50, p. 238.
[26] Michael Sadler, 'The Story of Education in Manchester', in Brindley, ed., *The Soul of Manchester*, pp. 39–61, p. 52.
[27] John Boyd Baxter, quoted in *Builder* 90 (1881), p. 58.
[28] SUA, UCS/SEN/1 University College Minutes of Senate, I (1897–1905), p. 274.
[29] SUA, US/CHA/4/8/1, Building Fund (1901–05), Sir Henry Stephenson.
[30] Lewis Campbell, *On the Nationalisation of the Old English Universities* (London, 1901), p. 236.

1830, he observed, the empire had possessed only eight universities; now there were nearly sixty. More than this, it was clear that the nature of higher education had changed. 'Whereas formerly', he explained,

> Had new Universities been founded, the founders would probably have chosen the sequestered solitude of some cathedral city... the new Universities are totally different. They meet the demand of great cities which require that they shall be situated in their midst, and that their Universities shall meet the demands of their community... every great city seems to consider it a matter of pride and a necessary appanage of its own position that it should hold a University within its walls.[31]

It was an astute point to make, for Redbrick continued to be the product of a particular sort of local patriotism.[32] The *Sheffield Daily Telegraph* was not unusual in stating that its university was 'the Institution in which the city takes most pride, from which it is entitled to expect most, and which it will most gladly maintain at the highest point of efficiency'.[33]

The foundation of colleges in Wales and the re-organization of the universities in Ireland only makes this point more clearly. For the newly nationalist Welsh, it was vital to be able to call on a properly national university.[34] Not only was higher education needed in the principality, argued its advocates, but that education must be properly Welsh. Even after the university's establishment, rival towns competed furiously to become its home, and its ethnic authenticity was constantly questioned.[35] We must, asserted one typically critical commentator in 1905, 'make secure for ever the foundations of a national institution which, alas! has no more appropriate title to-day than that of "The English University in Wales"'.[36] Likewise in Ireland, the arguments over higher education showed the importance of the university as both a symbol and a constituent of the nation itself.[37]

In England, university promoters were playing for lower stakes. Nonetheless, the way in which the possession of a local university became a vital part of local, regional, and national identity is noteworthy.[38] Indeed, as the historian Michael Sanderson has pointed out, 'for cities over 300,000 in population in the 1900s it became a matter of civic disgrace not to have a university'.[39] This was partly

---

[31] *Congress of the Universities of the Empire* (London, 1912), p. 3.
[32] P. J. Waller, *Town, City, and Nation: England 1850–1914* (Oxford, 1983), pp. 82–4.
[33] *Sheffield Daily Telegraph*, 7 January 1913.
[34] Gordon W. Roderick, '"A fair representation of all interests"? The Aberdare report on intermediate and higher education in Wales, 1881', *History of Education* 30 (2001), pp. 233–50. More generally, see Gareth Elwyn Jones, 'Education and Nationhood in Wales: an historiographical analysis', *Journal of Educational Administration and History* 38 (2006), pp. 263–77, p. 263.
[35] Williams, *University Movement*, ch. 5.
[36] T. Marchant Williams, *The University of Wales: its past, its present, and its future* (Cardiff, 1905), p. 35.
[37] Generally, see Märtha Norrback, Kristina Ranki, Helga Robinson-Hammerstein, and Rainer Knapas, eds, *University and Nation: the university and the making of the nation in Northern Europe in the 19th and 20th centuries* (Helsinki, 1996).
[38] William Whyte, 'Building the Nation in the Town: architecture and national identity in urban Britain, 1848–1914', in William Whyte and Oliver Zimmer, eds, *Nationalism and the Reshaping of Urban Communities, 1848–1914* (London, 2011), pp. 204–33.
[39] Michael Sanderson, *The Universities and British Industry, 1850–1970* (London, 1971), p. 79.

Fig. 20. Gender at work: the Liverpool Guild of Students uses a Baroque idiom for the men's side and a more refined Regency for the women's

University of Liverpool Special Collections.

because it was felt that a university would be of economic benefit to its locality. As J. E. G. De Montmorency ornately expressed it, 'An educational area that possesses a University is an entity of a self-sufficient type: it can develop to the fullest degree its economico-educational possibilities.'[40] It was also because people believed that a university would raise the cultural tone of the place, putting it properly on the map. 'A great city without a University', observed the principal of Liverpool in 1900, 'is like an uncrowned Queen.' (Figure 20)[41] Above all, as this suggests, universities were built because locals were convinced that their city would decline in status without one. 'The secret of it all', observed the *Bristol University College Gazette*, 'is that the name and dignity of a University captivates the imagination of a great city.'[42]

The belief that the Redbrick universities were by definition local universities was critical in shaping how they operated and whom they served. At Birmingham in 1898, for example, one commentator argued it should be 'not necessarily a Birmingham or Midland University, but a University *for* Birmingham and the Midlands'.[43] It was also central when it came to paying for them. The Redbricks

---

[40] J. E. G. De Montmorency, 'Local Universities and National Education', *Contemporary Review* 95 (1909), pp. 609–18, p. 612.
[41] *Sphinx*, 8 (1900–1), p. 1.
[42] *Bristol University College Gazette* 1 (1908), p. 31.
[43] R. H. Pickard, 'The Proposed University', *Mason College Magazine* 17 (1898–9), pp. 17–20, p. 20.

relied for their foundation and their survival on three sources of income: student fees, government aid, and the generosity of private benefactors. Each of these depended on local links.

The first source of income, student fees, was vital for each university or college—but also never enough. The cost of teaching always exceeded the amount an institution could charge for it. 'Every University College in England', wrote Michael Sadler in 1905, 'is working at a loss for every student it teaches.'[44] In 1901, indeed, Bristol calculated that each undergraduate cost the university £4 a year.[45]

The second of these sources of funding—state aid—consequently grew increasingly important. Few universities or colleges were like Nottingham, a place that was founded, and almost wholly funded, by the local ratepayers.[46] But just about all the colleges and universities received some sort of subsidy. By the turn of the century, Leeds was getting £5,500 a year from the City Council, £5,125 from the West Riding County Council, £505 from the East Riding Council, and £4,080 from the Yorkshire Council for Agricultural Education. Liverpudlian local government was just as generous: all in all, the City, County, and District councils granted over £12,000 annually.[47] Increasingly, too, national government got involved, providing an annual sum of £2,000 to the Victoria University from 1887 and, from 1889, awarding a yearly treasury grant which was divided between the ten English colleges and University College Dundee.[48] Initially set at £15,000, it had risen to £100,000 by 1901, and was increased again to £150,000 in 1910.[49] Central government also funded research, with different departments disbursing thousands of pounds between them. By 1918, the Board of Agriculture was awarding £10,000 a year, whilst the Board of Education gave £60,000 annually for work on technology and professional training.[50] All this meant that the Redbricks became increasingly dependent on the state. In 1890, 43 per cent of Manchester's income came from tuition fees and 45 per cent from endowments. Twenty years later, 39 per cent came from fees, 15 per cent from investments, and 32 per cent came from the government.[51]

Even so, the importance of private benefactors never went away. For one thing, the size of the main government grant was determined by the amount raised each year by the institutions themselves. It was matched funding, not a hand-out.[52] It could equally not be forgotten that whilst the government would support the day-to-day running of the place, it was primarily through the gifts of local worthies that

---

[44] Michael Sadler, *Report on Secondary Education in Newcastle-upon-Tyne* (Newcastle, 1905), p. 58.
[45] *The Magnet* 3 (1900–1), p. 36.
[46] Edith M. Beckett, *The History of University College, Nottingham* (Nottingham, 1928), p. 40.
[47] Sadler, *Newcastle*, p. 59.
[48] Robert O. Berdahl, *British Universities and the State* (Berkley and London, 1959).
[49] Keith Vernon, 'British Universities and the state, 1880–1914', *History of Education* 30 (2001), pp. 251–71, p. 265.
[50] TNA, UGC 5/8, Correspondence Leading to the Deputation to the Chancellor of the Exchequer, 23 November 1918.
[51] Charlton, *Portrait of a University*, pp. 149–50.
[52] See also, *History of the Royal Albert Memorial University College, Exeter* [Exeter, 1911], pp. 10–12 and E. J. Brown, *The Private Donor in the History of the University* (Leeds, 1953).

improved facilities and new posts could be created. Manchester, for example, would have been a very much poorer university without the £151,000 it managed to solicit from subscribers between December 1919 and March 1920.[53] At Bristol, it was really only the sudden decision of the rich tobacco-selling Wills family to support the local college that enabled it to escape financial difficulty. In 1904 the

Fig. 21. 'The majesty of learning' embodied in the Wills Tower at the University of Bristol
University of Bristol Library, Special Collections (DM485).

---

[53] SUA, US/CHA/4/9, University Buildings and Endowment Fund, 2 March 1920.

endowment was £4,000; five years later—thanks to the Wills—it was £203,000.[54] Moreover, to mark their generosity, they also gave over £500,000 to erect a grand new building. (Figure 21)[55] Nor were the only important patrons rich merchants and millionaires. 'In England to-day', wrote De Montmorency in 1909, 'we are witnessing the rapid creation of groups of local Universities, accumulating endowments not only from the very rich, but—a most notable sign of the times—from the well-to-do'.[56]

Naturally, this did not mean that the universities were always content with the generosity of their benefactors. Leeds began without the endowment it had hoped to raise, and discovered that any downturn in trade further immiserated the college. The principal complained that in times of plenty local worthies sent money elsewhere, and in times of dearth claimed to have no cash to spare.[57] Even in Manchester, not all gifts were equally valuable. Whilst they welcomed the local bishop's donation of his £1,000 wedding present, intended to pay for a scholarship in classics,[58] it was with some relief that the curator of the university museum was able to rid the place of other, less advantageous bequests: 'The two-headed lamb was sold; the mummy of Miss Beswick was buried; and other unsuitable objects were disposed of.'[59]

Fortunately for Redbrick, other benefactions proved more useful. The gap between ambition and reality at Birmingham, for example, was only bridged because a number of 'patriotic citizens' were willing to stump up the £650,000 needed to turn the college into a university.[60] At Reading, the support of local industrialists and local gentry was similarly significant—though on a smaller scale. A donation from Lady Wantage helped build a first hall of residence, whilst money from the local biscuit-makers Huntley and Palmer kept the college solvent.[61] Mary Ann Baxter, whose endowment founded University College Dundee, was even hailed in verse by the world's worst poet, William McGonnagall:

> I hope Miss Baxter will prosper for many a long day
> For the money that she has given away,
> May God shower his blessing on her wise head,
> And may all good angels guard her while living and hereafter when dead.[62]

---

[54] Sanderson, *Universities and British Industry*, p. 71.
[55] Sarah Whittingham, *Sir George Oatley: architect of Bristol* (Bristol, 2011), p. 219.
[56] De Montmorency, 'Local Universities and National Education', p. 610.
[57] *Yorkshire College Annual Report* 19 (1892–93), p. 24.
[58] Joseph Thompson, *The Owens College: its foundation and growth* (Manchester, 1886), p. 598.
[59] [J. Taylor Kay], *The Owens College: a descriptive sketch* (Manchester, 1891), p. 19.
[60] Eric Ives, 'What is a University?', in Ives et al., *First Civic University*, pp. 70–88, pp. 82–3. See also Diane K. Drummond, 'The University of Birmingham and the Industrial Spirit: reasons for the local support of Joseph Chamberlain's campaign to found the university, 1897–1900', *History of Universities* 14 (1995–6), pp. 247–63.
[61] W. M. Childs, *Making a University: an account of the university movement at Reading* (London, 1933).
[62] William McGonagall, *Last Poetic Gems*, ed., James L. Smith (Dundee and London, 1968), pp. 86–8.

He may have been a dismal poet, but McGonnagall was no slouch when it came to cash. As was stressed at the opening of the college, Dundee was entirely dependent on the generosity of the Baxter family.[63]

Not all benefactors were local. Andrew Carnegie, who also gave money to Dundee, and whose £50,000 donation made all the difference at Birmingham was, of course, a Pittsburgh steel magnate. The City of London Livery Companies, like the Clothworkers and Skinners, who supported Leeds; the Cutlers, who established a small scholarship at Sheffield; the Drapers, who gave money to Bangor, Sheffield, and Battersea Polytechnic: these were metropolitan groups with a national perspective, seeking—under pressure from the Charities Commission—to justify their existence by becoming major educational charities.[64] The money the Clothworkers gave made them by far the biggest donors to the University of Leeds, and turned an institution notorious for its poverty and poor facilities into a leading centre for textile research.[65] Nor were all the gifts the product of a purely local patriotism. At Leeds in the early 1880s a group of five Yorkshire women donated £1,050 to mark the fact that the college had always been coeducational.[66]

Reconciling the divergent interests of the different people who funded the universities and colleges would always prove difficult, however. Benefactors could prove quixotic in their enthusiasms, hence the fact that Liverpool ended up with four professors of archaeology at a time when most universities could not boast one.[67] City councils were also unpredictable. By the late-1890s the overwhelming majority were raising taxes to pay for technical education, with only one—Preston—holding out and refusing to levy a rate. But the amount they were willing to spend differed widely, as did the ways in which they spent it. Not all were prepared to use the money for higher education rather than more vocational training. In Manchester, for example, the council spent almost all of its hypothecated tax on the local technical school. The university got next to nothing.[68] The intervention of national government only complicated the picture further. As Michael Sanderson has shown, the advisory committee which doled out state grants 'was highly suspicious of institutions claiming to be university colleges when they were little more than local technical colleges, and it insisted that a fair range of subjects to degree level should be a criterion for the bestowal of a grant'.[69] Those academics who claimed to welcome the government's quinquennial inspections

---

[63] DUA, Recs A/807, *University College Dundee: the opening ceremony* (Dundee, 1883), p. 17.

[64] Tom Girtin, *The Mark of the Sword: a narrative history of the Cutlers' Company, 1189–1975* (London, 1975), p. 392, *The Golden Ram: a narrative history of the Clothworkers' Company, 1528–1958* (London, 1958), pp. 15–16, and *The Triple Crowns: a narrative history of the Drapers' Company, 1364–1964* (London, 1964), pp. 360–1. W. H. Armytage, *Civic Universities: aspects of a British tradition* (London, 1955), p. 229.

[65] Sanderson, *Universities and British Industry*, p. 67.

[66] *Yorkshire College Annual Report* 9 (1882–3), pp. 14–15.

[67] Thomas Kelly, *For Advancement of Learning: the University of Liverpool, 1881–1981* (Liverpool, 1981), p. 149.

[68] E. P. Hennock, 'Technological Education in England, 1850–1926: the uses of a German model', *History of Education* 19 (1990), pp. 299–331.

[69] Sanderson, *Universities and British Industry*, p. 105.

undoubtedly did so because they were able to use them as a device to challenge people who wished to narrow the curriculum—and that almost certainly included any local councillors who preferred a technical to a liberal education.[70]

Academics did not have it all their own way, however—and it is here that any notion that importing professors from Oxford necessarily implies importing notions derived from Oxbridge falls down. Whilst the ancient universities were governed by their dons, the Redbricks followed the example of Manchester by dividing control in three: a Senate made up of the professors, who determined academic policy; a 'large (and largely inert) Court', which was filled with local worthies and former students; and a smaller, executive Council made up of town councillors and benefactors, who oversaw financial matters.[71] Such an arrangement, argued Oliver Lodge, was intended to give benefactors and especially the government confidence that their money would be well spent. 'Their finances', he explained, 'are administered not by the professors, not by the Senate, that is, but by a lay body, the citizens of the town or city where they are at work'.[72]

In reality, of course, the distinction between financial and academic questions was not clear-cut and in many universities the academics chafed against the restrictions their Councils imposed upon them. At Liverpool, the leading professors founded a caucus to insist on the primacy of 'academic rights', seeking to accrue the authority of their equivalents in 'the great Continental Universities'.[73] The 'New Testament', as the group was called, exercised a growing influence on the university—and was a sign of the increasing self-confidence of the staff.[74] But the battle was long and hard, and the Council retained its financial control even in Liverpool, giving it an ultimate veto for any proposal. Moreover, there remained those who welcomed this lay involvement, seeing it as essential for the institution's success. 'Do not seek for independence or isolation', counselled Lodge on a visit to Liverpool; 'Encourage the leading men to take a living and personal interest in college government, and give them plenty of real power. Welcome civic control.'[75]

The divergent interests of local and national government, a lay Council and an academic Senate played themselves out across the whole range of university life. But one field in which these tensions were most evident was the question of who should be a student and what they should study. For many commentators, the real value of a civic university continued to be its presumed capacity to solve skills shortages in technological and industrial companies. This after all, was the great defence of the whole enterprise offered by such influential figures as the Liberal politician Lord Haldane.[76] For many involved in running the universities, by contrast, their

---

[70] TNA, ED/24/567, University Education, Unification of Grants, Nathan Boddington (24 July 1910).
[71] Graeme C. Moodie and Rowland Eustace, *Power and Authority in British Universities* (London, 1974), p. 29.
[72] TNA, UGC 5/8.
[73] John Simpson, *In Lighter Moments: a book of occasional verse and prose* (Liverpool, 1934), p. 112.
[74] C. H. Reilly, *Scaffolding in the Sky* (London, 1938), ch. 8.
[75] Oliver Lodge, 'An Address', *Sphinx* 9 (1901–2), pp. 11–14, p. 12.
[76] Eric Ashby and Mary Anderson, *Portrait of Haldane at Work in Education* (London, 1974).

institution could not afford solely to serve the interests of business, otherwise it risked becoming little more than 'a glorified night school'.[77] The support of the local community was also, some feared, a potentially limiting factor. As one Liverpool student put it, there was always the danger that it would become 'merely a local institution, generously supported, no doubt, by the citizens, but little known, and less respected, beyond the town's limits. A "local University"', he concluded, 'is a contradiction in terms.'[78]

Yet the people who attended Redbrick were overwhelmingly locals.[79] Even as late as 1908, nearly 90 per cent of Bristol's undergraduates were drawn from within thirty miles of the city. Nor was this wholly exceptional: at Leeds the figure was 78 per cent; at Liverpool 75; at Manchester 73.[80] In Wales the proportion of local students was even higher.[81] They tended to live at home and some also worked nearby. After all, throughout this period evening classes remained an important source of students and of revenue. At Birmingham, for example, the 1881 session saw 95 day students and about the same number of visitors in the evening. Ten years later, there were 492 day students and another 274 who attended after dark.[82] Less wealthy and prestigious institutions like Southampton saw a preponderance of part-time scholars. In 1886 there were 110 day students, but another 340 came in the evening.[83] Living locally, working—or hoping to work—for local firms, these people helped to root the universities and university colleges in their community. They also presented a challenge to those who wanted the place to be a national institution.

What made someone choose Redbrick? For many, no doubt, it was parental pressure. '"Going to College"', recalled F. H. Spencer of his boiler-maker father, 'appealed to him, and he hardly discriminated between Balliol or Trinity and a Training College for Teachers then in the back streets of London.'[84] For Spencer, it turned out to be the latter, and he attended Borough Road teacher training college from 1892 onwards. Parental poverty might also play its part in discouraging people from applying to Oxbridge. Whilst Oxford remained socially and economically exclusive in this period—indeed, if Albert Mansbridge, founder of the Workers' Educational Association, is to be believed, more exclusive than ever before—Redbrick was relatively more open.[85] Of course, it was still hard for the very poor to get in, but it was no longer completely impossible for the lower-middle

[77] John Macdonald Mackay, quoted in Sampson, *In Lighter Moments*, p. 112.
[78] R. Roscoe in *Sphinx* 8 (1900–1), p. 330.
[79] *Board of Education Reports for the Year 1913–14 from those universities and university colleges which are in receipt of grant* [sic] *from the Board of Education* Cd 8137 (1915), pp. xi–xii.
[80] A. H. Halsey, 'Oxford and the British Universities', in Brian Harrison, ed., *The History of the University of Oxford, vol. viii: the twentieth century* (Oxford, 1994), pp. 577–606, p. 580.
[81] Gareth Elwyn Jones, *The Education of a Nation* (Cardiff, 1997), p. 45.
[82] *Mason College Magazine* 10 (1892), p. 120.
[83] *The Hartley Institution and Its Proposed Extension as a Local University College* (Southampton, 1887), p. 5.
[84] F. H. Spencer, *An Inspector's Testament* (London, 1938), p. 75.
[85] Albert Mansbridge, *The Older Universities of England* (London, 1923), p. 109. On this, see especially M. C. Curthoys and Janet Howarth, 'Origins and Destinations: the social mobility of Oxford men and women', in Curthoys and Brock, *History of Oxford, vol. vii*, pp. 571–95.

and working classes to obtain a university education. As Robert Anderson has shown, nearly 40 per cent of the students studying in the civic universities were the children of small businessmen, clerks, or manual workers.[86] This was a figure reflected in the bursaries offered by local education authorities. In 1911, of £57,000 spent on university scholarships, two-thirds went to Redbrick.[87] Age was also a factor in admissions. Although it gradually went up, with fewer than 4 per cent of undergraduates aged under 17 by 1913, it remained the case that civic universities and colleges would accept people as young as 16 to study for the University of London's matriculation exams.[88] Redbrick thus provided a bridge to higher education that Oxbridge did not allow.

For women there was a particular reason to choose the new universities: it was only there that they could obtain a degree. In contrast to Oxford and Cambridge, Redbrick was open to women, almost from the first, with London leading the way in 1878 and Durham the last to go mixed in 1895.[89] This did not mean equality, of course. In most places, men and women had separate common rooms; at Manchester, until the turn of the century they entered lecture halls through different doors. Even after this was abandoned, differences still remained. When, in 1909, Manchester's Students' Union Building was opened, the creation of a shared refectory prompted some male undergraduates to suggest that their female counterparts should be hidden behind a screen.[90] The men's and women's student unions would remain segregated until the 1950s.[91] At Liverpool, at about the same time, the distinctions were embodied even more strongly in architecture. There, the Students' Guild was sharply divided, with the difference between the men's and women's halves marked by two completely contrasting façades—Baroque for the boys and a more refined Regency for the girls (Figure 20).[92]

What women were permitted to do also differed from place to place, and from subject to subject. At Bristol, women could join the debating society but were excluded from the engineering club.[93] In Leeds—at least until 1899—whilst the debating society was closed to women, the scientific society was open to them.[94] In 1901, the University of Birmingham rather smugly celebrated the fact that

> our authorities do not find it advisable to make regulations such as the following, made at Bangor:—'Men students may not (a) meet women students by appointment or walk

---

[86] Anderson, 'Elites and Universities', table 3.
[87] Roy Lowe, 'English Elite Education in the Late Nineteenth and Early Twentieth Centuries', in Werner Lonze and Jürgen Kocka, eds, *Bildungsbürgertum in 19. Jahrhundert*, vol 1. (Stuttgart, 1985), pp. 147–62, p. 159.
[88] *Report for the Year 1913–14* Cd. 8137, p. xiv; J. C. Maxwell-Garnett, 'The Universities and Technical Education', *Second Congress of the Universities of the Empire* (London, 1921), pp. 204–13.
[89] The standard work on this is Carol Dyhouse, *No Distinction of Sex? Women in British Universities, 1870–1939* (London, 1995).
[90] Mabel Tylecote, *The Education of Women at Manchester University* (Manchester, 1941).
[91] Alex B. Robertson and Colin Lees, *The University of Manchester, 1918–50: new approaches and changing perspectives* (Bulletin of the John Rylands University Library 84:1–2 [2012]), pp. 282–3.
[92] LivUA, S300, Students' Union Building Committee, 1905–13.
[93] *The Magnet* 1 (1898–9), pp. 30–1; 2 (1899–1900), p. 7.
[94] *The Gryphon* vol. 1, no. 3 (1898), pp. 47, 51; vol. 2, no. 4 (1899), p. 71.

with them; (b) accompany women students to and from the college; (c) walk with women students in the grounds; (d) visit women students in their lodgings or receive visits from them'.[95]

Yet despite the difficulties and in spite of the obstacles women students soon became an important part of Redbrick. By 1901, almost one in five undergraduates in the civic universities was female.[96] At some Colleges, like Dundee, there was even a majority of women students.[97]

By the outbreak of the First World War, Redbrick had become an important part of Britain's educational system. Indeed, in terms of the numbers educated by the civic universities and university colleges, it had outpaced Oxbridge. In 1914, there were 10,000 Redbrick students, and only 7,000 at the two ancient universities combined. True enough, this still meant that only about 1 per cent of the age group was actually attending university.[98] But given what had gone before—or, rather, what had not happened before—this can fairly be described as a remarkable change. It was the product of negotiation rather than planning; a series of improvised solutions to local circumstances. The result was a patchwork of local projects, places where people from the surrounding region were given opportunities that had previously been reserved for the elites.

Marjory Todd is a case in point. Growing up in Gateshead in the early years of the twentieth century, she was a working-class girl with ambitions. But, as she recalled,

> I had known nothing about universities in my early youth. No one I had ever heard of had been to one... When I was at the grammar school I heard of sixth-form girls who 'went on to College'. This usually meant a 'Normal' Teaching College, from which they emerged as teachers.[99]

Yet she would overcome these hurdles—and her rejection from Cambridge. Aged 23, she bought a cap and gown and college blazer and headed off to Hull.[100] By then, she was just one of thousands making a similar journey, following the road to Redbrick.

---

[95] *University of Birmingham Magazine* 2 (1901–2), p. 49.
[96] Carol Dyhouse, *Students: a gendered history* (London and New York, 2006), p. 4.
[97] *The College* NS 1 (1903–4), p. 2.
[98] T. W. Heyck, 'The Idea of a University in Britain, 1870–1970', *History of European Ideas* 8:2 (1987), pp. 205–19, pp. 207–10.
[99] Marjory Todd, *Snakes and Ladders: an autobiography* (London, 1960), p. 166.
[100] Todd, *Snakes and Ladders*, p. 168.

6
Life in a Modern University

Marjory Todd's purchase of clothes represents a rite of passage that all students experienced. Changed clothes marked a changed status. As Freda Young recalled of her first day at the Bedford Physical Training College in 1903: 'I had put up my hair and donned my first long skirt the day I arrived. Miss Petit had bought her first pair of boned corsets to help her through the great adventure.'[1] Coming to college—especially for those whose families had no experience of higher education—was undoubtedly a nerve-wracking time. It was made all the more remarkable by the need to dress appropriately. Thus, when Mary Craddock went to Durham she was given a hand-knitted scarf 'So's you'll have something decent to wear at College, like.'[2] Academic dress meant more than just a suit or a scarf, though. College or university colours were also adopted—although they were frequently changed, moving from claret and amber to blue and gold at Birmingham, for instance, in a matter of a few years.[3]

As Marjory Todd discovered, the search for appropriate clothing also often meant acquiring a mortarboard and academic gown. In some universities and colleges, the decision to mark the students out by enforcing the adoption of this gear was taken by the authorities. Reading the minutes of the Sheffield University senate in early 1908, one would be forgiven for thinking that they discussed little else.[4] In other institutions, however, the pressure to adopt—and compel the wearing of—academic gowns came from the students.[5] It would, suggested one writer in 1902, 'raise the "tone" of Birmingham, and also it would stamp all members with what one might call a "Varsity stamp".'[6] Five years later, a similar point was made again. Undergraduates, it was argued, should be required to wear gowns both inside and outside the university, 'as is done in the Welsh Universities'. 'We should thus', it was stated, 'be distinguished from the Townsmen.'[7] Necessarily, not everyone agreed. At Bristol it was observed that the scientists only wore

---

[1] Quoted in Richard Smart, *On Other's Shoulders: an illustrated history of the Polhill and Lansdowne Colleges, now De Montfort University, Bedford* (Bedford, 1994), p. 60.
[2] Mary Craddock, *A North Country Maid* (1960; Maidstone, 1995), p. 157.
[3] *Mason College Magazine* 9 (1891), p. 81; 15 (1897–8), pp. 97–8. See also F. H. Spencer, *An Inspector's Testament* (London, 1938), p. 127.
[4] SUA, US/SEN/2 (1907–8).
[5] See also the *Pupil Teachers' Monthly* 1 (November 1887), p. 13.
[6] *University of Birmingham Magazine* 2 (1901–2), p. 97.
[7] *The Mermaid* 3 (1906–7), p. 76.

their gowns on the very coldest of days, and then only to keep warm.[8] But the assumption that special clothes marked out students as special people was universal.

New clothes, though, were just part of the process of becoming a student. There was a new routine and a new life to absorb too. Take Mark Grossek, for example. The son of Jewish immigrants from Poland, he won a scholarship to East London College, the forerunner of Queen Mary College. 'Every morning', he recalled, 'I started off at about the same time as of old. I wore much the same clothes as of old too. But instead of carrying my books tied up in a strap, I sported an attaché case. And my school cap... was laid aside for a bowler hat.'[9] Small differences, perhaps; no doubt invisible to his professors. Yet for Grossek and for others, they symbolized the start of a new life.

For many female students, it may be inferred, the change was greater still; so great, in fact, that it could be terrifying. The Leeds magazine *The Gryphon* attempted to recapture this sense in 1899. 'Describe your state of mind', it asked,

> on the opening day of College when you (a lone female student) find yourself in the hall lined with professors in little desks, and filled with male students of every description. Which of the two plans of action would you pursue—to struggle through the crowd surrounding the Principal, or to bolt by the nearest exit?[10]

Some did bolt, no doubt, and who can blame them? Their subsequent treatment, in many cases, justified any decision to leave. For as students at Sheffield found out, many lecturers were ill-equipped and unprepared to deal with women. C. G. Moore Smith, professor of English from 1896 to 1924, was notorious in this respect. 'If a woman turned up late,' it was recalled, 'he listened with icy courtesy and impassive face to her stammering apologies. If a man was late he gave him a rare and friendly smile, recognising, as one man to another, that a man sometimes has to be late.'[11] Small wonder that some female undergraduates seem to have existed in a sort of internal exile: 'they hold themselves entirely aloof from their fellow students of the male persuasion', complained a Manchester undergraduate in 1892.[12]

But for most students, this understandable nervousness was mixed with genuine excitement. It was a combination well captured by D. H. Lawrence in *The Rainbow*. No doubt drawing on his own experience as a student at Nottingham, he pictured his heroine Ursula Brangwen's first day at college. Not everything and not everyone was wonderful. 'Still, it was lovely to pass along the corridor with one's books in one's hands, to push the swinging, glass-panelled door, and enter the big room where the first lecture would be given.' Although she was soon to be disappointed, for Ursula, as for others, this was 'a magic land'; indeed, it was 'holy ground'.[13] Moreover, many

---

[8] *The Bristol Nonesuch* 2 (1912), p. 47.
[9] Mark Grossek, *First Movement* (London, 1937), p. 270.
[10] *The Gryphon*, vol. 2, no. 3 (1899), pp. 46–7.
[11] Dover Wilson, quoted in Helen Mathers, *Steel City Scholars: the centenary history of the University of Sheffield* (London, 2005), p. 16.
[12] J. Harold Bailey, 'The Lady Student', *Owens College Magazine* 2 (1892–3), pp. 24–5, p. 25.
[13] D. H. Lawrence, *The Rainbow* (1915; London, 1995), p. 428. For similar views see R. Menzies Fergusson, *My College Days* (Paisley and London, 1887), pp. 41–2.

women did not fear to tread in this masculine environment. They were keen to meet men—and soon found spaces to do so. The main staircase at Liverpool; the peculiar roofed courtyard at Aberystwyth; the library in innumerable other institutions: these all played host to what Aberystwyth students called 'quadding', discrete and chaste encounters—apparently chance meetings—that might get more serious later on elsewhere.[14] Women also took on the men at games that were still regarded as exclusively male. In a mock election at Liverpool in 1900 it was a woman, E. L. Shallcross, who won—and what's more, she did so as a Liberal in a dreadful year for the party.[15]

The students were, of course, there to work; to obtain the qualifications that would get them jobs on graduation. For those on scholarships, this was an imperative. Trainee teachers on Board of Education Scholarships, who made up the majority of students at smaller colleges like Exeter and who dominated arts departments elsewhere, were only funded on condition that they continued to pass the exams which equipped them for their future career.[16] Even for those with a less clear path to follow, a solid round of lectures and a succession of tests marked the milestones on the way through college. For some it was undoubtedly all a bit much. In subjects like medicine the failure rate was extraordinarily high.[17] And almost all disciplines demanded a serious attention to work. Abel Jones went to Aberystwyth in 1898, and trained be a teacher. Rereading his diary he found that it seemed to be 'a record of almost continuous work, with occasional recreation periods and smoking concerts, literary and debating and other societies, and other college functions'. With forty-five hours a week of classes to attend, it is little wonder that the phrase 'The work is really overwhelming', occurred again and again.[18] Nor was this unusual. At Sheffield A. E. Dunstan recalled that 'Work was hard and incessant—lectures mainly from 9 to 10, laboratories 10 till 1 and 2 till 5, followed by further lectures from 5 till 6.... The evenings up to midnight were taken up with reading and the writing up of notes.'[19] Night-school and evening-class students, who were often attending after a full day's work must have found it still more exhausting and anxiety-provoking.[20]

This anxiety, and the fear of failure which underwrote many people's experience of Redbrick, also affected relationships between students and staff. Professors tended to rely on tuition fees, and as they were paid for each student they took

---

[14] J. Gwynne Williams, *The University Movement in Wales* (Cardiff, 1993), p. 102.
[15] *Sphinx* 8 (1900–1), p. 90.
[16] B. W. Clapp, *The University of Exeter: a history* (Exeter, 1982), p. 35.
[17] A. L. Mansell, 'Examinations and Medical Education: the preliminary sciences in the examinations of London University and the English Conjoint Board, 1861–1911', in Roy MacLeod, ed., *Days of Judgement: science, examinations, and the organization of knowledge in late-Victorian England* (Driffield, 1982), pp. 87–108.
[18] Abel Jones, *I Was Privileged* (Cardiff, 1943), p. 17.
[19] Quoted in Mathers, *Steel City Scholars*, p. 12.
[20] Sheila Rowbotham, 'Travellers in a Strange Country: working class students, 1873–1910', *History Workshop Journal* 12 (1981), pp. 62–95.

on, they often taught more than they should.[21] This could create serious overcrowding. At Dundee, in 1888, 110 science students worked in three relays each hour in an attempt to use facilities designed for thirty.[22] In Liverpool at about the same time, the problem was such that the professor of engineering 'was driven to the undignified expedient of having to crawl under the table before the students in order to reach his proper place'.[23] Packed classes could also lead to some strikingly uninspired teaching. At Nottingham, D. H. Lawrence wrote, 'I came to feel that I might as well be taught by gramophones as by these men, for all the interest and sincerity they felt.'[24] As a result, the relationship between staff and students could be difficult. At Liverpool in 1892 it even provoked protests, with the opening of a grand new building interrupted by an innovative prank. As the Chancellor tried to speak, he found himself obscured by a huge, specially-baked, three-foot biscuit which proclaimed it was for the university Senate, which 'took the biscuit for its impertinence in trying to exclude the students'.[25]

Yet the gap between academics and their undergraduates could be overcome. At Birmingham, the grandeur of graduation day at Birmingham was undercut by singing. To the tune of 'My Bonnie Lies Over the Ocean' Brummy students chorused: 'Speak up, speak up, speak up/Sir Oliver Lodge, Lodge, Lodge'.[26] Likewise, in winter, women students '"made" Sir Oliver Lodge in snow'.[27] The inauguration of the Sheffield University Chemical Society in 1905 provided a similar opportunity for humour. The lecturer in chemistry, W. E. S. Turner had arranged to start proceedings off with a bang. Mixing volatile materials together, he and his assistant hoped to produce a deafening explosion and ducked behind the desk to escape it. But—alas—something had gone wrong, and no explosion happened. 'There was tremendous applause', he recalled, 'as Jarrad and I sheepishly raised our heads again above bench level with coils of cotton wool streaming from our ears.'[28]

These were, it must be admitted, rather special occasions. No doubt for much of the time the relationship between staff and students was characterized by some formality—although even this must have been mitigated at institutions like Dundee where male undergraduates shared a common room with their tutors.[29] But most of all what should not be forgotten is that each Redbrick community was small and that many of its members were inspired by a shared sense of being

[21] F. T. Mattison, 'Government and Staff', in P. H. J. H. Gosden and A. J. Taylor, eds, *Studies in the History of a University: to commemorate the centenary of the University of Leeds, 1874–1974* (Leeds, 1975), pp. 181–245.
[22] *The College* 1 (1888), pp. 58–9.
[23] *University College Magazine* 2 (1886–7), p. 161.
[24] D. H. Lawrence, *Letters of D. H. Lawrence*, ed., James T. Boulton et al. (8 vols; Cambridge, 1979–2000), vol. i, p. 72.
[25] Eric Ashby and Mary Anderson, *The Rise of the Student Estate in Britain* (London and Basingstoke, 1970), pp. 45–6.
[26] BUA, UC/8/vi/2/16, 'Degree Day Song Book', no. iii.
[27] Margery Fry, quoted in Dyhouse, *No Distinction of Sex*, p. 109.
[28] Quoted in Mather, *Steel City Scholars*, p. 58.
[29] *The College* 2 (1904–5), p. 8.

pioneers. Such an ethos could often overcome divisions of age, experience, and education. As one former student recalled of his time at Bristol: 'Professors and students were then all young together, fresh to the work of teacher and pupil... and they brought a vigour, an enthusiasm, a robustness into those early days of study, with which the plain, grim College building seemed quite in keeping'.[30] This was, of course, a sentimental reminiscence, but it captured something that was probably true for many.

Despite the pressures, then, teaching at Redbrick was, potentially, an attractive proposition. For women, in particular, it could be highly desirable.[31] Not only did it offer the possibility of interesting work. It could also be potentially remunerative. In 1914 Edith Morley estimated that the few individuals heading women's colleges were making as much as £1,000 a year. True enough, most were on much less, perhaps as little as a tenth of that for lecturers. Others were ruthlessly exploited: teaching twenty or thirty hours a week. But it remained the case, as she put it, that, 'A competent girl who can bide her time can usually get a footing in some University.'[32] More than this, once employed, she might even be able to marry and keep her job.

Nor was the work wholly off-putting for men. When, in 1881, Nathan Bodington tired of teaching in Oxford, he moved first to Birmingham and then to Leeds as professor of Greek. The inadequacy of his stipend led him—repeatedly—to consider leaving, and he applied for a whole variety of other jobs. Yet, in the end, he chose to remain in Yorkshire and eventually became vice-chancellor of the University. What kept him there was a number of factors. In the first place, there was pure practicality: he could not get—much less think of—a better job. Secondly, Bodington was committed to the ideal of a Redbrick university, a local institution providing, as he put it, education for 'any man who wanted to be a leader in his calling'.[33] But, above all, he stayed and thrived because Leeds, like other modern universities, provided an environment in which he could thrive. As an Oxonian colleague had observed when Bodington thought of leaving for Redbrick, it was a place that 'gives an energetic man more and healthier scope for his energies than the curious, unnatural, spasmodic kind of life we lead in Oxford'.[34]

Doubtless, some would have disagreed with these sentiments. As the universities increased in size, so they came to include large numbers of people—junior lecturers and the like—who did not gain the salaries, the prestige or the power of the professoriate. Women, however gifted, could never rise to the highest ranks. Academic hierarchies were even reinforced by architecture. At Cardiff, for example,

---

[30] 'Recollections by an Old Student', *The Magnet* 2 (1899–1900), pp. 91–2, p. 92.

[31] Fernanda Perrone, 'Women Academics in England, 1870–1930', *History of Universities* 12 (1993), pp. 339–68. See also her, 'University Teaching as a Profession for Women in Oxford, Cambridge and London, 1870–1930' (DPhil Thesis, University of Oxford, 1991).

[32] Edith J. Morley, 'Women at the Universities and University Teaching as a Profession', in Edith J. Morley, ed., *Women Workers in Seven Professions: a survey of their economic conditions and prospects* (London, 1914), p. 21.

[33] William H. Draper, *Sir Nathan Bodington: first Vice Chancellor of the University of Leeds* (London, 1912), p. 192.

[34] T. H. Fowler, quoted in Draper, *Sir Nathan Bodington*, p. 62.

staff social space was strictly demarcated: the all-male professors' common room (with its easy chairs); the common room for female academics (with its two umbrella stands); and the study for junior members of staff.[35] But Bodington's words were not just wishful thinking. They would have made sense to many of his colleagues. These were determined individuals, who worked hard and had a clear goal in sight. Local people, they were rooted in their community and made their universities and colleges part of their environment. Yet they also distinguished themselves from 'townsmen' with new clothes, new routines, and a new way of life. For women in particular, this was a challenge. For both staff and students, the pressures could be enormous. But although some were unhappy, some felt short-changed, and some simply could not take the pace, they were breaking new ground—and they knew it.

ON THE MAKING OF TRADITIONS

The problem with being pioneering is that pioneers can get lost. Redbrick academics and their pupils were acutely aware of that risk. They worried that their institutions would become nameless, faceless places; that they would lose their *esprit de corps* and their energy. The solution, they concluded, was to create organizations, events, and ideals that would hold their institution together. They wanted, in other words, to invent tradition.[36] It was an attempt made both officially and unofficially. Vice-chancellors and professors sought to institutionalize identity through elaborate ceremony, the foundation of approved societies, and the provision of appropriate facilities. Students were similarly keen to create clubs, to establish conventions, and to display their distinctiveness.

Historians have been keen to suggest that this sort of invention is inauthentic—even duplicitous. Eric Hobsbawm, writing in *The Invention of Tradition*, makes the process sound a little like false consciousness, in which a sort of cultural hegemony is achieved by sleight of hand.[37] In Redbrick, however, the attempt to invent traditions was entirely open and wholly self-conscious. It was also often repeated. The call to create what Reading students called '"corporate consciousness"' echoed throughout this period.[38] Thus, when in 1906 the undergraduates of Birmingham wrote 'On the Making of Traditions', they were far from unusual. 'One of the greatest advantages the older Universities, such as Oxford and Cambridge and Paris, enjoy is their wealth of tradition', they wrote; 'In the new universities tradition has to be made.'[39] That is precisely what the Redbricks sought to do.

---

[35] CUA, UCC/Sn/M4, Senate Minutes 1902–9, pp. 437–8 (25 January 1909).
[36] Joyce Senders Pedersen, 'Enchanting Modernity: the invention of tradition at two women's colleges in late nineteenth- and early twentieth-century Cambridge', *History of Universities* 17 (2001–2) pp. 162–91.
[37] Eric Hobsbawm, 'Inventing Traditions', in Eric Hobsbawm and Terence Ranger, eds, *The Invention of Tradition* (Cambridge, 1983), pp. 1–14.
[38] *Tamesis* 23 (1923–34), p. 45.
[39] *The Mermaid*, Supplement 1906, p. 17.

Following the example of Owens, which was seen to have become a university precisely because of its success in creating clubs, societies, and a sense of community, they too attempted to invent their own traditions.

What, though, was that tradition to comprise? How was it to be invented? The answers to these questions can be found in various places at various times, but forty years of discussion found its apotheosis at Loughborough Technical College in 1920. 'Was it impossible to create a worthy tradition at this College?' enquired W. J. Morgan, the brand new president of their brand new students' union. 'Emphatically no!' he replied. Comparing the scholars of Loughborough with Kitchener's army, he reminded his fellow students that these soldiers had likewise possessed 'no tradition to look back to in 1914, but in a few short years of war they had created traditions worthy to be compared with the oldest and best cherished in the land'.[40] The challenge was to do the same in Loughborough and the solution was a programme of reform that would have been familiar in many older institutions. Indeed, it was a programme copied from them. First, the Student Representative Council would charge a subscription for membership. Secondly, it would use the monies raised from this to establish a student fund. Thirdly, it would found an annual Rag event, to raise money for charity. Fourthly, it would organize a yearly procession for students, who would join with the academic staff to walk in state to the local parish church. Fifthly, and finally, it would lobby for the wearing of academic dress by all members of the college. This combination of the practical and the ceremonial, the dignified and the efficient, was universally adopted by civic colleges and universities throughout the period.

Such student action mirrored the decisions made by their teachers. Even as the undergraduates of Loughborough drew up their plan of campaign, their principal, the enterprising and ambitious Herbert Schofield, was engaged in a similar process of invention. Between 1919 and 1921 he obtained a college coat of arms, ordered caps and gowns, commissioned a college hymn, and founded a college magazine. He established the first halls of residence and started the first canteen. College Sunday, the day on which the students proposed to process to the parish church, was also invented by Schofield in 1920.[41] Loughborough came late to the game. It was a technical college, which specialized in engineering. It was a small and unfashionable institution and had only been founded in 1909. Little wonder that it was not until 1966 it became a university. Nevertheless, the work done at Loughborough by both students and staff was typical, indeed archetypal. In seeking to construct a college they invented tradition. In inventing tradition they created a Redbrick culture of their own. Loughborough's solutions encapsulated the approach that had been evolved by all the colleges and universities in the generation before.

A key to this culture was the creation of student societies. Discouraged—even prohibited—in the 1830s, and fitfully experimented with in the 1860s, these

---

[40] *The Limit* 3 (1920), pp. 48–9.
[41] Leonard M. Cantor and Geoffrey F. Matthews, *Loughborough from College to University: a history of higher education at Loughborough 1909–1966* (Loughborough, 1977), pp. 50–4.

undergraduate clubs became a *sine qua non* for the civic universities, long before they were officially sanctioned at Oxbridge. Indeed, students' unions or representative councils proliferated. They were not, it must be said, always hugely popular. In 1904, it was complained that 'Birmingham students resemble nothing so much as that ephemeral body known as "The Liberal Party," both in their lack of cohesion and their ineffectual efforts to attain their aims'.[42] Yet they remained an important part of college life—especially valued because they provided a social base for the many students living at home or in lodgings.[43]

Other clubs were also founded: some based on the subjects being studied, and others intended to allow students to pursue their own independent interests. A debating society was a must. As the students at Loughborough observed, again in 1920: 'A Debating Society is an essential part of a College.... The country looks rightly to its educated men to lead its thought, and expects from them their advice and guidance, and it is at the meetings of debating societies that one learns the art of presenting one's cause.'[44] Sport was similarly central. A playing field was acquired in Leeds as early as 1888 in an attempt to cultivate a college life, and a generation later the vice-chancellor was still placing games at the heart of the college experience.[45] 'Nothing', declared Nathan Bodington, 'would in my opinion tend more to create a bond of common feeling among the students than the extension of facilities for sports.'[46] This emphasis on physical fitness, which echoed a similar enthusiasm at Oxbridge and in the public schools, even applied to female students.[47] As one contemporary observed: 'It is almost always the case that the girl who is first in the hockey-field and champion player at tennis is also the most keenly intellectual, most interested in the things of the mind.'[48]

Student societies needed proper facilities—and the playing fields at Leeds were just the first instalment. Cricket pitches required pavilions. Debating societies necessitated places in which to debate. Above all, it was recognized that students needed unions, or at least common rooms, in which to relax. Not all of these were nice, and not all of them were used appropriately. 'We learn from official sources', wrote a Dundee student in 1904, 'that the reason of the closing of the telephone room is "that the weemin have been usin' it for coortin"!'[49] But the creation of this special space set aside for students was undoubtedly important, creating as it did a new world of responsibility and freedom for its inhabitants. This was particularly the case for female students, granted—often for the first time—a room of their own. Its significance was reflected in the care the women took over it, creating a pleasant and welcoming environment often in the most adverse circumstances.[50]

---

[42] *The Mermaid* 1 (1904–5), p. 2.   [43] *The Magnet* 2 (1899–1900), pp. 45–6.
[44] *The Limit* 4 (1920), p. 177.   [45] *Yorkshire College Annual Report* 15 (1888–9), p. 16.
[46] Draper, *Sir Nathan Bodington*, p. 149.
[47] H. S. Jones, 'University and College Sport', in M. G. Brock and M. C. Curthoys, eds, *The History of the University of Oxford, vol. vii: the nineteenth century part II* (Oxford, 2000), pp. 517–44; J. A. Mangan, *Athleticism in the Victorian and Edwardian Public Schools: the emergence and consolidation of an educational ideology* (London, 2000).
[48] *The Magnet* 1 (1898–9), p. 103.   [49] *The College* NS 2 (1904–5), p. 33.
[50] See also, Carole Dyhouse, *No Distinction of Sex? Women in British universities, 1870–1939* (London, 1995), p. 108, and Jane Hamlett, '"Nicely Feminine, Yet Learned": student rooms at

Thus, although the women's common room was considerably smaller than the men's, female students at Dundee ensured that theirs was 'more comfortably furnished'.[51] Similarly at Bristol, the women's reading room was called 'the most comfortable room in the building'. Fitted out through the generosity of the students themselves, it was finished off by a collection of photographs of eminent women.[52]

From these unions and common rooms poured forth a plethora of ideas, and words, and disputed resolutions. At Borough Road College, as F. H. Spencer recalled, the students voted annually on college colours—though they never actually changed them.[53] At Birmingham, the call for a 'Varsity Song' was repeated again and again.[54] In Bristol, the success or failure of student social events was a matter of earnest debate.[55] There were also student publications—from regular magazines to ornate, well-published one-offs. So prolific were the student societies that some found it hard to keep up. Indeed at Birmingham there were complaints that there were too many competing clubs, that their meetings clashed, and that they inadvertently distracted attention from the main event, which was creating a more general corporate ethos. Nonetheless, such societies continued to proliferate.[56] Just as the people of Loughborough were confronted with 'College Sunday' and a regular 'Rag', so in Reading there was a version called 'Jantaculum' and in Manchester an annual Shrove Tuesday celebration.[57] Dating back to the 1880s, these were important invented traditions, which—like degree day—stressed the centrality of these colleges and universities to the cities that housed them.[58] They also revealed the way in which Redbrick was successfully pioneering its own, distinctive way of life—for Rag Weeks were invented there, and eventually imitated by Oxbridge.

Inevitably, not everyone was happy with all this. Nor was it always successful, even within its own terms.[59] The combination of poverty and parochialism found in some colleges was bitterly recalled by Ramsay Muir, who arrived at Liverpool in 1889: 'There was, indeed, a common-room,' he wrote,

> but it was a dark, comfortless cellar which few ever entered; there was a Refectory, but it was only another cellar where you could buy poached eggs and meat pies and cups of coffee. There was a debating society, but scarcely anybody ever joined it. There were no cricket or football teams, for all the good players played for their local clubs.[60]

Royal Holloway and the Oxford and Cambridge Colleges in the late-nineteenth century', *Women's History Review* 15 (2006), pp. 137–61.

[51] *The College* NS 2 (1904–5), p. 8.   [52] *The Magnet* 1 (1898–9), p. 161.

[53] Spencer, *Inspector's Testament*, p. 127.

[54] See, for example, *University of Birmingham Magazine* 1 (1900–1901), p. 156; *The Mermaid* 7 (1910–11), p. 116.

[55] See *The Magnet* 1 (1898–9), p. 85, 2 (1899–1900), pp. 44–5, 3 (1900–1901), pp. 86–7.

[56] *The Mermaid* 1 (1904–5), p. 92.

[57] Carole Dyhouse, *Students: a gendered history* (London and New York, 2006), pp. 186–203.

[58] Edward Fiddes, *Chapter in the History of Owens Colleges and of Manchester University 1851–1914* (Manchester, 1937), p. 144.

[59] H. S. Jones, 'Student Life and Sociability, 1860–1930: comparative reflections', *History of Universities* 14 (1995–6), pp. 225–46, p. 236.

[60] Ramsay Muir, *An Autobiography and Some Essays* (London, 1943), p. 24.

As this suggests, invented traditions and new facilities could only do so much. Redbrick always threatened to collapse into its component parts. Divisions between students were often pronounced, whether caused by class or gender or simply by subject. At Birmingham in the 1890s, the scientists ganged up on the others. 'There is, perhaps, no one in this wide world more deserving of commiseration than the Arts student in a science college... his rapt expression, placid brow, dreamy demeanour and neatly-brushed hair are regarded as the signs of a torpid intellect and undeveloped physical constitution'.[61] At Dundee in 1910, by contrast, it was the engineers that were patronized. 'Engineering, as any medical student will tell you, is a pastime', wrote one undergraduate. 'You do it in leisure moments when you might be doing something better. It is about bridges and docks and gas engines and sewers, and things like that, you know. There is not much work in it.'[62] Small wonder, then, that the call to unite, to produce a true '*University Spirit*', was so frequently repeated.[63]

It was the desire to create collegiality which, more than anything else, inspired the move to construct halls of residence.[64] To be sure, there was always the suspicion that these too created divisions amongst the students; after all, at pioneering Manchester, the first halls were established on denominational lines.[65] Nonetheless, there was a widespread belief that, on the whole, a resident population was more likely to cohere.[66] It was also hoped that halls would prove attractive to parents, worried about the safety of their daughters and the morality of their sons.[67] As the founders of University Hall in Liverpool unanswerably argued in 1900: 'The reasons against women students living in lodgings are so obvious that they need not be stated.'[68] For those places, like Reading, with a local population too small to sustain the college, providing accommodation was equally a matter of economic necessity.[69] Even here, however, more than merely mercenary considerations played a part. A hall of residence, wrote W. M. Childs, the principal of Reading,

> is a safeguard against the grosser forms of indiscipline. It deepens *esprit de corps* and offers no encouragement to cliques; it is the place where intimate friendships are made, where constant discussion and intercourse with fellow-students rounds off the corners of egotism, and where the lesson of corporate responsibility is best learned.[70]

---

[61] *Mason College Magazine* 8 (1890), p. 103.   [62] *The College* NS 8 (1910), p. 67.
[63] *The Mermaid* 7 (1910–11), p. 115.
[64] See also William Whyte, 'Halls of Residence at the British Civic Universities, 1870–1970', in Jane Hamlett, Lesley Hopkins, and Rebecca Preston, eds, *Residential Institutions in Britain, 1725–1950: inmates and environments* (London, 2013), pp. 155–66.
[65] See G. A. Sutherland, *Dalton Hall: a Quaker venture* (London, 1963), pp. 16, 30, 37–8.
[66] *Tamesis* 10 (1910–11), pp. 5–6.
[67] *Yorkshire College Annual Report* 15 (1888–9), p. 28; SUA, US/CHA/5/3, 'Notes for the Deputation to the Tramways Committee' (16 August 1913).
[68] *University College Liverpool Hall of Residence for Women Students* (Liverpool, 1900), p. 8.
[69] W. M. Childs, 'A New Residential University', *University Bulletin* 3:1 (June 1924), pp. 92–4, p. 93.
[70] W. M. Childs, 'The Essentials of a University Education', *Hibbert Journal* 10 (1912), pp. 581–98, pp. 595–6.

Thus it was that residence became increasingly accepted as 'an essential part of the best kind of University training', even by night-school students.[71] Thus it was that by 1909 any Leeds undergraduate who could not travel into college daily was required to live in halls.[72] In many respects, the hall of residence was to be one of the most important traditions that Redbrick ever invented.

LIKE AN ILLEGITIMATE CHILD OF THE LONDON LAW COURTS

Just as the students and staff of Redbrick hoped to build a new sort of university, so they sought to construct a new type of university building. This did not mean that they broke radically with the past, of course. Building in an age of historicism, they chose historic styles to house their modern institutions. Nor did it mean that they rejected wholesale the examples of their forerunners. Comparison with the ancient universities was always at the very least implicit.[73] But what is striking was the extent to which this period saw not just the creation of a Redbrick identity, but also the dissemination of an archetypally Redbrick architecture.

This was, of course, precisely what the architects and builders of the new universities hoped to achieve. Seeking to establish the importance of their new foundations, they built big. Hoping to attract students and impress potential benefactors, they built boldly. Above all, in an effort to institutionalize the traditions they had invented, they built distinctively.[74] True enough, lack of money and changing tastes could leave these institutions embarrassed. Improvisation and making do were often the order of the day. Nonetheless, the programme of building that this period witnessed was impressive. Arriving at the thinly-disguised University College Nottingham, Ursula Brangwen found herself moved by the architecture, however 'foolish' she had been taught to find it by her father. 'It was different from that of all other buildings' she thought; and 'amorphous as it might be, there was in it a reminiscence of the wondrous, cloistral origin of education.'[75] Ursula—and her creator D. H. Lawrence—were not alone. The impact of Redbrick architecture was deeply felt—and was meant to be (Figure 25).[76]

It is for that reason that subsequent criticism of these buildings so often misses the mark. Some writers have perplexingly read into Redbrick nothing more than a reworking of Oxbridge idioms. For Roy Lowe and Rex Knight, for example, the architecture of this era was characterized by a 'fruitless imitation of Oxbridge'.

---

[71] *The Oxford University Extension Gazette* 4 (1893–4), p. 122.
[72] A. N. Shimmin, *The University of Leeds: the first half century* (Cambridge, 1954), p. 35.
[73] See also Alex Duke, *Importing Oxbridge: English residential colleges and American universities* (New Haven and London, 1997), for an American example.
[74] William Whyte, '"Redbrick's unlovely quadrangles": reinterpreting the architecture of the civic universities', *History of Universities* 21 (2006), pp. 151–77.
[75] Lawrence, *Rainbow*, p. 428.
[76] See also William Whyte, 'Building the Nation in the Town: Architecture and National Identity in Urban Britain, 1848–1914', in William Whyte and Oliver Zimmer, eds, *Nationalism and the Reshaping of Urban Communities, 1848–1914* (Basingstoke, 2011), pp. 204–33.

The result, they claim, 'was a monument to the conservatism of English academic life'; a concrete, brick, and stone embodiment of 'the way in which universities were to sustain the traditionalism of English society during the twentieth century.'[77] Other historians have been apparently less dismissive, but reached broadly similar conclusions, seeing the Redbrick buildings erected in this period as a manifestation of the fact that things were going wrong. For Sarah Barnes, for instance, the architectural influence of Oxford and Cambridge was much more ambivalent and far less direct.[78] Yet even she concludes that ultimately Redbrick failed. 'The provincial universities', Barnes writes 'were defined—and redefined—first as pioneering alternatives to England's ancient institutions, then as second-class substitutes.'[79] These conclusions are highly contentious. In the first place, they do not reflect what we have already seen of the Redbricks: their pioneering spirit, their determination to be different, their attempt to create a distinctively modern university. In the second place, these arguments ignore or misunderstand the realities of Redbrick building. This was a new architecture for a new sort of institution. This was emphatically not what Sarah Barnes has depicted as a 'story of unrealised possibilities and the triumph of tradition'.[80]

It is nonetheless undeniable that many of these buildings did not live up to the hopes and expectations of their builders. Poverty, in particular, proved a problem: a big problem, with the University of Wales a particularly useful case in point. At Aberystwyth the college was housed within a bankrupt railway hotel. All turrets and staircases, it was later described by H. V. Morton looking 'like an illegitimate child of the London Law Courts'. (Figure 22)[81] In Bangor, staff and students were accommodated within 'a decrepit hostelry above the Menai Straits', whilst Cardiff's first home was 'an abandoned infirmary surrounded by Nissen huts'.[82] At the turn of the century, in fact, classes were still being held inside what even the most dedicated students had to admit were little more than 'unhygienic sheds'.[83] The college, complained another, less enthusiastic undergraduate, looked like 'a combination of a workhouse and a prison reformatory'.[84]

Other places often had a similarly unprepossessing start. At Dundee the college was squeezed into a small row of four houses on the way out of town, imbued with

---

[77] R. A. Lowe and Rex Knight, 'Building the Ivory Tower: the social functions of late-nineteenth century collegiate architecture', *Studies in Higher Education* 7:2 (1982), pp. 81–91, pp. 88, 90–1. See also, Roy Lowe, 'Anglo-Americanism and the Planning of Universities in the United States', *History of Education* 15 (1986), pp. 247–59.

[78] Sarah V. Barnes, 'Lessons in Stone: architecture and academic ethos in an urban setting', in Debra N. Mancoff and D. J. Trela, eds, *Victorian Urban Settings: essays on the nineteenth century city and its contexts* (New York and London, 1996), pp. 214–29.

[79] Sarah V. Barnes, 'England's Civic Universities and the Triumph of the Oxbridge Ideal', *History of Education Quarterly* 36 (1996), pp. 271–305, p. 305.

[80] Barnes, 'England's Civic Universities', p. 305.

[81] Lord Elwyn-Jones, *In My Time: an autobiography* (London, 1983), p. 23.

[82] Geraint H. Jenkins, *'The finest old university in the world': the University of Wales 1883–1993* (Cardiff, 1994), p. 4.

[83] *Cap and Gown* 5 (1907–8), p. 103; J. H. Howard, *Winding Lane: a book of impressions and recollections* (Carnarvon, 1938).

[84] *Cap and Gown* 5 (1907–8), p. 75.

Fig. 22. 'Like an illegitimate child of the London Law Courts': University College Aberystwyth

all the grandeur, as a student put it, of a 'procession of caravans'.[85] The effect, recalled one, 'was unobtrusive, undistinctive—so much so that I could never visualize it even when seeing it everyday'.[86] Plans kept in the university archive show how ingenious the institution had to be: with a laboratory made out of a drawing room and a common room made out of a cellar.[87] No wonder that in 1892 the local newspaper argued that 'the comparatively unimposing nature of our architectural pretensions' was seriously damaging the college's reputation.[88] At Newcastle, in 1883, things seemed even worse, and the principal threatened to resign unless better accommodation was provided.[89] The University of Liverpool was founded in a disused lunatic asylum, with laboratories converted out of old padded cells and a dining room that had begun life as a mortuary.[90] Even after expansion, extension, and really radical rebuilding, many would agree with a historian of Leeds that there was often 'more Etruscan fortitude than Roman beauty in the general design' of the civic universities.[91] Certainly, the principal of Reading was not alone in being forced to conclude that 'beautiful and stately

---

[85] *The College* 2 (1889), p. 160. [86] *The College* 6 (1908–9), p. 44.
[87] DUA, UC/PL/1/7, UCD in 1885 (1987).
[88] Donald Southgate, *University Education in Dundee: a centenary history* (Edinburgh, 1982), pp. 80, 140–2.
[89] E. M. Bettenson, *The University of Newcastle upon Tyne: a historical introduction, 1834–1971* (Newcastle, 1971), p. 24.
[90] Oliver Lodge, *Past Years* (London, 1931), p. 153; *Sphinx* 9 (1901–2), p. 185.
[91] Shimmin, *University of Leeds*, p. 18.

architecture was beyond our reach'.[92] Nonetheless, the acknowledgement was not an admission of defeat; nor should it be taken to mean that Redbrick architecture was little more than an attempt to ape Oxbridge. Even when poverty frustrated ambition, the desire to create a distinctive architecture remained.

The result was a fitful but nonetheless vibrant series of architectural experiments which were conducted all across the country. Liverpool and Leeds had followed Manchester in employing Alfred Waterhouse as their architect, and soon his Gothic Revival buildings became synonymous with the civic universities.[93] They set the standard that would be imitated everywhere. Even teacher training colleges, like F. H. Spencer's Borough Road, adopted what he later called 'the worst possible modern pseudo-Gothic style, which, I am afraid, we rather admired'.[94] This admiration is noteworthy. For although later generations were to condemn the Gothic extravagance of Waterhouse, the reality is that contemporaries did admire the architecture of Redbrick.[95] It is fair to say that as the medieval revival waned in popularity, Gothic universities came to seem problematic.[96] New styles started to appear. But it was Gothic that made Redbrick in this period: from Bristol to Newcastle, and from Devon to Dundee.

The Gothic of Redbrick was not, however, the Gothic of Oxbridge. Manchester was not just a sort of bargain-basement Balliol. Liverpool was not a knocked-off copy of King's College Cambridge. In the first place, by the 1880s Oxford and Cambridge were no longer bastions of revived medieval building. There, tastes had changed, with Renaissance architecture coming into the ascendant.[97] If simple imitation had been the goal, the founders of the civic universities would have followed this example. They emphatically did not. Secondly, and still more importantly, it is clear that to the people who built Redbrick, Gothic did not equal Oxbridge. Rather, it evoked education itself. Many of these buildings were built in a style known to contemporaries as 'Popular Perpendicular Gothic Collegiate Style'.[98] Originating in the 1820s, it was an approach seen to be 'rich in a sort of learned ease', and by the 1860s it was noted that nearly all schools were now built in the 'Collegiate Gothic'.[99] This had an obvious impact on the new universities. At Bristol, for example, the university's first architect was Charles Hansom, who had used Collegiate Gothic at a nearby public school. Sure enough, when commissioned to build for the university college, he imported the same style; doing no

---

[92] W. M. Childs, *Making a University: an account of the university movement at Reading* (London, 1933), p. 56.
[93] Colin Cunningham and Prudence Waterhouse, *Alfred Waterhouse, 1830–1905: biography of a practice* (London, 1992).
[94] Spencer, *Inspector's Testament*, p. 123.
[95] Lowe and Knight, 'Building the Ivory Tower', pp. 87–91.
[96] 'A. F.' [Austin Farrar Barker], *Leaves From a Northern University* (London, 1926), pp. 1–2.
[97] William Whyte, *Oxford Jackson: architecture, education, status and style, 1835–1924* (Oxford, 2006).
[98] Quoted in F. H. G. Percy, *A History of the Whitgift School* (London, 1976), p. 181.
[99] *Builder* 37 (1879), p. 929; *British Almanac* 1866, p. 172.

more, as the historian Andor Gomme puts it, than 're-arrange the motifs which had occupied him for twenty years at Clifton'.[100]

What developed, in fact, was not a naïve reworking of old, Oxbridge themes, but a sophisticated architectural rhetoric which was indirectly inspired by the buildings of the ancient universities, but which was never subservient to them. At Sheffield, for example, in 1903, the college was rebuilt in what its architects described as 'the Tudor Style, of which there are many examples in the Colleges of Oxford and Cambridge, and which by association and appropriateness gives a Collegiate character to the building'.[101] But, in truth, this owed little to Oxbridge and much to a more generalized idea of educational architecture—one that the colleges had learnt from the public schools.[102] The same can even be seen in the winning design for a University Extension College, designed by C. R. Ashbee in 1891.[103] This was a building explicitly intended to symbolize the work of Oxford University in the community: 'to carry out the idea of expansion expressed in actual stone' (Figure 23). Yet even this was more than just a narrowly Oxonian piece of architecture. The idea was, Ashbee made plain, to make 'reference to that earlier and greater extension of the Universities when Colet lectured at Oxford and Erasmus led the new learning of Europe from his little cell at Queens'.' (Figure 26)[104] Here was a universal vision rather than a piece of parochial imitation.

The same process can be seen in the plans of many of these new institutions. Once again, it would be a mistake to understand the quadrangles and courtyards of Redbrick as an attempt to ape Tom Quad at Oxford's Christ Church or Great Court at Trinity, Cambridge. Unsurprisingly enough, comparisons were often made. But analogy did not imply uncritical imitation. Thus W. D. Caroë described his work at Cardiff as drawing on the library at Trinity College Dublin; 'the charm and *quiet dignity* and scale' of Trinity College Cambridge; and the 'picturesque balance and delightful proportions' of Oxford. His Baroque confection, however, bore almost no resemblance to any of these institutions (Figure 24). Not only was it larger: 'longer than the Court of King's, Cambridge, or the Quads of Christ Church or Keble—the two largest at Oxford'. Caroë had also, he stressed, avoided all 'elements of direct likeness'.[105] His rhetoric was traditional, and emphasized similarity with Oxbridge. The reality was not and did not. In fact, the quadrangular

---

[100] Andor Gomme, Michael Jenner, and Bryan Little, *Bristol: an architectural history* (London, 1979), p. 323.
[101] SUA, US/CHA/5/2(1), Erection of Buildings in Western Bank (1901–6), Gibbs and Flockton, Plans (1903), 11.
[102] William Whyte, 'Building a Public School Community, 1860–1910', *History of Education* 32 (2003), pp. 601–26.
[103] See also, H. W. Moore's plans in H. J. Mackinder and M. E. Sadler, *University Extension, its past, present, and future* (London, 1891), pp. 123–5.
[104] *Oxford University Extension Gazette* 2 (1891–2), p. 32.
[105] Dewi-Prys Thomas, '"A Quiet Dignity...": William Douglas Caroë and the visual presence', in Gwyn Jones and Michael Quinn, eds, *Fountains of Praise: University College, Cardiff, 1883–1983* (Cardiff, 1983), pp. 54–70, pp. 58–67.

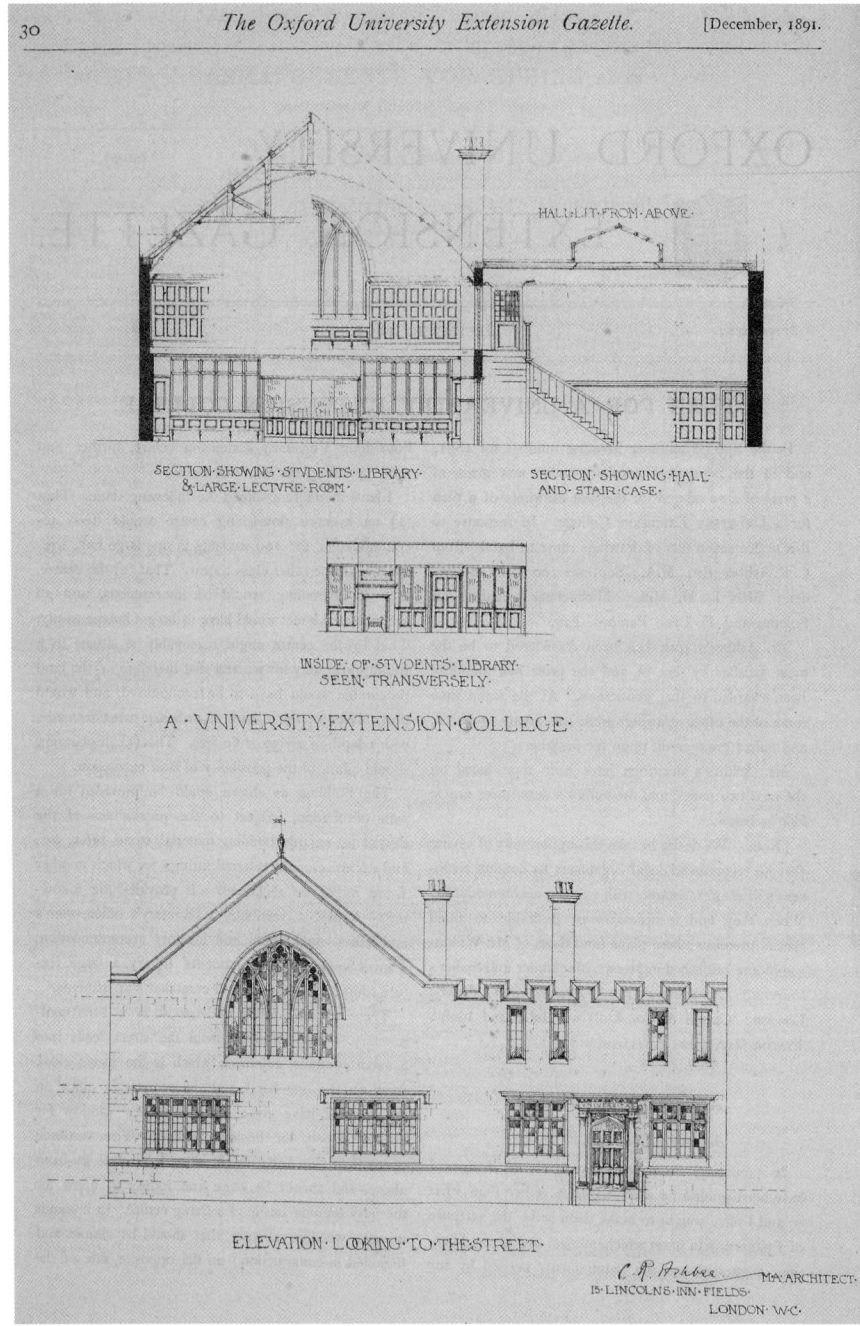

Fig. 23. A 'reference to that earlier and greater extension of the Universities when Colet lectured at Oxford and Erasmus led the new learning of Europe from his little cell at Queens'': C. R. Ashbee's design for a University Extension College

Oxford University Extension Gazette 2 (1891–2), Per. G.A. Oxon 4A 124, p. 30. Bodleian Libraries, University of Oxford.

Fig. 24. 'The court-yard—sacred to the collegers themselves': University College Cardiff
The Builder 15 May 1909, pp. 2–3. Per. N1863 c.1. Bodleian Libraries, University of Oxford.

plans adopted at the Redbrick universities and colleges owed less to Oxford and Cambridge than to the example of other, more urban universities.[106]

Indeed, just as the need to withstand industrial pollution required harder-wearing materials that would have been needed in Oxbridge, so the problem of building within crowded and expensive cities also generated its own architectural momentum—a momentum which had little to do with the example of the ancient universities.[107] As Sarah Barnes quite correctly notes, Waterhouse's quadrangle at Manchester was not a crude imitation of an Oxbridge college, 'but rather a solution, arrived at after prolonged argument, to particular problems of space, light, ventilation, noise and cost'.[108] The result was a building that faced onto Oxford Road, but which had very little to do with the University of Oxford itself.

The teaching accommodation at Redbrick was also inevitably rather different from the rooms used in Oxford and Cambridge, and not just because the civics taught in classes and lectures whilst Oxbridge increasingly emphasized the value of one-to-one tutorials. After all, the late-nineteenth century saw a move in Oxford and Cambridge to institutionalize larger lectures and laboratory teaching too.[109]

---

[106] Carol Severino, 'The Idea of an Urban University: a history and rhetoric of ambivalence and ambiguity', *Urban Education* 31:3 (1996), pp. 291–313, p. 299. See also Oliver Lodge, *The City University* (Liverpool, 1903), esp. pp. 5, 9.

[107] Catherine Bowler and Peter Brimblecombe, 'Environmental Pressures on Building Design and Manchester's John Rylands' Library', *Journal of Design History* 13 (2000), pp. 175–91.

[108] Barnes, 'Lessons in Stone', p. 225.

[109] William Whyte, '"Rooms for the Torture and Shame of Scholars": the new Examination Schools and the architecture of reform', *Oxoniensia* 66 (2001), pp. 85–101; J. W. Clark, *Endowments of the University of Cambridge* (Cambridge, 1904).

THE NEW UNIVERSITY COLLEGE, NOTTINGHAM.—SEE NEXT PAGE.

Fig. 25. 'Amorphous as it might be, there was in it a reminiscence of the wondrous, cloistral origin of education': University College Nottingham

Illustrated London News 2 July 1881.

More importantly, the fact that the Redbrick universities sought to concentrate their teaching in a single site rather than do it in halls of residence or separate science areas meant that the challenge for architects was to integrate a whole series of different functions within one or two coherent forms. This was even more troublesome when, as in Nottingham, the building erected attempted to combine a college, technical schools, natural history museum, and public library (Figure 25).[110] The architectural challenges presented by the multiple different buildings erected in Oxford and Cambridge were nothing compared to this.

Lowe and Knight's survey suggests that the attempt to integrate a multiplicity of different functions within a single form ultimately failed, with the colleges coming to distinguish sharply between science and arts, technical and liberal education. This again, they imply, would suggest an inability to reconcile the realities of Redbrick life with an Oxbridge architectural ideal.[111] And it is true that in one or two places, laboratories and classrooms were strikingly different. Take Sheffield, for example. Here the main building on Western Bank was Tudor (Figure 26), whilst the Engineering Department in nearby St George's Square was 'Queen Anne'.[112] It is also true that the principal of Reading made it clear that laboratories

[110] *The Builder* 15 October 1881.
[111] Lowe and Knight, 'Building the Ivory Tower', p. 90.
[112] SUA, US/CHA/4/8 (1), 'University College Sheffield' (1903), pp. 5–7.

Fig. 26. 'The Tudor Style, of which there are many examples in the Colleges of Oxford and Cambridge, and which by association and appropriateness gives a Collegiate character to the building': Western Bank, University of Sheffield

Reproduced with the permission of the University of Sheffield.

and workshops did not need elaborate architecture; indeed, he argued, any elaboration might make further development difficult.[113]

Once again, however, what was built bore little relationship to what was said about it. Even at Sheffield, the conventionally collegiate Western Bank building included a wing of labs and classrooms, a wing for the medical school, and another wing for administration and ceremonial purposes, and all in the same Gothic style. Likewise at Liverpool, Leeds, Manchester, Bristol, and even in Reading—whatever its Principal claimed—technical and scientific wings were barely distinguishable from the rest of the other buildings. Nor was any distinction between science and art necessarily made in the latter's favour. At Dundee, for example, 'the only part of the College which [had] any architectural pretensions at all' in the late 1880s was the chemistry laboratory.[114] In other words, the particular challenges of providing buildings for teaching and research created a variety of solutions which had little or nothing to do with the Oxbridge model or with the stark division between the scientific and the liberal that Lowe and Knight suggest. Rather, Redbrick was constructing a new sort of architecture: something *sui generis*.

[113] Childs, 'The Essentials of a University Education', p. 594.
[114] *The College* 1 (1888), p. 56.

Fig. 27. 'Give people something to see, and I will get...half a million without delay': Joseph Chamberlain at the University of Birmingham

Cadbury Research Library: Special Collections, University of Birmingham.

Of course it would be wrong to suggest that the builders and benefactors of these new institutions were solely motivated by a disinterested aesthetic enthusiasm for fine architecture. So, when Joseph Chamberlain defended the expense of Birmingham's new buildings at the turn of the century, he did so in two very different ways (Figure 27). First, he tried a Ruskinian argument: that good buildings would create good people. 'The architectural beauty of the University precincts' he declared, 'has an intellectual value not less than that of the intellectual training and practical skill which the University imparts.'[115] Secondly, he took a more mercenary tack, justifying the £25,000 red-brick bell-tower he proposed to put at the heart of the campus in the following terms: 'Every railway traveller passing the tower would ask, "What's that?"'[116] This, he claimed, could only help with fund-raising. 'Give people something to see, and I will get...half a million without delay.'[117] And which of these two arguments did Chamberlain believe, or his audience accept? Perhaps neither; perhaps both. For the architecture of Redbrick was the product of many different interests and many divergent agendas. Buildings could be personal memorials and public monuments; symbols of education in general and expressions of a very particular agenda.

---

[115] *The Mermaid* 2 (1905–6), Supplement, p. 13.

[116] Quoted in A. P. D. Thomson, 'The Chamberlain Memorial Tower, University of Birmingham', *University of Birmingham Historical Journal* 4 (1953–4), pp. 167–79, p. 176.

[117] Quoted in Eric Ives, 'A new campus', in Eric Ives, Diane Drummond, and Leonard Schwartz, eds, *The First Civic University: Birmingham, 1880–1980* (Birmingham, 2000), pp. 111–31, p. 126.

Chamberlain's combination of high-mindedness and low cunning can be seen throughout the Redbrick system. At Bristol, for example, the magnificent Wills Tower was, like the rest of the building, intended to 'remind the beholder of the majesty of learning'.[118] But at 215 feet high, this soaring Gothic structure was also surely intended to remind the city of the importance of the family who had paid for it. Similarly, in Ireland, at Maynooth, the professors found when celebrating the college's centenary in 1895 'that, whereas we should get fifteen thousand pounds for a tower and spire, we should not get one-fifth of the sum for library endowment'.[119] The mixed motives for erecting such striking and imposing buildings were perhaps most clearly summed up in, of all places, *The Oxford University Extension Gazette*. 'Local organisations', it advised,

> should secure their work by putting it inside bricks and mortar. When a building is devoted to any public work, the work itself gains dignity and importance. It impresses itself more on the general attention. People are less apt to forget its claims.... It reminds benevolent persons of their good intentions. It jogs the memories of many friends whose good-will might otherwise be distracted by newer, though not more valid, claims.[120]

In other words, these buildings should be seen as part of the wider process of inventing traditions, creating culture, and expressing identity. They were the outward and visible sign of the university, designed to impress, to attract admiration, to inspire benefaction, and—just like graduation processions or the wearing of gowns—intended to mark this as a special and significant place.

It is for that reason that these buildings are best understood as great municipal monuments as well as homes for educational institutions.[121] Indeed, the civic aspect could predominate—as at Bristol, where a student was approached by a child outside the imposing entrance to the university in 1912 and asked, 'Please, miss, is this 'ere the Children's 'Orspital?'[122] Less problematically, at Nottingham, as in many other places, the college building was greeted by the *Builder* as 'a pile which will in future go far to redeem the unusual poverty of the town as regards municipal architecture'.[123] It was natural, then, that when looking for architects, the builders and benefactors of Redbrick often turned to local men. Now, some of these men were also national names: Waterhouse worked at Manchester, and also at the Natural History Museum in London; Rowand Anderson added a quadrangle to Dundee, but was mainly known for his National Portrait Gallery in Edinburgh. Yet it was, on the whole, as locals that even these high-flyers were employed.[124]

---

[118] Sarah Whittingham, *The Wills Memorial Building* (Bristol, 2003) and her *Sir George Oatley: architect of Bristol* (Bristol, 2011), ch. 14. See also Roger Gill, 'The Buildings of the Main Precinct', in J. G. Macqueen and S. W. Taylor, eds, *University and Community: essays to mark the centenary of the founding of University College, Bristol* (Bristol, 1976), pp. 15–28.
[119] Walter McDonald, *Reminiscences of a Maynooth Professor* (London, 1925), p. 188.
[120] *Oxford University Extension Gazette* 1 (1890–91), p. 38.
[121] Sanderson, *Universities and British Industry*, p. 81.
[122] *The Bristol Nonesuch* 3 (1913), p. 18.   [123] *Builder* 11 (1881), p. 786.
[124] MUA, Owens College Extension, Minutes of Committee, vol. 1 (1867–71), p. 184. See also Sam McKinstry, *Rowand Anderson: 'the premier architect of Scotland'* (Edinburgh, 1991), pp. 167–8.

Moreover, in most other cases, a combination of poverty and propinquity led to the appointment of figures who would not have been known outside the region. Thus, at Sheffield, when the firm of Gibbs and Flockton were employed, it was undoubtedly their experience as architects of the local art gallery, city courts, and a variety of factory buildings that got them the job.[125] Indeed, it was as much to municipal as to educational buildings that they made reference in their reports. Whilst the men's cloakrooms were 'a size dictated by the experience of the Yorkshire College at Leeds', the main corridors were designed to be 'the same width as the Corridors to the Reception Rooms at the Town Hall', with subsidiary passages 'the same width as the Corridor to the City Surveyor's Department in the Town Hall'.[126] Local men building a local college for local people with local money: here was Redbrick incarnate.

Yet here too were the tensions that ran through the whole Redbrick project. Whilst some were more than happy to embrace idioms associated with civic buildings, others were determined to be distinctively different. 'There is an essential difference between municipal and academical architecture—or there should be', observed Caroë, in an article for the Cardiff students' newspaper. 'That does not imply that municipal buildings should not be academic, but that collegiate architecture should not readily be mistaken for that which has come to be associated with town halls.' What's more, he went on, universities should be exclusive in form and function—forming communities by resisting outsiders. His planned quadrangle was in that sense not merely an architectural feature, but a central part of his vision for the college. 'The court-yard—sacred to the collegers themselves', he wrote, 'is destined to be its chief claim to architectural consideration, our private property in architecture, as it were, from which the public can at will be wholly excluded, save for a narrow peep through iron screens just to whet the appetites.'[127] A generation before, the founders of public libraries had worried that too grand a building would frighten off the working classes.[128] No such concern was ever presented when considering university buildings—and the result was predictable. They were not only exclusive, they were excluding. Looking round the Salford Technical Institute, a young and ambitious millwright was clear. This 'wasn't for people like me'.[129]

By the end of the nineteenth century, however, a Redbrick style—or, more precisely, a distinctive architectural approach—had undoubtedly developed. Characterized by collegiate Gothic, by quadrangular plans, and by an attempt to integrate the parts of the college within the whole, it was instantly recognizable. To be sure, Gothic was never hegemonic, with both Birmingham and Cardiff, for example, coming to embrace the Byzantine and the Baroque respectively. There were also those who disliked the monumentality of this municipal mode of design,

---

[125] SUA, UCS/CNL/1/1, Council Minutes 1901–5, p. 92.
[126] SUA, US/CHA/5/2(1), 2–11.
[127] W. D. Caroë, 'The New College Buildings', *Cap and Gown* 7 (1909–10), pp. 23–6, pp. 23–4.
[128] Alistair Black, *A New History of the English Public Library: social and intellectual contexts, 1850–1914* (Leicester and New York, 1996), p. 243.
[129] Robert Roberts, *The Classic Slum* (1971; London, 1990), p. 147.

with W. M. Childs objecting to 'the erection of buildings of a characteristic city type—buildings of imposing frontage, storey above storey, rising from the pavement edge, full of echoing corridors and stone stairways—which are not particularly well-suited to University purposes'.[130] Oliver Lodge, doubtless articulating his own dissatisfaction with the grandiosity of Birmingham, likewise complained—and to the Chancellor of the Exchequer, of all people—that universities were 'cursed in many cases with monumental architecture totally unsuited to modern needs.' He called instead for 'buildings far more of the type of factories—spacious, light, capable of adaptation to changing uses, uses which none of us can really fully foresee'.[131] It was a call that would be repeated throughout the twentieth century. But the attraction of the substantial, civic university architecture which became synonymous with Redbrick in this period would prove hard—almost impossible—to resist.

The extent to which architects still struggled to agree on precisely the appropriate plan for these new sorts of universities was revealed in the 1911 competition to rebuild Southampton. Reviewing the entries, the *Builder* expressed bemusement: 'The competitors', it wrote,

> seem to have taken different views of the precise meaning to be attached to the term University College. Some seem to place the accent on the University, and show the departments arranged in separate buildings with carriage drives between them; others place it on the college and, connecting their departments, group them as a single building round one or more quadrangles.[132]

Nevertheless, if the architects were confused, then the authorities at Southampton had a much clearer sense of what they wanted. Like the other civic institutions, they hoped to create neither an old-style university, divided into separate buildings, nor an old-fashioned, small-scale college. Rather, taking the existing Redbricks as their model, they chose a design which brought together a variety of disparate functions—from labs to libraries, dining rooms to lecture halls—within a single, sprawling, monumental, university edifice.[133] Just like Cardiff or Birmingham, Southampton sought to express the comprehensiveness of its curriculum and the cohesiveness of the community it aspired to create through a unified building (Figure 28). Just like Bristol or Sheffield, it hoped also to impress visitors with its importance through the scale of its edifice. In that sense, it too—like all the other civic institutions—differed greatly from the dispersed and multifarious architectural environment produced by the ancient universities, and the federal university of London.

This was even true in the sole Scottish outpost of the Redbrick tradition: Dundee. Impoverished, and—frankly—ill-housed for much of its existence, it

---

[130] Childs, 'The Essentials of a University Education', p. 594.
[131] Universities Bureau of the British Empire, *Deputation to the President of the Board of Education and Chancellor of the Exchequer* (London, 1918), p. 16.
[132] *Builder* 100 (1911), p. 638.
[133] USA, 1/2/5/11, Block Plan. See also *Builder* 100 (1911), p. 638.

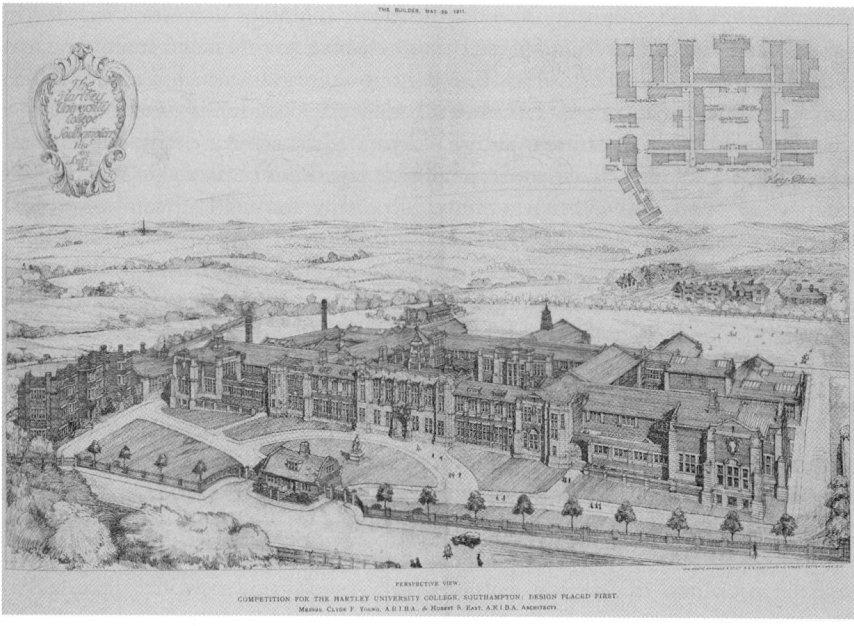

Fig. 28. 'The competitors seem to have taken different views of the precise meaning to be attached to the term University College. Some seem to place the accent on the University, and show the departments arranged in separate buildings with carriage drives between them; others place it on the college and, connecting their departments, group them as a single building round one or more quadrangles': Clyde and East's winning design for University College Southampton

The Builder, 26 May 1911, p. 646. Per. N1863 c.1, Bodleian Libraries, University of Oxford.

nonetheless celebrated its eclectic architectural heritage. As the student press put it, comparing Dundee with the Bodleian Library's entrance gateway:

> Though Oxford's Tower, of orders five,
> Gives scope for many a learnéd lecture,
> Yet Dundee College is alive
> With every kind of architecture.[134]

This, it was argued, gave the college its unique spirit, its particular charm. The same could be said of many rival Redbrick institutions. For whilst Oxbridge was a point of comparison, it was not—and never could be—something to be imitated. The colleges did not have the money to do so; nor did they have the desire. They were seeking to achieve something very different indeed. And they built some remarkable things as a result.

[134] *The College* 6 (1908–9), p. 44, quoting *The Meal Poke* (1903), p. 90.

Conclusion

All of which brings us back to Birmingham. For in many ways, it is here—in the first unitary university—that the Redbrick system of this era reached its apotheosis. The degree day of 1901 was undeniably exciting and also highly significant, marking, as it did, the University's coming of age. Those being filmed and those who later watched the film all knew that. But it was also just one part of Birmingham's transformation. For in 1905 it moved to its wholly new site and into its entirely new buildings. In 1909 Edward VII himself came to inaugurate what was the single largest and most striking example of a Redbrick university yet built.[1] This was in some respects a remarkably innovative development: built on a campus outside town in an assertive Byzantine style. But however new it looked, it was nonetheless a development which grew out of a living, Redbrick tradition. Here was a local university, sustained by civic pride and displaying its identity for all to see. Above the main door were statues to Darwin and Faraday; Watt and Newton; Shakespeare and Plato; Michelangelo, Virgil, and Beethoven. The sons of the Midlands took their place with the fathers of literature, art, and philosophy.[2] Each pavilion, too, was ornamented with friezes reflecting the industrial achievements of central England: pattern-making, pipe-laying, and cable-laying, amongst other activities. With its imposing great hall, its inspiring great tower, and its obvious self-belief, Birmingham represented the embodiment of the Redbrick tradition; the acme of civic university building.

The campus opened by the king in 1909 was unfinished. It was also the result of compromise as well as of conviction. Some—including the vice-chancellor, of course—actively opposed this move to the suburbs. Nor were Birmingham's benefactors as one on the future of the college. Andrew Carnegie, whose money underwrote the development, wanted to establish 'a first class modern Scientific College . . . not necessarily big, but perfect of its kind'.[3] Joseph Chamberlain, by contrast, imagined something far more ambitious, a federal university for the Midlands, bringing Birmingham together with Bristol and Nottingham on the

---

[1] Eric Ives, 'A New Campus', in Eric Ives, Diane Drummond, and Leonard Schwartz, eds, *The First Civic University: Birmingham, 1880–1980* (Birmingham, 2000), pp. 111–31; J. W. R. Whitehead, 'Institutional Site Planning: the University of Birmingham, 1900–69', *Planning History* 13:2 (1991), 29–35.

[2] BUA, UC/7/iv/8/39, Oliver Lodge, 'Preliminary Statement Concerning the Proposed Nine Statues on the Outside North Front of the Great Hall' (10 April 1905).

[3] BUA, UC/4/iii/10, Report of a Visit to Colleges and Universities in the United States and Canada made in November 1899 on the Suggestion of Mr Carnegie, p. 11.

model of the northern, Victoria University.⁴ Yet, with time, a clearer picture emerged of something rather different from each man's own idea—the image of a Redbrick University. This was, Chamberlain made clear, to be an institution that was not 'like Oxford and Cambridge'.⁵ And, not being like Oxford and Cambridge, he concluded, it should not look like Oxford and Cambridge. To that end he commissioned the President of the Royal Institute of British Architects, Aston Webb—a national name with local connections—who designed, as he himself put it, 'an entirely fresh type of building'. 'Our old universities', Webb wrote, 'are the result of centuries of care and labour and cannot be reproduced, nor do I take it that you would wish to do so.'⁶ Hence the Byzantine style, the radial plan, and the campus concept.

Birmingham was not Gothic and it was not quadrangular and it was not crammed into a site in the centre of town. But it was a Redbrick university: a single, coherent plan for a unified, comprehensive institution. In that sense what we are studying is variations on a theme rather than the creation of a fixed and unchanging type. This was a self-consciously modern university studying self-evidently modern subjects. It was a local university, drawing its students, its identity, and much of its funding from amongst the local people. It sought to impress a 'varsity stamp' on its students and to construct community by inventing tradition. And all this was housed in something that was immediately recognizable and designed to impress.

More than that: it worked. Redbrick was not as egalitarian as some hoped it would be. It remained a bastion of the bourgeoisie. Some prospective students were repelled by its image; others could not even afford appropriate clothes. Moreover, Redbrick was dependent on the generosity of bourgeois patrons and city councillors. As Michael Sanderson has observed, those colleges which failed to attract middle-class students thus failed to attract substantial financial support.⁷ At the other end of the social scale, class differences also meant that Oxbridge continued to claim greater social and educational cachet. Nor did Redbrick's money troubles ever wholly dissipate. There remained unresolved, if scarcely suppressed tensions between the local and the national, the civic and the academic: fault lines which would become ever more pronounced in later years. Yet, nonetheless, we can say that it worked. For in the decades after 1880 these institutions had developed and then disseminated a new concept, a new sort of university. Responding to the foundation of the Imperial College of Science in 1907, Arthur Headlam, principal of King's College London, was unsparing in his criticism of the Board of Education which had drawn up the plan. 'The Board', he wrote, 'appears to have picked up the old-fashioned German ideas ... and has entirely ignored the new and better ideas represented by the Universities of Leeds, of Sheffield, and of Birmingham'.⁸

⁴ Eric Ives, 'What is a University?', in Ives et al., eds, *First Civic University*, pp. 70–88, pp. 76–8.
⁵ Quoted in Diane Drummond, 'The New University', in Ives et al., eds, *First Civic University*, pp. 131–57, p. 142.
⁶ Ian Robert Dungavell, 'The Architectural Career of Aston Webb (1849–1930)' (University of London PhD, 1999), p. 218.
⁷ Michael Sanderson, *The Universities and British Industry, 1850–1970* (London, 1972), p. 99.
⁸ Arthur C. Headlam, *Universities and the Empire: a paper read at the Imperial Conference on Education, May 1907* (London, 1907), p. 9.

Twelve years later, we have another example. For it was then, in 1919, that Vero Garrett, the boy who had been so impressed by Oliver Lodge, went to university himself. It was not Birmingham, but London; and not Redbrick, but the icy—if still tragically incomplete—classicism of University College London. His experiences, however, were representative, and were proof that the processions, the lectures, and the hard work done by Lodge and his colleagues had paid off. They had inspired Garrett, who had left school at fourteen for employment in a gas-meter factory, to go to university himself. Wearing a new suit, bought specially for the occasion, he set out for UCL:

> I remember gazing on the façade of this imposing building before ascending the steps and feeling a sort of apostolic succession to the old classical scholars who passed through similar portals in ancient Greece and Rome.[9]

Here was the invention of tradition indeed.

---

[9] V. W. Garrett, *A Man in the Street* (London, 1939), p. 265.

PART IV

1914–1949

Prologue

'Mummy, there's a terrible old man in the hall, who won't take his hat off.'[1] Percy Morley Horder is not now a name to be conjured with. A mostly forgotten architect, he made it into the *Dictionary of National Biography*, but significantly does not rate an entry on *Wikipedia*.[2] In his day, however, Morley Horder was a phenomenon; a source of wonder and often infuriation to both his family and his friends. To his pupils he was 'Holy Murder'. To his daughter 'he was the most remarkable man I have ever met, the most dedicated, the most charming (when he chose to be) and the most awful'.[3] Pushing the artistic temperament to its limits, Morley Horder looked and behaved like a cantankerous Old Testament prophet. He quarrelled and he cavilled and he jibed. He was popularly supposed to have 'suffered from a superiority complex'.[4] And yet, despite all this, he was trusted by that most enterprising of businessmen, Jesse Boot, first Baron Trent, founder and motive force behind Boot's Cash Chemists. It was he who commissioned Horder to design not just a series of High Street shops, but also the building by which Boot hoped to be remembered.[5] For it was Morley Horder who erected the remarkable and palatial home of Nottingham University (Figure 29). Now named the Trent Building in Boot's honour, Morley Horder's success in embodying the aims and ambitions of the institution was so complete that his work remains an icon of the place to this day.

Horder's buildings remain important at Nottingham because he gave the university exactly what it wanted and precisely what it needed. The Trent Building is a striking piece of architecture: starkly classical, its white stone façade is almost too perfect; perched at the top of a gentle hill, it dominates the surrounding site. 'Its palatial dimensions, its majestic appearance, its grand spaciousness and its delightful surroundings', wrote one academic, 'enchant us and make us feel in the midst of

---

[1] An anonymous reminiscence of Morley Horder, quoted in Clyde Binfield, 'Holy Murder at Cheshunt College. The formation of an English architect: P. R. Morley-Horder, 1870–1944', *Journal of the United Reformed Church History Society* 4:2 (1988), pp. 103–34, p. 105.

[2] Though he is mentioned in the article on Nottingham's Trent Building. <http://en.wikipedia.org/wiki/Trent_Building> (accessed 3 August 2006). See also M. S. Briggs, 'Horder, Percy Richard Morley (1870–1944)', rev. Catherine Gordon, *ODNB*.

[3] Binfield, 'Holy Murder', p. 107.

[4] A. Peter Fawcett and Neil Jackson, *Campus Critique: the architecture of the University of Nottingham* (Nottingham, 1998), p. 43.

[5] For details, see A. Stuart Gray, *Edwardian Architecture: a biographical dictionary* (London, 1985), pp. 214–16.

Fig. 29. Built 'most grand and cakeily': the new University College Nottingham
© Martine Hamilton Knight.

something strange'.[6] Even *The Times* was impressed, and Frank Granger, an expert on Vitruvius and vice-principal of Nottingham, grew wildly over-excited about the edifice.[7] 'The visible beauty of the new work', he wrote, 'is the garment of the intellectual beauty which it is the aim of the University to disclose.' Boot's generosity, he went on, had been crowned 'by the attainment of superb architectural beauty'.[8]

Predictably, not everyone agreed. D. H. Lawrence, whose own time at Nottingham College had been far from enjoyable, attacked the new building even before it was finished.[9]

> In Nottingham, that dismal town
> Where I went to school and college
> They've built a new university
> For the new dispensation of knowledge.
>
> Built it most grand and cakeily
> Out of the noble loot
> Derived from shrewd cash-chemistry
> By good Sir Jesse Boot.

---

[6] J. H. West, 'Editorial' in *The Gong* 18:1 (1928), p. 3.
[7] *The Times*, 9 July 1928, p. 20.
[8] Frank Granger, *Memorials of University College Nottingham* (Nottingham, 1928), pp. 24–5, 30.
[9] Frank Barnes, *Priory Demesne to University Campus: a topographic history of Nottingham University* (Nottingham, 1993), p. 404. See also John Worthen, *D. H. Lawrence: the early years, 1885–1912* (Cambridge, 1991), ch. 7.

> Little I thought, when I was a lad
> And turned my modest penny
> Over on Boot's Cash Chemist's counter,
> That Jesse, by turning many
>
> Millions of similar honest pence
> Over, would make a pile
> That would rise at last and blossom out
> In grand and cakey style
>
> Into a new university
> Where smart men would dispense
> Does of smart cash-chemistry
> In language of common-sense!
>
> That future Nottingham lads would be
> Cash-chemically BSc
> That Nottingham lights would rise and say
> —By Boots I am MA!
>
> From this I learn, though I knew it before
> That culture has her roots
> In the deep dung of cash, and love
> Is a last offshoot of Boots.[10]

Twenty years later, the words still stung and local poets were provoked to respond in still more execrable verse.[11]

Yet even though Lawrence condemned the building, he evidently could not ignore it. However egregious, however gross, however absurd—and even Granger admitted that some might find it repellent—Morley Horder had undeniably built a striking new structure; a 'grand and cakey', but nonetheless unforgettable home for a new university college. Morley Horder was praised by others for having produced all that was needed for a university: a stately building, fine facilities, and room to grow.[12] Moreover, he was believed to have done so in an appropriate—and appropriately contemporary—way. 'Mr Morley Horder', wrote the *Architects' Journal*, 'recognised . . . from the outset that he was building a modern university, and not an imitation of medieval university'.[13] Situated in thirty-five acres of parkland and sustained by a massive benefaction, Nottingham was truly in an enviable position. Within twenty years, it did not just look like a university, it had actually become one, obtaining its charter in 1948.

Whilst Morley Horder's architecture made Nottingham noteworthy, he did not make it unique. Nottingham's evolution over this period was typical—even stereotypical. All across Britain in the years after the First World War, other universities and university colleges sought to strike the same sort of note. They big built and

---

[10] D. H. Lawrence, *Complete Poems of D. H. Lawrence*, ed., Vivian de Sola and Warren Roberts (2 vols; London, 1972), vol. i., p. 488.
[11] 'H. S. E.', 'To the New University', *The Gong* 36:3 (1947), pp. 4–5.
[12] *Universities Review* 1:1 (October 1928), p. 63.
[13] 'M. A.', 'Nottingham's New University', *Architects' Journal* 68 (1928), pp. 256–62, p. 256. See also, 'A. C. T.', 'the New University Building', *The Gong* 28:1 (1928), pp. 5–6.

they built to impress. In London, the massive, monumental Senate House went up; a suitably substantial home for an ever-growing institution, with 'the kind of soil pipes that one expects to see in the courts of heaven'.[14] The civic universities were not far behind.

They built to express two fundamental truths: that Redbrick was here to stay, and that Redbrick was getting bigger. This was establishment architecture for established institutions—institutions which built to last. In 1927, Leeds began work on a massive, £350,000 building programme.[15] In 1936, Sheffield began raising money for an even greater, £450,000 project, which would—had the war not intervened—have transformed the place completely.[16] The aftermath of conflict was marked by still more ambitious plans, with the Chancellor of the Exchequer promising that £50 million would be found for new sites and new buildings.[17] Even contemporary critics acknowledged that the civic universities in this period were responsible for 'a number of really striking and beautiful buildings, surpassed neither by Oxford or Cambridge nor even by the more materially prosperous universities of the United States'.[18]

Morley Horder's plans for Nottingham reflected other trends too. This was to be a campus university. In following the example of Birmingham, which had brought the campus model to Britain, Nottingham was just one of many. Nearby Leicester acquired one in 1921; Exeter bought one in 1922; and even Hull, the smallest and newest of them all, started out in 1927 with plans for 'a complete campus, exactly half a mile long', a suitable 'centre of culture' for the city.[19] These were formally, axially planned affairs; far removed from the picturesque planning that would characterize many post-war developments. The aim was to provide unity and dignity to an increasingly diverse group of buildings; to harmonize the library with the laboratory, rooms for teaching with places to live.[20] Like all the other civic colleges and universities, too, Nottingham was determined to increase the proportion of its students living within halls of residence. To that end, Morley Horder also designed Florence Boot Hall, a hostel for women in a pared-down domestic Georgian style.

This choice is worth noting. For Nottingham also reflects the way in which Redbrick came to renounce medieval models for its buildings.[21] Sure enough, there

---

[14] H. M. Fletcher, quoted in J. Mordaunt Crook, 'The Architectural Image', in F. M. L. Thompson, ed., *The University of London and the World of Learning, 1836–1986* (London, 1990), pp. 1–34, p. 25.

[15] M. W. Beresford, 'Red brick and Portland stone: a building history', in P. H. J. H. Gosden and A. J. Taylor, eds, *Studies in the History of a University 1874–1974* (Leeds, 1975), pp. 133–80.

[16] SUA, US/CHA/4/11 Building and Endowments Fund (1936–42).

[17] UGC, *University Development from 1935 to 1947* (London, 1948), 77.

[18] Bruce Truscot [E. Allison Pears], *Red Brick University* (London, 1943), p. 18.

[19] A. E. Morgan, 'The Project of a University of Hull', *University Bulletin* 5:2 (April 1927), pp. 52–6, p. 54.

[20] B. S. Townroe, *Nottingham University College: a record of its history and an appreciation of the new buildings* (privately printed, 1928), p. 45.

[21] See also William Whyte, 'Neo-Georgian: the other style in Britain's twentieth-century university architecture', in Julian Holder and Elizabeth McKellar, eds, *Re-appraising Neo-Georgian Architecture, 1850–1970* (Swindon, 2015).

RUTLAND HALL.—View from the air showing surrounding country and new stadium and athletic track in course of construction.

Fig. 30. 'In every respect modern': Rutland Hall, Loughborough
Reproduced with the permission of the archivist, Loughborough University.

were those like Bristol which retained a fondness for the Gothic, defended as late as 1925 in purely Ruskinian terms as 'the architecture of freedom'. Elsewhere, even when Gothic was chosen, it was rarely a revived Ruskinian sort with all the moral as well aesthetic baggage that this implied.[22] Rather, the Tudoresque additions to places like Loughborough were quite rightly seen as 'in every respect modern' (Figure 30).[23] Electrically-heated, electrically-lit: this was a mass-produced Tudor manor house without any chimneys. More popular still was a solid, even stolid neo-classicism, 'rather reminiscent of the town-hall architecture of the period'.[24] No doubt this reflected changing architectural fashions, as the universities strove once again to keep up. But it also marked a renewed attempt to stress the importance of the institutions to the towns that housed them; to keep them a crucial part of the cityscape. This was as true for Nottingham in 1928 as it was for Leicester twenty years later, where it was hoped that redevelopment would make the college the centrepiece of 'the city's finest civic building centre.'[25]

---

[22] Hubert C. Corlette, 'Bristol University: the new buildings', *Bristol Nonesuch* 10 (1924–26), pp. 127–34, p. 128.
[23] *The Limit* 15:1 (1932), p. 5.
[24] Lionel Brett and others, 'Leeds University', *Architects' Journal* 127 (1958), pp. 53–4, p. 53.
[25] LeiUA, ULA/AD/D5/1, Transcript of the City Council Debate, T. Rowland Hill (7 January 1947).

This civic pride and classical revivalism did not make for revolutionary architecture. The occasional cries for 'something new—a great memorial, not of antiquity and the legendary past, but of this time and this world' went unheeded.[26] Although some students claimed that 'Brains trying to escape the bonds of Medievalism are subtly held back by [the] strange, artificial environment they found themselves in', benefactors and university builders tended to disagree.[27] Thus the Sheffield alumnus who looked at T. A. Lodge's neo-classical proposals for the university and asked 'Was Stockholm Town hall built in vain? Are Mallet-Stevens and le Corbusier (sic.) voices crying in the wilderness?' should have known the answer to his own question.[28] Respectability was the keynote; a ponderous Palladianism the result.

Partly for that reason, it has been argued even by their advocates that the civic universities finally, fatally stalled and hit stasis after about 1920.[29] No longer struggling, and much less marginal than they had been, they are somehow less appealing to many writers, less in need of defence than the pioneering institutions of previous periods. Indeed for the sociologist A. H. Halsey, this was the moment when Redbrick settled for second-best, becoming a cheaper Oxbridge rather than a distinctively different and consciously radical approach to higher education.[30] Many contemporaries seemed to share these fears. Student magazines consistently complained about undergraduate apathy. The cynical Bristol student who sneered in the early 1920s that the labels in undergraduate gowns should not read 'Made In Oxford', but 'Made In Imitation of Oxford', represented a general complaint.[31] Even as Redbrick grew and apparently thrived, commentators were increasingly keen to argue that it had failed in its purpose. Contemporaries and subsequent historians both perceived a crisis in the civic university during this period: a crisis of finance, a crisis about standards, and a crisis of identity. Above all, it has been suggested, Redbrick universities faced a crisis of confidence. Were they nothing more than technical schools, producing under-educated and soulless graduates? Was the only solution to abandon their old ways and to adopt mock-Oxbridge models? Was the joke of the day 'that the modern University is a place where artificial pearls are cast before real swine' really true?[32]

The evidence suggests that this sense of alarm was overstated. In many respects, indeed, the fact that anyone thought that Redbrick could or should overtake Oxbridge actually reflected success, rather than failure. A careful examination of

---

[26] G. R. A. Antobus-Watson, 'After Ten Years', *Bristol Nonesuch* 67 (Autumn 1935), pp. 17–18, p. 17.
[27] W. Y. Willets, 'Design in University Buildings', *Bristol Nonesuch* 83 (Spring 1939), pp. 40–3, p. 41.
[28] SUA, US/CHA/4/11, Buildings and Endowment 1936–42, Hedley Heaton (5 August 1938).
[29] The key exception is Michael Sanderson, *The Universities and British Industry 1850–1970* (London, 1972). See esp. p. 313.
[30] A. H. Halsey, 'Oxford and the British Universities', in Brian Harrison, ed., *The History of the University of Oxford, vol. viii: the twentieth century* (Oxford, 1994), pp. 577–606. See also Elizabeth J. Morse, 'English Civic Universities and the Myth of Decline', *History of Universities* 11 (1992), pp. 177–204.
[31] *Bristol Nonesuch* 9 (1923–24), p. 95.
[32] *Tamesis* 33 (1934–5), p. 39.

the state of the civic universities and colleges in the era of the two world wars shows that these were, in the main, doing well. They were growing and thriving and becoming increasingly important. But, because of this, they were suffering from growing pains. No longer experimental institutions, seeking to define an identity and articulate an ethos, they were confronted with the perennial problems presented by permanence. Discussions about their failings were predicated now on the assumption that they would survive. Ironically, of course, by stressing their centrality, this debate highlights their achievement. The civic universities and colleges had never been bigger, richer, or more successful. Yet they and their critics were filled with concern. Talk of a crisis in the university wildly over-exaggerated the problems they faced. But the anxiety this reflected was, nonetheless, all too real. Morley Horder, with all his angst and all his bravado, with all his aggression and all his talent, was thus the ideal architect for a new university college. Self-confident to the point of caricature, he designed big, bold buildings which could not be ignored. This was exactly what Nottingham needed—and Nottingham was not alone. Growing in importance, yet coming increasingly under attack, the Redbricks used architecture to assert their significance, to solve their problems, and to encourage their supporters.

7

Redbrick Attacked

Criticism of the civic universities and colleges as mere imitations of Oxford and Cambridge was not new. The belief that they were second-rate, that it was always a case of 'Oxbridge if I can and Redbrick if I can't', had been articulated before.[1] The years after the First World War, however, saw an intensification of this old argument and a new focus on the failings of Redbrick. No longer were these institutions simply damned by comparison, they were now believed to have developed a set of problems all their own. The question 'What is wrong with the modern universities?' was asked again and again, and, rather quickly, a canon of complaints was drawn up.[2]

Whilst some stuck to the simple accusation that the standard of work was too low, others developed often lengthy and sometimes sophisticated critiques.[3] Mass education, argued some, meant too many lecturers, too little contact between students and staff, and too much focus on vocational rather than liberal education.[4] The lack of sufficient residential accommodation and the consequent need for students to live at home were attacked by others. It meant, they claimed, that 'Not a few of those who attend courses in city Universities seem to regard their life as just a sequel to "attendance" at a municipal school.'[5] Even the main state funding body, the University Grants Committee (UGC), which painted a generally rosy picture of the system it was charged with sustaining, had periodic bursts of apparent panic. In the mid-1930s it was concerned that accommodation was inadequate, that halls of residence were too few, that students were not receiving a wide enough education, and that tuition fees were too low to pay for high-quality teaching.[6] A dozen years later, it said very much the same.[7] More strikingly still, in the intervening period so did the National Union of Students.[8]

---

[1] Bruce Truscot [Edgar Allison Peers], *Red Brick University* (London, 1943), p. 54.
[2] E. R. Dodds, 'What is Wrong with the Modern Universities?', *Universities Review* 4:1 (October 1931), pp. 9–20. See also, F. A. Cavanagh, 'What is Wrong with Modern Universities?', *Universities Review* 4:2 (April 1932), pp. 99–106, and P. Mansell Jones, 'Where Modern Universities are Wrong', *Universities Review* 5:1 (October 1932), pp. 6–10.
[3] John Carruthers [J. Y. T. Grieg], *Adam's Daughter* (London, 1926), p. 154.
[4] See, for example, L. C. Knights, 'Problems of the Modern Universities', *TES* 15 February 1941, p. 71 and Ernest Simon, *The Development of British Universities* (London, 1944), pp. 18–20.
[5] J. J. Findlay, 'The Aim of a Modern University Education', in Hugh Martin, ed., *The Life of the Modern University* (London, 1930), pp. 21–30, p. 27.
[6] UGC, *Returns from Universities and University Colleges in receipt of Treasury Grant 1934–5*, pp. 12–19.
[7] UGC, *University Development from 1935 to 1947* (London, 1948).
[8] NUS, *The Challenge to the University* (London, 1938).

The general consensus about the failings of Redbrick was summed up in a notable book of 1928: H. G. G. Herklots' *The New Universities: an external examination*.[9] Herklots was a recent graduate of Cambridge; socially somewhat superior, if not downright condescending, he was quite reasonably attacked by one reader for his 'spirit of arrogance and smooth self-satisfaction'.[10] Relying, in the main, on secondary sources, it is little wonder that even more sympathetic critics saw his book as 'truer of the recent past than of the present and future'.[11] But whatever his failings as a researcher, Herklots was an accurate barometer of contemporary opinion. He fulsomely acknowledged the importance of the Redbrick universities; uncontroversially, even conventionally, suggesting that their foundation represented a 'revolution' in the life of the nation.[12] Yet, he went on to imply, this was an unfinished revolution. Conventional, too, was his concern at a dearth of residential accommodation and at what he saw as the apathy of the student body. Too many lectures and too little leisure time, he alleged, meant that 'the languid art of conversation—nay, the mental gymnastic—plays but a small part' in the life of these undergraduates. An absence of commitment on the part of its members meant that the students' union was 'rather a cloak-room than a club', he went on.[13] Wanting culture and lacking facilities, he concluded, it was little wonder that the new universities were in trouble. Herklots, in other words, painted a picture of places that were not really universities at all—at least not universities as a former editor of *Granta* and past President of the Cambridge Union understood them.

By the time the Liverpool professor Edgar Allison Peers took up his pen, took on the identity of Bruce Truscot, and sat down to write his now famous *Red Brick University*, there was thus a pretty clear conception of what the civic universities were and where they had gone wrong.[14] Much of what he wrote merely re-echoed these general criticisms of a student culture and a university system that seemed undeniably impoverished. Even his points of apparent originality had a pedigree. Truscot's emphasis on the need for these universities to undertake more research repeated the argument made by Abraham Flexner over a decade before.[15] His call for a broader curriculum and for students to be introduced to a wider world echoed Newman, but also surely drew on the work of José Ortega y Gasset,[16] which, as a professor of Spanish, Peers was well-placed to know.[17] In that sense *Red Brick* had

---

[9] H. G. G. Herklots, *The New Universities: an external examination* (London, 1928). Herklots acknowledged that he had a personal reason for writing the book: he had gone to Cambridge, whilst his brother went to Leeds. LivUA, D265/1/2/6 Herklots to Truscot (5 September 1943).

[10] F. C. Jones, in *Universities Review* 1:2 (1929), p. 139. Though see also *The Times* 21 May 1971, p. 16 for a more sympathetic account.

[11] WMRC, AUT MSS 27/3/55, F. E. Sandbach (15 May 1928).

[12] Herklots, *New Universities*, pp. 3, 26.

[13] Herklots, *New Universities*, p. 13.

[14] See also Harold Silver, *Higher Education and Opinion-Making in Twentieth-century England* (London, 2003) for some further contextual analysis.

[15] Abraham Flexner, *Universities: American, English, German* (New York, 1930).

[16] José Ortega y Gasset, *Mission of the University*, trans. Howard Lee Nostrand (Princeton, 1944).

[17] Although *The Times* 13 September 1946, p. 5 saw the two authors as polar opposites, this is to ignore Truscot's commitment to teaching in ch. 5 of *Red-Brick*.

little new to offer. Nevertheless, it made more of an impact than any of the volumes that preceded it. Its anonymity, its evident insider-knowledge, and the breadth of its criticisms made it an instant hit.[18] Unsurprisingly, it was soon followed by other publications: *Redbrick and these vital days* (1945); *First Year at the University* (1946); and occasional essays and reviews.[19] 'Mr Truscot has had his say—and it was a good say', observed one reviewer in 1945, 'and [he] should now be silent'.[20]

The debate, nonetheless, went on, intensified by the war and wider discussions about post-war reconstruction.[21] Brian Simon, the future historian of education and former president of the NUS, also published *A Student's View of the Universities* in 1943. Based on surveys and interviews and his own recent experience of both Cambridge and the Institute of Education, it reached essentially the same conclusions as other, less ostentatiously radical commentators.[22] What marked it out were two relatively original elements. In the first place, it gave voice to student criticisms of the higher education system, articulating the complaints of a group that was often ignored and generally patronized by other commentators. Secondly, amongst the familiar attacks on student apathy, the narrowness of the curriculum, the superficiality of the teaching, and the dangers of a 'nine-to-five' university in which everyone went home at the end of teaching day, leaving the university destitute of life and a sense of community, Simon also mounted a much more far-reaching attack on bourgeois liberalism.[23] Not everyone liked it; bourgeois liberals, of whom there were not a few in the universities, were especially scathing.[24] But the book's acceptance by a major publisher reflected the growing concern from all sectors of society about the place, the role, and the development of the civic universities. Similar anxieties prompted a series of twelve pamphlets on higher education by leaders of the Student Christian Movement in 1946[25] and a 1948 report on *The Problem Facing British Universities* by members of the newly founded Nuffield College, Oxford.[26]

---

[18] *Times Educational Supplement*, 7 August 1943, p. 374.
[19] See, Ann L. Mackenzie, 'Introduction', to E. Allison Peers, *Redbrick University Revisited*, ed., Ann L. Mackenzie and Adrian R. Allen (Liverpool, 1996), p. 495 for a list. Other articles include, 'Bruce Truscot' [E. Allison Peers], 'Nine to One: a study in demobilisation', *Universities Review* 19:1 (1946), pp. 28–31; 'From School to University', *Times Educational Supplement* 18 September 1943, p. 452; 'Contact with the Student Mind', *Conference of the Association of University Professors and Lecturers of the Allied Countries* (Oxford, 1944), pp. 17–20.
[20] D. G. James, Review in *Universities Review* 18:1 (1945), pp. 18–20, p. 18.
[21] See also J. H. Burns and D. Sutherland-Graeme, *Scottish University* (Edinburgh, 1944), for a Hibernian equivalent to this literature.
[22] Brian Simon, *A Life in Education* (London, 1998), p. 34.
[23] Brian Simon, *A Student's View of the Universities* (London, 1943).
[24] N.F., Review, in *Universities Review* 16:2 (1944), p. 69.
[25] These were all published in 1946 and comprised: John Baillie, *The Mind of the Modern University*; H. A. Hodges, *Objectivity and Impartiality* and *The Christian in the Modern University*; Dorothy M. Emmett, *The Foundations of a Free University*; A. R. Vidler, *Christianity's Need of a Free University*; Colin Forrester-Paton, *Universities Under Fire*; Paul White, *Calling All Freshmen*; Daniel T. Jenkins, *The Place of a Faculty of Theology in the University of To-day*; W. G. Symons, *Work and Vocation*; L. A. Reid, *Vocational and Humane Education in the University*; *Halls of Residence in Modern Universities: a group report*.
[26] Nuffield College, *The Problem Facing British Universities* (London, 1948).

The crowning point of this debate came with the publication of Walter Moberly's *Crisis in the University* in 1949. If Truscot represented the voice of the dissatisfied don and Simon echoed the discontents of disillusioned students, then Moberly personified the establishment itself. As his *Times* obituary put it, he was simply 'an educational statesman'.[27] A former fellow of two Oxford colleges, Moberly had taught at Aberdeen and Birmingham and had become principal of Exeter and then vice-chancellor of Manchester. In 1934 he took over as president of the UGC, and it was from this personal and professional pre-eminence that he surveyed the failings of the modern universities.

Moberly's was an explicitly Christian critique.[28] The universities, he argued, were failing to give their students the sort of values and moral uplift that the modern world required. A fragmented curriculum, a false neutrality, a neglect of moral and spiritual matters: all this meant that graduates were not emerging from their studies with any real vision of how the world ought to be. Although he recognized that there were problems in Oxbridge, Moberly believed that the Redbricks laboured under a set of particular disadvantages. These were, it should come as no surprise to learn, the lack of residential accommodation, the separation between staff and students, the over-specialization of studies, and the failure of the civic universities to function as real communities.[29] Although many objected to his cure—the reintroduction of explicit Christian teaching—far fewer disagreed with his diagnosis.[30] By the end of the 1940s, it seemed, people were pretty much agreed on the problems of Redbrick at all levels of the system.[31] A generation's debate found its fulfilment, its consummation, in Moberly.

The apparent consistency of this critique and the common anxieties of which it spoke should surely give us pause. Yet it is possible to acknowledge the sincerity of this sense of crisis whilst also questioning it. That Redbrick continued to be regarded as second best by many contemporaries is undeniable.[32] But the criteria by which the civic universities were judged do need further examination. It is clear, for example, that attacks on Redbrick were as much social as educational. In the early 1920s, the German commentator Wilhelm Dibelius had noted that the higher education system in England continued to be shaped by the class system. 'In Oxford and Cambridge the aristocratic spirit rules', he wrote. 'In the new schools of the North, trade and industry dominate.'[33] What was true then remained the case twenty years later. It is hard not to feel that similar social assumptions informed most criticisms of Redbrick. In reality, it proved almost impossible for Moberly of Oxford, or Herklots of Cambridge, or even Truscot of Cambridge and Liverpool to

---

[27] *The Times*, 2 February 1974, p. 14.
[28] In this he drew on the SCM pamphlets and Arnold Nash, *The University and the Modern World* (London, 1945).
[29] Walter Moberly, *The Crisis in the University* (London, 1949), pp. 206–16.
[30] Though see Michael Oakshott, 'The Universities', *Cambridge Journal* 2 (1948–9), pp. 515–42 and L. C. Sykes, *A Philosopher for the Modern University* (Leicester, 1951).
[31] See *Universities Quarterly* 4:1 (1949) for a series of responses to *The Crisis in the University*.
[32] UGC, *Returns from Universities 1934–5*, p. 12.
[33] Wilhelm Dibelius, *England*, trans., Mary Agnes Hamilton (1922; London, 1930), p. 441.

conceive that 'poor Bill Jones' of 'Drabtown' was capable of enjoying university as much as they had. The issue was always, as Truscot himself put it, how to turn 'the poor girl or boy from Lower Back Street... into a worthy member of a university'.[34] Such assumptions invariably implied a level of condescension and even disdain; a fact recognized by at least one contemporary, writing as one of Truscot's students and condemning the author of *Red Brick University*, not entirely unfairly, as a snob, a pedant, and a bore.[35]

With this in mind, it is possible to see that much contemporary criticism of the civic universities and colleges was simply prejudice. Despite these widely-canvassed doubts, attending a civic university was transformational—and was recognized as such by those that did so. It was still a shock to move from school to college; a rite of passage marked, as before, by the acquisition of new and grown-up clothes.[36] Arriving at Leicester in 1925, the first boy from his school to have gone directly to university, C. P. Snow proudly swapped his old uniform for the college cricket blazer in white with thin green and brown stripes.[37] Twenty years later, nothing had changed, as a Leicester alumnus who kept his own college scarf for the rest of his life recalled.[38] For the minority who lived in hall, life changed completely as they had to adapt to new rules and new people; and to find a way to live with 'cigarette card collectors... the horrid people who whistle through their teeth... the Marmite fiends, the morning hikers, and the apple enthusiast'.[39] Life in hall also meant new opportunities—especially for those for whom living away from home was a novel experience. 'One's own little nest', observes a character in D. W. Hackman's novel of training college life, *First Year Up*; 'I intend to make mine very cosy indeed—piles of cushions and one very impressive picture.'[40] Nor did staying at home necessarily mean that students were semi-detached. Indeed, as Richard Hoggart recalled,

> The fact that many of the Leeds students went back each night to the streets of the city or the townships around, or slipped at weekends to their homes in the Ridings, ensured that the University was felt to be part of the area in a way not easy to bring about today; its affairs and events were talked about in homes all around and became part of the folklore and fabric of day-to-day life.[41]

Here, clearly was a university that functioned as more than the technical school of Bruce Truscot's nightmares or Herklots' sneers.

Smugly to assume that because these students were not in Oxbridge or living the lives of undergraduates in the ancient universities that they were impoverished or culturally bereft is equally wrong. Redbrick was different: it was poorer, less

---

[34] Truscot, *Red Brick University*, pp. 33–4.
[35] *Universities Review* 19:2 (1947), p. 198.
[36] Jennie Lee, *This Great Journey* (London, 1963), p. 62; George Ewart Evans, *The Strength of the Hills: an autobiography* (London, 1983), p. 55.
[37] Philip Snow, *Stranger and Brother: a portrait of C. P. Snow* (London, 1982), p. 26.
[38] LeiUA, Uncat., John Winterburn, 'Recollections of University College, Leicester, 1947–50', p. 27.
[39] *The Gong* 22:1 (Christmas 1932), p. 37.
[40] D. W. Hackman, *First Year Up* (London, 1951), p. 19.
[41] Richard Hoggart, *A Local Habitation: life and times, 1918–1940* (Oxford, 1989), p. 187.

prestigious, more provincial, and less posh. But it was not necessarily inferior in ways that really mattered. Comparing Exeter to its trans-Atlantic equivalents, Margaret Halsey, the wife of a visiting American lecturer, observed in 1936 that it was 'more serious and less silly than American institutions customarily are. The students are better mannered and less flauntingly adolescent and all the activities connected with the establishment are pursued with a great deal of dignity.'[42] Such a comparison might also have been made with the ancient universities—and, as their critics suggested, Redbrick undergraduates would not necessarily have come off worse. As one Leeds professor put it, the great delight of teaching in a civic university was the 'freedom from luxurious idlers' of the sort that clustered round Cambridge and Oxford.[43]

That all this was described as a crisis reflected the familiar anxieties which continued to attend university life rather more than it helped to articulate the reality of Redbrick. True enough, in the years immediately after the First World War, some expressed the fear that the very existence of the civic institutions was under threat. In 1921, indeed, the vice-chancellor of Leeds rather melodramatically questioned whether his university or that of Sheffield would survive.[44] Cuts in government funding in 1922 reduced income for a time. The impact of the depression of the 1930s was likewise felt by staff as some local education authorities tried to force a reduction in academic salaries.[45] But it would be wrong to see even this as a real—much less as an existential—crisis. Leeds and Sheffield survived; indeed, they thrived. Government cuts were relatively quickly rectified. The universities became more and more independent from the influences of their local communities. Instead of collapse, there was a debate about the nature of Redbrick life conducted in crisis-ridden terms. As one level-headed contemporary observed, just as each generation has witnessed the cry of the Church in Danger, so every few years academics and others would point to the University in Crisis.[46] The truth was that, despite all the talk about disaster, the civic universities and colleges were in fact still growing.

Redbrick's rising profile was reflected, too, in its position on the national stage. After 1918, the civic universities were, like Oxford, Cambridge, and London, represented by their own MPs.[47] As time went on, it also became clearer and clearer that expansion within the university system—both in Britain and in the empire—would be based upon the Redbrick model.[48] So it was that the Barlow Report on Scientific Manpower of 1946 envisaged the civic universities as the key

[42] 'Margaret Halsey' [Mrs H. W. Simon], *With Malice Towards Some* (New York, 1938), p. 150.
[43] Arthur Smithells, *From a Northern University* (London, 1921), p. 22. See also J. Home, 'A Criticism of Oxford by an Undergraduate', *Universities Review* 7:2 (April 1935), pp. 151–6.
[44] Jack Simmons, 'The Last Forty Years', *The Twentieth Century* 159 (1956), pp. 112–22, p. 115.
[45] WMRC, CVCP, MS 399/1/1/1, Minutes 1931–35, 12 December 1931.
[46] Oakshott, 'The Universities', p. 515.
[47] Joseph S. Meisel, *Knowledge and Power: The Parliamentary representation of universities in Britain and the Empire* (Chichester, 2011).
[48] A. P. Newton, *The Universities and Educational Systems of the British Empire* (London, 1924), p. 119.

institutions which would increase the number of scientists taught by 86 per cent.[49] So too, it was Redbrick that formed the model for a reformed University of Calcutta in 1919,[50] and Redbrick which inspired the foundation of universities in the colonies after the Second World War.[51] In the words of the historian and university administrator Eric Ashby, underlying British policy 'was one massive assumption: that the pattern of university development appropriate for Manchester, Exeter and Hull was *ipso facto* appropriate for Ibadan, Kampala and Singapore'.[52]

As this suggests, the 'crisis' in the modern universities was a curious business. On the one hand, there were some very real problems; on the other, there was palpable growth and progress. This combination is best captured in the annual reports issued by the UGC. These regularly drew attention to the problems that it believed Redbrick faced: its comparatively low salaries and poor facilities; its allegedly narrow curriculum and supposedly uncultivated students.[53] In this, it echoed the complaints—and the language—of all those who perceived a crisis. Yet the UGC remained optimistic, and continued to be impressed. 'We should be sorry' they wrote,

> if in drawing attention to what seem to us shortcomings we should have given the impression that the life of University students in the populous urban centres is a drab or dreary thing. A visit to any one of them would quickly correct any such impression.[54]

In the generation after 1914, Redbrick laboured under many disadvantages and confronted many challenges. Nonetheless, as the UGC recognized, and as we can now affirm, this was not a period of collapse or decline. Rather, it was one of development—albeit development tempered by anxiety. Previous writers have tended to focus on the anxiety. It is important not to forget the development.

REDBRICKBATS

For those who perceived a crisis, what Truscot described as 'Redbrick's unlovely quadrangles' were the embodiment of all that was wrong.[55] Amongst those seeking to reform the system, it was widely believed that new buildings would resurrect Redbrick. Architecture, it was hoped, would solve many of the problems raised by

---

[49] *Scientific Manpower: Report of a Committee appointed by the Lord President of the Council* 1946 (cmd. 6824), p. 15.
[50] *Calcutta University Commission, 1917–19* (17 vols; Calcutta, 1919–20), vol. iv, pp. 422–30.
[51] *Report of the Commission on Higher Education in West Africa* 1945 (cmd. 6655), p. 74. See also *Report of the Commission on Higher Education in the Colonies* 1945 (cmd. 6647), pp. 34–5; 38–42.
[52] Eric Ashby, *Universities: British, Indian, African, an ecology of higher education* (London, 1966), p. 224.
[53] UGC, *Returns from Universities and University Colleges in receipt of Treasury Grant 1929–35*, p. 12.
[54] UGC, *Returns from Universities 1929–35*, p. 43.
[55] Truscot, *Redbrick and these vital days*, p. 13.

writers like Truscot or Moberly. Halls of residence would generate the community life that the civic universities were perceived to lack. Campuses and suburban sites would take the colleges away from the pollution and temptations of the busy city. New facilities would enable better teaching and the creation of a vibrant university culture. Buildings also remained an important draw for donors and a symbol of the university's success. More than this, although nineteenth-century assumptions about the ethical value of Gothic architecture came increasingly to seem old-fashioned, the belief that good buildings could make good people—and even better universities—never went away. 'From Plato downwards', wrote Moberly, 'educators have recognized the powerful indirect influence of physical surroundings'.[56] This combination of pragmatism and idealism was to shape the architecture of Redbrick irrevocably.

Visitors to Leeds or Liverpool, Exeter or Nottingham could not fail to be struck by an apparent paradox. On the one hand, these universities and colleges were building bigger and grander structures than ever before (Figure 31). On the other hand, much of their other accommodation was old and often frankly inadequate. The Victorian and Edwardian buildings which had been so admired in their day were now unfashionable. Truscot described Waterhouse's work for Liverpool as 'something between a super council-school and a holiday home for children.'[57] A Nottingham student visiting Birmingham in 1945 thought it lacked 'symmetry, grace and dignity'. 'It is not an attractive building', he wrote, 'having been erected at the turn of the century when the reaction against the Victorian Gothic Revival had set in, but had not been replaced by the more classical modern style architecture.'[58] The newer, neighbouring hospital was much more to his—and his contemporaries'—liking.

If this were not bad enough, many of the older buildings were simply insalubrious, coated in grime and shrouded in soot.[59] Inside, writers described rooms with 'dirty distempered walls and ... framed prints dating from the middle years of Queen Victoria.'[60] As Redbrick expanded, so it had continued to improvise. 'Roofs have been raised and stories added,' wrote the UGC; 'large rooms have been divided, cellars and garages have been turned into laboratories, wooden army huts ... have been made to serve as lecture rooms, and whole departments have found temporary homes in dwelling-houses adjoining the main university buildings.'[61] In one case this meant employing rooms that 'were condemned as unfit for human habitation as long ago as the last decade of the nineteenth century.'[62] In another, it meant re-using an old army hospital hut as a refectory, with diners

[56] Moberly, *Crisis in the University*, p. 218.
[57] Truscot, *Red Brick University*, p. 17.
[58] *Gongster*, 20 April 1945, p. 3.
[59] William Whyte, '"Redbrick's unlovely quadrangles": reinterpreting the architecture of the civic universities', *History of Universities*, 21 (2006) pp. 151–77. See also Kathleen Freeman, *Martin Hanner: a comedy* (London, 1926), pp. 32, 273.
[60] Bruce Truscot, 'A Red-Brick Tea-Party', *Universities Review* 17:2 (May 1945), pp. 38–40, p. 38.
[61] UGC, *Returns from Universities*, p. 4.
[62] UGC, *University Development from 1935 to 1946* (London, 1948), p. 52.

Fig. 31. 'A tremendous departure in style and tradition': the New Arts Faculty at the University of Liverpool

greeted for years by a sign reading 'Dysentery' on the door.[63] At Aberystwyth in 1937 the needs of the new Dairy department meant that any central heating in the college had to be discontinued—for, as the principal wrote, 'if we keep the students warm in a cold April or May, we melt the cheeses'.[64]

[63] *Wessex News*, 2 July 1957, p. 2.
[64] E. L. Ellis, *The University College of Wales, Aberystwyth, 1872–1972* (Cardiff, 1972), p. 263.

Students complained—understandably—that this make-do-and-mend approach was spoiling their experience of higher education. At Southampton, they hurled 'Redbrickbats' at their surroundings,[65] insisting on 'the psychologically deterrent effect of the large block of unattractive huts' and the practical difficulties of working in laboratories in which 'the floors were loose, half the windows would not open, and in-efficient fume cupboards were fitted'.[66] Not only was this problematic for work, it also caused complications when, in the absence of better accommodation, laboratories and lecture room were used for social events. 'To dance the Yale Blues around Cantor's pendulum or to engage in social chat surrounded by Wheatstone's Bridges', wrote one student, 'is good neither for the apparatus nor for the success of the function.'[67] Seeking to overcome such problems, in fact, at least one professor took the matter into his own hands. In the mid-1930s, Douglas Laurie built a new laboratory in Aberystwyth himself, aided only by £200 from the college, and assistance from his gardener, another lecturer, and a helpful MSc student.[68] For most of his colleagues, however, the solution was not so simple.

It was this combination of simply unfashionable and clearly inadequate architecture which led so many universities to build in the years after 1914. In so doing, they almost always abandoned previous plans and often sought to conceal the temporary, substandard, and outmoded accommodation that they could not afford to replace. At Leeds, such an attempt led to massive architectural enterprise. The buildings it began to erect in the late-1920s clearly served a three-fold purpose. First, they were intended to provide new and better lecture-rooms, laboratories, and libraries. Secondly—and just as importantly—they were designed to hide Waterhouse's now unfashionable neo-Gothic buildings which had become an embarrassment.[69] Finally, this new development was intended to express the success and the importance of the institution it housed. To this end, the university ran a competition to find the most appropriate architect. The three top entries were all neo-classical: a style, the *Architects' Journal* observed, 'suggestive of the character of the building'.[70] But the winner, H. V. Lanchester, offered much the grandest and most imposing edifice. As the competition assessor, Percy Worthington, put it, its tower was intended to 'dominate the neighbourhood and be seen from all directions and symbolise the University'. Its dome was likewise meant to be 'symbolic of the idea for which the University stands'. Its 'long series of fine buildings' would, it was hoped, give 'the idea of a complete homogenous and dignified University'. With its crisp white classicism, its Palladian pretensions, and its Portland Stone solidity, this was, Worthington claimed, a first class building; an 'ideal modern university' (Figure 32).[71]

---

[65] *Wessex News*, 2 March 1948, p. 3.
[66] USA, 1/4/76/29/2, Committee on the Decline in Student Numbers (1938).
[67] Edwin Barker, 'Social Life', in Hugh Martin, ed., *The Life of the Modern University* (London, 1930), pp. 43–55, p. 44.
[68] WMRC, AUT, MS 27/A16.7, Douglas Laurie 'The Life of a University Teacher', section 1, p. 22.
[69] Beresford, 'Red Brick and Portland Stone', p. 169.
[70] *Architects' Journal* 65 (1927), pp. 197–8, p. 197.
[71] *Builder* 122 (1927), p. 156.

Fig. 32. 'To dominate the neighbourhood and be seen from all directions and symbolise the University': the Parkinson Building, University of Leeds

Special Collections, University of Leeds.

Smaller, poorer, and less well-established places could not hope to match this 'unrivalled' model of a 'modern university'.[72] But they could try to follow its example. At Exeter, for example, the move out of town and on to a campus marked just such a bid for university status. The existing building, wrote the principal, was 'not exactly of University quality'. On the new site, he declared, 'The University note must be struck.' This meant erecting solid and substantial new structures. For, as he put it, 'the frank makeshift is forgivable: but a lapse in permanent [sic.] at this stage would nullify the struggle to rise.'[73] The result was series of developments by the architect Vincent Harris: new laboratories, new hostels, a new library; and all in the same revived Renaissance style.[74]

As this suggests, the 'university note' could be struck by a remarkably large range of buildings. At Southampton, as the college developed, it employed R. F. Gutteridge to build both 'a library worthy of a University institution' (Figure 33)[75] and, more

---

[72] *Builder* 122 (1927), p. 156.
[73] EUA, UA/26/16/1b, Senate Minutes (1936–1941), 19 November 1936, p. 2.
[74] B. W. Clapp, *The University of Exeter: a history* (Exeter, 1982), p. 84.
[75] *Wessex* 2:3 (1933), p. 87.

Fig. 33. 'How can we achieve a University atmosphere with a motley collection of buildings better suited to a factory yard?': the Turner Sims Library, Southampton

Special Collections, University of Southampton.

remarkably, 'a [cricket] pavilion worthy of a University Institution'.[76] The latter building formed a focus for the college's playing fields. The library served a still more important dual role: not only housing books, but also in the process hiding from passers-by the abandoned army huts that the college was still forced to use. Even this, though, was not enough, with one Southampton student left complaining 'How can we achieve a University atmosphere with a motley collection of buildings better suited to a factory yard?'[77]

Above all, Redbrick proved ever-keener to build halls of residence.[78] These, as the authorities at Southampton recognized, were 'the key to University status'.[79] In the words of the National Union of Students: 'A University without hostels is not a University.'[80] The proportion of students able to live in halls varied widely between institutions—ranging, in the mid-1930s, from 74 per cent at Exeter to 10 per cent at Sheffield.[81] The consensus on the crisis in the university, however, highlighted

---

[76] *Wessex* 2:2 (1932), p. 7.
[77] *Wessex News*, 24 February 1948, p. 3.
[78] William Whyte, 'Halls of Residence at the British Civic Universities, 1870–1970', in Jane Hamlett, Lesley Hopkins, and Rebecca Preston, eds, *Residential Institutions in Britain, 1725–1970: inmates and environments* (London, 2013), pp. 155–66.
[79] USA, 1/7/291/26, Opening of Highfield Hall (1930).
[80] NUS, *The Challenge to the University*, p. 44.
[81] UGC, *Returns from Universities 1934–35*, p. 57.

the need for residential accommodation. Such student housing was popular; at Sheffield it was acknowledged that 'there is ample evidence to show the University has lost a considerable number of able men and women... through the absence of such opportunities for residence in a Hall'.[82] But halls were also, of course, believed to have a still more important contribution to make. All Redbrick's critics—from Herklots to Moberly—agreed that the real weakness of the modern universities was their failure to create a proper sense of community. If this was the problem, then residence was widely understood to be the solution.[83] What had sometimes been seen as not much more than an attractive addition—a sop to the fears of parents about their daughters' safety, or a purely pragmatic response to the fact that the local population was not large enough to sustain an institution on its own—now became a matter of high policy. The founders and funders, the critics of and the advocates for the Redbrick universities: all of them came to conclude that residence was a central part of civic university life.[84]

Growing enthusiasm for these quasi-colleges inevitably prompted comparisons with England's two ancient universities. Architecturally, the construction of quadrangular buildings, complete with hall, library, common rooms and even chapel; sometimes built on the characteristically Oxbridge 'staircase system', with sets of rooms running off separate stairwells, but more frequently laid out along corridors: all this sent mixed messages. The decision to choose neo-classicism for some and neo-Gothic for others likewise muddied the waters.

Nonetheless, even in those places most obviously modelled on the ancient universities, the distinction between Oxbridge and Redbrick was always clear. Sometimes this was because the students were dismissed as incapable of living like true undergraduates. At Exeter, one especially superior academic observed that

> Very few... of the students in the modern Universities have had experience of living away from home, and therefore, their residential problems resemble those of the school boarding-house rather than those of an Oxford College.[85]

In other places, it was assumed that the residential system of the civics was simply preferable to that of the ancient universities. At Reading, as one student recalled, 'We rather looked down on Oxford and Cambridge'. These were, it was felt, institutions where university unity had been compromised by collegiate autonomy.[86] Above all, the distinction between the two sorts of universities—one modern and unitary, the other old and federal—meant that however collegiate the Redbrick halls of residence looked, they never functioned as colleges. They did

---

[82] SUA, US/CHA/4/11, Buildings and Endowments (1936–42), 'University of Sheffield: appeal for funds' (1936), p. 1.

[83] Harold Silver, '"Residence" and "Accommodation" in Higher Education: abandoning a tradition', *Journal of Educational Administration and History* 36 (2004), pp. 123–33.

[84] See, for example, UGC, *Returns from Universities 1934-5*, pp. 16–19; CVCP, *The Planning of Halls of Residence* (London, 1948).

[85] EUA, 26/10b, 'Notes on the Residential System at the University College of the South West, Exeter' (1935/6?), p. 3.

[86] Professor P. Allen, quoted in RUA, Uncat. Sidney Smith, 'Wantage Hall, 1927–1933' (n.d.), p. 25.

not admit students, nor were they primarily responsible for teaching them. Even Anselm Hall in Manchester, perhaps the closest attempt made to evoke 'the kind of atmosphere which Colleges provide at Oxford or Cambridge', was limited by its exclusive Anglicanism, relative poverty, and lack of influence within the university from doing any such thing.[87]

An increasing enthusiasm for campus universities distinguished suburban Redbrick halls from urban Oxbridge colleges still further. This move out of town similarly reflected a desire for reform. The smoky industrial environment in which many civic universities were situated had always been notable—a matter of concern for some, and the subject of humour for others. In the years after the First World War, it became a cause of genuine unease. Not only did high city property prices made expansion expensive; but more importantly still, it was increasingly felt that metropolitan life and academic development were incompatible. Even those, like the Leeds professor Arthur Smithells, who valued the university's connection with the city, nonetheless regretted 'the ugliness of our surroundings'.[88] For critics like Truscot, the pernicious influence of the 'slums' that encircled Redbrick seriously undermined the institution as a whole.[89] 'Only in attractive surroundings', wrote Herklots, 'will Dental Jones be encouraged to discuss his own problems and the problems of metaphysics with Anthropological Robinson and Architectural Smith.'[90] The UGC made the point less condescendingly, but nonetheless echoed the argument when it asked:

> How is the traditional British belief that education consists in the development of the whole man, and not merely of the intellect, to be made effective in a pre-dominantly non-residential University at the heart of a great industrial population?[91]

It was in answer to this question that so many civic universities and colleges struck out in the suburbs, acquiring green-field sites and seeking to escape the limitations of city life.

Redbrick architecture thus evolved in a response to criticisms. This was true generally, and also in particular. Seeking to defend its independence, Newcastle Medical School had to build new and better premises in the 1930s.[92] Reflecting on its comparative lack of success, a leading figure at Dundee reiterated the—by now perennial—call to rebuild the place. With a facade 'not worthy either of the college or the city', he declared, it was little wonder that Dundee was so under-rated.[93] The campuses of Southampton and Hull; the hostels of Exeter and Sheffield: all these were similarly designed and built to solve specific problems and address more general anxieties.

But the architecture of Redbrick was also born of optimism, ambition, and hope. Even apparently utilitarian projects had important rhetorical roles to play; as at

---

[87] T. E. Lawrenson, *Hall of Residence: Saint Anselm Hall in the University of Manchester, 1907–1957* (Manchester, 1957), p. 26.
[88] Smithells, *Northern University*, p. 21.   [89] Truscot, *Red-Brick University*, p. 27.
[90] Herklots, *New Universities*, p. 55.   [91] UGC, *Returns from Universities 1934–5*, p. 12.
[92] E. M. Bettensen, *The University of Newcastle upon Tyne: a historical introduction 1834–1971* (Newcastle, 1971), p. 50.
[93] Donald Southgate, *University Education in Dundee: a centenary history* (Edinburgh, 1982), p. 174.

Birmingham, where the Biology department was celebrated as an 'exceedingly noble one which will add materially to the general aspect of the University'.[94] Formal spaces were more important still; as at Leeds, where one benefactor gave money for 'an entrance hall which would leave an indelible impress on the mind of the student which he would remember in after-years with affection'.[95] What were needed, argued the literary scholar Bonamy Dobrée, were buildings 'which will be models of the best style of their day ... expressive of the grace of living'.[96] In some universities, some of the time, that was exactly what they got.

Building what Southampton students termed a world of 'Bricks and mortar-boards' undoubtedly came at a cost.[97] As the Redbricks grew bigger, as their needs grew greater, as their critics grew louder and as their ambitions grew more intense, so they required higher and higher levels of funding. As the building of Nottingham's new campus or the creation of Leeds' Brotherton Library each suggest, the civic universities and colleges remained reliant on generous benefactors in this period. In Scotland, indeed, the whole higher education system was dependent on money from the Carnegie Trust.[98] But figures like Jesse Boot, Lord Brotherton, and Andrew Carnegie were necessarily rare. In their place, Redbrick was forced back to the smaller donations of rather poorer people. In one sense, this reflected the perennial problem that had been faced by the universities since their foundation: they were always unable to attract as much money as they thought they needed. It was also, perhaps, evidence of a renewed unwillingness on the part of the very rich to give generously in an age of increasing taxation.[99] But the willingness of large numbers of middle-class subscribers to give money to their local universities in this period is noteworthy. It reflects the continued importance of these institutions to their region—and particularly to its bourgeois inhabitants.

Exeter provides a good example of a typical fund-raising campaign in this era. Seeking to turn the University College of the South West into the University of Exeter, it set up a remarkably efficient operation, employing agents who toured the region in search of cash. It was not always easy and not always successful, and the long list of 'Bad or Doubtful Promises' included such disconcerting figures as W. H. H. Lane of Exeter, who had promised £2 but was listed simply as 'Disappeared. Wanted by police'.[100] Nonetheless, the campaign raised £250,000 in all. Nor was this the largest benefaction received in this period.[101] Bigger and better-established institutions achieved still greater gifts: between 1929 and 1935

---

[94] *University Bulletin* 4:3 (June 1925), p. 107.

[95] A. N. Shimmin, *The University of Leeds: the first half century* (Cambridge, 1954), 55.

[96] Bonamy Dobrée, *The Universities and Regional Life* (Newcastle, 1943), p. 16.

[97] *Wessex News*, 16 March 1948, p. 1.

[98] J. R. Peddie, *The Carnegie Trust and the Universities of Scotland—the first fifty years (1901–1951)* (Edinburgh, 1951).

[99] Though see David Cannadine, *The Decline and Fall of the British Aristocracy* (London, 1992), pp. 573–5, 584–5 for the continued social significance of the upper classes at civic universities.

[100] EUA, UA/26/10, Buildings and Endowment Committee 1932–36, 20 January 1932. See also UA/26/11, Endowment Fund, 1920–26.

[101] For Manchester, which ran successful appeals in 1919 and 1937, see Alex B. Robertson and Colin Lees, *The University of Manchester, 1918–50: new approaches and changing perspectives* (*Bulletin of the John Rylands University Library* 84:1–2 [2012]), pp. 77–8, 98–101.

Leeds was given over £400,000, and in the years between 1945 and 1948 obtained over £1 million.[102] Visiting England in 1926, H. J. Bhaba, Inspector General of Education for Mysore, was amazed by the achievements of the universities. 'When I think of the princely gifts given by the industrial magnates of Bristol to their rising University', he declared, 'I feel the sort of admiration which puts me, as a Bombay man, to great shame.'[103]

Donors were cajoled into donating in a variety of ways. But as the need grew greater and the institutions became more ambitious, universities and colleges were increasingly willing to employ experts in order to maximize their income. Almost wholly ignored by previous writers, and completely disregarded by those who now argue that twentieth-century universities too quickly abandoned fund-raising and became dependent on the state, the decision by Bristol, Liverpool, and Southampton to hire a professional fund-raiser in 1920 reflects the seriousness with which these institutions approached the issue (Figure 34).[104] The man in question was A. F. Shepherd, founder of 'Business-Builders', specialists in 'Publicity Science-Craft', and subsequently author of *Business First Principles: an exposition, in simple terms, of the force which germinates all knowledge, all activity, all progress and all achievement* (1923).[105] Shepherd came fresh from his success promoting firms like the Eagle Star and British Dominions Insurance Company and raising money for hospitals like Barts. He was brash, slick, self-confident—almost a caricature of the PR man; quick to condemn the slow pace of university decision-making and contemptuous about the lack of imagination he encountered amongst academics. 'Really, one expects from those associated with the University (please do not take this as personal) that breadth of view and that insight into human nature which their better education is supposed to give them', he wrote to the vice-chancellor of Liverpool. Determined to prove his point, and in the process earn a percentage of the takings, Shepherd proposed what the *Advertiser's Weekly* described as 'a Death-blow to tradition', using what he admitted were 'moderately aggressive methods' to achieve his goal. Letters, pamphlets, articles in newspapers, and canvassers 'of a superior class' were all deployed to raise money. Public meetings were held, but Shepherd counselled that in order to achieve the desired effect, the universities should seek to turn hundreds away by inviting two or three times as many people as the hall could possibly hold.[106]

The dual nature of the universities and colleges as genuinely local but incipiently national institutions was made evident in the 'duplex campaign' that they ran.[107] Civic pride remained an important draw. Comparing itself to Liverpool in 1922,

---

[102] UGC *Returns from Universities 1934–5*, p. 59; *Yearbook of the Universities of the Empire* 1948, p. 36.
[103] *Third Congress of the Universities of the Empire* (London, 1926), p. 38. See also S. R. Dongerkery, *A History of the University of Bombay, 1857–1957* (Bombay, 1957), p. 87.
[104] The one exception is Morse, 'English Civic Universities', pp. 188–9.
[105] A. F. Shepherd, *Business First Principles: an exposition, in simple terms, of the force which germinates all knowledge, all activity, all progress and all achievement* (London, 1923). This includes his own—glowing—description of the campaign.
[106] *Advertising World*, March 1917; *Advertiser's Weekly*, 1 April 1920, pp. 7–9; LivUA, P.411, Appeal 1920, A. F. Shepherd, 'Note to Appeal Committee' (22 April 1921); Shepherd to vice-chancellor (1 December 1920; 24 June 1920).
[107] *Advertiser's Weekly*, 1 April 1920, p. 8.

Fig. 34. 'Help Youth to Realise Ambition,—Therein Lies Efficiency and the Nation's Destiny': appeal poster, University of Liverpool, 1920

University of Liverpool Special Collections.

the University of Bristol challenged local patrons to keep pace with their northern rival. 'Already', it declared, Liverpool 'is to-day making a supreme effort for leadership among the modern Universities of the world. Will the West again be content to remain inert?'[108] At Liverpool, by contrast, the comparison was with Canadian cities, where more than a million pounds had recently been raised for higher education. 'The Dignity, Prestige and Well-being of Liverpool at stake' claimed a leaflet. 'Shall it be said that the Citizens of Liverpool are possessed of less patriotism, less acumen, less generosity, or less unselfishness than those of Montreal?'[109] At the same time, the universities made an appeal to a wider, national audience, claiming, as Bristol did, that 'BRAINS ARE OUR FIRST LINE OF NATIONAL DEFENCE'.[110] In the great struggle for international survival,

---

[108] *Our First Line of National Defence* (Bristol, 1922), p. 5.
[109] LivUA, P.411, 'The Dignity, Prestige and Well-being of Liverpool at stake'.
[110] *Our First Line of National Defence*, p. 1.

Shepherd exclaimed, 'our Professor-Generals are at grips with the Pursuit of Truth for the Advance of Knowledge'.[111] Nor was it just his clients who articulated such ideas. At Manchester, a still more demanding goal was set out, with the university's fund-raising effort sustained by the ambition 'To supplant Bonn or Jena as one of the recognised centres of the most complete intellectual training obtainable in the world.'[112] Smaller colleges could not claim this, but it was practically the only argument that they did not try.

At Southampton, a whole variety of tacks were taken. 'Alfred the Great, king of Wessex, encouraged education. Follow his lead and help found a University of Wessex', cried a full-page advertisement in the *Hampshire Advertiser* in late 1928.[113] 'Commerce and Industry are moving south. They will move to those places which provide a welcome', explained another; 'A University is not merely a welcome, it is a beacon guiding them from far off. Help to light the beacon which shall guide them to the Great Port of Southampton.'[114] If potential benefactors were not persuaded by history and geography, it was reasoned, perhaps they might fall for something else. 'Why should Manchester, Liverpool and Leeds have a university, and not Southampton?' asked an advertisement in the *Southern Daily Echo*.[115] Surely, suggested another piece, employers needed the 'Expert Knowledge—Initiative—Salesmanship' that university graduates could uniquely offer?[116] Should even this not work, then a still more basic bottom line was brought up. Students, claimed the principal, drew between £40,000 and £50,000 into the local economy a year. A larger university would perhaps bring even more.[117]

The Southampton campaign was not a great success. It turned out that too few people wanted to emulate Alfred the Great, and only £20,000 was raised. Bristol similarly failed to raise its target amount, and Shepherd's relationship with the authorities at Liverpool descended into mutual antipathy, with the disgruntled public relations expert left infuriated that academics simply did not understand his job—or, he felt, really comprehend their own.[118] The problem was this: although the methods had changed, the basic realities of university fund-raising had not. Rich men and women could be persuaded to give money for buildings and scholarships—particularly when they were named after themselves. But they continued to be far less generous when asked to pay for the day-to-day running of the place. Nor did tuition fees and endowment income bring in the sort of money that could allow most universities and colleges to rest easy. Some could raise cash through a bond issue, with contemporaries expressing understandable envy at the £500,000 obtained by Manchester in this way in 1920.[119] The majority of

---

[111] LivUA, P.411, 'Ambassadors of Progress'.
[112] SUA, US/CHA/4/9, University Buildings of Manchester Appeal Fund (1919).
[113] USA, 1/2/1/8/1, *Hampshire Advertiser*, 24 November 1928.
[114] USA, 1/2/1/8/1, *Hampshire Advertiser*, 27 October 1928.
[115] USA, 1/2/1/8/1, *Southern Daily Echo*, 19 November 1928.
[116] USA, 1/2/1/8/1, *Southern Daily Echo*, 28 November 1928.
[117] USA, 1/2/1/8/1, *Southern Daily Echo*, 15 October 1928.
[118] LivUA, P.411, Shepherd to vice-chancellor (21 December 1921).
[119] LivUA P.411/3, Appeal 1920.

institutions, however, could not aspire to such *richesse*, so they ran big deficits and remained dependent on state aid to keep them going.[120] This was not through choice, much less through lassitude; it was the result of simple necessity.

Support from government came in three forms. In the first place, there was research funding.[121] Although not much of this reached Redbrick, by 1939 the Department of Scientific and Industrial Research was alone disbursing £1 million a year for technological research.[122] In the second place, there continued to be grants from local authorities. Yet whilst this money amounted to many thousands of pounds, it was also increasingly problematic. In many places, universities ended up paying more in rates than they received in support from the council.[123] Thus it was that Redbrick became ever-more reliant on the third source of state funding: cash allocated by the UGC. Founded in 1919 to underwrite the expansion of the modern universities, it became the key player in their development.[124] The £250,000 treasury grant of 1914 became £3,750,000 at end of the First World War; and by 1948 it had risen to £7,160,000.[125] Not all of this went to the Redbricks, of course, but its impact was remarkable.[126] In the mid-1930s, 36 per cent of civic university income came from the UGC; ten years later, this had risen to 54 per cent.[127]

Naturally, this growing dependence on the state led to questions.[128] The foundation myth of British higher education was, as the government itself put it, that 'the Universities of the United Kingdom have been, since their origin, independent of State control.'[129] That this was palpably false did not matter. The power of the myth was too strong—and the result a series of anxious questions. Was it possible, asked many, for the universities to retain their freedom, their vigour, and their identity if they were reliant on government support?[130] 'A university', observed the principal of Exeter in 1935, 'may gain the whole world and lose its own soul.'[131] Nonetheless, most commentators were pretty sanguine about the impact of the UGC. Writing in 1930, the vice-chancellor of Birmingham, Charles Grant Robertson cheerily observed, 'Should it turn out that the choice lay between a dominated affluence and a free if cramping poverty, there

---

[120] Christine Helen Shinn, *Paying the Piper: the development of the University Grants Committee, 1919–1946* (London and Philadelphia, 1986).
[121] See David Edgerton, *Warfare State: Britain, 1920–1970* (Cambridge, 2006), ch. 3.
[122] Michael Argles, *South Kensington to Robbins: an account of English technical and scientific education since 1851* (London, 1964), p. 80.
[123] Ross McKibbin, *Classes and Cultures: England, 1918–51* (Oxford, 1998), p. 254.
[124] Eric Hutchinson, 'The Origins of the University Grants Committee', *Minerva* 13 (1975), pp. 583–620.
[125] Shinn, *Paying the Piper*, p. 136.
[126] Truscot, *Red Brick University*, p. 55 complains at the amount given to Oxbridge which began receiving money in 1922.
[127] UGC, *University Development 1935–1946*, p. 79.
[128] Robert O. Berdahl, *British Universities and the State* (Berkeley and Los Angeles, 1959).
[129] Board of Education, *The Universities of the United Kingdom of Great Britain and Ireland* (London, 1918), p. 4.
[130] W. M. Childs, *Universities and their Freedom* (London, 1921), p. 50.
[131] *Universities Review* 8:1 (October 1935), p. 25.

is no question as to what the answer of the universities would be.' It would be—he was confident—the latter.[132] Indeed, the UGC itself made clear that guaranteeing university autonomy was a central part of its brief. To that end, it continued to encourage the colleges to rely not on grants, but on increasing endowment income.[133] So it was that one critic imagined a new university being granted arms showing on one side a Chancellor of the Exchequer and the other a private donor. The motto, he said, would be one approved by the UGC: 'A Pound for a Pound'.[134]

The relationship between the universities and central government did, however, grow closer in this period. The quinquennial visitations that had begun in the 1880s now assumed a new importance as the UGC began to make a significant impact on how the universities were run. For the students, these could be comic occasions, with undergraduates at Nottingham enjoying the half-term holiday and mocking the recall of 'dog-eared and well-thumbed volumes ... to form imposing ranks on the usually depleted library shelves'.[135] For the staff, however, they were rather more serious—and much harder work, requiring months of preparation. The relationship between universities and UGC remained a cosy one, nonetheless, with issues as often settled in the clubs of Pall Mall as they were in the offices of Whitehall.[136] Until the war, indeed, the UGC continued to see its job as 'the interpretation to the Government of the policies and financial needs of the universities'.[137] It was only in 1946 that the body came to conceive of itself as anything like the instrument for the creation of a national policy—and even then, it continued to stress the centrality of university autonomy.[138]

The existence of a national funding body could not help but shape a more comprehensive—and, potentially, a more coherent—system of higher education.[139] The need for further funding brought the heads of the universities together and, for the first time, in 1918 they lobbied the government for greater support.[140] Their institutions, they maintained, 'are national, they are not local'.[141] Arguably untrue at the time, this became more and more accurate as the years passed. Negotiations with the state heightened the need for principals and vice-chancellors

---

[132] Charles Grant Robertson, *The British Universities* (London, 1930), p. 71.
[133] E.g. UGC, *Returns from Universities 1923–4*, p. 29; *Returns from Universities 1928–9*, p. 52.
[134] J. A. Ewing, 'University Finance', *Second Congress of the Universities of the Empire* (London, 1921), pp. 295–303, p. 296.
[135] *The Gong* 13:2 (Easter 1934), p. 31.
[136] Charles Illingworth, *University Statesmen: Sir Hector Hetherington* (Glasgow, 1971), pp. 19–20.
[137] UGC, *University Development from 1935 to 1947*, p. 8.
[138] UGC, *University Development from 1935 to 1947*. On this, see also Michael Shattock, *Making Policy in Higher Education 1945–2011* (Maidenhead, 2012) and Gerard James Taggart, 'A Critical Review of the Role of the English Funding Body for Higher Education in the Relationship Between the State and Higher Education in the Period 1945–2003' (PhD Bristol, 2004).
[139] Hector Hetherington, *The British University System, 1914–1954* (Edinburgh and London, 1955), p. 1.
[140] TNA, UGC 5//8, Correspondence Leading to the Deputation to the Chancellor of the Exchequer 23 November 1918.
[141] Universities Bureau of the British Empire, *Deputation to the President of the Board of Education and Chancellor of the Exchequer* (London, 1918), p. 15.

to collaborate—and so, in 1919 the Committee of Vice-Chancellors and Principals (CVCP) was formally established. Significantly, amongst its first jobs was the attempt to establish a national scale of fees for student courses.[142] In the same year, the Association of University Teachers (AUT) was also founded, and it too sought national solutions to local problems, pushing repeatedly for universal pay scales.[143] Three years later, in 1922, the National Union of Students (NUS) was established.[144] Although initially confined to England and Wales, it too attempted to take a wider view, with regular congresses, publications, and campaigns. In 1926 it had 30,000 members. By 1945 there were 68,000.[145] Like the AUT, the NUS had its origins at, and was strongest in, the civic universities; they both had little connection with Oxbridge and for some students, at any rate, membership of the National Union was seen as 'The Hall-Mark of Provincialism'.[146]

In this way, the civics began to reshape university life in Britain, creating structures and forming links that links would eventually come to encompass the older foundations too. It was a slow, but seismic shift. 'Time was when, through the scantiness of the means of communication, each English University was an island', wrote Michael Sadler in 1922. 'The British Universities now realise that they are an archipelago with some of the characteristics of a continent.'[147] The tectonic plates were beginning to move, the landscape of higher education was being reformed, and Redbrick was a driving force behind this new world of universities.

---

[142] WMRC, CVCP, MS 399/1/16/1, CVCP Minutes, 1918–24, 24 January 1919.
[143] Harold Perkin, *Key Profession: the history of the Association of University Teachers* (London, 1969).
[144] Ivison S. Macadam, *Youth and the Universities* (London, 1922), p. 9.
[145] WMRC, NUS, MS 280/144/7, 'NUS: the first forty years, 1922–1962' (1962); Eric Ashby and Mary Anderson, *The Rise of the Student Estate in Britain* (London and Basingstoke, 1970), p. 91.
[146] R. G. Coward, 'The Hall-Mark of Provincialism', *Wessex News* 9 June 1942, pp. 1–2.
[147] Michael Sadler, 'A Threefold Allegiance', *University Bulletin* 1:1 (January 1922), p. 2.

8
Redbrick Inhabited

Who were the students who had joined this new world? There were more and more of them, that much was clear. The 10,000 undergraduates of 1914 had become 20,000 in 1948—and were set to grow still further in number.[1] This represented a tiny percentage of the population, of course; only about 3 per cent of people ever got the chance to go to university, and even the wildest plans for expansion envisaged only a marginal increase, with the influential 1946 Barlow Report on scientific training suggesting that ultimately one in twenty might be capable of undertaking higher education.[2] Nonetheless, the doubling of student numbers had an un-ignorable impact on the universities and colleges themselves. If there was a crisis, suggested the philosopher Michael Oakeshott in 1948, it was one which sprang from an 'altogether excessive number of undergraduates'.[3] Many of the obstacles faced by these institutions were indeed the result of growth. For whilst expansion undoubtedly equalled success, it also caused difficulties which ranged from the practical problems of overcrowding to a nagging but persistent concern that the universities had become too big for their own good. Growth both legitimated and threatened to undermine Redbrick.

The civic universities and colleges had, of course, been founded to educate local people who were, for whatever reason, excluded from the ancient universities. They remained local; in 1948 it was still the case that over 60 per cent of Redbrick students came from within 30 miles of the university they attended.[4] But they nonetheless found it ever harder to effect what the Southampton theologian Claude Montefiore had called a 'union of classes'.[5] The expansion in student numbers was not matched by an increase in the proportion of impecunious people attending university.[6] The growth of government grants and the tendency of local authorities to push the very brightest of the poorest towards Oxbridge meant that in fact Redbrick remained every bit as middle-class as it ever had been.[7] At the end of the 1920s, 53 per cent of provincial university students were supported by the state,

---

[1] UGC, *Returns from Universities and University Colleges in receipt of Treasury Grant 1947–8*, p. 3.
[2] *Scientific Manpower: Report of a Committee appointed by the Lord President of the Council* 1946 (cmd. 6824), p. 9. See also *Conference of the Home Universities* 1947 (London, 1947), p. 41.
[3] Michael Oakeshott, 'The Universities', *Cambridge Journal* 2 (1948–9), pp. 515–42, p. 533.
[4] Nuffield College, *The Problem Facing British Universities* (London, 1948), p. 54.
[5] *Wessex* 1 (June 1928), p. 9.
[6] See Carol Dyhouse, 'Going to University in England between the Wars: access and funding', *History of Education* 31:1 (2002), pp. 1–14, for the context of this.
[7] *Scientific Manpower*, p. 16.

compared to 38 per cent at Oxford and Cambridge. By the mid-1930s, however, the figures were 46 per cent at Redbrick and 43 per cent at the ancient universities.[8] After the Second World War, it is true, three-quarters of civic university undergraduates had some sort of scholarship. But this was now less than the 80 per cent of students in receipt of aid at Oxbridge.[9]

Such a shift did not mean that Redbrick wholly lost its role for the aspirational and impoverished. Nor did it mean that Oxbridge had lost its social cachet or the social elite that created it. For the children of ordinary middle-class families, life at Redbrick was a much more realistic possibility than Oxford or Cambridge, especially if they could find some of the fees themselves.[10] The cost of living, after all, was much lower there than in the ancient universities: on average 30 per cent less in the English civics,[11] and cheaper still in Wales.[12] But it did mean that the stark social differences between Oxbridge and Redbrick were less evident than hindsight would suggest.

Indeed, whilst Oxbridge spanned an increasingly wider social spectrum, Redbrick became the natural home to a rather narrower group of people: what one Reading undergraduate described as, 'the fairly intelligent and poorer section whom economic pressure thrusts out into the world where we must get a job.'[13] Richard Hoggart's experience at Leeds, where he arrived in 1936, is probably typical. Here he encountered three types of students. In the first place, there were 'those whose presence recalled the origins of the University'; the sons and daughters of mill-owners and manufacturers, 'the gilded youth of West Yorkshire coming in from the hills each day in two-seater sports coupés'. A second group consisted of the lower-middle- and upper-working-class students who were scraping together all or part of their fees. Finally, there were the poorer students; scholarship boys, like Hoggart himself, who 'tended to carry pressed cardboard attaché cases from Woolworth's or a market stall, to wear sports jackets, flannels and pullovers'.[14]

Within Redbrick, each group had different expectations, different ambitions, and different interests. 'He will want to keep a hunter, if he has learnt to regard hunting as the essential of a decent life', observed the vice-chancellor of Birmingham in 1930:

> He will dress for dinner, or have 'high tea', drink cocktails or wear silk underclothing, look at bar maids as social equals, or as the incidents of a gentleman's passage through life—according to the home from which he comes and the means that it provides for his University education.[15]

---

[8] UGC, *Returns from Universities and University Colleges in receipt of Treasury Grant 1934–35*, p. 55.
[9] UGC, *Returns from Universities 1947–8*, p. 5.
[10] G. S. M. Ellis, *The Poor Boy and the University* (London, 1925).
[11] E. A. G. Caroe, 'The Cost of Living at English Universities', *University Bulletin* 7:1 (April 1928), pp. 33–8, pp. 37–8.
[12] M. F. P. Joliffe, 'Comparison between the cost of living in English and Welsh universities', *Universities Review* 1:2 (April 1929), pp. 97–101.
[13] *Tamesis* 32 (1933–34), p. 106.
[14] Richard Hoggart, *A Local Habitation: life and times, 1918–1940* (Oxford, 1989), pp. 184–5.
[15] Charles Grant Robertson, 'Religion', in Hugh Martin, ed., *The Life of the Modern University* (London, 1930), pp. 61–82, p. 65.

But divisions amongst the undergraduates were not simply socio-economic; rather, age and wealth and education were inter-related, so that as Redbrick grew bigger, the differences between the students grew still greater.

The result was a complex, anxiety-provoking environment which was sometimes hard to navigate. At Reading in the 1920s there was a highly sophisticated hierarchy to be negotiated, as Elspeth Huxley recalled:

> To be an 'agri' was all right, and so was a 'horti'; pure scientists occupied a middle range, and at the bottom, I regret to say, came the future teachers... 'Edus' tended to cluster together looking earnest, pallid (probably from malnutrition) and even more drearily dressed than the rest of us; to dodge coffees in the Buttery because two pence was beyond their means, and, if girls, to live in a remote hall called St George's that no-one ever visited. The smart hall was St Andrew's, just as among the men it was Wantage, with St Patrick's in the second place.[16]

No wonder some found it difficult.[17] The nervous undergraduate in Kathleen Freeman's novel *Martin Hanner* spoke for many in seeing the whole civic university system as one enormous party to which she was not really invited. Taking a deep breath, she complained:

> The second year and third year people sit on the freshers, and the Honours people won't look at them, or if they do they try to draw them out and make asses of them; and yet the freshers don't pull together at all. And there seem to be such a lot of groups and cliques, and you never know whether, if you barge in anywhere, you mayn't get snubbed. And the staff—they seem so far off and aloof.... And the students are at you trying to get you to go to meetings and things in the evenings, and telling you not to be a swot... and if you do go you find it's run by the big pots and you don't get a look in.[18]

However parochial and parodic, these complaints do hint at a wider point. Redbrick students were not homogenous, however much their critics might imply they were. Nor was their social life undifferentiated. In fact, life in the civic universities and colleges was just as complex as at Oxbridge or in London.

What about differences of gender? The proportion of women at university actually declined after the First World War.[19] But relations between men and women nonetheless were permitted to become a little less icy. Originally, of course, colleges had strictly policed the interactions between men and women, with separate rooms and doors and spaces set aside for each. Until the mid-1930s, women at Exeter had to conform to a dress code which insisted they wore 'costumes of plain colour and cut, or dresses of plain colour and cut which have long sleeves'.[20] Whilst this rule was abolished there, at Sheffield the tutor for women continued to insist that her students were always 'suitably' dressed and wearing

---

[16] Quoted in Carol Dyhouse, *No Distinction of Sex? Women in British universities, 1870–1939* (London, 1989), p. 120.
[17] See also, Annotina, 'Problems of a Fresher', *The Gong* 7:3 (1928), pp. 18–19.
[18] Kathleen Freeman, *Martin Hanner: a comedy* (London, 1926), p. 114.
[19] Carol Dyhouse, *Students: a gendered history* (London and New York, 2006), ch. 1.
[20] Clapp, *University of Exeter*, p. 135.

stockings.[21] At Liverpool, the students' union building remained segregated. Any woman who wished to speak to a man was meant to approach the matron who guarded the door to the women's side. She would then carry the message across the hall to the men's steward who would seek out the individual in question and bring him back to meet his interlocutor under the watchful eye of a chaperone.[22] Some no doubt appreciated this enforced decorum; certainly one Reading student later possessed only fond memories of a time when 'We had no worries about alcohol, drugs, women or gays.'[23] But for many, including some other students at the same institution, restrictions on intercourse—of all sorts—between the students seemed irksome.[24] Just as in previous periods, within a co-educational establishment even the library might become 'a breeding-ground of whispering, giggling, and flirtation'.[25]

Though the halls of residence continued strictly to restrict contact between men and women, opportunities for encounters continued to proliferate, aided, not least, by a rise in the number of mixed social spaces within the university more generally. At Bristol, in the men's hall of residence, 'ladies were allowed to tea, but only on Sundays between 3 and 5pm and only if the man's study door was left open'.[26] Yet inside the main university building things were rather different. 'A few years ago', complained one dissatisfied Bristolian, 'when students came up one of the first things they learned was that one did not go to the General Common Room in the evening because of the couples inside.' Now, he went on, 'necking couples' could be found at all times. 'It is rather a poor state of affairs when students are overheard saying, "Don't go to the Common Room, there are too many over-sexed couples up there," and this at twelve forty-five in the morning!'[27] The same was true at Nottingham, where the well-planted campus provided additional opportunities for private indiscretions.[28] Often, though, contact between male and female students was less likely to alarm.[29] It was organized and monitored—and sometimes rather sweet. A social event at Leicester in 1947, for example, involved women sewing patches of coloured cloth on the seat of their (male) partner's trousers.[30] But even this would have been unthinkable a generation or so before. The official, rather rigid restrictions of the past were gradually being loosened. Those who moved from co-educational Redbrick to 'totally monastic' Oxbridge were often disappointed by the experience.[31]

---

[21] Helen Mathers, *Steel City Scholars: the centenary history of the University of Sheffield* (London, 2005), p. 103.
[22] *The Students' Union, University of Liverpool* (Liverpool, 1965).
[23] RUA, Uncat. Sidney Smith, 'Wantage Hall, 1927–1933' (n.d.), p. 2.
[24] *Tamesis*, 31 (1932–33), p. 4. See also NUS, *The Challenge to the University* (London, 1938), p. 48.
[25] *Wessex News*, 9 February 1936, p. 4.
[26] M. J. Crossley Evans and A. Sulston, *A History of Wills Hall, University of Bristol* (Bristol, 1994), pp. 25–6.
[27] *Bristol Nonesuch*, 83 (Spring 1939), p. 39.
[28] *Gongster*, 5 June 1939, p. 6.
[29] See also *Wessex News*, 16 June 1936, p. 4; 23 June 1936, p. 4.
[30] LeiUA, Uncat., John Winterburn, 'Recollections of University College, Leicester, 1947–50', p. 5.
[31] Lord Elwyn-Jones, *In My Time: an autobiography* (London, 1983), p. 24.

Where the ancient universities did appear to score was in their undergraduates' social lives. A contrast between the gilded youth of Oxbridge, effortlessly triumphing in sport and in debate, and the poor, harassed, and uncultured civic university student was even drawn by Redbrick undergraduates themselves. At Reading, for example, a complaint along these lines was made practically every other year.[32] And there is also some evidence of the apathy that critics claimed to have found. At Bristol in 1924 it was noted that only about 6 per cent of men and 20 per cent of women attended student union meetings.[33] At Nottingham in 1936 it was complained that only one in five students regularly appeared at official functions.[34] For critics—and, indeed, for supporters—the problem was simple: Redbrick students were too obsessed with getting a degree and finding a job to spend time on extra-curricular activities. Defending his students from the charge that they were intellectually insipid, one Southampton professor wrote to a newly appointed colleague in just these terms. 'I suspect the dullness to which you refer is in part due to the financial worries at home', he wrote. 'I cannot help feeling that you, not having been here so very long, are hardly aware how very acute is the economic insecurity of most of our students' home affairs, and that is why they are so desperately anxious with regards to getting jobs.'[35]

There is some suggestion that this insight was right. Students worked hard, with arts undergraduates sitting through as many as twenty-three hours of lectures a week, and engineers spending up to thirty-five hours in lecture-rooms or laboratories.[36] They worked hard because they needed good qualifications to get a job. It remained the case that for those students whose passport to university was the promise that they would teach, there was simply no way out.[37] As 90 per cent of those in the arts faculty were on such school teacher scholarships, this meant a lot of people having to pass exams—or risk a financially precarious future.[38] For many others, employment after graduation was also an over-riding consideration. In 1920, a survey showed that the overwhelming majority of Oxbridge students had little or no sense of what they would do after their degree, whilst Redbrick undergraduates were clearly focused on their future career, with jobs in chemistry and engineering being the most popular prospective destination.[39] Practical, sensible, eminently employable: it was little wonder that these students should be something of a disappointment to their lecturers.

---

[32] E.g. *Tamesis*, 25A (1925–6), p. 100; 25B (1926–7), p. 225; 31 (1932–3), p. 4; 32 (1933–34), p. 106; 36 (1937–8), pp. 3–4.
[33] *Bristol Nonesuch* 9 (1923–24), p. 84.
[34] *The Gong* 26:1 (Christmas 1936), p. 13.
[35] USA, 1/4/76/29/1, Committee on Declining Student Numbers, A. A. Cock to N. K. Adam (30 November 1938).
[36] Leonard Schwartz, 'In an unyielding hinterland: the student body, 1900–1945', in Eric Ives, Diane Drummond, and Leonard Schwarz, eds, *The First Civic University: Birmingham, 1880–1980* (Birmingham, 2000), pp. 237–70, p. 242.
[37] Dyhouse, *Students*, pp. 22–7.
[38] A. H. Stewart and V. de S. Pinto, 'The Training of the Teacher of English', in Vivian de Sola Pinto, ed., *The Teaching of English in Schools: a symposium* (London, 1946), pp. 149–66, p. 158.
[39] WMRC CVCP, MS 399/1/16/1, Minutes, 1918–24, 25 March 1920.

It is clear however that a student culture did exist and that student life at Redbrick could be attractive. It was both embodied and fostered in the increasing numbers of self-contained, and often rather grand, union buildings that were erected: at Birmingham (1925–30), Sheffield (1934–6), and elsewhere. Nor were most undergraduates obsessed with job-hunting to the exclusion of all other activities. In 1937, in fact, another survey showed that only 2 per cent of civic university students knew what career they wanted to pursue when they arrived at university.[40] Even prospective teachers, like George Ewart Evans, who had a busy schedule and a clear path to pursue, found time for sport, singing, and flirting with women in the students' union.[41]

Moreover, as the continual complaints about student apathy from the students themselves suggest, there was an ideal—a belief in the need for an active life beyond the library or laboratory—that they held in common. A debate at Exeter in 1925 was typical in concluding that 'a "Varsity must turn out sound, sane men", rather than becoming a degree factory'.[42] This principle found its expression in a plethora of clubs and societies. 'The notice-boards of every University,' wrote one commentator, 'are hardly large enough to contain the announcements of the various sectional societies.'[43] The proliferation of these clubs was a result of the increasing size of the student body. But it also reflected the success of previous generations of undergraduates; it was proof that their invented traditions had indeed become traditional. A student who had left Southampton, say, in 1920 and returned thirty years later would have recognized the annual 'Rag', the various political clubs, the students' union, and much else besides.[44] Even the symbols of Southampton student life remained the same, with 'Kelly'—a skeleton brought to the college in the nineteenth century—paraded at all Rags and displayed in most other events from the 1880s to the 1950s.[45]

There were two noteworthy developments in Redbrick life which mark out the period after about 1914. The first was a product of the newly, officially sanctioned familiarity between male and female students. It was dancing. Undergraduates from Oxbridge were shocked and amazed at the centrality of the 'hop' or the 'social'.[46] Civic university professors were even more appalled. Yet the 'excessive cult of dancing', as one described it, went on—indeed, it grew all but ubiquitous.[47] The second shift in student culture had a still more transformative role. For, increasingly, contact between members of different colleges and universities began to

---

[40] NUS, *Graduate Employment* (London, 1937), p. 21.
[41] Evans, *Strength of the Hills*, pp. 59–68.
[42] UEA UA/26/17d, Debating Society Minutes, 1912–25, 20 March 1925.
[43] A. J. Grant, 'Academic Life', in Martin, ed., *Modern University*, pp. 31–42, p. 41.
[44] Though see, *Wessex* 2.2 (June 1932), p. 97.
[45] Though he was briefly replaced: *Wessex News* 21 October 1952, p. 3. See also Southampton University Archives 1/7/292/22/1 and 1/7/291/22/3.
[46] Herklots, *New Universities*, p. 100.
[47] WMRC, AUT, 27/3/55, F. E. Sandbach, Comments on 'New University Prospects' (1928). See also Truscot, *Redbrick University*, pp. 212–13.

create a wider sense of identity, a 'student estate' in embryo.[48] The Intervarsity Christian Union, the Student Christian Movement, the NUS, and many other organizations all increased in importance and helped to forge links between institutions.[49] The Inter-varsity Ball used the supremely popular appeal of dancing to draw yet more students together.

Sporting fixtures functioned in a similar way. Just as nineteenth-century public schools defined themselves by playing sport against each other—and in so doing created a public school system, so twentieth-century civic universities used sport both to create college loyalty and to mark their university identity.[50] Matches between the rival Redbrick institutions saw crowds on the touchline mark their differences by shouting apparent nonsense, unintelligible to all but initiates: 'Dala fa! / Sprago fa! / Kicko fa! / I wara! I wara! I wara! / Pui? Pui? Pui?' sang Exeter in the 1920s;[51] 'Ah! Rah! Chickerah roo / Oni, Poni, Ping pong pyni, / Tara, wara, waxi richi poo, / Ah! Rah! Chickerah roo', sang Nottingham in the 1940s.[52] At the same time, though, the fact that they were meeting—and meeting as equals—demonstrated an equivalence. It was, as the undergraduates of Exeter had resolved, vital not to damage the interests of their college by competing with inappropriate teams.[53] Through playing other universities, they proved their university status.

The same was true of debating. Teams of Redbrick students toured the provincial universities, and even in the far southwest Exeter was able to draw in representatives of almost all universities, except Oxbridge.[54] In 1933, the National Union of Students attempted to mobilize this constituency to conduct a national debate on pacifism. Following the Oxford Union's notorious vote that 'This House will in no circumstances fight for its King and Country', the students at Redbrick were encouraged to make their views known.[55] To be sure, not everyone wanted to participate. The London College of Medicine for Women refused, arguing that 'the whole subject is not truly relevant to a women's college', and going on to suggest that 'it would be unwise for younger Universities to interfere or associate themselves . . . and thereby alienate that public sympathy which they have with such difficulty acquired'.[56] Nor was everyone permitted to join in. At Nottingham and Sheffield, the authorities prevented a debate.[57] But there was an enthusiastic response elsewhere, and, in the end, a dozen colleges discussed the motion. At Belfast and Birmingham, the students voted against pacifism. This was also the case

---

[48] Eric Ashby and Mary Anderson, *The Rise of the Student Estate in Britain* (London and Basingstoke, 1970).
[49] Robin Boyd, *The Witness of the Student Christian Movement* (London, 2007).
[50] J. R. de S. Honey, *Tom Brown's Universe: the development of the Victorian public school* (London, 1977).
[51] UEA, UA/26/12a, box 3313, Guild of Undergraduates Handbook, 1923–24, p. 60.
[52] *Gongster*, 14 February 1940, p. 3.
[53] UEA, 26/17d, Guild Council Minutes, 1909–21, 11 October 1920.
[54] UEA, UA, 26/17d, Debating Society Minutes, 1925–34, pp. 213–16, 248.
[55] Martin Caedel, 'The King and Country Debate: student politics, pacifism, and the dictators', *Historical Journal* 22 (1979), pp. 397–422.
[56] WMRC, NUS, MSS280/3/KC/9, Margaret Donald (4 March 1933).
[57] WMRC, NUS, MSS280/3/KC/26, Results of Debates (26 March 1933).

at Newcastle, where, 'with the Union Jack and the Engineering faculty in great evidence', the students voted 316 to 130 for King and Country.[58] In Aberystwyth and Leicester, Manchester, and Cardiff, however, hundreds turned out to support the Oxford motion. It was an important moment: not because these votes signify a widespread support for pacifism, but because it was believed to be an important moment. It was one that was widely reported, and which—more significantly still—signified the growing consciousness of a genuinely national student body.[59]

PROFESSOR DEADWOOD

In 1928, the University of Liverpool appointed Alan Dorward as professor of philosophy. He was to remain there until 1954, drinking steadily, taking at least three months' holiday a year, and publishing nothing but a single short booklet just before he retired.[60] Forgotten by posterity and disregarded by philosophy, he was, however, to find himself immortalized in polemic, becoming in Bruce Truscot's work Professor Deadwood, the archetypal dead-beat Redbrick academic. His opposite number was Professor Livewire, thinly—transparently—based on Truscot's creator Edgar Peers.[61] Deadwood did nothing. He taught as little as possible, administered as little as possible, and did no research whatsoever. His typical day was described thus:

> He has a leisurely breakfast at half-past-eight, followed by pipe and paper; reaches the University between ten and half-past; reads his letters and perhaps writes one; saunters into the Common Room for a cup of coffee; calls on a colleague, or the Bursar, or the Clerk to the Senate; returns to his room, glances through the latest issue of a learned review, has a few words with a pupil—and lo, it's lunch-time. After lunch in the refectory, followed by a chat about the day's news in the Common Room, he gives a lecture at half-past-two, and immediately afterwards hurries home lest he should be late for tea. After tea comes the day's exercise (unless it happens to be a day when he has no lecture, in which case he plays golf in the afternoon) and after dinner he spends a couple of hours with a new book on his special subject (or a book from the circulating library on something else), after which, the paper again, a nightcap, and bed at eleven after a somewhat tiring but thoroughly well-spent day.[62]

Livewire, by contrast, wrote and taught and administered—but, above all, researched. He, in Truscot's terms, was what Redbrick should be (but was not), whilst Deadwood embodied what Redbrick was (but should not be).

Both Deadwood and Livewire were, of course, caricatures. Truscot's sharp dichotomy should not be taken too seriously: its intention was polemical, and his

---

[58] WMRC, NUS, MSS280/3/KC/21, Ella Peacock (19 March 1933).
[59] WMRC, NUS, MSS280/3/KC, press cuttings.
[60] Cécile Dorward and Ron Davidson, *Anything But Ordinary: the nine lives of Cécile* (Fremantle, Western Australia, 2000), pp. 74, 77, 104, 134.
[61] Truscot, 'A Red-Brick Tea-Party'.
[62] Truscot, *Redbrick in these Vital days*, p. 96.

work—especially the books and articles that followed *Red Brick University*—should be read with this in mind. There were Deadwoods, of course; men like the professor who complained about his teaching load, yet only did two and a half hours work a day.[63] There were also Livewires; men like the Nobel Prize-winning physicist P. M. S. Blackett, who left Cambridge for London and then Manchester and refused all blandishments proffered to make him return. But there was also a whole spectrum of other men—and, though Truscot did not really seem to have noticed them, a small and diverse group of women.[64] Even within a single institution, the teaching staff ranged from the active to the languid, and from the charismatic to the cripplingly shy. At Sheffield in the 1920s, for example, physics produced a passionate and popular lecturer in J. R. Clarke, whilst metallurgy was run by the painfully introverted professor C. H. Desch, a man so obsessed with his work that he courted his wife with drawings of the internal structure of various metals. And if neither of these was Deadwood, nor—must it be said—were they Livewire. Though Clarke did little research, he overcame horrific war wounds to become an immensely gifted teacher. Whilst Desch was an important man in the world of metallurgy—a much-published author and a Fellow of the Royal Society—he was so frightened of human contact that he hid from his own dinner guests.[65]

The important structural distinction amongst university staff was not the subjective one between Deadwood and Livewire. It was the manifest difference between professors and lecturers. The reality was that most Redbrick lecturers were disempowered, underpaid, and over-worked. They started relatively young—the average age for a first appointment was 27—and only very few could hope to rise to the lofty heights of a Chair.[66] It remained the case that women, in particular, stood almost no chance of progressing that far.[67] Yet it was the professors who ran the departments and the universities; lecturers had almost no say. What had been tolerable when the professoriate made up the bulk of the teaching staff came to seem like an unacceptable abuse when they were able to lord it over a large number of lecturers. Worse still, this imbalance in power was reflected in pay. Whilst the average annual salary for professors rose to £1,115 by 1939, assistant lecturers saw a minuscule increase, from £307 a year to £313.[68] Little wonder that many were forced to take second jobs, nor that their teaching suffered.[69] Required to teach too many students, too much, too often, lecturers could find the experience frustrating. Undergraduates, too, also complained.[70] 'It is strongly felt', students at Southampton

---

[63] For the complaints, see USA, 22/17/A944, F. C. Scott. For the excuses, USA 1/4/76/7/1, Development Committee Minutes 1930–36, W. R. Sherriffs (5 February 1931).

[64] Margherita Rendel, 'How Many Women Academics? 1912–76', in Rosemary Deem, ed., *Schooling for Women's Work* (London, 1980), pp. 142–61.

[65] Mathers, *Steel-City Scholars*, pp. 108–9, 117–18.

[66] WMRC, AUT, 27/A16.7, Laurie, 'Average age of appointments'.

[67] Dyhouse, *No Distinction of Sex?*, ch. 4.

[68] Perkin, *Key Profession*, p. 79.

[69] Shinn, *Paying the Piper*, p. 235.

[70] See also the complaints of John Allaway at Sheffield in Ronald Goldman, *Breakthrough: autobiographical accounts of the education of some educationally disadvantaged children* (London, 1968), pp. 1–18, pp. 15–16.

observed, 'that all the lecturing staff ought to be able to teach and that too many cannot teach; and all ought to be definitely interested in their subjects, and some appear to be interested in a minute proportion of their subjects.'[71] Yet despite these problems, and despite the uncertainties of an academic career, the profession nonetheless continued to grow. In 1919, there were 2,277 university teachers outside Oxbridge; in 1939, there were 3,819.[72] As this suggests, the job remained attractive to many, at least some of whom—as one Sheffield scholar put it—may even have found the teaching 'mentally and spiritually refreshing'.[73]

This focus on teaching is worth noting. Today, Truscot's assumption that research is the main duty of a university might seem axiomatic to many. Then, it certainly did not. Indeed, his contemporaries were far from convinced that this was the case.[74] Some went further still, arguing that universities were 'making a fetish of research',[75] whilst the Bishop of Ripon urged scientists 'to take a ten year's holiday' from it.[76] 'So many men and women', observed Dorwood's very eminent predecessor, the Liverpool philosopher Alexander Mair, 'are induced to spend one or two important years doing pedestrian work that could equally be performed by an intelligent mechanic or clerk after a few weeks preliminary training'.[77] This was certainly a view shared by some colonial critics. 'If you try to give the degree of PhD for a thesis on the marriage customs in Madras, it passes my comprehension', declared one Indian academic in 1931. 'I think it really is not doing any credit to any academic body to encourage that type of work in British Universities,—and I hope they will make a note of that.'[78] He was preaching to the converted. At Oxbridge, as one don divulged, 'It might almost be said that in certain circumstances a good college tutor has no business to waste his time in research.'[79] In many Redbrick institutions, too, little real research was done. The money granted by the government or other groups for specific research projects was undeniably helpful. Some publications were needed to secure tenure, others were required to obtain promotion; but the attitude expressed by a junior lecturer in *Martin Hanner* was almost certainly not uncommon. 'Perhaps next winter we had better do a little Research', he observes to his wife; 'It's a good parlour game for winter evenings, I believe.'[80] This was not Deadwood talking. Rather, it expressed a truth: that for most of the Redbricks, for most of the time, it was teaching that mattered because it was teaching that paid.

---

[71] USA, 1/4/76/29/2, Committee on the Decline in Student Numbers (1938).
[72] Perkin, *Key Profession*, p. 49.
[73] A. W. Chapman, *The Story of a Modern University: a history of the University of Sheffield* (Oxford, 1955), p. 299.
[74] M. H. Carré, Review in *Universities Review* 16:1 (November 1943), pp. 34–6.
[75] Lord Meston, in *Fourth Congress of the Universities of the Empire* (London, 1931), p. 110.
[76] Perkin, *Key Profession,* p. 60.
[77] Alexander Mair, 'Research', *University Bulletin* 1:2 (May 1922), pp. 21–3, p. 21.
[78] S. V. Puntambekar in *Fourth Congress of the Universities of the Empire*, p. 102.
[79] R. B. McCallum, 'The Tutorial System at Oxford', *Universities Quarterly* 2 (1947–8), pp. 26–30, p. 29.
[80] Freeman, *Martin Hanner*, p. 239.

For the difference between those institutions that did research and those that did not was clear. It was the same difference that distinguished those lecturers who had time for research from those who did not. It was money. The lifestyles and the career opportunities of Redbrick academics depended almost entirely on the wealth of the universities they served. The poorer they were, the more the tutors taught and the less they tended to be paid. Overwhelmingly dependent on income from the UGC and the money received from tuition fees, there was little space for luxuries like research time or a decent staff room. In richer and better-supported institutions the quality of life was superior and there was money set aside for research. This, more than anything else, reflected the importance of links between the universities and their regions. The contrast between poor impoverished Southampton and fortunate, expansive Birmingham makes this plain. At Southampton in the early 1920s, precisely no money was spent on research. Worse still, 'a small room was described as "Senior Common Room", but it was seldom used and indeed was so detested that one member of the staff treated it as a private study room'.[81] In Birmingham, by contrast, civic pride had funded a lectureship in Russian, a fellowship in mechanical engineering, research into oil refining, and much more besides. Such largesse was not wholly altruistic. It was the Birmingham Chamber of Commerce that recognized the need for Russian; the Cycle and Motor Manufacturers' Union that wanted work on engineering; and the Anglo-Persian Oil Company that paid for much of the research on petroleum.[82] But it did allow Birmingham to expand and to grow in prestige. The links between the university and its community were further exemplified in the welcome given to academics by the Union Club in the centre of the city.[83] The same was true in Liverpool, where the University Club provided a similarly 'excellent meeting ground for City and University'.[84]

Increasingly, however, these disparities of wealth and opportunity began to be eroded. The process was not sudden, nor was it ever complete.[85] But the creation of an increasingly national system of higher education had its effect on the staff as well as the students. The Association of University Teachers (AUT) played an important part in this, campaigning for national pay grades, for pensions, and for equal rights in university governance.[86] It was not an easy or an uncomplicated campaign. M. T. Smiley, a classics professor at Aberystwyth, had nightmares about it, recalling a dream in which 'He was fighting for his life in a stormy sea and struggled to a raft which he saw afar off. Having reached it, he was about to grasp it when he read on it a notice which ran "Reserved for Vice-Chancellors only".'[87] Nonetheless, the AUT

---

[81] USA, 1/2/5/42, Report by the Principal, 'Looking Back and Looking Forward' (1942), pp. 7 and 5.
[82] Diane Drummond, 'The Interwar Years', in Ives ed., *The First Campus University*, pp. 191–215, p. 198–9.
[83] Diane Drummond, 'The New University', in Ives ed., *The First Campus University*, pp. 131–57, p. 146.
[84] WMRC, AUT, 27/A16.7, Laurie, 'University Teacher', p. 15.
[85] The consequences of this are very ably brought out in Jeremy Black's forthcoming history of Exeter. I am enormously grateful to Professor Black for allowing me to read a draft copy.
[86] See Perkin, *Key Profession*.
[87] Perkin, *Key Profession*, section 3, p. 2.

was not alone in its campaign. The University Grants Committee had similarly identified pay and conditions as an important issue and in 1948 a national pay scheme was conceded.[88] Individual institutions also sought to integrate the non-professorial staff a little more. In 1948 at Birmingham, for example, this meant the vice-chancellor announcing a 'declared policy' of bringing lecturers into all levels of university government.[89] The universal desire to provide adequate recreational facilities for academics even influenced the famously anti-social vice-chancellor of Sheffield, Irvine Mason, to open a Staff Club. The man who refused to serve refreshments of any sort at receptions, now apparently wanted his colleagues to get together for a drink or two.[90] This was not, however, inexplicable behaviour, nor were these isolated events. In fact, this was part of a more general process, as the convergence of the universities changed the lifestyles of the staff, just as it was changing the lives of the students.

[88] Shinn, *Paying the Piper*, pp. 244–5.
[89] Eric Ives, 'Stress, Hope, and Frustration', in Ives ed., *First Civic University*, pp. 294–315, p. 297.
[90] Mathers, *Steel City Scholars*, p. 130.

Conclusion

'During the last twenty years', wrote the historian Denis Mack Smith in 1953, 'the older universities have both of them moved far towards Redbrick, a direction symbolised by unexciting and efficient laboratory architecture'.[1] It was true. Oxford and Cambridge, which had long sneered at the practical research done by the modern universities, increasingly came to see the value of such work—and the need for buildings in which to do it. So it was, for example, that Lanchester and Lodge, winners of the 1927 Leeds University competition, came to Oxford's science area in buildings of 1946, 1948, and 1949. As this suggests, far from seeing the period between 1914 and 1948 as one of failure and decline, it is possible to see it as one of quite remarkable success, as even the two ancient English universities came to imitate many of Redbrick's founding principles. Certainly, it is true to say that the national system of higher education which began to grow had its roots in Redbrick. It was the grant to the civic colleges which evolved into the UGC; it was the battle to obtain that grant that created the Committee of Vice-Chancellors and Principals; and it was the fight for lecturers' representation which necessitated the creation of the AUT. To switch metaphors: the civic universities were thus the crucible in which the structures of modern university life were forged.

Redbrick was even strong enough to survive two world wars. Both were potentially cataclysmic for the universities and colleges. The first saw their buildings taken over and used as hospitals, their students called up, and their studies, in many cases, almost completely halted.[2] The second had a less catastrophic effect, but was still significant.[3] Bristol and Liverpool were bombed. Other institutions became home to evacuated government departments and other universities. This could mean overcrowding—at Loughborough, for example, 1,600 were catered for each day by kitchens fit for 600.[4] But it did not mean collapse. Remarkably, indeed, the real struggle came after the wars, as student numbers rose to previously unimaginable levels. Bristol, like many others, had to erect temporary accommodation to provide rooms for twice as many undergraduates in 1918 as in 1914.[5] At Hull, in 1947, Professor Bynmor Jones complained, 'my department is now 3.3 times as

---

[1] Denis Mack Smith, 'The Changing University: a report on Cambridge today', *Encounter* 6:5 (1953), pp. 53–8, p. 54.
[2] *British Universities and the war: a record and its meaning* (London, 1917).
[3] *TES*, 15 February 1941, pp. 72–3; 22 February 1941, pp. 84–5; 1 March 1941, pp. 96–7. See also, UGC, *University Development 1935–47*, pp. 16–22.
[4] WMRC, NUS, MS280/139/7, I. M. Thomas (30 October 1942).
[5] *Yearbook of the Universities of the Empire* 1921, p. 27.

large as it was in 1939. This October I shall have to house nearly half my students in two huts, one of which has still to be furnished.'[6]

As this suggests, the peculiar image of Redbrick—with its temporary buildings contrasting so strikingly with neighbouring new, neo-classical façades—represented both failure and success. It expressed their need for more money and their recurrent reliance on improvisation and expedient. But it also showed that they were growing—and suggested that they would grow greater still. By 1947 Hull had joined those institutions in receipt of a UGC grant, and would, in 1954, become a university in its own right. It had done so by following a familiar route: the path that had already been laid-out by Manchester, Birmingham, Nottingham, and a dozen others in their turn. The importance of these modern universities was reflected in the controversy they aroused and the criticism to which they were subject. No longer simply seen as a second-rate version of Oxbridge, they were believed to have generated problems all of their own.

Unsurprisingly, perhaps, it was argued that many of these solutions could be solved by building. So they built. They built grand new buildings, designed to house impressive new institutions. They built fashionably, too; abandoning the now outmoded neo-Gothic architecture of the past in favour of a cool classicism, a striking stylistic shift. They also hoped to create a stronger, richer, more cohesive student culture with halls of residence, students' unions, and the like. Hiding the temporary, the expedient, and the old-fashioned behind the contemporary, the striking, and the imposing, the builders of the modern universities created some truly impressive edifices.

The criticism did not go away—indeed, it was to influence university development for years to come. But for all the worry and the anxious debate, there was no real crisis here. By the end of the 1940s, two things were clear: first that the national system of higher education would continue to expand; secondly, that it would expand along Redbrick lines. This did not mean that the civic universities ceased to change. Nor did it mean that the new universities of the 1950s and 1960s were nothing more than clones. But it does mean that Redbrick both survived and thrived. In 1951 the historian and Cambridge professor D. W. Brogan declared: 'Let the rulers of the civic universities of England (and Scotland) reflect that they, not Oxford or Cambridge (or Yale or Princeton) are the normal universities of the modern world.'[7]

---

[6] *Conference of the Universities of the Empire* (London, 1947), p. 29.
[7] D. W. Brogan, 'Redbrick Revisited: II', *Cambridge Journal* 5 (1951–2), pp. 199–210, p. 210.

PART V

1949–1973

Prologue

'The past ten years', wrote Kingsley Amis in 1960, 'have been the worst, falsest, most cynical, most apathetic, most commercialised, most Americanised, richest in cultural decline of any in Britain's history.' It was a problem that the novelist, Oxford graduate, and Swansea academic explicitly identified with the expansion of the nation's universities. 'Nobody who has not seen it in all its majesty—I speak as a university lecturer—can imagine the pit of ignorance and incapacity into which British education has sunk since the war.'[1] The fact of growth was indeed undeniable in this period and the pace was in fact beginning to quicken even as Amis produced his jeremiad. Whether this amounted to decline, however, was contentious. For many of those involved in this expansion, the growth of the universities enabled them to overcome precisely the sorts of problems that had been identified in the 1930s and 1940s. New institutions and improved facilities, they believed, would end the crisis in the universities, inspiring stronger scholarly communities and equipping students to be better citizen than before. But Amis' rant is worth noting nonetheless, because it reveals the persistent doubts many commentators had about the growth of higher education, doubts that would become more pronounced as the sector continued to grow. If this was a revolution in higher education—and few doubted at the time that it was just that—then it amounted to an ambiguous one, and it was certainly not without its critics.

Never was this clearer than in the experiment that took place in the Staffordshire Potteries after 1949. Now, at first sight, Staffordshire may seem an unlikely location for a new chapter in the history of Britain's universities.[2] True enough, as far back as 1814 Charles Kelsall had imagined his *Phantasm of an University* taking shape on 'in the county of Stafford'. It is true, too, that by the 1940s, the six towns of Longton, Fenton, Burslem, Tunstall, Hanley, and Stoke-upon-Trent had become the largest conurbation in the country without some sort of permanent university provision. But the area scarcely bore any resemblance to the 'healthy and cheerful spot' that Kelsall imagined, where 'the silver Trent' would 'mænder at the end of the University Grove'.[3] Rather, as the historian W. G. Hoskins observed in 1951, the area amounted to 'seven miles of concentrated ugliness and dirt'; indeed,

---

[1] Kingsley Amis, 'Lone Voices: views of the 'fifties', *Encounter* 15 (1960), pp. 6–11.
[2] 'The Keele Experiment', *Planning* 22:372 (18 October 1954), pp. 249–51, p. 249.
[3] Charles Kelsall, *Phantasm of an University* (London, 1814), p. 170.

he went on, it had become a place where the 'ugliness is so demonic that it is fascinating.'⁴

Despite these apparently unpropitious surroundings, however, the foundation of the University College of North Staffordshire in 1949 should be seen as a key moment in the evolution of Britain's higher education. It reflected, on the one hand, the outcome of many of the debates that had consumed academics and commentators in the two decades that preceded it. On the other hand, however, it marked a new beginning for British universities. In that sense, and however surprising it may now seem, the post-war history of higher education actually begins in the 'dirty, rough industrial country' round the little village of Keele in Staffordshire.⁵

The University College of North Staffordshire, which became the University of Keele in 1962, owed its existence to a pair of remarkable men and one noteworthy moment.⁶ The men were Thomas Horwood and A. D. Lindsay; the moment was the immediate post-war period, when the debate over the 'crisis in the university' was at its height, and optimism about reconstruction was in full spate.⁷ Horwood, who rejoiced in the Ruritanian title of vicar of Etruria, was a committed Christian Socialist and powerful local politician. His ally, the equally baroquely ennobled Lord Lindsay of Birker, Master of Balliol College Oxford, was a still more high-profile and no less high-minded figure. Indeed, he was almost a parody of the socially conscious academic.⁸ A university reformer and a passionate advocate of adult education, he had stood as the anti-appeasement candidate in the Oxford by-election of 1938 and led the commission to democratize German universities in 1946. His public service was rewarded by the Labour Government, which elevated him to the peerage. Together, they were a remarkable team, with Horwood whipping up local support, and Lindsay able to exert a more national influence.⁹ To a certain extent, what the master and the vicar sought to do was not new—in fact, it was highly traditional. Just like other university founders in the late-nineteenth century, both men sought to build on the Oxford Extension lectures that had been staged in the Potteries since the 1890s. But their vision—and particularly Lindsay's plan for the university—was also profoundly contemporary, the product of recent debates and events.

Lindsay's tendency to promise everything to everyone meant that his ambitions for North Staffordshire were not always self-evident. He was wont to describe himself as 'a conservative, a liberal, and a socialist', and his claims for Keele were

---

⁴ W. G. Hoskins, quoted in John R. Gold, *The Practice of Modernism: modern architects and urban transformation, 1954–1972* (London and New York, 2007), p. 177.

⁵ Cedric Price, quoted in Samantha Hardingham and Kester Rattenbury, eds, *Supercrit #1: Cedric Price, Potteries Thinkbelt* (Routledge, 2007), p. 117.

⁶ The best introduction to the history of Keele is J. M. Kolbert, *Keele: the first fifty years, 1950–2000* (Keele, 2000).

⁷ For the context to these debates, see Michael Shattock, *Making Policy in British Higher Education, 1945–2011* (Buckingham, 2012), pp. 9–18.

⁸ See John Betjeman, *Summoned By Bells* (London, 1960), p. 91.

⁹ Including a House of Lords debate: HL Deb 14 May 1947 vol. 147 cc. 696–742.

often equally all-encompassing, tending to change according to his audience.[10] To local listeners, he argued that the college would serve local needs. To other groups, he stressed the more general need for radical reform—an end to over-specialization, an expansion in student numbers, the development of wholly residential universities, and much more besides.[11] Sometimes, he sounded as though he was simply arguing for change for its own sake, claiming that he just wanted 'a University College on new lines, or at any rate not just a repetition of Southampton, Exeter, etc.'.[12] Sometimes, he sounded utterly utilitarian, simply stressing the need for more teachers and better-trained social workers.[13]

There was, however, a unifying thread to all this rhetoric.[14] In making his arguments, Lindsay drew on the critique of the universities that had been made throughout the 1930s and 1940s. Indeed, he echoed his old friend Walter Moberly in the *Crisis in the University*, which was also published in 1949.[15] In developing the curriculum for his college, Lindsay likewise drew on the work of Karl Mannheim and he quoted Ortega y Gasset—who had, of course, influenced Bruce Truscot's books—in his inaugural address to the first 159 students.[16] In 1946, the government's Barlow Report on Scientific Manpower had argued that a new university should be founded, 'which would give to the present generation the opportunity of leaving to posterity a monument of its culture'.[17] Despite the opposition of powerful groups like the Committee of Vice Chancellors and Principals (CVCP), and the concerns of the University Grants Committee (UGC), Keele was, from the first, intended to be just that.[18]

The 'Keele Experiment' came to encompass three key elements.[19] In the first place, Lindsay sought to create a proper university community. He attempted to avoid undue subject specialization by insisting that students study for four, rather than the more normal three years. The first of those years would be taken up with a common curriculum, which was intended to 'inculcate a sense of the unity of Knowledge'.[20] This Foundation Year, which, as the undergraduates put it, took them in great bounds 'From Plato to NATO', was followed by three years studying joint degrees, with each student required to take at least one science and one non-science subject. At the same time, in a bid to overcome the 'nine-to-five' university, Keele was to insist upon 'total residence': both students and staff

---

[10] Drusilla Scott, *A. D. Lindsay: a biography* (Oxford, 1971), p. xiv.
[11] W. B. Gallie, *A New University: A. D. Lindsay and the Keele experiment* (London, 1960), p. 60.
[12] A. D. Lindsay to Walter Moberly (1946), quoted in W. A. C. Stewart, *Higher Education in Postwar Britain* (Houndmills, 1989), p. 51.
[13] Scott, *Lindsay*, p. 317.
[14] KUA, Lindsay Papers, L226, H. E. Teale, 'Memorandum on the Aims of the Founders of the College' (1960).
[15] See Chapter 4.
[16] Gallie, *A New University*, p. 101; Scott, *Lindsay*, p. 315.
[17] *Scientific Manpower: Report of a Committee appointed by the Lord President of the Council* 1946 (cmd. 6824), p. 17.
[18] WMRC CVCP, MS 399/1/1/4, Minutes, 1942–48, 28 March 1947; UGC, *University Development from 1935–1947* (London, 1948), p. 42.
[19] See James Mountford, *Keele: an historical critique* (London, 1972), p. 9.
[20] Kolbert, *Keele*, p. 58.

would live on site.[21] In the second place, Lindsay wanted to break the monopoly held by the University of London on the oversight of new university colleges. This, he believed, had fettered 'the initiative and the experimenting of the smaller institutions'.[22] Instead, 'sponsorship' by Oxford, Cambridge, and Birmingham would allow greater flexibility. There was, as the UGC observed, also 'a third respect in which the establishment of the college [was] experimental. Never before [had] the founders of a university institution in this country been in a position to dispense with an endowment and put their plans into effect with the backing of the state.'[23]

Each of these aspects of the Keele Experiment were to be formative for the postwar development of higher education. The idea of creating a broader and better curriculum for students—of 'drawing a new map of knowledge'—was to dominate university development in the 1950s and 1960s.[24] The increasing provision of residential accommodation was also to become an obsession for academics and policy-makers alike.[25] Equally, the University of London was slowly, but surely, to lose its role as the nursemaid to future institutes of higher education. Although it was to remain profoundly influential, not least as the midwife to several colonial universities, London was essentially uninvolved in the wave of new foundations that swept across Britain from the late-1950s onwards.[26] Most importantly of all, the state's role in establishing Keele was to change the landscape of British universities forever. Of course, this was only one part of a wider trend, as universities looked ever more at national rather than local government for support. But it was significant in its own right, nonetheless. For the foundation of Keele established for the first time that the UGC could, would, and perhaps even should, take a proactive role in shaping the development of higher education and—more specifically—in the creation of new institutions. As events were to show, this was a revolutionary doctrine.[27] Indeed, it was probably Keele's most important contribution to Britain's new world of universities.

This had not been Lindsay's intention. He thought that the UGC was a 'wonderful institution', and fully expected the state to underwrite university expansion.[28] But he could not have expected—and would not have wanted—his work to help produce a more uniform national system of higher education. Yet it did just that. Nor could Lindsay have foreseen Keele's other significant influence on Britain's universities—and its most powerful effect on their architecture.

---

[21] Gallie, *New University*, p. 62.
[22] HL Deb 14 May 1947 vol. 147 cc. 701–2.
[23] UGC, *University Development 1947–1952* 1953 (cmnd. 8875), p. 10.
[24] Asa Briggs, 'Drawing a New Map of Learning', in David Daiches, ed., *The Idea of a New University: The Experiment in Sussex* (London, 1964), pp. 60–80.
[25] Harold Silver, '"Residence" and "Accommodation" in Higher Education: abandoning a tradition', *Journal of Education Administration and History* 36:2 (2004), pp. 123–33, p. 126.
[26] Bruce Pattison, *Special Relations: the University of London and new universities overseas, 1947–1970* (London, 1984).
[27] Though see also Michael Shattock, *The UGC and the Management of British Universities* (Buckingham, 1994), p. 3.
[28] HL Deb 14 May 1947 vol. 147 c. 709.

Fig. 35. 'A physical environment so mediocre that it belies the experiment of the university itself': Keele in the early 1960s

Reproduced with the permission of the archivist, University of Keele.

Keele's site initially comprised a semi-derelict Victorian mansion, more than 100 army huts, and 'a blasted heath of brambles, tree stumps, old tin huts and petrol cans'.[29] (Figure 35) Working in a period of post-war austerity, Lindsay and his fellow founders did what they could to ameliorate matters. The hall was restored; the huts made habitable, the grounds were cleared.[30] There was, however, neither the money nor the will to impose a coherent plan on future developments.[31] The appointment of a succession of ever-more impressive architects charged with drawing up development plans after the foundation—H. W. Marmorek in 1951, J. A. Pickavance in 1954, Sir Howard Robertson in 1956, Peter Shepheard in 1962—did little to improve matters.[32] The result, claimed Tony Birks in 1972, was 'a physical environment so mediocre that it belies the experiment of the

---

[29] Kolbert, *Keele*, p. 35.
[30] Stanley Beaver, 'The Keele Campus and its Environment', in Christopher Harrison, ed., *Essays on the History of Keele* (Keele, 1986), pp. 155–68.
[31] See the report by Sir Howard Robertson, KUA, Senate Minutes 1955–57, pp. 99 (14 March 1956) and 146–9 (30 April 1956); and the landscape report by S. M. Haywood, in KUA, Senate Minutes 1955–57, pp. 245–52 (December 1956).
[32] KUA, Senate Minutes 1950–51, 16 May 1951; Senate Minutes 1955–57, p. 83 (15 February 1956); Senate Minutes 1961–62, 16 May 1962. Marmorek and Pickavance were the Stoke borough architects.

university itself'.³³ Nor was this view confined to outsiders: even the university's own architects acknowledged that they had been responsible for 'haphazard ribbon development',³⁴ whilst the students bemoaned the 'scrappy, formless agglomeration of ill-conceived boxes' that they found on the campus.³⁵ Such was the universal acceptance of Keele's architectural failure that other institutions were determined not to replicate its mistakes.³⁶

For good—and, for that matter, for ill—Keele consequently deserves far more attention than it has previously been paid. It was at one and the same time the culmination of half a century's efforts at university extension, the embodiment of a generation's debates about higher education, and a sign of things to come. For within a few years of its foundation, Keele was no longer the only truly new university. Sussex was chartered in 1961; York and the University of East Anglia (UEA) in 1963; Lancaster in 1964; and Essex, Kent, and Warwick in 1965. In the following years, a stream of technological universities was established—from Bath to Bradford and from Salford to Surrey. Each of these institutions, even when they denied it, shared a family resemblance with Keele.³⁷ Many similarly experimented with widening the curriculum. Most sought to secure residential accommodation for the majority of their students. All were utterly dependent on the state for their establishment. Like Keele, too, these new universities were often founded on country estates some distance from any large town. Yet unlike Keele, they took architecture seriously from the start: commissioning development plans, publishing reports, hiring distinguished architects, and publicly discussing their design.³⁸ 'The life of a Vice Chancellor', claimed Fred Dainton of Nottingham, 'is largely made up of bricks, mortar and money.'³⁹ Malcolm Bradbury diagnosed the condition in *The History Man*, his depiction of a thinly disguised UEA.⁴⁰ It was 'building mania ... an Edifice Complex'.⁴¹ No visitor to Keele, with its Nissen huts and its utility architecture, could ever say that Lindsay had suffered from that.

The forces that helped create Keele similarly reshaped the older universities and colleges in this period. They grew in number, with Southampton, Hull, Exeter, and Leicester progressing to university status in the years between 1954 and 1957. They also grew in size and wealth. Indeed, it was the old civic universities that expanded most. Leeds grew from just over 3,000 to just under 10,000 students between 1949 and 1973.⁴² Manchester went from around 5,000 to almost 15,000

---

³³ Tony Birks, *Building the New Universities* (Newton Abbot, 1972), p. 10. See also *Times Educational Supplement*, 22 April 1955.
³⁴ J. A. Pickavance, 'University of Keele: architecture', in *University of Keele, chapel guide* (n.p., 1965), pp. 7–8, p. 8.
³⁵ Bernard Martin, 'Where else?', *Cygnet*, 27 November 1970, p. 8.
³⁶ Mountford, *Keele*, p. 225.
³⁷ See John Pratt and Tyrell Burgess, *Polytechnics: a report* (London, 1974); Peter Venables, *Higher Education Developments: the technological universities, 1956–76* (London and Boston, 1978).
³⁸ *TES*, 9 December 1966, p. 1416.
³⁹ *Gongster*, 20 November 1964, p. 1.
⁴⁰ *THES*, 14 November 1975, p. 7.
⁴¹ Malcolm Bradbury, *The History Man* (1975; London, 2000), p. 50.
⁴² P. H. J. H. Gosden, 'The Student Body', in P. H. J. H. Goseden and A. J. Taylor, eds, *Studies in the History of a University, 1874–1974* (Leeds, 1975), pp. 43–82, p. 48.

at the same time.[43] All this necessitated massive building, what the Germans at the same time called a 'Hochshulbau-Boom'.[44] Manchester, indeed, became known as 'an empire on which the concrete never set', whilst Leeds found itself with a megastructure that was believed to possess the longest corridor in Europe.[45] Not a single university escaped—or wanted to escape—the trend. Bradbury, again, analysed the phenomenon well in his *Eating People is Wrong*, begun when he was still a student at Leicester. 'Vice chancellors,' he wrote, 'all share in common a Platonic ideal for a university. For one thing it should be *big*. . . . There should be big sports grounds, a science building designed by Basil Spence, and more and more students coming every year.'[46]

What made all this expansion possible was ever-increasing state support. In 1946 just over half of the income received by the Redbrick universities came from the UGC.[47] By 1961, that figure had risen above 70 per cent. Indeed, including tuition fees, which were overwhelmingly paid by the government, and research funding, the majority of which was also granted by the state, by the end of this period more than 90 per cent of the universities' income came from the Treasury.[48]

This growth in numbers and in state funding helped to confirm the trends which had emerged before the Second World War, producing what one well-placed commentator described as 'a new formal coherence' to higher education in Britain.[49] Indeed, as David Edgerton has argued, it was in this period that the universities were finally fully 'nationalized'.[50] This did not make them all equal or identical. As the Secretary to the UGC observed, to look at the Grants List even in 1965 was to encounter a document which bore some resemblance to a description of the Holy Roman Empire—'for Oxford was no more like Bradford than Bavaria was like Hesse-Darmstadt'.[51] But it did mean that they were now part of a truly national system, responsible more and more to the central state. Each, however, was determined to stand out—and all used their buildings to do just that. The result was, as the *Architectural Review* hyperbolically explained, 'a great new university building movement . . . somewhat similar to, and perhaps as exciting as, the cathedral movement of the twelfth century'.[52] And, certainly, as even their critics admitted, the results were large and grand, 'monumental'

---

[43] Brian Pullan and Michele Abendstern, *A History of the University of Manchester, 1951–73* (Manchester, 2000), p. 265.
[44] Stephanie Endlich, *Hochschulbau im Spannungsfeld zwischen Bildingsplannung und Bauproduktion: exemplarische Untersuuchung zur Enstehung eines bautyps* (Dresden, 1980), p. 9.
[45] Pullan and Abendstern, *University of Manchester*, p. 106; William Whyte, 'The Modernist Moment at the University of Leeds, 1957–1977', *Historical Journal* 51 (2008), pp. 169–93.
[46] Malcolm Bradbury, *Eating People is Wrong* (London, 1959), p. 170.
[47] UGC, *University Development from 1935 to 1946* (London, 1948), p. 79.
[48] UGC, *University Development 1957–1962* 1964 (cmnd. 2267), p. 45.
[49] John Carswell, *Government and the Universities in Britain: programme and performance, 1960–1980* (Cambridge, 1985), p. 55.
[50] David Edgerton, *Warfare State: Britain, 1920–1970* (Cambridge, 2006), p. 106.
[51] Carswell, *Government and the Universities*, p. 55.
[52] *Architectural Review* 136 (1964), p. 9.

and 'cathedral-like'.⁵³ Paradoxically, however, this architectural elaboration only served to deepen the universities' dependence on government support. Put plainly, they could not afford to build statements of their individuality without all relying on the same single source of funding: the state.⁵⁴ In that sense, the buildings and plans of the period were both the product and the precondition for radical change within higher education.

---

⁵³ Ian Brown, 'The Irrelevance of University Architecture', *Higher Education Review* 2:1 (1969), pp. 31–55, p. 38. See also, Richard P. Dober, *The New Campus in Britain: ideas of consequence for the United States* (New York, 1965).

⁵⁴ Carswell, *Government and the Universities*, p. 93.

9

The Expansion of Redbrick

'The state and the universities' John Carswell once observed,

> are like a discontented couple who cannot live without each other: he rich, busy, self-important, preoccupied with the office; she proud, independent and in her own opinion beautiful. The state-husband will always complain about her extravagance and inconsistency, and the university-wife will endlessly denounce his stinginess, jealousy and philistinism.... But they would not dream of parting: because of the children.[1]

As a former Treasury civil servant and secretary to both the University Grants Committee (UGC) and the British Academy, Carswell was well placed to comment. Indeed, his history of the relationship between higher education and the government is—remarkably enough—one of the most interesting books on universities in this period. Nonetheless, his vivid metaphor is potentially misleading. However true his characterization was when he wrote it in 1985, things had not always been so. Like a great many unhappy marriages, the relationship between the university and the state had begun with great hopes and no little affection on either side, and only gradually deteriorated. In the 1940s, after all, the Committee of Vice Chancellors and Principals (CVCP) had asked for more government involvement in the universities, not less.[2]

Moreover, there were always at least three people in this marriage: the state, the universities, and the University Grants Committee.[3] The UGC was, of course, a part of government, and—from 1946—it was charged with coordinating higher education. But it conceived its role as being 'a channel of communication between the state and the universities', rather than an instrument of direct control.[4] This did not mean that it was opposed to intervention or entirely *laissez faire*. Indeed, it stressed the fact that the 'unprecedented' increase in government spending after the war meant that 'the universities were called upon to accept guidance from the centre to an extent which was also unprecedented'.[5] Nevertheless, the principle of 'academic freedom'—which essentially translated as institutional autonomy—remained paramount in its thinking. The UGC even resisted attempts by the Auditor General and the Public Accounts Committee to view its records, or

---

[1] John Carswell, *Government and the Universities in Britain: programme and performance, 1960–1980* (Cambridge, 1985), p. 168.
[2] Eric Ashby, *Hands Off the Universities* (London, 1968), p. 7.
[3] For a rather different characterization, see Michael Shattock, *Making Policy in British Higher Education, 1945–2011* (Buckingham, 2012).
[4] UGC, *University Development from 1935 to 1946* (London, 1948), p. 8.
[5] UGC, *University Development 1952–57* (1958), cmnd 534, p. 8.

those of the universities, on the grounds that it 'would raise a real danger of interference with academic freedom'.[6] It was not until the late-1960s that the Committee publicly accepted it had any role in 'making positive judgements' rather than merely advising,[7] and even then it continued to conceive itself as much as an advocate for the universities as their paymaster.[8] In this institutional *ménage à trois* it was sometimes hard to see who was the dominant partner.[9]

This period, then, was one in which the relationship between the universities and the state was transformed—but it was transformed in ways that were ambiguous even at the time. In some respects, in fact, it all looked like business as usual. The basic pattern of practice remained unchanged from before the Second World War—even the quinquennial visitations and reports carried on, although as the number of institutions rose so the process of inspecting them became ever more arduous. The UGC continued to offer two forms of funding to universities: recurrent and non-recurrent grants.[10] The bulk of university finance came from the recurrent grants which covered basic operating costs. In 1966–7, at the very peak of university expansion, they amounted to some £139 million—or three-quarters of the universities' total annual income. The non-recurrent grants, by contrast, were for special, one-off payments. In most cases, this meant money for buildings, or sites, or furnishings and fittings. In 1966–7, £77 million was granted for this sort of spending.[11] Recurrent grants were calculated every five years and given as a block grant, not specifying exactly how the money should be spent; non-recurrent grants were offered annually and were highly specific. This created a familiar rhythm to university life and university planning. More than this, as Lord Wolfenden, head of the Committee from 1963 to 1968 observed, it ensured that the UGC operated 'as a septic tank, through which filthy Treasury money passed and emerged as a crystal-clear liquid which even a professor might drink without risk'.[12]

From the late-1950s onwards, however, this apparent continuity concealed genuine change. Pressure to expand and growing public attention forced the universities, the state, and the UGC to alter their relationship. As expenditure grew, so the position of the UGC within the Treasury came to seem more and more anomalous. It turned the Treasury into a spending department, and left the universities isolated from other parts of the education system.[13] In 1964, therefore, the Committee was placed under the control of the newly formed Ministry of

---

[6] UGC, *University Development 1957–1962* 1964 (cmnd. 2267).p. 122.
[7] UGC, *University Development 1962–1967* (1968), cmnd 3820, p. 179. The key moment came with the 'Memorandum of General Guidance' issued in November 1967. See Shattock, *Making Policy*, ch. 5.
[8] UGC, *University Development 1967–1972* (1973), cmnd 5728, p. 51.
[9] See also Michael Shattock, *The UGC and the management of British Universities* (Buckingham, 1994).
[10] The best introduction to the operation of the UGC in this period remains Anthony Kerr, *The Universities of Europe* (London, 1962), pp. 205–25.
[11] UGC, *University Development 1962–1967*, pp. 36, 39, 44.
[12] Lord Wolfenden, *Turning Points* (London, 1976), p. 151.
[13] Noel Annan, 'The Universities', *Encounter* 20:4 (April 1963), pp. 3–14, p. 4.

Education.[14] Not only did this mean the universities' funding body was now run by a department with increasingly firm views about the need to systematize education and make it serve socially responsible ends.[15] It also meant that from 1965 until 1967 they became the responsibility of the irascible but brilliant Tony Crosland, the first minister ever willing to say to the vice-chancellors 'they can stuff themselves'. He was, he said, 'not frightfully interested in the universities'. He was not much more interested in the UGC, which was not consulted over his decision, in April 1965, to create a whole new class of higher education providers—the Polytechnics; nor was it given prior warning about his highly controversial plan to raise the tuition fees for overseas' students in 1967.[16] Yet, as student numbers grew, universities became more important as a political issue. Greater attention was paid to them in parliament and in the press, and in 1967 the UGC's accounts, together with those of the institutions that it funded, were finally opened to the Auditor General.[17] Here was tangible proof that higher education could no longer hide behind the authority and discretion of the Treasury.

Wider changes—both political and social—also affected the relationship between the universities and their main source of funding. The first breach in the system came in 1961, when it became clear that in response to government pressure the universities had over-recruited. The UGC decided, as it euphemistically put it, to 're-open the settlement', and increase the recurrent grants.[18] It seems like a small change, but it set an important precedent. If quinquennial grants could be 'reopened', then they were no longer really quinquennial. Subsequent events were to bear this out. Government cuts, pay pauses, inflation, devaluation, new taxes, and a determination to increase numbers: all of these led to an incessant tinkering with the UGC's grants.[19] By 1968, the Committee was writing to revise its plans almost monthly.[20] This made it very hard to plan—and the economic crisis of the 1970s soon made it impossible.[21]

To make matters worse, these significant alterations in the link between the universities and the state coincided with a new and more turbulent relationship between the universities and their students. Given the closeness of the connection between the government and the universities, it was not unreasonable for radicals to think that an attack on the latter was in fact a way of subverting the former.[22] More specifically, the Ministry of Education's unilateral and entirely unexpected decision

---

[14] The move from the Treasury having happened at the end of 1963: see UGC, *University Development 1962–1967*, pp. 1–2.
[15] See, Carswell, *Government and the Universities*, pp. 53–4.
[16] Susan Crosland, *Tony Crosland* (London, 1982), p. 147.
[17] UGC, *University Development 1967–1972*, p. 51.
[18] UGC, *University Development: Interim report of the UGC for the years 1957 to 1961* (1962), cmnd 1691, p. 14.
[19] UGC, *University Development 1967–1972*, pp. 12–13.
[20] EssUA, Development Committee 1967–70, 29 January, 11 March, 6 May, 17 June, 16 September 1968.
[21] Carswell, *Government and the Universities*, p. 145; Shattock, *Making Policy*, pp. 122–3. See also, Michael Cassidy, 'Pressure on University Building', *Official Architecture* 30 (1967), pp. 503–11.
[22] Alexander Cockburn 'Introduction', to Alexander Cockburn and Robin Blackburn, eds, *Student Power: problems, diagnosis, action* (Harmondsworth, 1969), pp. 7–21, p. 14.

to raise overseas student fees sparked protests which were often directed less at the government than at the universities themselves.[23] And the UGC did not escape this turn against authority. The quinquennial visitations thus became at one and the same time both increasingly pointless and evermore unpleasant. In November 1973, indeed, the Committee found themselves locked in a room by protesting Southampton students. It was only after the vice-chancellor squeezed through the window and ran off to fetch the police that they were freed.[24]

The UGC, on this occasion at least, could escape the students and the universities. The universities and the students, however, could not escape the UGC. In reality, although the relationship was imperfect—and subject to continual modification—it was now also the single most important influence in university development. Without money from the state, the existing universities could not have expanded, and no new universities would have been founded at all.

This did not mean that universities abandoned attempts to search out benefactors, nor that they ceased to receive financial support from local authorities. Between 1952 and 1962, nearly £37 million was raised nationwide through appeals and fund-raising campaigns. Still more was granted by councils in annual subsidy.[25] University officials could be comically particular in their search for support. In 1961, for example, the registrar of Exeter was reduced to writing begging letters in the hope of acquiring an organ for the university. 'There must, somewhere, be a rich man or a rich institution—a trust fund or a foundation—which is particularly interested in such matters as this, and would help by providing, if not the whole cost, at least a substantial part of it', he wrote to the conductor Malcolm Sargent. 'Unfortunately, we do not know of such a person or body, either in this country or America. If you do, and could put me in touch with him (or it) the University would be more than grateful.'[26] Local authorities could be similarly precise with their donations—as at Keele, where Stoke-on-Trent Council gave not just money, but also a billiard table.[27] These gifts and grants, however, only ever amounted to a tiny fraction of the universities' income. To build big, and still bigger, and yet bigger again, higher education needed help from central government.

All this begs the obvious question of why the government was so consistently keen to provide ever more financial support—especially as both political parties proved to be equally enthusiastic about investing in the universities. In part, it was the product of a consensus on the civilizing effects of education: 'the transmission of a common culture and common standards of citizenship'.[28] In part, too, as David Edgerton has argued, this reflected a shared sense of the universities' practical importance. To be sure, he somewhat overstates his case, claiming that 'the warfare

---

[23] Colin Crouch, *The Student Revolt* (London, 1970), pp. 99–21.
[24] Lord Dainton, *Doubts and Certainties: a personal memoir of the twentieth century* (Sheffield, 2001), p. 296.
[25] UGC, *University Development, 1957–1962*, pp. 45, 54.
[26] EUA, UA/26/1c, Great Hall 1961–65, Roderick Ross to Malcolm Sargent (18 October 1961).
[27] KUA, Senate Minutes 1950–51, 24 January 1951.
[28] *Higher Education: report of the committee appointed by the Prime Minister under the chairmanship of Lord Robbins* (1963), cmnd 2154, vol. i., p. 7.

state, not the welfare state, had a decisive influence on the... post-war development of the British university'.[29] In reality, as Edgerton goes on to admit, British universities had very little to do with military research.[30] But the sense that they were increasingly seen as serving a strategic purpose is worth noting.

More important even than this, however, was the continuing—indeed, the revitalized—belief that the universities had a vital role to play in the country's economy, especially in training a workforce able to compete with Britain's commercial rivals. Just as in the 1870s, therefore, anxieties about national decline prompted a focus on university development. Commissions in the 1940s argued first for an increase of 20,000, then of 50,000 graduates—especially scientists.[31] By 1960, the cry had become even more shrill and was no longer addressed only at the demands of science: 'the nation urgently needs the greatest possible number of highly educated men and women', declared the businessman Sir Colin Anderson, a director of P&O and the Midland Bank.[32] The publication of books like John Vaizey's *Economics of Education* (1962), which appeared to provide evidence that highly-educated workforces were more productive, only confirmed an existing attitude.[33]

At the same time, too, the government was also responding to pressure from the electorate. Two great forces came to dominate debate on higher education from the 1950s onwards: the 'bulge' and the 'trend'. The bulge was the post-war baby boom; the trend was the increasing propensity of pupils to stay on at school and thus achieve the qualifications necessary for university entry.[34] The product of the two was tens of thousands more potential undergraduates—what the French were conterminously to call '*l'explosion scolaire*'.[35] The state had to do something about it.

But this was not just a debate between the government and forces outside the universities—be they military, economic, cultural, or simply middle-class parents determined that their child would obtain the competitive advantages of a higher education. The universities themselves exerted considerable pressure on the state. To a certain extent, this was merely because they were after money, and were not altogether concerned about where it came from. The inescapable reality was that central government had more cash than local government, and considerably more than any benefactor. More importantly, it is clear that the leaders of the universities were also convinced that a move towards even greater state funding represented a form of liberation. For one thing, they had faith in the University Grants Committee and its willingness to confront the government, to act as 'a watchdog trained to bark at what were once its masters'.[36] Equally importantly, reliance on Whitehall freed them from dependence on the local town hall. Experience showed that city

---

[29] David Edgerton, *Warfare State: Britain, 1920–1970* (Cambridge, 2006), p. 148.
[30] Edgerton, *Warfare State*, p. 160.
[31] *Scientific Manpower: Report of a Committee appointed by the Lord President of the Council* 1946 (cmd. 6824). p. 15; *Universities and the Increase in Scientific Manpower* (London, 1947), p. 11.
[32] *Grants to Students* (1960), cmnd 1051, p. 3.
[33] John Vaizey, *The Economics of Education* (London, 1962).
[34] UGC, *University Development 1957–62*, p. 65.
[35] [Robbins], *Higher Education*, vol. i., p. 45.
[36] Noel Annan, 'Higher Education', in Bernard Crick, ed., *Essays on Reform* (London, 1967), pp. 24–43, p. 33.

councillors were often less sympathetic to the universities than university-educated civil servants and cabinet ministers. Indeed, the cosiness of the relationship between the vice chancellors and members of both government and the UGC is remarkable. When, in 1962, the Committee of Vice Chancellors and Principals went to lobby Henry Brooke, the chief secretary to the Treasury, they were greeted as old friends because that was precisely what they were: 'One of the Vice Chancellors present was my tutor at Oxford', he observed. 'Another Vice Chancellor present was the most dangerous hockey-player I ever associated with.'[37] Likewise, when the CVCP met in London, the chairman of the UGC always ensured that he dined at the Athenaeum that evening, 'just to see the chaps'.[38] Nor was it only the administrators who cultivated these connections. When seeking a new Chancellor, the academics at Reading were determined to ensure that 'in the event of a real crisis in the University's affairs he should be able to lift his telephone and speak to the Chancellor of the Exchequer, whatever Party was in power, on Christian-name terms'.[39] By electing Lord Bridges, a former cabinet secretary, they ensured that this would indeed be so.

Small wonder that Selwyn Lloyd as Chancellor of the Exchequer had a list of all the universities' Chancellors drawn up: he risked unwittingly encountering them over dinner, in a club, in parliament or in the Treasury itself. Little wonder, too, that universities continued to put up with the growing weaknesses in the system and the increasing *dirigisme* of the UGC. The vice-chancellors were a deeply impressive lot—'what Admirals had been before the war of 1914', according to the Treasury mandarin Otto Clarke.[40] They were powerful men, confident that they could work the system and fend off any unwanted demands made by the state. So long as the universities were still able to control whom they employed and what they taught, argued Sir Hector Hetherington of Exeter, Liverpool, and then Glasgow, 'we need not be feverishly anxious about anything else'.[41] As a result the universities came to treat the UGC as a benevolent benefactor, relying on it for advice as well as money. 'They want', explained Noel Annan, 'to know what the UGC's policy is on any particular subject, and are vexed if told that the UGC does not consider that it should have a policy.'[42]

Through the CVCP, the universities also came to adopt a much more self-consciously national profile, seeking to speak as one group, and—to some extent, at least—surrendering individual university autonomy 'in the interests of a corporate autonomy of them all'.[43] In that way, the government, the UGC, and the universities themselves sought to formalize the national system that had begun to

---

[37] CVCP, *Report of a Deputation Received by the Chief Secretary to the Treasury, 26 January 1962* (1962), p. 7.
[38] Keith Murray, quoted in Shattock, *Making Policy in Higher Education*, p. 16.
[39] Wolfenden, *Turning Points*, p. 126.
[40] Wolfenden, *Turning Points*, pp. 37, 34.
[41] Hector Hetherington, *The British University System, 1914–1954* (Edinburgh and London, 1955), p. 13.
[42] Annan, 'Higher Education', p. 33.
[43] UGC, *University Development 1962–67*, pp. 191–2.

emerge in the interwar period. This was also something that was experienced by students, who, from 1963 onwards, applied to a central clearing-house for places instead of writing to individual universities.[44]

This system building was embodied in the Robbins Report, published in 1963. Now, it must be said that rather too much has been made of its originality and its importance for shaping the future.[45] In fact, Robbins did little more than reinforce existing assumptions. It is noteworthy, for example, that the decision to expand the university sector had already been made.[46] That the report was almost immediately accepted *in toto* by both government and opposition similarly suggests that Robbins was not a break with the past, much less a herald of controversial change in the future. But the central significance of the Report was the fact that this was first time that higher education had been considered as a whole. It was, in that sense, as important for what it represented as for what it actually achieved. Its many volumes and its invaluable data—the first genuinely national collection of quantified information on higher education—are a monument to what the strange marriage of the universities and the state achieved in the years between 1949 and 1973.

THE WRITING ON THE REDBRICK WALL

Robbins revealed just how big and how complex this newly nationalized system had become. On average, student numbers rose by 10 per cent every year, with a sudden speeding up in the 1960s.[47] Nor was it just the universities that expanded. All further and higher education establishments grew in number and in size. By 1967 there were about 200,000 university students and another 179,000 at a bewildering range of different institutions.[48] Put another way, of the 407,000 members of the National Union of Students in 1969, only 42 per cent were at university.[49] The alternatives to university were several: teacher training colleges, of which there grew to be around 150; technical colleges and art schools, of which there were about 600; and other, more specific and idiosyncratic institutions, like the Rycotewood College for Rural Crafts or the Waterperry Horticultural School for Women in Oxfordshire.[50] In 1956 ten CATs, or Colleges of Advanced Technology, were founded, created out of the larger and more successful technical

---

[44] Ronald Kay, *UCCA: its origins and development, 1950–85* (Cheltenham, 1985).
[45] For a good analysis, see the special edition of the *Oxford Review of Education* 14:1 (1988).
[46] Shattock, *Making Policy*, p. 43.
[47] Richard Layard, John King, and Claus Moser, *The Impact of Robbins* (Harmondsworth, 1969), p. 13.
[48] Carswell, *Government and the Universities*, pp. 169–71; A. H. Halsey, 'Further and Higher Education', in A. H. Halsey and Josephine Webb, eds, *Twentieth Century British Social Trends* (Basingstoke, 2000), pp. 221–53, pp. 225, 231.
[49] Eric Ashby and Mary Anderson, *The Rise of the Student Estate in Britain* (London, 1970), p. 91.
[50] Sir Peter Venables, 'Technical Education in Great Britain: second thoughts on the Robbins Report', *International Review of Education* 11:2 (June 1965), pp. 151–64; William Whyte, 'Twentieth-Century Education', in Kate Tiller, ed., *A Historical Atlas of Oxfordshire* (Oxford, 2011), pp. 71–2.

colleges.[51] Ten years later they became technological universities.[52] The proposals to create an even more unlikely acronym—SISTERs, or Special Institutions for Scientific and Technological Education and Research—came to nothing. Nonetheless, the decision, in 1965, to establish more than two-dozen Polytechnics (known as Central Institutions in Scotland), helped to diversify the ecology of higher education still further.[53] The polytechnics were funded by local government and the universities, of course, got their money from the UGC.[54] But these distinctions were to become increasingly less important—and, indeed, as we will see in the next section, the polytechnics came ever more to resemble the universities.

This system of higher education offered untold opportunities to the young people of post-war Britain. True enough, going to university—or an equivalent institution—remained a possibility for only a small elite. As late as 1970, less than 14 per cent of 18 to 19 year-olds made it into higher education. This, however, represented a huge increase on the 3 per cent which experienced some form of tertiary education before the war, and was an appreciable rise on the 6 per cent of the early 1950s.[55]

Money became less and less of a problem too. In 1951 80 per cent of Redbrick students received some sort of financial assistance—nearly double the number before the war.[56] Ten years later, in 1961, all but 8 per cent of students at the civic universities had a grant.[57] Official documents, like the Anderson Report on *Grants to Students* in 1960 and the Robbins Report in 1963 both affirmed the principle that any person qualified to attend university had the right to do so—and to receive the money that would make this possible. The result was a now unimaginably generous regime of state-sponsored higher education. Even radicals of the late-1960s were forced to admit that 'university students in this country have things a lot easier, academically and materially, than students in the US, France, almost any other country in fact'. It was this, they complained, that made it so hard to generate a genuinely revolutionary situation within the universities.[58]

The combination of an ever-growing network of institutions and an apparently ever-more generous system of funding meant that, for the first time as well, the universities outside Oxbridge and London were able to attract a really national constituency of students. Of course, some places had always been reliant on luring people from far afield—indeed, colleges in smaller towns and cities only survived because of their appeal to people from out of town. But even they were often more regional than genuinely national in their focus, whilst the larger Redbrick institutions had always been truly civic, recruiting chiefly from their local communities.

---

[51] Tyrell Burgess and John Pratt, *Policy and Practice: the colleges of advanced technology* (London, 1970).
[52] Venables, *Higher Education Developments*.
[53] Eric Robinson, *The New Polytechnics: the people's universities* (Harmondsworth, 1968), pp. 243–5.
[54] John Pratt and Tyrrell Burgess, *Polytechnics: a report* (London, 1974), p. 4.
[55] Halsey, 'Further and Higher Education', pp. 226, 230.
[56] UGC, *University Development 1947–52*, p. 23.
[57] UGC, *University Development 1957–62*, p. 29.
[58] Bill Hooper, 'The Free University of Liverpool', *Sphinx*, Autumn 1968, pp. 10–12, p. 10.

Signs of change began to be noticed in 1953, when the UGC observed that fewer than half of students now came from within thirty miles of the civic universities.[59] Ten years later, the statistics were stark: at Leicester 97 per cent of students came from more than 30 miles away; at Liverpool, fewer than one in ten came from within the city.[60] At Leeds, too, the trend was undeniable, with two-thirds of students coming from within a thirty mile radius in 1938 and two-thirds coming from outside it twenty years later.[61] The new universities were completely reliant on students' ability and willingness to travel. Keele, after all, was founded in a village of only a few dozen houses. Essex, Sussex, Lancaster, Kent, and the others, were all established on green-field sites outside relatively small towns. From the first, as the UGC put it, each one was intended to be 'a national rather than a regional or local institution'.[62]

But if there were more students, with more choice, and more money, travelling further to study than ever before, this did not necessarily mean that they escaped the sorts of anxieties experienced by those who went before them. Although the 1950s and 1960s are now viewed as a halcyon era for undergraduates, this was not exactly how it was seen at the time. Choice brought with it dilemmas. Opportunity brought with it some measure of accountability. Ferdynand Zweig's survey *The Student in the Age of Anxiety* (1963) is deeply flawed in many respects, but nevertheless does capture a sense of young people who were 'taking their studies very seriously, with a sense of responsibility and a sense of duty'. Indeed, he worried that there was little *joie de vivre* in Redbrick.[63] This was to go too far—the dancing and Rag weeks and drinking and talking that traditionally characterized student life had not gone away. There were still lazy or disengaged students, and many who had ended up at university by default, with no real sense of commitment to academic study. There were also many who had a whale of a time.[64] Indeed, if anything, the undergraduate pranks of the period outdid anything that had gone before, with Stonehenge frequently filled with fetishes and the British army actually mobilized in 1967 to fight off a student-created and entirely fantastic alien invasion.[65] Yet, for most, the hours in laboratories and lecture rooms remained long; and, although some of the financial worries had dissipated, improving results and the pressure to compete led some academics to worry that the modern university was becoming 'less fun and more fuss'.[66] This was also almost certainly an exaggeration—after all, surveys showed that some students only attended a couple of classes every week.[67] But the need to pass tests and prove oneself on paper was ever-present. Certainly, students at Manchester described their

---

[59] UGC, *University Development 1947–52*, p. 24.
[60] Brian Burch, *The University of Leicester: a history, 1921–96* (Leicester, 1996), p. 37; Thomas Kelly, *For Advancement of Learning: the University of Liverpool, 1881–1981* (Liverpool, 1981), p. 330.
[61] *University of Leeds Development Plan* (Leeds, 1960), p. 9.
[62] UGC, *University Development 1957–1962*, p. 93.
[63] Ferdynand Zweig, *The Student in the Age of Anxiety* (London, 1963), pp. xiii–iv.
[64] Carol Dyhouse, *Students: a gendered history* (London and New York, 2006), ch. 10.
[65] *Guardian*, 11 August 2008; *Daily Telegraph*, 3 March 2011.
[66] Hetherington, *British University System*, p. 10.
[67] P. H. Mann and G. Mills, 'Living and Learning at Redbrick: a sample survey at Sheffield University', *Universities Quarterly* 16 (1961–62), pp. 19–35, p. 21.

experience as 'death by a thousand exams'.[68] Some could not cope—and there was a drop-out rate of 14 per cent by the end of the 1960s.[69] This was low by continental standards, and in comparison to some technical colleges, where 40 per cent of students left without a qualification, yet it was considerably higher than the 5 per cent at Oxbridge.[70]

Growing numbers of students coming from further afield also meant greater competition for accommodation, and in some towns this became a real problem. The start of the academic year at Nottingham in the 1960s, for example, almost always saw students having to sleep on floors whilst they engaged in the desperate rush for empty rooms.[71] By 1963, the UGC was considering the possibility of buying guesthouses, whilst the University of Exeter pondered whether it could put people up in hotels.[72] Students in the larger cities often had to live miles away in digs, and even in smaller towns, whilst those renting rooms were never far from the university, they were less involved in the place than those who lived in halls of residence. The lucky few with a place in halls were found to have 'studied more, conversed more frequently with their fellow students on their subject, read more non-fiction books, attended more university societies and clubs, and entertained a member of the opposite sex in their room more frequently'.[73] There were haves and have-nots even in this brave new world of universities.[74]

The divisions amongst students were not confined to those living in halls and those living in digs. There were also, of course, some who still lived at home— nearly 10 per cent in the English civic universities and over 40 per cent in Scotland even as late as 1961.[75] Just as in the past, different halls had different atmospheres—and different clientele. By 1968, for example, Leicester had six halls, yet it was only one—Digby—that was recognized as the home for the 'social aristocracy of Leicester'.[76] Within the halls, too, students divided into cliques which were determined by such arbitrary factors as which floor, or block, or staircase they lived on.[77] The layout of the dining hall served as a map of the different groups within the community: 'the "lads" congregated on a particular table; the "Christians" or "God Squad" occupied another; the sensitive sandal-wearing and

---

[68] Quoted in Brian Pullan and Michelle Abendstern, *A History of the University of Manchester, 1951–73* (Manchester, 2000), p. 45.
[69] V. H. H. Green, *The Universities* (Harmondsworth, 1969), p. 239.
[70] Roy Douglas, *Surrey: the rise of a modern university* (Guildford, 1991), p. 86.
[71] *Gongster*, 9 October 1969, p. 1.
[72] EUA, 26/1c, Building Files: Development Programme 1963–69, 5 November 1963.
[73] Joan Brothers and Stephen Hatch, *Residence and Student Life: a sociological enquiry into residence in higher education* (London, 1971), p. 311; M. C. Albow, 'The influence of accommodation upon 64 Reading University students—an ex post facto study', *British Journal of Sociology* 17:4 (1966), pp. 403–18, p. 409.
[74] See also, Doris Thoday, 'Halls of Residence', *Universities Quarterly* 12 (1957–8), pp. 45–56; C. L. Jones, P. M. McMichael, and A. F. McPherson, 'Residence and the First Year Student', *Universities Quarterly* 28 (1973–74), pp. 111–22.
[75] UGC, *University Development 1962–1967*, p. 21.
[76] *Ripple*, 1 October 1968, p. 3.
[77] Anthony Giddens, 'Aspects of the Social Structure of a University Hall of Residence', *Sociological Review* 8 (1960), pp. 97–108, p. 100.

wrought-iron aesthetes avoided the "lads"; and the "nonentities" gravitated to their own table'.[78] In most places, hierarchies were also expressed through a complicated set of codes. At one all-male hall in Hull, the young Anthony Giddens found that freshers not only had to give up their seats to their seniors, but were forbidden from growing facial hair.[79]

Overlying and underpinning these distinctions there remained three crucial differences: class, gender, and academic discipline.[80] Strikingly, expansion did not bring in a larger proportion of new working-class students.[81] The Robbins Report showed that in 1961 middle-class pupils were still eight times more likely to get to university than their working-class counterparts. Indeed, the relative chance of children from the manual working class reaching higher education had not changed since the 1920s.[82] Sociologists in the early 1960s observed that even the brightest working-class students at grammar schools were often woefully unprepared for university entry: only discovering in the sixth form, for example, that it was impossible to study English without Latin; or simply assuming that 'the universities belonged to the upper and middle class', and that there would, as a result, be no room for them. Their parents' lack of interest or simple lack of knowledge only compounded the matter: 'some mothers and fathers found difficulty in even physically imagining a university'.[83]

If anything, indeed, the next ten years saw this problem become even more pronounced. At universities like Birmingham, for example, the end of the 1960s witnessed a smaller working-class presence amongst the student body than at the beginning of the decade—'in fact,' as one historian points out, the students may have been 'the most select in the University's history'.[84] The new universities like Sussex and York were still more socially exclusive.[85] This inevitably meant that, to some extent, working-class students still stood out. They were more likely to live at home; less likely to find a place in halls of residence. They almost all had to work to support themselves in the vacation.[86] Working-class students were consequently seen as a particular problem by university officials—and the wider public.[87] Yet, intriguingly, even as the proportion of working-class students declined, so the undergraduates' self-conscious rejection of these bourgeois universities became

---

[78] Maurice Punch, 'The Student Ritual', *New Society* 10 (1967), pp. 811–13, p. 812.
[79] Giddens, 'University Hall of Residence', p. 98.
[80] See also Peter Marris, *The Experience of Higher Education* (London, 1964), p. 185.
[81] Joan Abbott, *Student Life in a Class Society* (Oxford, 1971).
[82] *Higher Education: appendix one*, cmnd. 2154–1, pp. 46, 52–3.
[83] Brian Jackson and Dennis Marsden, *Education and the Working Class* (London, 1962), pp. 99, 136–8, 148.
[84] Leonard Schwarz, 'The Escape from the Hinterland, 1945–80', in Eric Ives, Dianne Drummond, and Leonard Schwartz, *The First Civic University: Birmingham, 1880–1980* (Birmingham, 2000), pp. 375–88, p. 385.
[85] Malcolm Cross and R. G. Jobling, 'The English New Universities—a preliminary enquiry', *Universities Quarterly* 23 (1968–69), pp. 172–82, p. 177.
[86] Jackson and Marsden, *Education and the Working Class*, p. 147.
[87] See Brothers and Hatch, *Residence and Student Life*, p. 135. The hit film of 1962, *The Wild and the Willing* is, for example, as much an exploration of class and the university as anything else.

more pronounced.[88] By the mid-1960s, this paradox was pointed out by an observant student at Keele: 'The upper and upper-middle class are the easiest to recognise, their accents are invariably cockney'.[89]

Gender and subject were, in many ways, interrelated issues. For the first half of this period, the universities became more and more masculine as they became more and more scientific.[90] Between 1949 and 1961, the number of humanities undergraduates increased by 30 per cent, whilst the number of science and technology students rose by 63 per cent. The overwhelming majority of scientists were men, and women were not always welcome amongst them. At Sheffield, in 1965, for example, two women were expelled from a Physics lecture for wearing trousers.[91] The result was a massive re-masculinization of universities in general—and especially of Redbrick.[92] Manchester, Liverpool, Birmingham, Sheffield, Swansea, and other civic universities all had a minority of arts students by the early 1960s, and consequently also had a diminishing minority of women.[93] Moreover, scientists stood out as a privileged group even amongst the male students, not least because until the abolition of National Service in 1960, they alone were exempt from conscription.[94]

It was 1960 that represented the high watermark for both science and male domination. The expansion of the university system in the years that followed saw a massive increase in the number of non-scientists. With grants available for all, it was now no longer necessary for poorer students to train as teachers in order to be able to study the humanities. 'Like lemmings', complained the educationalist W. H. G. Armytage in 1968, 'the majority of 18-year-olds have been plunging under some compulsive hallucination into the already over-crowded waters of the arts and social sciences, leaving the dry lands of the pure and applied sciences'.[95] What became known as the 'swing away from science' inspired concern, debate, and a number of official enquiries prompted by the fear that this would make Britain still more uncompetitive, but it became apparently unstoppable.[96] The social science bias of the new universities not only exacerbated the problem, but also provided an opportunity for women, who came to comprise nearly half the student body in Kent, York, and UEA.[97]

---

[88] Richard Hoggart, 'Higher Education and Personal Life: changing attitudes', in W. R. Niblett, ed., *Higher Education: demand and response* (London, 1969), pp. 211–30, p. 218.

[89] *Cygnet*, October 1966, p. 1.

[90] Edgerton, *Warfare State*, is especially good on this, see pp. 178–9.

[91] Helen Mathers, *Steel City Scholars: the centenary history of the University of Sheffield* (London, 2005), p. 234.

[92] See, UGC, *University Development 1952–57*, pp. 19, 14; *University Development 1957–62*, p. 24.

[93] J. Gwyn Morgan, 'What the Students Want', *New Statesman* 61:1564 (3 March 1961), pp. 344–5, p. 344.

[94] Pullan and Abendstern, *Manchester1951–73*, p. 41.

[95] W. H. G. Armytage, 'Thoughts After Robbins', in John Lawlor, ed., *The New University* (London, 1968), pp. 77–100, p. 96.

[96] *Enquiry into the Flow of Candidates in Science and Technology into Higher Education* (1968), cmnd 3541.

[97] Dyhouse, *Students*, p. 102.

Rising numbers of women students and changing social mores provoked questions about sexual politics in the university. In most places, gender boundaries continued to be rigidly enforced at the halls of residence. At Sheffield, as late as 1967, no men were permitted to enter the so-called 'Virgins' Retreat' of Halifax Hall.[98] Two years later, a survey showed that the hours at which students could have visitors of the opposite sex were still restricted at universities from Belfast to Bradford to Bristol.[99] The absurdity of much of this was made clear at Keele, where men and women who shared a bed were punished, but no disciplinary action was taken against a student who kept a pig in his room—for the rules did not forbid him from entertaining animals, only female humans.[100]

Yet, in their defence, the universities could point to the fact that they were, until 1970 when the age of majority was lowered to 18, legally *in loco parentis*. They had—and believed themselves to have—a moral and legal responsibility for their students' welfare. At Nottingham in 1949, for example, the vice-chancellor was not unusual in opening the university year with a speech which included advice on relationships.[101] A decade later, he insisted that couples found kissing in the common room should be disciplined.[102] The same was true in many other institutions and attempts to challenge this paternalism were strongly resisted.[103] Keele was only one of many institutions convulsed over the issue of student sexuality in the mid-1960s, with the vice-chancellor publicly describing one pregnant woman as 'a reproach to the University'.[104] For the traditionalists, like the Kantian philosopher A. E. Teale, it was clear that Keele needed to take action— 'Has not the vice chancellor made it clear', he wrote, 'that in his view students should not contemplate marriage until the man has secured employment for the support of his wife, and should not engage in sexual intercourse before marriage?'[105] Reformers, by contrast, like the young utilitarian Alan Ryan, believed that whether the students engaged in premarital sex ought to be a matter of no consequence to university.[106] By the end of the 1960s, it was this approach that had become increasingly widespread and universities like Essex thus abandoned single-sex accommodation as 'against the whole spirit of the day'.[107]

As this suggests, questions about gender and sexuality were only one part of a wider debate over the role of the modern university in the modern world. Much of this was admittedly familiar stuff. Well into the 1960s, the habitual rhetoric of crisis and calls for the invention of tradition were repeated again and again. At Exeter, in

---

[98] Mathers, *Steel City Scholars*, p. 196.
[99] Exeter, UA/26/10e, Exeter University Guild of Students, Survey on Visiting Hours in British Universities (1969).
[100] J. M. Kolbert, *Keele: the first fifty years, 1950–2000* (Keele, 2000), p. 147.
[101] *Gongster*, 11 October 1949, p. 1.
[102] *Gongster*, 9 May 1958, p. 1.
[103] This is very well illustrated by cc 4–5 in Jeremy Black's forthcoming history of Exeter. I am grateful to Professor Black for showing me a copy of his draft manuscript.
[104] *Cygnet*, June 1964, p. 1.
[105] KUA, Senate Minutes 1963–4, 'Professional Etiquette' (9 January 1964), p. 3.
[106] Alan Ryan, 'The New Monasticism', *Cygnet*, January 1964, pp. 1–3.
[107] Albert Sloman, *A University in the Making* (London, 1963), p. 59.

1949 and again in 1952, students were still trying to find college colours and establish a proper college 'yell'.[108] At Southampton in 1957, the student newspaper called—once more—for the wearing of gowns to be made compulsory in order to create a corporate spirit.[109] Nor was this all-too recognizable anxiety confined to places like Exeter and Southampton. Some of the older universities, like Birmingham, remained equally keen to foster tradition—with complaints coming in 1950 that, because of rationing, it was proving hard to obtain appropriate academic dress.[110] Even the newest and most self-confident institutions, like Sussex, also dredged up well-worn worries about their failure to develop a proper university character. The campus was empty at weekends and at nights, one writer claimed.[111] It was full of apathy, wrote another, and of 'young people whose only concern is for a pint, a game of darts or cards'.[112] Nonetheless, it is notable that only two pages after this article in the student paper came another about Apartheid, written by the young Thabo Mbeki. As this suggests, if the cries of apathy and calls for community were not new, then neither was the fact that some students remained very seriously engaged in politics.

As higher education and student life were nationalized, the local loyalties and institutional particularities which had underwritten these complaints of apathy and crisis came to have less purchase. Naturally, fears that the university was not doing its job never went away. Quotidian grievances about the quality or cost of food continued to motivate complaints in even the most highly politicized of institutions.[113] Yet the idea that what the university needed was a clear institutional image—with colours, teams, scarves, and idiosyncratic songs—was increasingly mocked. 'At last', sneered one Essex student in 1965, 'we can truly take our place in the ranks of student society. At last we can all express our corporate identity. One scarf, one Essex.'[114] Indeed, the notion that the university should separate itself off from the community, marking the distinction between students and non-students with special clothes and traditions, came to be seen as highly dubious by many. For radicals, the idea was a university open to everyone—not a closed and autonomous community.[115]

In part, this analysis reflected the influence of new leftist ideologies.[116] In part, it was produced by the growing importance of youth politics more generally.[117] In part, too, it owed something to changing notions about authority, and the right of students to determine their own rules.[118] But, perhaps most of all, this

---

[108] EUA, UA/26/17d, Guild Council Minutes 1940–65.
[109] *Wessex*, 28 February 1957, p. 9.   [110] Schwarz, 'Escape from the Hinterland', p. 387.
[111] *Wine Press*, 12 October 1967, p. 4.   [112] *Wine Press*, 6 May 1963, n.p.
[113] See, for example, *Wyvern*, 10 November 1967.   [114] *Wyvern*, 5 March 1965, p. 2.
[115] See Cockburn and Blackburn, *Student Power*, for a good account of this.
[116] For a far from balanced—but nonetheless full—account, see Julius Gould, *The Attack on Higher Education: Marxist and radical penetration* (ISC Special Report, 1977).
[117] Nick Thomas, 'Challenging the Myths of the 1960s: the case of student protest in Britain', *Twentieth Century British History* 13:3 (2002), pp. 277–97.
[118] Thomas Nicholas Thomas, 'The British Student Movement 1965–72' (Warwick PhD, 1996); Caroline M. Hoefferle, *British Student Activism in the Long Sixties* (New York and London, 2013).

abandonment of an older rhetoric and the development of a different set of demands reflected a new reality: students were now by definition different from the inhabitants of the towns in which their universities were situated. They came from far afield, and had less and less contact with local communities. 'The first year student on arrival will have soon found that the 2s 6d he spent on a street plan of Nottingham was money wasted', observed one undergraduate publication. 'There is no need for him to leave the campus at all during his period of residence.'[119] The creation of universal, national grants also helped to create a sense amongst students that they were a single, national class—people earning a sort of wage, instead of receiving a social benefit.[120] 'Yes, we are privileged,' declared a Liverpool radical, 'but the state will also be privileged to have the use of our virile, developed minds in the future; it is a two-sided agreement, but one side is dictating the terms. Crazy!'[121] Given this, there is little wonder that the old attempts to distinguish town from gown seemed old fashioned. It was simply no longer needed.

These changes inevitably prompted comment and complaint. The growth of higher education—in terms of size and cost—led to increased public interest in it; for as Michael Beloff put it in 1968, 'Universities which yesterday were ivory towers are today goldfish bowls.'[122] Growth also provoked doubts. Had the universities expanded too quickly?[123] Had the quality of education and the average ability of students declined? Certainly, Kingsley Amis's view that 'MORE WILL MEAN WORSE'[124] was shared by philosophers like Michael Oakeshott,[125] sociologists like Bryan Wilson, and novelists like Malcolm Bradbury.[126] By the early-1960s, undergraduates were also becoming more vocal in their criticisms that the size of the universities made contact between staff and students perfunctory.[127] In a remarkable precursor to *The History Man*, published more than a decade later, Bradbury and Wilson suggested that expansion risked dilution—a dilution of quality and of community. Students, they said, would become alienated; already 'there has grown up in redbrick universities a distinctive student culture which manifests a number of the disturbing aspects of our modern anomic youth culture'.[128] By 1962, then, there were already those who believed that they could read 'The Writing on the Redbrick Wall'.[129]

---

[119] *Gongster*, 19 October 1967, p. 4.
[120] Carswell, *Government and the Universities*, p. 25.
[121] *Sphinx*, Spring 1968, p. 5.
[122] Michael Beloff, *The Plateglass Universities* (London, 1968), p. 152.
[123] Christopher Driver, *The Exploding University* (London, 1971), p. 33.
[124] Kingsley Amis, 'Lone Voices: views of the "fifties"', *Encounter* 15 (1960), pp. 6–11, p. 8.
[125] Michael Oakeshott, 'The Universities', *Cambridge Journal* 2 (1948–9), pp. 515–42, p. 537.
[126] Bryan Wilson and Malcolm Bradbury, 'The Writing on the Redbrick Wall', in Bryan Wilson, *The Youth Culture and the Universities* (London, 1970), pp. 73–85.
[127] Ashby and Anderson, *Student Estate*, p. 101.
[128] Wilson and Bradbury, 'The Writing on the Redbrick Wall', p. 83.
[129] Wilson and Bradbury, 'The Writing on the Redbrick Wall'.

THE UNEASY DON

Criticism also extended to the staff of the expanding universities. Bradbury and Wilson were not alone in pointing to the problems produced by a sudden rise in the demand for university teachers. Indeed, as one lecturer complained, 'Kingsley Amis's *Lucky Jim* has spread the impression that Redbrick is peopled by beer-drinking, scholarship louts, who wouldn't know a napkin from a chimney-piece and whose one ideal is to end their sex-starvation in the arms of a big-breasted blonde.' No wonder journalists discussed 'The Uneasy Don', or that academics responded by joking that, *contra* Amis, 'Redbrick prides itself on the production of delicate sodomites with the right vocabulary'.[130] At the same time, however, the growth of the universities meant that lecturers and professors in this period gained a greater sense of national, as well as purely local, importance—and an enhanced sense, too, of their place within a profession.[131] The 'remote and ineffectual' academic was now increasingly replaced in the popular press by the 'Don in scarlet, Don in tails, / Don advertising Daily Mails, / Don in Office, Don in power, / Don talking on the Woman's Hour' satirized by A. N. L. Munby.[132] This change was acknowledged in 1949, when—for the first time—a genuinely national pay scale for academics was created. It was also seen in the significant increase in numbers of university teachers. The 9,000 academics at the start of the 1950s became 25,000 by the end of the 1960s.[133] The small section of the *Times Educational Supplement* that covered university matters grew ever larger and eventually transmuted into the stand-alone *Times Higher Educational Supplement* in 1971. To that extent, at least, criticism of Redbrick academics was an acknowledgement of their increased prominence more generally in this period.

This is not to say that the criticism was always undeserved, of course. The growth of the universities did mean that it was sometimes necessary to employ people who would not previously have been thought qualified. Before 1958, 54 per cent of lecturers at large civic universities and 62 per cent of those at smaller Redbrick institutions had obtained first-class degrees. After that, however, the trend was downwards, with fewer than half of those appointed possessing a top mark.[134] At the same time, the old problem of poor teaching had not gone away. Memories of Manchester suggest that, in some subjects at least, the lecturers were 'bloody awful teachers for the most part'.[135] By 1968 Richard Hoggart was not alone in complaining that students found 'most teaching simply dull'.[136] This was certainly not true everywhere—and experiences differed even within institutions. If electrical engineering was boring at Manchester, then other students recalled history teaching

---

[130] J.-G. Weightman, 'The Uneasy Don', *Twentieth Century* 159 (1956), pp. 130–41, p. 139.
[131] A. H. Halsey and Martin Trow, *The British Academics* (London, 1971).
[132] Quoted in Jasper Rose and John Ziman, *Camford Observed* (London, 1964), p. 216.
[133] Harold Perkin, *Key Profession: the history of the Association of University Teachers* (London, 1969), p. 160. These figures do not include academics in Oxford, Cambridge, or Northern Ireland.
[134] *Higher Education: appendix three*, p. 22.
[135] Quoted in Pullan and Abendstern, *Manchester 1951–73*, p. 61.
[136] Hoggart, 'Higher Education and Personal Life', p. 219.

at the same place as extraordinarily intellectually demanding, with tutorials in which 'no quarter was given' (though it might be observed that it was the historians who gathered this testimony).[137] It should also be noted that initially at any rate, class sizes were smaller than they had been before the war. Nonetheless, even this advantage was gradually lost as the universities expanded.[138] There is a sense that, even if it did not mean worse, more might sometimes mean less—with less highly-qualified teachers seeing less and less of their students. This was not true at small and cosy Strathclyde, where everyone—staff and student alike—gathered round the tea-trolley each afternoon.[139] But was certainly the case in larger institutions. By 1957, a majority of Nottingham students complained that they never met staff in a social capacity, and nearly 50 per cent claimed that they rarely even spoke to their tutors.[140]

The life of the university lecturer undoubtedly changed. A growing emphasis on the need for research gave more people more opportunity to do it. Slowly, but surely, the amount of time spent teaching was reduced and the amount of time spent doing research rose. By the early 1960s, the Robbins Report found that across the universities, even in term, slightly more time was given up to research than to teaching. Indeed, the average lecturer now only taught for seven and a half hours a week.[141] The result was a highly flexible timetable for academics, allowing even much-published heads of department, like Exeter's Frank Barlow, a tremendous freedom to do their own thing. For Barlow this meant a weekly schedule of teaching or administration in the morning, research and writing in the evening, leaving the afternoons free for gardening.[142] At the same time, salaries went up too—and, although pay differentials remained significant, lowly assistant lecturers found themselves both a little better off and a lot less badly-paid than their bosses. In the middle of the 1940s, professors received at least three and a half times as much as assistant lecturers.[143] Just over twenty years later, however, the post of assistant lecturer had been abolished, and professors earned, on average, only one and a half times more than lecturers.[144]

Increasing equity of pay was paralleled by improving university democracy. Of course, professors remained powerful, but their stranglehold on university government was gradually relaxed. In the early 1960s, faced by the fact that only 12 per cent of staff now held chairs, the University of Manchester opened its Senate to some elected lecturers too.[145] Most other institutions followed suit—and the new universities were founded on this basis. Indeed, the self-consciously egalitarian

---

[137] Quoted in Pullan and Abendstern, *Manchester 1951–73*, p. 59.
[138] *Higher Education: appendix three*, pp. 4, 7–8.
[139] Calum G. Brown, Arthur J. McIvor, and Neil Rafeek, *The University Experience 1945–1975: an oral history of the University of Strathclyde* (Edinburgh, 2004), p. 220.
[140] Mike Scammell, 'Tutorial System—a failure?', *Gongster*, 1 March 1957, p. 1.
[141] *Higher Education: appendix three*, pp. 55–6.
[142] David Bates, 'Frank Barlow, 1911–2009', *Proceedings of the British Academy* 172 (2010), pp. 3–26, p. 18.
[143] UGC, *University Development 1935–47*, pp. 46–8.
[144] Perkin, *Key Profession*, p. 192.
[145] Pullan and Abendstern, *Manchester 1951–73*, pp. 141, 144.

Essex created a 'General Assembly' at which all academics were entitled to speak.[146] That the balance of power had been shifted—if not entirely transformed—was made clear at Lancaster in 1973, when a battle between the professor of English and one of his lecturers led to complete stalemate. The professor, W. A. Murray, insisted on his right to determine the department's curriculum; the lecturer, D. M. Craig, asserted his right to autonomy over what he taught. Neither man won; but the fact that Craig retained his job, and even achieved promotion, was proof that the day of the all-powerful professor had apparently passed for good.[147]

The struggle between professors and lecturers was generational. It was also—as at Lancaster—often ideological. This much was not all that new. What did change in the 1950s and 1960s was the composition of this academic community—although, again, there were some continuities even here. In particular, women remained marginal members of the universities, not even allowed access to senior common rooms in some institutions.[148] The proportion of female lecturers remained pretty stable at about 10 per cent; the same figure it had been before the war. If anything, numbers came to look like they were on the decline. As the old university colleges were turned into universities, so the percentage of male lecturers increased. The turn to science also, doubtless, had a similar impact.[149]

Yet if gender was a remarkably stable category, then the same was not true for class. As Malcolm Bradbury pointed out most famously, what really changed in this period were the social origins of those teaching in the universities. *The History Man*, Howard Kirk, is thus not just an anti-hero but an epitome: 'the scholarship boy, serious and severe, well-read in the grammar-school library, bad at games and humanity, who had got in to Leeds University, in 1957, by pure academic effort—a draining effort that had, in fact, left him for a time pallid in features and in mind'.[150] Empirical research sustains this suggestion. The proportion of grammar school educated academics rose and rose in this period. By 1964, nearly two-thirds of lecturers at the larger Redbrick universities shared this educational background. Civic university teachers were also less likely to come from professional or white-collar homes: only just over half did at Redbrick, compared to 68 per cent at London and nearly three-quarters at Oxbridge.[151] The truth was, as Harold Perkin put it in 1969, that becoming a lecturer was 'especially attractive to first-generation grammar and other secondary school pupils, and to first-generation university students, the children of less-educated but socially ambitious fathers'.[152] What this meant was that the Redbrick lecturers of the 1950s and 1960s were more likely to come from working-class backgrounds than either their students or their

---

[146] Sloman, *University in the Making*, p. 84.
[147] *The Craig Affair: the background to the case of Dr David Craig, and others, University of Lancaster* (London, 1972). See also, Marion E. McClintock, *The University of Lancaster: quest for innovation* (Lancaster, 1974), p. 393.
[148] Dainton, *Doubts and Certainties*, p. 129.
[149] Margherita Rendel, 'How Many Women Academics, 1912–76?', in Rosemary Deem, ed., *Schooling for Women's Work* (London, 1980), pp. 142–61, pp. 148–9; *Higher Education: appendix three*, pp. 18, 172.
[150] Bradbury, *The History Man*, p. 20.   [151] Halsey and Trow, *British Academics*, p. 216.
[152] Perkin, *Key Profession*, p. 240.

professors. The social distinction between teachers and taught had not been as sharply pronounced for more than a century.

The social origin of the lecturers was a matter of concern to commentators of both left and right. For Bryan Wilson (and Malcolm Bradbury, for that matter), the perceived proletarianization of Redbrick dons risked creating alienated, radicalized intellectuals.[153] 'Rapid growth in some disciplines', Wilson went on, 'has led to the recruitment of junior staff who have themselves suffered all the inadequacies of the expanding universities: they cannot transmit university values because they have never really received them'.[154] This, in many ways, was of course the message of *The History Man*. From a completely divergent position, the sociologist A. H. Halsey was alarmed at just how conservative the academics of his age turned out to be. A passionate egalitarian, he was shocked to find that, despite their often relatively humble social origins, his colleagues were, on the whole, opposed to university expansion and the democratization of the academy.[155] The reality was that class gave only a crude guide to people's views about university life. After all, both Bryan Wilson and A. H. Halsey were themselves from working-class families. The former embraced the values of his Oxford College, reactionary All Souls, and opposed change within the universities. The latter espoused the values of his Oxford College, progressive Nuffield, and pushed for reform.

To that extent, it is impossible to say for certain whether the arrival of so many working-class and petit-bourgeois lecturers radicalized the profession. Nevertheless, the existence of these different perspectives, and the presence of these new voices amongst university teachers was significant, and undeniably added an edge to the struggle between lecturers and professors. When, at the end of the 1960s, the hierarchies of the university began to be challenged, a significant number of those pushing for change would be lecturers themselves.[156]

Redbrick academics consequently shared some of the same experiences as those they taught. Indeed, with the exception of those at entirely new foundations, they were likely to be teaching in the same sort of institution as they themselves had studied. Even in the late-1960s, only 2 per cent of lecturers moved between universities each year.[157] Nevertheless, like their students, academics found themselves part of a newly, truly national system. Just as the students came to receive a nationally-determined grant, so their teachers became part of a national pay scheme. Just as growing numbers of students led to fears about lowering standards, so the increase in the size of the faculty prompted questions about their qualifications too. In each case, the expansion of the university provoked anxiety about the nature and function of the academy—an anxiety that was to be articulated ever more often and still more furiously as time went on.

---

[153] Wilson and Bradbury, 'The Writing on the Redbrick wall', pp. 78–9.
[154] Bryan Wilson, 'The Youth Culture, the Universities, and Student Unrest', in Wilson, *Youth Culture and the Universities*, pp. 218–33, p. 224.
[155] Halsey and Trow, *British Academics*, ch. 11.
[156] See, for example, University of Essex, *Report of the Annan Enquiry* (Colchester, 1974), p 6.
[157] Halsey and Trow, *British Academics*, p. 228.

10
Buildings and Battles

Buildings became synonymous with these changes in higher education. Following Bruce Truscot, writers used architecture as shorthand. According to Jimmy Porter, in John Osborne's *Look Back in Anger* (1957), his university was 'not even red brick, but white tile'.[1] It was a sobriquet that stuck, becoming ineluctably associated with the old university colleges like Leicester, Southampton, and Hull. An attempt was made to identify the new polytechnics as 'Blackbrick Universities',[2] and in keeping with this theme, it was suggested that the other new universities of the 1960s should be known as 'whitebricks', 'whitestone', or even 'pinktile'. Having dismissed these—and the more accurate 'greenfields'—the writer Michael Beloff hit on 'Plateglass Universities', and the phase quickly took off.[3] Architecture, though, was more than just a convenient metaphor. It was also seen as a way to resolve the tensions that the expanding universities inspired. It was intended to create the communities that commentators feared were being lost. It was meant to provide an exciting environment in which to teach and research. It was used to signal the importance of the university to the wider world.

In all these respects, the developments of the 1950s and 1960s can look a little like business as usual. And it is true that many architectural projects in this period drew on debates that had been going on for decades. The sense that better planning would create stronger university communities and thus solve the perceived problems of Redbrick had been articulated for decades. Nonetheless, the changed circumstances of the post-war era did also affect architecture. For one thing, new ideas about planning and design reshaped university buildings. The somewhat belated advent of modernism, with its distinctive ideological and aesthetic agendas, in that way, did not just alter the façades but also the very nature of university architecture.[4] In the second place, the massively increased size of these institutions—and the creation of entirely new universities—meant that their planning became more complex, more expansive, and more expensive. It also meant that both the public and the architectural profession took a greater interest

---

[1] John Osborne, *Look Back in Anger* (London, 1957), p. 34.
[2] Caroline Cox, Maurice Meaking, and Julia Witburn, 'The Blackbrick Universities', *Times Higher Education Supplement*, 5 November 1971, p. 16.
[3] Michael Beloff, *The Plateglass Universities* (London, 1968), pp. 11, 13; W. Boyd Alexander, 'England's New Seven: an American view', in John Lawlor, ed., *The New University* (London, 1968), pp. 25–48, p. 47.
[4] See Diane Chablo, 'University Architecture in Britain, 1950–75' (Oxford DPhil, 1987); Stefan Muthesius, *The Postwar University: utopianist campus and college* (New Haven and London, 2000).

in university buildings than ever before. Indeed, for writers like Joseph Rykwert, universities had become the archetypal architecture of the age.[5] Finally, the fact that these institutions became part of a national system and were almost entirely dependent on state funding for their development meant that the government—in the form of the University Grants Committee (UGC)—was ever-more involved in the physical form of higher education.[6] It also meant that the architects employed would be national, even international names, rather than the local figures who had often previously been employed. This mixture of academic anxiety, architects' ambitions, university expansion, growing public interest, and state funding was an inherently unstable one. Little wonder that by the early 1970s, commentators were beginning to ask where it had all gone wrong.

This, though, is to pre-empt matters. In reality, the 1950s and 1960s were filled with hope about the possibilities that modern architecture offered.[7] True enough, there were always limits. At Loughborough in 1957, for example, it was reluctantly accepted that 'it may well be true that public opinion is not at the present time ready to accept a Nuclear Plant in close proximity to established residential districts'.[8] This aside, however, the ambitions of the universities and their designers seemed almost unlimited. Architects, in particular, became increasingly optimistic and adventurous. 'I wish I was as certain of the value of my educational plan as you are of your architecture', the director of education for Ghana once observed to the architect Maxwell Fry. 'You are going to mould their lives the more because not a word will be said. It will all be absorbed unconsciously.'[9] What was true in West Africa was also true in Britain.[10]

Architects were immensely keen to secure university jobs. To a large extent, this was because of public interest. As the *Architectural Review* commented in 1963, work at a university had become highly desirable because 'in terms of prestige and architectural significance it is . . . one of the dominant areas of design'.[11] Architects, in other words, hoped to use the universities as an advertisement for what they could do. Universities were not only examples of a how architecture could remake the post-war world, test cases for the production of the ideal urban environment; they also provided an opportunity to persuade people about the virtues of modern

---

[5] *Architectural Review* 147 (1970), p. 242.
[6] John Carswell, *Government and the Universities in Britain: programme and performance, 1960–1980* (Cambridge, 1985), p. 93.
[7] John R. Gold, *The Practice of Modernism: modern architects and urban transformation, 1954–1972* (London and New York, 2007).
[8] ULouA, LCT/G4/M1, Minutes of Buildings Development Sub-Committee, 1954–61, 11 July 1957.
[9] Quoted in Ulli Beier, *Art in Nigeria, 1960* (Cambridge, 1960), p. 18. On Fry's university work, see Iain Jackson, 'Post-war Modernism: Maxwell Fry's buildings at the University of Liverpool', *Journal of Architecture* 16 (2011), pp. 675–702.
[10] See also Rhodri Windsor Liscombe, 'Modernism in Late-Imperial British West Africa: the work of Maxwell Fry and Jane Drew, 1946–1956', *Journal of the Society of Architectural Historians* 65:2 (2006), pp. 188–215; William Whyte, 'Modernism, Modernisation, and Europeanization in West African Architecture, 1944–1994', in Martin Conway and Kiran Klaus Patel, eds, *Europeanization in the Twentieth Century: Historical Approaches* (Basingstoke, 2010).
[11] *Architectural Review* 134 (1963), p. 231.

architecture.[12] For the *Architects' Journal*, the issue was self-evident: 'If the opportunity is given to modern architects to carry out the universities' building programmes, future students will be familiar, early on in their lives, with the potentialities of modern architecture, and they, in their turn, when acting as clients, will help ensure that the principles of modern architecture are spread throughout the nation'.[13] Hence, the intrinsic interest of the universities, as well as their status as high-profile projects, made them so desirable for architects that they were even willing to work on them at a loss.[14]

Architects were also attracted by the remarkable degree of freedom that many universities granted them. Keen to secure the best, and dependent on specialist advice, vice-chancellors allowed the leading names in the profession to dole out jobs like so many sweets.[15] Key figures, like the Cambridge professor of architecture Leslie Martin, proved to be highly successful kingmakers, determining choices at Essex,[16] Leicester,[17] Leeds,[18] East Anglia, and elsewhere.[19] Once appointed, universities proved willing to tolerate some remarkably high-handed behaviour— with Basil Spence providing a particularly good set of examples. When slated by students at Southampton for the poor acoustics of his Union building, he was dismissive: 'After all,' he said, 'you can hardly tell an Architect—who has had no little success—his job.'[20] At Liverpool, by contrast, he was simply absent. 'Basil Spence was perfectly accurate when we interviewed him for our Physics building,' observed the university's staff architect; 'he said he would do the initial design, but that thereafter we would not see him.'[21] And at Sussex, where he gained the nickname 'Sir Basil-Expense', because of his cost over-runs, he over-ruled the experts and insisted on his own ideas for the new chemistry laboratories, explaining to the professor in charge that he had not ignored, but simply rejected, his criticisms. When the academic complained, the vice-chancellor responded: 'there is only one Basil Spence; I can get any number of Professors of Chemistry.'[22]

For many contemporaries—and some subsequent historians—this licence created nothing more than 'architects' universities'. 'What we are seeing', wrote the Sussex professor Boris Ford in 1964, 'is a confrontation between academics— conservative, slow, non-planners by tradition, but now trying desperately to change their intellectual gear, and a generation of younger architects—predominantly urban in experience, efficient planners and specifiers, and above all confident in

[12] Muthesius, *Postwar University*, pp. 2, 90.
[13] *Architects' Journal* 127 (1957), p. 2.
[14] EssUA,1(b), Wivenhoe Park, A. E. Sloman, 'Architects' (19 January 1966).
[15] Gold, *Practice of Modernism*, p. 58.
[16] EssUA, 1(b), Wivenhoe Park, 21 September 1962.
[17] LeiUA, Minutes 1958–59, Buildings Advisory Committee, 15 July 1959.
[18] LeeUA, Lodge Committee, 23 May, 5, 25, 27 June, 1 July 1958.
[19] Peter Dormer and Stefan Muthesius, *Concrete and Open Skies: architecture at the University of East Anglia, 1962–2000* (London, 2001), p. 50. See also, Mark Girouard, *Big Jim: the life and work of James Stirling* (London, 1998), pp. 103–4.
[20] *Wessex*, 7 February 1961, p. 1.
[21] SussUA, SxMs45/1, Staff Architect's Papers Box 1, J. F. Cory Dixon to T. C. Green (14 February 1961).
[22] SussUA, SxUOSI/3/3/1, Colin Eaborn, 'Autobiography'.

themselves.'[23] Yet it would be wrong to assume that these plans reflected only the thoughts and ambitions of architects. Academics also saw architecture as important. Like their predecessors, they believed that 'the universities have the duty to set standards in matters of taste'.[24] Like their predecessors, too, they used architecture 'to give physical and visual expression to... academic ideals'.[25] Universities worked hard to make sure that they got the right architects. Leeds spent months looking in the late-1950s, consulting widely and interviewing thoroughly.[26] At Liverpool, in 1957, the Development Committee spent three days interrogating no fewer than a dozen different designers.[27] At York, the architect and the vice-chancellor continued a debate about university architecture that lasted six months.[28] It was, recalled the latter, a 'process of the closest collaboration imaginable between architects and university, a process of architectural dialectic, often exhausting, always stimulating, but in the end deeply educative', and the result was that 'the material form of the university... reflects its educational ideals'.[29] If the universities allowed their architects a lot of latitude, this was because they came to trust them; not because they did not care.[30]

Moreover, the relationship between university and architect was not exclusive. There were a number of mediating bodies. Local authorities had to approve plans. Student Unions were sometimes involved in design decisions.[31] The Royal Fine Arts Commission intervened in an attempt to modernize university architecture.[32] Above all, the UGC exercised a decisive role: as it was paying for most of these buildings, it could hardly not. The UGC consequently created a code of practice that universities found themselves bound to follow.[33] It also evolved a standard system for approving plans and a standard formula for assessing costs.[34] Halls of residence were measured against the SBU (or 'study-bedroom unit'); laboratories were laid out according to a fixed price for bench space. In 1957 the UGC acquired a small architects' department of its own, which set to work overseeing the expansion of the universities. Even buildings built by benefactors did not escape

---

[23] Boris Ford, 'Learning in a Beehive', *New Statesman* 68 (1964), pp. 919–20, p. 920. See also, J. W. R. Whitehead, 'Institutional Site Planning: the University of Birmingham, England, 1900–69', *Planning History* 13:2 (1991), pp. 29–35.
[24] EUA, UA/26/1c, Great Hall 1961–65, Vice Chancellor to UGC (31 July 1962).
[25] Sloman, *A University in the Making*, p. 64.
[26] Whyte, 'Modernist Moment', pp. 174–80.
[27] LivUA, S.236, Development Committee, 1946–57, pp. 218–21 (13, 15, 16 July 1957).
[28] Andrew Saint, *Towards a Social Architecture: the role of school building in post-war England* (New Haven and London, 1987), p. 217.
[29] Lord James, 'The University of York', in Murray G. Ross, ed., *New Universities in the Modern World* (New York, 1966), pp. 32–52, p. 38.
[30] For an intriguing, though only partial exception, see Miles Glendinning, *Modern Architect: the life and times of Robert Matthew* (London, 2008), ch.10.
[31] *Architectural Review* 133 (1963), pp. 267–70.
[32] Alan Powers, *Britain: modern architectures in history* (London, 2007), p. 149.
[33] *Methods Used by Universities of Contracting and of Recording and Controlling Expenditure* (1956), cmnd 9.
[34] *Methods Used by Universities of Recording and Controlling Expenditure* (1965), cmnd 1235.

their attention: if the maintenance costs seemed abnormally high, then the Committee would veto the project.[35]

It must be said that not all the members of the UGC were equally interested in architecture. At least one complained that 'I seem to have spent many of the best hours of my life wandering round brick and plants labelled "Physics Block, Stage 2".'[36] The system was never all-encompassing, either.[37] The importance of the Committee to university architecture in this period should not, however, be underestimated; for it went far beyond simple administrative oversight. The UGC promoted particular plans, approaches, and architects.[38] Many found this intrusion insufferable. 'Is it really necessary for any state organization to know exactly how each room of known size in every university is used?' asked the university architect and administrator J. F. Cory Dixon.[39] Predictably, Spence was even more coruscating: '"Buildings" are put up for as little as £3.17.0d per square foot,' he wrote, 'but not permanent University buildings where the more intelligent members of the nation's youth are brought to the highest standard of learning.... Universities must surely enjoy the best of architecture and buildings which can be provided.'[40] Yet he was forced to toe the line. When faced by the implacable demands of the UGC, even Sir Basil-Expense knew when he was beaten.

This consortium of idealists, educationalists, bureaucrats, and prima donnas was confronted by a series of interlinked issues. It was quite clear that no university could grow or survive, for that matter, on the cramped and over-crowded sites that had grown up over the previous half century. It was also vitally important to replace the many shoddy buildings that still clustered round numerous campuses. At Leeds, in the 1950s, there was no Senior Common Room—just a wooden hut where lunch could be taken.[41] At Leicester, in the 1960s, many staff still had offices in temporary nurses' accommodation put up in the First World War.[42] And some of the permanent buildings were also showing their age. In Reading, as Frank Kermode recalled, 'Surveyors had limited classes in some of the rooms to a maximum of five persons; they recommended that one should head for the chimney if the floor showed signs of collapse.'[43] At the same time, too, Redbrick sought to overcome the sense that it had embraced a 'raw, uneasy, bogus style of

---

[35] UGC, *University Development 1957–62*, pp. 123–7.

[36] Lord James in *RIBA Journal* 71 (1964), p. 303.

[37] Robert Proctor, 'Social Structures: Gillespie, Kidd, and Coia's Halls of Residence at the University of Hull', *Journal of the Society of Architectural Historians* 67 (2008), pp. 106–29.

[38] Whyte, 'Modernist Moment', p. 186.

[39] J. F. Cory Dixon, *Building For and By Degrees: a clients [sic] experience on [sic] building for Universities* (Guildford, 1978), p. 15.

[40] SussUA, IB/IV/6, Sussex House Admin Box 23, Building Committee Correspondence 1959–63, Spence to Fulton (13 May 1960).

[41] Dainton, *Doubts and Certainties*, p. 129.

[42] LeiUA, ULA/AD/D5/7, development Plans, 1962–7, Report of Development Board (6 October 1964).

[43] Frank Kermode, *Not Entitled: a memoir* (London, 1996), pp. 182–3.

architecture'.[44] This was especially important for the new universities, but the older civics also embraced the idea.[45]

The need for more space was perhaps the most pressing concern for the universities. Some, of course, already possessed suburban sites with room to grow. Others hoped to move. At Reading, in 1947 the acquisition of an estate on the outskirts of town enabled the university to abandon some of its decaying buildings.[46] At Birmingham, in 1960, the university was finally unified on the Egbaston campus, as the very last of the faculties moved out of the centre of town, a mere six decades late.[47] But not all the universities could do this—and not all wanted to. In 1946 Liverpool appointed Lord Holford as its planning consultant. It was clear, he concluded, that the university's current site was too small—indeed, he estimated that at least 200 acres was now required. Nonetheless, he rejected any suggestion that the campus should be relocated. 'He thought it was wrong, in principle that the University should remove from the centre of Liverpool. Apart from the loss entailed by the abandonment of buildings and the long time over which transfer would be spread, he thought that public bodies like the University had an obligation to remain at the centre.'[48] This combination of pure practicality and simple sentiment proved convincing; Liverpool stayed put. The same was true at Leeds and Manchester, and at Leicester, which resolved that 'A civic university must grow up in the heart of the city, alive to its commercial and industrial needs and taking full advantage of its cultural resources. It must be readily accessible to the city'.[49] Instead of moving themselves, many places planned to remove the terraced houses that surrounded them, plunging those departments at Leeds which inhabited them into a 'competition to get oneself demolished'.[50]

It would be wrong, however, to suggest that there was a fundamental difference between urban and suburban universities—much less a big gap between old Redbrick and new Plateglass. In reality, the whole sector shared similar preoccupations and assumptions. Even Holford's use of language was significant. Although not the first to use it, he nonetheless helped to popularize the word 'campus' in Britain.[51] More importantly, his argument that a modern university required a 200-acre site was seminal. It became the standard by which the UGC assessed all possible locations for new universities.[52] The Redbrick universities also provided a useful test case for other institutions. Thus, the 1953 Sheffield University competition

---

[44] Mary Scrutton [Midgley], 'Newcastle: comments on a case-history', *Twentieth Century* 159 (1956), pp. 159–68, p. 159.
[45] *Architectural Review* 134 (1963), pp. 237–8.
[46] Wolfenden, *Turning Points*, p. 111.
[47] Eric Ives, 'Waiting for Robbins', in Eric Ives, Dianne Drummond, and Leonard Schwartz, *The First Civic University: Birmingham, 1880–1980* (Birmingham, 2000), pp. 316–32, p. 322.
[48] LivUA, S.236, development Committee 1946–57, p. 6 (27 November 1946). See also William Holford, *Proposals for the Development of a Site for the University of Liverpool* (Liverpool, 1949), p. 8.
[49] LeiUA, ULA/ADS/D5/1, 'A Note on Sites and Full Development' (1950). See also ULA/ADS/D5/1, H. Percy Gee, Alfred A. Ironside, F. L. Attenborough, 'The Siting of University College', 22 Oct. 1946.
[50] Maurice Beresford, *Walks Round Red Brick* (Leeds, 1980), p. 26.
[51] Holford, *University of Liverpool*, p. 13.
[52] UGC, *University Development 1957–62*, p. 99.

was to be highly influential—not least because it revealed the radical thinking of Alison and Peter Smithson, whose unplaced entry, with its walkways and decks and unified structure, was to inspire much imitation.[53] The 1960 Leeds *Development Plan*, by Chamberlin, Powell, and Bon, was even more important. It was based upon fifteen months of questions and questionnaires, and, with its organizational diagrams, flowcharts, and time and motion studies, it proved formative for every other subsequent proposal, whether intended for an old, urban institution or a new, green-field site.[54]

These developments were somewhat different from those at Oxford and Cambridge—and not just because the greater wealth of those two institutions freed them to some degree from the constraints imposed by theUGC; though the licence that some Oxbridge colleges exercised certainly made them incomparable with the strictly regulated civic institutions.[55] Rather, the various projects undertaken by both Redbrick and Plateglass universities reveal a shared set of assumptions about their nature and function. The debates of the 1940s had yielded some very clear criticisms of the civics and some equally explicit solutions. Concerns about Redbrick's perceived failure to create an academic community, for example, had an important impact on discussions about building. How to turn the 'nine-to-five' university (in which everyone went home at the end of the day)[56] into a 'ten-minute' university (in which all departments were no more than a short walk apart) became a constant refrain.[57] Experience of life at Redbrick was also formative. It was, for instance, Albert Sloman's period in Liverpool, where he served on the committee overseeing development, rather more than his time at Oxford, where he had been a student, that shaped his plans as the founding vice-chancellor of Essex.[58] In that way, even though the Plateglass universities were new, and innovative, and very conscious of that fact, they were not created *ex nihilo*, nor were they a sort of ersatz Oxbridge. Indeed, with their insistence on residence, their escape from the city, and their attempts to create a coherent, modern campus, they can be seen as a product of the same reforming impulse that had begun within Redbrick.

All the universities and would-be universities of this period consequently shared in the common experience of planning and building on a grand scale, with the lessons learnt—or believed to have been learnt—at Redbrick filtering through the system and shaping even the most avant-garde of new institutions. From the 1950s onwards, this increasingly meant employing modern architects to build self-consciously modernist campuses. Indeed, modernism became synonymous with university status. Thus at Leicester, there was a deliberate effort to abandon the

---

[53] Alison and Peter Smithson, *Urban Structuring* (London, 1967), pp. 46–8.
[54] Whyte, 'Modernist Moment', pp. 182–6.
[55] See, William Whyte, '"A pastiche or a packing case": building in twentieth-century Oxford and Cambridge', *Twentieth-Century Architecture* 11 (2013), pp. 16–29.
[56] J. A. Brennan, *Redbrick University: a guide for parents, sixth-formers and students* (Oxford, 1969), p. 10.
[57] Birks, *New Universities*, p. 18.
[58] Jules Lubbock, 'The Counter-Modernist Sublime: the campus of the University of Essex', *Twentieth-Century Architecture* 6 (2002), pp. 105–18, pp. 109, 111.

neo-classicism that had characterized the place since it was founded.[59] Instead, they sought 'plain, severe, clean lines'; 'a science building of red brick and glass'; 'buildings...in contemporary style'. Whilst the principal 'said this might not be desirable for a women's hall', the general point was taken and in 1955 the traditionalist Shirley Worthington was sacked in favour of the ubiquitous modernist Leslie Martin.[60] Leicester became a university two years later. Even at Nottingham, which hung on to neo-classicism longer than most, the science park was given over to Basil Spence, and by the mid-1960s the first modernist halls were being built.[61] Little wonder. Pressure from the architectural profession, which named and shamed universities guilty of producing 'old-fashioned' architecture;[62] encouragement from the UGC, which seems to have persuaded the cabinet secretary, no less, to confront Nottingham's vice-chancellor over his unwillingness to employ 'new style architects';[63] the demands of students, who wanted a 'building designed for our time and built with modern techniques and materials':[64] all these factors forced even the most recalcitrant into the embrace of modernism, leaving Nottingham's undergraduates to greet one of Spence's first new buildings as '60,000 square feet of progress. Progress which will itself induce progress and achievement'. (Figure 36)[65]

As this suggests, modern architecture was seen as a way of reforming as well as rehousing the university. At Birmingham, successive new plans broke up the formality of Aston Webb's vision, and overturned the axial planning of the interwar period.[66] The idea was to create a more free-flowing, open community and 'break down the imperforate nature' of what had gone before.[67] At Manchester, the creation of an enormous 'Education Precinct', incorporating technical colleges, and university, and what was to become the polytechnic, was intended to re-unite town with gown.[68] The work at Leeds was even more ambitious. With its emphasis on high-density accommodation and with its attempt to create a sense of place through the use of a standardized architectural vocabulary, the *Development Plan* sought a complete transformation in the university's environment (Figure 37).[69]

The new universities, too, shared in this experience of architectural experimentation. At Sussex and Warwick, the architects hoped to inspire community through the creation of a single social structure—'a building which should father and

[59] William Whyte, '"A Hell of a Job": Building the University of Leicester', 50th Anniversary Lecture to the University of Leicester (19 February 2008), <http://www2.le.ac.uk/offices/press/pdf-files/A%20Hell%20of%20a%20Job.doc> (accessed 30 April 2010).
[60] LeiUA, Minutes 1955–56, Buildings Advisory Committee, 3 November 1955.
[61] A. Peter Fawcett and Neil Jackson, *Campus Critique: the architecture of the University of Nottingham* (Nottingham, 1998), ch. 4.
[62] Lionel Brett, 'Universities: today', *Architectural Review* 122 (1957), pp. 240–51.
[63] Derek Winterbottom, *Bertrand Hallward: the first vice-chancellor of the University of Nottingham* (Nottingham, 1995), p. 160.
[64] Tony Barker, 'The New University Church', *Gongster*, 11 November 1960, p. 13.
[65] *Gongster*, 11 March 1960, p. 7.
[66] Whitehead, 'Institutional Site Planning', pp. 29–30.
[67] Casson and Conder, quoted in Ives, 'Expansion', in Ives, *First Civic University*, pp. 333–52, p. 335.
[68] Pullan and Abendstern, *Manchester, 1951–73*, pp. 103–5.
[69] Whyte, 'Modernist Moment', pp. 182–6.

Fig. 36. '60,000 square feet of progress. Progress which will itself induce progress and achievement': the Electrical Engineering and Architecture Building, University of Nottingham

Henk Snoek/RIBA Library Photographs Collection.

mother the undergraduate', as Spence put it;[70] a place that would turn 'frightened schoolchildren' into 'healthy, intelligent adults' and 'good citizens'.[71] For Kent, Lancaster, and York, by contrast, the solution was modernist colleges—'like some Dalek stronghold in Doctor Who'—which would, they hoped, inspire a sense of corporate life (Figure 38).[72] These were not of course colleges in the Oxbridge sense. Rather, they were a renewal—and an extension—of the old Redbrick hall of residence, intended to ensure that every member of the university had at least some

---

[70] Basil Spence, 'Building a New University', in David Daiches, ed., *The Idea of a New University: an experiment in Sussex* (London, 1964), pp. 201–16, p. 202.
[71] SussUA, UnivSx Coll IV/IV, 'Sussex in the 1960s' (film), interview with Basil Spence.
[72] Beloff, *Plateglass Universities*, p. 133.

Fig. 37. 'Our First Contemporary Urban University': Mathematics, Earth Sciences and Computer Sciences Building, University of Leeds

John Maltby/RIBA Library Photographs Collection.

experience of corporate life. Still more ambitiously, at Essex and UEA—like Leeds—decks and high-density building were intended to create a vibrant and ever-expanding university.[73] At Essex, in particular, everything was apparently up for grabs: the students would live in tower blocks, the density of population would be higher than ever before; even the bedding was new—with students trialling (and then, it must be said, rejecting) ultra-modern sleeping bags.[74] This was, in Stefan Muthesius' words, a genuinely 'utopianist' moment.[75]

Yet utopia cannot be built quickly—and cannot be built on the cheap. In the 1940s, rationing and government building controls severely restricted the universities' ambitions.[76] In the 1950s, there were complaints that although the materials were now available, the money simply was not.[77] Even in the boom times of the 1960s, the stop-go of government finance and the sudden increases in numbers that the UGC demanded made it hard to stick to a coherent plan. The 1960 proposal for Leeds envisaged a student population of 7,200 by 1970. Even as it was

---

[73] EssUA, University 1(b), Winvenhoe Park, Kenneth Capron to Albert Sloman (27 November 1962).
[74] EssUA, Development Committee 1965/66, 27 September 1965.
[75] Muthesius, *Postwar University*, p. 6.
[76] HL Deb 14 May 1947 vol 147, cc. 727–31.
[77] University of Liverpool, *Report of the Development Committee 1949–54* (Liverpool, 1955), p. 12.

Fig. 38. 'Like some Dalek stronghold in Doctor Who': Langwith College, University of York
Architectural Press Archive/RIBA Library Photographs Collection.

published, however, it was clear that this was at least 1,000 too few. Within a few more years, it was speculated that it might be 10,000 under—and by 1964, people were talking about a university of 20,000.[78] In the determination to keep up, quality was often sacrificed to speed.[79] At Sussex, buildings were designed before it was actually clear how many would inhabit them or even what they would use them for.[80] At Essex, the pace was such that only by the time the fourth tower block was built could the problems encountered in the design of the first be rectified (Figure 39).[81]

When the architectural historian John Summerson was called in to advise the University of Leicester on an architect, he cautioned the vice-chancellor, who had invited him to lunch: 'Some other time I will gladly lunch with you—but not—please not—in any spirit of celebration! From long and bitter experience I know that one should never be optimistic about a building enterprise until the roof is on;

---

[78] Whyte, 'Modernist Moment', pp. 186–7.
[79] EssUA, Development Committee 1966/7, Review of first major building project (31 October 1966).
[80] SussUA, SxMs45/1, Staff Architect's Papers Box 1, Fulton to D. G. Christopherson (7 March 1959).
[81] EssUA, Development Committee 1963–5, 30 November 1964.

Fig. 39. 'The writer receiving the most votes was Kafka': Towers at the University of Essex by Rwendland
Source: Wikipedia. CC BY-SA. 30 Rwendland.

then one should celebrate quickly before the rain begins to come in.'[82] His words were sadly prophetic: many of Leicester's buildings leaked; the lecture theatre subsided; and the Physics block roof collapsed.[83]

The strain that this placed on the relationship between architect and client was understandably extreme. The University of Leeds began taking legal advice on

---

[82] LeiUA, Uncat. Bursarial notes, Summerson to Vice Chancellor (19 March 1956).
[83] LeiUA, Uncat. Files on Rattray Lecture Theatre, 1 July 1968; Bursary Files, 'Reinstatement, 1974–8', 20 March 1974.

whether its architect could be sacked only a few years after appointing him.[84] Peter Chamberlin himself was often 'on the point of resigning in disillusionment'.[85] As his letters grew longer and still more irate, members of the University mocked him behind his back, comparing his letters to the rants of Communist orators, to the lengthy sermons of 'Wee Free' preachers, and finally to 'those periods in "the Ring" when Fricka upbraids Wotan for about two hundred bars whilst the Conductor stirs the orchestral pudding sleepily.' 'What puzzles me', one writer concluded, 'is whether Chamberlin really thinks that his letter will achieve [his goal] or whether the letter is largely reflex combined with an element of the sleepwalker. In either case psychiatric treatment seems advisable.'[86] This was, however, at least a private complaint. In Essex, the architect Kenneth Capon was confronted at a public meeting by furious students,[87] and faced by a motion passed by the General Assembly of academics, which reported 'the impression that the architects appeared to subordinate the wishes of the ultimate users of any building to their own views and . . . the existence of serious defects and technical problems in buildings which had not been foreseen or corrected by specialist consultants'.[88] In 1965 Hugh Casson observed 'most universities are the cemeteries of architects' reputations'.[89]

ALMA MATER REJECTA

It would be wrong to assume from this, however, that the building programmes of the 1950s and 1960s were simply failures. To be sure, there were real problems. Roofs leaked.[90] Sound travelled between rooms, down corridors, and up lift shafts.[91] Universities also found it hard to keep up with the steadily improving conditions that students experienced at home. With wall-to-wall carpets, attractive furnishings, larger and more comfortable houses, the gap between private affluence and public buildings grew greater every year. Homes even grew warmer, with the average living room temperature rising by over 5°F between 1950 and 1970.[92] The results were hugely problematic for the universities. Indeed, a survey at Sussex in 1972 concluded that 'students' expectations with regard to the pure mechanics of existence are consistently higher than is catered for', and it seems likely that this was

---

[84] LeeUA, B Architects and Consultants: CPB 1966–74 (12 July 1966).
[85] LeeUA, Administration, Bursar: Edmund Williamson, unpublished memoir, p. 321.
[86] LeeUA, B Architects and Consultants: CPB 1966–74, Arthur Dower to Vice Chancellor (31 December 1968).
[87] *Wyvern*, 14 November 1969, p. 7.
[88] EssUA, Development Committee 1967–70, 10 December 1969.
[89] Hugh Casson, 'Living, Learning, and Leisure—the planning of the new universities', *Journal of the Royal Society of Arts* 113 (1964–5), pp. 556–71, p. 556.
[90] LeeUA, B Buildings, Development Plan (General) Geoffrey Wilson to Peter Chamberlin (7 August 1973).
[91] Paul Thompson, 'Essex University: what it's like to live there', *Architects' Journal* 145 (1967), pp. 4–6.
[92] Brian Harrison, *Seeking a Role: the United Kingdom 1951–1970* (Oxford, 2009), p. 334.

a more general experience.[93] Certainly, this also proved to be the case at Essex, where the initial enthusiasm of students for their new tower-block living accommodation was replaced by dissatisfaction at a remarkable speed.[94]

Still more importantly, architecture continued to possess symbolic significance. Just as all this new building had signalled a new era in university life, so challenges to that life found their expression in attacks on new buildings. This meant that even those edifices which obviously worked could be seen as complicit in a more general failure. So it was at Liverpool, where a bitter article of 1968—'Alma Mater Rejecta'—decried the 'concrete and glass jungle now arising around us', and objected to the 'centrally-heated, cloyingly comfortable university buildings', that the writer saw as synonymous with a corrupt and corrupting institution.[95]

This attack on university architecture was often driven by a dislike for a building's particular function. Places of worship, in particular, became ever more unpopular.[96] At Keele, for example, the new chapel was described as 'luxuriously and largely unnecessary',[97] 'Phallic symbolism gone mad'.[98] Its site, at the heart of the university, was similarly condemned as conveying an entirely unrepresentative—indeed, a dishonest—sense of Keele as a fundamentally Christian community.[99] The same was true at Sussex, where the chapel and its location, again at the centre of the campus, was seen as 'a symbol of all this University *doesn't* stand for'.[100] Even when renamed—called a 'Meeting House' instead of a chapel—it riled some working there, with one Sussex professor claiming that the very sight of the building from his office window would make it quite impossible for him to do any work whatsoever (Figure 40).[101]

Increasingly, halls of residence, which had only recently been considered the heart of Redbrick university life, also came in for the same sorts of criticism. Their rules became increasingly irksome; 'It's like living with a maiden aunt', complained students at Leicester.[102] Their traditions became harder to maintain.[103] Their very existence was challenged. 'A university which does not aim to segregate its students from the ordinary business of life can have little or no use for halls of residence', declared a Liverpool academic in 1964.[104] By 1969 even the Federation of Conservative Students believed that halls had become 'obsolete'.[105]

---

[93] SussUA, UoS Architecture, Box 2, 'Survey of Student Attitudes to Accommodation' (May 1972).
[94] Marie Clossick, *Student Residence: a new approach at the University of Essex. A Study of the Rayleigh Tower, 1965–8* (London, 1967); University of Essex, *Report of the Annan Enquiry* (Colchester, 1974), p. 32.
[95] *Sphinx*, Spring 1968, pp. 5–6. [96] See also, *Wessex*, 25 November 1958, p. 5.
[97] *Concourse*, 10 December 1965, p. 3. [98] *Cygnet*, January 1968, p. 3.
[99] *Cygnet*, March 1963, p. 1. [100] *Wine Press*, 4 June 1964, p. 1.
[101] Lord Shawcross, *Life Sentence* (London, 1995), p. 267.
[102] *Ripple*, 25 February 1964, p. 1.
[103] M. J. Crossley Evans and A. Sulstan, *A History of Wills Hall, University of Bristol* (Bristol, 1994), pp. 49–50; Mathers, *Steel City Scholars*, p. 197.
[104] *Sphinx*, January 1964, p. 12.
[105] PP 1968–9 (449-I), *Select Committee on Education and Science: Report on Student Relations*, vol. i, p. 100.

Fig. 40. 'A symbol of all this University doesn't stand for': Meeting House, University of Sussex

Architectural Press Archive/RIBA Library Photographs Collection.

More important than these particular critiques was a general sense that university architecture had taken a wrong turning.[106] Architectural critics, academics, and students came increasingly to condemn the pretensions of the post-war university. The megastructures and the massive development plans came to be seen as evidence not of ambition, but of hubris.[107] Incomplete, almost certainly uncompletable, the new universities became particular targets of scorn: the home of 'an idiosyncratic and largely frivolous style of architecture', in the words of one critic.[108] Yet the attack also reached out to the older civic institutions, too. 'The architects and planners have pronounced our doom', observed one Manchester historian in 1965. 'It is to spend the rest of our days in this university... in identical cells, forever wandering down long, dark, tunnels, lurching against doors that will always open

---

[106] For a very early example, see J. K. Page, 'Academic Goals and University Buildings', *Universities Quarterly* 18 (1963–4), pp. 301–8.
[107] Brown, 'The Irrelevance of University Architecture', pp. 31–55.
[108] Cassidy, 'Pressure on University Building', p. 508.

the other way, searching for the numbers that alone will distinguish one cell from another'.[109]

Nor was it just details that were attacked. The whole approach taken—with its emphasis on unity, on density, on monumentality—soon stood condemned. 'Where is the vice-chancellor with sufficient self-confidence to say, "We won't commit ourselves to permanent buildings until we see how it works"', asked Reyner Banham in 1966. 'And in the absence of such paragons of academic modesty, where is the architect who has the guts to say, "Don't do it. Call me back in three quinquennia, when you begin to know what you're doing".'[110] Perhaps the most damning comment came from Essex, where the department of literature was asked to suggest names for a new tower block: 'The writer receiving the most votes was Kafka'.[111]

The increased isolation of university campuses added a particular resonance to these objections. It was not just the new universities with their green-field sites, nor the institutions which moved to the suburbs that became increasingly separated from local, urban communities. The sheer scale of developments at Liverpool, Manchester, and Leeds inevitably distanced town from gown, with the demolition of hundreds of homes creating a sort of *cordon sanitaire* around the campus.

Even smaller universities, like Leicester, also saw a slow but inexorable estrangement.[112] Its development plan of 1948 was predicated on the belief that it would create 'the city's finest civic building centre'.[113] Leslie Martin's revisions of 1957 similarly acknowledged that as 'whatever was built would become a dominating feature of the district; we needed to show the city that we were taking the responsibility seriously'.[114] To that end both plans—however different in form—sought to preserve a similar sense of place and stress the university's connection with Leicester: using local bricks, low-rise buildings, and retaining the view of the city from the neighbouring park. Not everyone approved. 'I cannot possibly believe that you can have a healthy mind in the great Neo-Urinal Halls of Residence and the Physics and Chemistry blocks', declared one student.[115] But the attempt to preserve what was seen as a civic site continued. Nevertheless, within just a few years, this vision had been lost—replaced by a series of three high-rise, high-profile towers, each dramatically symbolizing the university's detachment from its locality. First came Stirling and Gowan's famous Engineering Building,[116] described by the local paper as 'Bizarre...angry...controversial...rubbery and man-hating'

---

[109] Brian Manning, quoted in Brian Pullan and Michelle Abendstern, *A History of the University of Manchester, 1951–73* (Manchester, 2000), p. 106.
[110] Reyner Banham, 'The Outhouses of Academe', *New Society* 8 (1966), pp. 546–7, p. 547.
[111] EssUA, UoE, Box 3(b), Development Plan, File on Residential Towers.
[112] Though cf. Mark Crinson, *Stirling and Gowan: architecture from austerity to affluence* (New Haven and London, 2012), p. 259.
[113] LeiUA, ULA/AD/D5/1, Transcript of City Council Debate (7 January 1947).
[114] LeiUA, Uncat Minutes 1955–56, Buildings Advisory Committee, 13 March 1956.
[115] Edward Teague, 'The New Tradition', *Ripple*, 8 Feb. 1963, p. 3.
[116] John McKean, *Leicester University Engineering Building: James Stirling and James Gowan* (London, 1994).

Fig. 41. 'Bizarre... angry... controversial... rubbery and man-hating': James Stirling's engineering department, Denys Lasdun's Charles Wilson Building, and Ove Arup's Attenborough Building at the University of Leicester

John Donat/RIBA Photographs Collection.

(Figure 41).[117] Then there was Denys Lasdun's lumpen concrete Charles Wilson building.[118] Finally came Ove Arup's Attenborough Building. Looking at its scale and size, observing its profile and bearing in mind its name, students pointedly enquired, 'should it be called "Dick"?'[119] With each building, the university came to look less and less like Leicester and more and more like the other institutions within a national system.

For sixties' student radicals, already upset at the gap they perceived between the university and the world, this growing physical and symbolic separation was intolerable.[120] In that respect, it is worth quoting at length the complaints made by Dave Robertson, a leading Liverpool agitator, in 1969:

> Over the last ten years, Liverpool University has undergone a face-lift, concrete surgery. Moving with the times and because the city had plenty left, they proceeded to smash every available pre-1930 building into rubble, and erect new, shiny, intellectual structures, with simple lines—90° angles; and intersecting forms—boxes. Over acres of old Liverpool, over roads, over footpaths, over the shops and houses, where

---

[117] *Leicester Mercury*, 2 April 1963.
[118] LeiUA, Bursarial Files, Charles Wilson Building (3 March 1961).
[119] *Ripple*, 30 Oct. 1969, p. 5.
[120] Trevor Fisk, 'Student Power', *Architectural Review* 147 (1970), pp. 292–4, p. 294.

once there had been people, they built long and white. (Is it so dissimilar to covering your poor pubic hair with adhesive tape?)

Leaving that unanswerable question hanging, he went on:

> Into the vacuum, they poured, ink into milk, 6000 students—4800 scientists, 1200 artists, 4800 men, 1200 women. The fences went up. No cars allowed on the campus: all roads across the campus to be closed: entry and exit permits under review. Halls of residence—palaces of luxury, incubators for the sterile, prefabricated ovens for the insipid, complacent and congenitally dull—were built far enough away from anybody's problems—except their own—in intellectually stimulating greenery, whilst those who could not receive technological, hygienic, bisexual, asexual incarceration were sent to mellifluous suburbs and lace-curtain landladies.[121]

In slightly fewer than two hundred words, Roberston—who went on to become a professor at the neighbouring John Moores University—encapsulated every one of the objections that radicals made against the new university architecture. He damned its design, condemned its effects on the city, drew attention to the way in which it isolated the university from its neighbourhood, and attacked the halls of residence as a way of separating students further from real life.[122] This sense that there was something rotten at the heart of the university—something that found its expression in its physical form—was articulated again and again. No wonder that buildings became such a central part of student protest in the late-1960s and early-1970s.

The architecture of the universities did not just inspire contempt; it also aided student agitation. The range of designs was of course huge—from the 'grids' of Loughborough to the 'nodes' of Kent;[123] from the corridors of Leeds to the precinct of Manchester; 'from Sussex's swinging pseudo-Corbusian vaults... to York's ever-so-'umble prefabricated units'.[124] What united this effort was the widespread acceptance that university planning was analogous to town planning, that the university was 'a special kind of town'.[125] Nor was this view confined only to architects, for academics shared it too. At Essex, for example, the vice-chancellor hoped to inspire the 'variety and liveliness of town life';[126] the historian Paul Thompson celebrated the fact that 'the Essex student is treated like an adult in an intellectual city';[127] and the poet Donald Davie compared the university plan variously to the townscapes of Genoa, Venice, Warsaw, and Budapest, exclaiming

---

[121] *Sphinx*, Summer 1969, p. 9.
[122] On the background to this, see the excellent website: <http://senatehouseoccupation.wordpress.com/> (accessed 21 May 2014).
[123] Michael Brawne, 'The New Universities: an appraisal', *Architectural Review* 147 (1970), pp. 250–4, 283–5, p. 253.
[124] Banham, 'Outhouses', p. 546.
[125] Lionel Brett, 'Site, Growth and Plan', *Architectural Review* 134 (1963), pp. 257–64, p. 264. See also Nicholas Bullock, Peter Dickens, and Philip Steadman, *A Theoretical Basis for University Planning* (Cambridge, 1968), p. 1; Edward Williamson, 'New University Development in the Sixties', *Era* 1 (1968), pp. 38–43, p. 38.
[126] Sloman, *University in the Making*, p. 69.
[127] Paul Thompson, 'Essex University: what it's like to live there', *Architects' Journal*, 4 January 1967, pp. 4–6, pp. 5–6.

'if there is still time to try one more throw of this noble European concept of the civic, who should make the attempt, if not a university?'[128] Yet, as events at Essex were to show, such a conception offered problems as well as opportunities.[129] An urban environment lacked the clearly defined boundaries that had characterized much previous university building, creating a sense of 'homelessness'.[130] 'The conception of a university city', wrote Noel Annan in a report on Essex, 'depersonalises students still further', fostering a sense of *anomie*.[131] Moreover, as John Carswell was later to reflect, the homogenous and expansive sites of the universities made 'a perfect campaigning ground for the imaginative strategist'. A new campus 'lacked any permanent garrison by the opposition, and it could be cut off, picketed and exhibited. It was in fact an ideal theatre of war.'[132]

From 1968 events at Essex bore out this analysis, as the university experienced a remarkable level of student—and staff—unrest. Sit-ins, protests, vandalism, even physical threats: the university grew so used to fights over the campus that the student newspaper greeted the opening of one new building with the simple headline: 'Ready for occupation soon.'[133] The whole world watched as buildings became battlegrounds, and messages of support for student militants were sent from Jean-Paul Sartre, Bertrand Russell, Joseph Needham, Alex Comfort, and Jo-Jo La Boot—'the people's porno performer'—who wrote, 'You are doing a funnerful groovey thing.'[134]

Nor was this confined to Essex: there were sit-ins across the university system from the summer of 1966 onwards. At the LSE, fights took place over the use of lecture theatres and the erection of steel gates designed to divide up the buildings. In the ensuing struggle, a porter died.[135] At Warwick, the struggle was over access to university offices—and especially to the locked files kept in the registry.[136] In sympathy with this, Southampton students also occupied their registry, expelling a secretary with the immortal words: 'What are you doing here, Daddy-O? This is ours.'[137] Copycat occupations took place at Leicester, Birmingham, Bristol, Manchester, Nottingham, and beyond.

Once again, Liverpool provides a good example of what went on even in the older universities. Here, in March 1970, students occupied the newly built Senate House: 'a symbol', as Dave Robertson put it, 'of all that the university has stood for in this society—an edifice of bureaucratic insensitivity, technocratic isolation, of plain old-fashioned indifference to external problems'. Part of the appeal was the

---

[128] Donald Davie, 'The Merits of City Culture', *New Statesman* 68 (1964), p. 920.
[129] See also, Crouch, *Student Revolt*, p. 174; E. P. Thompson, *Warwick University Ltd: industry, management and the universities* (Harmondsworth, 1970), p. 43.
[130] Mary Douglas, *The Times*, 3 August 1974, p. 13.
[131] University of Essex, *Report of the Annan Enquiry* (Colchester, 1974), p. 31.
[132] Carswell, *Government and the Universities*, p. 122.
[133] *Wyvern*, 31 January 1969, p. 6.
[134] Richard Boston, 'The Essex Affair', *New Society*, 26 May 1968, pp. 745–6, p. 746.
[135] Crouch, *Student Revolt*, pp. 48–85.
[136] Thompson, *Warwick University*, pp. 51–4. See also, p. 59.
[137] USA, MS 224/7/A914, Sit in At Southampton: February 1970. Fact-Finding Committee Report, p. 14.

fact that 'From the outside it looks like a fortress'; partly, the sit-in was simply fun.[138] In the words of another student, 'I was stuck out in digs in Bootle and paid over £5 5 shillings each week for full board, so the opportunity to occupy the Senate was not just a political act but an amazing social opportunity: girls, dope, music.'[139] Perhaps the primary motivation for the occupation was about control of space—or, more accurately, about the possession of places which were familiar, but had previously been tightly policed. As Dave Robertson went on: 'I found it pleasantly amusing to walk and sleep in a room from which I had been asked to leave some months before.'[140]

In that way, university buildings provided the means, motive, and opportunity for student protest. Far from being an outright failure, post-war university architecture was a victim of its own success: the size and scale of the project helped create a counter-reaction which was impossible to contain. What was intended to be a utopian environment—one designed to solve the perceived problems of the civic universities—was now, as a contemporary put it, 'the elite, separate, breeding ground of an unreal discontent'.[141]

---

[138] *Sphinx*, Summer 1970, p. 14.
[139] <http://senatehouseoccupation.wordpress.com/reflections-and-recollections/waking-to-the-sound-of/> (accessed 16 April 2010): punctuation added.
[140] *Sphinx*, Summer 1970, p. 14.
[141] John McKean, 'The English University of the 1960s: built community, model universe', in Iain Boyd Whyte, ed., *Man-Made Future: planning, education and design in mid-twentieth-century Britain* (London, 2007), pp. 205–33, p. 208 (quoting his own article of 1970).

Conclusion

Predictably enough, little attention has been paid to how all these developments—architectural, social, academic, and political—affected the University of Keele. Yet here too, the changes that swept across the world of higher education had important consequences. Expansion produced problems with accommodation.[1] A reduction in government funds made it harder to sustain the university's expensive four-year course; in any event by the mid-1960s complaints were growing, even amongst the staff recruited to teach it, that although the intention of the curriculum was 'laudable, the effect... [was] almost always trivial and may be worse'.[2] Total residence was abandoned in 1967, and the common curriculum of the foundation year ceased to be compulsory in 1973. Student radicalism also reshaped relationships. By 1970, there had been occupations, marches, and even arson, with firebombs thrown at a series of university buildings.[3] One protest took the form of nude sunbathing, and although one senior staff member welcomed the display on the grounds that it allowed him to distinguish between male and female undergraduates for the first time in years, others proved less amused.[4] Staffordshire County Council stopped its annual grant until student behaviour was improved.[5] The Keele experiment stood condemned as the construction of what students in the 1970s called a 'concentration campus'.[6]

This was, of course, a gross exaggeration, not much less offensive than UEA students who described their accommodation as 'Auschwitz with carpets' (Figure 42).[7] But it spoke of a general sense of failure; of opportunities not taken and hopes not realized. By the end of this period, indeed, a number of people were abandoning their belief in the Redbrick tradition in favour of something more flexible, more nebulous even. For some, the problem was state control, and the answer a private university, founded in Buckingham in 1976.[8] For others, the problem was the inherent limitation of a physical site and the solution a 'University

---

[1] *Cygnet*, 15 October 1971, p. 1.
[2] Andor Gomme, 'Publicity or Promise: the new universities', *Delta* 34 (Autumn 1964), pp. 2–19, p. 17.
[3] KUA, Senate Minutes 1970–71, p. 3: Report of the Committee on the Events of the Summer Term 1970.
[4] J. M. Kolbert, *Keele: the first fifty years, 1950–2000* (Keele, 2000), pp. 149–50.
[5] *Cygnet*, 19 June 1970, p. 1.
[6] *Cygnet*, 29 May 1970, p. 1.
[7] John Lowe, 'Bark I Worse than it's [*sic.*] Bite', *Octopus* 20 (Autumn, 1974), pp. 10–11, p. 11.
[8] John Clarke, 'The University of Buckingham: an historical perspective', in James Tooley, ed., *Buckingham at 25: freeing the universities from state control* (London, 2001), pp. 189–210.

Fig. 42. 'Auschwitz with carpets'? The University of East Anglia Campus, Norwich
Architectural Press Archive/RIBA Library Photographs Collection.

of the Air': higher education offered solely by radio and television. One of the most interesting contributions to the debate came from the avant-garde architect, Cedric Price. In the place of what he believed to be the 'failed higher education experiment' at Keele, he drew up plans for a 'Potteries ThinkBelt': a rolling university, carried on the railway lines that snaked through Staffordshire (Figure 43).[9] This would be, he argued, 'a major industrial undertaking, not a service run by gentleman for the few'.[10] It was, without doubt, a visionary proposal. Yet it came to nothing, and had no impact on the development of higher education in Britain.[11] The monumental mode remained dominant. Planners still aimed at permanence.

---

[9] Paul Barker in Samantha Hardingham and Kester Rattenbury, eds, *Supercrit #1: Cedric Price, Potteries Thinkbelt* (Routledge, 2007), p. 63.

[10] Cedric Price, 'Potteries ThinkBelt: a plan for an advanced educational industry in North Staffordshire', *Architectural Design* 36 (1966), pp. 484–97, p. 484.

[11] Tellingly, the only purchaser of the full documentation was the Ministry of Housing rather than the Department of Education: Royston Landau, 'A Philosophy of Enabling', in Cedric Price, *The Square Book* (Chichester, 2003), p. 9–15, p. 15.

Fig. 43. 'A major industrial undertaking, not a service run by gentleman for the few': Cedric Price's Potteries Thinkbelt

© 1964–66, Museum of Modern Art/Scala, Florence.

The University of Buckingham did at least become a reality, but it remained small and undercapitalized, and failed to inspire imitation.[12] And whilst the Open University—as the University of the Air was eventually named—did become a major provider of higher education, it could not quite escape the expectations that had grown up in the century since Owens College received its charter. From the first it was more than just a virtual institution; it spent time and money on building appropriately impressive accommodation. Initially based in Belgrave Square and equipped with a grand chandelier so ostentatiously opulent that it pulled the ceiling down, it soon acquired a home in Milton Keynes designed by the same Maxwell Fry whose West African ideas had so intimidated the education officer for Ghana.[13] Despite all the critics, and in spite of all the problems that it faced, the old Redbrick university model had life in it yet.

---

[12] Clarke, 'The University of Buckingham', p. 210.
[13] Walter Perry, *Open University: a personal account by the first vice chancellor* (Milton Keynes, 1976), pp. 37–9.

PART VI

1973–1997

Prologue

From a distance, the University of Lowlands was a striking and substantial edifice:

> In a certain light, from a certain angle, viewed in later afternoon from the far side of the lake, it looks like a modern version of a medieval fortified town, with its subtly interlocked towers and flat roofs and buttresses casting patterns of light and shadow, its elegantly brutal concrete walkways and bridges crisscrossing the facades, creating unexpected teasing links between tower and piazza, refectory and boiler room, Arts and Cybernetics, in an endless labyrinth of multi-level interfacing.

Viewed close-up, however, it was clear: 'The University of Lowlands is a dump'.[1] Indeed, worse than that, by the mid-1980s it was in terminal decline, a patchwork of 'flaking concrete', a wind tunnel that funnelled 'dust, dust and grit along the sad abandoned walkways, into the cracks and fissures of the empty towers'.[2] Of course, Lowlands University did not actually exist. It was created by Andrew Davies for his television comedy, *A Very Peculiar Practice*. But despite the fact that it was fiction, it is not hard to see the germs of truth in this account. *A Very Peculiar Practice* was based on Davies' own experiences as a lecturer at Warwick; the university was inspired by the campus at UEA; and the series was filmed at both Birmingham and Keele.[3] In that sense, at least, the decaying carcass of Lowlands was intended to be every British university in an age of apparently manifest crisis.

For many in higher education, this period was experienced as one of anger as well as anxiety and acute difficulty. The 1970s witnessed the impact of inflation, the 1980s saw swingeing reductions in funding, the 1990s was a decade of quite remarkable uncertainty in universities. More long-lasting influences also contributed to the sense of turmoil, as rising student numbers and growing government involvement continued radically to reshape the academy. Yet, if this was an era of traumatic and infuriating change for some, it was also a golden age for the university novel and the university film; and, indeed, for a new genre: the university television series.[4] The year 1981—a year of dramatic cuts in the higher education budget—was also marked by the roaring successes of first *The History Man* on BBC2 and then *Brideshead Revisited* on ITV. Three years later, Willy Russell's Open University comedy, *Educating Rita*, won the BAFTA for best film.

---

[1] Andrew Davies, *A Very Peculiar Practice* (London, 1986), p. 5.
[2] Andrew Davies, *A Very Peculiar Practice: the new frontier* (London, 1988), p. 4.
[3] Paul Fisher, 'A Very Peculiar Playwright', *THES*, 15 September 1989, p. 16.
[4] <http://www.independent.co.uk/arts-entertainment/tv/features/how-tv-drama-became-university-challenged-1811485.html> (accessed 21 October 2010).

Colleges and universities had been fictionalized before—but never so prolifically or successfully.

As the sociologist Ian Carter complained in 1990, the campus novel had been a predominantly Oxbridge enterprise for years.[5] Now, however, Redbrick struck back in terms of quantity as well as quality—starting with David Lodge's trilogy of books on the University of Rummidge, a place 'which occupies, for the purposes of fiction, the space where Birmingham is to be found on maps of the so-called real world'.[6] Nor was it just the civic universities that found themselves depicted. The polytechnics were playfully satirized in Posy Simmonds' *Guardian* cartoons and mercilessly mocked in Howard Jacobson's first novel, *Coming from Behind*.[7] The technical colleges were aggressively attacked in Tom Sharpe's increasingly scabrous, increasingly obscene *Wilt* series.[8] And this is to say nothing of *The Young Ones*, a cult TV comedy of the early 1980s, which depicted student life as utterly squalid and students themselves as socially and intellectually inadequate.[9] It is still justly famous for its parody of the quiz show *University Challenge*, in which the ghastly undergraduates of Scumbag College came face to face with the appalling snobs of Footlights College, Oxbridge.

A widespread sense of crisis in higher education pervades even the most humorous of these books and TV serials, with Jacobson and Sharpe in particular each painting an equally depressing picture of both the students and staff: the incapable in full pursuit of the unteachable. Nor were novels set in universities any more cheery. The Kent sociologist Frank Parkin's deservedly little-known novel, *The Mind and Body Shop* is simply the most extreme of its type, describing, as it does, a dystopian university in which students are forced to sleep rough, Shi'ite terrorists populate the campus, and the philosophy department can only survive by running a brothel on the side.[10] In other books, characters echoed the complaints of David Lodge's anti-hero, the Rummidge English lecturer Philip Swallow:

> I feel as if, by the time I retire, I shall have lived through the entire lifecycle of post-war higher education. When I was a student myself, provincial universities were a very small show. Then in the sixties, it was all expansion, growth, new building. Would you believe our biggest grouse in the sixties was about the noise of construction work? Now it's all gone quiet. Won't be long before they're sending in the demolition crews, no doubt.[11]

---

[5] Ian Carter, *Ancient Cultures of Conceit: British university fiction in the post-war years* (London and New York, 1990), p. 4.

[6] David Lodge, *Nice Work* (1988; London, 1989), p. 7. See also his *Changing Places* (1975; London, 1978) and *Small World: an academic romance* (1984; London, 1985).

[7] Posy Simmonds, *Pick of Posy* (London, 1982), *Very Posy* (London, 1985), *Pure Posy* (London, 1987); Howard Jacobson, *Coming from Behind* (London, 1983). See also *THES*, 12 August 1983, p. 8.

[8] Tom Sharp, *Wilt* (London, 1976), *The Wilt Alternative* (London, 1979), *Wilt on High* (1984; Oxford, 1986).

[9] Ben Elton, Rik Mayall, and Lise Mayer, *Bachelor Boys: the Young Ones Book* (London, 1984).

[10] Frank Parkin, *The Mind and Body Shop* (London, 1986).

[11] Lodge, *Nice Work*, p. 65.

Indeed the notion that higher education was in terminal decline, and that universities might find themselves bulldozed to the ground, was a popular one—and it was not confined to fiction. In 1975 the Tory MP—and future universities minister—Rhodes Boyson proposed that the troubled University of Essex should be turned into a sugar beet refinery.[12] Six years later, in 1981, Keith Joseph was made secretary of state for education, and almost his first question was 'How do you close a University?'[13]

Perhaps the best insight into the mentality of higher education in this period comes in the source with which this section began: Andrew Davies' *A Very Peculiar Practice*. Although Davies is now better known for his costume dramas and sexually-charged adaptations of classic novels, in many respects he deserves his place in history—and certainly earns his place in this history—for this piece of work, which remains a strikingly insightful, and amusing, account of universities under strain, threatened by financial ruin and philistine managerialism.[14] The first series, broadcast in 1986, sees the University of Lowlands face a 25 per cent drop in funding and forcible merger with Hendon Police College. The second series, shown two years later, concludes with a student riot, the vice-chancellor's collapse into insanity, and the University's re-establishment as a mental hospital. Throughout it all, decay is the *Leitmotif*; in the words of one central character, the equally degenerate Dr Jock McCannon, it was 'The Sick University'. Indeed, that is the title of his latest book manuscript—a worthy successor to his previous works, *The Therapeutic Village* and *Sexual Anxiety and the Common Cold*. Looking over the campus one morning, a hung-over McCannon sees the problems with unusual clarity: 'the constipated administrative structure, the clogged and flooded walkways, the puny stature of its leader'; 'the University', he concludes, 'is a swamp of fear and loathing'.[15]

But was Davies fair? Was this the era of the Sick University? And what of the others? What of writers like Peter Scott, editor of the *Times Higher* and a future vice-chancellor, who talked disparagingly of the 'menopausal university' in 1981?[16] Were they, too, correct to suggest that this was an era of not just change but also decay, a time in which Britain's higher education lost its energy and began a slow process of decline? As we will see, in many ways this period was extraordinarily challenging for the university. But it was also an era of accelerated growth and remarkable creativity. Moreover, the world of the universities was not merely defended—it was actually expanded, as the forty-six universities of 1974 became 115 by 1997. Once again, talk of a crisis conceals as much as it reveals.

There is, then, no simple answer to the question of whether higher education was demeaned or redeemed, debased or reformed in this period. Indeed, it is doubtful whether that is even a question worth asking. More interesting than the existence of

---

[12] *THES*, 3 January 1975, p. 2.
[13] Andrew Denham and Mark Garnett, *Keith Joseph* (Chesham, 2001), p. 368.
[14] *THES*, 21 October 2010, p. 33.
[15] Davies, *A Very Peculiar Practice*, pp. 125, 12.
[16] *THES*, 14 August 1981, p. 24; See also Peter Scott, *The Crisis of the University* (London, 1984), p. 8.

this all-too familiar—if, perhaps, especially shrill—cry of crisis in the university is the fact that the debate about higher education now involved an even larger public than it had done before. It was discussed in numerous books, filled pages in the newspapers, and was considered sufficiently interesting to be broadcast on prime-time TV. What this reflected was an apparently significant change in the nature of higher education—and, more than that, an ostensibly striking shift in perceptions.

To a certain extent, this critique of higher education represented little more than the by-product of a more general sense of cultural, social, and—especially—economic crisis. Just as the fears of the 1870s and 1950s had prompted expansionism, so now declinism provoked attacks on the universities which had been founded or enlarged in the hope of solving Britain's problems. The 1970s and 1980s, in particular, gave voice to the widespread conviction that Britain was experiencing not just relative decline, but perhaps even economic collapse.[17] In this context, all forms of established authority—from politicians to clerics, the trades unions to the civil service—were open to attack.[18] And the universities were not immune from this general sense of pessimism; indeed, they were linked to it, with a much broadcast belief that higher education was not only degenerate but also implicated in a more national degeneration.[19] As Noel Annan observed in 1982: 'The decline in the esteem of higher education is linked to the decline in the performance, indeed in some cases, the extinction, of British industry.'[20]

For some, like the historians Martin Weiner and Corelli Barnett, the case was clear: British universities had failed in their duty to inculcate entrepreneurialism and inspire economic growth. Oxbridge, they argued, was mired in amateurism and an anti-business ethos.[21] The Redbrick universities 'never threw off the lower status that went with their task',[22] and, as a result, simply ended up imitating Oxbridge.[23] The consequences, they concluded, were disastrous for universities and economy alike. For other commentators, higher education had failed not because it was alienated from capitalism, but because it was too closely connected to it. The sociologist Michael Rustin, for example, argued—not inaccurately—that the class structure still mapped directly on to the university system: with Oxbridge for the aristocracy, Redbrick and Robbins creating 'the "bourgeois" university', and a desperate need for the creation of a genuine 'Popular University' for the working classes to attend.[24]

---

[17] David Edgerton, *Warfare State, Britain, 1920–1970* (Cambridge, 2006), pp. 5–6, 301–3.
[18] Brian Harrison, *Finding a Role? The United Kingdom, 1970–1990* (Oxford, 2010), pp. 514–15, 543–6.
[19] See, for example, Ivor Crewe, in *THES*, 14 February 1975, p. 5.
[20] Noel Annan, 'British Higher Education, 1960–80: a personal retrospect', *Minerva* 20 (1982), pp. 1–24, 17.
[21] See also Bernard Crick, in *THES*, 28 January 1977, p. 1, for an early intimation of this theme.
[22] Martin J. Weiner, *English Culture and the Decline of the Industrial Spirit, 1850–1980* (1981; Harmondsworth, 1985), p. 23.
[23] Corelli Barnett, *The Audit of War* (1986; London, 1987), p. 222.
[24] Michael Rustin, 'The Idea of the Popular University: a historical perspective', in Janet Finch and Michael Rustin, eds, *A Degree of Choice: education after eighteen* (Harmondsworth, 1986), pp. 17–66.

Despite the pioneering work of scholars like Michael Sanderson, who sought to overturn both the accounts of national decline and of the universities' part within it, the belief that British higher education was uniquely problematic—especially cut off from the realities of economic life or particularly oblivious to the demands of social justice—remained powerful throughout this period.[25] Politicians of the right, like the Conservative Chancellor Nigel Lawson, were impressed by the arguments adduced by Corelli Barnett—and backbench Tory MPs were willing to go further still, urging the government: 'Why don't we just make them give up this Shakespeare nonsense and do something useful?'[26] Politicians of the centre, like the Social Democrat Shirley Williams, condemned universities which, in her view, 'lived comfortably in their ivory towers, blissfully disregarding the world outside'.[27] Politicians of the left, like the Labour leader Neil Kinnock, increasingly believed that the universities had been instrumental in thwarting social mobility—and threatened fines for those institutions which admitted too many products of the public schools.[28] So powerful and pervasive was this discourse of failure that historians were tempted uncritically to perpetuate it well into the 1990s: repeating, on the basis of very little evidence, the old story of a university system in which innovation was invariably—perhaps inevitably—crushed beneath the weight of aristocratic, Oxbridge, tradition.[29]

But if there was a widespread agreement that something was wrong with higher education, there was no consensus on what should be done to put it right. Attempts by government to make the universities more responsive to business led to accusations of unwarranted interference and a corruption of the academy. With ever-increasing frequency the politicians responsible admitted that they were concerned about the impact of their actions too.[30] Even Margaret Thatcher came to doubt the wisdom of her own government's higher education policy, accepting that some of her critics 'had a stronger case than I would have liked. It made me concerned that many distinguished academics thought that Thatcherism in education meant a philistine subordination of scholarship to the immediate requirements of vocational teaching.'[31] Within institutions, as well, changes in the culture of higher education were fiercely contested. Attempts to radicalize the curriculum at North London Polytechnic in 1970s, for example, were described as the *Rape of Reason* by discontented members of staff.[32]

---

[25] See, in general, Michael Sanderson, *Education and Economic Decline in Britain, 1870s to the 1990s* (Cambridge, 1999) and especially his 'The English Civic Universities and the "Industrial Spirit", 1870–1914', *Historical Journal* 61 (1988), pp. 90–104.

[26] Nigel Lawson, *The View From No 11: memoirs of a Tory radical* (London, 1992), p. 607; quoted in George Walden, *Lucky George: memoirs of an anti-politician* (London, 1999), p. 270.

[27] Shirley Williams, *Climbing the Bookshelves* (London, 2009), p. 239.

[28] Fred Dainton, *British Universities: purposes, problems, and pressures* (Cambridge, 1981), p. 18.

[29] Sarah V. Barnes, 'England's Civic Universities and the Triumph of the Oxbridge Ideal', *History of Education Quarterly* 36 (1996), pp. 271–305; Elizabeth J. Morse, 'English Civic Universities and the Myth of Decline', *History of Universities* 11 (1992), pp. 177–204.

[30] George Walden, *We Should Know Better: solving the education crisis* (London, 1996).

[31] Margaret Thatcher, *The Downing Street Years* (London, 1993), p. 599.

[32] Caroline Cox, Keith Jacka, and John Marks, *Rape of Reason: the corruption of North London Polytechnic* (London, 1975).

At the end of this period, the journalist Melanie Phillips summed up these ostensibly conflicting complaints in her book, *All Must Have Prizes*. Phillips condemned policies which had, she claimed, created universities where 'free intellectual enquiry was all but snuffed out by business imperatives'. She was equally scathing about the cultural relativism of academics, who in the name of equality and access to university had actually—or so she said—contributed to a pronounced deterioration in standards.[33] Phillips was unusually catholic in her hatreds, but she undoubtedly spoke for many who were dissatisfied with attempts to make higher education either more relevant to the economy or more representative of society as a whole.[34]

The historian of higher education between 1974 and 1997 is consequently presented with a series of intractable paradoxes. On the one hand, there were those who argued that this period saw too much change; on the other, there were those who said that change did not go far enough. Some maintained that the universities admitted too many students; others that they admitted too few. Critics of the British higher education system were inclined to accuse it of being at one and the same time anti-entrepreneurial and too beholden to big business. The universities had never been more criticized; yet they had never been more popular either. The reality was that higher education in Britain was radically changed in these two decades—growing to an unprecedented size at unprecedented speed, becoming ever-more tightly circumscribed by government control, and doing all this against the backdrop of hostile comments and a poor financial environment. Little wonder that many academics recurred, once again, to talk of a crisis in the university. 'Nostalgia is a big thing in academia', observed Diana Warwick, head of the Committee of Vice Chancellors and Principals in 1996; 'everything is worse today.'[35]

Yet, amidst all this talk of decline, debasement, and even of betrayal, what was often missed was the remarkable strength of older ideas about the nature and function of the university. Although the scale of the system changed almost beyond all recognition, Redbrick remained the basis of British higher education—and the transformation of the polytechnics into universities in 1992 was simply further proof that no genuine alternative to the civic university model had been evolved. This crisis, just like the other crises we have explored, thus exposes surprising continuities as well as changes. Above all—and this is perhaps the greatest surprise—it reveals the continuing importance of a university tradition begun nearly 200 years before.

---

[33] Melanie Phillips, *All Must Have Prizes* (London, 1996), pp. 300, 302.
[34] For a good survey of criticisms, see David Watson, 'The New Attack on Higher Education', *Perspectives* 4 (2000), pp. 90–4.
[35] Diana Warwick, 'Sunset or New Dawn for the Universities?', *Perspectives* 1 (1997), pp. 2–5, p. 2.

11
Reshaping Higher Education

Two factors reshaped the world of higher education in this period: a growth in student numbers and an increase in direct government intervention. Yet the relationship between the two is not as uncomplicated as this categorical statement might suggest. Writing in 1996, the political scientist Anthony King observed that in the previous three decades Britain had been governed, in effect, by 'a tribe of hyper-active children'.[1] Higher education policy certainly bore this out, and the years after 1974 were marked by a bewildering range of policies, initiatives and reforms, whilst the number of students and of institutions grew and grew. It would be wrong, however, to suggest that government intervention was the only key to explaining this growth. For one thing, it is vital not to ignore the mediating institutions that acted between the state and the general public. The universities and polytechnics themselves were also agents of change, as were the organizations (like the University Grants Committee) charged with overseeing them.

Moreover, not only were politicians extremely ambivalent about many of the changes they were nominally responsible for, they were also ill-equipped to understand the impact of their decisions in the first place. As a senior civil servant later recalled, for much of the 1980s, for example, at the Department for Education 'there was lacking, even in the most general terms, any policy on student numbers'.[2] Even when policies were made, they were often based on inadequate information and were still more frequently changed. The explanation was simple: politicians found it as hard to keep up with changes in higher education as those who were experiencing them. Indeed, policy was often made on the basis of very little tangible evidence or considered reflection. The 1991 White Paper, for example, which transformed higher education by abolishing the distinction between polytechnics and universities, was drafted in only six weeks.[3] Nor was this unusual. In 1976, as the government moved to change student funding, the prime minister's advisor, Bernard Donoughue, rejoiced that the issue would not need to go to Cabinet 'where nobody would understand the details'.[4] That ministers very

---

[1] Quoted in David Watson and Rachel Bourden, 'Why Did They Do It? The Conservative Government and Higher Education', *Journal of Education Policy* 14 (1999), pp. 243–56, p. 246.
[2] Richard Bird, 'Reflections on the British Government and Higher Education', *Higher Education Quarterly* 48 (1994), pp. 73–85, p. 74.
[3] Roger Brown with Helen Carasso, *Everything For Sale? The marketization of UK higher education* (London and New York, 2013), p. 34.
[4] Bernard Donoughue, *Downing Street Diaries, vol. ii: with James Callaghan in No 10* (London, 2008), p. 41.

rarely understood the details explains much about the development of higher education from 1974 to 1997.

One fact is indisputable, however: the fact of growth. In the summer term of 1974 there were around 250,000 full-time students and just over 30,000 academics in British universities as a whole.[5] In addition, there were about 180,000 students and 13,000 lecturers in polytechnics.[6] By 1997 there were 1.8 million students and over 100,000 full-time staff—all of them in what were now called universities.[7] This was a staggering change, and it meant that by the end of the century, nearly one in three of all 18-year olds attended university—up from one in eighteen in the 1960s, and one in a hundred only a few decades before that.[8] It also meant that higher education had become a major industry in its own right: employing nearly 2 per cent of the UK's workforce,[9] and with a combined turnover of £9.3 billion a year.[10]

Yet the pattern of development was not constant. In the mid-1970s, expansion slowed and student demand declined.[11] In the early 1980s, something like 4,000 university staff were made redundant.[12] Then, in the six years from 1987 to 1993, there was a sudden dash for growth, with the number of full-time students rising by almost 85 per cent, from nearly 600,000 to 1.1 million.[13] And even this account conceals important variations in the system. The polytechnics made only a limited contribution to rising student numbers until the 1980s, when they suddenly very nearly doubled in size. Student numbers in university, by contrast, stalled at the start of the 1980s, and it was not until the end of that decade that they started to pick up again.[14] Growth, then, was an undeniable fact—but it was neither universal nor continuous. It was sporadic and sometimes patchy in its effects.

What growth did achieve was the slow but steady erasure of the difference between universities and polytechnics. From the late-1960s onwards, attempts had been made to articulate a particular polytechnic ethos. For the director of Lancashire Polytechnic, Eric Robinson, they were to be 'the people's universities', open to all, part of a comprehensive higher education system.[15] For Tyrrell Burgess, an educationalist and lecturer at North East London Polytechnic, they were the

---

[5] *UGC Annual Survey 1973–74* 1975 (cmnd. 6024), p. 6.

[6] Julia Whitburn, Maurice Meaking, and Caroline Cox, *People in Polytechnics* (Guildford, 1979), pp. 7, 12.

[7] HESA, *Students in Higher Education Institutions 1997–98*, table 0a; *Resources of Higher Education Institutions 1997–98*, table 12.

[8] National Committee of Enquiry into Higher Education, *Higher Education in the Learning Society* (London, 1997), 3.9.

[9] National Committee of Enquiry into Higher Education, *Higher Education in the Learning Society*, 14.4.

[10] Diana Warwick, 'Sunset or New Dawn for the Universities?', *Perspectives* 1 (1997), pp. 2–5, p. 3.

[11] John H. Farrant, 'Trends in Admissions', in Oliver Fulton, ed., *Access to Higher Education* (Guildford, 1981), pp. 42–88, p. 47.

[12] *UGC Annual Survey 1983–84*, 1985 (cmnd 9489), p. 7.

[13] David Watson and Rachel Bowden, *Ends Without Means: the Conservative stewardship of UK higher education, 1979–1997* (Brighton, 1997), p. 12.

[14] John Pratt, *The Polytechnic Experiment, 1965–1992* (Buckingham, 1992), p. 29.

[15] Eric Robinson, *The New Polytechnics: the people's universities* (Harmondsworth, 1968).

only alternative to the old, outmoded, conservative university tradition: democratic places relevant to modern society.[16] The local authorities which controlled them were also keen to preserve their distinctiveness. In many cases, the polytechnic was the largest single institution for which a council had responsibility.[17] It was a source of pride—and also, potentially, of revenue, not least in the rates that the authority could charge on its buildings. Canny polytechnic directors knew that they were more likely to obtain additional funding if they named buildings after civic worthies.[18] As a consequence, although polytechnics often found local authorities over-bearing and even incompetent—sometimes taking months to achieve the simplest administrative changes—they did benefit from their largesse.[19] Indeed, until the mid-1980s, when a centralized system of funding was introduced for polytechnics, the additional grants made by councils ensured that some were better off than nearby universities.[20]

This financial good fortune enabled some students and staff to imagine that the polytechnics were indeed redrawing the map of higher education. Institutional newspapers of the 1970s, in particular, used the accusation that the polytechnic in question was attempting to imitate the universities as an all-purpose insult. Commenting on the Oxford Polytechnic Development Plan of 1973, the staff newspaper, *Octopus*, condemned it because it offered 'little to distinguish us from a University.... Would it not be wiser to produce a real Higher Education *alternative* to the universities?' it asked.[21] Six years later, Oxford Polytechnic students made an even more pointed objection, complaining that 'several members of the Admin[istration] want to turn this place into the great University down the road, where many of them failed to get jobs'.[22]

There was more than hint of truth to these accusations, and, with time, the distinctiveness of the polytechnic tradition proved to be largely illusory.[23] It was a process signified in a hundred different ways. Terminology changed: Sheffield polytechnic, for example, refused to appoint professors in 1979 for fear that this would look too much like an aping of universities; yet only nine years later they changed their mind and began creating Chairs. The balance of subjects also shifted: with ever more students doing degrees rather than diplomas and proportionally fewer taking the technical and practical subjects for which the polytechnics had ostensibly been created.[24] In 1985, the National Advisory Board, which oversaw polytechnic development, also began to encourage selected institutions to engage in research—just like universities.[25] And although little was made of it, the absorption

---

[16] See Tyrrell Burgess and John Pratt, eds, *Polytechnics: a report* (London, 1974).
[17] Pratt, *Polytechnic Experiment*, p. 285.
[18] Tyrrell Burgess, Michael Locke, John Pratt, and Nick Richards, *Degrees East: the making of the University of East London* (London, 1995), pp. 204, 3.
[19] *THES*, 19 December 1986, p. 1.
[20] *THES*, 15 July 1983, p. 9; 3 February 1984, p. 10; 24 May 1984, p. 1.
[21] *Octopus* 17 (Autumn, 1973), p. 3.
[22] *The Last Edition*, 5 January 1979, p. 3.
[23] Peter Scott, *The Meanings of Mass Higher Education* (Buckingham, 1995), p. 31.
[24] Pratt, *Polytechnic Experiment*, pp. 53–5.
[25] *THES*, 25 January 1985, p. 1; Brown, *Everything For Sale?*, pp. 76–7.

of residential teacher-training colleges in the 1970s also involved the acquisition of accommodation that not only looked like old university buildings, but also often functioned in similar ways.[26] So it was that Leicester Polytechnic obtained the Georgian Scraptoft Hall and Sheffield Polytechnic came to own the magnificent, Palladian Wentworth Woodhouse.[27] As the students of Oxford Polytechnic discovered when their own institution merged with the Lady Spencer-Churchill College of Education, teacher-training colleges had often modelled themselves after the civic universities and operated like traditional halls of residence, with formal dining, high tables, and even academic gowns.[28]

This change of culture and the tremendous increase in polytechnic student numbers combined in the 1980s to erode any fundamental functional difference between the universities and their younger rivals. In 1979, Edward Boyle, the vice-chancellor of Leeds University, looked out of his window across the motorway towards the Polytechnic and remarked 'that the chasm between the two institutions was even greater than the deep cutting the road ran in'.[29] Even as he said it, his statement was already inaccurate—indeed, for the students at the two institutions, it had not been true since at least 1973 when they created a unified newspaper, the *Leeds Student*. By the mid-1980s, the gap between polytechnics and universities had actually narrowed so much that Keele and nearby Staffordshire Polytechnic began discussing a merger.[30] At about the same time, at least one London polytechnic was considering whether to append the word University to its title—making it Middlesex Polytechnic University. After all, it was argued, the majority of Middlesex students were now studying for degrees.[31] By 1991 there was even speculation that the Polytechnic and University in Leeds would themselves unite to form a single institution.[32]

From the start of the polytechnic experiment, its proponents had worried about 'academic drift'—a move away from the ideal of inclusive, comprehensive, popular higher education towards the exclusivity of the university tradition.[33] By the late-1980s academic drift was complete and at the beginning of the 1990s surveys showed that more than half of polytechnic directors wanted to rename their institutions universities.[34] Little wonder: in some places, like Manchester, the polytechnic was producing a thousand more graduates than the neighbouring

---

[26] Michael Locke, John Pratt, and Tyrrell Burgess, *The Colleges of Higher Education, 1972–1982* (Croydon, 1985), p. 1.

[27] Karen Gold, 'The House-Proud Polys', *THES*, 24 August 1985, p. 9.

[28] *Lady Spencer-Churchill College of Education: a history* (Oxford, 1994); see also, *Octopus* 20 (1974); *Breed* 5 (1973).

[29] Richard Hoggart, 'Hopes and Fears of Twenty Years', *THES*, 28 October 1983, pp. 10–11, p. 11.

[30] J. M. Kolbert, *Keele: the first fifty years, 1950–2000* (Keele, 2000), pp. 222–3.

[31] *THES*, 5 October 1984, p. 1. On the pressure from London polytechnics to change status, see also Michael Heller, 'The Institute and the Polytechnic', in Helen Glew, Anthony Gorst, Michael Heller, and Neil Matthews, eds, *Educating Mind, Body, and Spirit: the legacy of Quintin Hogg and the Polytechnic, 1864–1992* (London, 2013), pp. 45–77, pp. 71–3.

[32] *Leeds Student*, 24 May 1991, p. 1.

[33] Pratt and Burgess, *Polytechnics* explores this theme most fully.

[34] *THES*, 22 February 1991, p. 1.

university each year.³⁵ In 1989, Eric Robinson was driven out of his post as director of Lancashire Polytechnic. It was a symbolic moment, as the man who, more than anyone else, had tried to overturn the hegemony of the universities was pushed aside. Four years earlier, in 1985, he had argued that 'the Polytechnic did not wish to evolve... into a University'. In 1991, it was announced that Lancashire, like the other polytechnics, would now become just that.³⁶

The instrument for this change, which nearly doubled the number of universities in Britain, was a hastily-written White Paper.³⁷ It was the government, too, that restructured the funding of universities and polytechnics: creating the National Advisory Board (NAB) for polytechnics in 1982 and then replacing it by the Polytechnics Funding Council (PFC) six years later; abolishing the University Grants Committee (UGC) in 1988 and replacing it with the Universities Funding Council (UFC). Both the PFC and the UFC were themselves abolished four years afterwards, in 1992, and succeeded by Higher Education Funding Councils for England (HEFCE), Scotland (SHEFC), and Wales (HEFCW). With each new acronym, the state's direct involvement in and control of higher education grew greater.

But this process was not as simple as it may at first appear. For one thing, as the rapid changes in the names and nature of higher education funding bodies suggest, government policy was constantly in flux. In the 1970s, economic crisis meant that planning—much less state control—was almost impossible.³⁸ In the 1980s, the Thatcher administration changed its position on higher education every other year, and when Keith Joseph was asked what policy drove these changes, he responded, 'we've got no policy. Indeed government should not have a policy.'³⁹ The 1990s witnessed similar statements and equally inexplicable about turns by the government.⁴⁰ It was, for example, the Education Secretary Kenneth Clarke who abolished the binary divide between universities and polytechnics. Yet, only a few months after the publication of this policy, it was the same Kenneth Clarke who appeared to want to re-impose a distinction between the two sorts of institution, warning former polytechnics that they should avoid imitating universities by engaging in research and concentrate on their real purpose: teaching.⁴¹ And, again, when his successor John Patten was asked in 1994 what his vision for the future of higher education amounted to, he replied that 'it was not his job to have one'.⁴²

Underlying this ambiguity was the hard reality of financial difficulty.⁴³ The Robbins Report had assumed that the expansion of higher education would be paid

---

³⁵ Pratt, *Polytechnic Experiment*, pp. 3–4.
³⁶ Rex Pope and Ken Phillips, *University of Central Lancashire: a history of the development of the institution since 1828* (Preston, 1996), pp. 161–5.
³⁷ Department of Education and Science, *Higher Education: a new framework*, 1991 (cm 1541).
³⁸ Michael Shattock, *The UGC and the Management of British Universities* (Birmingham, 1994).
³⁹ Quoted in Joseph A. Soares, *The Decline of Privilege: the modernization of Oxford University* (Stanford, 1999), p. 220.
⁴⁰ See Michael Shattock, *Making Policy in Higher Education 1945–2011* (Maidenhead, 2012), p. 68.
⁴¹ *THES*, 2 August 1991, p. 1.
⁴² Quoted in Watson and Burden, 'Why Did They Do That?', p. 254.
⁴³ This is brilliantly analysed by Shattock, *Making Policy*, ch 3.

for by annual growth in GDP of 4 per cent. This had never happened.[44] Although Britain's economic performance was not as dire as many critics claimed, nor was it as good as the optimists had hoped it would be.[45] More than this, the shock of the oil crisis, rising prices, and industrial downturn destroyed the ambitions for fully funded expansion that had even underwritten Margaret Thatcher's 1972 White Paper *Education: a framework for expansion*.[46] Within less than twelve months of its publication, the quinquennial plan due to run from 1972 to 1977 had, in the words of the UGC's chairman, been 'largely abandoned'.[47] In place of a system that stretched back a century, universities now lived 'year to year, hand to mouth, often not fully knowing their money for a current year until that year was well under way or almost over'.[48]

The 1980s were to be even more traumatic, as the government remorselessly drove down the costs of higher education. Funding was based on a notional 'unit of resource'—the amount of money that each student brought into the institution. Each year it declined: by 1989, the unit of resource at polytechnics was only 79 per cent of what it had been a decade earlier.[49] The universities and the UGC fought against this erosion for much of the 1980s, but in the 1990s the unit of resource collapsed even in that part of the sector, with a decline of something like 37 per cent between 1989 and 1997.[50] All in all, this meant that overall the unit of resource had more than halved: more students were being educated for much less money.[51]

Falling funding was not simply the product of economic crisis. After all, it continued to decline even when the stock market began to rise. This trend was pre-eminently the product of changes in the way government approached the issue of higher education. In the first place, the unit of resource had reached a historic highpoint by the beginning of the 1980s; indeed it was 50 per cent higher than it had been twenty years earlier, and was considerably more generous than most international competitors.[52] This seemed especially anomalous because at the same time demographic change appeared to necessitate reform. For much of this period, it was widely accepted that a declining birth rate would necessarily result in decreasing demand for university and polytechnic places.[53] The squeeze on

---

[44] Annan, 'British Higher Education', p. 7.
[45] Jim Tomlinson, *The Politics of Decline: understanding post-war Britain* (Harlow, 2000), ch. 1.
[46] *Education: a framework for expansion*, 1972 (cmnd. 5174), pp. 34–40.
[47] Fred Dainton, *Doubts and Certainties: a personal memoir of the twentieth century* (Sheffield, 2001), p. 299.
[48] Denys Wilkinson, 'The Lean Years, 1976–1986', in Roger Blin-Stoyle and Geoff Ivey, eds, *The Sussex Opportunity: a new university and the future* (London, 1986), pp. 23–35, p. 23.
[49] Gareth Williams, *Changing Patterns of Finance in Higher Education* (Buckingham, 1992), p. 5.
[50] National Audit Office, *The Financial Health of Higher Education Institutions in England* 1994 (HC 13 [1994–5]), 3.10.
[51] Robert Stevens, *University to Uni: the politics of higher education in England since 1944* (London, 2004), p. 56.
[52] Ken Mayhew, Cecile Deer, and Mehak Dua, 'The Move to Mass Higher Education in the UK: many questions and few answers', *Oxford Review of Education* 30 (2004), pp. 65–82, p. 67. Though cf. Andrew McGettigan, *The Great University Gamble: money, markets, and the future of higher education* (London, 2013), p. 19.
[53] Department of Education and Science, *Higher Education into the 1990s: a discussion document* (London, 1978).

finances of the early-1980s would almost certainly have been instigated whichever party was in power because it was believed that the number of students would drop by nearly one-third over the next decade.[54]

Nonetheless, ideology proved to be even more important than demography in shaping policy. Tory governments from 1979 to 1997 looked with suspicion on higher education as yet another public-sector monopoly that needed to be broken up. Margaret Thatcher believed that the system had expanded too far and too fast and that standards had declined.[55] Keith Joseph believed that there were too many institutions offering too little real choice.[56] Kenneth Baker, his successor as Secretary of State, thought that academics were over-paid and under-worked.[57] The fact that each of these politicians had been physically assaulted by students—Keith Joseph no fewer than half a dozen times even before he took on the universities—presumably did not help endear higher education to them either.[58] Above all, the Conservatives were determined to make universities more responsive to the perceived needs of industry and less preoccupied with what was seen as intellectual abstraction at best, and near sedition at worst. 'I certainly became alarmed', recalled Rhodes Boyson, 'when I found that the Social Science Research Council was funding 200 doctoral students in sociology and 230 in planning.'[59] The Tories thus wanted to make higher education more efficient and less dependent on the state for funding.[60] In addition, it is clear that higher education was an easy target for a government committed to reducing spending, but conspicuously failing to do so in areas like health or social security.[61]

As it turned out, events appeared to justify some of the Conservatives' assumptions. Efficiency gains were made within the higher education sector: between 1991 and 1995, for instance, productivity went up 6 per cent per annum, compared to an average of 2 per cent across the public sector as a whole.[62] Class sizes rose, but so did degree results.[63] More research was published; more private finance was obtained. Universities reached out to business in ways that had never happened before.[64] Cynics might complain that this was all smoke and mirrors.[65] Well-informed analysts have concluded that 'it is virtually certain that quality declined as the growth in resources fell seriously behind the growth in student numbers'.[66]

---

[54] Gareth Williams and Tessa Blackstone, *Response to Adversity: higher education in a harsh climate* (Guildford, 1983), p. 19. See also Edward Parker, quoted in *THES*, 17 December 1982, pp. 10–11.
[55] Margaret Thatcher, *The Path to Power* (London, 1995), p. 186.
[56] Denham and Garnett, *Keith Joseph*, p. 368.
[57] Kenneth Baker, *The Turbulent Years: my life in politics* (London, 1993), p. 233.
[58] Denham and Garnett, *Keith Joseph*, p. 293.
[59] Rhodes Boyson, *Speaking My Mind* (London, 1995), p. 151.
[60] Department for Education and Science, *The Development of Higher Education into the 1990s*, 1985 (cmnd. 9254).
[61] Martin McLean, 'Higher Education in the United Kingdom into the 1990s: shopping mall or reconciliation with Europe?', *European Journal of Education* 25 (1990), pp. 157–70.
[62] *Independent Review of Higher Education Pay and Conditions* 1999 (C25 6/99), p. 16.
[63] CVCP, *Academic Standards in Universities* (London, 1988).
[64] Scott, *Meanings of Mass Higher Education*, p. 69.
[65] Stevens, *University to Uni*, p. 48.
[66] Brown, *Everything For Sale?*, p. 172.

Even higher education ministers would come to bemoan the 'progressive degradation' of the universities.[67] But instead of the financial and intellectual collapse predicted by so many, higher education survived, adapted—and even grew.[68]

This was not the only way in which the commentators were surprised. The government's projections of demand for student places turned out to be hopelessly wrong. Instead of a decline in the 1980s, falling to a trough by the mid-1990s, the number of people qualified for, and keen to participate in, higher education simply escalated. Rising numbers of successful A level students and the growing tendency of women to stay on for further study more than counteracted any fall in the birth rate. Towards the end of 1986, the Department of Education and Science was forced to admit that the model it had been using for nearly a decade was based on false premises and needed to be replaced.[69] The government's analysis of higher education more generally was, in many respects, similarly problematic. As the political scientist Elie Kedourie pointed out in 1989, far from being 'an extortionate academic monopoly', universities were, in fact, a 'government-operated monopsony': there was not one higher education provider serving a lot of customers, but one customer—the state—buying places from a large number of providers.[70] This was symptomatic of a wider failure to understand higher education—and it was one reason that meant ministers often pursued policies which did not achieve the goals they intended.

In his recollection of life at the UGC, John Carswell rebukes those who saw the inhabitants of higher education as unworldly dons or cloistered academics. 'Far from being separated from the currents of ordinary life', he observed, 'universities are almost excessively sensitive to them and reflect them in a thousand ways.'[71] As a man who devoted his whole career to the sector, he knew whereof he spoke; and the events of the 1980s and 1990s were to bear out his assertion: revealing the universities and polytechnics as far more dynamic and infinitely more enterprising than their critics—including those within parliament—imagined.

Indeed, it would be a mistake to assume that the government's reforms of higher education were always imposed on a reluctant and recalcitrant set of institutions. For many university and polytechnic leaders these changes were in fact distinctly welcome. It was notable, in particular, that the language of rationalization, efficiency, and intensified research deployed by the government and funding bodies alike was pioneered by vice-chancellors rather than ministers.[72] So too, the reduction in funding enabled senior management to restructure—closing unwanted

---

[67] Robert Jackson, quoted in Peter Scott, 'Higher Education', in Dennis Kavanagh and Anthony Seldon, eds, *The Thatcher Effect* (Oxford, 1989), pp. 198–212, p. 206.
[68] Watson and Bourden, *Ends Without Means*, p. 26, 'Why Did They Do That?', pp. 245–7, 251.
[69] *THES*, 2 November 1986, p. 1.
[70] Elie Kedourie, *Perestroika in the Universities* (London, 1989), p. 5.
[71] John Carswell, *Government and the Universities in Britain: programme and performance, 1960–1980* (Cambridge, 1985), p. 167.
[72] A. Ian Glendon, 'Radical Change Within a British University', in Dian Marie Mosking and Neil Anderson, eds, *Organizational Change and Innovation: psychological perspectives and practices in Europe* (London, and New York, 1992), pp. 49–70, p. 65.

departments and subjecting academics to regular research assessment.[73] In public, observed the well-connected Tory MP Robert Rhodes-James, vice-chancellors 'constantly criticised the cuts and so on, but privately their only criticism was that we hadn't gone far enough'.[74] Equally, an absence of coordinated government policy enabled higher education institutions to play off different parts of the state against each other. In the late 1980s, for example, it became a moot point whether over-recruitment by polytechnics should be punished, because it jeopardized central planning, or rewarded, because it represented an efficiency gain. In the absence of a clear direction from the government, individual institutions were able to evolve a policy on their own.[75]

The surprising conservativism of the ostensibly radical Thatcher governments also meant that ministers had to reform universities and polytechnics at one remove. Although they tinkered with the funding bodies, eroded their independence, and even contemplated the abolition of the Social Science Research Council on the grounds that it supported that suspiciously socialist-sounding subject sociology, they never assumed direct control of the higher education system.[76] This provided the opportunity for organizations like the UGC, UFC, and even HEFCE—which was often regarded as little more than the government's stooge—to reshape policy and impose their own agenda.[77] After the drift of the 1970s, the government's cuts, especially a sudden drop in funding in 1981, actually revitalized the UGC, enabling it to reassert itself as an active agent of change.[78] Remarkably, Margaret Thatcher herself was unaware that the Committee had drawn up its own criteria for making cuts instead of imposing the government's uniform reduction. She found out when listening to the radio a full day after the UGC had announced its decision to the universities.[79] Towards the end of the century, indeed, the supposedly supine HEFCE was capable of displaying some signs of independence—as it did when it invented a new 'rating of research quality' as a way of seeing off the government's plans to create a premier league of universities which would be funded separately.[80]

Moreover, pressure on these agencies did not simply come from the government. It also came from higher education itself. The polytechnics' National Advisory Board was fatally damaged by the polytechnics' own rejection of its policies.[81] The

---

[73] John M. Roberts, 'Recollections of a Pre-Revolution', *Oxford Review of Education* 24 (1998), pp. 99–110.
[74] *THES*, 21 February 1986, p. 13.
[75] Peter C. Knight, 'The National Advisory Planning Exercise, 1987–88: a shot in the foot', *Higher Education Quarterly* 41 (1987), pp. 317–28, p, 326.
[76] Stuart Weir, 'Sentence of Death on the SSRC?', *New Society* 7 January 1982, pp. 11–12.
[77] Stevens, *University to Uni*, p. 126.
[78] Michael Shattock, 'British Higher Education Under Pressure: politics, budgets, and demography, and the acceleration of ideas for change', *European Journal of Education* 19 (1984), pp. 201–16, p. 210.
[79] Michael Shattock, 'The Change from Private to Public Governance of British Higher Education: its consequence for higher education policy-making, 1980-2006', *Higher Education Quarterly* 62 (2008), pp. 181–203, p. 189.
[80] Peter Scott, 'Mass Higher Education—Ten Years On', *Perspectives* 9 (2005), pp. 68–73, p. 70. The new rating was the 5* category in the 2001 Research Assessment Exercise.
[81] Knight, 'The National Advisory Planning Exercise', p. 318.

universities similarly conspired to destroy the UGC.[82] Even in the early 2000s, higher education showed that it could still thwart the state. The government's attempts to regulate teaching quality, for example, were consistently undermined by institutional resistance. Established in 1997, within less than a decade the Quality Assurance Agency had become essentially toothless.[83]

Above all else, it is important to remember that government policy had to respond to huge public demand for—and increasing interest in—higher education. The growing expectation amongst a growing middle class that their children would attend university or, failing that, polytechnic contrived to thwart any attempts to reduce student numbers. This trend was also almost certainly instrumental in pushing the government to abolish the distinction between universities and polytechnics.[84] There was a social and intellectual cachet to obtaining a university degree that other institutions could not offer. When Birmingham Polytechnic became the University of Central England, its vice-chancellor proudly revealed that 'Students who left ten years ago are 'phoning to ask if they can change their degree certificate.'[85] Although few would now argue—as some did at the time—that the binary system was abolished in a 'fit of absentmindedness', the extent to which public pressure rather than political principle led to this change is noteworthy.[86] And the way in which government policy could be shaped by extra-parliamentary, non-university agitation was revealed in the mid-1980s, when Keith Joseph contemplated introducing tuition fees. The proposal was met with horror by the middle classes.[87] Two hundred and fifty Tory MPs turned up for a meeting held to oppose the measure—the largest gathering of their number since the Falklands War. Joseph was forced into a retreat, he even contemplated resignation; his attempt to marketize higher education was lost, so far as he could see, for good.[88] It was precisely the opposite of what the government had intended.

For many commentators, like the Conservative thinker Shirley Robin Letwin, this failure was emblematic of a wider problem. Indeed, she was to argue that higher education policy was the most obvious disappointment of the Thatcher years, producing a system in which centralization and state power had, quite contrary to Thatcherite principles, actually increased, rather than being reduced.[89] For others, what was even more remarkable was the government's inability to use its growing power to change the fundamental nature of higher education. Here was the biggest increase in student numbers ever recorded—an expansion as 'unanticipated as it was unprecedented', but it was one that involved 'the creation of no

---

[82] Stevens, *University to Uni*, pp. 41–2.
[83] Ourania Filippkapu, Brian Salter, and Ted Tapper, 'Compliance, Resistance and Seduction: reflections on 20 years of the funding council model of governance', *Higher Education* 60 (2010), pp. 543–57; Brown, *Everything For Sale?*, ch. 6.
[84] Peter Scott, '1992–2002: where next?', *Perspectives* 7 (2003), pp. 71–5, p. 72.
[85] *Newsline* 58 (September 1992), p. 1.
[86] Scott, 'Mass Higher Education', p. 70. For the original comment, see Scott, '1992–2002', p. 71. See also Denis Lawton, *Education and Politics in the 1990s: conflict or consensus?* (London, 1992), p. 74.
[87] Lawson, *View from No 11*, p. 309.
[88] Denham and Garnett, *Keith Joseph*, pp. 391–3.
[89] Shirley Robin Letwin, *The Anatomy of Thatcherism* (London, 1992), pp. 264–9.

alternative institutions, few mergers or amalgamations, and without the culture change normally associated with the shift to a mass system'.[90] The reality is that both conclusions were spot on—and that each reflects the absence of effective policy-making by government in this period. As a result, the higher education system grew larger than anyone had intended and more homogenous than anyone wanted.[91] The demand for university places increased exponentially, and the hunger for university status similarly intensified. Both impulses found their fulfilment in the early 1990s. All government could do was try to keep the costs down. Yet even as the unit of resource declined, the attraction of the universities remained high. As Martin McLean puts it, 'Despite the obloquy against higher education, governments in the 1980s seemed as mesmerized by university mystique as their predecessors since the 1920s.'[92] In more ways than one this reflected the remarkable resilience of Redbrick.

---

[90] Gareth Parry, 'Reform of Higher Education in the United Kingdom', in Brendan Nolan, ed., *Public Sector Reform: an international perspective* (Basingstoke, 2001), pp. 117–32, p. 127.

[91] Shattock, *UGC*, p. 68.

[92] McLean, 'Higher Education in the United Kingdom', p. 161.

12

Students and Staff

'We have in this college', wrote a Birmingham Polytechnic undergraduate in 1983, 'students who (hopefully) have been selected as the most intelligent representatives of their generation.'[1] The 'hopefully' is a nice touch—and the doubt it signalled was one shared by many. Three years earlier, for instance, the principal of Westfield College London had joined the ranks of those bemoaning what they saw as declining standards. 'The student of today', he said, 'is less knowledgeable, and less intellectually competent than his counterpart after the last war.'[2] More than a decade later, the criticism was, if anything, still more pointed—and all the more so because it focused on the system as well as the undergraduates themselves. 'Our best students', observed one Surrey academic, 'are probably as good as they've ever been. But we're giving 2:1s to people who shouldn't be awarded a degree at all.'[3] In many respects, such rhetoric was simply an amplification of the old 'more means worse' argument—something given greater impetus by the fantastic growth in student numbers.[4] But this traditional concern about the maintenance of standards was also accompanied by a broader critique of students and the subjects they studied. For many commentators—not least successive ministers—the real issue was that students were both unprepared and unwilling to study the sorts of subjects that would contribute to economic growth. For other people, the problem was that students were themselves not sufficiently well supported—either financially or intellectually.

A key problem for ministers was the continuation of a trend that had begun in the 1960s. The 'swing away from science' that so worried governments twenty years before intensified in this period, with more and more people opting for the humanities and social sciences. Worse still, in the 1980s, the tendency for prospective undergraduates to shun science was inadvertently exacerbated by the Thatcher administration's own policies. Indeed, attempts to rationalize and improve efficiency in higher education had the perverse effect of undermining efforts to create a more technologically capable workforce.

This was most obviously the case in the savage cuts of 1981. Having been ordered to reduce expenditure by more than 10 per cent, the University Grants Committee (UGC) outwardly followed the government's agenda of encouraging

---

[1] Dave H. Beerer in *Polygon* 125 (January 1983), p. 8.
[2] Bryan Thwaite in *THES*, 3 October 980, p. 2.
[3] Derek McCulloch, quoted in Melanie Phillips, *All Must Have Prizes* (London, 1996), p. 302.
[4] George Walden, *We Should Know Better: solving the education crisis* (London, 1996), p. 171.

science and cutting social science.[5] Yet the methodology it used to determine where the axe should fall did not always achieve this. In making decisions, it relied on two measures: quality of research (calculated by the amount of grant income generated) and the quality of students (calculated by their average A Level grades). The consequences were not what the government had hoped: with technological universities like Salford and Aston receiving cuts of 44 and 31 per cent respectively.[6] That they had pioneered industrial engagement and vocational degrees; that they consistently had the highest post-graduation employment rates in the country: none of this mattered.[7] More important was their failure to recruit high-achieving applicants.[8] Nor was this surprising: the falling number of students applying to study science meant that almost all universities struggled to find suitably able candidates. Across the Pennines from Salford, as the historian Simon Dixon observes, 'it was only by rejecting strong candidates in the arts and admitting less well qualified scientists' that Leeds could achieve its desired undergraduate mix, ensuring a preponderance of students studying science.[9]

The decision to squeeze numbers in the universities and increase them in the polytechnics had a similarly unexpected outcome.[10] The cuts of 1981 assumed a reduction in the number of university students of about 5 per cent. Yet there was, in fact, an ever-increasing number of qualified candidates—and they had to go somewhere. By the end of 1982, therefore, applications to Bristol Polytechnic had gone up by 80 per cent, and to the Polytechnic of Central London by 120 per cent.[11] Naturally, not everyone was pleased with such a situation, and the Student Union president at Leicester Polytechnic felt compelled to welcome incoming students with the encouraging words: 'those of you who feel that you've failed to get into University will, I hope, look back in a few years [sic] time and thank fate'.[12] Nor did this growth in polytechnic numbers help achieve the government's ambitions. True enough, it ensured that higher education became cheaper.[13] But it was a far from effective way of increasing the number of scientific and technological graduates. What happened was quite the reverse, with significant growth in the polytechnics confined to the very subjects—social sciences and humanities—that were being cut in the universities. By 1987, only a third of polytechnic students were doing degrees in science or technology, compared to 43 per cent in the universities.[14]

---

[5] *THES*, 3 July 1981, p. 1.
[6] Geoffrey Walford, *Restructuring Universities: politics and power in the management of change* (London, 1987), pp. 49–52.
[7] Michael Shattock, *The UGC and the Management of British Universities* (Birmingham, 1994), p. 66.
[8] Henry Miller, 'Academics and the Labour Process', in Chris Smith, David Knights, and Hugh Willmott, eds, *White-Collar Work: the non-manual labour process* (Basingstoke, 1996), pp. 109–38, p. 129.
[9] Simon Dixon, 'The University of Leeds and the British Higher Education System, 1963–2004', *Northern History* 43 (2006), pp. 303–25, p. 210.
[10] *THES*, 27 August 1982, p. 1.
[11] Maurice Kogan and David Kogan, *The Attack on Higher Education* (London, 1983), p. 130.
[12] *LPSU Student Handbook 1981/2*, p. 1.
[13] Kenneth Baker, *The Turbulent Years: my life in politics* (London, 1993), p. 234.
[14] John Pratt, *The Polytechnic Experiment, 1965–1992* (Buckingham, 1992), p. 55.

Reductions in funding coupled with rising student numbers also reshaped the ways in which undergraduates were taught. In many institutions, size became everything—with new lecturers at one polytechnic greeted by the director's cheering words: 'In the next few years, forget quality, think about bums on seats!'[15] This inevitably—indeed, deliberately—resulted in larger classes. It was widely agreed that the ideal upper limit for groups in the humanities was twelve—'Jesus got it about right', as one academic put it. But by the 1990s, seminars and tutorials were often four times that size, whilst in places like Cardiff it was not unusual to have thirty in a room designed for twenty, with some sitting on the floor.[16] Such a significant increase in scale inevitably affected the dynamics of the class—and for some it was just too much. 'Tutorials had 25+ students only enabling the very self-confident to dominate the proceedings', complained one drop-out from a social science degree.[17] In the sciences it was a practical problem in every sense: 'We simply can't get 80 students into the lab and we only have one slot. It's impossible.'[18] Yet, the impossible had to be achieved. And it had to be achieved with ageing equipment as well as larger classes. Little wonder that by 1998 chemistry lecturers were complaining that they simply could not prepare their students for a career in science. To make matters worse, the gap between school and university also seemed to be widening, so that almost all chemistry departments in the country now provided remedial maths classes for their first years.[19] In every way, this was the reverse of what the government had hoped to achieve.

These changed conditions were accompanied by some changes in the make-up of the study body. Not the least important of these was the escalation of a trend that had begun in the 1960s: the dramatic rebalancing of gender within higher education.[20] Just as the rise of science had tipped the scales against women, so its relative decline helped them become proportionately more important. That the polytechnics admitted more female students—not least for teacher training courses—also meant that, when the sectors merged, the number of women in university immediately went up. In 1974, something like a third of undergraduates were female. Just over twenty years later, more than half were women. Less spectacular, though no less significant, was the rising number of mature students. In 1986, only 15 per cent of full-time undergraduates entered higher education aged 21 or over; yet by 1995 this figure had nearly doubled to 29 per cent. The average student by the end of the 1990s, therefore, was rather different from her predecessors a generation earlier—she was more likely to be female, and increasingly likely not to be a school-leaver. She was, however, still almost certainly middle class, for higher

[15] Chris Rust, *Surviving the First Year: the experiences of new teaching staff in higher education*, SECD paper 65 (1991), p. 13.
[16] Colin Evans, *English People: the experience of teaching and learning English in British Universities* (Buckingham, 1993), p. 63.
[17] Mantz Yorke, *Leaving Early: undergraduate non-completion in higher education* (London, 1999), p. 40.
[18] Quoted in Graham Gibbs, Roy Gregory and Ivan Moore, *Labs and Practicals with More Students and Fewer Resources* (Oxford, 1997), p. 6.
[19] Harriet Swain, 'Chemists Fail Industry's Acid Test', *THES*, 20 March 1998.
[20] Carol Dyhouse, *Students: a gendered history* (London and New York, 2006), ch. 5.

education expansion exacerbated existing problems of access, with new student places taken up by middle-class applicants.[21] Even mature students were just as likely to be middle class as their younger colleagues.[22] The result was that by 1997 fewer than a third of full-time students came from working-class homes.[23] Growth had created what Peter Scott has termed 'a middle-class mass system', with a student body that was, on the one hand, somewhat feminized and sometimes older; but on the other hand, every bit as bourgeois as ever.[24]

The students who inhabited this mass, middle-class system could take for granted many of the reforms their parents had fought for. There was student representation on many university committees. The students' views about the institution in which they studied and the ways in which they were taught became ever-more important. By the late-1980s it was becoming clear that—in the words of Leicester Polytechnic's director—'we are increasingly moving into a **buyers** [sic] **market**. The 18–21 cohort knows what it wants and knows how to find whether we provide it.'[25] At the same time, mixed halls and increasingly liberal attitudes about sex meant that the old rules about private behaviour and public discussion were steadily abandoned. When Cardiff planned new accommodation in 1973, for example, it was keen to emphasize that it would not be a traditional hall of residence. '*Every effort is made to treat tenants as adults*', asserted the Domestic Bursar. '*No restriction is placed on their way of life.*'[26]

Not everyone took advantage of this licence, of course, and surveys consistently showed that the great majority of students were, in the words of one sociologist, 'sober, hard-working, responsible and more sexually restrained than the majority of their age group'.[27] But this was, as one female student—writing 'in praise of casual sex'—observed, now a matter of choice or disposition rather than regulation. 'I think a lot more students would be promiscuous if they knew how to go about it. For example the Engineers tend to hang around in groups boozing and watching the women whilst they are dancing, but they never actually go up and ask them to dance.'[28] And within a very little time, even asking someone to dance would seem charmingly old-fashioned at clubs which advertised themselves with the slogan 'Get Laid'. Indeed, etiquette changed to such an extent that the same places welcomed students because, instead of fighting like others of their age, 'if one pukes on another they turn round and laugh about it'.[29]

---

[21] Jo Blanden and Stephen Machin, 'Educational inequality and the expansion of UK higher education', *Scottish Journal of Political Economy* 51 (2004), pp. 230–49.
[22] Alison Gallagher and Michael Locke, *Mature Students in Higher Education: how institutions can learn from experience* (London, 1992), p. 9.
[23] *Higher Education in the Learning Society*, 7.1–4, 3.12. See also the same document's Report 6.
[24] Peter Scott, '1992–2002: where next?', *Perspectives* 7 (2003), pp. 71–5, p. 73.
[25] *Staff*, October 1987, p. 3.
[26] *Gair Rhydd*, May [1973], p. 1. Italics in the original text.
[27] Hugh Livingstone, *The University: an organizational analysis* (Glasgow, 1974), p. 80. See also Claire Callender and Elaine Kempson, *Student Finance: income, expenditure, and take-up of loans* (London, 1996), p. 47.
[28] Fiona Haughton, *Leeds Student*, 6 October 1977, p. 11.
[29] Quoted in Paul Chatterton, 'University Students and City Centres—the formation of exclusive geographies. The case of Bristol', *Geoforum* 30 (1999), pp. 117–33, pp. 127, 123.

For some, there was a political edge to this hedonism. Given the increasing number of women attending university, it raised questions about female sexuality—and empowerment. Women at Cardiff in 1980 campaigned against the rugby club's decision to book a stripper for an event being held at the university.[30] The same was true in the ancient Scottish universities, where, in the same year, the men's and women's unions at Glasgow finally merged, though the men continued to show free pornographic films every Thursday lunchtime until they were finally forced to stop four years later.[31] As this suggests, although freed from the formal rules imposed by the university, throughout the 1980s and early-1990s, Students' Unions increasingly imposed their own restrictions on undergraduate behaviour, formally condemning sexist language and banned supposedly sexist publications like the *Sun*, the *Star*, the *Daily Mirror*, and *Amateur Photography*.[32]

Nor was it just heterosexuality that inspired debate. Gay liberation burst into university life, provoking fierce hostility as well as passionate commitment from a minority.[33] It was hardly a revolution. Students at Birmingham Polytechnic complained in 1984 that 'One of the common problems with all gay soc[ietie]s is building up a membership of three or four people!'[34] Anecdotally, at any rate, it remained easier to find sexual partners in cottages than colleges: 'it would be nice not to have to mix Jeyes Lavatory Fluid with the great smell of Brut', mused one undergraduate.[35] But the increased visibility of gay life and its increasing acceptability, even on traditionally conservative campuses, did mark a moment in which student attitudes appeared to be running ahead of wider public opinion.[36] This was certainly the case at Leeds, where in 1985 university security guards refused to hand over the key to the gay switchboard—a student-run help-line—for fear of contracting AIDS.[37]

In part, this push to make higher education a more equal and accommodating place was the outworking of the student campaigns in the 1960s to break down the barriers between university and society. The same impulse informed attempts to make campuses more accessible for the disabled and more welcoming to different ethnicities and faiths.[38] More than this, the growth of special interest groups and single-issue organizations reflected the impossibility of creating a single community out of the massively-increased student population at each institution. By 1997,

---

[30] *Gair Rhydd*, 10 December 1980, p. 1.
[31] *THES*, 11 May 1984, p. 7.
[32] *Gair Rhydd*, 30 October 1985, p. 3; *Polygon*, 19 May 1992; *Leeds Student*, 24 February 1984, p. 1.
[33] Frances Gibb, 'Out of the Commune and Into the Community', *THES*, 14 February 1975, p. 7; 20 November 1987, p. 1. See also, Caroline M. Hoefferle, *British Student Activism in the Long Sixties* (New York and London, 2013), pp. 193–6.
[34] *Polygon*, March 1984, n.p.
[35] *Leeds Student*, 1 March 1985, p. 9.
[36] *Salford Student*, March 1990. See also Margaret Sutherland, *Women Who Teach in Universities* (Stoke-on-Trent, 1985), p. 24.
[37] *Leeds Student*, 22 February 1985, p. 1.
[38] Hillary Stephens, 'Fit to Study', *National Student*, May 1986, pp. 6–10; *Leeds Student*, 2 November 1984, p.1.

there were 24,000 students at the University of Manchester alone—4,000 more than there had been in the whole of England 70 years before.[39] To be sure, universities had always been divided by subject, social background, interest, and age. Just as they always had done, student newspapers continued to mock the 'rowdy' medics; hard-drinking athletes; ambitious student politicians, or 'hacks'; and the 'arty type'—'with a tendency towards berets, earrings and a well-scrubbed general appearance'.[40] But the sheer size of the student population meant that increasingly these groups rarely even met one another.[41]

The other changes affecting higher education also exaggerated these divisions. Although the proportion of part-time students declined in this period, their growth in numbers—up 66 per cent between 1988 and 1996—was notable.[42] Similarly, although the proportion of overseas students barely changed—rising from nearly 12 to almost 13 per cent—their number greatly increased, from nearly 59,000 to more than 143,000.[43] Both part-timers and non-natives could feel marginalized and actually be marginal. The same was true for the ever-increasing number of mature students, many of whom had families and homes of their own.[44] All these 'non-traditional' types of students had always struggled to integrate. Now there were so many of them that they often did not even have to try. And as they entered overwhelmingly bourgeois institutions, they sometimes felt that they would not be welcomed even if they did. 'If you're not white and middle class', observed one Asian mature student, 'you're not accepted. There's nothing overt, you just sense it.'[45]

Student politics consequently changed, becoming more preoccupied with issues of identity, and more concerned about welfare.[46] There were still marches, and still frequent sit-ins, of course. In the mid-1970s, the recurrent threat that senior officials at Sheffield might find themselves imprisoned within the University's main meeting room led to the creation of a trapdoor into the basement to facilitate escape.[47] In the winter of 1991, twenty institutions were occupied.[48] Rising student numbers resulted in larger student protests—with 1986 witnessing what was then the biggest NUS march in the organization's history, with no fewer than 300,000 attending.[49] Nonetheless, there was no return to the rebellions of

---

[39] HESA, *Student Statistics 1997–98*; UGC, *Returns from Universities 1920–21*, p. 4.
[40] *Gair Rhydd*, 2 October 1984, p. 17.
[41] Chatterton, 'University Students and City Centres', p. 126.
[42] *Higher Education in the Learning Society*, Report 2.
[43] David Watson and Rachel Bowden, *Ends Without Means: the Conservative stewardship of UK higher education, 1979–1997* (Brighton, 1997), p. 28.
[44] Veronica McGivney, *Staying On or Leaving the Course: non-completion and retention of mature students in further and higher education* (London, 1996).
[45] Marion Bowl, 'Experiencing the Barriers: non-traditional students entering higher education', *Research Papers in Education* 16 (2001), pp. 141–60, p. 145.
[46] David Holmes, 'Universities and their Students', in Stuart Bosworth, ed., *Beyond the Limelight: essays on the occasion of the silver jubilee of the Conference of University Administrators* (Reading, 1986), pp. 107–14, p. 109.
[47] Helen Mathers, *Steel City Scholars: the centenary history of the University of Sheffield* (London, 2005), p. 253.
[48] *National Student Extra*, Summer 1992, pp. 13–14.
[49] *Guardian*, 4 March 1986.

the late-1960s and early-1970s. Institutions became more successful at serving injunctions on recalcitrant students.[50] Public figures started to fight back—with the SDP's David Owen giving chase to protestors at Sussex who threw eggs and tomatoes at him in 1981.[51] More importantly still, it became harder and harder to mobilize a significant proportion of students for any sort of mass protest. Indeed, one of the largest meetings ever held at the University of Leeds was a vote of more than 1,500 undergraduates against a sit-in in 1977.[52]

As this suggests, increasingly student politics became more moderate. At some places, like Leicester Polytechnic, the Conservative Association became the largest society in the place.[53] This growing moderation was accompanied by greater professionalization, as Student Unions became big businesses: managing accommodation and running an entertainments budget amounting to tens of thousands of pounds. At impecunious Salford, students bought and ran a pub and established a profit-making subsidiary.[54] At Birmingham City University in 1997 the Student Union went one step further, turning itself into a limited company.[55] Unsurprisingly, a MORI poll at the turn of the millennium showed that 58 per cent of students valued Student Unions for their facilities and only 9 per cent for their political functions.[56]

This process of professionalization reshaped student politicians as well as student politics. Successive Presidents—from Charles Clarke (1975–6) to Phil Woolas (1984–5), Stephen Twigg (1990–92) to Jim Murphy (1994–6)—used the National Union of Students as the way of establishing a political career. Indeed, Jim Murphy was elected an MP only a year after he demitted office, before he had even finished his degree.[57] Nor was it just the politicians who increasingly saw student life as a professional training. Anyone reading student journalism in this period cannot help but be struck by the growing convergence in form and content of university newspapers, which became less and less distinctive and more and more modelled on the tabloid press. This was a bad thing for future historians, who would find these sources far less informative about student life and opinion than their more homespun predecessors. But it was undoubtedly a good thing for putative journalists, who could now increasingly use time on the student newspaper as a staging post on the way to their chosen career. The inauguration in 1978 of the *Guardian* Student Media Awards provided a national platform for their work—and those chosen as 'best journalist', like Andrew Rawnsley (1982) and Mark Frith (1992), went on to write for publications from the *Observer* to *Heat* magazine.[58]

---

[50] *Staff*, 26 May 1983, p. 1.
[51] SussUA, 2B/1/7/J, Occupations and Other Events, David Owen Incident, 1981.
[52] *Leeds Student*, 18 March 1977, p. 1.
[53] *LPSU Student Handbook 1982–3*, p. 53.
[54] *Salford Student*, 4 October 1983, p. 1; 11 October 1983, p. 1.
[55] *Newsline*, May 1997, p. 3.
[56] Unite/MORI, *Student Living Report, 2001* (London, 2001), p. 22.
[57] <http://www.guardian.co.uk/education/2002/mar/06/students.studentpolitics> (accessed 9 November 2010).
[58] <http://www.guardian.co.uk/media/2010/mar/15/guardian-student-media-awards-where-are-they-now> (accessed 9 November 2010).

This emphasis on university as a preparation for future work was not, of course, novel. But it was given a new intensity by the changed environment in which students found themselves—and it was not confined to apprentice politicians or journalists. The slow but steady erosion of the student grant, which fell by 20 per cent between 1979 and 1990; the removal of a range of benefits—from the dole in the vacation to a travel allowance during term; the rising cost of rent even for those able to live within university accommodation: all of these factors made student life more precarious for the impecunious than it had been in the 1960s.[59] The introduction of student loans in 1990 helped to bridge the gap between an expected income of £3,615 and estimated expenditure of £5,091 a year.[60] Nonetheless, as the average amount borrowed each year was only a little over £860, much of the burden undoubtedly fell on the undergraduates' family and on the cheap credit offered by banks.[61] It also meant that students themselves had to get jobs. In 1982 just over half of students surveyed undertook some employment over the summer, and 60 per cent claimed social security in the vacation.[62] By end of the century, however, almost a third were in paid employment during term.[63]

To add to the pressure, the rising number of graduates was accompanied by increased levels of graduate unemployment and declining salaries for those who did manage to obtain work. In 1986 it was reported that 10 per cent of university and 16 per cent of polytechnic graduates were unemployed—up from something like 6 per cent in 1970.[64] Five years later, it was observed that the financial advantage graduates held over those who had not been to university was beginning to decline.[65] Moreover, it became clear that the chances of securing employment and a decent wage were becoming critically dependent on degree results. Graduates, the NUS reported gloomily, were ten times more likely to be unemployed with a third than with an upper second.[66] As the modal result moved from a 2:ii to a 2.i, and the number of first-class degrees increased by more than half over the 1980s, this placed students in a double bind—simultaneously needing to work for money and for their degree in order to be able to obtain a job that would enable them to pay off the debts they had accrued doing both.[67] It was a sign of the times when, in 1994, the National Union of Students' in-house paper began offering careers advice and hints on how to write the perfect CV.[68] Things had certainly changed.

---

[59] NUS, *Undergraduate Income and Expenditure Survey 1982/3* (London, 1984), pp. x–xi.
[60] Callender and Kempson, *Student Finance*, p. 95.
[61] Watson and Bowden, *Ends Without Means*, pp. 17–19; *Higher Education in the Learning Society*, 18.10.
[62] NUS, *Undergraduate Income and Expenditure Survey*, pp. x–xi.
[63] Unite/MORI, *Student Living Report*, p. 14.
[64] Scott, *Crisis in the University*, p. 101.
[65] Malcolm Bee, 'What Do Graduates Earn? The starting salaries and earning prospects of university graduates, 1960–1986', *Higher Education Quarterly* 45 (1991), pp. 78–90, p. 81.
[66] *National Student*, March 1986, pp. 32–3.
[67] David Watson and Rachel Bourden, 'Why Did They Do It? The Conservative Government and Higher Education', *Journal of Education Policy* 14 (1999), pp. 243–56, p. 251; Mathers, *Steel City Scholars*, p. 321.
[68] *National Student Extra*, March 1994, pp. 27–30.

For many commentators, this was a disaster. True enough, there was little evidence that the majority of students themselves agreed. The dropout rate remained low in international terms and the overwhelming majority expressed a favourable view of their university experience.[69] Yet, radicals on both sides of the debate found the students disappointing. For the right, there continued to be the problem that too few studied subjects like engineering, and too many had failed to embrace the 'enterprise consciousness' that the government wanted to instil. They may have been working—but they were working at the wrong subjects in the wrong way.[70] For the left, the problem was still more profound. The new student culture seemed like a betrayal. 'In the 60s I wasn't worrying about a career', complained one academic to the linguist Colin Evans. Worse still, he went on,

> Between me and the students there is a gap that is widening all the time. It seems to me that the students I am teaching at the moment are far more conservative, with a small c and a big C, than I am now and certainly more conservative than I was as an undergraduate.... Everything that we teach has to be relevant to their achievement of their goal and their goal is very well defined—the getting of a job.[71]

It was a fair comment—and it explained not only how student life changed since the 1960s, but also why so many people, from so many different perspectives, were dissatisfied with the results.

THRUSTING, FORTHRIGHT, DOING IT, GETTING THE MONEY IN

The self-proclaimed 'museum piece' who offered Colin Evans such a jaundiced view of students in the mid-1980s surely spoke for many. But he did not speak for all. Another lecturer Evans interviewed took a very different view, revealing an almost comic pride in his university's receptivity to change. 'Our department', he enthused, 'is ... thrusting, forthright, doing it, getting the money in, getting the students in, getting the prestige in.'[72] In 1974 Hugh Livingstone had identified 'a new stereotype of the university world, that of the academic entrepreneur'.[73] As the cuts bit deeper, as the scope of higher education grew and grew, and as sources of funding changed, ever more entrepreneurs would be needed—and not all of them would be lecturers.[74] The expansion of the university system and the demands of government created whole new categories of employment: the number

---

[69] Scott, 'Mass Higher Education', p. 70; Unite/MORI, *Student Living Report*, p. 10.
[70] James Curan and Robert A. Blackburn, 'Youth and the Enterprise Culture', *Journal of Education and Work* 4 (1990), pp. 31–45.
[71] Colin Evans, *Language People: the experience of teaching and learning modern languages in British universities* (Milton Keynes, 1988), p. 122.
[72] Quoted in Evans, *Language People*, p. 95.
[73] Livingstone, *University*, p. 74.
[74] Rudolf Klein, 'Universities in the Market Place', *Universities Quarterly* 33 (1978–9), pp. 306–20.

of administrators increased exponentially, as did the quantity of people employed solely to undertake research.

Inevitably, there were winners and losers in this process. For many of the losers—and, indeed, for some of the winners—the changes were deeply painful, compared by one to a 'Latter-Day Dissolution' of the monasteries.[75] Yet, although it is undeniable that there was significant change, this was not quite the apocalypse that many commentators discerned. For large numbers of lecturers, as the sociologist Henry Miller observed in 1996, 'the academic labour process remain[ed] in its core activities remarkably constant. Little of the activity of teaching, research, scholarship, counselling and administration ha[d] changed.' What had altered, as he went on, was more subtle: 'the context and the pressures on these activities'.[76]

To be sure, for many of those individuals—especially those who lost their jobs—this was a period of genuine crisis. The cuts of the early 1980s, for example, led to thousands of redundancies.[77] In those institutions, like Aston, which were hit especially hard, more than half the academic staff were eased out.[78] Even at less unlucky universities like Leeds, more than one in ten were let go.[79] The abolition of tenure as a part of the 1988 Education Act also made an academic career apparently less secure. At the same time, university lecturers experienced a relative drop in pay of 18 per cent compared to other public sector employees and 30 per cent compared to workers in the economy as a whole.[80] By the early 1990s, lecturers were on average earning £5,000 less than many schoolteachers.[81] Given this, it was scarcely surprising that morale declined; that, for the first time, lecturers went on strike;[82] and that, by 1989, nearly 40 per cent of staff had seriously considered leaving the profession.[83] For some, indeed, it had ceased to be a profession, with academics slowly, but steadily, becoming proletarianized.[84]

In reality, however, the picture was somewhat more complicated than this suggests. The abolition of tenure had almost no effect. Its practical insignificance was made clear by the fact that, although polytechnic lecturers had never possessed permanent contracts of employment, they were no less hard to dismiss than their university equivalents.[85] Most redundancies were, in actuality, generous early-retirement packages.[86] Some staff were almost immediately re-employed,

---

[75] P. B. Fellgett, 'A Latter-Day Dissolution', *THES*, 15 August 1986, p. 11.
[76] Miller, 'Academics and the Labour Process', p. 111.
[77] *UGC Annual Survey 1983–84* 1985 (cmnd. 9489), p. 7.
[78] Walford, *Restructuring Universities*, p. 1.
[79] Dixon, 'University of Leeds', p. 317.
[80] *Independent Review of Higher Education Pay and Conditions* 1999, p. 51.
[81] AUT-NTAFHE Confederation, *Bursting at the Seams* (1993), p. 6.
[82] *THES*, 17 January 1986, p. 1.
[83] A. H. Halsey, *Decline of Donnish Dominion: the British academic profession in the twentieth century* (Oxford, 1995), p. 333.
[84] Tom Wilson, 'The Proletarianisation of Academic Labour', *Industrial Relations* 22 (1991), pp. 250–62.
[85] Pratt, *Polytechnic Experiment*, p. 162.
[86] Michael Shattock, 'The Academic Profession in Britain: a study in the failure to adapt to change', *Higher Education* 41 (2001), pp. 27–47, p. 37.

and others were only ever redundant on paper.[87] In 1988, for example, the vice-chancellor of Salford announced a dozen redundancies solely for the purposes of satisfying the UGC's expectations of a balanced budget. There was no intention of actually laying anyone off.[88] On further analysis, pay also presents a less overwhelmingly dismal aspect. The 1970s was a period of growing prosperity for polytechnic lecturers.[89] The 1980s witnessed a slow but steady rise in university salaries.[90] And the 1990s saw the—now unified—higher education system increase academics' wages through improved promotion prospects.[91] Lecturers did see their relative advantage decline from the high point of the late-1960s, but in real terms, they were still better off. The truly important changes in academic employment, therefore, were not really those that made the headlines. Rather, life for those working in the universities was reshaped most profoundly by apparently less dramatic shifts.

Perhaps the most important of these was the gradual restructuring of university finance: not least the increasing emphasis on tuition fees, which had recently been such an insignificant part of a university's income that they were very nearly abolished altogether. The government's decision in 1976 to increase these fees was intended to tighten the state's direct control of the universities. It meant that the amount paid directly by Whitehall became almost as important as the sums laid out by the UGC.[92] In time, and as the cutbacks bit, however, this purely administrative change produced unexpected outcomes. It provided the key incentive for universities to recruit more—and in 1989, as the tuition fee more than doubled, that temptation proved impossible to resist, with the proportion of money from this source very suddenly rising from 8 to 30 per cent of most universities' income.[93] Simply to sustain its existing revenue—and thus maintain staffing levels—the university of Leeds made the decision in September 1989 to increase its admissions by first 500, then 790; leaving a month to prepare for an influx nearly a third higher than originally anticipated.[94]

Leeds was not alone in experiencing this growth, nor the consequences that came with it.[95] The polytechnics, of course, increased their own numbers faster and sooner, and for somewhat different reasons—not least their ambition of becoming large enough to achieve university status.[96] But the result was equally dramatic for lecturers in either sort of institution. In 1990, for example, the Oxford Polytechnic

[87] Peter G. Moore, 'University Financing, 1979–86', *Higher Education Quarterly* 41 (1987), pp. 25–42, p. 32.
[88] Salford, Council Minutes 1976–1990, 7 June 1988.
[89] Pratt, *Polytechnic Experiment*, p. 191.
[90] Conor Cradden, '"Old" University Academic Staff Salary Movement Since 1949', *Higher Education Quarterly* 52 (1998), pp. 394–412, p. 402.
[91] *Higher Education in the Learning Society*, 14.44.
[92] John Carswell, *Government and the Universities in Britain: programme and performance, 1960–1980* (Cambridge, 1985), p. 155.
[93] Roger Brown with Helen Carasso, *Everything For Sale? The marketization of UK higher education* (London and New York, 2013), p. 76.
[94] LeeUA, 195/L, Housing and Estates Committee 1987–90, 12 September 1989.
[95] National Audit Office, *Financial Health of Higher Education Institutions*, appendix 2.
[96] Pratt, *Polytechnic Experiment*, pp. 322–3.

tutor Margaret Price discovered that 400, rather than the anticipated 250, first-years had enrolled for her course. As she ruefully noted, it took a quarter of an hour just to distribute hand-outs for each lecture.[97] Naturally, such a significant growth did not just affect the students themselves. Academics now had to cope with previously unimaginable numbers of undergraduates. Indeed, the ratio of teaching staff to students declined dramatically in this period, from around 1:10 to something closer to 1:20, or even worse.[98]

To make university life still more complicated, these demanding conditions for teaching were accompanied by an increased emphasis on research. In 1979, more than a third of professors felt under no pressure to publish at all.[99] All this was to change, for in 1984, the UGC announced that it would institutionalize the selective approach it had taken to the cuts of 1981. 'Research selectivity', as it called the process, would allocate money based on something called 'research excellence'. Two years later, the first Research Selectivity Exercise was carried out in the universities. It was undertaken again in 1989; then repeated, in both universities and former polytechnics, as a Research Assessment Exercise in 1992 and 1996.[100] Although the particular methodologies used in each exercise differed, the overall approach was the same: with the disciplines in each university subject to a form of peer review. High-scoring departments were rewarded with higher levels of funding.[101] True enough, most institutions were themselves selective in how they dealt with the consequences of this selectivity. Many ignored the 1989 exercise, for example, when distributing money between departments.[102] Nonetheless, continued financial pressure made the emphasis on research increasingly unavoidable. Individuals who did not perform—who did not produce enough publications, attract enough grant income, or who were otherwise seen to fail this regular series of tests—soon came to be seen 'as "a problem"', and efforts were made to ease them out.[103] Departments that persistently under-performed faced the threat of closure. By the same token, those individuals or subjects seen as stars were rewarded. Academics got promotion and departments grew larger.[104] In an atmosphere of financial stringency, and an environment in which promotion was the only effective way to improve income, this undoubtedly concentrated the mind on publishing.

---

[97] *Independent*, 19 July 1990.
[98] National Audit Office, *Financial Health of Higher Education*, 3.30–31.
[99] Richard Startup, *The University Teacher and His World: a sociological and educational study* (Farnborough, 1979), p. 57.
[100] Valerie Bence and Charles Oppenheim, 'The Evolution of the United Kingdom's Research Assessment Exercise: publications, performance, perceptions', *Journal of Educational Administration and History* 37 (2005), pp. 137–55.
[101] Ted Tapper and Brian Salter, 'Interpreting the Process of Change in Higher Education: the case of the Research Assessment Exercise', *Higher Education Quarterly* 57 (2003), pp. 4–23.
[102] *THES*, 12 April 1991, p. 1.
[103] Hugh Willmott, 'Managing the Academics: commodification and control in the development of university education in the United Kingdom', *Human Relations* 48 (1995), pp. 993–1027, p. 1014.
[104] Mark Baimbridge, 'Institutional Initiatives for the 1996 Research Assessment Exercise', *Journal of Further and Higher Education* 22 (1998), pp. 125–34.

One obvious outcome from the twin demands of pressure to publish and rising numbers of students was longer working hours for lecturers. At the start of the 1970s, it was estimated that academics worked, on average, just over 50 hours a week. By the mid-1990s, it was more like a 55-hour working week.[105] More intangibly, though no less importantly, the culture of academic life subtly changed. It had always been competitive, of course. Bruce Truscot's sneers against 'Professor Deadwood' are an instructive reminder that a division between the 'research active' and 'inactive' had existed before. But this institutionalized competition—in which 'problem' staff were side-lined and 'problem' departments shrunk or closed—had a profound effect on attitudes as well as university finances. Poorly-rated institutions reported declining morale.[106] Academics complained that there were increasing 'divisions between "fast track" and "other" members of staff'.[107]

Nor was this the only important development. In a process which was neither designed nor desired by a government devoted to rationalizing higher education, the growth in student numbers, the mounting need to plan for research assessment, and the increasing demands made by funding bodies to account for the money they granted inadvertently led to a rise in bureaucracy. By 1996 academics spent more time on administration than on any other single activity—with up to a third of their week devoted to it.[108] Not only was this far removed from the lean, hungry, entrepreneurial university of the government's imagination. It was also not what most academics themselves wanted to be doing.[109] 'The system is killing me', complained one lecturer. 'There's too much teaching, too much admin, too much research, too much everything.'[110]

Something had to give—and gradually it meant that full-time, permanent lecturers became proportionately less prevalent than part-time and fixed-term staff. By the end of the century, in fact, about half of all academics were on temporary contracts.[111] Many were teaching, often at an hourly rate; something like 30 per cent of sociology teachers, for example, were part-time.[112] Still more of these people were engaged in research, with the number of temporary researchers rising four-fold after 1980. In 1998, this meant that there were nearly 29,000 people employed on research contracts, 96 per cent of whom were paid by the

---

[105] Stephen Court, 'The Use of Time by Academic and Related Staff', *Higher Education Quarterly* 50 (1996), pp. 237–60.

[106] Arifin Zainal and Michael Gruneburg, 'Dissatisfaction Guaranteed', *THES*, 2 October 1987, p. 18.

[107] Willmott, 'Managing the Academics', p. 1014.

[108] Court, 'The Use of Time', p. 245.

[109] Titus Oshagbemi, 'Job Satisfaction of UK Academics', *Educational Management, Administration and Leadership* 24 (1996), pp. 389–400, p. 395.

[110] Evans, *English people*, p. 111.

[111] Colin Bryson and Nikki Barnes, 'The casualisation of Employment in Higher Education in the UK', in Malcolm Tight, ed., *Academic Work and Life: what it is to be an academic and how this is changing* (Amsterdam, 2000), pp. 187–241.

[112] Andrea Abbas and Monica McLean, 'Becoming Sociologists: professional identity for part-time teachers of university sociology', *British Journal of the Sociology of Education* 22 (2001), pp. 339–52, p. 343.

hour.[113] Blurring the increasingly sharp distinction between research-only and teaching-only staff, postgraduate students were also increasingly drawn into both roles.[114] In many respects, this was the natural result of the massive expansion of postgraduate numbers: in 1974 there were 46,000 of them, almost all full-time. Numbers then fell some 15 per cent, before recovering in the years after 1983.[115] By 1997 there were 387,000 research students in the country, two-thirds of whom were part-time.[116] But their employment as teachers and contract researchers was also the product of the universities' insatiable need for people to teach more students and produce still more research.

Temporary workers and postgraduates often felt under-appreciated and could be treated shabbily.[117] The average length of each contract was 26 months; long enough to settle down, but not long enough to become comfortable—and certainly not an encouraging basis on which to plan a career. In the competitive world of the modern university—with its division between the 'stars' and the 'problems', the 'fast track' and the 'other' staff—not to be employed on a permanent contract was also symbolically significant. 'At the back of my mind,' observed one contract researcher, 'there's always the thought that I am not a full member of the university, and then jumps up the invidious thought, "Why? Why have I not been made permanent, why am I not good enough?"'[118] Nonetheless, nearly half of all academics passed through this stage before being successfully hired on a more permanent basis.[119] Temporary contracts could consequently be a life raft as well as a life sentence, at least for some.

The increasing number of academics employed solely to carry out research or undertake teaching was paralleled by an equally remarkable rise in the quantity and importance of university administrators. In the 1960s, they had been few in number and strictly limited in their authority.[120] Famously, one Registrar was reputed to look in the mirror every morning and say 'I know I am evil—but am I necessary evil?'[121] Yet, by the end of the 1990s, administrators—or managers, as they were increasingly (and tellingly) known—had become a sizeable and significant part of the university workforce, amounting to nearly 40,000 people and possessing an influence well in excess of this number.[122] True enough, not all

[113] Jacquelyn Allen Collinson, 'Occupational Identity on the Edge: social science contract researchers in higher education', *Sociology* 38 (2004), pp. 313–29, p. 314.
[114] Sara Delamont, Odette Parry, Paul Atkinson, and Andy Hiken, 'Suspended Between Two Stools: doctoral students in British higher education', in Amanda Coffey and Paul Atkinson, eds, *Occupational Socialization and Working Lives* (Aldershot, 1994), pp. 138–53.
[115] Brown, *Everything For Sale*, p. 61.
[116] *UGC Annual Survey 1973–4*, p. 6; *Students in Higher Education 1997/8*, table 0a.
[117] Adele Graham and Barbara Grant, *Managing More Postgraduate Research Students* (Oxford, 1997), pp. 5–6; Abbas and McLean, 'Becoming Sociologists', pp. 345–7.
[118] Quoted in Collinson, 'Occupational Identity on the Edge', p. 322.
[119] Bryson and Barnes, 'Casualization of Employment', pp. 207, 213.
[120] Mike Shattock, 'Managing Modern Universities', *Perspectives* 4 (2000), pp. 33–4.
[121] Stuart Bosworth, 'Introduction', to Stuart Bosworth, ed., *Beyond the Limelight: essays on the occasion of the Silver Jubilee of the Conference of University Administrators* (Reading, 1986), pp. ix–xi, p. ix.
[122] Celia Whitchurch, '"Who Do they Think They Are?" the changing identities of professional administrators and managers in UK higher education', *Journal of Higher Education Policy and Management* 28 (2006), pp. 159–71; *Professional Managers in UK Higher Education: preparing for complex futures* (London, 2008), p. 7.

administrators were equally important. In 1990, it was reported that 62 per cent of university clerical staff were employed below the Council of Europe's 'decency threshold' of £163 a week.[123] Junior administrators—often on short-term contracts, and sometimes undertaking the role because they could not find an academic post—frequently complained of being marginalized.[124] For senior managers, however, the increasing demands of government and the growing complexity of the university each provided an opportunity to expand the power and importance of the administration.[125] What even administrators described as a period of 'audititus' resulted in a truly Weberian process, as bureaucracy begat bureaucracy.[126] Moreover, it was not just the need to demonstrate that the government's money was being spent wisely, nor the necessity of preparing for Research Assessment Exercises, Teaching Quality Audits, and the like that drove this trend.[127] Other legislation—like the 1974 Health and Safety at Work Act—unexpectedly demanded the creation of new departments to oversee aspects of the university that had up till then been quietly neglected or managed by no more than one or two members of staff.[128]

Above all, the move towards greater centralized control was the result of a deliberate attempt to rebalance power within the university.[129] In hindsight, the 1970s would turn out to be the high watermark for academic democracy: decision-making was decentralized; university senates were open to ordinary academics and tended to play an important role in shaping the institution; the authority of the vice-chancellor was at its lowest ebb.[130] Professors, too, were no longer all-powerful; indeed at many universities the professor had become, in the words of Manchester's Brian Pullan, nothing more than 'an administrative can-carrier'.[131] Nor were heads of department the 'lords of creation' they had been a generation before. Now, according to Exeter's Frank Barlow, they were simply 'dogsbodies'.[132] Yet this egalitarian system proved to be less effective at responding to change than the more *dirigiste* polytechnics, with their clear lines of command and administrative hierarchies.[133] University heads seized the opportunity given by straitened

---

[123] *THES*, 18 May 1990, p. 7.
[124] Jacquelyn Allen Collinson, '"Get yourself some nice, neat, matching box files!" Research administrators and occupational identity work', *Studies in Higher Education* 32 (2007), pp. 295–309, p. 297.
[125] Rosemary Deem, Sam Hillyard, and Mike Reed, *Knowledge, Higher Education and the New Managerialism: the changing management of UK universities* (Oxford, 2007), p. 35.
[126] David Allen, 'A Tale of Two Universities', *Perspectives* 5 (2001), pp. 98–101.
[127] Cris Shore and Susan Wright, 'Coercive Accountability: the rise of audit culture in higher education', in Marilyn Strathern, ed., *Audit Cultures: anthropological studies in accountability, ethics and the academy* (London, 2000), pp. 57–89.
[128] John Lawrence, 'The Future of the Profession of University Administration and Management', *Perspectives* 6 (2002), pp. 93–7, p. 93.
[129] Scott, *Meanings of Mass Higher Education*, p. 62.
[130] John Hayward, 'University Councils in Times of Change', in Bosworth, ed., *Beyond the Limelight*, pp. 91–8; Geoffrey Lockwood, 'Continuity and Transition in University Management: the role of professional administrative service', *Higher Education Management* 8 (1996), pp. 41–52, p. 43.
[131] *THES*, 15 February 1974, p. 7.   [132] *THES*, 6 August 1997, p. 5.
[133] Jon Sizer, 'British Universities' Responses to Events Leading to Grant Reductions Announced in July 1981', *Financial Accountability and Management* 4 (1988), pp. 79–98.

circumstances to reassert their authority—and they were helped in this by a government which was, of course, determined to make higher education more business-like.[134] The publication of the Committee of Vice Chancellors and Principals' Jarratt Report on 'Efficiency Studies in Universities' (1985) marked the moment when vice-chancellors assumed the mantel of 'chief executive of the university'.[135] This was often a divisive process, producing polarized universities with staff divided 'into "us" and "them"'—academics and administrators—each suspicious of the other.[136] But it was also decisive in changing how the universities worked.

For some—especially those eased out of their jobs or unable to find stable employment—this was an undeniably traumatic time. Even those who apparently thrived in this competitive environment sometimes expressed regrets, bemoaning what they saw as increased instrumentalization and a decreased interest in the pastoral responsibilities of lecturers towards their students. The demands of larger classes and the insistent need to publish, they argued, meant that there was no longer time to care.[137]

The negative effects of these changes were also most strongly felt by the least well-integrated members of staff. Women, in particular, continued to find it hard to get on in academia. Although they amounted to nearly 40 per cent of academics by the late-1990s—up from only 16 per cent twenty-five years before, they continued to be considerably less likely to obtain promotion or higher pay.[138] Indeed, the gap in income between men and women widened as the century came to a close.[139] In part, this was to do with the continuing problem of managing a career and childcare. 'For most academic women', observed Colin Evans in 1988, 'the sensible choice is not to have children.'[140] Throughout this period, the research selectivity exercises took no account of maternity leave—ensuring that many women who had taken it became a 'problem' for their departments. In a notorious case in the 1990s, the LSE refused to re-employ one female member of staff who had taken sick leave following a miscarriage.[141] More subtly, the growing competitiveness of academic life may have disadvantaged women, who were more likely to

---

[134] John M. Roberts, 'Recollections of a Pre-Revolution', *Oxford Review of Education* 24 (1998), pp. 99–110, p. 106.

[135] CVCP, *Report of the Steering Committee for Efficiency Studies in Universities* (London, 1985), recommendation 5.5.

[136] Walford, *Restructuring Universities*, p. 70. For an international comparison, see Ian R. Dobson, '"Them" and "Us"—General and Non-General Staff in Higher Education', *Journal of Higher Education Policy and Management* 22 (2000), pp. 203–10.

[137] Miller, 'Academics and the Labour Process', p. 119; Willmott, 'Managing the Academics', pp. 1013–14.

[138] Margharita Rendel, 'Women Academics in the Seventies', in Sandra Archer and David Warren Piper, eds, *Is Higher Education Fair to Women?* (Guildford, 1984), pp. 163–79; Alison Park, 'Women, Men, and the Academic Hierarchy: exploring the relationship between rank and sex', *Oxford Review of Education* 18 (1992), pp. 227–39.

[139] David Knights and Wendy Richards, 'Sex Discrimination in UK Academia', *Gender, Work, and Organization* 10 (2003), pp. 213–38, p. 213.

[140] Evans, *Language People*, p. 151.

[141] Knights and Richards, 'Sex Discrimination in UK Academia', pp. 214, 222.

be caught up in the pastoral problems their male colleagues increasingly avoided. 'Somehow the men's doors are always closed,' complained one female lecturer; 'they've got important things to do. It's always my door and my shoulder.'[142]

Despite it all, however, academia remained an attractive career for many. There were vociferous complaints about workload and about the changes in academic life. In 1996, more than half of academics surveyed were dissatisfied with their current salary, for example.[143] But, what is even more striking is the fact that this did not prevent lecturers from enjoying their job. Indeed, the proportion satisfied with their teaching conditions was reported to have risen—from 70 per cent in the 1970s to 80 per cent in the 1990s.[144] By the end of the century, nearly 80 per cent also found their work either challenging or exciting, compared to only one per cent who found it dull. Despite the perception of a gap between administrators and lecturers, 81 per cent said they had a good relationship with their manager.[145]

What this suggests is two conclusions. First, like the institutions for which they worked, academics proved to be more flexible and adaptable than their reputation would lead us to expect. This was particularly true for new generations of lecturers, who got used to change as a fact of academic life. Secondly, and still more importantly, it begs the question of whether that change was as dramatic as contemporaries believed. The scale of university life was dramatically transformed in this period. But was its nature similarly altered?

---

[142] Quoted in Evans, *Language People*, p. 152.
[143] Oshagbemi, 'Job Satisfaction of UK Academics', p. 395.
[144] Startup, *University Teacher and His World*, p. 25; Oshagbemi, 'Job Satisfaction of UK Academics', p. 395.
[145] Bryson and Barnes, 'Working in Higher Education', pp. 164, 169.

13

Towards a New Architecture?

In October 1993 *The Sunday Times* carried a long article by the critic Hugh Pearman about a new university building in Leicester.[1] This was not, of course, the first time that the city's academic architecture had been the focus of attention. After all, James Stirling's Engineering Laboratory was listed grade II* that same year.[2] What was remarkable was the fact that this was a new building for a new university. Indeed, it was the first new building for De Montfort University, as Leicester Polytechnic was now called. Not surprisingly, therefore, Pearman played up the 'battle of buildings' between the old university and the new, contrasting Stirling's lab for the former with the Queens Building, by Alan Short and Brian Ford, for the latter. In this battle, he concluded, honours were even. Looking at the striking red brick and shingle walls of the Queens Building, he summed up: 'Its self-appointed task is to gobsmack. It means little to say that it is utterly different from the Stirling building—everything is utterly different from the Stirling building—but in its way it is just as distinctive.' Nor was he alone in his admiration. When the Royal Fine Art Commission held a symposium on higher education buildings three years later, experts and Lord St John of Fawsley alike competed in their praise.[3] The Queens Building was part of a wider plan to 'create a coherent visual identity for the University', to overcome the fact that 'the excellent academic reputation enjoyed by De Montfort University was not reflected in the quality of its buildings and their surroundings'.[4] It seemed to have done just that—and was later nominated as one of the ten most significant buildings of the 1990s.[5]

At one level, this battle of the buildings undoubtedly signals change. Functionally, the Queens Building's environmentally friendly principles stand in sharp distinction to the leaky, heat-exuding, light-polluting engineering laboratory up the road. Educationally, it speaks of an end to the old binary line, which had not just divided polytechnics from universities in terms of their governance, sources of funding, and names, but had also restricted the polytechnics to public sector architects. The whimsy of the Queens Building—all gables and chimneys outside, all angles and atria within—was a million miles away from the pragmatic, cost effective structures that Leicester Polytechnic had previously erected: buildings like the central Students'

---

[1] Hugh Pearman, 'The Battle of the Buildings', *Sunday Times*, 10 October 1993.
[2] Arthur Lyons, *The Architecture of the Universities of Leicester* (Leicester, 2010), p. 51.
[3] Royal Fine Art Commission, *Design Quality in Higher Education Buildings* (London, 1996), pp. 5, 22–9.
[4] Livingstone Eyre Architects, *De Montfort University Masterplan* (December, 1992), p. 1.
[5] *Architecture Today*, July 1999, p. 62.

Fig. 44. 'Its self-appointed task is to gobsmack'. The Queens Building, De Montfort University Leicester

© Martine Hamilton Knight.

Union, designed as an experimental prototype by the Department of Education, and known simply as 'the shed',[6] or its equivalent on the outlying Scraptoft campus, which stood condemned as 'Leicester Polytechnic's equivalent' of the no-frills 'Laker Airways'.[7] With the construction of the Queens Building (Figure 44), De Montfort took a step towards the civic university model—and especially towards its tradition of expressing institutional identity in substantial and arresting bricks and mortar. The comparison Hugh Pearman made between the city's old and new institutions of higher education was, in that respect, spot on. Their buildings revealed that the city had acquired two literally Redbrick universities.

Buildings and things thus present us with a useful way of answering the question of how much had changed in higher education. Even apparently insignificant details exposed cultural shifts. More temporary lecturers and fewer offices, for example, meant increasing numbers of people lugging luggage around the university: 'Every time it's raining you come in ringing wet, you've got your bag across your shoulder and your marking everywhere and you look like a dithering secondary school teacher', complained one. 'You have no status; you haven't got an office, you haven't got your name on a door.'[8] The rising numbers of managers who

---

[6] *Leicester Polytechnic Student Handbook, 1975–6*, p. 8.
[7] *Leicester Polytechnic Student Handbook, 1983–4*, p. 23.
[8] Quoted in Andrea Abbas and Monica McLean, 'Becoming Sociologists: professional identity for part-time teachers of university sociology', *British Journal of the Sociology of Education* 22 (2001), pp. 339–52, p. 347.

wanted to bridge the gap between themselves and the academics with whom they worked was marked by more and more administrative offices stacked with scholarly books and journals—and even with degree certificates. 'I guess what I'm saying is "Look, I'm more than just a person who just happens to be working in administration at the moment. I have interests too, like you lot".'[9]

At a larger scale, the growing student population reshaped whole areas of university cities, as terraced houses and old council estates were bought up and turned into lodgings.[10] Indeed, middle-class students showed themselves able to price out poorer families in the search for housing as early as the 1970s.[11] With students making up more than one in ten of the population in places like Newcastle, Manchester, and Salford by the mid-1990s, their impact on these towns simply grew greater still. Whole areas of the city centre were given over to student clubs and pubs and entertainment.[12] Critics talked about 'student ghettos' being formed—and, in Oxford, one resident went so far as to attribute a reduction in the number of owls to the concentration of rowdy polytechnic students.[13]

Declining support from the state also had an impact on university sites. Cutbacks meant that they undoubtedly grew shabbier in the 1970s and 1980s.[14] Maintenance budgets were slashed—and by the early-1990s, there was a backlog of almost £2 billion worth of work to be done.[15] In Leeds, a spate of fires was blamed on reductions in regular repair work.[16] Nor was this just a problem for universities. A survey in 1989 suggested that every one of Liverpool Polytechnic's buildings was unsafe, whilst at Thames Polytechnic there had been no new building work since 1965.[17] Campuses also grew less comfortable, as the heating was turned down—and sometimes off.[18] At Surrey, by 1988, rooms were kept at a constant 16°C.[19] Elsewhere, it was even colder: visiting the new principal of cash-strapped Stirling, a journalist observed that his office seemed 'barely heated'.[20] More poignantly, campuses were scattered with memorials to plans that had been killed off for lack of cash. At the University of Hull the concrete piles of an unbuilt arts building provided the foundations for a car park.[21] At Leeds Polytechnic, the abandonment of the master plan left rusting reinforcing rods sticking out of

---

[9] Quoted in Jacquelyn Allen Collinson, '"Get yourself some nice, neat, matching box files!" Research administrators and occupational identity work', *Studies in Higher Education* 32 (2007), pp. 295–309, p. 302.

[10] Brian Pullan and Michael Abendstern, *A History of the University of Manchester, 1873–90* (Manchester, 2004), p. 272; Mathers, *Steel City Scholars*, p. 373; *THES*, 10 August 1990, p. 3.

[11] David Morgan and Linda McDowell, *Patterns of Residence: costs and options in student housing* (Guildford, 1979), ch. 3.

[12] Paul Chatterton, 'University Students and City Centres—the formation of exclusive geographies. The case of Bristol', *Geoforum* 30 (1999), pp. 117–33.

[13] *Leeds Student*, 12 October 1990, pp. 6–7; *Oxford Mail*, 28 January 1992.

[14] *THES*, 1 January 1982, p. 1.

[15] National Audit Office, *Financial Health of Higher Education*, 4.28.

[16] *Leeds Student*, 29 January 1988, p. 1.   [17] *THES*, 21 July 1989, p. 3.

[18] *Leeds Student*, 17 May 1975, p. 1.

[19] 'Office Temperatures During Heating Season' (1988), in AUDE Building Officers' Handbook (?1992/3).

[20] *THES*, 8 January 1982, p. 8.   [21] *THES*, 27 November 1987, p. 9.

the concrete on several floors.[22] The same was also true across the road at the university.[23]

This reduction in finance was accompanied by new duties imposed by the state. Grants for building fell by three-quarters between the late-1970s and early-1990s, yet higher education was expected to cope with a rising burden of responsibility.[24] 'In financial terms', complained the surveyor of Sheffield University in 1980, 'the consequences of "complying with legislation" could well be catastrophic'.[25] He was not exaggerating: it was estimated in 1975 that it would take £40 million to satisfy the requirements of new health and safety laws.[26] Moreover, there were additional, hidden, knock-on costs to be accounted for. It turned out that fitting new safety devices to that 1960s icon, the paternoster, actually left the lift more prone to mechanical failure, for example.[27] But this was not the only important development.[28] Increasingly, universities were required to improve conditions for students, staff, and even laboratory animals. They were also compelled to treat some of their buildings better, too.

Working on a limited budget, it must be admitted, attempts to provide enhanced facilities for the disabled were not always encouraging. At Surrey in the 1970s, one student observed that, had he used the steep ramps provided, 'I would have ended up more disabled than when I had arrived'.[29] Nonetheless, improving access would become an increasing cost for institutions. Raising the standards of housing for experimental animals to satisfy Home Office requirements likewise led to the expenditure of millions of pounds.[30] Indeed, at Liverpool, records suggest that the 'Official Opening of the Experimental Pig House' was one of the few major celebrations of the 1970s.[31] As the state took a greater interest in architectural preservation, universities also found themselves responsible for large numbers of old buildings that they had previously expected to demolish. The massive Manchester Education Precinct consequently stuttered to a halt when faced by newly listed cinemas, pubs, and nineteenth-century houses.[32] The university—like so many others—was left responsible for what one director of estates plangently described as a well-recognized type: 'Ancient Property too Costly to Maintain but Grade II Listed'.[33]

---

[22] Patrick Nuttgens, 'Sixties Hit of the Mods', *THES*, 16 May 1986, p. 13.

[23] William Whyte, 'The Modernist Moment at the University of Leeds, 1957–1977', *Historical Journal* 51 (2008), pp. 169–93.

[24] Brian Salter, Tony Rich, and David Bird, 'Managing the Private Finance Initiative', *Perspectives* 4 (2000), pp. 68–73, p. 68; Chairmen of University Councils Group, 'The Maintenance of the Estate' (1991), in AUDE Building Officers' Handbook (?1992/3), p. 3.

[25] TNA, UGC 7/1621, A. R. Hill (7 February 1980).

[26] *UGC Annual Survey 1975–6*, p. 5.   [27] *Staff*, 10 October 1980.

[28] MUA, USG/4/9, Building Committee 1975–8, p. 154.

[29] N. Shaban, 'A Graduate's Viewpoint', in Richard Holmes and Francis Aprahamian, eds, *The Disabled Student in Higher Education: access and support* (Milton Keynes, 1981), pp. 19–24, p. 21.

[30] LeeUA, 195/L, House and Estates Committee Minutes 1990–94, 25 February 1991.

[31] Liverpool University, *Official Opening of the Experimental Pig House* (1974).

[32] MUA, USG/4/8, Building Committee 1973–75, Hugh Wilson and Lewis Womersley, 'Report on Listed Buildings' (1975).

[33] Richard Metcalfe, 'How to Survive in Estates', in Helena Thorley, *Take a Minute: reflections on modern higher education administration* (Lancaster, 1998), pp. 39–44, p. 40.

Unfortunately, the pressures of declining funds, rising expectations, and increasing numbers of students came at exactly the moment when the buildings erected in the 1960s—which often made up the majority of a campus—began to need renewal or replacement.[34] In 1974, the Cornwallis Building at Kent collapsed.[35] In 1975, Manchester discovered that the materials used in its precinct were defective.[36] In 1982, a tower block at Cardiff started shedding lumps of concrete.[37] Some of these problems were the product of incompetent design and slipshod workmanship. Others were undoubtedly due to poor maintenance. But they were also the consequence of cutbacks made at the time the buildings were erected.[38] The plain concrete walls at Leeds, which were compared unfavourably to Victorian prison cells—where 'the bricks are at least painted'—were bare because the university had not been able to pay for them to be plastered and painted when they were first built.[39] Many student rooms at Lancaster were cold because the university had been unable to rise to the cost of installing central heating.[40] It must be said that there were those who could look beyond these issues. A survey in 1977, for example, showed staff at Leeds divided in their attitudes—with some describing the 1960s lecture block as 'awful in every possible way' and others calling it 'excellent'. The students, however, were almost universally unhappy, with the university detecting 'an undercurrent of opposition to concrete and lack of colour'.[41] 'I have had a number of strongly worded requests from students', wrote one lecturer, 'to have the lectures elsewhere.' They even, he went on, preferred the basement of the once-despised 1930s buildings.[42]

It would be wrong, however, simply to see this as an era of stasis or neglect. 'My ambition', stated the deputy principal of Manchester Polytechnic in 1977, 'is to produce the very best sort of buildings at the very worst sort of time'.[43] He was far from alone. Even in the 1970s, amidst a collapse in funds for buildings that the UGC itself compared to the darkest days of the Great Depression, many universities and polytechnics were still building.[44] They were making additions to the now-listed Victorian villas they could not demolish—as at Bristol, where the Faculty of Arts employed Richard MacCormac to build a series of inter-connected, low-cost pavilions.[45] New medical schools were established, like the Building

---

[34] AUDE, *The Legacy of 1960s University Buildings* (Milton Keynes, 2008), 2.3.
[35] Graham Martin, *From Vision to Reality: the making of the University of Kent at Canterbury* (Canterbury, 1990), p. 261.
[36] MUA, USG/4/9, Building Committee 1975–78, pp. 3, 86.
[37] *Gair Rhydd*, 4 October 1982, p. 1.
[38] Idris Pearce, 23 May 1991, in AUDE Buildings Officers' Handbook; TNA, UGC 7/1621, F Taylor (17 March 1980).
[39] LeeUA, B67, Housing and Estates Committee, Buildings R, February 1977, G. M. Rees.
[40] Robert M. Smart, 'Loan Finance Straitjacket', *Official Architecture and Planning* 34 (1971), pp. 660–6, p. 663.
[41] LeeUA B67, Housing and Estates Committee, Buildings R, May 1977.
[42] LeeUA, B67, Housing and Estates Committee, Buildings R, February 1977, G. M. Rees.
[43] *THES*, 26 November 1976, p. 9.
[44] *UGC Annual Survey 1975–6*, p. 5.
[45] Margaret Richardson, 'The Architecture of Learning', in Ian Latham, ed., *Building Ideas: MJP architects* (London, 2010), pp. 108–41, pp. 112–14.

Fig. 45. One of 'The very best sort of buildings at the very worst sort of time': the Arts and Social Sciences Library, University College Cardiff

Architectural Press Archive/RIBA Library Photographs Collection.

Design Partnership's Queen's Medical Centre at Nottingham (1971–5).[46] A whole series of new libraries were also erected—at Cardiff (Figure 45), Loughborough, Strathclyde, and elsewhere. True enough, even these massive, monolithic structures were affected by economies. At Leicester, for example, a whole bay was removed from the library extension at the very last minute, suddenly reducing capacity by a quarter.[47] But libraries kept on being planned, nonetheless, and the 1980s would

---

[46] A. Peter Fawcett and Neil Jackson, *Campus Critique: the architecture of the University of Nottingham* (Nottingham, 1998), pp. 119–21; *UGC Annual Survey 1976–7*, p. 6.
[47] Library Association, *New Library Buildings* 1976, pp. 242–4.

Fig. 46. 'The most significant building in Britain for a quarter of a century': the Sainsbury Centre for the Visual Arts, University of East Anglia

RIBA Photographs Collection.

see a series of readily recognizable open-plan, modular, boxy buildings arise from Exeter to Dundee.[48]

Private benefactions also resulted in some remarkable projects—not least Norman Foster's spectacular Sainsbury Centre at the University of East Anglia (1977–8).[49] It was the winner of the RIBA Building of the Year Award and was greeted as 'the most significant building in Britain for a quarter of a century' (Figure 46).[50] Its users were not always persuaded of its merits, observers were not always convinced that it was an appropriate university building, and the architect's freedom from financial constraint certainly made it atypical of other academic projects.[51] It is, however, more than just a striking anomaly; it was a sign of the renewed importance of private money for university building.

The increasing need for universities to supplement the income they received from the state also led them to change the ways they used their property. In 1971

---

[48] Anthony Quinsee, 'After Atkinson: British university library planning since 1976' (1995), <http://webdoc.gwdg.de/ebook/aw/liber96/quin.htm> (accessed 20 November 2010).
[49] Witold Rybczynski, *The Biography of a Building: how Robert Sainsbury and Norman Foster built a great museum* (London, 2011).
[50] Martin Pawley, *Norman Foster: a global architecture* (London, 1999), p. 63; Ted Happold in *Architectural Design* 49 (1979), *AD Profile* 19, p. 30.
[51] Peter Dormer and Stefan Muthesius, *Concrete and Open Skies: the architecture of the University of East Anglia, 1962–2000* (London, 2001), pp. 34–5; Peter Cook, in *Architectural Review* 164 (1978), pp. 355.

Heriot-Watt opened the first-ever British science park, modelled on one at MIT.[52] This pioneering move was soon followed by others. By 1987, there were thirty-four university science parks and four others developed by polytechnics.[53] Rarely great architectural statements, these were places where 'trendiness is not sought, the more traditional appearance of brick and tile is preferred'.[54] Beneath this banality, however, these were important signs of evolution within higher education.

The same was true of the rising number of conference centres and hotels opened by universities—from Radcliffe House at Warwick to Black Horse House at Reading to Wivenhoe Park at Essex.[55] As early as 1973, a group of institutions established University Holidays Ltd to let out rooms in the summer vacation.[56] This was just the start. By 1991, the conference and tourist trade brought universities a combined total of £65 million a year—an increase of 250 per cent in a decade.[57]

The growing recognition of the cost as well as the value of accommodation within the campus was also acknowledged by the development in the 1990s of new 'space charging' methods, in which departments paid a rent for the rooms that they occupied. Designed to maximize occupancy rates, they were also intended to reward subjects that had succeeded in acquiring large research grants.[58] At Leeds, for instance, some of the Senior Common Room was lost to the 'South American Gravity Project' in 1991, because gravity paid and the common room could not.[59]

The commercialization of the higher education estate was not always successful. Space charging had almost no effect on efficiency.[60] Like many attempts to make higher education more entrepreneurial, science parks very rarely produced the desired results: only 9 per cent of their cost was born by the private sector and the universities who established them almost never turned a profit.[61] In many respects, they were little more than an expensive way of the state—which provided the bulk of the finance—equipping local business with superior space for their cars. After all, a survey of 1989 showed that 24 per cent of tenants valued them for their parking, and only 15 per cent for their links to the university.[62] The vice chancellor of Salford was not simply being cynical when he scoffed at ministers who 'go up and down the country giving the impression that new technology-based companies

---

[52] Patrick N. O'Farrell, *Heriot-Watt University: an illustrated history* (Harlow, 2004), pp. 353, 386–91.
[53] Peat Marwick McLintock, *Science Parks and the Growth of Hi-Technology Firms* (London, 1988), p. 79.
[54] Norma Carter, *Science Parks: development and management* (London, 1989), p. 21.
[55] LeeUA, 195/L House and Estates Committee 1987–90, Weetwood Hall Business Plan (1989).
[56] *THES*, 23 August 1973, p. 4.
[57] *THES*, 26 August 1911, p. 1.
[58] National Audit Office, *Space Management in Higher Education: a good practice guide* (London 1996).
[59] LeeUA, 195/l, House and Estates Committee 1990–94, 20 September 1991.
[60] Mary Lou Downie, 'Efficiency Outcomes from Space Charging in UK High Education', *Property Management* 23 (2005), pp. 33–42. See also, Auditor General, *The management of Building Projects at English Higher Education Institutions* 1998 (HC 452), 16.
[61] Peat Marwick McLintock, *Science Parks*, p. 82; *THES*, 24 April 1987, p. 10.
[62] Carter, *Science Parks*, p. 21. See also *THES*, 18 May 1984, p. 16.

founded by entrepreneurial professors and housed in pastel coloured incubator units in Science Parks attached to universities will play a major role in bringing down next month's unemployment'.[63] Indeed, higher education arguably benefited just as much from firms failing as succeeding. As Coventry's John Gledill put it: 'Very often the modern universities found themselves waiting for local businesses to go bankrupt so as to release large "brownfield" sites for acquisition.'[64]

But commercialization was not all bad either. For students, it undoubtedly improved their living conditions, which, by the 1980s, had become a genuine problem. It was not merely that much was substandard; nor that rising numbers of undergraduates put pressure on existing housing stocks.[65] It was also that the supply of rooms was drying up. The start of each academic year was greeted by first-years living in temporary caravans (as at Leeds) and holiday camps (as at Cardiff and Lancashire Polytechnic), the Senior Common Room (as at Manchester), and even in their own cars (as at Oxford Polytechnic).[66] Yet universities, which had to fund accommodation out of loans, were initially unable—and unwilling—to do much about it. Notoriously, one institution was rumoured to have entitled its discussion of student housing: 'How Little Can We Get Away With?'[67] The development of the conference trade, however, made accommodation suddenly seem much more important. Rooms were smartened up. Carpets, curtains, and other furnishings were improved. Washbasins were installed.[68] Whole blocks were built with conferences as well as students in mind.[69] The growing competition for students—and the fees they brought with them—also drove up standards. Between 1990 and 1995 higher education consequently spent £1 billion on student residences.[70]

In that respect at least, the pressures of financial downturn and student growth actually prompted institutions to rediscover the old idea of residence as an important part of university life. To be sure, this was not the return of the old hall of residence. Save for a few isolated examples—Wills Hall in Bristol or Aberdare Hall in Cardiff, for example—the gated, gowned, and single-sex halls of the past were almost completely abandoned; and even the defiantly traditional Wills went co-educational eventually.[71] The new residences—and the reformed versions of the old halls—were self-catering, informal, and unisex. They no longer tended to have

[63] Quoted in Peat Marwick McLintock, *Science Parks*, p. 89.
[64] John Gledhill 'The Modern English Universities', in David Warner and David Palfreyman, eds, *The State of UK Higher Education: managing change and diversity* (Buckingham, 2001), pp. 95–102, pp. 98–9.
[65] Morgan and McDowell, *Patterns of Residence*, p. 16; Allan Doig, 'Flat-units are the best bet in the student housing stakes', *THES*, 25 October 1974, p. 9.
[66] *THES*, 20 October 1989, p. 7 and 28 September 1990, p. 4; *Gair Rhydd*, 4 October 1982, p. 1; *Oxford City Courier*, 16 October 1987.
[67] Martin Blakey, 'Student Accommodation', in Susanne Haselgrove, ed., *The Student Experience* (Buckingham, 1994), pp. 72–81, p. 74.
[68] LeeUA, B67, Housing and Estates Committee, Sou-Te, Tetley Hall, 7 November 1978.
[69] Hugh Pearman, *Rick Mather: urban approaches* (London, 1992), p. 63.
[70] Blakey, 'Student Accommodation', p. 77.
[71] M. J. Crossley-Evans, *A History of Wills Hall, University of Bristol* (Bristol, 1994); Joan N. Harding, *Aberdare Hall, 1885–1985* (Cardiff, 1986).

academics as wardens.[72] But the continued demand for campus accommodation reflected the continuing strength of the tradition that the civic universities had created: students still expected to be able to leave home and live at university—just as they had been doing since the first hall of residence was opened a century before. This process was even more striking at the polytechnics, as they reshaped themselves in imitation of the civic universities. Far from remaining purely local institutions for solely local students, they became national—even international—in their focus.[73] They, too, built halls of residence, and even the most radical of students could see no alternative to them.[74]

In the same way, instead of re-imagining the architecture of higher education, polytechnics quickly sought to recreate the eye-catching campuses they associated with university life.[75] At the start of the polytechnic experiment, writers like Tyrell Burgess had been hopeful that the new institutions would develop a new architecture.[76] They celebrated 'the dispersed polytechnic', with its split-site, multifunctional, low-key buildings—well adapted, or so they argued, to the more human scale of a non-elite institution.[77] No ivory tower, the polytechnic would look and feel totally different from the imposing, monolithic structures that characterized Redbrick.[78] Yet even as Burgess and his allies dreamt of reforming the architecture of higher education, individual institutions drifted back to more familiar ideas. The government, too, assumed that a single campus was the ideal and this attitude was widely accepted—even within Burgess' own institution, the Polytechnic of North East London.[79] Inevitably, limited funding restricted these intentions. The desire to create something that seemed somehow like a university nevertheless only grew stronger with time.[80] On the verge of acquiring university status, indeed, it was often argued that the biggest change the polytechnics needed to make was architectural. 'The polytechnics come to the new sector with a range of immediate handicaps', wrote one commentator in 1992. 'Most do not *look* like universities; environmentally many remain a quantum leap from a university campus culture.'[81]

---

[72] LeeUA 195/L, House and Estates Committee 1987–90, Organisation and Management of Halls of Residence (13 October 1987).

[73] John Pratt, *The Polytechnic Experiment, 1965–1992* (Buckingham, 1992), pp. 89–93; Pamela Lewis, 'Finance and the Fate of Polytechnics', in Tyrrell Burgess and John Pratt, eds, *Polytechnics: a report* (London, 1974), pp. 110–48, pp. 132–42.

[74] DMU, City of Leicester Polytechnic, 'Report on Student Residences' (1972); BCU, *The Worst Poly in the Country* (1974), pp. 32–4.

[75] Edward Jones, 'The University and the City: to case studies', in Royal Fine Art Commission, *Design Quality*, pp. 12–16, p. 12.

[76] Tyrrell Burgess, 'Polygenesis', *Architectural Review* January 1971, pp. 3–4.

[77] Ian Brown, 'The Dispersed Polytechnic', *Higher Education Review* 3 (1971), pp. 25–45.

[78] DES, Design Note 8, *Polytechnics: planning for development* (1972), section 7.

[79] DES, *Design Note 8*; Burgess et al., *Degrees East*, pp. 210–11. See also *THES*, 6 January 1984, p. 10.

[80] David Warner, 'A Corporate Identity case study: grasping the nettle', in Clive Keen and David Warner, eds, *Visual and Corporate Identity: a study of identity programmes in the college, polytechnic and university environment* (Banbury, 1989), pp. 35–45, pp. 35–6.

[81] Christopher Price, 'Elegant and Democratic: how will the new English Universities gel?', *Higher Education Quarterly* 46 (1992), pp. 243–51, p. 247.

In response, the polytechnics developed a slew of master-plans, iconic buildings, and award-winning designs, as they embraced the monumental traditions of civic university architecture.[82] Far from seeking anonymity, places like the newly created University of Portsmouth enthusiastically sought to create an impressive urban landmark.[83] Far from celebrating the 'dispersed polytechnic' ideal, institutions like the University of East London attempted to centralize, creating massive new campuses which integrated a variety of different functions.[84] Just as Owens College in the 1860s had worried that its poor location and cramped buildings deterred future applicants, so institutions in the 1990s sought to 'improve undergraduate and postgraduate recruitment', by employing high-profile architects to design buildings with what became known as the 'wow factor'.[85]

Fig. 47. The first entirely new university campus created since the 1960s: the University of Lincoln

© Martine Hamilton Knight.

[82] *THES*, 4 January 1991, p. 5.
[83] Ian Latham and Mark Swenarton, eds, *Jeremy Dixon and Edward Jones: buildings and projects, 1959–2002* (London, 2002), p. 188.
[84] Brian Edwards, *University Architecture* (London, 2000), pp. 10–11.
[85] University of Sunderland quoted in CABE, *Design with Distinction: the value of good building design in higher education* (London, 2005), p. 11.

In 1995, the process of assimilation was brilliantly exemplified at the University of Lincoln—the former Humberside Polytechnic—which produced plans for a wholly new campus on a sixteen-hectare site, the first entirely new university campus created since the 1960s (Figure 47).[86] Yet its inspiration actually stretched further back than the Plateglass institutions; back all the way to Redbrick. This was intended to be a major intervention in the city: symbolizing its importance and linking the university to the urban community which gave it its name.[87] Even more than Leicester's Queens Building, this massive, landmark project was a symbol of dramatic change—and remarkable continuity. The civic university tradition was being rediscovered and renewed.

[86] Brian Edwards, *University Architecture* (London, 2000), pp. 31–2.
[87] Robert Maxwell, Tim Macfarlane, and Patrick Bellew, *Rick Mather Architects* (London, 2006), pp. 25–7.

Conclusion

The years between 1974 and 1997 witnessed a genuine revolution in higher education—or, rather, a series of revolutions. The scale of the enterprise was transformed beyond recognition. The number of universities and, above all, the number of students increased at an unprecedented rate. At the same time, the involvement of the state was evolving, often in ways that observers found disconcerting. Governments had of course always been interested in higher education. But the direct involvement of ministers as it developed in this period was understood to be something new; and it is certainly the case that one has to look back to the early years of the University of London to find anything quite as *dirigiste* as the system that developed in the 1980s and 1990s.

Once again, it is worth being a little sceptical about the extent to which this actually amounted to a crisis. True enough, there were moments when the universities and their staff struggled to cope with change, especially when they seemed threatened by acute financial problems. The emotional response evoked by these changes—especially the anger obviously felt by so many—was real. In the strictest sense, however, this was not a crisis—not, that is, a moment of decision—for, in fact, it was the absence of a clear decision or even a coherent set of policies on higher education that led to these lurches from one expedient to another. More than this, what is striking about the history of the universities after 1974 is the extent to which this change ran along some familiar tracks. As Michael Shattock observes in his undeniably definitive account of post-war higher education policy, in spite of everything, British universities still cling to an old conception of their function and purpose. For Shattock, this older notion is the 'Humboldtian concept of universities which incorporate research with teaching', and it is surely the case that this is part of the story.[1] The nineteenth-century reforms embodied by Von Humboldt at the University of Berlin did indeed remain inspirational. But it is evident that it was the Humboldtian model mediated by and through Redbrick that actually predominated even in this time of great change.

As the steady assimilation of the polytechnics showed, the British proved incapable of rethinking the nature or the form of higher education. Even though an elite system was giving way to mass university access, the old symbols and old assumptions retained their purchase. The result was not the highly-differentiated system that the government hoped to create, but a set of strikingly similar

---

[1] Michael Shattock, *Making Policy in Higher Education 1945–2011* (Maidenhead, 2012), p. 186.

institutions—all of them modelled on the civic universities, whose structure, working practices, and architectural forms were the implicit points of comparison throughout. Critics at the time were inclined to blame an inherent conservatism for this, and they were half right. Higher education proved to be both more innovative and more conservative than one might expect. But it was conservative in aping Redbrick, not Oxbridge.

14
Epilogue
Redbrick since 1997

British universities are now, once again, widely believed to be in crisis. They are, it should be stressed, scarcely unique in that respect. Familiar anxieties about higher education have recurred throughout this book, as the university formed the focus of personal, political, and economic fears for successive generations. The last decade and a half has been no different. Indeed it has witnessed a proliferation of books and articles proclaiming a state of emergency in universities across the world.[1] In good times and in bad, at moments that were genuinely problematic and in periods that seem apparently more propitious, there has always been someone willing to stand up and prophesy disaster.

Yet, it does seem true to say that there is a new feel, a new texture, to the current concern about Britain's universities.[2] For the first time since the early nineteenth century, when it was literally a life and death matter for a prime minister, higher education policy has become a central part of high political debate beyond the department and the minister responsible for it. Universities were the single issue, as Tony Blair recalled, that came closest to destroying New Labour and forcing him to resign.[3] They are, wrote another well-informed commentator in 2011, the 'laboratory of the current Government's social ambitions'.[4] More than this, and still more than was the case even in the 1870s, 1950s, or 1980s, higher education is seen as central to the nation's development, and especially to its economic success.[5] As the historian James Vernon observed in December 2011, 'Never before has the idea of the university been so feverishly debated.'[6]

---

[1] See, for example, Erhard Stölting, *Die Krise der Universitäten* (Berlin, 2001); Nicolas Obin, Patrick Vassort, and Jean-Marie Brohm, *La Crise de l'Université française: traité contre une politique de l'anéantissement* (Paris, 2005); James E. Cote and Anton L. Allahar, *Ivory Tower Blues: a university system in crisis* (Toronto, 2007); Mark C. Tylor, *Crisis on Campus: a bold plan for reforming our colleges and Universities* (New York, 2010). The blog of the International Sociological Association is called 'Universities in Crisis' and provides good global coverage of this sort of debate. See <http://www.isa-sociology.org/universities-in-crisis/> (accessed 22 May 2014).

[2] Stefan Collini, *What are Universities For?* (London, 2012), p. 118.

[3] Tony Blair, *A Journey* (London, 2010), p. 480.

[4] Matthew D'Ancona, 'Within Our University System, the Revolution is Under Way', *Sunday Telegraph*, 21 August 2011, p. 22.

[5] For a polemical survey of this rhetoric, see Stefan Collin, *Common Reading: critics, historians, publics* (Oxford, 2008), ch. 24.

[6] James Vernon, 'Canary in the Coal Mine', *THES*, 1 December 2011.

That Britain's universities should be the subject of such comment is hardly surprising. Higher education has become an ever-bigger business and student numbers have never been greater. By the end of the first decade of the twenty-first century, there were nearly 2.5 million students in the United Kingdom, and universities were estimated to contribute more than £3 billion to the national economy.[7] The financial consequences of all this expansion were remarkable, with the income for the higher education sector rising over this period from under £12 billion to almost £27 billion.[8] There were more institutions too. From 2001 onwards, a further thirty-one new universities were created, as a series of further education colleges were enlarged and upgraded. This meant that by 2012 there were 115 chartered universities in the United Kingdom, some forty foundations that possessed varying sorts of university status, and another 150 colleges offering some higher education courses.[9]

The forces of change were not solely insular. Although only a dozen or so British universities acquired overseas campuses, many others began offering overseas degrees; just one sign of a definite and self-conscious process of globalization in British higher education, and one that was further exemplified in the vice chancellor of Reading's comments of February 2012: 'A university like this should have a presence somewhere else in the world. It shows that you are a serious international player.'[10]

This globalization also helped reshape the profile of the student body as a whole.[11] By 2010, nearly one in five of all students was from outside the UK and amongst postgraduates a clear majority were not British.[12] Nor was this the only way in which student life was transformed, as trends which had emerged in the 1980s and 1990s were amplified. The universities of the early-twenty-first century, where women made up rather more than 50 per cent of undergraduates, were strikingly dissimilar from the male-dominated institutions of just a generation before. The number of mature students also continued to rise, and there was greater variation in the ways in which students studied. In 2010 more than a fifth of all undergraduates were over 30, and more than a quarter were taking part-time courses. This still left an overwhelming preponderance of students aged around 18 and studying full-time; given that 45 per cent of all school-leavers went straight to university, it could hardly be otherwise. Nonetheless, it gave Britain a considerably older student body than neighbouring countries, with an average age of nearly 30 compared to France's 22.[13] It also meant that the patterns

---

[7] <http://www.hesa.ac.uk> (accessed 21 February 2012); HEFCE, *Higher Education Business and Community Interaction Survey 2009–10* (London, 2011).
[8] <http://www.hesa.ac.uk> (accessed 21 February 2012).
[9] <http://www.universitiesuk.ac.uk/Publications/Documents/PatternsAndTrendsinUKHigher Education.pdf> (accessed 21 February 2012).
[10] *THES*, 9 February 2012.
[11] This paragraph relies on data from <http://www.hesa.ac.uk> (accessed 21 February 2012).
[12] Lorraine Brown and Steven Richards, 'The British Host: just how welcoming are we?', *Journal of Further and Higher Education* 36 (2012), pp. 57–79.
[13] Brian Ramsden, 'Euro Student 2000: comparisons with the United Kingdom', in Maria Slowey and David Watson, eds, *Higher Education and the Life Course* (Maidenhead, 2000), pp. 3–19, p. 8.

of student life became ever more highly differentiated, with a diminishing number of undergraduates conforming to what had become a sort of ideal type. Indeed, as only a quarter of students were able to live on campus and a third were engaged in paid employment during term,[14] there were growing fears that even the traditional type of undergraduate was missing out on the all-consuming experience that these universities had tried to create over the previous century.[15]

Driving these developments in student life was a significant change in English university funding. By the end of the 1990s, it had become clear that higher education as a whole was in serious financial trouble. A number of institutions teetered on the verge of bankruptcy. Others had expanded beyond their capacity. Buildings were falling apart and some universities were finding it hard to recruit staff.[16] It was calculated in 2001 that universities needed £2.7 billion for remedial work on their laboratories alone.[17] After several decades of declining resources and increasing demands—both in terms of teaching and research—higher education seemed, as one expert put it, 'permanently on the verge of financial crisis'.[18] In response, a succession of controversial reforms was enacted: each one designed to increase university income; each one fiercely resisted; and each one, as a result, only partially successful in achieving this aim.

The 1998 Higher Education Act introduced an up-front £1,000 a-year tuition fee for all students. It was not what the government's enquiry—the Dearing Committee—had recommended, it was not what universities wanted, and it was fiercely fought by many students and some academics alike.[19] Nor did it bring the additional resources required; indeed, as one well-placed source observed, it left 'some parts of the sector...close to meltdown'.[20] So in 2004 another act was introduced, which enabled universities to charge undergraduates as much as £3,000 a-year. It was this legislation which Tony Blair feared would drive him from government, and this additional money which helped bring most universities back into the black for the first time in years.[21] Yet three-quarters of this new income went on staff salaries, whilst the amount spent on each student remained as

---

[14] NUS/HSBC, *Student Experience Full Report 2010/11* (London, 2011), pp. 26, 80.
[15] RIBA, *Growing By Degrees: universities and the future of urban development* (London, 2009), p. 17.
[16] Brian Salter, Tony Rich, and David Bird, 'Managing the Private Finance Initiative', *Perspectives: policy and practice in higher education* 4 (2000), pp. 68–73; Hilary Metcalfe, Heather Rolfe, Philip Stevens, and Martin Weale, *Recruitment and Retention of Academic Staff in Higher Education* (London, 2005), p. 21.
[17] Roger Brown with Helen Carasso, *Everything For Sale? The marketization of UK higher education* (London and New York, 2013), p. 59.
[18] Gerry Webber, 'Funding in UK Universities: living on the edge', *Perspectives: policy and practice in higher education* 7 (2003), pp. 93–7, p. 93.
[19] National Committee of Enquiry into Higher Education, *Higher Education in the Learning Society* (London, 1997).
[20] David Watson, 'New Labour and Higher Education', *Perspectives: policy and practice in higher education* 10 (2006), pp. 63–8, p. 63. See also, David Greenaway and Michelle Haynes, 'Funding Higher Education in the UK', *Economic Journal* 113 (2003), pp. 150–64.
[21] HEFCE, *The Financial Health of the Higher Education Sector* (London, 2011), p. 6.

low, in real terms, as it had been in 1989.[22] It quickly became clear, therefore, that even this most fiercely contested of changes had proved to be inadequate. The result was another enquiry, another set of recommendations, and—in 2010—another act of parliament. The Browne Review reported that universities should be able to determine their own fees. In a party political compromise, fees were in fact capped at £9,000; a figure that will doubtless have to be revised upwards relatively soon. The critical point was this: that tuition fees, which, a generation before had become an utterly insignificant part of any university's income were, now, once again, a core source of funding for undergraduate teaching. This was, in Roger Brown's terms, a revolution: 'from subsidizing institutions to subsidizing students'.[23]

This turn back to tuition fees was not designed solely to solve the problems of higher education funding, of course. It was also intended to reshape the universities and the system they are part of. The two acts of 2004 and 2010, in particular, were designed to create a sliding scale of charges, one that would, it was hoped, inspire a market in higher education.[24] But the results of these reforms were not all that their progenitors had imagined they would be. No market emerged after 2004; almost all the universities simply charged the maximum fee. The one exception—Leeds Met—abandoned the attempt to cap charges after a couple of years, with its chief executive ruing the millions of pounds that the experiment had lost them.[25] Nor did the outcome of the later legislation seem to satisfy its promoters. Although the government expected the average fee to be around £7,500 a-year, almost all institutions once again raced to the top end of the scale,[26] with the most expensive university, on at least one reckoning, lowly-ranked Middlesex rather than highly-rated Oxbridge.[27] The University of Derby, which set the lowest fees, was rewarded by a drop in the number of applications.[28] In an attempt to introduce further competition, whilst also preserving standards and seeking to defend the expensive and vulnerable science subjects that ministers considered so important, a succession of apparently ad-hoc changes was introduced, from premiums for students with high A level grades to cut-price places in further education colleges.[29]

Not for the first time in the recent history of universities, an attempt to reduce government control was followed by a period of tinkering as ministers sought to rein in a system that was not behaving in the way that they had hoped—and predicted—it would.[30] Little wonder that a long-promised new higher education act was repeatedly, indeed indefinitely, delayed;[31] nor that attempts to restrain

---

[22] UCEA, *Where are We Now? The benefits of working in HE* (London, 2008), pp. 64–7; *Securing a Sustainable Future for Higher Education* (London, 2010), p. 22.

[23] Brown, *Everything For Sale?*, p. 93.

[24] Ingrit Lunt, 'Beyond Tuition Fees? The legacy of Blair's government to higher education', *Oxford Review of Education* 34 (2008), pp. 741–52.

[25] *THES*, 1 October 2009.

[26] Andrew McGettigan, *The Great University Gamble: money, markets, and the future of higher education* (London, 2013), p. 23.

[27] *The Times*, 13 July 2011.

[28] McGettigan, *The Great University Gamble*, p. 36.

[29] John Morgan, 'Hefce chief stands by policy comments', *THES*, 5 April 2012.

[30] *Daily Telegraph*, 6 April 2011.   [31] *Daily Telegraph*, 23 January 2012.

student numbers in 2012 were followed, just a year later, by a series of contorted about-turns, as, first, the cap on places was apparently abolished,[32] and then the government wrote to hundreds of private colleges, begging them to cease recruitment.[33]

These changes took place within a wholly new political environment. The 1992 Higher Education Act divided university funding along national lines for the first time since the nineteenth century, creating separate bodies for England, Scotland, Wales, and Northern Ireland.[34] Devolution further entrenched this development. Although there has been less divergence in practice between the four nations than might be expected, one clear point of difference has been over tuition fees.[35] Scotland, Wales, and Northern Ireland each developed systems of student funding that were more generous than the English, with Scotland abolishing fees altogether in 2008.[36] This financial variation was symbolic as well as practical, reflecting a greater confidence in the power of the state to intervene directly in higher education.[37] Thus in Scotland generosity was linked to structural reform, with a commission established that was designed to make universities more responsive to the perceived needs of the nation as determined by the government.[38] In Wales, too, the desire to eschew the English market model led the government—and its instrument, the Higher Education Funding Council for Wales—to adopt a series of increasingly *dirigiste* policies, designed to reshape the sector completely.[39] The collapse of the 118 year-old federal University of Wales, destroyed by a scandal over its poorly-managed move into the international market for degrees, was not part of this process. But it effectively signalled the way in which the apparently fixed points of the higher education world were being moved even in those parts of the UK which otherwise seemed to be clinging on to older ways of doing things.[40]

These shifts in policy and practice had human consequences as well as institutional ones. For the staff in universities, this continued to be a time of striking, and often dismaying instability. Some developments were unarguably positive: pay went up by more than a third; the percentage of people on permanent rather than temporary or renewable contracts rose to almost three-quarters; the sector as a whole began to offer benefits like generous maternity (and paternity) leave. There were also some claims that, on average, the working week grew shorter, with the English funding council maintaining that it had fallen to little more than 35 hours.[41] Were this true, it would have been a remarkable turnaround, with lecturers

---

[32] <http://www.bbc.co.uk/news/education-25236341> (accessed 15 January 2014).
[33] *Guardian*, 18 November 2013.
[34] Michael Shattock, *Making Policy in Higher Education 1945–2011* (Maidenhead, 2012), p. 82.
[35] Jim Gallacher and David Raffer, 'Higher Education Policy in post-Devolution UK: more convergence than divergence?', *Journal of Education Policy* 27 (2012), pp. 467–90.
[36] Ølivind Bratberg, 'A Long Path to Divergence: English and Scottish policies on tuition fees', *Higher Education Policy* 24 (2011), pp. 285–306.
[37] David Matthews, 'The price of avoiding the market: your freedom', *THES*, 19 April 2012.
[38] <http://www.scotland.gov.uk/Resource/0038/00386780.pdf> (accessed 24 February 2012).
[39] See *THES*, 20 December 2011, 19 January 2012.
[40] David Matthews, 'Boom and Bust', *THES*, 5 January 2012.
[41] UCEA, *Where are We Now?*, pp. 5–6, 12; HEFCE, *The Higher Education Workforce Framework 2010* (London, 2012), pp. 27, 107. Though see Metcalfe et al, *Recruitment and Retention*.

very suddenly working less hard than they had at any point in last 200 years. Other—more convincing—figures suggested that, on the contrary academics managed an average 47–48 hour week.[42] But this was still lower than a few decades before, and it was noteworthy that the turnover rate for staff more than halved, falling to only 6 per cent.[43] There evidently was a general sense that conditions were tolerable.

Yet, in other ways, the demands placed on university employees grew still more exacting. Research Assessment Exercises, Student Satisfaction Surveys, and a variety of other means of measuring 'output', all piled on the pressure. With universities increasingly run like businesses—and businesses, in the words of one vice-chancellor, which had 'to make the bottom line of every year, and . . . have to have some profit at the bottom line'—staff experienced a limited sort of marketization.[44] Indeed, the government's own research showed that universities were falling over themselves to capitalize on their discoveries and work in harness with local enterprises.[45] Only the consistent failure of British businessmen to take advantage of this enthusiasm stood in the way of a still more dramatic change in the way that the country did research and development.[46]

The burgeoning market within—though never really between—universities steadily reshaped the experience of being an academic. True enough, the process was not uniform or universal. Staff in newer institutions experienced more uncertainty and more change than those in older ones.[47] The general trends, nonetheless, were unmistakable: a growing centralization of control within universities and a corresponding decline in academic autonomy; greater overt competition between staff; and an ever-rising quantity of bureaucracy.[48] These changes were not new. They reflected a transition that had begun years before. Taken together, however, they effected a remarkable reversal of the moves towards a democratic university community which had culminated in the 1970s, and they transformed working conditions. In at least one university, academics found themselves required to clock in and out, ensuring that they were on site for a full 35-hour week.[49] In others, they lost their own offices, and found themselves working in open-plan spaces—a development that was seen as, and was often meant to be, a symbolic loss of

---

[42] Metcalfe et al, *Recruitment and Retention*, p. 31.
[43] Melcalfe et al., *Recruitment and Retention*, p. 12; HEFCE, *Higher Education Workforce Framework*, p. 74. On working hours see also Josh Howgego, '"Beyond the call of duty": lecturers top overtime figures', *THES*, 24 February 2012.
[44] Rosemary Deem, Sam Hillyard, and Mike Reed, *Knowledge, Higher Education, and the New Managerialism: the changing management of UK universities* (Oxford, 2007), p. 53.
[45] Michael Kitson, Jeremy Howells, Richard Braham, and Stian Westlake, *The Connected University: driving recovery and growth in the UK economy* (London, 2009), esp. pp. 17, 36.
[46] *The Lambert Review of Business–University Collaboration* (London, 2003), pp. 1–3.
[47] Seng-Kiat Kok, Alex Douglas, Bob McClelland, and David Bryde, 'The Move Towards Managerialism: perception of staff in "traditional" and "new" UK universities', *Tertiary Education and Management* 16 (2010), pp. 99–113.
[48] Deem et al., *Knowledge*, p. 35.
[49] Rebecca Attwood, 'Edict Curtailing Freedom to Work at Home "Appals" Staff', *THES*, 2 July 2009.

status.[50] Everywhere, the number of managers increased year by year;[51] and their authority increased too, as they came to see their job as being one of 'Herding the Academic Cats'.[52]

Undeniably, there were many who benefited from these changes: both academics who were successful in obtaining grants and managers who were successful in reforming the structures of their university. Each type was rewarded with a higher salary and greater status—and even given their own offices.[53] The universities' need to obtain research 'superstars' created a transfer market not unlike the Premier League, with bankable academics lured to leave their existing institutions with the promise of a significant pay rise and better working conditions.[54] The ever–rising number of scholars encouraged to turn their discoveries into marketable commodities also began to reap the rewards of a system which was determined to commercialize the university.[55] Vice-chancellors, who saw their pay and perks and power rise and rise again, were also obvious beneficiaries of this process.[56] Indeed, even economic crisis could not dent their confidence, with some observing that they were actually grateful for cuts which would enable them to achieve still greater efficiencies within their institutions.[57]

But these developments did leave British universities ever more divided within themselves: still more split between winners and losers, academics and managers, men and women. The pressure to publish and to obtain ever-more valuable research funding produced a highly segregated workforce: with one-quarter employed exclusively to teach, another quarter solely to research, and only half of all academics fulfilling a dual role of both teaching and research.[58] At the same time, the tensions between academic and non-academic staff became, if anything, more stark, with one vice-chancellor describing the distance between the two as one of 'almost "apartheid" proportions'.[59] The sociologist Maurice Glasman went even further still, vociferously complaining about managers at his own institution: 'I was told what to do by people who had no idea what they were doing. A shelf stacker at Waitrose has more power in corporate governance of the firm than I do as an academic at London Met.'[60] Many managers, in turn, were equally unhappy with

---

[50] Lee Taylor, 'Accommodating Change: a case study in planning a sustainable new Business School building', *Perspectives: policy and practice in higher education* 6 (2002), pp. 38–44. More generally, see Matthew Reisz, 'Space to Think', *THES*, 13–19 May 2010.
[51] *THES*, 7 October 2010.
[52] Rosemary Deem, 'Herding the Academic Cats', *Perspectives: policy and practice in higher education* 14 (2010), pp. 37–43.
[53] HEFCE, *Performance in Higher Education Estates 2010* (London, 2011), p. 16.
[54] John Gill, 'Spending Spree on RAE Stars may spark Cash Crisis', *THES*, 10 January 2008.
[55] Kitson, Howells, Braham and Westlake, *The Connected University*; <http://www.nesta.org.uk/library/documents/Report%2023%20-%20The%20Connected%20Uni%20v4.pdf> (accessed 21 February 2012).
[56] John Morgan, 'Identity Check: vice chancellors' education and pay revealed', *THES*, 24 March 2011.
[57] PA Consulting, 'A Passing Storm, or Permanent Climate Change?' (2010), <http://hedbib.iau-aiu.net/pdf/PAConsulting_2010_Passing_storm.pdf> (accessed 21 February 2012).
[58] William Locke, *The Changing Academic Profession in the UK; setting the scene* (London, 2007), 2.1.
[59] Locke, *Changing Academic Profession*, 2.
[60] *Guardian*, 20 July 2011, G2, p. 13.

academics who saw 'it as their job to make the life of the Administration, as they call it, "Hell"'.[61]

These divisions revealed the heightened significance of existing hierarchies within higher education. Administrators complained that they were 'always second best to academics'.[62] Staff on teaching-only contracts were similarly seen by some as 'A Lesser Breed' of lecturer.[63] In the competitive environment of the modern university such distinctions mattered. And they continued disproportionately to disadvantage women, who were more likely to work part-time, less likely to receive promotion, and consequently made up only 16 per cent of the professoriate.[64] These attempts at marketization thus produced quite distinct differences between those who gained and those who lost out, and the gap between the two grew ever greater.[65]

Given this rapid change and the apparently increasing insecurity of university life, it should come as little surprise that many commentators—especially academics—were tempted to contrast current conditions with some point in the past that seemed more appealing. This was of course not a new development; but it was one that certainly intensified in this period. Thus, when the *London Review of Books* turned its attention to the subject in December 2011, it found a variety of laments and a range of dates: from Keith Thomas' celebration of the mid-1950s as a 'golden age of academic freedom', to Rachel Malik's description of the mid-1990s as a 'wonderful' time to work in academia.[66] That both comments placed the glory days of higher education at the start of the commentator's own career is surely telling; but more important was the fact that each saw the past as a refuge. And they were not alone. Since 1997 different writers have favourably compared every post-war decade with the experience of life in the twenty-first century university.[67]

Most interestingly of all, this nostalgic rhetoric also came to embrace more distant periods. In particular, the last few years have witnessed an increasing celebration of Redbrick. Previously condemned by historians and social critics alike as an impoverished, inadequate tradition, forever in thrall to the elitism of Oxbridge, the civic universities are now back in fashion. When the then universities minister, David Willetts, gave his first keynote speech on higher education in 2010, he did so in the great hall of that great Redbrick institution, Birmingham. After observing that his great-grandfather had helped install the stained glass windows and that his grandfather had attended the opening ceremony in 1909, he went on

[61] Deem et al., *Knowledge*, p. 157.
[62] Celia Whitchurch, *Professional Managers in UK Higher Education: preparing for complex futures* (November, 2008), p. 32.
[63] Esther Oxford, 'A Lesser Breed', *THES*, 31 January 2008.
[64] Locke, *Changing Academic Profession*, 2.1.
[65] See also: <http://issuu.com/ncafc/docs/ncafchighpay?mode=window&backgroundColor=%23222222> (accessed 26 April 2012).
[66] Keith Thomas, 'Universities Under Attack', *London Review of Books*, 15 December 2011, pp. 9–10, p. 9; Rachel Malik, 'Universities Under Attack', <http://www.lrb.co.uk/2011/12/16/rachel-malik/universities-under-attack> (accessed 28 February 2012).
[67] See, for example, Richard Garner, 'David Lodge: a novelist's lament for the golden age of universities', *Independent*, 28 March 2011 (on the 1960s); Vincenzo Raimo, 'Golden Age of the Don is Not Entirely a Relic', *THES*, 2 May 1997 (on the 1970s); Cassandra Jardine, 'University is Not What it Used to Be', *Telegraph*, 9 July 2009 (on the 1980s).

to celebrate Birmingham's pioneering mission, what he called its 'bold departure from the Oxbridge model'.[68] Three years later, in a powerful critique of Willetts, the writer Andrew McGettigan argued that universities should reject a marketized model of higher education and instead 'be more concerned with local and civic society'.[69] Both the government and its fiercest opponents, therefore, and each for very different reasons, would like a return to Redbrick.

Nor has this trend been confined to politicians and their critics. Academics, like the Newcastle geographer John Goddard, have seemed similarly enthusiastic about the Redbrick model. 'Now', he wrote in 2009, 'is the time to re-invent the notion of the broadly based civic university that served the country so successfully in the nineteenth century.' Indeed, he claimed that this was already happening. 'Newcastle University', he went on, 'has been on a journey in which it has re-discovered its roots.'[70] As a welter of other institutions undertook similar journeys, so they too re-emphasized their Redbrick origins. At Manchester, for example, successive re-brandings took the university back to its past, with logos which first presented a stylized version of Alfred Waterhouse's 1874 main building, and then rather tenuously claimed that the place had been established in 1824.[71]

This Redbrick renaissance has provided more than just a point of comparison with present travails. As its official endorsement by both politicians and vice-chancellors suggests, there are those who see the civic university tradition as a highly attractive model for British higher education in the future. The government has seized on the idea of a university ostensibly focused on serving industry and the wider economy, with David Willetts declaring that he took comfort from the fact that both UCL and Birmingham were criticized at their foundation for being solely focused on vocational instruction because exactly the same charges were being levelled at his own reforms.[72] A return to the idea of the civic university—a place intended to play a pivotal role in its region—has also grown in appeal, with government advisers stressing the direct economic importance of such institutions in de-industrialized Britain. 'Fifteen years ago, Nottingham was a manufacturing centre... and the university had around 8,000 students', observed the 2003 Lambert Review into business–university collaboration. 'Today, much of the old manufacturing has gone and the city's universities have around 46,000 students. The same story is repeated all over the country.'[73] University leaders have likewise used the history of their own institutions not only to stress their importance—both to the country and the locality—but also to emphasize their legitimacy. 'Many modern universities are not the higher education upstarts that some would claim',

---

[68] <http://www.bis.gov.uk/news/speeches/david-willetts-keynote-speech> (accessed 8 March 2012).
[69] McGettigan, *The Great University Gamble*, p. 188.
[70] John Goddard, 'Reinventing the Civic University', <http://www.nesta.org.uk/publications/provocations/assets/features/re-inventing_the_civic_university> (accessed 8 March 2012).
[71] *Design Week*, 28 October 2004, p. 3. The claim was based on the merger with UMIST, which grew out of the medical school established in the mid-1820s. The branding consultants were Lloyd Northover.
[72] *THES*, 17 November 2011.
[73] *Lambert Review of Business-University Collaboration*, 5.1.

argued the vice-chancellor of Middlesex in 2012. 'A considerable number have their roots in 19th-century movements to expand opportunities for education.'[74] Small wonder, then, that numerous institutions have recently published their histories, nor that these accounts have tended to stress the importance of links between the university and the city in which it was founded.[75]

Predictably, much of this discussion was not so much history as mythology. In reality, as this book has shown, the relationship between civic universities and the cities they serve was often strained. Many leapt at the chance to escape their local communities and embrace the apparent freedoms offered by national funding and a national constituency. Redbrick was also never just about technical education. From the very first, there was always a desire to offer precisely those subjects, like history or classics, that would be condemned by the education secretary Charles Clarke as nothing more than 'ornamental' in 2003.[76] If anything, rather than relying on technical education for their success, many institutions in the late-nineteenth century were kept going by state subsidies for teacher training.

Nonetheless, a renewed interest in the origins of the Redbrick universities did reflect the continued importance of the tradition they had developed over the previous 200 years. Their system of governance, for example, with a sharp distinction between an academic senate and a lay-dominated council, is now seen as the normal way to run a British university. Indeed, for HEFCE, it is normative, with Oxford and Cambridge each criticized for perpetuating an apparently outmoded and inefficient system of self-government, and both urged to adopt the model first pioneered by Owens College back in the 1870s.[77]

More importantly still, the notion—first articulated by the Victorians—that civic pride finds its highest fulfilment in a local unitary university still lives on. Both the multiplication of institutions since 1992 and the strikingly small number of mergers in the same period undoubtedly owe much to this idea. The cries of outrage when Salford University added the word 'Manchester' to its logo are evidence of this, as are the words of advice offered by an expert to 'vulnerable' institutions which fear closure or loss of a separate identity.[78] If a university is in such danger, argues John Goddard, then its links to its local community will be crucial in defending its existence.[79] The same advice could have been given a hundred years ago.

The sense of place that these institutions developed has remained similarly influential. Universities have continued to seek architectural advantage, building substantial structures to symbolize their significance and advertise their identity. Just as their predecessors did, they also produce plans in the hope of enticing donors to support them.[80] Campuses, as a result, have grown ever larger and buildings have

---

[74] Michael Driscoll, 'Thoroughly Entitled', *THES*, 8 March 2012.
[75] John Goddard and Paul Vallance, *The University and the City* (London and New York, 2012).
[76] *THES*, 9 May 2003.
[77] See, for example, *Guardian*, 8 August 2007; *THES*, 26 March 2009.
[78] *Manchester Evening News*, 18 July 2011.
[79] David Matthews, 'What have they ever done for us?', *THES*, 24 November 2012.
[80] Colin Davies, ed., *Hopkins2: the work of Michael Hopkins and partners* (London, 2001), p. 218.

grown ever more grandiose.[81] In part, this was nothing more than the outgrowth of a more general process, which has seen universities across the world employ 'starchitects' to erect what critics have called 'the idols of the architecture world'.[82] In part, too, this building boom owes much to the new-found financial freedoms of British higher education, with universities now able to borrow huge amounts of money for big capital projects.[83] A bond-issue in Sheffield, for example, enabled the university to raise no less than £160 million to build a 'Student Village'.[84] But the form that all this building took continued to be shaped by the Redbrick tradition in important and enduring ways. Residence remains a fundamental part of university life, and has even grown in popularity, ensuring that British students are still more likely to live away from home than almost any other nationality in Europe.[85]

The model provided by the great civic university buildings of the past has likewise proved hard to escape. Commentators might bemoan the cost, analysts might doubt the tangible value of all this architecture, ministers might wishfully imagine that universities could be created by someone who would 'just rent an office block' and set up shop: it was all to no avail.[86] The popular image of the university remains the one that the Redbricks created, and prospective students explicitly contrast this ideal with the 'sad', 'concrete' inner-city institutions which they continue to characterize as the 'worst' universities.[87] Indeed, as the twenty-first century began, older foundations self-consciously embraced their origins—as at Birmingham, where Glenn Howells Architects were employed in 2010 finally to complete Aston Webb's Edwardian master plan.[88] At Nottingham, too, ambitious plans to create a whole new campus overseas involved recreating Morley Horder's interwar architecture. Condemned by some as nothing more than 'England with palm trees', the University of Nottingham, Ningbo, was in fact a little bit of Redbrick set down in China (Figure 48).[89]

As this suggests, and however surprisingly, the tradition that this book has sought to explore still retains its relevance. In fact, as people return to Redbrick and increasingly celebrate its legacy, it seems likely that it will become ever more

---

[81] University of Lincoln, Centre for Educational Research and Development, *Learning landscapes in Higher Education* (2010): <http://learninglandscapes.blogs.lincoln.ac.uk/files/2010/04/FinalReport.pdf> (accessed 12 March 2012).

[82] Jonathan Coulson, Paul Roberts, and Isabelle Taylor, *University Planning and Architecture: the search for perfection* (London and New York, 2011), p. 35.

[83] *The Management of Building Projects at English Higher Education Institutions*, PP. HC 452 1997–98, p. 13.

[84] McGettigan, *The Great University Gamble*, p. 146.

[85] Ramsden, 'Euro-Student 2000', p. 16.

[86] John Morgan, 'Salford's bold move to MediaCity's lights, camera and action', *THES*, 29 September 2011; Paul Temple, *Learning Spaces of the 21st century* (2007): <http://www.heacademy.ac.uk/assets/documents/research/Learning_spaces_v3.pdf> (accessed 12 March 2012); *THES*, 1 September 2011.

[87] Louise Archer, Merryn Hutchings, and Alistair Ross, *Higher Education and Social Class* (London and New York, 2002), p. 28.

[88] See <http://www.glennhowells.co.uk/content/education/103> (accessed 12 March 2012).

[89] RIBA, *Growing By Degrees*, p. 13.

Fig. 48. 'England with palm trees': the University of Nottingham Ningbo
© Martine Hamilton Knight.

seminal. Certainly, the resurrection of old traditions and the re-creation of old institutions like the hall of residence suggest that there is still life in the civic university model. The number of students who wish to live in university accommodation has increased in recent years, with only 6 per cent of prospective undergraduates surveyed in 2013 wanting to stay at home and study.[90]

Yet this rediscovery of Redbrick raises some important questions, especially in an age that seems increasingly impatient with vested interests and barriers to social mobility. The story of these innovative institutions is a heroic one: a history of universities which have overcome all manner of obstacles and individuals who have fought hard to reform higher education. But it remains the case that Redbrick did not succeed in transforming Britain's universities completely. Whilst it provided opportunities for those excluded from higher education by their religion or their gender, and whilst it opened universities up to the middle classes, it always struggled to do the same for the children of the less fortunate. As the polytechnics reshaped themselves in the Redbrick image, so they too became less egalitarian. The expansion of the university sector at the end of the twentieth century thus maintained rather than narrowed the gap between rich and poor, leaving the wealthiest more than twice as likely to find a university place.[91] Although the

---

[90] <http://www.bbc.co.uk/news/education-25493976> (accessed 15 January 2014).
[91] Fernando Galindo-Rueda, Oscar Marcenaro-Gutierez, and Anna Vignoles, 'The Widening Socio-Economic Gap in UK Higher Education', *National Institute Economic Review* 190 (2008), 75–88.

first decade of the twenty-first century saw some moves towards a greater openness, the proportion of working-class students remains low.[92] Moreover, the older and more prestigious the institution, the less likely it is that those from poorer backgrounds will manage to get in to it.[93]

It would be wrong to level all the blame at universities for this phenomenon. In a country with an ever-widening gap between rich and poor, educational unfairness begins at birth.[94] As Sir Martin Harris, then director of the government's Office for Fair Access observed in 2010: 'The picture... is of early inequality in attainment amongst pupils from disadvantaged backgrounds which increases incrementally through primary and secondary education.'[95] Yet, it is not merely this disparity in schooling that prevents potential students from poorer backgrounds going to university and, especially, from attending the most selective institutions. People from lower income families are simply less likely to apply for a place, even if they are qualified to obtain one.[96] For many, university is an alien and alienating environment; and the more impressive the university, the more off-putting it seems.[97]

This is a major problem for Oxbridge. But it is also a serious difficulty for those universities which pioneered or came to adopt the Redbrick model. The places which the civic universities created were built in the image of the urban middle class. This was true in the nineteenth century, and continued to be the case thereafter. As other, younger institutions increasingly imitated these older foundations, so this bourgeois ideal became universal. It has left a higher education landscape that is deeply unappealing to precisely those people who need most encouragement to apply to university.[98] 'What's a person like me going to do at a place like that?' asked one typical student on a visit to King's College London.[99] Similar emotions were expressed by another aspirant undergraduate visiting the dauntingly neo-classical UCL and the shiny new LSE: 'wonderful but just very off-putting', she observed; 'they are both very rich universities, not really my sort of places'.[100] It is exactly the same complaint that was made 50 and, indeed, 100 years ago. That the imposing campuses of Redbrick and its imitators have never

---

[92] Vikki Boliver, 'Expansion, Differentiation, and the Persistence of Social Class Inequalities in British Higher Education', *Higher Education* 61 (2011), pp. 229–42.
[93] *Higher Education: students at the heart of the system* (2011) Cm 8122, 5.7.
[94] Haroon Choudry, Claire Crawford, Lorraine Dearden, Alicia Goodman, and Anna Vignoles, 'Widening Participation in HE: analysis using linked administrative data', IFS Working paper W10/04 (2010), p. 20.
[95] Martin Harris, *What more can be done to widen access to highly selective universities?* (2010): <http://www.offa.org.uk/wp-content/uploads/2010/05/Report-on-access-to-highly-selective-universities.pdf> (accessed 12 March 2012).
[96] Harris, *What more can be done?*, p. 68.
[97] Diane Reay, Gill Crozier, and John Clayton, '"Fitting In" or "Standing Out": working-class students in UK higher education', *British Educational Research Journal* 32 (2009), pp. 1–19.
[98] HEFCE, *Teaching and Learning Infrastructure in Higher Education* (2002), p. 20.
[99] Quoted in Diane Reay, Jacqueline Davies, Miriam David, and Stephen J. Ball, 'Choices of Degree or Degrees of Choice? Class, "race", and the higher education choice process', *Sociology* 35 (2001), pp. 855–74, p. 864.
[100] Diane Reay, 'A Risky Business? Mature working-class women students and access to higher education', *Gender and Education* 15 (2003), pp. 301–17, p. 308.

Fig. 49. 'The building liberates modern university architecture from its redbrick, tower-block image, away from a tradition of mere functionality over form.' The Graduate Centre, London Metropolitan University

© Michele Nastasi.

seemed—and were never intended to be—the sorts of places that are open to everyone should give us pause.

What is to be done? Bold architectural statements like Daniel Libeskind's Graduate Centre for London Metropolitan University may aspire to liberate 'modern university architecture from its redbrick, tower block image'; but, in fact, their eye-catching idiosyncrasy does nothing but perpetuate it (Figure 49).[101] For some writers now, as in the 1970s and, indeed, the 1820s, 'the attainment of "real" widened participation...may well require a shift away from current notions of a fixed university site'.[102] The success of the Open University, which has become the country's largest provider of higher education, suggests that other ways of teaching are possible. Much is made, too, of the opportunities opened up by new technology.[103] Some have even speculated that 'the bricks-and-mortar elite will end up on the wrong side of history', replaced by cheaper, more easily accessible, ostensibly more democratic Massive Open On-Line Courses (or MOOCs).[104] But it is worth remarking that the 'E-University' set up

---

[101] <http://www.londonmet.ac.uk/services/conference-and-commercial-hire-services-/venues/north/graduate-centre/graduate-centre.html> (accessed 7 May 2013).
[102] Archer et al., *Higher Education and Social Class*, p. 200.
[103] Kevin Robins and Frank Webster, *The Virtual University? Knowledge, market, and managements* (Oxford, 2002).
[104] Jon Marcus, 'Cap and gown learning on a shoestring', *THES*, 23 February 2012.

by the government in 2003 cost £50 million and attracted only 900 students.[105] In the words of Michael Shattock, it was 'perhaps the biggest financial white elephant in Britain's higher education history'.[106] Moreover, even though MOOCs seem able to recruit many more students, their drop-out rate is tremendous, with fewer than one in ten finally completing the course.[107]

As this suggests, the idea of the university as a real rather than just a virtual place evidently retains some sort of purchase. 'One of the university's most remarkable features', concluded a report of 2006, 'is its durability as a...physical form'. Indeed, the same report went on to suggest that instead of being replaced by the internet, universities may yet become ever more physically distinctive, with other organizations tending to cluster around them.[108] Certainly, the recently renewed emphasis on the Redbrick tradition of civic and commercial engagement suggests that this scenario is as likely as any move away from what has become the conventional understanding of the university in Britain.[109]

There are a number of possible futures for Britain's universities, many of which bear more than a passing resemblance to experiments in the past. In recent years, the quasi-commercial, corporate model adopted in the early-nineteenth century by UCL has been rediscovered, with the University of Central Lancashire—once Eric Robinson's pioneering polytechnic—turning itself into a limited company. In Coventry, the University has established a low-cost subsidiary: a college which, just like its early London equivalents, provides no access to the sorts of social facilities most undergraduates have come to take for granted.[110] The rising number of private providers certainly suggests that a return to the start of our story—to a pre-Redbrick type of higher education—is yet possible.[111]

But it seems more likely that the story of the civics is not over yet. One way forward is perhaps to be found back by the banks of 'the silver Trent', where Charles Kelsall imagined his *Phantasm of an University* and where a rather new institution, Staffordshire University, is currently trying to build itself a very new home (Figure 50).[112] In almost every respect, the story of Staffordshire is a very familiar one. Founded as a Polytechnic in 1971, the product of mergers between local art schools and technical colleges, it was initially sure about its distinctive status, making it clear that 'polys were not set up to provide the universities of the future'.[113] Within a few years, however, it had expanded and extended and journalists were reporting

---

[105] <http://www.publications.parliament.uk/pa/cm200405/cmselect/cmeduski/205/205.pdf> (accessed 10 April 2013).
[106] Michael Shattock, *Making Policy in Higher Education 1945–2011* (Maidenhead, 2012), p. 102.
[107] Chris Parr, 'Mooc completion rates "below 7%"' *THES*, 8 May 2013.
[108] UK Higher Education Space Management Project, *Impact on Space of Future Changes in Higher Education* (2006): <http://www.smg.ac.uk/documents/FutureChangesInHE.pdf> (accessed 12 March 2012).
[109] See, for example, Fielden Clegg Bradley, *Education Architecture Urbanism: three university projects* (London, 2012).
[110] McGettigan, *The Great University Gamble*, pp. 150, 35.
[111] Brown, *Everything For Sale?*, pp. 39–40.
[112] Charles Kelsall, *Phantasm of an University* (London, 1814), p. 170.
[113] *THES*, 12 October 1973, p. 6.

Fig. 50. One answer to the question 'What is a civic university?' Staffordshire University Science Centre, Stoke on Trent

© Staffordshire University.

that 'it looks and feels like a regional university already'.[114] In 1992 it finally became one. Staffordshire's current plans to build at its Stoke campus are also, in some respects, entirely typical of the times. The glossy brochures, flashy website, and visions of 'an innovative education-led regeneration partnership which promises to create a new symbol of civic pride' can seem simply generic, echoing the words and images used by dozens of other institutions in a similar situation.[115] Nonetheless, the

[114] *THES*, 20 June 1986, p. 11.
[115] <http://www.uniq-stoke.org/> (accessed 13 March 2012).

UNIQ—or University Quarter— project, which envisages a rebuilt university in a re-planned city, is a genuinely ambitious undertaking.[116]

What's more, this development grows out of two impulses that tell us much about both the past and future of Redbrick. In drawing up proposals, the authorities at Staffordshire looked back to the example of its predecessors, places like Birmingham, with their commitment to local life. They asked 'What is a civic university?' and 'What are the civic responsibilities of a university?', and began to plan accordingly; conceiving a campus that was highly visible and clearly connected to the city.[117] But they went beyond the old idea of Redbrick, with its well-policed boundaries, its distinctions between insiders and outsiders, its bourgeois origins and inspiration, and sought to envisage a place that was open to everyone. Indeed, not only is the new site meant to form a key part of a re-planned city centre, the university's facilities are intended to be shared with a neighbouring further education college. In that way, the children of Stoke, many of whom have previously fought shy of higher education, will be exposed to university life. These laboratories, libraries, and lecture-rooms will be as familiar—and, it is hoped, as unthreatening—to them as their own classrooms.[118]

Predictably enough, the project has not gone smoothly. Lack of money and sudden changes in government policy have, as ever, slowed progress and threatened the more ambitious aspects of the enterprise.[119] It is clear that it will not be completed to plan. Nor can it be said that the self-consciously 'modern, vibrant' architecture proposed resembles anything of the sort that Charles Kelsall could have imagined.[120] Yet, to stand by the Trent—now, give or take the odd shopping trolley, clean and silvery once again—and to see the gleaming new science and technology centre filled with undergraduates and sixth-formers alike is to witness in some respects the fulfilment of his dream.

More than that, and much more importantly than that, Staffordshire University is further tangible evidence of the way in which Redbrick has continually reinvented itself. Despite the recurrent sense of crisis and perpetual feeling of anxiety, despite the problems bequeathed by the past and created by the present, despite the angst and even anger which always frames discussions of university life, this is a tradition that has proved both flexible and enduring. Here in Stoke we can witness, once again, a civic university taking shape—which is to say, taking place.

---

[116] I am very grateful to Ruth Thompson and Paul Richards for their help in explaining the UNIQ project.
[117] Interview with Paul Richards (deputy vice-chancellor), 21 December 2010.
[118] University Quarter Stoke-on-Trent, Development Strategy Final Report (2004).
[119] <http://www.bbc.co.uk/news/uk-england-stoke-staffordshire-11029634> (accessed 13 March 2012).
[120] *UNIQ: our future is now* (supplement to *The Sentinel*, 28 January 2011), p. 2.

Bibliography of works cited

MANUSCRIPT SOURCES

Birmingham

1. **Birmingham City University Archive**
   Uncatalogued collection of papers relating to the university's history.

2. **Birmingham University Archive**
   Uncatalogued Minutes of Council.
   UC/4/iii/10, Advisory Sub-Committee Minutes.
   UC/4/iii/11, Opening of New Building.
   UC/4/ii/27, Mason College Building Committee.
   UC/7/ii, Buildings Committee Reports.
   UC/7/iv/5/3, Deed of Foundation of Josiah Mason's Scientific College.
   UC/iv/5/5 Mason College, first session.
   UC/7/iv/8/39, Statement concerning the proposed statues.

3. **Queen's Foundation Archive**
   Introductory Remarks and Index to Mr Martin's Report.
   Council Minute Book.
   Minutes of Council and Governors.
   Register of Students.

Brighton
University of Sussex Archive.
1A/V/1, Chaplaincy and Meeting House.
2B/1/7, Occupations.
IB/IV/2 Sussex House.
IB/IV/4 Sussex House.
IB/IV/6 Sussex House.
SxMs45/1, Staff Architect's papers.
SxUOSI/3/3/1, Colin Eaborn, Autobiography.
UnivSx Coll IV.IV, 'Sussex in the 1960s' (film).
UoS Architecture, Boxes 1–2.
Uncatalogued sketches by Basil Spence.

Cardiff
Cardiff University Archive.
UCC/5n/M/1-4, Senate Minutes.
Uncatalogued Committee Minutes.

Colchester
Essex University Archive.
1(b) Architecture.
Box 2, Foundation Fund.

Box 3, The first three years.
Box 3(b), Development Plan.
Box 3(c), Registrar's papers.
Box 3(d), Construction of the University.
Uncatalogued Development Committee papers and press cuttings.
Uncatalogued papers and correspondence relating to the building programme.

Dundee
Dundee University Archives.
Rec A/96, Minute Book of the Governors.
Rec A/98, Council Minutes.
Rec A/121, William Paterson Scrapbook.
Rec A/807, Opening Ceremony.
UR-DUSA 646/1, 'The Meal Poke' (1903).
UR-DUSA 647/1 'The New Meal Poke' (1922).
UR-PL 1/2, Plans and drawings.
UR-PL 1/8, Plans and drawings.

Exeter
Devon County Record Office, University of Exeter Archive.
UA/10b, University History and Register of Staff.
UA/26/12a/box 3313, Undergraduate handbooks and College magazines.
UA/12/13e, Registrar's letter books.
UA/26/1b, Senate Minutes.
UA/26/1c, Building Development Programme.
UA/26/10b, University History.
UA/26/10c, Building and Endowment Committee.
UA/26/10d, Annual Reports.
UA/26/10e, Academic Dress.
UA/26/11, Endowment Fund.
UA/26/16, Building Files.
UA/26/17d, Debating Society and Guild Council Minutes.

Keele
Keele University Archive.
Annual Reports.
Council Minutes.
Oral History Project.
Lindsay Papers.
Senate Minutes.

Leeds
Leeds University Archive.
A4, Personalia.
B48, Roger Stevens Building.
B65, Council, Estates and Building Committee.
B66, Council, Estates and Building Committee.
B67, Council, Estates and Building Committee.
195/L, Council, House and Estates Committee.

Uncatalogued reports on development.
Uncatalogued records from the Planning Office.

Leicester

1. De Montfort University Archive

Livingston Eyre, Master-plan (1992).
Report on Student residence (1972).
Student handbooks.
Uncatalogued materials on buildings, staffing, and student services.
Uncatalogued collection of photographs.

2. University of Leicester Archive

PCB 6-8, 11-13, Press Cuttings.
ULA/AD/D5/1, Development Plan and correspondence (1948–51).
ULA/AD/D5/1D, Development Plan and correspondence (1970–).
ULA/AD/D5/11, Development Plan and correspondence (1957–62).
ULA/AD/D5/7, Development Plan and correspondence (1962–66).
Shepheard Epstein Hunter, 'University of Leicester development plan: draft final report' (2002).
Buildings Advisory Committee Minutes.
Buildings Committee Minutes.
Buildings and Sites Committee Minutes.
Council Minutes.
Uncatalogued building papers.
Uncatalogued Bursarial papers.
John Winterburn, 'Recollections of University College, Leicester, 1947–50'.

Liverpool

1. Liverpool University Archive

P411, University Appeal.
S236-7, Development Committee.
S275, Building Committee Minutes.
S278, New Arts Building.
S300, Students' Union Building.
S504, Development Committee.
S2444, Principal Rendell's Letter Book.
S2931, Development Committee.
Reports of the Development Committee.
Vice Chancellor's papers.

2. Liverpool University Special Collections

(i) Holford Papers
D147/UCL/4, Gower Street.
(ii) Peers papers
D265/1/2, Letters to Bruce Truscot.
D265/3/2/1, Redbrick: the beginnings.
D265/3/2/2-4, Recollections of Professor Peers.

London

1. Association of Commonwealth Universities Archive
Miscellaneous uncatalogued publications.

2. Blackheath, Morden College Archive
Papers of Charles Kelsall.

3. King's College Archive
KA/IC/A/2/1-3, Secretary's In-Correspondence.
KA/1C/B1-3, Secretary's In-Correspondence.
KA/1C/F1-7, Secretary's In-Correspondence.
KA/1C/H1-4, Secretary's In-Correspondence.
KA/1C/S1-14, Secretary's In-Correspondence.
KA/CS/M/1-3, Council and Special Committee Minutes.

4. The National Archive
DES, 'Polytechnics: planning for development' (1972).
DES, 'Space Utilization in Universities and Polytechnics' (1974).
DES, 'Polytechnics: planning for change' (1979).
ED24/567, Government assistance to universities.
UGC5/8, Correspondence leading to the deputation to the Chancellor.
UGC6/46, Annotated Building Norms.
UGC7/1194, Design and construct contracts.
UGC7/1597/1-2, Cardiff University.
UGC7/1598, Cardiff University.
UGC7/1616, Proposed abolition of capital controls.
UGC7/1621, Study of Maintenance and Interchangeability commitments in Universities.
UGC24/1970, Deputation to the Chancellor.

5. Senate House, University of London Archive
RO1/2/1-2, Letter Books.
RO1/7, Treasury Correspondence.
RO1/10/1, Home Office Letters.

6. University College Archive
MS Add. 56, Notes from the Minutes of General Meetings and Meetings of the Council.
College Correspondence.
Council Minutes.
Letter Books.
Miscellaneous Committee Minutes.

Loughborough
Loughborough University Archive.
G/M7, Governing Body Minutes.
LC/G/M8, Governors' Minutes.
LC/P/EV3/1-5, Commemorative guides.
LCT/AD1/6, Designs for Academic Dress.
LCT/AD1/21/5-9, Papers relating to development.
LCT/G1/M1-2, Minutes of Hostel Sub-Committee.
LCT/G4/M1-2, Buildings and Development Committee.
University Calendar.

Manchester
University of Manchester Archive.
HDH/9/1, Inventory of Dalton Hall.
OCA/1/6, Sale of Quay Street.
OCA/2/1-3, Examiners' papers and Principal's reports.
OCA/3, Prospectuses.
OCA/5/1/1-4, Trustees' Minutes.
OCA/7/1-2, Owens College Extension Committee.
OCA//7/1/3, Owens College Extension Sub-Committees.
OCA/7/2, Papers relating to the extension campaign.
OCA//7/2/9, Appeal for government aid.
OCA/16/1, Registrar's Letter Book.
OCA/23, Papers relating to the campaign for a university.
RA/1/1, Minutes of Council.
UA/1/57-59, Reports on new buildings.
UA/6/4/4, Proposed University of Manchester.
UA/6/4/5B, Letters in response to memorandum.
USG/4/1-10, Building Committee.
VCA/7/565/1-3, Vice chancellor's papers: buildings.
VCA/7/386/1-6, Vice chancellor's papers: Education Precinct.

Nottingham
Nottingham University Archive.
Not.5.E2.JEL, G. A. Jellicoe, landscape design (1955).
Not.5.EG, Portland Building.
Not.5.612.FLO, Florence Boot Hall.
'An outline of the scope of education provided' (1937)
Development Plans (1958, 1961).

Oxford

1. **Bodleian Library**
   MS.Top.Warw.d.1, Papers Relating to Queen's College, 1838–52.

2. **Oxford Brookes University Archive**
   Uncatalogued collection: Regional College, early material up to 1947.
   Uncatalogued collection of college and polytechnic plans.
   Uncatalogued files of press cuttings.

Reading
Reading University Archive.
Uncatalogued material.

Salford
Salford University Archive.
Faculty of Business, 'Centenary Building' (2002).
Council Minutes.
Uncatalogued files on buildings and plans.

Sheffield
University of Sheffield Archive.
SU/COU/19, Council Minutes.
UCS/CNL/1, Council Minutes.
UCS/SEN/1, Senate Minutes.
US/CHA/1/1, Firth College.
US/CHA/1/4, University College.
US/CHA/1/7, Pamphlets and posters.
US/CHA/4/8-11, University buildings and endowment fund.
US/CHA/5/2-3, Western Bank.

Southampton
Southampton University Archive.
1/2/1/8/1, Press cuttings.
1/2/5/54, Principal's Report.
1/2/12, Development Committee Minutes.
1/2/2/22, Library Building Committee Minutes.
1/2/5/11, Building plans.
1/4/76/29/1-2, Committee on declining student numbers.
1/7/291/22/1-4, Photograph albums.
1/7/291/24-25, Reminiscences of College Days.
1/7/291/26, Opening of Highfield Hall.
1/7/322/1, Society of Old Harteyans.
MSS224/7/A914, Report on Sit-in (1970).
MS1/2/1/8/7, Press cuttings.
MS1/3/451/445/1-2, Planning and Development subcommittee.
MS1/4/76/7/1-2, Development Committee Minutes.
MS224/12/A919/1-3, Betty Wicks papers.
MS224/17/A944, F. S. Scott letters.

University Modern Records Centre

1. **Association of University Teachers Archive**
   MSS27/3/55, Correspondence with the NUS.
   MSS27/3/186, AUT at Oxbridge.
   MSS27/A.16.7, papers of Professor Laurie.

2. **Committee of Vice Chancellors and Principals Archive**
   MSS399/1/1/1-4, Minutes.
   MSS399/1/6/16/1-2, Minutes.

3. **National Union of Students Archive**
   MSS280/3/KC, General Correspondence.
   MSS280/73/EC, Education Committee.
   MSS280/139, Loughborough.
   MSS280/144, Miscellaneous publications.

Bibliography of works cited

PRINTED

State Papers
Report of the Royal Commission of Enquiry into the State of the Universities of Scotland, PP 1831 (310).
Copies of the Correspondence and Communications which have passed between the Treasury and the Chancellor of the Exchequer and the University of London, PP 1842 (542).
Queen's Colleges, Ireland, PP. 1859 Session 1 (168) XXI Pt.II.
Report of the Commissioners Appointed for the Purposes of the Durham University Act, 1861, PP 1863 (3137).
Royal Commission on Scientific Instruction and the Advancement of Science, PP 1872 c. 536.
Report of the Committee Appointed to Inquire into the Condition of Intermediate and Higher Education in Wales, PP 1881 C.3047.
Board of Education Reports for the Year 1913–14 from those universities and university colleges which are in receipt of grant [sic] *from the Board of Education*, Cd 8137 (1915).
Report of the Commission on Higher Education in West Africa, 1945 (cmd. 6655).
Report of the Commission on Higher Education in the Colonies, 1945 (cmd. 6647).
Scientific Manpower: Report of a Committee appointed by the Lord President of the Council, 1946 (cmd. 6824).
University Development 1947–1952, 1953 (cmnd. 8875).
Methods Used by Universities of Contracting and of Recording and Controlling Expenditure, 1956 (cmnd. 9).
University Development 1952–57, 1958 (Cmnd. 534).
Grants to Students, 1960 (cmnd. 1051).
University Development: Interim report of the UGC for the years 1957 to 1961, 1962 (cmnd. 1691).
Higher Education: report of the committee appointed by the Prime Minister under the chairmanship of Lord Robbins, 1963 (cmnd. 2154).
University Development 1957–1962, 1964 (cmnd. 2267).
Enquiry into the Flow of Candidates in Science and Technology into Higher Education, 1968 (cmnd. 3541).
University Development 1962–1967, 1968 (cmnd. 3820).
Education: a framework for expansion, 1972 (cmnd. 5174).
PP 1968–9 (449-I), *Select Committee on Education and Science: Report on Student Relations*.
University Development 1967–1972, 1974 (cmnd. 5728).
UGC Annual Survey 1973–74, 1975 (cmnd. 6024).
UGC Annual Survey 1983–84, 1985 (cmnd 9489).
The Development of Higher Education into the 1990s, 1985 (cmnd. 9254).
Higher Education: a new framework, 1991 (cm 1541).
The Management of Building Projects at English Higher Education Institutions, 1998 (HC 452).
The Financial Health of Higher Education Institutions in England Independent Review of Higher Education Pay and Conditions 1999 (C25 6/99)d 1994 (HC 13 [1994–5]).
Higher Education: students at the heart of the system, 2011 (Cm 8122).

Periodicals
Annual Register.
Architects' Journal.
Architectural Design.
Architectural Review.

Beyond the Limit.
Birmingham Pictorial and Dart.
Birmingham Pictorial and Post.
Breed.
Bristol Nonesuch.
Bristol University College Gazette.
British Critic.
British Medical Journal.
Builder.
Cambridge Journal.
Cap and Gown.
College.
Concourse.
Contemporary Review.
Cum Grano.
Cygnet.
Ecclesiologist.
Edinburgh Review.
Encounter.
Examiner.
Ex-Communication.
Fortnightly Review.
Frazer's Magazine.
Gair Rhydd.
Gong.
Gongster.
Gryphon.
Guerilla.
Hampshire Advertiser.
John Bull.
Journal of the Royal Society of Arts.
King's College Calendar.
Last Edition.
Leeds Student.
Leicester University College Magazine.
Limit.
Literary Gazette.
London Medical and Surgical Journal.
Luciad.
Macmillan's Magazine.
Magnet.
Mason College Magazine.
Mermaid.
Mirror of Literature, Amusement and Instruction.
National Student.
New Monthly Magazine.
New Society.
New Statesman.
Nineteenth Century.

Octopus.
Old Owensian.
Owens College Calendar.
Owens College Magazine.
Oxford Magazine.
Oxford University Extension Gazette.
Perspectives.
Planning.
Polygon.
Pupil Teachers' Monthly.
Quarterly Review.
Resources of Higher Education Institutions.
Ripple.
Salford Student.
Saturday Magazine.
Sheffield Daily Telegraph.
Southern Daily Echo.
Sphinx.
Students in Higher Education Institutions.
Tamesis.
Times.
Times Educational Supplement.
Times Higher Education.
Times Higher Education Supplement.
Twentieth Century.
Universities Review.
University Bulletin.
University College London Annual Report.
University College Magazine.
University of Birmingham Magazine.
Viewpoint.
Wave.
Wessex.
Wessex News.
Westminster Review.
Wine Press.
Wyvern.
Yearbook of the Universities of the Empire.
Yorkshire College Annual Report.

BOOKS AND ARTICLES

Abbas, Andrea and McLean, Monica, 'Becoming sociologists: professional identity for part-time teachers of university sociology', *British Journal of the Sociology of Education* 22 (2001), pp. 339–52.

Abbott, Joan, *Student Life in a Class Society* (Oxford, 1971).

Alberti, Samuel J. M. M., 'Civic Cultures and Civic Colleges in Victorian England', in Martin Daunton, ed., *The Organisation of Knowledge in Victorian Britain* (Oxford, 2005), pp. 337–56.

Albow, M. C., 'The influence of accommodation upon 64 Reading University students—an ex post facto study', *British Journal of Sociology* 17:4 (1966), pp. 403–18.
Allchin, W. H., *An Account of the Reconstruction of the University of London. Part I: from the foundation to the appointment of the first Royal Commission, 1825 to 1888* (London, 1905).
Allen, Robert, *The Presbyterian College, Belfast, 1853–1953* (Belfast, 1954).
Allibone, Jill, *Anthony Salvin: pioneer of Gothic Revival architecture* (Cambridge, 1987).
An Answer to the Rev T. H. Maberly's Pamphlet on the Death of Lawrence Dundas, Esq (London, 1818).
Alter, Peter, *The Reluctant Patron: science and the state in Britain, 1850–1920* (Oxford, 1987).
Amery, Julian, *The Life of Joseph Chamberlain, vol. iv* (London 1951).
Anderson, Robert, *Education and Opportunity in Victorian Scotland; schools and universities* (Oxford, 1983).
Anderson, Robert, 'Universities and Elites in Modern Britain', *History of Universities* 10 (1991), pp. 225–50.
Anderson, Robert, *Universities and Elites in Britain since 1800* (Cambridge, 1992).
Anderson, Robert, *European Universities from the Enlightenment to 1914* (Oxford, 2004).
Anderson, Robert, *British Universities: past and present* (London, 2006).
Annals of Queen's College, Birmingham (4 vols; London, 1873).
Annan, Noel, 'Higher Education', in Bernard Crick, ed., *Essays on Reform* (London, 1967), pp. 24–43.
Annan, Noel, 'British Higher Education, 1960–80: a personal retrospect', *Minerva* 20 (1982), pp. 1–24.
Archer, Louise, Hutchings, Merryn, and Ross, Alistair, *Higher Education and Social Class* (London and New York, 2002).
Archer, Sandra and Piper, David Warren, eds, *Is Higher Education Fair to Women?* (Guildford, 1984), pp. 163–79.
Argles, Michael, *South Kensington to Robbins: an account of English technical and scientific education since 1851* (London, 1964).
Armytage, W. H., *Civic Universities: aspects of a British tradition* (London, 1955).
Arnold, Dana, *Reading Architectural History* (London and New York, 2002).
Arnold, Matthew, *Schools and Universities on the Continent* (London, 1868).
Arnold, Matthew, *Essays In Criticism: first series* (London, 1900).
Ashby, Eric, *Universities: British, Indian, African, a study in the ecology of higher education* (London, 1966).
Ashby, Eric, *Hands Off the Universities* (London, 1968).
Ashby, Eric and Anderson, Mary, *The Rise of the Student Estate in Britain* (London and Basingstoke, 1970).
Ashby, Eric and Anderson, Mary, *Portrait of Haldane at Work in Education* (London, 1974).
Ashley Smith, J. W., *The Birth of Modern Education: the contribution of the Dissenting Academies, 1660–1800* (London, 1954).
Ashton, Rosemary, *Victorian Bloomsbury* (New Haven and London, 2012).
AUDE, *The Legacy of 1960s University Buildings* (Milton Keynes, 2008).
AUT-NTAFHE Confederation, *Bursting at the Seams* (1993).
Bacon, Alan, 'English Literature Becomes a Subject: King's College, London, as pioneer', *Victorian Studies* 29 (1986), pp. 591–612.
Bailey, Alfred G., 'Early Foundations, 1783-1829', in Alfred G. Bailey, ed., *The University of New Brunswick: memorial volume* (Fredricton, NB, 1950).
Baimbridge, Mark, 'Institutional Initiatives for the 1996 Research Assessment Exercise', *Journal of Further and Higher Education* 22 (1998), pp. 125–34.

Baker, Alan R. H., *Geography and History: bridging the divide* (Cambridge, 2003).
Baker, J. H., *The Third University of England* (London, 1990).
Baker, Kenneth, *The Turbulent Years: my life in politics* (London, 1993).
Barker, Austin Farrar, *Leaves From a Northern University* (London, 1926).
Barnes, Frank, *Priory Demesne to University Campus: a topographic history of Nottingham University* (Nottingham, 1993).
Barnes, Sarah V., 'England's Civic Universities and the Triumph of the Oxbridge Ideal', *History of Education Quarterly* 36 (1996), pp. 271–305.
Barnes, Sarah V., 'Lessons in Stone: architecture and academic ethos in an urban setting', in Debra N. Mancroft and D. J. Trela, eds, *Victorian Urban Settings: essays on the nineteenth-century city and its contexts* (New York and London, 1996), pp. 214–29.
Barnes, Thomas, 'Proposals for Establishing in Manchester a Plan of Liberal Education for Young Men designed for civil and active life, whether in trade, or in any of the professions', *Memoirs of the Literary and Philosophical Society of Manchester* 2 (1789), pp. 30–41.
Barnett, Corelli, *The Audit of War* (1986; London, 1987).
Barry, J. C., 'The Legislation of the Synod of Thurles, 1850', *Irish Theological Quarterly* 26 (1959), pp. 131–66.
Bates, David, 'Frank Barlow, 1911–2009', *Proceedings of the British Academy* 172 (2010), pp. 3–26.
Bayly, C. A., *The Birth of the Modern World, 1780–1914* (Oxford, 2004).
Beattie, William, *Life and Letters of Thomas Campbell* (3 vols; London, 1849).
Beckett, Edith M., *The History of University College, Nottingham* (Nottingham, 1928).
Beckwith, E. G. C., *Samuel Wilson Warneford, LL.D (1763–1855): rector extraordinary* (Bourton-on-the-Hill, 1974).
Bee, Malcolm, 'What Do Graduates Earn? The starting salaries and earning prospects of university graduates, 1960–1986', *Higher Education Quarterly* 45 (1991), pp. 78–90.
Beier, Ulli, *Art in Nigeria, 1960* (Cambridge, 1960).
Belfast Academical Institution, *An Account of the System of Education in the Belfast Academical Institution* (Belfast, 1818).
Bell, Robert and Tight, Malcolm, *Open Universities: a British tradition?* (Buckingham, 1993).
Bellaigue, Christina de, *Educating Women: schooling and identity in England and France, 1800–1867* (Oxford, 2007).
Bellot, H. Hale, *University College, London, 1826–1926* (London, 1929).
Beloff, Michael, *The Plateglass Universities* (London, 1968).
Bence, Valerie and Oppenheim, Charles, 'The Evolution of the United Kingdom's Research Assessment Exercise: publications, performance, perceptions', *Journal of Educational Administration and History* 37 (2005), pp. 137–55.
Bender, Thomas, ed., *The University and the City: from medieval origins to the present* (New York and Oxford, 1988).
Bentham, Jeremy, *Crestomathia* (London, 1815).
Berdahl, Robert O., *British Universities and the State* (Berkley and London, 1959).
Beresford, Maurice, *Walks Round Red Brick* (Leeds, 1980).
Betjeman, John, *Summoned By Bells* (London, 1960).
Bettensen, E. M., *The University of Newcastle Upon Tyne: a historical introduction, 1834–1971* (Newcastle, 1971).
Beveridge, William, *The Physical Relation of a University to a City* (London, 1928).

Binfield, Clyde, 'Holy Murder at Cheshunt College. The formation of an English architect: P. R. Morley-Horder, 1870–1944', *Journal of the United Reformed Church History Society* 4:2 (1988), pp. 103–34.
Bingham, Caroline, *The History of Royal Holloway College, 1886–1986* (London, 1987).
Bird, Richard, 'Reflections on the British Government and Higher Education', *Higher Education Quarterly* 48 (1994), pp. 73–85.
Birks, Tony, *Building the New Universities* (Newton Abbot, 1972).
Black, Alistair, *A New History of the English Public Library: social and intellectual contexts, 1850–1914* (Leicester and New York, 1996).
Blair, Tony, *A Journey* (London, 2010).
Blakey, Martin, 'Student Accommodation', in Susanne Haselgrove, ed., *The Student Experience* (Buckingham, 1994), pp. 72–81.
Blanden, Jo and Machin, Stephen, 'Educational inequality and the expansion of UK higher education', *Scottish Journal of Political Economy* 51 (2004), pp. 230–49.
Board of Education, *The Universities of the United Kingdom of Great Britain and Ireland* (London, 1918).
Boliver, Vikki, 'Expansion, Differentiation, and the Persistence of Social Class Inequalities in British Higher Education', *Higher Education* 61 (2011), pp. 229–42.
Bosworth, Stuart, ed., *Beyond the Limelight: essays on the occasion of the silver jubilee of the Conference of University Administrators* (Reading, 1986).
Bourdieu, Pierre, *Homo Academicus* trans. Peter Collier (Cambridge, 1988).
Bourdieu, Pierre, *The State Nobility: elite schools in the field of power,* trans. Lauretta C. Clough (Cambridge, 1996).
Bourdieu, Pierre and Jean-Claude Passeron, *Reproduction in Education, Society and Culture*, trans. Richard Nice (2nd edn; London, 1977).
Bowl, Marion, 'Experiencing the Barriers: non-traditional students entering higher education', *Research Papers in Education* 16 (2001), pp. 141–60.
Bowler, Catherine and Brimblecombe, Peter, 'Environmental Pressures on Building Design and Manchester's John Rylands' Library', *Journal of Design History* 13 (2000), pp. 175–91.
Boyd, Robin, *The Witness of the Student Christian Movement* (London, 2007).
Boylan, Maureen, *The University of Sheffield: a pictorial history* (Sheffield, 1985).
Boyne, Don, *I Remember Maynooth* (London, 1937).
Boyson, Rhodes, *Speaking My Mind* (London, 1995).
Bradbury, Malcolm, *Eating People is Wrong* (London, 1959).
Bradbury, Malcolm, *The History Man* (1975; London, 2000).
Brake, Laurel and Demoor, Marysa, eds, *Dictionary of Nineteenth-Century Journalism in Great Britain and Ireland* (London, 2009).
Bratberg, Ølivind, 'A Long Path to Divergence: English and Scottish Policies on Tuition Fees', *Higher Education Policy* 24 (2011), pp. 285–306.
Brennan, J. A., *Redbrick University: a Guide for Parents, Sixth-Formers and Students* (Oxford, 1969).
British Universities and the war: a record and its meaning (London, 1917).
Brittain, John and Pugin, A. C., *Illustrations of the Public Buildings of London* (2 vols; London, 1828).
Brock, M. G. and Curthoys, M. C., eds, *The History of the University of Oxford: vol. vi, nineteenth-century Oxford, part I* (Oxford, 1997).
Brock, M. G. and Curthoys, M. C., eds, *The History of the University of Oxford, vol. vii, the nineteenth century part II* (Oxford, 2000).

Brockliss, Laurence, 'Gown and Town: the university and the city in Europe, 1200–2000', *Minerva* 38 (2000), pp. 147–70.
Brooks, Chris, *The Gothic Revival* (London, 1999).
Brothers, Joan and Hatch, Stephen, *Residence and Student Life: a sociological enquiry into residence in higher education* (London, 1971).
Brown, Calum G., McIvor, Arthur J., and Rafeek, Neil, *The University Experience 1945–1975: an oral history of the University of Strathclyde* (Edinburgh, 2004).
Brown, E. J., *The Private Donor in the History of the University* (Leeds, 1953).
Brown, Ian, 'The Irrelevance of University Architecture', *Higher Education Review* 2:1 (1969), pp. 31–55.
Brown, Ian, 'The Dispersed Polytechnic', *Higher Education Review* 3 (1971), pp. 25–45.
Brown, Kenneth D., *A Social History of the Nonconformist Ministry in England and Wales, 1800–1930* (Oxford, 1988).
Brown, Lorraine and Richards, Steven, 'The British Host: just how welcoming are we?', *Journal of Further and Higher Education* 36 (2012), pp. 57–79.
Brown, Roger, with Carasso, Helen, *Everything For Sale? The marketization of UK higher education* (London and New York, 2013).
Brown, Stewart J., *The National Churches of England, Ireland, and Scotland, 1801–1846* (Oxford, 2001).
Buchanan, Alexandrina, *Robert Willis and the Foundation of Architectural History* (Woodbridge, 2013).
Buchanan, Tom, *Britain and the Spanish Civil War* (Cambridge, 1997).
Burch, Brian, *The University of Leicester: a history, 1921–96* (Leicester, 1996).
Burgess, Tyrrell and Pratt, John, *Policy and practice: the colleges of advanced technology* (London, 1970).
Burgess, Tyrrell, Locke, Michael, Pratt, John, and Richards, Nick, *Degrees East: the making of the University of East London* (London, 1995).
Burke, Catherine, Cunningham, Peter, and Grosvenor, Ian, 'Putting Education in its Place: space, place, and materialities in the history of education', *History of Education* 39 (2010), pp. 677–80.
Burns, J. H. and Sutherland, Graeme, D., *Scottish University* (Edinburgh, 1944).
Burrows, Edwin G. and Wallace, Mike, *Gotham: a history of New York City to 1898* (New York, 1999).
CABE, *Design with Distinction: the value of good building design in higher education* (London, 2005).
Caedel, Martin, 'The King and Country Debate: student politics, pacifism, and the dictators', *Historical Journal* 22 (1979), pp. 397–422.
Calcutta University Commission, 1917–19 (17 vols; Calcutta, 1919–20).
Callender, Claire and Kempson, Elaine, *Student Finance: income, expenditure, and take-up of loans* (London, 1996).
Cameron, J. G. P., *A Short History of the Royal Indian Engineering College, Coopers Hill* (Coopers Hill, 1960).
Campbell, Lewis, *On the Nationalisation of the Old English Universities* (London, 1901).
Cannadine, David, *The Decline and Fall of the British Aristocracy* (London, 1992).
Cantor, Leonard M. and Matthews, Geoffrey F., *Loughborough From College to University: a history of higher education at Loughborough 1909–1966* (Loughborough, 1977).
Carleton, Don, *A University for Bristol: an informal history in text and pictures* (Bristol, 1984).
Carp, Benjamin L., 'The Night the Yankees Burned Broadway: the New York City Fire of 1776', *Early American Studies* 4 (2006), pp. 471–511.

Carruthers, John [J. Y. T. Grieg], *Adam's Daughter* (London, 1926).
Carswell, John, *Government and the Universities in Britain: programme and performance, 1960–1980* (Cambridge, 1985).
Carter, Ian, *Ancient Cultures of Conceit: British university fiction in the post-war years* (London and New York, 1990).
Carter, Jennifer J. and Withrington, Donald J., eds, *Scottish Universities: distinctiveness and diversity* (Edinburgh, 1992).
Carter, Norma, *Science Parks: development and management* (London, 1989).
Casey, Edward S., 'How to Get from Space to Place in a fairly Short Stretch of Time: phenomenological prolegomena', in Steven Feld and Keith H. Basso, eds, *Senses of Place* (Sante Fe, NM, 1996), pp. 13–52.
Casey, Edward S., *The Fate of Place: a philosophical history* (Berkeley, 1997).
Cassidy, Michael, 'Pressure on University Building', *Official Architecture* 30 (1967), pp. 503–11.
Casson, Hugh, 'Living, Learning, and Leisure—the planning of the new universities', *Journal of the Royal Society of Arts* 113 (1964–5), pp. 556–71.
Champ, Judith F., *Oscott* (Birmingham, 1987).
Chandler, Andrew, *'The Latter Glory of this House': a history of two Christian Commonwealths in Britain in the nineteenth and twentieth centuries, the Queen's and Handsworth Colleges in Birmingham, 1828–1980* (London, 2013).
Chapman, A. W., *The Story of a Modern University: a history of the University of Sheffield* (Oxford, 1955).
Charlton, H. B., *Portrait of a University, 1851–1951* (Manchester, 1951).
Chatterton, Paul, 'University Students and City Centres—the formation of exclusive geographies. The case of Bristol', *Geoforum* 30 (1999), pp. 117–33.
Childs, W. M., 'The Essentials of a University Education', *Hibbert Journal* 10 (1912), pp. 581–98.
Childs, W. M., *Universities and their Freedom* (London, 1921).
Childs, W. M., *Making a University: an account of the university movement at Reading* (London, 1933).
Choudry, Haroon, Crawford, Claire, Dearden, Lorraine, Goodman, Alicia, and Vignoles, Anna, 'Widening Participation in HE: analysis using linked administrative data', *IFS Working paper W10/04* (2010).
Church, Roy, *Economic and Social Change in a Midland Town: Victorian Nottingham, 1815–1900* (1966; London and New York, 2006).
Clapp, B. W., *John Owens: Manchester merchant* (Manchester, 1965).
Clapp, B. W., *The University of Exeter: a history* (Exeter, 1982).
Clark, John Willis, *Old Friends at Cambridge and Elsewhere* (London and Cambridge, 1900).
Clarke, John, 'The University of Buckingham: an historical perspective', in James Tooley, ed., *Buckingham at 25: freeing the universities from state control* (London, 2001), pp. 189–210.
Clawley, Alan, *John Madin* (London, 2011).
Clossick, Marie, *Student Residence: a new approach at the University of Essex. A Study of the Rayleigh Tower, 1965–8* (London, 1967).
Coates, Jerry, 'John Henry Newman's "Tamworth Reading Room": adjusting rhetorical approaches for the periodical press', *Victorian Periodicals Review* 24 (1991), pp. 173–80.
Cockburn, Alexander and Blackburn, Robin, eds, *Student Power: problems, diagnosis, action* (Harmondsworth, 1969).

Cockburn, W., *Strictures on Clerical Education in the University of Cambridge* (London, 1809).
Collini, Stefan, *Public Moralists: political thought and intellectual life in Britain, 1850–1930* (Cambridge, 1991).
Collini, Stefan, *Common Reading: critics, historians, publics* (Oxford, 2008).
Collini, Stefan, *What are Universities For?* (London, 2012).
Collinson, Jacquelyn Allen, 'Occupational Identity on the Edge: social science contract researchers in higher education', *Sociology* 38 (2004), pp. 313–29.
Collinson, Jacquelyn Allen, '"Get yourself some nice, neat, matching box files!" Research administrators and occupational identity work', *Studies in Higher Education* 32 (2007), pp. 295–309.
Colvin, H. M., *Unbuilt Oxford* (New Haven and London, 1983).
Colvin, H. M., *A Biographical Dictionary of British Architects, 1600–1840* (New Haven and London, 2008).
Committee of Vice Chancellors and Principals, *The Planning of Halls of Residence* (London, 1948).
Committee of Vice Chancellors and Principals, *Report of a Deputation Received by the Chief Secretary to the Treasury, 26 January 1962* (1962).
Committee of Vice Chancellors and Principals, *Academic Standards in Universities* (London, 1988).
Conference of the Association of University Professors and Lecturers of the Allied Countries (Oxford, 1944).
Conference of the Home Universities (London, 1947).
Conference of the Universities of the Empire (London, 1947).
Congress of the Universities of the Empire (London, 1912).
—— *Second Congress of the Universities of the Empire* (London, 1921).
—— *Third Congress of the Universities of the Empire* (London, 1926).
—— *Fourth Congress of the Universities of the Empire* (London, 1931).
Copleston, Edward, *A Reply to the Calumnies of the* Edinburgh Review *against Oxford* (Oxford, 1810).
Corish, Patrick J., *Maynooth College, 1795–1995* (Dublin, 1995).
Cory Dixon, J. F., *Building For and By Degrees: a clients* [sic] *experience on* [sic] *building for Universities* (Guildford, ?1978).
Cote, James E. and Allahar, Anton L., *Ivory Tower Blues: a university system in crisis* (Toronto, 2007).
Coulson, Jonathan, Roberts, Paul, and Taylor, Isabelle, *University Planning and Architecture: the search for perfection* (Abingdon, 2011).
Court, Stephen, 'The Use of Time by Academic and Related Staff', *Higher Education Quarterly* 50 (1996), pp. 237–60.
Cox, Caroline, Jacka, Keith, and John Marks, *Rape of Reason: the corruption of North London Polytechnic* (London, 1975).
Cradden, Conor, '"Old" University Academic Staff Salary Movement Since 1949', *Higher Education Quarterly* 52 (1998), pp. 394–412.
Craddock, Mary, *A North Country Maid* (1960; Maidstone, 1995).
The Craig Affair: the background to the case of Dr David Craig, and others, University of Lancaster (London, 1972).
Crinson, Mark, *Stirling and Gowan: architecture from austerity to affluence* (New Haven and London, 2012).

Crinson, Mark and Lubbock, Jules, *Architecture: art or profession? Three hundred years of architectural education in Britain* (Manchester and New York, 1994).
Crook, J. Mordaunt, *The Greek Revival: neo-classical attitudes in British architecture, 1760–1870* (London, 1972).
Crook, J. Mordaunt, *The Dilemma of Style: architectural ideas from the picturesque to the postmodern* (London, 1987).
Crook, J. Mordaunt, *The Rise of the Nouveaux Riches: style and status in Victorian and Edwardian Architecture* (London: John Murray, 1999).
Crook, J. Mordaunt and M. H. Port, *The History of the King's Works vol. vi: 1782–1851* (London, 1973).
Crosland, Susan, *Tony Crosland* (London, 1982).
Crossick, Geoffrey, 'From Gentlemen to the Residuum: languages of social class in Victorian Britain', in Penelope J. Corfield, ed., *Language, History, and Class* (Oxford and Cambridge, MA, 1991), pp. 150–78.
Crossley Evans, M. J. and Sulston, A., *A History of Wills Hall, University of Bristol* (Bristol, 1994).
Crouch, Colin, *The Student Revolt* (London, 1970).
Culler, A. Dwight, *The Imperial Intellect: a study of Newman's educational ideal* (New Haven, 1955).
Cunningham, Colin and Waterhouse, Prudence, *Alfred Waterhouse, 1830–1905: biography of a practice* (London, 1992).
Curan, James and Blackburn, Robert A., 'Youth and the Enterprise Culture', *Journal of Education and Work* 4 (1990), pp. 31–45.
Curthoys, Mark and Howarth, Janet, 'The Political Economy of Women's Higher Education in Late-Nineteenth and Twentieth-Century Britain', *Historical Research* 60 (1987), pp. 208–31.
Cuthbertson, Brian, *The First Bishop: a biography of Charles Inglis* (Halifax, NS, 1987).
Daiches, David, ed., *The Idea of a New University: The Experiment in Sussex* (London, 1964).
Dainton, Lord, *British Universities: purposes, problems, and pressures* (Cambridge, 1981).
Dainton, Lord, *Doubts and Certainties: a personal memoir of the twentieth century* (Sheffield, 2001).
Danziger, Elon, 'A University Building for New York', *Burlington Magazine* 150 (2008), pp. 444–51.
Daunton, Martin, ed., *The Cambridge Urban history of Britain, vol. ii: 1800–1950* (Cambridge, 2000).
Davies, Andrew, *A Very Peculiar Practice* (London, 1986).
Davies, Andrew, *A Very Peculiar Practice: the new frontier* (London, 1988).
Davies, Colin, ed., *Hopkins2: the work of Michael Hopkins and partners* (London, 2001).
Davies, Emily, *The Higher Education of Women* (London, 1866).
Deed of Settlement of the University of London (London, 1826).
Deem, Rosemary, Hillyard, Sam, and Reed, Mike, *Knowledge, Higher Education and the New Managerialism: the changing management of UK universities* (Oxford, 2007).
Delamont, Sara, Parry, Odette, Atkinson, Paul, and Hiken, Andy, 'Suspended Between Two Stools: doctoral students in British higher education', in Amanda Coffey and Paul Atkinson, eds, *Occupational Socialization and Working Lives* (Aldershot, 1994), pp. 138–53.
Denham, Andrew and Garnett, Mark, *Keith Joseph* (Chesham, 2001).
Dent, H. C., 'Bruce Truscot', *Universities Quarterly* 7 (1952–3), pp. 326–32.

Department of Education and Science, *Higher Education into the 1990s: a discussion document* (London, 1978).
de Sola Pinto, Vivian, ed., *The Teaching of English in Schools: a symposium* (London, 1946).
Desmond, Adrian, *The Politics of Evolution: morphology, medicine, and reform in radical London* (Chicago, 1989).
DeYoung, Ursula, *A Vision of Modern Science: John Tyndall and the role of the scientist in Victorian culture* (London and New York, 2011).
Dibelius, Wilhelm, *England*, trans. Mary Agnes Hamilton (1922; London, 1930).
Dill, Richard, *On the Importance and Necessity of establishing a Presbyterian College in Ireland* (Belfast, 1846).
Dill, Richard, *Prelatico-Presbyterianism: or, curious chapters in the recent history of the Irish Presbyterian Church* (Dublin, 1856).
Disraeli, Benjamin, *Vivian Grey* (2 vols; London, 1827).
Dixon, Simon, 'The University of Leeds and the British Higher Education System, 1963–2004', *Northern History* 43 (2006), pp. 303–25.
Dober, Richard P., *The New Campus in Britain: ideas of consequence for the United States* (New York, 1965).
Dobrée, Bonamy, *The Universities and Regional Life* (Newcastle, 1943).
Dobson, Ian R., '"Them" and "Us"—General and Non-General Staff in Higher Education', *Journal of Higher Education Policy and Management* 22 (2000), pp. 203–10.
Dongerkery, S. R., *A History of the University of Bombay, 1857–1957* (Bombay, 1957).
Donoughue, Bernard, *Downing Street Diaries, vol. ii: with James Callaghan in No 10* (London, 2008).
Dormer, Peter and Muthesius, Stefan, *Concrete and Open Skies: architecture at the University of East Anglia, 1962–2000* (London, 2001).
Dorward, Cécile and Davidson, Ron, *Anything But Ordinary: the nine lives of Cécile* (Fremantle, Western Australia, 2000).
Douglas, Roy, *Surrey: the rise of a modern university* (Guildford, 1991).
Dowland, David, *Nineteenth-Century Anglican Theological Training: the redbrick challenge* (Oxford, 1997).
Downie, Mary Lou, 'Efficiency Outcomes from Space Charging in UK High Education', *Property Management* 23 (2005), pp. 33–42.
D'Oyly, George [Christianus], *A Letter to the Right Hon. Robert Peel on the Subject of the London University* (London, 1828).
D'Oyly, Maria Francis, ed., *Sermons delivered at the Parish Church of St Mary, Lambeth by George D'Oyly DD FRS* (2 vols; London, 1847).
Draper, William H., *Sir Nathan Bodington: first Vice Chancellor of the University of Leeds* (London, 1912).
Driver, Christopher, *The Exploding University* (London, 1971).
Drummond, Diane K., 'The University of Birmingham and the Industrial Spirit: reasons for the local support of Joseph Chamberlain's campaign to found the university, 1897–1900', *History of Universities* 14 (1995–6), pp. 247–63.
Drummond, Henry Home, *Observations Suggested by the Strictures of the* Edinburgh Review *upon Oxford* (Edinburgh, 1810).
Duke, Alex, *Importing Oxbridge: English residential colleges and American universities* (New Haven and London, 1997).
Dunne, Tom, Coolahan, John, Manning, Maurice, and O Tuathaigh, Gearoid, eds, *The National University of Ireland: centenary essays* (Dublin, 2008).

Dyer, G., *Academic Unity; being the substance of a general discussion contained in the privileges of the University of Cambridge* (London, 1827).
Dyhouse, Carol, *No Distinction of Sex? Women in British universities, 1870–1939* (London, 1995).
Dyhouse, Carol, 'Going to University in England between the Wars: access and funding', *History of Education* 31:1 (2002), pp. 1–14.
Dyhouse, Carol, *Students: a gendered history* (London and New York, 2006).
Edgerton, David, *Warfare State: Britain, 1920–1970* (Cambridge, 2006).
Edwards, Brian, *University Architecture* (London, 2000).
Edwards, Eliezer, *Personal Recollections of Birmingham and Birmingham Men* (Birmingham, 1877).
Ellis, E. L., *The University College of Wales, Aberystwyth, 1872–1972* (Cardiff, 1972).
Ellis, G. S. M., *The Poor Boy and the University* (London, 1925).
Elton, Ben, Mayall, Rik, and Mayer, Lise, *Bachelor Boys: the Young Ones Book* (London, 1984).
Elwyn-Jones, Lord, *In My Time: an autobiography* (London, 1983).
Endlich, Stephanie, *Hochschulbau im Spannungsfeld zwischen Bildingsplannung und Bauproduktion: exemplarische Untersuuchung zur Enstehung eines bautyps* (Dresden, 1980).
Engel, A. J., *From Clergyman to Don: the rise of academic profession in nineteenth-century Oxford* (Oxford, 1983).
Evans, Colin, *Language People: the experience of teaching and learning modern languages in British universities* (Milton Keynes, 1988).
Evans, Colin, *English People: the experience of teaching and learning English in British Universities* (Buckingham, 1993).
Evans, David and Larmour, Paul, *Queens, an architectural legacy* (Belfast, 1995).
Evans, George Ewart, *The Strength of the Hills: an autobiography* (London, 1983).
Evans, G. R., *The University of Cambridge: a new history* (London, 2009).
Evans, G. R., *The University of Oxford: a new history* (London, 2010).
Facts and Observations Relating to the Popish College of St Patrick (London, 1845).
Fawcett, A. Peter and Jackson, Neil, *Campus Critique: the architecture of the University of Nottingham* (Nottingham, 1998).
Fergusson, R. Menzies, *My College Days* (Paisley and London, 1887).
Feriman, Z. D., *Some English Philhellenes vol. vi: Lord Guildford* (London, 1919).
Fiddes, Edward, *Chapters in the History of Owens College and of Manchester University, 1851–1914* (Manchester, 1927).
Fiddes, Edward, 'The University Movement in Manchester (1851—1903)', in J. G. Edwards, V. H. Galbraith, and E. F. Jacob, eds, *Historical Essays in Honour of James Tait* (Manchester, 1933), pp. 97–110.
Fielden Clegg Bradley, *Education Architecture Urbanism: three university projects* (London, 2012).
Filippkapu, Ourania, Salter, Brian, and Tapper, Ted, 'Compliance, Resistance and Seduction: reflections on 20 years of the funding council model of governance', *Higher Education* 60 (2010), pp. 543–57.
Fingard, Judith, *The Anglican Design in Loyalist Nova Scotia, 1783–1816* (London, 1972).
Fisher, Joseph R. and Robb, John H., *Royal Belfast Academical Institution: centenary volume, 1810–1910* (Belfast, 1913).
Fisher, Shirley and Hood, Bruce, 'The Stress of the Transition to University: a longitudinal study of psychological disturbance, absent-mindedness and vulnerability to homesickness', *British Journal of Psychology* 78 (1987), pp. 425–41.

Flexner, Abraham, *Universities: American, English, German* (New York, 1930).
Forgan, Sophie, 'The Architecture of Science and the Idea of a University', *Studies in the History and Philosophy of Science* 20 (1989), pp. 405–34.
Forgan, Sophie, 'Bricks and Bones: architecture and science in Victorian Britain', in Peter Galison and Emily Thompson, eds, *The Architecture of Science* (Cambridge, MA, and London, 1999), pp. 181–208.
Forgan, Sophie and Gooday, Graeme, 'Constructing South Kensington: the buildings and politics of T. H. Huxley's working environments', *British Journal for the History of Science* 29 (1986), pp. 435–68.
Fortescue, the Earl, *Public Schools for the Middle Classes* (London, 1864).
Fraser, Hamish, 'Municipal Socialism and Social Policy', in R. J. Morris and Richard Rodger, eds, *The Victorian City: a reader in British urban history* (London and New York, 1993), pp. 258–80.
Freeman, Kathleen, *Martin Hanner: a comedy* (London, 1926).
Friedland, Martin L., *The University of Toronto: a history* (Toronto, 2002).
Frost, Stanley Brace, *McGill University: for the advancement of learning: vol. i, 1801–1895* (1980; Kingston and Montreal, 1985).
Fulton, Oliver, ed., *Access to Higher Education* (Guildford, 1981).
Gaines, Thomas A., *The Campus as a Work of Art* (London, 1991).
Galindo-Rueda, Fernando, Marcenaro-Gutierez, Oscar, and Vignoles, Anna, 'The Widening Socio-Economic Gap in UK Higher Education', *National Institute Economic Review* 190 (2008), 75–88.
Gallacher, Jim and Raffer, David, 'Higher Education Policy in post-Devolution UK: more convergence than divergence?', *Journal of Education Policy* 27 (2012), pp. 467–90.
Gallagher, Alison and Locke, Michael, *Mature Students in Higher Education: how institutions can learn from experience* (London, 1992).
Gallie, W. B., *A New University: A. D. Lindsay and the Keele experiment* (London, 1960).
Gardner, W. J., *Colonial Cap and Gown: studies in the mid-Victorian universities of Australasia* (Canterbury, NZ, 1979).
Garland, Martha McMackin, *Cambridge Before Darwin: the ideal of a liberal education, 1800–1860* (Cambridge, 1980).
Garratt, V. W., *A Man in the Street* (London, 1939).
Gibbs, Graham, Gregory, Roy, and Moore, Ivan, *Labs and Practicals with More Students and Fewer Resources* (Oxford, 1997).
Gibson, Mary, *Warneford: being the life and times of Harriet Elizabeth Wetherell Warneford* (Bournemouth, 1966).
Giddens, Anthony, 'Aspects of the Social Structure of a University Hall of Residence', *Sociological Review* 8 (1960), pp. 97–108.
Gieryn, Thomas F., 'What Buildings Do', *Theory and Society* 31 (2002), pp. 35–74.
Girouard, Mark, *Life in the English Country House: a social and architectural history* (New Haven and London, 1978).
Girouard, Mark, *Town and Country* (New Haven and London, 1992).
Girouard, Mark, *Big Jim: the life and work of James Stirling* (London, 1998).
Girtin, Tom, *The Golden Ram: a narrative history of the Clothworkers' Company, 1528–1958* (London, 1958).
Girtin, Tom, *The Triple Crowns: a narrative history of the Drapers' Company, 1364–1964* (London, 1964).
Girtin, Tom, *The Mark of the Sword: a narrative history of the Cutlers' Company, 1189–1975* (London, 1975).

Gladstone, W. E., *The State in Its Relations with the Church* (London, 1838).
Gledhill, John, 'The Modern English Universities', in David Warner and David Palfreyman, eds, *The State of UK Higher Education: managing change and diversity* (Buckingham, 2001), pp. 95–102.
Glendinning, Miles, *Modern Architect: the life and times of Robert Matthew* (London, 2008).
Glendon, A. Ian, 'Radical Change Within a British University', in Dian Marie Mosking and Neil Anderson, eds, *Organizational Change and Innovation: psychological perspectives and practices in Europe* (London, and New York, 1992), pp. 49–70.
Goddard, John and Vallance, Paul, *The University and the City* (London and New York, 2012).
Gold, John R., *The Practice of Modernism: Modern architects and urban transformation, 1954–1972* (London and New York, 2007).
Goldman, Lawrence, *Dons and Workers: Oxford and adult education since 1850* (Oxford, 1995).
Goldman, Ronald, *Breakthrough: autobiographical accounts of the education of some educationally disadvantaged children* (London, 1968).
Gomme, Andor, 'Publicity or Promise: the new universities', *Delta* 34 (Autumn 1964), pp. 2–19.
Gomme, Andor, Jenner, Michael, and Little, Bryan, *Bristol: an architectural history* (London, 1979).
Gooday, Graeme, 'Lies, Damned Lies, and Declinism: Lyon Playfair, the Paris Exhibition and contested rhetorics of scientific education and industrial performance', in Ian Inkster, ed., *The Golden Age: essays in British social and economic history, 1850–1870* (Aldershot, 2000), pp. 105–20.
Gosden, P. H. J. H. and Taylor, A. J., eds, *Studies in the History of a University 1874–1974* (Leeds, 1975).
Gould, Julius, *The Attack on Higher Education: Marxist and radical penetration* (ISC Special Report, 1977).
Graham, Adele and Grant, Barbara, *Managing More Postgraduate Research Students* (Oxford, 1997).
Granger, Frank, *Memorials of University College Nottingham* (Nottingham, 1928).
Gray, A. Stuart, *Edwardian Architecture: a biographical dictionary* (London, 1985).
Green, V. H. H., *The Universities* (Harmondsworth, 1969).
Greenaway, David and Haynes, Michelle, 'Funding Higher Education in the UK', *Economic Journal* 113 (2003), pp. 150–64.
Grieg, James, *Leonard Horner FRSE* (Edinburgh, 1982).
Grier, Lynda, *Achievement in Education: the work of Michael Ernest Sadler, 1885–1935* (London, 1952).
Grossek, Mark, *First Movement* (London, 1937).
Guagnini, Anna, 'Worlds Apart: academic instruction and professional qualifications in the training of mechanical engineers in England, 1850–1914', in Robert Fox and Anna Guagnini, eds, *Education, Technology, and Industrial Performance in Europe, 1850–1939* (Cambridge, 1993), pp. 16–41.
Gunn, Simon, 'Ritual and Civic Culture in the English Industrial City, *c.* 1835–1914', in Robert J. Morris and Richard H. Trainor, eds, *Urban Governance: Britain and beyond since 1750* (Aldershot, 2000), pp. 225–41.
Gunn, Simon, *The Public Culture of the Victorian Middle Class: ritual and authority in the English industrial city, 1840–1914* (Manchester and New York, 2000).
Hackman, D. W., *First Year Up* (London, 1951).

Haliburton, Thomas Chandler, *A General Description of Nova Scotia* (London, 1823).
Halsband, Frances, 'Campuses in Place', *Places* 17 (2005), pp. 4–11.
Halsey, A. H., *Decline of Donnish Dominion: the British academic profession in the twentieth century* (Oxford, 1995).
Halsey, A. H. and Trow, Martin, *The British Academics* (London, 1971).
Halsey, A. H. and Webb, Josephine, eds, *Twentieth Century British Social Trends* (Basingstoke, 2000).
Halsey, Margaret [Mrs H. W. Simon], *With Malice Towards Some* (New York, 1938).
Hamilton, William, *Discussions on Philosophy and Literature, Education and University Reform* (London, 1853).
Hamlett, Jane, '"Nicely Feminine, Yet Learned": student rooms at Royal Holloway and the Oxford and Cambridge Colleges in the late-nineteenth century', *Women's History Review* 15 (2006), pp. 137–61.
Hammerton, Elizabeth and Cannadine, David, 'Conflict and Consensus on a Ceremonial Occasion: the diamond jubilee in Cambridge in 1897', *Historical Journal* 24 (1981), pp. 111–46.
Hanson, Brian, *Architects and the 'Building World' from Chambers to Ruskin: constructing authority* (Cambridge, 2003).
Harding, Joan N., *Aberdare Hall, 1885–1985* (Cardiff, 1986).
Hardingham, Samantha and Rattenbury, Kester, eds, *Supercrit #1: Cedric Price, Potteries Thinkbelt* (Routledge, 2007).
Hargreaves-Mawdsley, W. N., *A History of Academic Dress in Europe until the End of the Eighteenth Century* (Oxford, 1963).
Harlow, Vincent T., *The Founding of the Second British Empire, 1763–1793* (2 vols; London, 1964).
Harries, Susie, *Nikolaus Pevsner: the life* (London, 2011).
Harris, Reginald V., *Charles Inglis: missionary, loyalist, bishop (1734–1816)* (Toronto, 1937).
Harris, Robin S., *A History of Higher Education in Canada, 1663–1960* (Toronto and Buffalo, 1976).
Harrison, Brian, 'Philanthropy and the Victorians', *Victorian Studies* 9 (1966), pp. 353–74.
Harrison, Brian, ed., *The History of the University of Oxford: vol. viii, the twentieth century* (Oxford, 1994).
Harrison, Brian, *Seeking a Role: the United Kingdom 1951–1970* (Oxford, 2009).
Harrison, Brian, *Finding a Role? The United Kingdom, 1970–1990* (Oxford, 2010).
Harrison, Christopher, ed., *Essays on the History of Keele* (Keele, 1986).
Harte, Negley, *The University of London 1836–1986: an illustrated history* (London, 1986).
Harte, Negley and North, John, *The World of UCL, 1828–1990* (London, 1991).
The Hartley Institution and Its Proposed Extension as a Local University College (Southampton, 1887).
Hartog, P. J., *The Owens College Manchester (founded 1851): a brief history of the college and description of its various departments* (Manchester, 1900).
Harvie, Christopher, *The Lights of Liberalism: university liberals and the challenge of democracy* (London, 1976).
Headlam, Arthur C., *Universities and the Empire: a paper read at the Imperial Conference on Education, May 1907* (London, 1907).
Hearnshaw, F. J. C., *The Centenary History of King's College, London, 1828–1928* (London, 1929).
HEFCE, *Teaching and Learning Infrastructure in Higher Education* (London, 2002).

HEFCE, *The Financial Health of the Higher Education Sector* (London, 2011).
HEFCE, *Higher Education Business and Community Interaction Survey 2009–10* (London, 2011).
HEFCE, *Performance in Higher Education Estates 2010* (London, 2011).
HEFCE, *The Higher Education Workforce Framework 2010* (London, 2012).
Heller, Michael, 'The Institute and the Polytechnic', in Helen Glew, Anthony Gorst, Michael Heller, and Neil Matthews, eds, *Educating Mind, Body, and Spirit: the legacy of Quintin Hogg and the Polytechnic, 1864–1992* (London, 2013), pp. 45–77.
Henderson, G. P., *The Ionian Academy* (Edinburgh, 1988).
Henderson, J. L. H., 'The Founding of Trinity College, Toronto', *Ontario History* 44 (1952), pp. 7–14.
Hennock, E. P., *Fit and Proper Persons: ideal and reality in nineteenth-century urban government* (London, 1973).
Hennock, E. P., 'Technological Education in England, 1850–1926: the uses of a German model', *History of Education* 19 (1990), pp. 299–331.
Herklots, H. G. G., *The New Universities: an external examination* (London, 1928).
Hetherington, H. J. W., 'The History and Significance of the Modern Universities', in Hugh Martin, ed., *The Life of the Modern University* (London, 1930), pp. 9–20.
Hetherington, H. J. W., *The British University System, 1914–1954* (Edinburgh and London, 1955).
Heyck, T. W., 'The Idea of a University in Britain, 1870–1970', *History of European Ideas* 8 (1987), pp. 205–19.
Hill, Rosemary, *God's Architect: Pugin and the building of romantic England* (London, 2007).
Hilton, Boyd, *A Mad, Bad, and Dangerous People? England, 1783–1846* (Oxford, 2006).
Hind, Henry Yorke, *The University of King's College, 1790–1890* (New York, 1890).
Hinde, Thomas, *A Great Day School in London: a history of King's College School* (London: 1995).
History of the Birmingham Medical School, 1825–1915 (Birmingham, 1925).
History of the Royal Albert Memorial University College, Exeter (Exeter, 1911).
Hobsbawm, Eric, 'Inventing Traditions', in Eric Hobsbawm and Terence Ranger, eds, *The Invention of Tradition* (Cambridge, 1983), pp. 1–14.
Hodgskin, Thomas, *Travels in the North of Germany* (London, 1820).
Hoefferle, Caroline M., *British Student Activism in the Long Sixties* (New York and London, 2013).
Hofstetter, Michael J., *The Romantic Idea of the University in England and Germany, 1770–1850* (Basingstoke, 2001).
Hoggart, Richard, *A Local Habitation: life and times, 1918–1940* (Oxford, 1989).
Holford, William, *Proposals for the Development of a Site for the University of Liverpool* (Liverpool, 1949).
Hollingsworth, S., *An Account of the Present State of Nova Scotia* (London, 1786).
Holmes, Richard and Aprahamian, Francis, eds, *The Disabled Student in Higher Education: access and support* (Milton Keynes, 1981).
Honey, J. R. de S., *Tom Brown's Universe: the development of the Victorian public school* (London, 1977).
Hoppen, K. Theodore, *The Mid-Victorian Generation, 1846–1886* (Oxford, 1998).
Horner, Leonard, *Letter to the Council of the University of London* (London, 1830).
Horowitz, Helen Lefkowitz, *Alma Mater: design and experience in the women's college from their nineteenth-century beginnings to the 1930s* (Boston, 1984).

Horowitz, Helen Lefkowitz, *Campus Life: undergraduate cultures from the eighteenth century to the present* (Chicago, 1988).
Horwood, Tom, 'The Rise and Fall of the Catholic University College, Kensington, 1868–82', *Journal of Ecclesiastical History* 54 (2003), pp. 302–18.
Howard, J. H., *Winding Lane: a book of impressions and recollections* (Carnarvon, 1938).
Howson, Susan, *Lionel Robbins* (Cambridge, 2011).
Huber, V. A., *The English Universities*, abridged and translated by Francis W. Newman (2 vols; London, 1843).
Humberstone, Thomas Lloyd, *University Reform in London* (London, 1926).
Humphrey, David C., *From King's College to Columbia, 1746–1800* (New York, 1976).
Hurt, John, *Education in Evolution: Church, state, society and popular education, 1800–1870* (London, 1971).
Hutchinson, Eric, 'The Origins of the University Grants Committee', *Minerva* 13 (1975), pp. 583–620.
Huxley, T. H., *Education and Science: essays* (1893; n.p, 2008).
Illingworth, Charles, *University Statesmen: Sir Hector Hetherington* (Glasgow, 1971).
Inglis, Charles, *Letters of Papinian* (New York, 1779).
Inglis, Charles, *The Duty of Honouring the King* (New York, 1780).
Innes, Joanna, 'L'« éducation nationale » dans les îles Britanniques, 1765–1815: variations britanniques et irlandaises sur un thème européen' *Annales: Histoire, Science Sociales* 65 (2010), pp. 1087–116.
Ives, Eric, Drummond, Diane, and Schwartz, Leonard, *The First Civic University: Birmingham, 1880–1980* (Birmingham, 2000).
Jackson, Brian and Marsden, Dennis, *Education and the Working Class* (London, 1962).
Jackson, Iain, 'Post-war Modernism: Maxwell Fry's buildings at the University of Liverpool', *Journal of Architecture* 16 (2011), pp. 675–702.
Jackson, T. G., *Recollections: the life and times of a Victorian architect*, ed. Nicholas Jackson (London, 2003).
Jacobson, Howard, *Coming from Behind* (London, 1983).
James, Lord, 'The University of York', in Murray G. Ross, ed., *New Universities in the Modern World* (New York, 1966), pp. 32–52.
Jasanoff, Maya, *Liberty's Exiles: the loss of America and the remaking of the British Empire* (London, 2011).
Jenkins, Geraint H., *'The finest old university in the world': the University of Wales 1883–1993* (Cardiff, 1994).
Jevons, Harriet A., ed., *Letters and Journals of W. Stanley Jevons* (London, 1886).
Jones, Abel, *I Was Privileged* (Cardiff, 1943).
Jones, David R., *The Origins of Civic Universities: Manchester, Leeds, and Liverpool* (London, 1988).
Jones, Gareth Elwyn, *The Education of a Nation* (Cardiff, 1997).
Jones, Gareth Elwyn, 'Education and Nationhood in Wales: an historiographical analysis', *Journal of Educational Administration and History* 38 (2006), pp. 263–77.
Jones, Gwyn, and Quinn, Michael, eds, *Fountains of Praise: University College, Cardiff, 1883–1983* (Cardiff, 1983).
Jones, Harry Longueville, *Plan of a University for the Town of Manchester* (Manchester, 1836).
Jones, H. S., 'Student Life and Sociability, 1860–1930: comparative reflections', *History of Universities* 14 (1995–6), pp. 225–46.
Jordan, F. W., *Life of Joseph Jordan, Surgeon* (London, 1904).

Joyce, Patrick, *Visions of the people: industrial England and the question of class, 1848–1914* (Cambridge, 1991).
Joyce, Patrick, 'What is the Social in Social History?', *Past and Present* 206 (2010), pp. 213–48.
Kargon, Robert H., *Science in Victorian Manchester: enterprise and expertise* (Manchester, 1977).
Kay, J. Taylor, *The Owens College: a descriptive sketch* (Manchester, 1891).
Kay, Ronald, *UCCA: its origins and development, 1950–85* (Cheltenham, 1985).
Kedourie, Elie, *Perestroika in the Universities* (London, 1989).
Kelly, Thomas, *George Birkbeck: pioneer of adult education* (Liverpool, 1957).
Kelly, Thomas, *For Advancement of Learning: the University of Liverpool, 1881–1981* (Liverpool, 1981).
Kelsall, Charles, *The Last Two Pleadings of Marcus Tullius Cicero against Cauis Verres* (London, 1812).
Kelsall, Charles, *Letter from Athens* (London, 1812).
Kelsall, Charles, *Phantasm of an University* (London, 1814).
Kelsall, Charles, *Classical Excursion from Rome to Arpino* (Geneva, 1820).
Kelsall, Charles, *Remarks touching geography specially that of the British isles, comprising strictures on the hierarchy of Great Britain* (London, 1825).
Kelsall, Charles, *A Letter to the Society of the Dilettanti on the Works in Progress at Windsor Castle by Mela Britannicus* (London, 1827).
Kelsall, Charles, *Constantine and Eugene, or an evening at Mount Vernon* (Brussels, 1828).
Kelsall, Charles, *Esquisse de mes travaux, de mes voyages et de mes opinions* (London, 1830).
Kelsall, Charles, *Horæ Viaticæ* (London, 1836).
Ker, Ian, *John Henry Newman* (Oxford, 2009).
Kermode, Frank, *Not Entitled: a memoir* (London, 1996).
Kerr, Anthony, *The Universities of Europe* (London, 1962).
Kerr, Donal A., *Peel, Priests, and Politics* (Oxford, 1982).
King's College, Windsor, *The Statutes, Rules and Ordinances of the University of King's College at Windsor* (Halifax, 1821).
King's College, Windsor, *Memorial Received from the Governors of King's College at Windsor, Nova Scotia* (London, 1822).
'King's College and Episcopate in Nova Scotia', *Collections of the Nova Scotia Historical Society* 6 (1887–8), pp. 123–35.
Kitson, Michael, Howells, Jeremy, Braham, Richard, and Westlake, Stian, *The Connected University: driving recovery and growth in the UK economy* (London, 2009).
Knapas, Rainer, 'An Intellectual Space: codes of early-nineteenth-century university architecture in Northern Europe', in Märtha Norrback, Kristina Ranki, Helga Robinson-Hammertsein, and Rainer Knapas, eds, *University and Nation: the university and the making of the nation in Northern Europe in the 19th and 20th centuries* (Helsinki, 1996).
Knight, Peter C., 'The National Advisory Planning Exercise, 1987–88: a shot in the foot', *Higher Education Quarterly* 41 (1987), pp. 317–28.
Knight, William, ed., *The Poetical Works of William Wordsworth* (8 vols; London, 1896).
Knights, David and Richards, Wendy, 'Sex Discrimination in UK Academia', *Gender, Work, and Organization* 10 (2003), pp. 213–38.
Kogan, Maurice and Kogan, David, *The Attack on Higher Education* (London, 1983).
Kok, Seng-Kiat, Douglas, Alex, McClelland, Bob, and Bryde, David, 'The Move Towards Managerialism: perception of staff in "traditional" and "new" UK universities', *Tertiary Education and Management* 16 (2010), pp. 99–113.

Kolbert, J. M., *Keele: the first fifty years, 1950–2000* (Keele, 2000).
Kumar, Krishnan, 'The Need for Place', in Anthony Smith and Frank Webster, *The Postmodern University? Contested visions of higher education in society* (Buckingham, 1997), pp. 27–35.
Lady Spencer-Churchill College of Education: a history (Oxford, 1994).
Lambert Review of Business–University Collaboration (London, 2003).
Latham, Ian and Swenarton, Mark, eds, *Jeremy Dixon and Edward Jones: buildings and projects, 1959–2002* (London, 2002).
Latour, Bruno, *Reassembling the Social: an introduction to actor-network-theory* (Oxford, 2005).
Law, C. M., 'Growth of the Urban Population in England and Wales, 1801–1911', *Transactions of the Institute of British Geographers* 41 (1967), pp. 125–43.
Law, James, *Materials for a Brief History of the Advance and Decline of the Queen's College, Birmingham* (Lichfield, 1869).
Lawlor, John, ed., *The New University* (London, 1968).
Lawrence, D. H., *The Rainbow* (1915; London, 1995).
Lawrence, D. H., *Complete Poems of D. H. Lawrence*, ed., Vivian de Sola and Warren Roberts (2 vols; London, 1972).
Lawrence, D. H., *Letters of D. H. Lawrence*, ed., James T. Boulton, et al. (8 vols; Cambridge, 1979–2000).
Lawrence, Susan C., 'Private Enterprise and Public Interest: medical education and the Apothecaries' Act, 1780–1825', in Roger French and Andrew Wear, eds, *British Medicine in the Age of Reform* (London, 1991), pp. 45–73.
Lawrenson, T. E., *Hall of Residence: Saint Anselm Hall in the University of Manchester, 1907–1957* (Manchester, 1957).
Lawson, Nigel, *The View From No 11: memoirs of a Tory radical* (London, 1992).
Lawton, Denis, *Education and Politics in the 1990s: conflict or consensus?* (London, 1992).
Layard, Richard, King, John, and Moser, Claus, *The Impact of Robbins* (Harmondsworth, 1969).
Leach, Arthur F., *Educational Charters and Documents 598–1909* (Cambridge, 1911).
Leahy, A. H., *The Work of a University and of a College* (Sheffield, 1903).
Lee, Jennie, *This Great Journey* (London, 1963).
Lees, Andrew and Lees, Lynn Hollen, *Cities and the Making of Modern Europe, 1750–1914* (Cambridge, 2007).
Letwin, Shirley Robin, *The Anatomy of Thatcherism* (London, 1992).
Levitan, Kathrin, 'Redundancy, the "Surplus Woman" Problem, and the British census', *Women's History Review* 17 (2008), pp. 359–76.
Ley, David, *A Social Geography of the City* (London, 1983).
Liscombe, R. W., *William Wilkins, 1778–1839* (Cambridge, 1980).
Liscombe, R. W., 'Modernism in Late-Imperial British West Africa: the work of Maxwell Fry and Jane Drew, 1946–1956', *Journal of the Society of Architectural Historians* 65:2 (2006), pp. 188–215.
Livingstone, Hugh, *The University: an organizational analysis* (Glasgow, 1974).
Livingstone Eyre Architects, *De Montfort University Masterplan* (Leicester, 1992).
Locke, Michael, Pratt, John, and Burgess, Tyrrell, *The Colleges of Higher Education, 1972–1982* (Croydon, 1985).
Locke, William, *The Changing Academic Profession in the UK; setting the scene* (London, 2007).
Lockmiller, David A., *Scholars on Parade: universities, scholars, and degrees* (London, 1969).

Lockwood, Geoffrey, 'Continuity and Transition in University Management: the role of professional administrative service', *Higher Education Management* 8 (1996), pp. 41–52.
Lodge, David, *Changing Places* (1975; London, 1978).
Lodge, David, *Small World: an academic romance* (1984; London, 1985).
Lodge, David, *Nice Work* (1988; London, 1989).
Lodge, Oliver, *Address to Students During the First University Session* (Birmingham, 1900).
Lodge, Oliver, *University of Birmingham: University Development by the Principal* (Birmingham, 1902).
Lodge, Oliver, *The City University* (Liverpool, 1903).
Lodge, Oliver, *Past Years* (London, 1931).
Logan, William, *The Story of Magee College* (Londonderry, 1989).
Loudon, Irvine, *Medical Care and the General Practitioner, 1750–1850* (Oxford, 1986).
Loudon, Irvine, 'Medical Education and Medical Reform', in Vivian Nulton and Roy Porter, eds, *The History of Medical Education in Britain* (Amsterdam, 1995), pp. 229–49.
Lowe, Roy, 'English Elite Education in the Late-nineteenth and Early-twentieth Centuries', in Werber Lonze and Jürgen Kocha, eds, *Bildungsbürgertum in 19. Jahrhundert* (Stutggart, 1985), pp. 17–62.
Lowe, Roy, 'Anglo-Americanism and the Planning of Universities in the United States', *History of Education* 15 (1986), pp. 247–59.
Lowe, Roy, 'Structural Change in English Higher Education, 1870–1920', in Detlef K. Müller, Fritz Ringer, and Brian Simon, eds, *The Rise of the Modern Educational System: structural change and social reproduction, 1870–1920* (Cambridge and Paris, 1987), pp. 163–78.
Lowe, Roy, 'The Changing Role of the Academic Journal: the coverage of higher education in *History of Education* as a case study, 1972–2011', *History of Education* 41 (2012), pp. 103–15.
Lowe, Roy and Knight, Rex, 'Building the Ivory Tower: the social functions of late-nineteenth-century collegiate architecture', *Studies in Higher Education* 7 (1982), pp. 81–91.
Lubbock, Jules, 'The Counter-Modernist Sublime: the campus of the University of Essex', *Twentieth-Century Architecture* 6 (2002), pp. 105–18.
Lunt, Ingrit, 'Beyond Tuition Fees? The legacy of Blair's government to higher education', *Oxford Review of Education* 34 (2008), pp. 741–52.
Lyons, Arthur, *The Architecture of the Universities of Leicester* (Leicester, 2010).
Macadam, Ivison S., *Youth and the Universities* (London, 1922).
Macaulay, T. B., *The History of England from the Accession of James II* (1848–55; 3 vols, London, 1906).
McCarthy, Donal, *UCD: a National Idea, a history of University College, Dublin* (Dublin, 1999).
McCaughey, Robert A., *Stand, Columbia: a history of Columbia University in the city of New York, 1754–2004* (New York, 2003).
McClelland, Vincent Alan, *English Roman Catholics and Higher Education, 1830–1903* (Oxford, 1973).
McClintock, Marion E., *The University of Lancaster: quest for innovation* (Lancaster, 1974).
McDonald, Walter, *Reminiscences of a Maynooth Professor* (London, 1925).
McDowell, R. B. and Webb, D. A., *Trinity College, Dublin 1592–1952* (1982; Dublin, 2004).
McGettigan, Andrew, *The Great University Gamble: money, markets, and the future of higher education* (London, 2013).

McGivney, Veronica, *Staying On or Leaving the Course: non-completion and retention of mature students in further and higher education* (London, 1996).
McGonagall, William, *Last Poetic Gems*, ed. James L. Smith (Dundee and London, 1968).
McGrath, Fergal, *Newman's University: idea and reality* (London, 1971).
McKean, John, *Leicester University Engineering Building: James Stirling and James Gowan* (London, 1994).
McKean, John, 'The English University of the 1960s: built community, model universe', in Iain Boyd Whyte, ed., *Man-Made Future: planning, education and design in mid-twentieth-century Britain* (London, 2007), pp. 205–33.
McKibbin, Ross, *Classes and Cultures: England, 1918–51* (Oxford, 1998).
Mackinder, H. J. and Sadler, M. E., *University Extension, its past, present, and future* (London, 1891).
MacKinnon, Neil, *This Unfriendly Soil: the loyalist experience in Nova Scotia, 1783–91* (Kingston and Montreal, 1986).
McLachlan, H., *English Education Under the Test Acts: being the history of the Non-Conformist academies, 1662–1820* (Manchester, 1931).
Maclean, James Mackenzie, *A Guide to Bombay: historical, statistical, descriptive* (Bombay, 1889).
McLean, Martin, 'Higher Education in the United Kingdom into the 1990s: shopping mall or reconciliation with Europe?', *European Journal of Education* 25 (1990), pp. 157–70.
McLeod, Roy M., 'Resources of Science in Victorian England: the endowment of science movement, 1868–1900', in Peter Mathias, ed., *Science and Society, 1600–1900* (Cambridge, 1972), pp. 111–66.
McMenemey, W. H., 'William Sands Cox and the Stoicism of Elizabeth Powis', *Medical History* 2 (1958), pp. 109–13.
McNutt, Jennifer Powell and Whatmore, Richard, 'The Attempts to Transfer the Geneva Academy to Ireland and to America, 1782–1795', *Historical Journal* 56 (2013), pp. 345–68.
Macqueen, J. G. and Taylor, S. W., eds, *University and Community: essays to mark the centenary of the founding of University College, Bristol* (Bristol, 1976).
Maberly, F. H., *The Melancholy and Awful Death of Lawrence Dundas Esq* (London, 1818).
Machin, G. I. T., *The Catholic Question in English Politics 1820 to 1830* (Oxford, 1964).
Malan, S. C., *An Outline of Bishop's College* (London, 1843).
Mansbridge, Albert, *The Older Universities of England* (London, 1923).
Mansell, A. L., 'Examinations and Medical Education: the preliminary sciences in the examinations of London University and the English Conjoint Board, 1861–1911', in Roy MacLeod, ed., *Days of Judgement: science, examinations, and the organization of knowledge in late-Victorian England* (Driffield, 1982), pp. 87–108.
Marrett-Crosby, Anthony, *A School of the Lord's Service: a history of Ampleforth* (Ampleforth, 2002).
Marris, Peter, *The Experience of Higher Education* (London, 1964).
Martin, Graham, *From Vision to Reality: the making of the University of Kent at Canterbury* (Canterbury, 1990).
Martin, Hugh, ed., *The Life of the Modern University* (London, 1930).
Masefield, John, *There are Few Earthly Things More Splendid than a University* (Providence, RI, 1969).
Massey, Doreen, 'A Global Sense of Place', *Marxism Today* 38 (1991), pp. 24–9.
Mathers, Helen, *Steel City Scholars: the centenary history of the University of Sheffield* (London, 2005).

Matthew, H. C. G., *Gladstone, 1809–1898* (Oxford, 1997).
Maurice, F., *The Life of Frederick Denison Maurice*, (2 vols; London, 1884).
Maurice, F. D. 'London University and King's College', *Athenaeum and Literary Chronicle* 51 (15 October 1828), pp. 799–800.
Maxwell, Robert, Macfarlane, Tim, and Bellew, Patrick, *Rick Mather Architects* (London, 2006).
Mayhew, Ken, Deer, Cecile, and Dua, Mehak, 'The Move to Mass Higher Education in the UK: many questions and few answers', *Oxford Review of Education* 30 (2004), pp. 65–82.
Maynard, John, *Browning's Youth* (Cambridge, MA, 1977).
Meisel, Joseph S., *Knowledge and Power: The Parliamentary Representation of Universities in Britain and the Empire* (Chichester, 2011).
Meller, Helen, *Leisure and the Changing City, 1870–1914* (London, 1976).
Metcalfe, Hilary, Rolfe, Heather, Stevens, Philip, and Martin Weale, *Recruitment and Retention of Academic Staff in Higher Education* (London, 2005).
Metcalfe, Richard, 'How to Survive in Estates', in Helena Thorley, *Take a Minute: reflections on modern higher education administration* (Lancaster, 1998), pp. 39–44.
Miller, Henry, 'Academics and the Labour Process', in Chris Smith, David Knights, and Hugh Willmott, eds, *White-Collar Work: the non-manual labour process* (Basingstoke, 1996), pp. 109–38.
Miles, Frank and Cranch, Graeme, *King's College School: the first 150 years* (London, 1979).
Mitchell, James, 'Queen's College, Galway 1845–1858: from site to structure', *Journal of the Galway Archaeological and Historical Society* 50 (1998), pp. 49–89.
Moffatt, Michael, *Coming of Age in New Jersey: college and American culture* (New Brunswick and London, 1989).
Moodie, Graeme C. and Eustace, Rowland, *Power and Authority in British Universities* (London, 1974).
Moody, T. W. 'The Irish University Question of the Nineteenth Century', *History* 43 (1958), pp. 90–109.
Moody, T. W. and Beckett, J. C., *Queen's, Belfast, 1845–1949* (2 vols; Belfast, 1959).
Moore, Peter G., 'University Financing, 1979–86', *Higher Education Quarterly* 41 (1987), pp. 25–42.
Morgan, David and McDowell, Linda, *Patterns of Residence: costs and options in student housing* (Guildford, 1979).
Morison, Stanley, *The History of* The Times, *'The Thunderer' in the making, 1785–1841* (London, 1935).
Morley, Edith J., ed., *Women Workers in Seven Professions: a survey of their economic conditions and prospects* (London, 1914).
Morrell, J. B., 'London Institutions and Lyell's Career: 1820–41', *British Journal for the History of Science* 9 (1976), pp. 132–46.
Morris, R. J., 'Middle-Class Culture, 1700–1914', in Derek Fraser, ed., *A History of Modern Leeds* (Manchester, 1980), pp. 200–22.
Morrison, J. T. J., *William Sands Cox and the Birmingham Medical School* (Birmingham, 1926).
Morse, Elizabeth J., 'English Civic Universities and the Myth of Decline', *History of Universities* 9 (1992), pp. 177–204.
Mountford, James, *Keele: an historical critique* (London, 1972).
Muir, Ramsay, *An Autobiography and Some Essays* (London, 1943).
Mullin, James, *The Story of a Toiler's Life* (Dublin and London, 1921).
Munby, Alan E., *Laboratories, their plannings and fittings* (London, 1921).

Murray, Margaret, *My First Hundred Years* (London, 1963).
Musgrove, F., 'Middle-Class Education and Employment in the Nineteenth Century', *Economic History Review* 12 (1959), pp. 99–111.
Muthesius, Stefan, *The Postwar University: utopianist campus and college* (New Haven and London, 2000).
Nash, Arnold, *The University and the Modern World* (London, 1945).
National Audit Office, *Space Management in Higher Education: a good practice guide* (London 1996).
National Committee of Enquiry into Higher Education, *Higher Education in the Learning Society* (London, 1997).
National Union of Students, *Graduate Employment* (London, 1937).
National Union of Students, *The Challenge to the University* (London, 1938).
National Union of Students, *Undergraduate Income and Expenditure Survey 1982/3* (London, 1984).
New, C. H., *The Life of Henry Brougham to 1830* (Oxford, 1961).
Newell, J. Philip, 'The Other Christian Socialist: Alexander John Scott', *Heythrop Journal* 24 (1983), pp. 278–89.
Newman, John Henry, *The Tamworth Reading Room: letters on an address delivered by Sir Robert Peel Bart. MP on the establishment of a reading room at Tamworth* (London, 1841).
Newman, John Henry, *The Idea of a University: defined and illustrated*, ed. Ian Ker (Oxford, 1976).
Newton, A. P., *The Universities and Educational Systems of the British Empire* (London, 1924).
Niblett, W. R., ed., *Higher Education: demand and response* (London, 1969).
Nicholas, Thomas, *Middle and High Schools and a University for Wales* (London, 1863).
Nuffield College, *The Problem Facing British Universities* (London, 1948).
Nuttall, Geoffrey F., *The Significance of Trevecca College, 1768–91* (London, 1969).
Nuttall, Geoffrey F., *New College, London and its Library* (London, 1977).
Oakeshott, Michael, 'The Universities', *Cambridge Journal* 2 (1948–9), pp. 515–42.
Obin, Nicolas, Vassort, Patrick, and Brohm, Jean-Marie, *La Crise de l'Université française: traité contre une politique de l'anéantissement* (Paris, 2005).
O'Brien, Creide, *The Development of Accounting in Ireland—the accounts of Maynooth College, 1795–1832*, Maynooth Economics Department Working Papers N96/11/99 (1999).
O'Brien, P. K., 'British Incomes and Property in the Early-Nineteenth Century', *Economic History Review* 12 (1959), pp. 255–67.
O'Dwyer, Frederick, 'A. W. N. Pugin and St Patrick's College, Maynooth', *Irish Arts Review Yearbook* 12 (1996), pp. 102–9.
O'Dwyer, Frederick, *The Architecture of Deane and Woodward* (Cork, 1997).
'O'F, K.' 'Random Notes from QCC in the Fifties', *Cork University Record* 10 (1947), pp. 26–8.
O'Farrell, Patrick N., *Heriot-Watt University: an illustrated history* (Harlow, 2004).
O'Neal, William B., *Jefferson's Fine Arts Library for the University of Virginia* (Charlottesville, 1956).
Ortega y Gasset, José, *Mission of the University*, trans. Howard Lee Nostrand (Princeton, 1944).
Osborne, John, *Look Back in Anger* (London, 1957).
Oshagbemi, Titus, 'Job Satisfaction of UK Academics', *Educational Management, Administration and Leadership* 24 (1996), pp. 389–400.

Our First Line of National Defence (Bristol, 1922).
Owen, David, *English Philanthropy, 1660–1960* (London, 1965).
Owens College, *Introductory Lectures on the Opening of Owens College Manchester* (2nd edn; London, 1852).
Owens College, *Essays and Addresses by Professors and lecturers of the Owens College, Manchester* (London, 1874).
Owens College Jubilee (Manchester, 1901).
Page, G. G. H., *An Angel Without Wings: the history of University College School, 1830–1980* (London, 1981).
Panayotidis, E. Lisa and Storz, Paul, 'Intellectual Space, Image, and Identities in the Historical University campus: Helen Kemp's map of the University of Toronto, 1932', *Journal of the Canadian Historical Association* 15 (2004), pp. 123–52.
Parker, Charles Stuart, ed., *Sir Robert Peel from His Private Papers* (3 vols: 1899; New York, 1970).
Parker, Charles Stuart, ed., *Life and Letters of Sir James Graham* (2 vols; London, 1907).
Parkes, Susan, 'Higher Education, 1793–1908', in W. E. Vaughan, ed., *A New History of Ireland, vol. vi—Ireland under the Union ii, 1870–1921* (Oxford, 1996), pp. 539–70.
Parkin, Frank, *The Mind and Body Shop* (London, 1986).
Parry, Gareth, 'Reform of Higher Education in the United Kingdom', in Brendan Nolan, ed., *Public Sector Reform: an international perspective* (Basingstoke, 2001), pp. 117–32.
Parry, Jonathan, *The Politics of Patriotism: English liberalism, national identity and Europe, 1830–1886* (Cambridge, 2006).
Parry-Jones, Brenda, *The Warneford Hospital, Oxford, 1826–1976* (Oxford, 1976).
Parsons, Kermit C., 'The Quad on the Hill: an account of the first buildings at Cornell', *Journal of the Society of Architectural Historians* 22 (1963), pp. 199–216.
Pašeta, Senia, *Before the Revolution: nationalism, social change and Ireland's Catholic elite, 1789–1922* (Cork, 1999).
Pašeta, Senia, 'The Catholic Hierarchy and the Irish University question, 1880–1908', *History* 85 (2000) pp. 268–84.
Paterson, T. G. F., 'Proposals for a University of Armagh', *Ulster Journal of Archaeology* 3rd series 8 (1945), pp. 5–13.
Pattison, Bruce, *Special Relations: the University of London and new universities overseas, 1947–1970* (London, 1984).
Pattison, Mark, *Memoirs* (London, 1885).
Pawley, Martin, *Norman Foster: a global architecture* (London, 1999).
Pearce, Martin, *University Builders* (Chichester, 2001).
Pearman, Hugh, *Rick Mather: urban approaches* (London, 1992).
Peat Marwick McLintock, *Science Parks and the Growth of Hi-Technology Firms* (London, 1988).
Peddie, J. R., *The Carnegie Trust and the Universities of Scotland—the first fifty years (1901–1951)* (Edinburgh, 1951).
Pedersen, Joyce Senders, 'Enchanting Modernity: The Invention of Tradition at Two Women's Colleges in Late Nineteenth- and Early Twentieth-Century Cambridge', *History of Universities* 17 (2001–2) pp. 162–91.
Peel, Robert, *Address to the Electors of the Borough of Tamworth* (London, 1834).
Peel, Robert, *An Inaugural Address Delivered by the Right Hon Sir Robert Peel Bart. MP, President of the Tamworth Library and Reading Room* (London, 1841).
Percy, F. H. G., *A History of the Whitgift School* (London, 1976).
Perkin, Harold, *Origins of Modern English Society* (1969; London and New York, 1996).

Perkin, Harold, *Key Profession: the history of the Association of University Teachers* (London, 1969).
Perkin, Harold, *The Rise of Professional Society: England since 1880* (London and New York, 1989).
Perrone, Fernanda, 'Women Academics in England, 1870–1930', *History of Universities* 12 (1993), pp. 339–68.
Perry, Walter, *Open University: a personal account by the first vice chancellor* (Milton Keynes, 1976).
Pevsner, Nikolaus, *A History of Building Types* (London, 1976).
Pevsner, Nikolaus, et al., *The Buildings of England* (52 vols; London, 1951–).
Phillips, Melanie, *All Must Have Prizes* (London, 1996).
Pickavance, J. A., 'University of Keele: architecture', in *University of Keele, chapel guide* (Keele, 1965), pp. 7–8.
Playfair, Lyon, *On Teaching Universities and Examining Bodies* (Edinburgh, 1872).
Pope, Rex and Phillips, Ken, *University of Central Lancashire: a history of the development of the institution since 1828* (Preston, 1996).
Port, M. H., *600 New Churches: the Church Building Commission 1818–1856* (Reading, 2006).
Porter, Roy, 'Medical Lecturing in Georgian London', *British Journal for the History of Science* 28 (1995), pp. 91–9.
Powers, Alan, *Britain: modern architectures in history* (London, 2007).
Poynting, J. H., *Sir Oliver Lodge: a biographical sketch* (London, 1910).
Praeger, Robert Lloyd, *The way that I went: an Irishman in Ireland* (Dublin and London, 1937).
Pratt, John, *The Polytechnic Experiment, 1965–1992* (Buckingham, 1992).
Pratt, John, and Burgess, Tyrell, *Polytechnics: a report* (London, 1974).
Prest, John, *Lord John Russell* (London, 1972).
Prestwich, G. H., *Life and Letters of Sir Joseph Prestwich* (London, 1899).
Price, Cedric, *The Square Book* (Chichester, 2003).
Price, Christopher, 'Elegant and Democratic: how will the new English Universities gel?', *Higher Education Quarterly* 46 (1992), pp. 243–51.
Price, D. T. W., *A History of St David's College, Lampeter, volume one: to 1898* (Cardiff, 1977).
Prochaska, F. K., 'Philanthropy', in F. M. L. Thompson, ed., *Cambridge Social History of Britain, 1750–1950* (3 vols; Cambridge, 1990).
Proctor, Robert, 'Social Structures: Gillespie, Kidd, and Coia's Halls of Residence at the University of Hull', *Journal of the Society of Architectural Historians* 67 (2008), pp. 106–29.
Pugin, A. N. W., *Contrasts: or, a parallel between the noble edifices of the middle ages and the corresponding buildings of the present day; shewing the present decay of taste* (London, 1836).
Pullan, Brian and Abendstern, Michele, *A History of the University of Manchester, 1951–73* (Manchester, 2000).
Punch, Maurice, 'The Student Ritual', *New Society* 10 (1967), pp. 811–13.
Rafferty, Deidre, 'The Opening of Higher Education to Women in Nineteenth-Century England: "unexpected revolution" or inevitable change?', *Higher Education Quarterly* 56 (2002), pp. 327–450.
Ramsden, Brian, 'Euro Student 2000: comparisons with the United Kingdom', in Maria Slowey and David Watson, eds, *Higher Education and the Life Course* (Maidenhead, 2000), pp. 3–19.

Rappoport, Amos, *The Meaning of the Built Environment: a nonverbal communication approach* (Tucson, 1990).
Rashdall, Hastings, *Universities of Europe in the Middle Ages* (2 vols; Oxford, 1895).
Rashdall, Hastings, 'The Functions of a University in a Commercial Centre', *Economic Review* 12 (1902), pp. 60–79.
Reader, W. J., *Professional Men: the rise of the professional classes in nineteenth-century England* (London, 1966).
Reay, Diane, 'A Risky Business? Mature working-class women students and access to higher education', *Gender and Education* 15 (2003), pp. 301–17.
Reay, Diane, and Crozier, Gill, and Clayton, John, '"Fitting In" or "Standing Out": working-class students in UK higher education', *British Educational Research Journal* 32 (2009), pp. 1–19.
Reay, Diane, and Davies, Jacqueline, David, Miriam, and Ball, Stephen J., 'Choices of Degree or Degrees of Choice? Class, "race", and the higher education choice process', *Sociology* 35 (2001), pp. 855–74.
Reeks, Margaret, *Register of the Associates and Old Students of The Royal School of Mines and History of the Royal School of Mines* (London, 1920).
Reichel, H. R., *Some Interesting Features of American Universities* (Cardiff, 1905).
Reilly, C. H., *Scaffolding in the Sky* (London, 1938).
Remarks on the Objects of Public Education respectfully addressed to the provisional committee for conducting the intended establishment of King's College, London, by a subscriber (London, 1828).
Rendel, Margherita, 'How Many Women Academics? 1912–76', in Rosemary Deem, ed., *Schooling for Women's Work* (London, 1980), pp. 142–61.
Rendel, Margherita, 'Women Academics in the Seventies', in Sandra Acher and David Warren Piper, eds, *Is Higher Education Fair to Women?* (Guildford, 1984), pp. 163–79.
Report of a Public Meeting held at the Victoria Rooms, Clifton, on 11th of June 1874, to promote the establishment of a College of Science and Literature for the West of England and South Wales (Bristol, 1874).
RIBA, *Growing By Degrees: universities and the future of urban development* (London, 2009).
Richards, Eveleen, 'Huxley and Women's Place in Science: the "woman question" and the control of Victorian anthropology', in James R. Moore, ed., *History, Humanity, and Evolution: essays for John C. Greene* (Cambridge, 1989), pp. 253–84.
Richardson, Margaret, 'The Architecture of Learning', in Ian Latham, ed., *Building Ideas: MJP architects* (London, 2010), pp. 108–41.
Roach, John, *Public Examinations in England, 1850–1900* (Cambridge, 1971).
Robbins, Keith, *Foreign Encounters: English Congregationalism, Germany and the United States c.1850–c.1914* (London, 2006).
Roberts, John M., 'Recollections of a Pre-Revolution', *Oxford Review of Education* 24 (1998), pp. 99–110.
Roberts, Robert, *The Classic Slum* (1971; London, 1990).
Robertson, Alex B. and Lees, Colin, *The University of Manchester, 1918–50: new approaches and changing perspectives* (*Bulletin of the John Rylands University Library* 84:1–2 [2012]).
Robertson, Charles Grant, *The British Universities* (London, 1930).
Robins, Kevin and Webster, Frank, *The Virtual University? Knowledge, market, and managements* (Oxford, 2002).
Robinson, Eric, *The New Polytechnics: the people's universities* (Harmondsworth, 1968).

Roderick, Gordon W., '"A fair representation of all interests"? The Aberdare report on intermediate and higher education in Wales, 1881', *History of Education* 30 (2001), pp. 233–50.

Roper, Henry, 'Aspects of the History of a Loyalist College: King's College, Windsor, and Nova Scotian higher education in the nineteenth century', *Anglican and Episcopal History* 60 (1991), pp. 443–59.

Roscoe, Henry Enfield, *Record of Work Done in the Chemical Department of the Owens College, 1857–1887* (London, 1887),

Roscoe, Henry Enfield, *Life and Experiences* (London, 1906).

Rose, Hugh James, *The Tendency of Prevalent Opinions about Knowledge Considered* (Cambridge, 1826).

Rose, Jasper and Ziman, John, *Camford Observed* (London, 1964).

Rose, Michael E., 'Culture, Philanthropy, and the Manchester Middle Classes', in A. J. Kidd and K. W. Roberts, eds, *City, Class, and Culture: studies of cultural production and social policy in Victorian Manchester* (Manchester, 1985), pp. 102–19.

Rothblatt, Sheldon, *The Modern University and Its Discontents: the fate of Newman's legacies in Britain and America* (Cambridge, 1997).

Rothblatt, Sheldon and Trow, Martin, 'Government Policies and Higher Education: a comparison of Britain and the United States, 1630–1860', in Colin Crouch and Anthony Heath, eds, *Social Research and Social Reform: essays in honour of A. H. Halsey* (Oxford, 1992), pp. 173–216.

Rowbotham, Sheila, 'Travellers in a strange country: responses of working-class students to the University Extension Movement—1873–1910', *History Workshop Journal* 12 (1981), pp. 62–95.

Rowbotham, Sheila, *Edward Carpenter: life of liberty and love* (London, 2008).

Royal Fine Art Commission, *Design Quality in Higher Education Buildings* (London, 1996).

Rüegg, Walter, ed., *A History of the University in Europe: vol. iii—universities in the nineteenth and twentieth centuries (1800–1945)* (Cambridge, 2004).

Russell, Colin A., *Edward Frankland: chemistry, controversy and conspiracy in Victorian England* (Cambridge, 1996).

Rust, Chris, *Surviving the First Year: the experiences of new teaching staff in higher education*, SECD paper 65 (1991).

Rustin, Michael, 'The Idea of the Popular University: a historical perspective, in Janet Finch and Michael Rustin, eds, *A Degree of Choice: education after eighteen* (Harmondsworth, 1986), pp. 17–66.

Rybczynski, Witold, *The Biography of a Building: how Robert Sainsbury and Norman Foster built a great museum* (London, 2011).

Sack, Robert David, *Homo Geographicus: a framework for action, awareness, and moral concern* (Baltimore and London, 1997).

Sadler, Michael, *Report on Secondary Education in Newcastle-upon-Tyne* (Newcastle, 1905).

Saint, Andrew, *Towards a Social Architecture: the role of school building in post-war England* (New Haven and London, 1987).

Salter, Brian and Tapper, Ted, *The State and Higher Education* (London, 1994).

Sanderson, Michael, *The Universities and British Industry, 1850–1970* (London, 1972).

Sanderson, Michael, 'The English Civic Universities and the "Industrial Spirit", 1870–1914', *Historical Research* 61 (1988), pp. 90–104.

Sanderson, Michael, *Education and Economic Decline in Britain, 1870s to the 1990s* (Cambridge, 1999).

Sands Cox, William, *Reprint of the Charter; Supplemental Charter; the Warneford Trust Deeds; and the Act of Parliament of the Queen's College, Birmingham* (Birmingham, 1873).
Schmiechen, James A., 'The Victorians, the Historians, and the Idea of Modernism', *American Historical Review* 93 (1988), pp. 287–316.
Scott, Christine Kenyon, *The Council: a portrait* (London, 2007).
Scott, Drusilla, *A. D. Lindsay: a biography* (Oxford, 1971).
Scott, George Gilbert, *Personal and Professional Recollections*, ed. Gavin Stamp (1879; Stamford, 1995).
Scott, Peter, *The Crisis of the University* (London, 1984).
Scott, Peter, 'Higher Education', in Dennis Kavanagh and Anthony Seldon, eds, *The Thatcher Effect* (Oxford, 1989), pp. 198–212.
Scott, Peter, *The Meanings of Mass Higher Education* (Buckingham, 1995).
Searby, Peter, *A History of the University of Cambridge: vol. iii, 1750–1870* (Cambridge, 1997).
Severino, Carol, 'The Idea of an Urban University: a history and rhetoric of ambivalence and ambiguity', *Urban Education* 31:3 (1996), pp. 291–313.
Sewell, William, *A Second Letter to a Dissenter on the Opposition of the University of Oxford to the Charter of the London College* (Oxford and London, 1834).
Sharp, Tom, *Wilt* (London, 1976).
Sharp, Tom, *The Wilt Alternative* (London, 1979).
Sharp, Tom, *Wilt on High* (1984; Oxford, 1986).
Sharples, Joseph, *Liverpool* (New Haven and London, 2004).
Shattock, Michael, 'British Higher Education Under Pressure: politics, budgets, and demography, and the acceleration of ideas for change', *European Journal of Education* 19 (1984), pp. 201–16.
Shattock, Michael, *The UGC and the Management of British Universities* (Buckingham, 1994).
Shattock, Michael, 'The Academic Profession in Britain: a study in the failure to adapt to change', *Higher Education* 41 (2001), pp. 27–47.
Shattock, Michael, 'The Transformation of the Civic Universities', *History of Education* 31 (2002), pp. 623–34.
Shattock, Michael, The Change from Private to Public Governance of British Higher Education: its consequence for higher education policy-making, 1980–2006', *Higher Education Quarterly* 62 (2008), pp. 181–203.
Shattock, Michael, *Making Policy in Higher Education 1945–2011* (Maidenhead, 2012).
Shepherd, A. F., *Business First Principles: an exposition, in simple terms, of the force which germinates all knowledge, all activity, all progress and all achievement* (London, 1923).
Shimmin, A. N., *The University of Leeds the First Half Century* (Leeds, 1954).
Shinn, Christine Helen, *Paying the Piper: the development of the University Grants Committee, 1919–1946* (London and Philadelphia, 1986).
Shore, Cris and Wright, Susan, 'Coercive Accountability: the rise of audit culture in higher education', in Marilyn Strathern, ed., *Audit Cultures: anthropological studies in accountability, ethics and the academy* (London, 2000).
Silver, Harold, 'The Universities' Speaking Conscience: "Bruce Truscot" and Redbrick university', *History of Education* 28 (1999), p. 173–89.
Silver, Harold, *Higher Education and Opinion-Making in Twentieth-century England* (London, 2003).
Silver, Harold, '"Residence" and "Accommodation" in Higher Education: abandoning a tradition', *Journal of Educational Administration and History* 36 (2004), pp. 123–33.

Silver, Ira, 'Role Transitions, Objects, and Identity', *Symbolic Interaction* 19 (1996), pp. 1–20.
Simmonds, Posy, *Pick of Posy* (London, 1982).
Simmonds, Posy, *Very Posy* (London, 1985).
Simmonds, Posy, *Pure Posy* (London, 1987).
Simon, Brian, *A Student's View of the Universities* (London, 1943).
Simon, Brian, *The Two Nations and the Educational Structure, 1780–1870* (London, 1974).
Simon, Brian, *A Life in Education* (London, 1998).
Simon, Ernest, *The Development of British Universities* (London, 1944).
Simpson, John, *In Lighter Moments: a book of occasional verse and prose* (Liverpool, 1934).
Simpson, Ray and Sargeant, Peter, *Stamp Perforation: the Somerset House years, 1848–1880* (London, 2006).
Singer, Charles and Holloway, S. W. F., 'Early Medical Education in Relation to the Pre-History of London University', *Medical History* 4 (1960), pp. 1–17.
Sizer, Jon, 'British Universities' Responses to Events Leading to Grant Reductions Announced in July 1981', *Financial Accountability and Management* 4 (1988), pp. 79–98.
Sloman, Albert, *A University in the Making* (London, 1963).
Smart, Richard, *On Other's Shoulders: an illustrated history of the Polhill and Lansdowne Colleges, now De Montfort University, Bedford* (Bedford, 1994).
Smart, Robert M., 'Loan Finance Straitjacket', *Official Architecture and Planning* 34 (1971), pp. 660–6.
Smith, Adam, *An Inquiry into the Nature and Causes of the Wealth of nations* (1776; Indianapolis, 1981).
Smith, Barbara, ed., *Truth, Liberty and Religion: Essays Celebrating Two Hundred Years of Manchester College* (Oxford, 1986).
Smith, Crosbie and Agar, Jon, eds, *Making Space for Science: territorial themes in the shaping of knowledge* (Basingstoke, 1998).
Smith, Dennis, *Conflict and Compromise: class formation in English society, 1830–1914* (London, 1982).
Smith, Goldwin, *The Reorganization of Oxford University* (Oxford and London, 1868).
Smith, Harold, *The Society for the Diffusion of Useful Knowledge, 1826–1846: a social and bibliographical evaluation* (Halifax, NS, 1974).
Smith, J. W. Ashley, *The Birth of Modern Education: the contribution of the Dissenting Academies, 1660–1800* (London, 1954).
Smithells, Arthur, *From a Modern University, some aims and aspirations of science* (Oxford, 1921).
Smithson, Alison and Peter, *Urban Structuring* (London, 1967).
Snow, Philip, *Stranger and Brother: a portrait of C. P. Snow* (London, 1982).
Soares, Joseph A., *The Decline of Privilege: the modernization of Oxford University* (Stanford, 1999).
Southgate, Donald, *University Education in Dundee: a centenary history* (Edinburgh, 1982).
Spencer, F. H., *An Inspector's Testament* (London, 1938).
Startup, Richard, *The University Teacher and His World: a sociological and educational study* (Farnborough, 1979).
Statement by the Council of the University of London, explanatory of the nature and objects of the Institution (London, 1827).
Statement of Proceedings towards the establishment of King's College, London (London, 1830).
Steiner, Bruce E., *Samuel Seabury, 1729–1796: a study in the high church tradition* (Athens, OH, 1971).

Stevens, Robert, *University to Uni: the politics of higher education in England since 1944* (London, 2004).
Stewart, W. A. C., *Higher Education in Post-war Britain* (Houndmills, 1989).
Stölting, Erhard, *Die Krise der Universitäten* (Berlin, 2001).
Stone, Lawrence, ed., *The University in Society* (2 vols; London, 1975).
Strachan, John, *An Appeal to the Friends of Religion and Literature in* [sic] *behalf of the University of Upper Canada* (London, 1827).
The Students' Union, University of Liverpool (Liverpool, 1965).
Substance of the Speech of Sir Charles Wetherell before the Lords of the Privy Council on the subject of the Incorporating of London University (London, 1834).
Sumner, James, 'Halls of Resonance: institutional history and the buildings of the University of Manchester', *Studies in the History and Philosophy of Science* 44 (2013), pp. 700–15.
Sutherland, G. A., *Dalton Hall: a Quaker venture* (London, 1963).
Sutherland, Gillian, 'The Social and Intellectual Context of the Movement for Women's Higher Education', in P. J. Waller, ed., *Politics and Social Change in Modern Britain: essays for A. F. Thompson* (Brighton, 1987), pp. 99–116.
Sutherland, Gillian, *Faith, Duty, and the Power of Mind: the Cloughs and their circle, 1820–1960* (Cambridge, 2006).
Sutherland, L. S. and Mitchell, L. G., eds, *The History of the University of Oxford: vol. v, the eighteenth century* (Oxford, 1986).
Sutherland, Margaret, *Women Who Teach in Universities* (Stoke-on-Trent, 1985).
Sykes, L. C., *A Philosopher for the Modern University* (Leicester, 1951).
Tapper, Ted and Salter, Brian, 'Interpreting the Process of Change in Higher Education: the case of the Research Assessment Exercise', *Higher Education Quarterly* 57 (2003), pp. 4–23.
Taylor, Shephard T., *The Diary of a Medical Student During the Mid-Victorian Period, 1860–1864* (Norwich, 1927).
Tempest, N. R., 'An Early Scheme for an Undenominational University', *Universities Review* 32 (1960), pp. 45–9.
Temple Patterson, A., *The University of Southampton* (Southampton, 1962).
Thackeray, Arnold, 'Natural Knowledge in Cultural Context: the Manchester model', *American Historical Review* 79 (1974), pp. 672–709.
Thackeray, William Makepeace, *An Irish Sketchbook* (1843; New York, 1848).
Thatcher, Margaret, *The Downing Street Years* (London, 1993).
Thatcher, Margaret, *The Path to Power* (London, 1995).
Thelwall, A. S., ed., *Proceedings of the Anti-Maynooth Conference of 1845* (London, 1845).
Thomas, Imogen, *Haileybury, 1806–1987* (Hertford, 1987).
Thomas, Nick, 'Challenging the Myths of the 1960s: the case of student protest in Britain', *Twentieth Century British History* 13:3 (2002), pp. 277–97.
Thompson, E. P., *Warwick University Ltd: industry, management and the universities* (Harmondsworth, 1970).
Thompson, F. M. L., *The University of London and the World of Learning, 1836–1986* (London, 1990).
Thompson, F. M. L., ed., *Cambridge Social History of Britain, 1750–1950* (3 vols; Cambridge, 1990).
Thompson, Joseph, *The Owens College: its foundation and growth, and its connection with the Victoria University, Manchester* (Manchester, 1886).
Thomson, A. P. D., 'The Chamberlain Memorial Tower, University of Birmingham', *University of Birmingham Historical Journal* 4 (1953–4), pp. 167–79.

Thorpe, Edward, *The Right Honourable Henry Enfield Roscoe: a biographical sketch* (London, 1916).
Tight, Malcolm, 'The Golden Age of Academe: myth or memory?', *British Journal of Educational Studies* 58 (2010), pp. 105–16,
Tight, Malcolm, ed., *Academic Work and Life: what it is to be an academic and how this is changing* (Amsterdam, 2000).
Tomlinson, Jim, *The Politics of Decline: understanding post-war Britain* (Harlow, 2000).
Toulmin, Vanessa, *Electric Edwardians: the story of Mitchell and Kenyon* (London, 2006).
Toulmin, Vanessa, Russell, Patrick, and Popple, Simon, eds, *The Lost World of Mitchell and Kenyon: Edwardian Britain on film* (London, 2004).
Townroe, B. S., *Nottingham University College: a record of its history and an appreciation of the new buildings* (1928).
Transactions of the National Association for the Promotion of Social Science 1878 (London, 1879).
Truscot, Bruce [Edgar Allison Peers], *Red Brick University* (London, 1943 and 1951).
Truscot, Bruce [Edgar Allison Peers], *Redbrick University Revisited*, ed. Ann L. Mackenzie and Adrian R. Allen (Liverpool, 1996).
Tuan, Yi-Fu, *Space and Place: the perspective of experience* (Minneapolis, 1977).
Turner, Frank M., ed., *The Idea of the University: John Henry Newman* (New Haven and London, 1996).
Turner, Paul Venable, *Campus: an American planning tradition* (Cambridge, MA, and London, 1984).
Tyack, Geoffrey, *Sir James Pennethorne and the Making of Victorian London* (Cambridge, 1992).
Tyack, Geoffrey, *Oxford: an architectural guide* (Oxford, 1998).
Tyack, Geoffrey and William Whyte, eds, *George Gilbert Scott: an architect and his influence* (Donington, 2014).
Tylecote, Mabel, ed., *The Education of Women at Manchester University* (Manchester, 1941).
Tylor, Mark C., *Crisis on Campus: a bold plan for reforming our colleges and Universities* (New York, 2010).
UCEA, *Where are We Now? The benefits of working in HE* (London, 2008).
UCEA, *Securing a Sustainable Future for Higher Education* (London, 2010).
Unite/MORI, *Student Living Report, 2001* (London, 2001).
Universities Bureau of the British Empire, *Deputation to the President of the Board of Education and Chancellor of the Exchequer* (London, 1918).
University Grants Committee, *Returns from Universities and University Colleges in receipt of Treasury Grant* (London, 1920–48).
University Grants Committee, *University Development from 1935 to 1946* (London, 1948).
University College Liverpool Hall of Residence for Women Students (Liverpool, 1900).
University of Essex, *Report of the Annan Enquiry* (Colchester, 1974).
University of Liverpool, *Report of the Development Committee 1949–54* (Liverpool, 1955).
University of London: the historical record (London, 1912).
University of London. Proposed Plan for Future Management (London, 1832).
University of London Prospectus (London, 1826).
Vaizey, John, *The Economics of Education* (London, 1962).
Varley and Robinson's Guide for the Stranger in Manchester (Salford, 1857).
Vaughan, Thomas, *Christian Philanthropy Exemplified in a Memoir of the late Rev Samuel Wilson Warneford LLD* (London, 1856).

Venables, Peter, 'Technical Education in Great Britain: second thoughts on the Robbins Report', *International Review of Education* 11:2 (June 1965), pp. 151–64.
Venables, Peter, *Higher Education Developments: the technological universities, 1956–76* (London and Boston, 1978).
Vernon, Keith, 'British Universities and the state, 1880–1914', *History of Education* 30 (2001), pp. 251–71.
Vickery, Margaret Birney, *Buildings for Bluestockings: the architecture and social history of women's colleges in late Victorian England* (London, 2000).
Wadsworth, Kenneth W., *Yorkshire United Independent College* (London, 1954).
Wahrman, Dror, *Imagining the Middle Class: the political representation of class in Britain, c.1780–1840* (Cambridge, 1995).
Wainewright, Latham, *The Literary and Scientific Pursuits which are Encouraged and Enforced in the University of Cambridge* (London, 1815).
Wainwright, J. M., *Collegiate Education: an address pronounced before the House of Convocation of Trinity College, Hartford, August 4th, 1847* (Hartford, 1847).
Waite, P. B., *The Lives of Dalhousie University: vol. one, 1818–1925, Lord Dalhousie's university* (Montreal and Kingston, 1994).
Walden, George, *We Should Know Better: solving the education crisis* (London, 1996).
Walden, George, *Lucky George: memoirs of an anti-politician* (London, 1999).
Walford, Geoffrey, *Restructuring Universities: politics and power in the management of change* (London, 1987).
Waller, Philip, *Town, City, and Nation: England 1850–1914* (Oxford, 1983).
Waller, Philip, *Writers, Readers, and Reputations: literary life in Britain, 1870–1918* (Oxford, 2006).
Walsh, James Jackson, 'The University Movement in the North of England at the End of the Nineteenth century', *Northern History* 46 (2009), pp. 113–31.
Walsham, Alexandra, *The Reformation of the Landscape: religion, identity, and memory in early-modern Britain and Ireland* (Oxford, 2011).
Warner, David, 'A Corporate Identity Case Study: grasping the nettle', in Clive Keen and David Warner, eds, *Visual and Corporate Identity: a study of identity programmes in the college, polytechnic and university environment* (Banbury, 1989), pp. 35–45.
Watkin, David, 'Charles Kelsall: the quintessence of neo-classicism', *Architectural Review* 140 (1966), pp. 109–12.
Watkin, David, *Thomas Hope and the Neo-Classical Idea* (London, 1968).
Watkin, David, *The Life and Work of C. R. Cockerell* (Cambridge, 1974).
Watkin, David, ed., *The Age of Wilkins: the architecture of improvement* (Cambridge, 2000).
Watson, David and Bourden, Rachel, *Ends Without Means: the Conservative stewardship of UK higher education, 1979–1997* (Brighton, 1997).
Watson, David and Bourden, Rachel, 'Why Did They Do It? The Conservative Government and Higher Education', *Journal of Education Policy* 14 (1999), pp. 243–56.
Webster, Christopher and Elliott, John, eds, *'A Church as it should be': the Cambridge Camden Society and its Influence* (Stamford, 2000).
Weiner, Martin J., *English Culture and the Decline of the Industrial Spirit, 1850–1980* (1981; Harmondsworth, 1985).
Weiss, F. E., 'The University of Manchester', in W. H. Brindley, ed., *The Soul of Manchester* (Manchester, 1929), pp. 62–76.
Whitburn, Julia, Meaking, Maurice, and Cox, Caroline, *People in Polytechnics* (Guildford, 1979).

Whitchurch, Celia, '"Who Do they Think They Are?" the changing identities of professional administrators and managers in UK higher education', *Journal of Higher Education Policy and management* 28 (2006), pp. 159–71.

Whitchurch, Celia, *Professional Managers in UK Higher Education: preparing for complex futures* (London, 2008).

White, James F., *The Cambridge Movement: the Ecclesiologists and the Gothic Revival* (Cambridge, 1962).

Whitehead, J. W. R., 'Institutional Site Planning: the University of Birmingham, 1900–69', *Planning History* 13:2 (1991), 29–35.

Whitelaw, Marjory, ed., *The Dalhousie Journals* (Ottowa, 1978).

Whiting, C. E., *The University of Durham, 1832–1932* (London, 1932).

Whittingham, Sarah, *The Wills Memorial Building* (Bristol, 2003).

Whittingham, Sarah, *Sir George Oatley: architect of Bristol* (Bristol, 2011).

Whyte, William, '"Rooms for the torture and shame of scholars": the New Examination Schools and the architecture of reform', *Oxoniensia* 66 (2001), 85–103.

Whyte, William, 'Unbuilt Hertford: T. G. Jackson's contextual dilemma', *Architectural History* 45 (2002), 347–62.

Whyte, William, 'Building a Public School Community, 1860–1910', *History of Education* 32 (2003), 601–26.

Whyte, William, 'The Intellectual Aristocracy Revisited', *Journal of Victorian Culture* 10 (2005), 15–45.

Whyte, William, *Oxford Jackson: architecture, education, status and style, 1835–1924* (Oxford, 2006).

Whyte, William, 'How do Buildings Mean? Some issues of interpretation in the history of architecture', *History and Theory* 45 (2006) pp.153–77.

Whyte, William, '"Redbrick's unlovely quadrangles": reinterpreting the architecture of the civic universities', *History of Universities* 21 (2006) pp. 151–77.

Whyte, William, 'The Modernist Moment at the University of Leeds, 1957–1977', *Historical Journal* 51 (2008), pp.169–93.

Whyte, William, 'The Englishness of English Architecture: modernism and the making of a national International Style, 1927–1957', *Journal of British Studies* 48 (2009), pp. 441–65.

Whyte, William, 'Modernism, Modernisation, and Europeanization in West African Architecture, 1944–1994', in Martin Conway and Kiran Klaus Patel, eds, *Europeanization in the Twentieth Century: historical approaches* (London, 2010), pp. 210–28.

Whyte, William, 'Restoration and Recrimination: the Temple Church in the nineteenth century', in Robin Griffith-Jones and David Park, eds, *The Temple Church: history, art, and architecture* (Woodbridge, 2010), pp. 195–210.

Whyte, William, 'Twentieth-Century Education', in Kate Tiller, ed., *A Historical Atlas of Oxfordshire* (Oxford, 2011), pp. 160–1.

Whyte, William, 'Sacred Space as Sacred Text: church and chapel building in Victorian Britain', in Joe Sterrett and Peter Thomas, *Sacred Text-Sacred Space: architectural, literary, and spiritual convergences in England and Wales* (Brill, 2011), pp. 247–67.

Whyte, William, 'Building the Nation in the Town: architecture and national identity in urban Britain, 1848–1914', in William Whyte and Oliver Zimmer, eds, *Nationalism and the Reshaping of Urban Communities, 1848–1914* (London, 2011), pp. 204–33.

Whyte, William, 'Halls of Residence at the British Civic Universities, 1870–1970', in Jane Hamlett, Lesley Hopkins, and Rebecca Preston, eds, *Residential Institutions in Britain, 1725–1950: inmates and environments* (London, 2013), pp. 155–66.

Whyte, William, '"A pastiche or a packing case": building in twentieth-century Oxford and Cambridge', *Twentieth-Century Architecture* 11 (2013), pp. 16–29.

Whyte, William, 'Neo-Georgian: the other style in British twentieth-century university architecture?', in Julian Holder and Elizabeth McKellar, eds, *Re-appraising Neo-Georgian Architecture, 1850–1970* (Swindon, 2015).

Wilkie, Laurie, *The Lost Boys of Zeta Psi: a historical archaeology of masculinity at a university fraternity* (Berkeley, 2010).

Wilkinson, Denys, 'The Lean Years, 1976–1986', in Roger Blin-Stoyle and Geoff Ivey, eds, *The Sussex Opportunity: a new university and the future* (London, 1986), pp. 23–35.

Williams, Ben T., *The Desirableness of a University for Wales* (London, 1853).

Williams, Gareth and Tessa Blackstone, *Response to Adversity: higher education in a harsh climate* (Guildford, 1983).

Williams, Gareth, *Changing Patterns of Finance in Higher Education* (Buckingham, 1992).

Williams, J. Gwynn, *The University Movement in Wales* (Cardiff, 1993),

Williams, J. Gwynn, *The University of Wales 1893–1930* (Cardiff, 1994).

Williams, Shirley, *Climbing the Bookshelves* (London, 2009).

Williams, T. Marchant, *The University of Wales: its past, its present, and its future* (Cardiff, 1905).

Williamson, W. C., *Reminiscences of a Yorkshire Naturalist* (London, 1896).

Willmott, Hugh, 'Managing the Academics: commodification and control in the development of university education in the United Kingdom', *Human Relations* 48 (1995), pp. 993–1027.

Willson, F. M. G., *Our Minerva: the men and politics of the University of London, 1836–58* (London, 1995).

Willson, F. M. G., *The University of London 1858–1900: the politics of Senate and Convocation* (Woodbridge, 2004).

Wilson, Bryan, *The Youth Culture and the Universities* (London, 1970).

Wilson, Tom, 'The Proletarianisation of Academic Labour', *Industrial Relations* 22 (1991), pp. 250–62.

Winterbottom, Derek, *Bertrand Hallward: the first vice-chancellor of the University of Nottingham* (Nottingham, 1995).

Woods, Mary N., 'Thomas Jefferson and the University of Virginia: planning the academic village', *Journal of the Society of Architectural Historians* 44 (1985), pp. 266–83.

Wolfenden, Lord, *Turning Points* (London, 1976).

Worsnip, Judith, 'A Re-evaluation of "the problem of surplus women" in nineteenth-century England: the case of the 1851 census', *Women's Studies International Forum* 13 (1990), pp. 21–31.

Worthen, John, *D. H. Lawrence: the early years, 1885–1912* (Cambridge, 1991).

Wyse, Thomas, *Speech on the Extension and Improvement of Academic, Collegiate, and University Education in Ireland at the Meeting Held for the Purpose at Cork* (London, 1845).

Wyse, Winifride M., *Notes on Education Reform in Ireland During the First half of the Nineteenth Century: compiled from speeches, letters, &c contained in the unpublished memoirs of the Rt Hon Sir Thomas Wyse KCB* (Waterford, 1901).

Yacobi, Haim, 'Academic Fortress: the case of Hebrew University on Mount Scopus, Jerusalem', in Wim Wiewal and David C. Perry, eds, *Global Universities and Urban Development* (New York, 2008), pp. 257–72.

Yaneva, Albena, 'Is the Atrium More Important than the Lab? Designer buildings for new cultures of creativity', in Peter Meusberger, David N. Livingstone, and Heike Jöns, eds, *Geographies of Science* (Loughborough, 2010), pp. 19–50.

Yates, James, *Thoughts on the Advancement of Academical Education in England* (London, 1826).
Yorke, Mantz, *Leaving Early: undergraduate non-completion in higher education* (London, 1999).
Zimmer, Oliver, *Remaking the Rhythms of Life: German communities in the age of the nation state* (Oxford, 2013).
Zweig, Ferdynand, *The Student in the Age of Anxiety* (London, 1963).

WEBSITES AND OTHER UNPUBLISHED WORK

Aspin, Philip, 'Architecture and Identity in the English Gothic Revival, 1800–1850' (University of Oxford DPhil, 2013).
AUDE Building Officers' Handbook (?1992/3). <http://www.bis.gov.uk/news/speeches/david-willetts-keynote-speech>.
Black, Jeremy, 'The City on the Hill: A Life of the University of Exeter'.
Chablo, Diane, 'University Architecture in Britain, 1950–75' (University of Oxford DPhil, 1987).
Dungavell, Ian Robert, 'The Architectural Career of Aston Webb (1849–1930)' (University of London PhD, 1999).
Goddard, John, 'Reinventing the Civic University', <http://www.nesta.org.uk/publications/provocations/assets/features/re-inventing_the_civic_university>.
Harris, Martin, 'What more can be done to widen access to highly selective universities?'(2010) <http://www.offa.org.uk/wp-content/uploads/2010/05/Report-on-access-to-highly-selective-universities.pdf. http://www.hesa.ac.uk>.
Jones, Stuart, 'Mark Pattison and the Idea of the University Revisited'.
Nockles, Peter, 'Oriel's Religious History in an Era of Intellectual Ascendancy'.
Peronne, Fernanda, 'University Teaching as a Profession for Women in Oxford, Cambridge and London, 1870–1930' (University of Oxford, DPhil, 1991).
Quinsee, Anthony, 'After Atkinson: British university library planning since 1976' (1995), <http://webdoc.gwdg.de/ebook/aw/liber96/quin.htm>. <http://www.scotland.gov.uk/Resource/0038/00386780.pdf> <http://senatehouseoccupation.wordpress.com>.
Skinner, Simon A., 'Protestants Disunited: Britons and the Maynooth Grant'.
Taggart, Gerard James, 'A Critical Review of the Role of the English Funding Body for Higher Education in the Relationship Between the State and Higher Education in the Period 1945–2003' (PhD Bristol, 2004).
Thomas, Thomas Nicholas, 'The British Student Movement 1965–72' (Univeristy of Warwick PhD, 1996).
UK Higher Education Space Management Project, *Impact on Space of Future Changes in Higher Education* (2006) <http://www.smg.ac.uk/documents/FutureChangesInHE.pdf. http://www.uniq-stoke.org/>.
University of Lincoln, *Learning landscapes in Higher Education* (2010) <http://learninglandscapes.blogs.lincoln.ac.uk/files/2010/04/FinalReport.pdf>.
Whyte, William, ' "A Hell of a Job": Building the University of Leicester', 50th Anniversary Lecture to the University of Leicester (19 February 2008), <http://www2.le.ac.uk/offices/press/pdf-files/A%20Hell%20of%20a%20Job.doc.>.
Whyte, William, 'What Can Buildings Do?' (lecture at the Buildings in Society International Conference, Queen's University, Belfast, June 2014).

Index

Note: References in bold refer to the page numbers of illustrations.

Aberdeen:
   Marischal College 4
   University of 73
Aberystwyth, University College 110, 128, 135,
   149, 158, **159**, 192, 193, 212, 215
academies, dissenting, *see* dissenting academies
adult education 38, 98–9, 110–11, 113–14, 144
agricultural university, proposal for a 87
Amis, Sir Kingsley 221, 243–4
Ampleforth College, 30
Anderson, Sir Colin 233
Anderson Report 236
Anderson, Robert 74, 144
Anderson, Rowand 167
Anglo-Persian Oil Company 215
Annan, Noel, baron 234, 266, 276
architectural history 12–14
architecture, *see* buildings and sites
Armagh, plans for a university of 29
Armytage, W. H. G. 8, 239
Arnold, Matthew 106
Arup, Ove 264
Ashbee, C. R. 161–2
Ashby, Sir Eric 190
Association of University Teachers (AUT) 9–10,
   204, 215, 217
Aston, University 291
Athanasian Creed, influence on soft furnishings
   of 106
Atkinson, William 54
Auckland, George Eden, earl of 55
A Very Peculiar Practice 273–5

Baker, Kenneth, baron 285
Baldwin, Stanley, first earl 8, 9
Bangor, University College 128, 135, 142,
   145, 158
Banham, Reyner 263
Barnes, Sarah 158, 163
Barlow, Frank 245, 304
Barlow Report on Scientific Manpower
   189–90, 222
Barnett, Corelli 276–7
Barrington, Shute 24
Bath, proposals for a university of 31, 33
Battersea Polytechnic 142
Baxter, Ann 141
Baxter family of Dundee 141–2
Bedford Physical Training College 147
Belfast:
   Assembly's College 82

Queen's College (later University) 73, 81, 84,
   85, 101–2, **103**, 107, 109, 128–9,
   211–12, 241
Royal Academical Institution 30, 78, 82
Bell, Sir Charles 48
Beloff, Michael 243, 248
Bentham, Jeremy 37, 39, 91
Berlin, University of 30, 36, 53, 318
Bermuda, University of 22
Bhaba, H. J. 1926
Birkbeck, George 46
Birks, Tony 225
Birmingham:
   Chamber of Commerce 215
   City University 288, 296
   Guild of Students 126
   Mason College 120–1, **120**, 130, 133
   Polytechnic 288
   Queen's College 71–2, 74–5, **86**, 86, 89–92,
      96–7, 109, 121,
   Queen's Hospital 91, 96
   Syddenham College 97
   Union Club 215
   University of 12, 35, 120–1, 125–8, 130,
      133, 134, 135, 138, 144, 145–6, 147, 152,
      154, 155, 156, 166–7, **166**, 171–4, 180,
      191, 198, 202, 210, 211–12, 215, 216,
      224, 239, 255, 266, 273, 328–9, 330, 337
Blackett, Philip Maynard Stuart, baron 213
Blair, Tony 321, 323
Blomfield, Charles 65
Bodington, Nathan 151, 154
Bombay (Mumbai), University of 73, 101, **102**,
   105, 199
Bonn, University of 35
Boston, University 135
Bourdieu, Pierre 11
Boyle, Edward, baron 282
Boyson, Sir Rhodes 275, 285
Bradbury, Sir Malcolm 226, 227, 243–4, 246–7
Bradford, University of 227, 241
Brideshead Revisited 273
Bridges, Edward Ettingdene, baron 234
Bristol, University of 110, 112, 115, 117–18,
   118, 128, 132, 138, 140–1, **140**, 144, 145,
   147–8, 150, 151, 155, 160, 167, 182,
   199, 200, 208, 209, 217, 241, 253, 266,
   311, 315
British and Foreign School Society 38
Britton, John 51
Brogan, D. W. 218

382 Index

Brooke, Henry, baron 234
Brotherton, Edward first baron 198
Brougham, Henry, first baron Brougham and Vaux 37, 38, **42**, 46–7, 53, 65, 67, 80
Browne Review 324
Browning, Robert 63
Bryce, James, first viscount 129
Buckingham, University of 268–70
Building Design Partnership 311–12
buildings and sites:
    Byzantine 171–2
    campuses 6, 12, 18, 171–2, 180, 191, 194, 197, 253–4, 261, 263–7, 316–17, 318, 329–30
    chapels 1, **2**, 45, 56, 59, 60, 63, 109, 196, 261–2, **262**
    classicism 1, 25, 51–8, 145, 161–3, 180–2, 191–2, 196
    complaints about 26, 51–3, 56–7, 79, 99, 106–7, 150, 155–6, 157–9, 167, 168–9, 178–9, 182, 190–3, 197–8, 225–6, 252–3, 259–66, 262–70, 310–11
    gender and **138**, 145, 150–2, 154–5, 156, 238–9, 241, 255
    Gothic Revival 1–2, 57, 78, 104–6, 108–9, 121, 160–1, 165, 167, 168–9, 181, 191–2, 196
    halls of residence and accommodation 25, 40–1, 45, 59–60, 61–3, 100, 109, 156–7, 180, 188, 191, 195–7, 207, 208, 238–9, 241, 255–7, 261, 265, 293, 309, 315–16, 323, 330, 331–2
    hotels and conference centres 314–15
    modernism 181, 248–70
    occupied by students 232, 266–7, 268, 295
    repair of 26, 51–2, 107, 309–11, 323
    science parks 314–15
    sexuality 149, 154, 241, 267, 268, 293
    symbolism of 13, 51–60, 101–2, 106–10, 118, 130, 134, 145, 151, 157–8, 163–7, 169–70, 171, 177–82, 198, 217–18, 226–8, 254–5, 316–17, 326–7, 328–31, 333–7
    see also entries for individual institutions
Bunting, Percy 95
Burgess, Tyrell 280–1, 315
Burnett, Gilbert 65

Calcutta:
    Bishop's College 30–1
    University of 73, 190
Cambridge:
    Downing College 4, 54, 57
    extension lectures 113–14
    Fitzwilliam Museum, licentious pictures within 32, 39
    Footlights College, 274
    idleness of 189
    King's College 4

Peterhouse 4
St John's College, 4
Trinity College 3, 4
University 3, 31–2, 40, 43, 50, 73, 113–14, 128, 129, 132–3, 135, 136, 145, 160, 184, 189, 196, 206, 213, 217, 224, 254, 276, 329
Campbell, Lewis 136
Campbell, Thomas 35–9, 46, 53, 63, 64
Capon, Kenneth 260
Cardiff, University College 128, 151–2, 158, 161, **163**, 167, 212, 293, 294, 311, 312, **312**, 315
Carnegie, Andrew 142, 171, 198
Carnegie Trust 198
Caroë, W. D. 161, 167
Caroline, queen 47
Carpenter, Edward 114
Carswell, John 229, 266, 286
Carter, Edward 274
Casson, Sir Hugh 260
Casey, Edward 15
Catholic University, *see* Dublin, University College
Cavendish, Lord Frederick 111, 112
Central Institutions 236; *see also* Polytechnics
Chamberlain, Joseph 127, 130, 166–7, **166**, 171–2
Chamberlin, Peter 260
Chamberlin, Powell, and Bonn 254
Charities Commission 142
Childs, W. M. 156, 169
Clarke, Charles 296, 330
Clarke, J. R. 213
Clarke, Kenneth 283
Clarke, Sir Richard 'Otto' 234
class:
    middle class 21, 37–8, 41, 63, 76–7, 111–12, 114–15, 117–18, 120–1, 144–5, 172, 187–8, 198, 205–6, 239–40, 276, 288, 291–2, 332–7
    working class 38–9, 76, 79, 110–14, 144–5, 168, 187–8, 205–6, 239–40, 276, 332–7
Classics 3, 40, 45, 74, 94, 133, 141, 330
Clothworkers' Company 142
Clyde and East, architects 170
Cockerell, Charles Robert 34, 54
Colleges of Advanced Technology (CATs) 235–6
Columbia University 21; *see also* New York, King's College.
Coming From Behind 274
Committee of Vice Chancellors and Principals (CVCP) 9, 203–4, 217, 223, 229, 234, 278, 305
Cork, Queen's College 73, 81, 82, 85, 102, **103**, 107, 109, 128
Cornell University 5
Coventry, University of 315, 335
Cox, F. A. 53

Craddock, Mary 147
Craig, W. A. 246
Croker, John 53–4
Crook, J. Mordaunt 13
Crosland, Tony 231
Curtis, John 84
Cutlers' Company 142
Cycle and Motor Manufacturers' Union 215

Dainton, Frederick Sydney, baron 226
Dalek 256
Dalhousie, James Broun-Ramsay, first marquess of 26
Dalhousie University 26–27
Davie, Donald 265–6
Davies, Andrew 273–5
Davies, Emily 113
Deane, Sir Thomas Newenham 102
De Montfort University, *see* Leicester
De Montmorency, J. E. G. 138, 141
Derby, Edward Stanley, fourteenth earl of 80
Derby, University of 324
Derry/Londonderry, Magee College 82, 84
Desch, C. H. 213
Desmond, Adrian 90
devil, the 1, 39
Dibelius, Wilhelm 187
Disraeli, Benjamin, first earl of Beaconsfield 39, 99
Dissenting Academies 5, 29, 50, 54, 88, 94
Dixon, J. F. Cory 252
Dixon, Simon 291
Dobrée, Bonamy 198
Donoghue, Bernard, baron 279
Dorwood, Alan 212–13
Doyly, Geroge 42–3
Drapers' Company 142
Driver, Christopher 14
Dublin:
   Trinity College 4, 5, 31, 43, 45, 79, 93
   University College 72, 82–4, 128–9
duel, only one to be fought over higher education 45
Dumfries, proposals for university of 31
Dundee, University of 8, 129, 134, 135, 139, 141–2, 145, 150, 154, 155, 156, 158–60, 165, 167, 169–70, 197, 311
Dunstan, A. E. 149
Durham, University of 33, 35, 50, 57, 72, 73, 94, 128, 145, 147

East Anglia, University of, *see* University of East Anglia (UEA)
Eating People is Wrong 227
Ecclesiologist, The 105–7
Economics of Education 233
Edgerton, David 227, 232–3
Edinburgh:
   High School 53

National Memorial 54
University 4
Educating Rita 273
Education Act of 1988: 299
Education: a framework for expansion 284
Edward VII, king 190–9
Eliot, George 36, 133
emotions, history of 17–18
English literature 45
Essex, University of 226, 241, 242, 246, 250, 254, 257, 258, **259**, 260, 261, 263, 265–6, 275
Eton College 3
E-University 334–5
Evans Colin 298, 305
Evans, George Ewart 210
Exeter, University of 128, 180, 189, 194, 195, 196, 198, 202, 207, 210, 226, 232, 238, 241–2, 245, 311, 314
exhibitions, international:
   London 92
   Paris 114

Faulkner, George 93
Finance:
   central government 11, 17, 25, 27, 33, 49–50, 53, 73, 79–82, 84, 86, 97–8, 99, 101, 115–18, 127, 139, 142, 180, 202, 205–6, 214, 224, 226–7, 229–32, 257–8, 281, 283–6, 300, 330; *see also* Higher Education Funding Councils; University Grants Committee
   local government 76–7, 115–18, 120, 127, 137–9, 142–5, 232, 233–4, 268, 281
   philanthropy and fund-raising 41, 46, 71–2, 74, 76, 89–92, 92–3, 96, 100, 115–16, 121, 135–6, 139–42, 145, 167, 177–82, 198–202, 232, 251–2, 313
   tuition fees, scholarships, grants, and loans 46, 63, 86, 88, 94, 139, 145, 149–50, 184, 201, 204–6, 215, 227, 231–2, 236–7, 288, 297, 300, 323–5
Flexner, Abraham 185
Ford, Basil 250–1
Ford, Brian 307–8
Foster, Norman, baron 313
Frankland, Edward 99, 110
Fredericton, N. B., King's College 24
Frith, Mark 296
Fry, Maxwell 249, 270

Galway, Queen's College 73, 82, 85 102–4, **104**, 109, 128
Gandy, John 54, 55
Gardner, W. J. 78
Garrett, Vero 126–7, 173
George III, king 24
George IV, king 44, 47
Gibbs and Flockton, architects 168

Giddens, Anthony, baron 239
Gladstone, William 81
Glasgow, University of 105
Glasman, Maurice, baron 327
Gledhill, John 315
Glenn Howells Architects 331
Goddard, John 329
Gomme, Andor 161
Gower Street:
 anonymity of 54
 godlessness of 39–40, 43
Grafton, Anthony 10
Graham, Sir James 80
Granger, Frank 178
Grants to Students 236
Great Exhibition 92
Greenwood, John 75, 97–100
Grosseck, Mark 148
Guardian Student Media Awards 296
Guilford, Frederick North, fifth earl of 31
Gutteridge, R. F. 194

Hackman, D. W. 188
Haileybury College 54
Haldane, Richard, first viscount 143
Halsey, A. H. 182, 247
Halsey, Margaret 189
Hansom, Charles 160–61
Harris, Sir Martin 333
Harris, Vincent 194
Harvard University 135
Headlam, Arthur 172
Health and safety 304, 310
Heat Magazine 296
Hendon Police College 275
Heriot-Watt, University 314
Herklots, H. C. G., 185, 197
Hetherington, Sir Hector 234
Highbury, Dissenting Academy 54
Higher Education Act:
 1992: 283, 325
 1998: 321, 323
 2004: 323–4
 2010: 324
Higher Education: a new framework 279, 283
Higher Education Funding Councils:
 England (HEFCE) 283, 287, 325, 329
 Scotland (SHEFC) 283, 325
 Wales (HEFCW) 283, 325
Hirst, Thomas 110
History Man, The 226, 243, 246, 247, 273
Hobsbawm, Eric 152
Hoggart, Richard 188, 206, 244
Holford, William, baron 253
Horder, Percy Morley 177–80, 331
Horner, Leonard 46
Horowitz, Helen Lefkowitz 14
Horwood, Thomas 222
Hoskins, W. G. 221

Huber, V. A. 49
Hull, University of 146, 180, 217–18, 226, 239, 248, 309
Humberside Polytechnic 317, 318
Huntley and Palmer 141
Huxley, Elspeth 207
Huxley, Thomas Henry 106, 112, 133

Ice hockey, mythic origins of 27
Inglis, Charles 22–7, 72
Inter-Varsity Ball 211
Inter-Varsity Christian Union 211
Ionian Academy, Corfu 31
Ireland, Queen's, Royal, and National University of 82, 84–5, 101–4, 107–8, 128–9
Irving, Edward 40

Jacobson, Howard 274
Jarratt Report on Efficiency Studies in Universities 305
Jebb, Caroline, lady 113
Jefferson, Thomas 5, 36
Johns Hopkins University 106, 135
Jones, Abel 149
Jones, Sir Brynmor 217–18
Joseph, Sir Keith 275, 283, 284, 288
Joyce, Patrick 11

Keane, John Benjamin 102
Kedourie, Elie 286
Keele, University 221–6, **225**, 239, 241, 261, 268–70, 273, 282
Kelsall, Charles 1–5, 18, 31, 221, **335**–7
Kent, University of 226, 239, 256, 265, 311
Kenyon, James 125
Kermonde, Sir Frank 252
King, Anthony 279
Kinnock, Neil, baron 277
Kirwan, Francis 82
Knight, Rex 157–8, 164–5
Knox, William 24

La Boot, Jo-Jo 266
Lady Spencer-Churchill College of Education 282
Lambert Review 329
Lampeter, St David's College 33, **34**, 35, 37, 54, 57
Lancashire Polytechnic 280, 283, 315
Lancashire, University of Central 280, 283, 315, 335
Lancaster, University of 226, 246, 256, 311
Lanchester, H. V. 193
Lanchester and Lodge 217
Lane, W. H. H. 198
Lanyon Sir Charles 101–2
Latour, Bruno 11
Laurie, Douglas 193
Lasdun, Denys 264

Law, James 96
Lawrence, D. H. 148, 150, 157, 178–9
Lawson, Nigel, baron 276
Leeds:
  Leeds Student 282
  Metropolitan University 282, 309–10, 324
  Polytechnic 282, 309–10
  Proposals for a university 31
  University 12, 110, 111, 115, 116, 130, **131**, 134, 135, 136, 139, 141, 142, 144, 145, 148, 159, 160, 180, 188, 189, 193–4, **194**, 197, 198, 199, 206, 217, 226–7, 250–1, 252, 253, 254–5, 257–8, **257**, 259–60, 263, 265, 282, 291, 294, 296, 300, 309–10, 311, 314, 315
Leicester:
  De Montfort University 282, 291, 293, 296, 307–8, **308**, 318
  Polytechnic 282, 291, 293, 296
  University of 180, 188, 212, 248, 250, 252–3, 254–5, 258–9, 261, 263–4, **264**, 266, 311
Letwin, Shirley Robin 288
Libeskind, Daniel 334
Lincoln, University of 317–18, **317**
Lindsay, Alexander Dunlop, first baron 222–6
Liverpool:
  Polytechnic, later John Moores University 265, 309
  University 12, 110, 111, 114, 133, 134, 136, 138, **138**, 139, 143, 144, 145, 148, 150, 155–6, 159, 160, 191, **192**, 199–200, **200**, 208, 212–13, 239, 250–1, 253, 254, 261, 263, 264–7, 310
  University Club 215
Livingstone, Hugh 298
Lodge, David 274
Lodge, Sir Oliver 126–7, 133, 135, 143, 150, **166**, 169, 173
Lodge, T. A. 182
London:
  Battersea Polytechnic 142
  Bethlehem Hospital 54
  Borough Road Training College 144, 155, 160
  College of Health 106
  College of Medicine for Women 211
  East London College 148
  East London, University of 280, 317
  Government School of Mines 73, 75
  Imperial College 172
  Inns of Court 35
  Kensington University College 75
  King's College (KCL) 43–50, 56–63, 65–6, 67, 72, 74, 75, 78, 80, 94, 107, 333
  King's College School 47, 56
  Livery Companies 142
  London School of Economics 266, 305, 333

Marlborough House 52
Medical education in 35, 47–8, 60
Metropolitan University 277, 316, 327, 334, **334**
Middlesex Polytechnic 282
Middlesex University 282, 324, 329–30
National Gallery 57
North East London Polytechnic 280
North London Polytechnic 277, 316
Queen Mary College 148
Royal College of Chemistry 73
Royal Holloway College 115, **116**
Royal Indian Engineering College 73
Royal Institution 36
St George's Hospital 57
Senate House 180
Somerset House 51–2, 63
Thames Polytechnic 309
University College (UCL) 21, 35–41, 46–50, 53–5, 57–66, **62**, 72, 74, 78, 91, 94, 99, 110, 129, 172, 189, 329, 335; *see also* London, University of
University College Hospital 47–8
University of 6, 29, 48–50, 51–3, 67, 73, 110, 128, 134, 145, 213, 318
Webb Street School of Anatomy 90–1
Westfield College 290
Look Back in Anger 248
Loughborough, Technical College, Technological University, and University of 153–4, 155, 181, **181**, 217, 249, 265, 311
Louvain, University of 83
Lowe, Roy 129, 157–8, 164–5
Lowlands, University of 273–5
Lubbock, Sir John 51
Lucky Jim 244
Lydiard Millicent 90
Lyell, Sir Charles 45, 133

McCartney, Donal 83
Macaulay, Thomas Babington, first baron 38–9, 41, 81
Macaulay, Zachary 39, 46
McClean, Martin 289
MacCormac, Sir Richard 311
McGettigan, Andrew 329
McGonnagall, William Topaz 141–2
Mack Smith, Denis 217
Madison, James 3, 5
Madras, University of 73
Magee College 82, 84
Mair, Alexander 214
Malik, Rachel 328
Maltby, Edward 52
Manchester:
  cultural life within 87–8
  early proposals for a university of 31

Manchester: (cont.)
  education precinct 255, 265, 310
  Independent Academy (later Harris
    Manchester College) 88, 94
  Owens College 71–2, 74–5, 86, 92–6,
    97–100, 107–9, **108**, 112, 115, **117**,
    119–20, 136, 153, 317, 329
  Polytechnic 255, 282–3, 311
  University of 71–2, 74–5, 86, 92–6, 97–100,
    107–9, **108**, 110, 112, 115, **117**, 119–20,
    133, 135–6, 140, 141, 142, 144, 145, 148,
    153, 155, 156, 160, 163, 167, 197, 201,
    212, 213, 226–7, 239, 244–6, 253, 262–3,
    266, 283, 294–5, 311, 315, 329
  Women's College 119–20
  Working Men's College 98
Mannheim, Karl 223
Mansbridge, Albert 144
Marmoreck, H. W. 225
Martin Hanner 207, 214
Martin, Sir Leslie 250, 255, 263–4
Martineau, Harriet 81
Masefield, John 13
Mason, Irvine 216
Massachusetts Institute of Technology
  (MIT) 135, 314
Massey, Doreen 17
Massive Open On-Line Courses
  (MOOCs) 334–5
mathematics 40, 74, 94
Maurice, F. D. 75
Maynooth College 30, 33, 73, 79–82, 85,
  105–6, 167
Mechanics' Institutes 38
medical training 35, 47–8, 60, 88–90, 98, 110,
  149, 311
Melbourne, University of 85
Meller, Helen 117
Metternich, Prince Klemens Wenzel von 39
Mill, James 63
Miller, Henry 299
Milton Keynes 270
Mind and Body Shop 274
Mitchell, Sagar 125
Mitchell and Kenyon 125–6
Mkebi, Thabo 242
Moberly, Sir Walter 187, 191, 223
modern languages 40, 94
Montefiore, Claude 205
Montreal, University of 135
Morgan W. J. 153
Morley, Edith 151
Morley, Samuel 112
Mortan, H. V. 158
Muir, Ramsey 155–6
Mullin, James 104
mummies 39, 141
Munby, A. N. L. 244
Murphy, Jim 296
Murray, W. A. 246

Mursell, J. P. 81
Muthesius, Stefan 257

National Advisory Board (NAB) 281–2,
  283, 287
National Society for Promoting the Education of
  the Poor in the Principles of the Established
  Church 38
National Union of Students (NUS) 9, 186, 195,
  204, 211, 235, 295–6, 297
Needham, Joseph 266
Newcastle, Henry Pelham Fiennes Pelham-Clinton,
  fourth duke of 35
Newcastle:
  proposals for a university of 31
  University of 110, 159, 197, 212, 329
Newman, John Henry 15, 72, 80–1, 82–4, 85
'New Testament' 143
New York 21–4
  King's College (later Columbia), 21, 23
New Zealand, University of 73
Ningbo, University of Nottingham 331, **332**
North of England Council for Promoting the
  Higher Education of Women 113
Nottingham, University of 110, 114, 115, 128,
  149, 150, 157, 164, **164**, 167, 177–81,
  178, 191, 203, 208, 209, 211, 226, 238,
  243, 255, **256**, 266, 311–12, 329, 330, **332**

Oakeshott, Michael 205, 243
Office for Fair Access (OFFA) 333
Open University 268–70, 334
Ortega y Gasset, José 185, 223
Osborne, John 248
Oscott, St Mary's College 30
Owen, David, baron 296
Owens, John 71–2, 92–3, 100, 112
owls, effect of students on 309
Oxford:
  All Souls 247
  Christ Church 57, **58**, 102
  curious, unnatural, spasmodic life there 151
  encaenia 125
  extension classes 113–14, 161, **162**, 167, 222
  Footlights College, 274
  Harris Manchester College 88, 94
  Magdalen College 102
  Nuffield College 186, 247
  Polytechnic 281, 282, 300–1, 309, 315
  Union Society 211–12
  University 3, 31–2, 40, 43, 73, 78, 83,
    113–14, 115, 125, 128, 129, 132–3, 135,
    136, 145, 151, 160, 163, 182, 184, 189,
    196, 206, 217, 224, 227, 254, 276, 329
  University Press 57
  Warneford Hospital 89

Panizzi, Sir Antony 65–6
Paris international exhibition 114
Parkin, Frank 274

parliamentary representation 189
Patten, John, baron 283
Pattison, G. S. 64
Pearman, Hugh 307–8
Peel, Sir Robert 43, 44, 48, 79–82, 85, 101
Peers, Edgar Allison *see* Truscot, Bruce Perkin, Harold 246
Peterhouse, future agricultural college 4
Pevsner, Nikolaus 12
Phantasm of an University 1–4, **2**, 18, 335
Phillips, Melanie 278
Pickavance, J. A. 225
Picton, James 95
Pitt, William the younger 25
place as an analytical category 14–18
Playfair, Lyon, first baron 114, 115
Playfair, W. H. 59
polytechnics 226, 231, 236, 255, 280–4, 291, 300–1, 304–5, 315–16, 318–19
Polytechnics Funding Council (PFC) 282
Porno Performer, the People's, *see* La Boot Jo-Jo
Portsmouth, University of 317
Potteries Thinkbelt 269–70, **270**
Prestwich, Joseph 61
Price, Cedric 269–70
Price, Margaret 301
Pugin, Augustus 57, **58**, 105–6
Pullan, Brian 304

Quality Assurance Agency (QAA) 288

Rashdall, Hastings 134
Rawnsley, Andrew 296
Reading, University of 128, 133, 141, 155, 156, 159–60, 196, 207, 208, 209, 234, 252, 253, 314, 322
Redbrick University 7, 185–7
Reichel, H. R. 135
Research Assessment Exercise (RAE) 287, 292, 301–2, 304, 326
Rhodes-James, Sir Robert 287
Ripon, Edward Burroughs, fifth bishop of 214
Robertson, Sir Charles Grant 202–3
Robertson, Dave 264–7
Robertson, Sir Howard 225
Robbins Report 235–6, 245, 283–4
Robinson, Eric 280, 283
Rochdale 113
Roscoe, Sir Henry 98–9, 110, 133
Rose, James 43
Rosebery, Archibald Primrose, fifth earl of 136–7
Rothblatt, Sheldon 14
Royal Commission:
  on Scientific Instruction 115
  on the Scottish Universities 32, 93
  on the University of Durham 35, 72
Royal Fine Arts Commission 251, 307
Rummidge, University of 274
Ruskin, John 133

Russell, Bertrand, third earl 266
Russell, Lord John, later first earl 33
Russell, Willy 273
Rustin, Michael 276
Ryan, Alan 241
Rycotewood College for Rural Crafts 235

St Bees College 30
St John of Fawsley, Norman, baron 307
Sacks, Robert 15
Sadler, Michael 130, 135, 204
Salford Technical Institute, 168
Salford, University of 168, 291, 296, 300, 329
Sanderson, Michael 137, 142, 172, 277
Sands Cox, William 89–92, 96
Sargent, Sir Malcolm 232
Sartre, Jean-Paul 266
Schofield, Herbert 153
Scholemmer, Carl 133
Scott, A. J. 97
Scott, Sir George Gilbert 101, 105
Scott, Peter 275, 293
Scottish universities 4–5
  criticism of 32, 78
  funded by the state 33, 325
  influence on teaching methods 36, 58, 134–5, 136
  low average age of entry 36–7
  Royal Commission on 32, 93
Scraptoft Hall 282
Scumbag College 274
Seeley, Sir John 87
Selwyn-Lloyd, John, baron 234
Shallcross, E. L. 149
Sharpe, Tom 274
Shattock, Michael 318, 335
Sheffield:
  Polytechnic 281, 282
  University 13, 110, 128, 134, 135, 137, 142, 147, 148, 149, 150, 161, **165**, 164–5, 168, 180, 182, 189, 195, 196, 207, 210, 211, 213, 214, 216, 239, 240, 253–4, 295, 310, 330
Shepheard, Peter 225
Shepherd, A. F. 199, 201
Short, Alan 307–8
Simmonds, Posy 274
Simon, Brian 186
skeleton 210
Skinners' Company 142
Sloman, Sir Albert 254
Smiley, M. T. 215
Smirke, Sir Robert 56–7, 59
Smith, Adam 46
Smith, G. G. Moore 148
Smith, Goldwin 97, 112
Smith, Southwood 91
Smithells, Arthur 197
Smithson, Alison and Peter 254

Snow, Charles Percy, first baron 188
social history 11–12
Social Science Research Council 285, 287
Society for the Diffusion of Useful Knowledge 38
Society for the Propagation of the Gospel 26, 43
sociology 285, 287
Southampton:
  Hartley Institute 87
  University of 87, 128, 144, 169, **170**, 193, 194–5, **195**, 201, 209, 210, 213–14, 215, 226, 232, 241, 248, 250, 266
Southey, Robert 56, 63
Special Institutions for Scientific and Technological Education and Research (SISTERs) 236
Spence, Sir Basil 227, 250, 252, 256
Spencer, F. H. 144, 155, 160
staff, university:
  administrative and managerial 110, 303–4, 308–9, 326–8
  architectural involvement of 107–8, 260, 261, 311
  criticism of 244–7
  discouraged from doing research 64, 213–14
  divisions within 26, 212–15, 245–6, 302–6, 308–9, 325–8
  early deaths of 65
  encouraged to do research 64, 110, 185, 212–15, 245, 287, 301, 326–8
  gender of 63, 150–2, 213, 246, 305–6, 325–6, 328
  government of universities by 64–6, 120, 143, 245–6, 304–5, 326–7, 330
  incompetence of 64–5, 150, 244–5
  laziness of 212–13
  made redundant 299–300
  nostalgia of 15, 278, 328
  numbers of 214, 244, 302–3
  overwork of 45, 65, 149–51, 292, 302, 325–6
  part-time and temporary 302–4, 308–9, 325–6
  poor pay of 45, 63–4, 66, 96, 130, 189, 190, 213, 215–16, 244–5, 299–300, 304, 323–4
  poor education of 244–7
  revelling in indecency 91
  religious restrictions on 4–5, 25, 44–5, 72, 75
  social class of 63–6, 246–7, 299
  sexism of 148, 240
  stress and anxieties of 17–18, 189, 247, 299–302, 319, 321, 325–9
  surprisingly enterprising 298–9
  teaching-only contracts 302–3, 327–8
  tenure abolished 299
Staffordshire 4, 6, 221–2, 268–70
Staffordshire Polytechnic 282
Staffordshire, University of 282, 335–7, **336**
Stirling and Gowan 263–4, 307
Stirling, Sir James 307

Stirling, University of 309
Stone, Lawrence 11
Stoner 17
Stonyhurst College 50
Strathclyde, University 245, 312
Student Christian Movement (SCM) 186, 211
Student Satisfaction Survey 326
students:
  age of 36–7, 61, 119, 292–3, 322
  anxiety of 17–18, 148–9, 155, 207, 209, 237–8, 247, 297, 321
  clothes worn by 61, 101, 104, 125–6, 127, 146, 147, 155, 172, 182, 188, 242, 282
  complain about teaching 64–5, 150, 213–14, 244–5
  conscription of 217, 239
  disabled 310
  disappoint their teachers 209
  dislike university buildings 107, 109, 260–70, 311
  divisions within 60, 63, 114, 144, 156, 206–7, 238–9, 294–5, 323
  ethnicity of 295
  evening classes, attended by 98–9, 110, 144, 149, 157
  gender of 36, 76, 100, 112–13, 119–21, 126, 133, 142, 145–6, 148–9, 154, 196, 207–8, 239–42, 286, 292–3, 322
  graduations 32, 43, 60, 125–7, 150
  local 144, 205, 236–7, 316
  need for coffee 98
  numbers of 4–5, 26–7, 31, 35, 46–8, 49, 60, 72, 75, 84, 85, 95, 96, 98–9, 100, 110–11, 135, 144, 146, 204–6, 217–18, 226–7, 233, 235–6, 243, 280, 284–6, 291–2, 294–5, 300, 322
  overseas 231–2, 295, 322, 325
  part-time 45, 60, 98, 295, 303
  politics of 149, 150, 211–12, 232, 242–3, 293–6
  poor education of 95, 190, 222, 290–2
  postgraduate 214, 303
  Rag week 153, 155, 210, 237
  rebellion by 232, 242–3, 264–70, 295
  recreations and social life 59, 60–3, 76, 98–9, 109, 149, 153–4, 155–6, 193, 209, 210–11, 237–8, 241–2, 293–4, 335
  religion of 4–5, 25, 43, 85, 94
  restrictions on entry to university 4–5, 23, 25, 33, 36, 43–4, 71–2, 79, 94, 100, 144–5, 172, 332–7
  sexuality of 149, 208, 238–41, 267, 293–4
  social class of 63, 76, 79, 84, 94, 111–13, 144–5, 129, 172, 187–8, 196, 205–6, 209, 239–40, 246–7, 276, 292–3, 332–7
  sport 27, 61, 154, 211
  unions and guilds 126, 145, 153, 210, 251, 294, 296, 307–8
Summerson, Sir John 258–9
Surrey, University of 290, 309, 310

Sussex, University of 226, 239, 242, 250, 255–6, 258, 260–1, 261, **262**, 265, 296
Swansea, University College 128, 239
Sydney, University of 73, 78
Synthetic Society 133

teacher training 97–8, 149, 209, 235, 282, 292, 330
Teaching Quality Audit (TQA) 304
Teale, A. E. 241
technical education 3, 74, 92, 95–6, 98–9, 100, 115, 121, 133, 139, 142–4, 235–6, 281, 291, 330
Thackeray, William 79
Thatcher, Margaret, baroness 277, 283, 284
theology 37, 40, 48, 88, 91, 92, 94, 95, 99
Thomas, Arthur 125–6
Thomas, Sir Keith 328
Thompson, Paul 265
Thurles, Synod of 82, 85
Tilden, Sir William 133
Todd, Marjorie 146, 147
Toronto, University of 43–4, 135
Trent, Jesse Boot, first baron 177, 198
Trevecca, Dissenting Academy of 50
Truscot, Bruce 7, 185–7, 190, 197, 212–13, 302
Turner, Paul Venable 14
Turner, W. E. S. 150
Twigg, Stephen 296

Universities Funding Council (UFC) 283, 287
University Challenge 274
University Grants Committee (UGC) 10, 184, 190, 191, 197, 202–3, 216, 217, 223–4, 226–7, 229–32, 233–4, 238, 249, 251–2, 255, 257–8, 283, 284, 287–8, 290–1, 300, 311
University of East Anglia (UEA) 226, 239, 250, 257, 268, **269**, 273, 313, **313**
utilitarianism 37, 241

Vaizey, John Ernest, baron 233
Vassar College 115
Vernon, James 321
Victoria, queen 33
Victoria University 110, 119, 128, 139, 172; *see also* Leeds, Liverpool, and Sheffield Universities
Virginia, University of 5, 36
Vivian Grey 39

Wahrman, Dror 37
Wales, University of 73, 85, 128, 137, 144, 325; *see also* Aberystwyth, Bangor, Cardiff, and Swansea
Wantage, Harriet Loyd-Lindsay, lady 141

war:
    first world 189, 197, 202, 217
    second world 180, 186, 190, 206, 217, 229
'warfare state' 232–3
Warneford, Samuel 71–2, 89–90, 96
Warwick, Diana, baroness 278
Warwick, University of 226, 255–6, 266, 273, 314
Waterhouse, Alfred 107–8, 111, 160, 163, 167, 191, 193, 329
Waterperry Horticultural School for Women 235
Watkin, David 1
Webb, Aston 172, 255, 330
Weiner, Martin 276
Wellington, Arthur Wellesley, first duke of 44
Wentworth Woodhouse 282
Wetherell, Sir Charles 48
Wilberforce, William 46
Whyte, Jacob ix
Whyte, Nahum ix
Wilkins, William 54–5, 59
Willetts, David 328–9
William IV, king 89
Williams, John 17
Williams, Shirley, baroness 277
Williamson, W. C. 102
Willis, Robert 14
Wills family of Bristol 140–1
Wilson, Bryan 243–4, 247
Wilson, James 33
Wilt 274
Winchelsea, George William Finch-Hatton, tenth earl of 45
Windsor N. S., King's College 21–8, **22**, 35, 67
Wolfenden, John Frederick, baron 230
Woolas, Phil 296
Worden, Peter 125
Wordsworth, William 29
Workers' Educational Association (WEA) 144
Worthington, Percy 193
Worthington, Thomas Shirley 255
Wyatville, Sir Jeffry 54–5
Wyse, Sir Thomas 82

Yates, James 53, 67
York:
    proposals for a university 31
    University of 226, 239, 251, 256, **258**, 265; *see also* Toronto, University of
Yorkshire College of Science, *see* Leeds: University
Young, Freda 147
Young Ones, The 274

Zweig, Ferdynand 237